LISTENING
CLEAR

중학영어듣기
모의고사 20회

3

▎핵심만 골라 담은 중학 영어듣기능력평가 완벽 대비서 LISTENING CLEAR

- **더 완벽하게!** 최신 중학 영어듣기능력평가 출제 유형 100% 반영
- **더 풍부하게!** 유형별 문제 해결 전략 및 풍부한 기출 표현 수록
- **더 편리하게!** 1.0배속, 1.2배속, 받아쓰기용 QR코드로 학습 편의성 강화
- **더 정확하게!** 잘 안 들리는 영어 발음 현상과 영국식 발음 반복 훈련

학습자의 마음을 읽는 **동아영어콘텐츠연구팀**

동아영어콘텐츠연구팀은 동아출판의 영어 개발 연구원, 현장 선생님, 그리고 전문 원고 집필자들이 공동연구를 통해 최적의 콘텐츠를 개발하는 연구조직입니다.

원고 개발에 참여하신 분들

고미라   강윤희   이정은   이지현   김영선   전혜래나
유경연   박석완   배윤경   윤소영   김지형   강남숙

LISTENING
CLEAR
중학영어듣기
모의고사 20회

3

STRUCTURES 구성과 특징

STEP 1 유형별 기출문제로 기본 다지기

〈전국 16개 시·도 교육청 영어듣기능력평가〉에 출제된 유형별 기출문제를 학습하며 기본기를 다집니다.

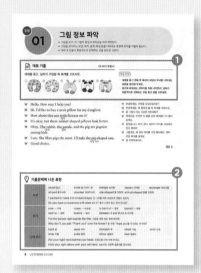

📄 대표 기출 | (해결 전략) ❶

유형별 대표 기출문제를 풀어 보며 유형에 대한 감을 익힐 수 있어요.
해결 전략에는 어느 부분을 집중해서 들어야 하는지, 무엇을 주의해야 하는지 설명되어 있어요.
문제 푸는 요령을 터득할 수 있으니 꼭 짚어 보세요.

💡 기출문제에 나온 표현 ❷

실제 시험에 출제되었던 필수 어휘와 필수 표현을 한눈에 볼 수 있어요.
매 시험마다 반복적으로 출제되는 표현이 많으므로 암기해 두는 것이 좋아요.

STEP 2 모의고사로 실전 감각 기르기

실제 시험과 유사한 소재와 유형, 출제 경향을 완벽히 반영한 모의고사 20회를 풀며 실전 감각을 기릅니다.

실전 모의고사

실제 시험보다 약간 어려운 난이도로 구성되어
있어서 실전에 효과적으로 대비할 수 있어요.

고난도 모의고사

실전 모의고사보다 어려운 문제를 통해 실력을
더욱 향상시킬 수 있어요.

★ 1.0배속 / 1.2배속 녹음 파일: 각자 수준에 맞는 속도를 선택하여 문제를 풀어 보세요.

1.0배속

1.2배속

STEP 3 받아쓰기로 실력 높이기

모의고사 문제를 다시 듣고 받아쓰면서 듣기 실력을 향상시킵니다.

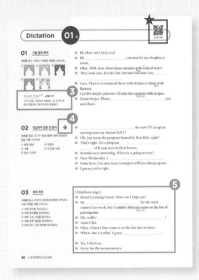

Sound Clear ☆ ③

듣기 어려운 발음과 주의해야 하는 발음 현상을 학습할 수 있어요.

🇬🇧 영국식 발음 ④

매회 다섯 문항이 영국식 발음으로 녹음되어 있어서 영국식 발음에 익숙해질 수 있어요.

정답 단서 / 함정 ⑤

정답 단서와 함정이 표시되어 있어서 문제를 더욱 잘 이해할 수 있고, 반복되는 출제 패턴을 파악할 수 있어요.

★ 받아쓰기용 녹음 파일: 문장마다 받아쓰기 시간이 확보되어 있어서 편리하게 학습할 수 있어요.

STEP 4 필수 어휘·표현 정리하기

모의고사에 나온 필수 어휘와 표현을 점검하며 학습한 내용을 마무리합니다.

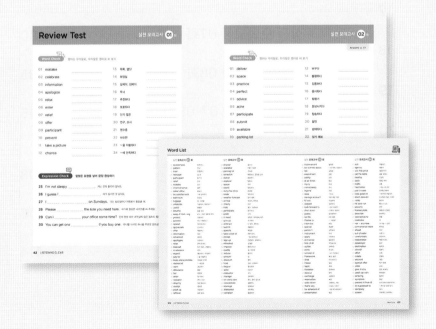

Review Test

모의고사에 나온 단어, 숙어, 관용 표현 문제를 풀며 복습할 수 있어요.

Word List

부록으로 제공된 어휘 목록을 암기장으로 활용해 보세요.

CONTENTS 차례

PART
3
**고난도 모의고사
19-20회**

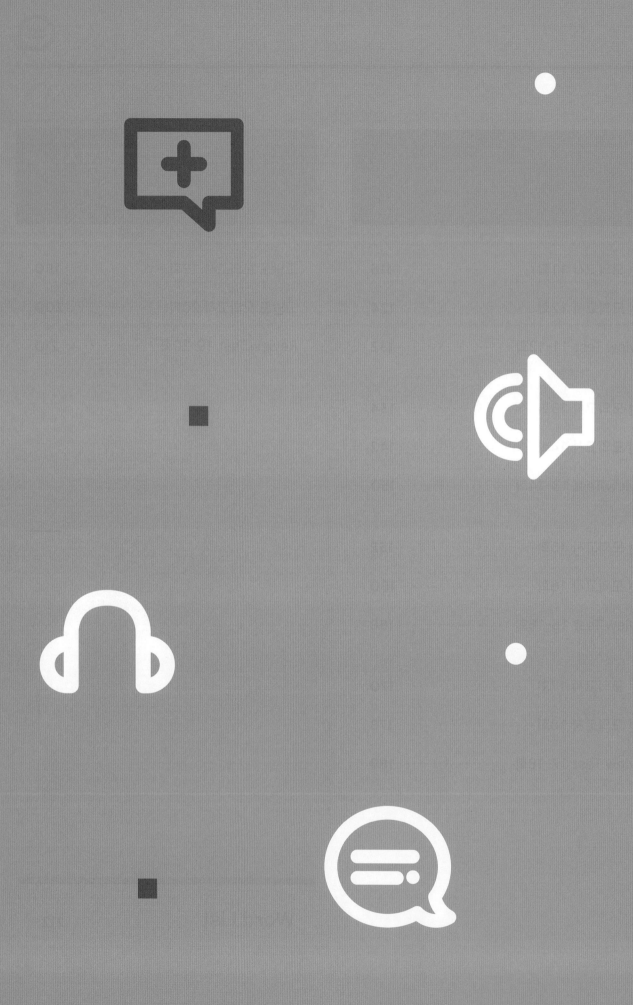

PART

1

유형 분석 &
주요 표현

그림 정보 파악

- 그림을 보고, 각 그림의 특징과 차이점을 미리 파악한다.
- 그림을 묘사하는 모양, 위치, 동작, 특징 등을 나타내는 표현에 주의를 기울여 듣는다.
- 대화 속 인물이 최종적으로 선택하는 것을 답으로 고른다.

📄 대표 기출

🔊 MP3 유형 01

대화를 듣고, 남자가 구입할 목 베개를 고르시오.

①   ②   ③   ④   ⑤

W Hello. How may I help you?

M Hi. I'd like to buy a neck pillow for my daughter.

W How about this one with flowers on it?
              한정

M It's okay, but these animal-shaped pillows look better.

W Okay. The rabbit, the panda, and the pig are popular
         한정   한정
   among kids.

M I see. She likes pigs the most. I'll take the pig-shaped one.
                                        정답 단서

W Good choice.

(해결 전략)

- 대화를 듣기 전에 목 베개의 모양과 무늬를 나타내는 표현을 생각해 두세요.
- 중간에 제외되는 선택지를 지워 나가면서, 남자가 최종적으로 선택하는 것을 듣고 답을 고르세요.

여 안녕하세요. 무엇을 도와드릴까요?

남 안녕하세요. 제 딸에게 줄 목 베개를 사려고요.

여 꽃 그림이 있는 이것은 어떠세요?

남 괜찮네요. 하지만 이 동물 모양 베개들이 더 좋아 보여요.

여 알겠습니다. 토끼, 판다, 돼지가 아이들 사이에서 인기 있어요.

남 그렇군요. 제 딸은 돼지를 가장 좋아해요. 돼지 모양 베개를 살게요.

여 잘 선택하셨어요.

정답 ⑤

💡 기출문제에 나온 표현

모양	round 둥근	circle 동그라미, 원	triangle 삼각형	square 사각형	rectangle 직사각형
	striped 줄무늬의	checked 체크무늬의	star-shaped 별 모양의	animal-shaped 동물 모양의	
	I wanted to make it in a heart shape. 난 그것을 하트 모양으로 만들고 싶었어.				
	Do you have a round one with stars on it? 별이 그려진 둥근 것이 있나요?				
위치	over ~ 위에	under ~ 아래에	in front of ~ 앞에	behind ~ 뒤에	
	next to ~ 옆에	beside ~ 옆에	between A and B A와 B 사이에		
	Put the picture right beside the title. 그림을 제목 바로 옆에 배치해.				
	Why don't you add "Thank you" over the flower? 꽃 위에 'Thank you'를 추가하는 게 어때?				
신체 부위	back 등	waist 허리	stomach 배	chest 가슴	wrist 손목
	knee 무릎	ankle 발목	elbow 팔꿈치	heel 발꿈치	
	Put your right hand behind your head. 오른손을 머리 뒤에 두세요.				
	Hold your right elbow with your left hand. 왼손으로 오른쪽 팔꿈치를 잡으세요.				

목적 파악

- '전화·방문한 목적'이나 '방송의 목적'을 고르는 두 가지 형태로 출제된다.
- 인사말 바로 뒤나 대화의 앞부분에서 목적을 밝히는 경우가 많으므로 처음부터 집중해서 듣는다.

📄 대표 기출
🔊 MP3 유형 02

대화를 듣고, 남자가 여자에게 전화한 목적으로 가장 적절한 것을 고르시오.

① 식당을 예약하려고
② 영업시간을 문의하려고
③ 식당 위치를 물어보려고
④ 근무 조건을 알아보려고
⑤ 게시판 설치를 요청하려고

(해결 전략)

- 전화한 사람이 남자이므로 남자의 말을 주의 깊게 들으세요.
- 남자의 첫 번째 말에서 식당에서 일할 사람을 구하는 것과 관련해서 문의하려는 것임을 알 수 있어요.

(*Telephone rings.*)

W Tom's Restaurant. Can I help you?

M I heard that you need workers for your restaurant.

W Yes. We're still looking for a waiter. Do you have any experience?

M Yes, I've worked in a restaurant for six months. Can I ask how much you pay?

W 15 dollars an hour.

M How many hours do I have to work a day?

W You'll have to work six hours every day, Monday through Friday.

M I see. Thank you.

(전화벨이 울린다.)

여 Tom's Restaurant입니다. 도와드릴까요?

남 식당에서 일할 사람이 필요하다고 들었어요.

여 네. 아직 웨이터를 찾고 있어요. 경험이 있으신가요?

남 네, 6개월 동안 식당에서 일했어요. 급여가 얼마인지 여쭤봐도 될까요?

여 시간 당 15달러입니다.

남 하루에 몇 시간 일해야 하나요?

여 월요일부터 금요일까지 매일 6시간 일하셔야 합니다.

남 알겠습니다. 감사합니다.

정답 ④

💡 기출문제에 나온 표현

전화·방문한 목적	I'm sorry, but the T-shirts you ordered will be delayed for a few days. 죄송하지만, 주문하신 티셔츠가 며칠 지연될 것입니다. I was wondering if I can change my time. 시간을 바꿀 수 있는지 궁금했어요. Why don't we go visit him this afternoon? 오늘 오후에 그를 보러가는 게 어때? That's why I'm calling you. Can you give me a ride? 그래서 너한테 전화하는 거야. 나 좀 태워 줄 수 있니?
방송의 목적	Let me tell you how you can ask for the songs you want to hear. 듣고 싶으신 노래들을 어떻게 신청하는지 알려 드리겠습니다. The heating system has some problems, so we changed the location. 난방 시스템에 문제가 있어서 장소를 변경했습니다.

그림의 상황에 적절한 대화 찾기

- 그림 속 상황을 빠르게 파악하고, 특히 그림에서 강조하는 부분에 주목한다.
- 대화를 하나씩 들으면서 그림과 관련 없는 선택지를 지워 나간다.
- 그림과 관련된 대화의 선택지에 표시해 두었다가 끝까지 듣고 나서 알맞은 답을 골랐는지 확인한다.

📄 대표 기출

🔊 MP3 유형 03

다음 그림의 상황에 가장 적절한 대화를 고르시오.

①   ②   ③   ④   ⑤

(해결 전략)

- 대화를 듣기 전에 그림에서 강조하고 있는 화살표 부분을 미리 확인하세요.
- 가방을 싸는 상황과 관련 없는 대화를 순서대로 지워 나가세요.
- 가방을 싸는 상황과 관련된 대화의 선택지에 답을 표시한 후, 마지막 대화까지 듣고 답을 고르세요.

---

① **W**   You should not run here.

   M   Sorry. I won't do it again.

② **W**   Can I borrow this book?

   M   Sure. Please give me your library card.

③ **W**   Where can I buy some cookies?

   M   You can buy them on the second floor in this mall.

④ **W**   Are you still packing your bag?

   M   Yes, I am. I have so many things to pack.

⑤ **W**   I'd like to send this letter by express mail.

   M   Okay, it'll cost $5.

① **여** 여기서 뛰면 안 된단다.

   남 죄송합니다. 다시는 그러지 않을게요.

② **여** 이 책을 빌려도 되나요?

   남 네. 도서관 카드를 주세요.

③ **여** 과자를 어디에서 살 수 있나요?

   남 이 쇼핑몰 2층에서 사실 수 있습니다.

④ **여** 아직 가방을 싸고 있니?

   남 네. 쌀 짐이 너무 많아요.

⑤ **여** 이 편지를 빠른우편으로 부치고 싶어요.

   남 네, 5달러입니다.

정답 ④

⭐ 기출문제에 나온 표현

슈퍼마켓에서 물건을 찾는 상황	**A** Where can I find the candy? 사탕을 어디에서 찾을 수 있나요?
	B They're over there, in section three. 저쪽 3번 구역에 있어요.
세탁기 사용법을 묻는 상황	**A** Can you tell me how to use this washing machine? 이 세탁기를 어떻게 사용하는지 알려 주시겠어요?
	B Okay. Let me show you how. 네. 제가 사용법을 보여 드릴게요.
애완동물 출입을 금지하는 상황	**A** Sorry, but dogs are not allowed here. 죄송하지만, 이곳에 개는 들어갈 수 없습니다.
	B Oh, I'm sorry. I didn't know that. 오, 죄송합니다. 그걸 몰랐어요.
버스에서 자리를 양보하는 상황	**A** You can have my seat, ma'am. 제 자리에 앉으세요. 부인
	B Thanks. How kind of you! 고맙습니다. 정말 친절하시네요!

특정 정보 파악

- 날짜, 요일, 물건 등 다양한 소재가 출제된다.
- 대화의 앞부분에서 오답을 유도하는 경우가 많으므로 주의해야 한다.
- 끝까지 집중해서 들으면서 대화 속 인물이 최종적으로 선택하는 것을 답으로 고른다.

📄 대표 기출

🔊 MP3 유형04

대화를 듣고, 여자가 치과에 가기로 한 날짜를 고르시오.

① 5월 4일　　② 5월 6일　　③ 5월 7일
④ 5월 9일　　⑤ 5월 11일

(*Telephone rings.*)

M　Hello. This is Riverside Dentist.

W　Hello. This is Emma Parker. I'd like to make an appointment to get a checkup.

M　Okay. When would you like to visit?

W　Is May 4 in the afternoon possible?

M　Wait a minute. (*Typing sound*) I'm sorry. The doctor is fully booked that day. How about May 7?

W　I'm afraid I can't.

M　Are you available on May 9? We have a time at 11 o'clock.

W　May 9? Hmm, that's good. I'll visit then.

M　Okay, see you then.

해결 전략

- 예약이 가능하지 않은 날짜를 하나씩 지워 나가세요.
- 끝까지 집중해서 들어야 최종적으로 결정한 날짜를 고를 수 있어요.

(전화벨이 울린다.)

남　안녕하세요. Riverside Dentist입니다.

여　안녕하세요. 저는 Emma Parker입니다. 진료 예약을 하고 싶은데요.

남　네. 언제 방문하고 싶으세요?

여　5월 4일 오후 가능한가요?

남　잠깐만요. (*타이핑하는 소리*) 죄송합니다. 그날은 선생님께서 예약이 꽉 차 있어요. 5월 7일은 어떠세요?

여　저는 안 될 것 같아요.

남　5월 9일은 가능하신가요? 11시에 시간이 있어요.

여　5월 9일이요? 음, 좋아요. 그때 방문할게요.

남　네, 그때 뵙겠습니다.

정답 ④

💡 기출문제에 나온 표현

날짜	We'll deliver it at 9 a.m. on May 10. 5월 10일 오전 9시에 배달해 드리겠습니다.
	How about June 2 or June 7? 6월 2일이나 6월 7일은 어떠세요?
	Let's leave on July 20 and come back on July 23. 7월 20일에 떠나서 7월 23일에 돌아오자.
요일	Yes, you can use it on Thursday. 그래, 넌 그것을 목요일에는 사용할 수 있어.
	Thursday is not good for me, but I'll be free on Friday. 나한테 목요일은 좋지 않지만, 금요일에는 한가할 거야.
	Can I sign up for Thursday lesson now? 지금 목요일 수업에 등록해도 될까요?
물건	Why don't we buy him a new helmet? 그에게 새 헬멧을 사 주는 게 어때?
	I forgot to get some mushrooms for the topping. 나는 토핑으로 얹을 버섯을 사는 걸 잊었어.
장소	Can we meet at the computer lab and work on it? 우리가 컴퓨터실에서 만나서 그것을 작업할 수 있을까?

장소·관계·직업 추론

- 장소를 묻는 문제는 장소를 짐작할 수 있는 특정 어휘, 표현, 전체적인 상황을 통해 추론한다.
- 관계를 묻는 문제는 대화의 앞부분에 결정적인 단서가 나오는 경우가 많으므로 처음부터 집중해서 듣는다.
- 직업을 묻는 문제는 누구의 직업을 묻는 문제인지 확인하고 화자가 말한 내용을 종합하여 추론한다.

📄 대표 기출

🔊 MP3 유형 05

대화를 듣고, 두 사람이 대화하는 장소로 가장 적절한 곳을 고르시오.

① 서점
② 치과
③ 식당
④ 은행
⑤ 우체국

해결 전략

- 여자의 첫 번째 말에 나오는 the food is great here를 통해 음식과 관련된 장소임을 짐작할 수 있어요.
- 이어서 나오는 음식 관련 표현을 통해 두 사람이 대화하는 장소를 알 수 있어요.

W Paul, I heard that the food is great here.　　*정답 단서*

M Yeah. This place is famous for its beef dishes.

W What are you going to have for lunch today?

M Let's take a look at the menu first.

W Well, I'd like to try the beef-fried rice.

M Okay, and I'll have the beef soup.

W Good. Do you want something to drink? I just want some water.

M I'd like some apple juice. Let me call the waiter.

여 Paul, 이곳 음식이 아주 괜찮다고 들었어.
남 맞아. 이곳은 소고기 요리로 유명해.
여 너는 오늘 점심으로 뭐 먹을래?
남 먼저 메뉴를 한번 보자.
여 음, 난 소고기 볶음밥을 먹고 싶어.
남 그래. 그러면 나는 소고기 수프를 먹을래.
여 좋아. 마실 것을 원하니? 난 그냥 물을 원해.
남 난 사과 주스를 마실래. 내가 웨이터를 부를게.

정답 ③

💡 기출문제에 나온 표현

장소	식당	I'd like a hamburger and a coke, please. 햄버거 하나와 콜라 하나 주세요.
	미술관	The person in this picture seems to be looking at me. 이 그림 속의 사람이 나를 보고 있는 것 같아.
	서점	I'm looking for the book *The American Tourists*. 저는 〈The American Tourists〉라는 책을 찾고 있어요.
	도서관	When do I have to return this book? 언제 이 책을 반납해야 하나요?
관계	진행자 – 작가	Thank you for being a guest on our show, *New Books Weekly*. 저희 프로그램 〈New Books Weekly〉에 초대 손님으로 나와 주셔서 감사합니다.
	택배 기사 – 물품 구매자	I'm going to drop by your house in ten minutes to deliver your order. 주문하신 물건을 배달하기 위해 10분 후에 고객님 댁에 들를 예정입니다.
	우체국 직원 – 고객	Let's see how much it weighs. It's about 500 grams, so it'll cost 4,000 won. 무게가 얼마나 나가는지 봅시다. 500그램 정도니까 4,000원입니다.
직업	사서	The book is in section D, on the second floor. 그 책은 2층 D 구역에 있습니다.
	의사	My nurse will help you get your medicine before you leave. 가시기 전에 저희 간호사가 약을 가져가시도록 도와드릴 것입니다.
	교사	You'd better go see the school nurse right now. 너는 지금 당장 보건 선생님께 가 보는 게 좋겠구나.

유형 06 언급되지 않은 것 찾기

- 선택지 순서대로 내용이 언급되는 경우가 많다.
- 선택지와 비교해 가면서 언급된 내용을 하나씩 지워 나간다.
- 끝까지 들은 후에 남아 있는 선택지를 답으로 고른다.

📄 대표 기출

🔊 MP3 유형 06

다음을 듣고, 미술 전시회에 관해 언급되지 <u>않은</u> 것을 고르시오.

① 목적　　　② 제목　　　③ 작품 수
④ 기간　　　⑤ 개최 장소

해결 전략

- 미술 전시회의 목적, 제목, 기간, 개최 장소가 언급될 때마다 선택지를 하나씩 지우세요.
- 마지막에 남아 있는 하나의 선택지를 답으로 고르세요.

M　Hi, students. This is Andrew from the art club. As you know, June 5 is the World Environment Day. In order to celebrate this day, the art club will hold an art exhibition. *(정답 단서)* The title is *Nature and Art*. *(정답 단서)* The exhibition will be from June 5 to 10. *(정답 단서)* It's going to be held in the art classroom. *(정답 단서)* I hope many of you can come and enjoy the artworks. Thank you.

남　안녕하세요, 학생 여러분. 저는 미술 동아리의 Andrew입니다. 아시다시피, 6월 5일은 세계 환경의 날입니다. 이 날을 기념하기 위해, 미술 동아리는 미술 전시회를 열 계획입니다. 제목은 〈Nature and Art〉입니다. 전시회는 6월 5일부터 10일까지입니다. 전시회는 미술실에서 열릴 것입니다. 많은 분들이 오셔서 예술품들을 즐기시기를 바랍니다. 감사합니다.

정답 ③

💡 기출문제에 나온 표현

제목	A: What's the title of this song? 이 노래의 제목은 무엇이니? B: It's *The Fall*. 그것은 〈The Fall〉이야.
시간·날짜	I'm happy to tell you that we'll have the annual event on May 13, 2017. 2017년 5월 13일에 연례행사를 개최한다는 것을 알려드리게 되어 기쁩니다. We are closed every Sunday. 저희는 일요일마다 문을 닫습니다.
개최 장소	It'll be held at Lake Park next Friday at 8 p.m. 그것은 다음 주 금요일 저녁 8시에 Lake Park에서 열릴 것입니다.
행사 내용	We have a variety of programs including swimming and painting. 수영과 그림 그리기를 포함한 다양한 프로그램들이 있습니다.
참가비	There is a $5 registration fee for sellers. 판매자에게는 5달러의 등록비가 있습니다.
등록 방법	If you are interested, please register through our school website. 관심이 있으시면, 저희 학교 웹사이트를 통해 등록하십시오.
가격	They are $30. 그것들은 30달러입니다.
사이즈	I wear a size 7. 저는 7 사이즈를 신습니다.
색상	How about this pair of green boots? 이 초록색 부츠는 어떠세요?

심정 추론

- 지시문을 읽고, 누구의 심정을 묻는 문제인지 확인한다.
- 화자의 어조에 주목하면서 전체적인 상황과 분위기를 통해 심정을 추론한다.
- 선택지가 영어로 출제되므로 심정을 나타내는 영어 단어를 익혀둔다.

📄 대표 기출

🔊 MP3 유형 07

대화를 듣고, 남자의 심정으로 가장 적절한 것을 고르시오.

① bored   ② jealous   ③ regretful
④ excited   ⑤ surprised

(해결 전략)

- 남자의 심정을 묻는 문제이므로 남자의 말을 주의 깊게 들으세요.
- 남자의 말을 통해 이사한 것을 후회하는 심정을 파악할 수 있어요.

W Hey, Brian. I heard you've moved to a new apartment. Congratulations!

M Well, thanks, but I should have thought about it more 한정 before moving. 정답 단서

W Why? What's the matter?

M I can't sleep well because the heavy traffic makes lots of noise at night.

W Oh, really? That's too bad.

M If I had known that it was going to be noisy like this, I would have never moved here. 정답 단서

W That's a pity. I don't know what to say.

여 이봐, Brian. 네가 새 아파트로 이사했다고 들었어. 축하해!

남 음, 고마워. 하지만 이사 가기 전에 좀 더 생각해 봤어야 했어.

여 왜? 무슨 문제가 있니?

남 밤에 교통 체증으로 소음이 많아서 잠을 잘 못 자.

여 오, 정말? 정말 안됐구나.

남 이렇게 시끄러울 줄 알았더라면, 나는 여기로 절대 이사 오지 않았을 거야.

여 안됐구나. 무슨 말을 해야 할지 모르겠다.

정답 ③

💡 기출문제에 나온 표현

긍정적 심정	happy 행복한	pleased 기쁜	delighted 기쁜	relaxed 여유 있는
	relieved 안도한	excited 신이 난	satisfied 만족하는	thankful 고맙게 생각하는
	That's wonderful. I can't wait! 정말 굉장해. 정말 기다려져!			
	You're very lucky to get it back. 그것을 다시 찾다니 넌 정말 운이 좋구나.			
부정적 심정	bored 지루해하는	frustrated 좌절한	shy 부끄러운	jealous 질투하는
	worried 걱정하는	regretful 후회하는	scared 무서워하는	nervous 초조한
	I should have been more careful. 제가 좀 더 조심했어야 했어요.			
	I wish I hadn't bought them. 내가 그것들을 사지 않았더라면 좋았을 텐데.			
	Oh, no! I can't believe that I made such a big mistake. 아, 안 돼! 제가 그렇게 큰 실수를 했다니 믿을 수가 없어요.			

어색한 대화 찾기

■ 대화를 하나씩 들으면서 자연스러운 대화를 지워 나가다가 끝까지 듣고 나서 답을 고른다.
■ 의문문으로 시작하면 그에 호응하는 응답을 하는지 확인한다.
■ 평서문으로 시작하면 상황에 알맞은 응답을 하는지 확인한다.

📄 대표 기출

🔊 MP3 유형 08

다음을 듣고, 두 사람의 대화가 <u>어색한</u> 것을 고르시오.

①   ②   ③   ④   ⑤

① **W**   I have a terrible headache.

   M   You should go to see a doctor.

② **W**   Michael, it's time to have dinner.

   M   Okay, I'm coming.

③ **W**   Excuse me. How can I get to the station? *정답 단서*

   M   I'm sorry. Our T-shirts are all sold out. *정답 단서*

④ **W**   You played the flute really well.

   M   Thank you. I practiced a lot.

⑤ **W**   Can I talk to you for a minute?

   M   Sure. What is it?

(해결 전략)

• 길을 묻는 표현과 특정 상품이 매진되었다는 응답은 서로 호응하지 않아요.

① **여** 나 두통이 심해.
  남 넌 병원에 가야 해.
② **여** Michael, 저녁 먹을 시간이야.
  남 네, 갈게요.
③ **여** 실례합니다. 역에 어떻게 가야 하나요?
  남 죄송합니다. 저희 티셔츠는 모두 매진됐어요.
④ **여** 넌 플루트를 정말 잘 연주했어.
  남 고마워. 난 많이 연습했어.
⑤ **여** 잠깐 얘기해도 되니?
  남 물론이야. 뭔데?

정답 ③

💡 기출문제에 나온 표현

의문문	A Where can I find men's clothing? 남성복을 어디에서 찾을 수 있나요?
	B It's on the second floor. 2층에 있습니다.
	A How often do you go to the movies? 너는 얼마나 자주 영화를 보러 가니?
	B Once or twice a month. 한 달에 한두 번.
	A Can you take care of my dog this afternoon? 오늘 오후에 내 개를 돌봐 줄 수 있니?
	B I'm afraid I can't. 미안하지만 안 돼.
	A Would you prefer a weekday or weekend? 평일이 좋은가요, 주말이 좋은가요?
	B Anytime will be fine. 아무 때나 괜찮아요.
평서문	A I'd like to exchange this book for a new one. 이 책을 새것으로 바꾸고 싶어요.
	B Is there anything wrong with it? 거기에 무슨 문제라도 있나요?
	A I failed the singing audition again. 나는 노래 오디션에 또 떨어졌어.
	B Don't give up. You'll do better next time. 포기하지 마. 너는 다음번엔 더 잘할 거야.

09 의도 파악

- 지시문을 읽고, 마지막 말을 하는 사람이 누구인지 확인한다.
- 마지막 말에 담긴 의도를 파악하는 문제이므로 특히 마지막 말을 집중해서 들어야 한다.
- 의도를 나타내는 다양한 상황별 표현을 미리 익혀 둔다.

📄 대표 기출

🔊 MP3 유형 09

대화를 듣고, 여자의 마지막 말에 담긴 의도로 가장 적절한 것을 고르시오.

① 동의   ② 충고   ③ 거절   ④ 요청   ⑤ 위로

(해결 전략)

- 마지막 말을 하는 사람이 여자이므로 여자의 말을 주의 깊게 들으세요.
- You can say that again.은 상대방의 말에 동의할 때 쓰는 표현이에요.

M   It seems like everybody has a smartphone these days.

W   Yeah. Even my eight-year-old nephew owns one.

M   Really? Using smartphones is not good for young children's health.

W   Right. I've heard that smartphones can also be harmful to their studies at school.

M   I think parents should limit their children's smartphone use.

W   You can say that again.
       정답 단서

남   요즘 모든 사람들이 스마트폰을 가지고 있는 것 같아.

여   그래. 심지어 여덟 살짜리 내 조카도 하나 가지고 있어.

남   정말? 스마트폰을 사용하는 것은 어린아이들의 건강에 좋지 않아.

여   맞아. 스마트폰은 학교 공부에도 해로울 수 있다고 들었어.

남   난 부모들이 자녀들의 스마트폰 사용을 제한해야 한다고 생각해.

여   동감이야.

정답 ①

💡 기출문제에 나온 표현

동의	You can say that again. 동감이야. I agree (with you). (네 말에) 동의해. That could be a good idea. 좋은 생각이야.
반대	I'm against it. 나는 그것에 반대해. I don't think so. 난 그렇게 생각하지 않아. I don't think that's a good idea. 그것은 좋은 생각이 아닌 것 같아.
거절	I'm afraid not. It would be too late. 난 못 갈 것 같아. 너무 늦을 거거든. I wish I could, but I've already finished my homework. 그러고 싶지만, 난 이미 숙제를 끝마쳤어. I'd love to, but I have to take my mother to the hospital now. 그러고 싶지만, 난 지금 엄마를 모시고 병원에 가야 해.
제안	Why don't you ask her to email it to you? 너에게 그걸 이메일로 보내 달라고 그녀에게 부탁하는 게 어때?
감사	Thank you for the tip. I'll try. 조언 고마워. 노력해 볼게. There couldn't be a better present for me. 저에게 더 좋은 선물은 없을 거예요. I don't know how to thank you enough for your help. 선생님의 도움에 어떻게 감사드려야 충분할지 모르겠어요.
축하	Wow, congratulations! 와, 축하해!

할 일·한 일·부탁한 일 파악

■ 할 일을 묻는 문제는 미래를 나타내는 동사에 유의하여 듣는다.
■ 한 일을 묻는 문제는 과거를 나타내는 동사에 유의하여 듣는다.
■ 부탁한 일을 묻는 문제는 주로 마지막 부분에 부탁하는 내용이 드러나므로 뒷부분을 주의 깊게 듣는다.

📄 **대표 기출**　　　　　　　　🔊 MP3 유형 10

대화를 듣고, 여자가 할 일로 가장 적절한 것을 고르시오.

① 자동차 고치기
② 식료품 구입하기
③ 자동차 청소하기
④ 청소용품 가져가기
⑤ 자동차 주차하기

W　Honey, aren't we supposed to clean our garage today?

M　Oh, I forgot all about it.

W　You told me we could clean it today. Let's do it now. I've already prepared the brushes and towels for cleaning.

M　Sure. Oh, wait! The car is in the garage. I parked it there after returning from the store.

W　Then we can't start until the car is moved outside.

M　Don't worry. I'll move it now.

W　Okay. Then I'll take the cleaning items to the garage.
　　　　　　　　　　　정답 단서

解決 전략

· 여자가 할 일이므로 여자의 말을 주의 깊게 들으세요.
· 할 일은 주로 마지막 부분에 나오므로 끝까지 듣고 나서 답을 고르세요.

여　여보, 오늘 우리 차고를 청소하기로 하지 않았나요?
남　오, 완전히 잊고 있었어요.
여　오늘 우리가 그곳을 청소할 수 있다고 당신이 말했잖아요. 지금 청소해요. 난 벌써 청소하기 위해 빗자루와 타월을 준비했어요.
남　알았어요. 오, 잠깐만요! 차가 차고 안에 있어요. 내가 가게에서 돌아온 후에 그곳에 주차를 했어요.
여　그러면 차가 밖으로 옮겨질 때까지 우리는 시작할 수 없어요.
남　걱정 말아요. 내가 지금 옮길게요.
여　좋아요. 그러면 내가 차고에 청소용품들을 가져갈게요.

정답 ④

💡 **기출문제에 나온 표현**

할 일	A　Sure. Let me get the cake. 물론이야. 내가 케이크를 살게.
	B　Then I'll buy the flowers. 그러면 난 꽃을 살게.
	A　Then why don't you ask her? 그러면 그녀에게 물어보는 게 어때?
	B　Okay, I will. I'm going to see her in class this afternoon. 좋아, 그럴게. 나는 오늘 오후 수업 시간에 그녀를 만날 거야.
한 일	A　What did you do with your friend yesterday? 너는 어제 친구와 무엇을 했니?
	B　We visited the traditional houses in Seoul. 우리는 서울에 있는 전통 가옥들을 방문했어.
부탁한 일	Can you buy some oil from the supermarket? 슈퍼마켓에서 기름 좀 사다 줄래?
	Before you leave, can you feed the cat? 나가기 전에 고양이에게 먹이를 줄 수 있니?
	Could you choose the clothes for the play? 연극 의상 좀 골라 주시겠습니까?
	Could you pass this letter to Susan for me? 저를 위해 이 편지를 Susan에게 전해 주시겠어요?
	I have to return this book today, but I don't have any time. 내가 오늘 이 책을 반납해야 하는데, 시간이 없어.

위치 찾기

- 배치도를 보고, 입구와 각 공간의 위치를 확인한다.
- 제외되는 위치에 표시하면서 대화 속 인물이 최종적으로 선택하는 위치를 답으로 고른다.
- 위치를 나타내는 표현을 미리 익혀 둔다.

대표 기출

🔊 MP3 유형 11

대화를 듣고, 두 사람이 사용할 회의실을 고르시오.

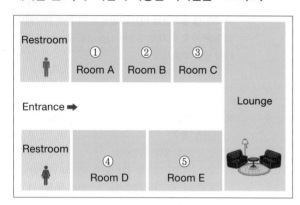

M Mary, which room is good for our meeting this Thursday?

W What about Room D?

M I heard that Robert will use it on that day.

W Hmm... how about using one of the rooms next to the lounge? They're convenient.

M But the lounge is often crowded, so those rooms may be noisy.

W You're right. Then we have two rooms left, Room A and Room B. *정답 단서*

M Let's not use the room next to the restroom. *정답 단서*

W Okay. Let's use this room.

해결 전략

- 두 사람이 사용하지 않기로 한 방을 지워 나가세요.
- 앞부분에서 여러 방을 언급하다가 마지막에 하나의 방을 선택하므로 끝까지 주의 깊게 들으세요.

남 Mary, 이번 주 목요일 우리 회의에 어떤 방이 좋니?

여 D룸은 어때?

남 Robert가 그날 그 방을 쓸 거라고 들었어.

여 음… 라운지 옆에 있는 방들 중 하나를 사용하는 게 어때? 그 방들이 편리해.

남 하지만 라운지는 종종 붐벼. 그래서 그 방들은 시끄러울 수도 있어.

여 네 말이 맞아. 그럼 A룸과 B룸 두 개가 남았어.

남 화장실 옆에 있는 방은 사용하지 말자.

여 알았어. 이 방을 사용하자.

정답 ②

기출문제에 나온 표현

위치	front 앞	back 뒤	near ~ 근처	close to ~에 가까운	far from ~에서 먼
	next to ~ 옆에	central 중앙의	section(area) 구역	site(place) 장소, 곳	

위치 정하기	What about a place next to the pool? 수영장 옆에 있는 곳은 어때?
	What about taking seats near the entrance? 입구 근처 좌석에 앉는 게 어때?
	Then only one section is left. Let's go sit. 그러면 한 구역만 남아. 가서 앉자.
	Let's avoid both sites directly next to the showers. 샤워실 바로 옆에 있는 두 곳은 피하자.
	Unfortunately, the central section is already full. 안타깝게도, 그 중앙 구역은 이미 꽉 찼어.

유형 12 도표 정보 파악

- 다섯 가지 중에서 하나를 고르는 유형과 대화의 내용과 일치하지 않는 선택지를 고르는 유형이 있다.
- 표에 제시된 항목의 순서대로 언급되는 경우가 많으므로 한 번에 한 항목씩 집중하며 듣는다.
- 들은 내용을 하나씩 표시하면서 답을 좁혀 나간다.

📄 대표 기출   🔊 MP3 유형 12

다음 표를 보면서 대화를 듣고, 두 사람이 선택할 수업을 고르시오.

	Class	Time	Food Style	Dessert Making
①	A	9:00 ~ 11:00 a.m.	Italian	×
②	B	9:00 ~ 11:30 a.m.	French	○
③	C	2:00 ~ 4:30 p.m.	Italian	○
④	D	2:00 ~ 4:00 p.m.	Italian	×
⑤	E	2:00 ~ 4:00 p.m.	French	×

해결 전략

- 두 사람이 수업 시간대, 음식의 종류, 후식 만들기 여부를 하나씩 결정할 때마다 표에 표시하세요.
- 끝까지 듣고 나서 모든 항목에 표시된 선택지를 답으로 고르세요.

M Honey, look at this schedule for next Saturday. There are one-day cooking classes.

W Why don't we take a class together? It'll be fun.

M Great. Which do you prefer, a morning or afternoon class?

W An afternoon class. We're going to attend Tom's wedding in the morning. *정답 단서*

M Right. What about learning how to cook Italian food?

W Sounds good. Do you also want to make dessert? *정답 단서*

M Sure. Then let's take this class. *정답 단서*

W Okay.

남 여보, 다음 주 토요일 스케줄 좀 봐요. 일일 요리 수업들이 있어요.

여 함께 수업을 듣는 게 어때요? 재미있을 거예요.

남 좋아요. 오전 수업과 오후 수업 중 어느 것이 더 좋아요?

여 오후 수업이요. 오전에 우리는 Tom의 결혼식에 참석할 거잖아요.

남 맞아요. 이탈리아 음식을 요리하는 법을 배우는 게 어때요?

여 좋아요. 후식도 만들기를 원하나요?

남 물론이죠. 그럼 이 수업을 들어요.

여 좋아요.

정답 ③

💡 기출문제에 나온 표현

시간대 고르기	Wouldn't a two-hour show be too long for us? 우리에게 두 시간짜리 쇼는 너무 길지 않을까? There are one-hour shows at 12 p.m. and 3 p.m. 오후 12시와 오후 3시에 한 시간짜리 쇼가 있어. Let's see the show after lunch. 점심 식사 후에 쇼를 보자.
날짜 고르기	I have a dance class every Wednesday, so I can't take it then. 난 매주 수요일에 댄스 수업이 있어서 그때는 그걸 들을 수 없어.
가격대 고르기	I'll take the cheaper class. 난 더 저렴한 강좌를 들을래. You can get clearer pictures with the more expensive one. 너는 더 비싼 것으로 더 선명한 사진을 얻을 수 있어.

유형

13

화제·주제 파악

- 화제를 묻는 문제는 담화에서 설명하는 'this'가 무엇인지 고르는 문제로, 사물이나 동물의 특징을 종합하여 답을 고른다.
- 주제를 묻는 문제는 주로 앞부분에 주제가 언급되는 경우가 많으므로 처음부터 집중해서 듣는다.

📄 대표 기출

🔊 MP3 유형 13

다음을 듣고, 무엇에 관한 설명인지 고르시오.

① 기린　　　② 독수리　　　③ 타조
④ 사자　　　⑤ 북극곰

W　This is a wild animal, but you can also see it in a zoo. This animal is usually found in Africa. It has long legs and a long neck. This is the largest living animal of its kind. It's a bird, but it cannot fly. It can run very fast at a speed of about 70 kilometers per hour when necessary.

(정답 단서)

(해결 전략)

- Africa, long legs and a long neck, a bird 등 언급된 모든 특징에 해당하는 동물을 답으로 고르세요.
- 중간에 한두 단어만 듣고 답을 고르지 않도록 주의하세요.

여　이것은 야생 동물이지만, 동물원에서도 볼 수 있습니다. 이 동물은 보통 아프리카에서 발견됩니다. 이것은 긴 다리와 긴 목을 가지고 있습니다. 이것은 그 종류 중에서 살아 있는 가장 큰 동물입니다. 이것은 새지만 날 수 없습니다. 이것은 필요한 경우 약 시속 70킬로미터의 속도로 매우 빠르게 달릴 수 있습니다.

정답 ③

💡 기출문제에 나온 표현

화제	헬멧	This is something you wear on your head. 이것은 머리에 쓰는 것이다. You need this when you ride bicycles, explore caves, or skates on ice. 당신은 자전거를 타거나, 동굴을 탐험하거나, 얼음 위에서 스케이트를 탈 때 이것이 필요하다.
	아이스하키	This is a team sport. Players play this on ice with skates on. 이것은 팀 스포츠이다. 선수들은 스케이트를 신고 얼음 위에서 이 경기를 한다.
	체온계	It's used to measure body temperature for medical purposes. 이것은 의학적인 목적으로 체온을 재는 데 사용된다.
	저울	It is a machine for measuring the weight of an object. 이것은 물체의 무게를 재는 기계이다.
주제	수영장 안전 수칙	This is an announcement from the *Green Community Swimming Pool*. Let me tell you three things to follow for your safety. Green Community Swimming Pool에서 알려드립니다. 여러분의 안전을 위해 다음의 세 가지를 말씀 드리겠습니다.
	학교 도서관 휴관	We're sorry to announce that the library will be closed next week from Monday to Wednesday. 도서관이 다음 주 월요일부터 수요일까지 휴관하게 된 것을 알려 드리게 되어 죄송합니다.

숫자 정보 파악

- '지불할 금액'이나 '~할 시각'을 고르는 두 가지 형태로 출제된다.
- 금액을 묻는 문제는 물건의 가격이나 개수, 할인, 쿠폰, 무료 제공 등의 정보를 종합하여 총액을 계산한다.
- 시각을 묻는 문제는 시각 정보가 여러 번 등장하므로 필요한 정보의 시각을 주의 깊게 듣는다.

📄 대표 기출

🔊 MP3 유형 14

대화를 듣고, 남자가 지불할 금액을 고르시오.

① $5   ② $10   ③ $15
④ $20   ⑤ $25

(해결 전략)

- 대여할 자전거 대수, 대여 시간, 가격을 메모하면서 들으세요.
- 헬멧은 무료이고 할인에 대한 정보는 없으므로 앞에서 계산한 금액을 답으로 고르세요.

W   Hello. How may I help you?

M   Hi. I'd like to rent two bicycles. How much are they?

W   Each bicycle is $5. How long are you going to ride?

M   For an hour.

W   Then it's $10 in total.

M   Okay. I need some helmets, too. Do I need to pay extra for them? <small>정답 단서</small>

W   No, they're free. The helmets are over there.

M   Good. Here's my credit card. <small>정답 단서</small>

여   안녕하세요. 무엇을 도와드릴까요?

남   안녕하세요. 자전거 두 대를 빌리고 싶어요. 얼마인가요?

여   자전거당 5달러입니다. 얼마 동안 타실 건가요?

남   1시간 동안요.

여   그러시면 총 10달러입니다.

남   알겠습니다. 헬멧도 필요합니다. 추가 요금을 지불해야 하나요?

여   아니요, 그것들은 무료입니다. 헬멧은 저쪽에 있습니다.

남   좋네요. 여기 제 신용 카드 있습니다.

정답 ②

💡 기출문제에 나온 표현

금액	가격	This is the most popular design and it's just $20. 이것이 가장 인기 있는 디자인인데 겨우 20달러입니다.
		$30 for 10 copies, and $100 for 50 copies. 10장은 30달러이고, 50장은 100달러입니다.
		It's $30 a month, but if you sign up for three months, it's only $70. 한 달에 30달러이지만, 3개월을 등록하시면 단 70달러입니다.
	할인· 무료 제공	We offer you $5 off the total price. 총액에서 5달러 할인해 드립니다.
		You get 10% off if you pay with this card. 이 카드로 결제하시면 10퍼센트 할인해 드립니다.
		Can I use this five-dollar discount coupon? 이 5달러 할인 쿠폰을 사용할 수 있나요?
		If you buy two cups, then you can get an extra one for free. 컵 두 개를 사시면, 추가로 한 개를 무료로 드립니다.
시각		Do you want one seat for 1 p.m.? 오후 1시 좌석 하나를 원하세요?
		Are there any seats available at 1 p.m. then? 그러시면 오후 1시에 좌석이 있나요?
		Please wake me up at 8. 저를 8시에 깨워 주세요.
		I'll book a table for three people at 7 p.m. 오후 7시에 3명 테이블을 예약할게요.
		Doors open at 6 p.m., but the musical begins at 7 p.m. 객석 문은 오후 6시에 열지만, 뮤지컬은 오후 7시에 시작해.

마지막 말에 대한 응답 찾기

- 지시문을 읽고, 마지막 말을 하는 사람이 누구인지 확인한다.
- 각 선택지 문장에서 핵심이 되는 단어를 미리 파악해 둔다.
- 마지막 말에 대한 응답을 찾는 문제이므로 마지막 말을 놓치지 않도록 주의한다.

📑 대표 기출

🔊 MP3 유형 15

대화를 듣고, 남자의 마지막 말에 대한 여자의 응답으로 가장 적절한 것을 고르시오.

Woman: _____

① Sure. I'd love to.
② That's too bad. Cheer up!
③ I didn't mean to bother you.
④ No, that's not my favorite movie.
⑤ You can join our band if you want.

(해결 전략)

- 대화의 흐름을 따라가다가 뒷부분으로 갈수록 남자가 하는 말을 더욱 집중해서 들으세요.
- 남자의 마지막 말이 제안하는 말이므로 수락하거나 거절하는 응답을 답으로 고르세요.

M   Karen, guess what? I watched the movie, *The Joy*, last week.

W   You mean the movie you had asked me to watch together? How was it?

M   Fantastic! The music in the movie was amazing.

W   Oh, I should have joined you. What about the story?

M   The story was touching. In fact, I want to watch the movie again.

W   Really? I'd like to go with you if it's okay.

M   <u>Then why don't we go watch it together?</u>

W   _____ *정답 단서*

남   Karen, 있잖아? 나 지난주에 영화 〈The Joy〉를 봤어.

여   네가 나에게 함께 보자고 말했던 그 영화 말이니? 어땠니?

남   정말 좋았어! 영화 음악이 굉장했어.

여   오, 너와 같이 봤어야 했는데. 이야기는 어땠니?

남   이야기가 감동적이었어. 사실, 나는 그 영화를 또 보고 싶어.

여   정말이니? 괜찮다면 너와 함께 가고 싶어.

남   그러면 함께 보러 가는 게 어때?

여   <u>물론이야. 그리고 싶어.</u>

정답 ①

💡 기출문제에 나온 표현

수락하기	**A** I'd like to take a look around at the comic books. Can I join you? 난 만화책을 둘러보고 싶어. 내가 함께 가도 되니? **B** Why not? Let's go together. 물론이지. 같이 가자.
약속 시간 정하기	**A** Of course. You can come at around 5 o'clock. 물론. 너는 5시쯤에 오면 돼. **B** Okay. See you then. 좋아. 그때 보자.
허락하기	**A** I feel like reading this book. Can I borrow this now? 난 이 책을 읽고 싶어. 내가 지금 이것을 빌려도 되니? **B** Sure. You can take it with you. 물론이야. 네가 가져가도 돼.
동의하기	**A** You should do something to get up early. 너는 일찍 일어나도록 무언가를 해야 해. **B** Right. I need to set the alarm for an earlier time. 맞아. 나는 더 이른 시간에 알람을 맞춰야 해.

상황에 적절한 말 찾기

- 인물이 처한 문제 상황을 듣고, 이를 해결하기 위해 무슨 말을 해야 할지 고르는 문제이다.
- 각 선택지 문장에서 핵심이 되는 단어를 미리 파악해 둔다.
- 상황 설명을 끝까지 듣고 나서 답을 고른다.

📄 대표 기출
🔊 MP3 유형 16

다음 상황 설명을 듣고, Crystal이 Brian에게 할 말로 가장 적절한 것을 고르시오.

Crystal: Brian, _____

① you should read more books.
② don't be late for practice again.
③ stop eating snacks while talking.
④ why don't we take a look at the menu?
⑤ will you go and watch a movie with me?

W　Crystal and Brian are practicing for a singing contest as a team. Their contest is just a week away. Crystal doesn't think that they are ready yet. However, Brian often comes late for practice, and Crystal is unhappy about it. Today, Brian is 30 minutes late again. Crystal is upset about it. So, Crystal decides to tell Brian not to be late for practice again. In this situation, what would Crystal most likely say to Brian?

정답 단서

Crystal　Brian, _____

(해결 전략)

- 앞부분은 Crystal이 어떤 상황에 처해 있는지를 파악하는 데에 집중하세요.
- 뒷부분의 Crystal decides to tell Brian ~.에서 Crystal이 Brian에게 할 말이 무엇일지 드러나요.

여　Crystal과 Brian은 한 팀으로 노래 경연 대회를 위해 연습하고 있다. 그들의 경연 대회는 겨우 1주일 남아 있다. Crystal은 그들이 아직 준비가 되어 있지 않다고 생각한다. 그러나, Brian은 연습에 자주 늦게 오고, Crystal은 그것 때문에 기분이 안 좋다. 오늘. Brian은 또 30분 늦었다. Crystal은 그것 때문에 화가 났다. 그래서, Crystal은 Brian에게 다시는 연습에 늦지 말라고 말하기로 결심한다. 이 상황에서, Crystal은 Brian에게 무엇이라고 말할 것 같은가?

Crystal　Brian, 다시는 연습에 늦지 마.

정답 ②

💡 기출문제에 나온 표현

조언하기	Why don't you take a warm jacket with you? 따뜻한 재킷을 가져가는 게 어때?
위치 묻기	Could you tell me where the music room is? 음악실이 어디에 있는지 알려 주시겠어요? Where can I find a vending machine? 자동판매기는 어디에 있나요?
부탁·요청하기	Could you exchange this bill into coins? 이 지폐를 동전으로 바꿔 주시겠습니까? Would you wrap this necklace for me? 이 목걸이를 포장해 주시겠어요?
도움 주기	Hey, wait! It is out of order. 이봐요, 기다리세요! 그것은 고장 났어요. I'm afraid you forgot your sunglasses. 선글라스를 잊으신 것 같아요.
사과하기	I apologize for the late response. 답변이 늦어서 죄송합니다.
위로하기	Cheer up! You will do better next time. 기운 내! 다음번엔 더 잘할 거야.

PART

2

실전
모의고사
01-18회

01 대화를 듣고, 여자가 구입할 커튼을 고르시오.

①   ②   ③

④   ⑤

02 대화를 듣고, 새 TV 프로그램에 관해 언급되지 <u>않은</u> 것을 고르시오.

① 방송 채널   ② 진행자
③ 내용   ④ 첫 방송 요일
⑤ 방송 시간대

03 대화를 듣고, 여자가 남자에게 전화한 목적으로 가장 적절한 것을 고르시오.

① 대회 참가를 취소하려고
② 대회 준비물을 문의하려고
③ 대회 수상 사실을 알리려고
④ 대회 등록 방법을 문의하려고
⑤ 대회 참가 신청 여부를 확인하려고

04 대화를 듣고, 두 사람이 만나기로 한 시각을 고르시오.

① 6:00 p.m.   ② 6:30 p.m.   ③ 7:00 p.m.
④ 7:30 p.m.   ⑤ 8:00 p.m.

05 대화를 듣고, 두 사람이 대화하는 장소로 가장 적절한 곳을 고르시오.

① 극장   ② 오락실   ③ 야구장
④ 운동용품점   ⑤ 버스 정류장

06 다음 그림의 상황에 가장 적절한 대화를 고르시오.

① ② ③ ④ ⑤

07 대화를 듣고, 남자가 여자에게 부탁한 일로 가장 적절한 것을 고르시오.

① 전화 걸기   ② 탁자 옮기기
③ 물건 정리하기   ④ 휴대 전화 찾기
⑤ 휴대 전화 빌려주기

08 다음을 듣고, 바다 축제에 관해 언급되지 <u>않은</u> 것을 고르시오.

① 개최 장소   ② 개최 기간
③ 입장권 가격   ④ 입장권 구입 방법
⑤ 행사 내용

09 다음을 듣고, 무엇에 관한 설명인지 고르시오.

① 모자   ② 장갑   ③ 귀마개
④ 마스크   ⑤ 체온계

10 다음을 듣고, 두 사람의 대화가 <u>어색한</u> 것을 고르시오.

① ② ③ ④ ⑤

11 대화를 듣고, 여자가 할 일로 가장 적절한 것을 고르시오.

① 주차 연습하기   ② 이메일 보내기
③ 호텔 예약하기   ④ 여행 계획 세우기
⑤ 웹 사이트 확인하기

12 다음 표를 보면서 대화를 듣고, 두 사람이 선택할 수업을 고르시오.

	Time	Level	Day
①	9:00~9:50 a.m.	Advanced	Saturday
②	10:00~10:50 a.m.	Advanced	Saturday
③	11:00~11:50 a.m.	Advanced	Sunday
④	2:00~2:50 p.m.	Beginner	Saturday
⑤	3:00~3:50 p.m.	Beginner	Sunday

13 대화를 듣고, 남자의 생일을 고르시오.

① 7월 8일   ② 7월 9일   ③ 7월 10일
④ 7월 17일   ⑤ 7월 18일

14 대화를 듣고, 남자가 대화 전에 한 일로 가장 적절한 것을 고르시오.

① 약 먹기   ② 샤워하기
③ 간식 먹기   ④ 커피 마시기
⑤ 따뜻한 우유 마시기

15 다음을 듣고, 방송의 목적으로 가장 적절한 것을 고르시오.

① 글쓰기 강좌를 개최하려고
② 새로운 서점을 홍보하려고
③ 작가 초청 행사를 알리려고
④ 신간 도서 목록을 소개하려고
⑤ 유명 인사 초청 강연을 알리려고

16 대화를 듣고, 남자가 지불할 금액을 고르시오.

① $5   ② $10   ③ $15
④ $20   ⑤ $30

17 대화를 듣고, 여자의 마지막 말에 대한 남자의 응답으로 가장 적절한 것을 고르시오.

Man: _____

① Sure. I will tell you later.
② You shouldn't have done that.
③ Please tell me how to make it.
④ I wish you the best of luck with that.
⑤ Thank you for giving me another chance.

18 대화를 듣고, 남자의 마지막 말에 대한 여자의 응답으로 가장 적절한 것을 고르시오.

Woman: _____

① It's a great pleasure to meet you.
② Is it possible to change the topic?
③ Cheer up! You'll do better the next time.
④ I have no time now. How about after school tomorrow?
⑤ Don't forget to finish your book by tomorrow.

19 대화를 듣고, 여자의 마지막 말에 대한 남자의 응답으로 가장 적절한 것을 고르시오.

Man: _____

① Cheer up! You can do better.
② It's wrong to talk loudly here.
③ Why not? You're welcome any time.
④ Make sure you always do your best.
⑤ I'm surprised that you came to see me.

20 다음 상황 설명을 듣고, Kate가 종업원에게 할 말로 가장 적절한 것을 고르시오.

Kate: _____

① Can I pay by credit card?
② Could I have a receipt, please?
③ Can I book a table for four tonight?
④ Could you pack up these leftovers, please?
⑤ Will I be able to get a refund on this pizza?

Dictation 01회

받아쓰기용

01 그림 정보 파악

대화를 듣고, 여자가 구입할 커튼을 고르시오.

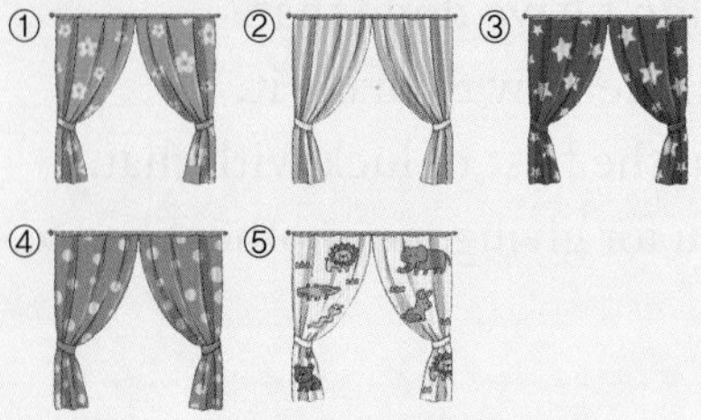

Sound Clear ☆ **a lot of**

[t]가 모음 사이에서 약화되고 뒤 단어의 모음과 연음되어 [얼라러브]로 발음된다.

M Hi. How can I help you?
W Hi. ________ ________ ________ curtains for my daughter's room.
M Okay. Well, how about these curtains with a lot of stars?
W They look nice, but her last curtains had stars, too. ________ ________ ________ ________.
M I see. Then I recommend these with stripes or these with flowers.
W I prefer simple patterns. I'll take the curtains with stripes.
M Good choice. Please ________ ________ ________ ________ you need here.

02 언급되지 않은 것 찾기

대화를 듣고, 새 TV 프로그램에 관해 언급되지 않은 것을 고르시오.

① 방송 채널　② 진행자
③ 내용　④ 첫 방송 요일
⑤ 방송 시간대

W ________ ________ ________ ________ the new TV program starting soon on channel KNT?
M Oh, you mean the program hosted by Ken Kim, right?
W That's right. It's a program ________ ________ ________ ________ of K-pop stars in their homes.
M Sounds very interesting. When is it going to start?
W Next Wednesday. I ________ ________ ________ ________.
M Same here. I'm sure many teenagers will love this program.
W I guess you're right.

03 목적 파악

대화를 듣고, 여자가 남자에게 전화한 목적으로 가장 적절한 것을 고르시오.

① 대회 참가를 취소하려고
② 대회 준비물을 문의하려고
③ 대회 수상 사실을 알리려고
④ 대회 등록 방법을 문의하려고
⑤ 대회 참가 신청 여부를 확인하려고

(*Telephone rings.*)
M Smart Learning Center. How can I help you?
W Hi. ________ ________ ________ ________ for the math contest last week, but I couldn't find my name on the list of participants.
M Oh, really? ________ ________ ________ ________ ________?
W Anna Choi.
M Okay. (*Pause*) Your name is on the list that we have.
W Whew, that's a relief. I guess ________ ________ ________ ________.
M Yes, I think so.
W Sorry for the inconvenience.

04 숫자 정보 파악 ✳

대화를 듣고, 두 사람이 만나기로 한 시각을 고르시오.

① 6:00 p.m.　　② 6:30 p.m.
③ 7:00 p.m.　　④ 7:30 p.m.
⑤ 8:00 p.m.

Sound Clear ☆ **What's up?**
앞 단어의 끝 자음과 뒤 단어의 모음이 만나 연음되어 [왓첩] 또는 [왓썹]으로 발음된다.

(*Cellphone rings.*)

M Hello, Mina. It's me, Sam.
W Oh, hi, Sam. What's up?
M I'm going to the hip-hop concert this Saturday. Do you want to go there together?
W That would be great. What time and _____ _____ _____ _____?
M The concert starts at 8. _____ _____ _____ at 7:30 near the ticket office? 함정
W Well, why don't we meet earlier and eat dinner together _____ _____ _____?
M Sounds good. Then what about at 6:30? 정답 단서
W Okay, see you then.

05 장소 추론

대화를 듣고, 두 사람이 대화하는 장소로 가장 적절한 곳을 고르시오.

① 극장　　② 오락실
③ 야구장　　④ 운동용품점
⑤ 버스 정류장

M Claire, why are you so late? You've missed _____ _____ _____ _____ _____.
W Sorry. I _____ _____ _____. What's the score?
M Three to one. Our team is winning now. Player number four is batting extremely well.
W Great! I hope our team will win today's game.
M Me, too. _____ _____ _____ _____ when our team lost yesterday.
W Don't worry. Our pitcher is the best.
M Right. He throws the fastest ball in the world.
W Look! He just _____ _____ _____ _____!

06 그림의 상황에 적절한 대화 찾기

다음 그림의 상황에 가장 적절한 대화를 고르시오.

① ② ③ ④ ⑤

① W Are you _____ _____ _____ _____?
　 M Of course, I love it.
② W Do you like _____ _____ _____?
　 M Yes, I'm interested in playing it.
③ W Excuse me. Where is the bathroom?
　 M It's _____ _____ _____.
④ W Can I send my luggage to Incheon?
　 M Okay, let me help you with that.
⑤ W Where can I _____ _____ _____ to the city center?
　 M There's a bus stop in front of gate number 7. 정답 단서

07 부탁한 일 파악

대화를 듣고, 남자가 여자에게 부탁한 일로 가장 적절한 것을 고르시오.

① 전화 걸기 ② 탁자 옮기기
③ 물건 정리하기 ④ 휴대 전화 찾기
⑤ 휴대 전화 빌려주기

W Peter, what are you looking for?
M I'm looking for my cellphone. I don't know ________ ________ ________.
W Don't you remember where you put it?
M I thought I ________ ________ ________ ________ ________ after calling Jiho, but it's not there.
W Did you look anywhere else?
M Sure. Well, can you call me? (정답 단서) Then I think I can hear it ring.
W No problem. ________ ________ ________.

08 언급되지 않은 것 찾기

다음을 듣고, 바다 축제에 관해 언급되지 않은 것을 고르시오.

① 개최 장소 ② 개최 기간
③ 입장권 가격 ④ 입장권 구입 방법
⑤ 행사 내용

M Hello, everyone. This year, the city of Busan is celebrating its 12th Sea Festival at Haeundae Beach! (정답 단서) This festival ________ ________ ________ from July 19 to 30. (정답 단서) You can buy tickets online at www.sfestival.org. (정답 단서) There will be ________ ________ ________ such as a jazz concert, a dance contest, and a fishing trip. (정답 단서) Come and ________ ________ ________ at the Sea Festival!

09 화제 파악

다음을 듣고, 무엇에 관한 설명인지 고르시오.

① 모자 ② 장갑 ③ 귀마개
④ 마스크 ⑤ 체온계

Sound Clear ☆ **breathe**
breathe(숨을 쉬다)는 [브리드]로, breath(숨)는 [브레쓰]로 발음된다.

W This is a useful thing when you ________ ________ ________ ________. As you know, in order to get better, ________ ________ ________ ________ ________ not to breathe☆ in cold air. This can help you get well because it keeps cold air from reaching your throat. Therefore, you can ________ ________ ________ even though you are outside. Also, this can be helpful in ________ ________ ________ ________ spreading to others.

10 어색한 대화 찾기

다음을 듣고, 두 사람의 대화가 어색한 것을 고르시오.

① ② ③ ④ ⑤

① **M** Can you ________ ________ ________ ________?
W I'm sorry, but I'm very busy.
② **M** What's your plan for this year?
W I'm thinking of studying Chinese.
③ **M** Do you mind if I ________ ________ ________?
W Not at all. Go ahead.
④ **M** I'm afraid you can't take pictures in here.
W I really ________ ________ ________.
⑤ **M** I have an important test tomorrow.
W I'll ________ ________ ________ ________ for you.

11 할 일 파악

대화를 듣고, 여자가 할 일로 가장 적절한 것을 고르시오.

① 주차 연습하기 ② 이메일 보내기
③ 호텔 예약하기 ④ 여행 계획 세우기
⑤ 웹 사이트 확인하기

M Somi, are the preparations for your trip going well?
W Well, everything is fine _____ _____ _____.
M Oh, what's the problem?
W I'm going to _____ _____ _____ for the trip, but I'm not sure if the hotel _____ _____ _____ _____ _____.
M Did you check the website?
W I did, but _____ _____ _____ _____ about it.
M Then why don't you send an email to the hotel?
W That's a great idea. I'll send an email right now.

12 도표 정보 파악

다음 표를 보면서 대화를 듣고, 두 사람이 선택할 수업을 고르시오.

	Time	Level	Day
①	9:00~9:50 a.m.	Advanced	Saturday
②	10:00~10:50 a.m.	Advanced	Saturday
③	11:00~11:50 a.m.	Advanced	Sunday
④	2:00~2:50 p.m.	Beginner	Saturday
⑤	3:00~3:50 p.m.	Beginner	Sunday

Sound Clear ☆ **schedule**
미국식은 [스케쥴]로, 영국식은 [셰쥴]로 발음된다.

M Jisu, I have the schedule for swimming lessons at our city community center.
W Really? Let's look at it together.
M _____ _____ _____ _____, a morning or an afternoon lesson?
W A morning lesson is better, but there are _____ _____ _____ in the morning.
M Then we can choose an afternoon lesson for beginners.
W Yeah, I think so. Which day is _____ _____ _____, Saturday or Sunday?
M As for me, Saturday is better. How about you?
W Me, too. _____ _____ _____ _____ on Sundays.

13 특정 정보 파악

대화를 듣고, 남자의 생일을 고르시오.

① 7월 8일 ② 7월 9일 ③ 7월 10일
④ 7월 17일 ⑤ 7월 18일

W Hi, Woojin. I _____ _____ _____ _____ _____.
M Why?
W Well, I'm so sorry that I _____ _____ _____.
M What do you mean?
W Yesterday was your birthday, but _____ _____ _____.
M What are you talking about? My birthday hasn't come yet.
W Really? Then _____ _____ _____ on July 8?
M I'm not sure. But mine is tomorrow.
W Oh, sorry. I thought it was yesterday.

14 한 일 파악

대화를 듣고, 남자가 대화 전에 한 일로 가장 적절한 것을 고르시오.

① 약 먹기 ② 샤워하기
③ 간식 먹기 ④ 커피 마시기
⑤ 따뜻한 우유 마시기

Sound Clear ☆ **at all**
[t]는 모음 사이에서 약화되고 뒤 단어의 모음과 연음되어 [애롤]로 발음된다.

W Jacob, it's already 11 p.m. Aren't you going to bed?
M ________ ________ ________ at all.
W Did you drink some coffee?
M No, you know I don't like coffee.
W Well, how about ________ ________ ________ ________? It'll make you relax.
M I already took one.
W Then why don't you drink some hot milk? I've heard that ________ ________ ________ ________ ________.
M Okay, I'll try that right now.

15 목적 파악

다음을 듣고, 방송의 목적으로 가장 적절한 것을 고르시오.

① 글쓰기 강좌를 개최하려고
② 새로운 서점을 홍보하려고
③ 작가 초청 행사를 알리려고
④ 신간 도서 목록을 소개하려고
⑤ 유명 인사 초청 강연을 알리려고

M Hello, book lovers. One of the world's ________ ________ ________ Andrew Lee will visit our bookstore next Tuesday, at 3 p.m. This is an event to ________ ________ ________ ________, *A Peaceful Mind*. First, he will be signing copies of the book. After that, he will read his favorite parts of the book to visitors who registered on our website ________ ________. Thank you.

16 숫자 정보 파악

대화를 듣고, 남자가 지불할 금액을 고르시오.

① $5 ② $10 ③ $15
④ $20 ⑤ $30

M I'd like to buy a stuffed animal for my 5-year-old niece.
W How about ________ ________ ________? It's very popular among that age group and it's only $10.
M It's cute, but she already ________ ________ ________ ________.
W Then what about this elephant? You can get one for free if you buy one.
M Oh, it's cute, too. How much is it?
W It's $15.
M ________ ________ ________ I expected. I'll buy two.
W Well, remember you only need to pay for one.
M Oh, that's right. Thanks.

17 마지막 말에 대한 응답 찾기

대화를 듣고, 여자의 마지막 말에 대한 남자의 응답으로 가장 적절한 것을 고르시오.

Man: ____________________

① Sure. I will tell you later.
② You shouldn't have done that.
③ Please tell me how to make it.
④ I wish you the best of luck with that.
⑤ Thank you for giving me another chance.

W Noah, you didn't ________ ________ ________.
M Mom, what do you mean?
W Don't you remember? You promised to hang your jacket in the closet ________ ________ ________ ________ on the floor.
M Oh, I totally forgot about it. I'm so sorry.
W It's too late. ________ ________ ________ ________, I'm not going to give you any allowance for two weeks.
M Mom, please let it go just this once.
W (*Sighs*) Okay, but remember this will be the last time.
M Thank you for giving me another chance.

18 마지막 말에 대한 응답 찾기

대화를 듣고, 남자의 마지막 말에 대한 여자의 응답으로 가장 적절한 것을 고르시오.

Woman: _____

① It's a great pleasure to meet you.
② Is it possible to change the topic?
③ Cheer up! You'll do better the next time.
④ I have no time now. How about after school tomorrow?
⑤ Don't forget to finish your book by tomorrow.

Sound Clear ☆ **the end**
모음 앞의 the는 [디]로 발음해서 [디엔드]로 발음된다.

M Minji, _____ _____ _____ _____ _____ _____!
W Me? For what?
M You know there will be a science fair, right?
W Yes, at the end of the month.
M Will you _____ _____ _____ _____ _____?
W Yes, of course. I'd love to. Do you have a project topic yet?
M Actually, I haven't decided yet. Why don't we go to the library and _____ _____ _____ _____ _____?
W I have no time now. How about after school tomorrow?

---

19 마지막 말에 대한 응답 찾기

대화를 듣고, 여자의 마지막 말에 대한 남자의 응답으로 가장 적절한 것을 고르시오.

Man: _____

① Cheer up! You can do better.
② It's wrong to talk loudly here.
③ Why not? You're welcome any time.
④ Make sure you always do your best.
⑤ I'm surprised that you came to see me.

(*Cellphone rings.*)
M Hello?
W Hello, Mr. Jones. This is Rachel, your student from last year. _____ _____ _____ _____ _____?
M Of course! Is there anything wrong, Rachel?
W No, I was just looking at some pictures of my middle school days, and they _____ _____ _____ _____.
M I see. So how's everything going? Are you doing well in high school?
W Pretty well. _____ _____ _____ _____, can I drop by your office some time? I would like to say hi.
M Why not? You're welcome any time.

---

20 상황에 적절한 말 찾기

다음 상황 설명을 듣고, Kate가 종업원에게 할 말로 가장 적절한 것을 고르시오.

Kate: _____

① Can I pay by credit card?
② Could I have a receipt, please?
③ Can I book a table for four tonight?
④ Could you pack up these leftovers, please?
⑤ Will I be able to get a refund on this pizza?

W Kate and her friend are having dinner at a popular Italian restaurant. Now Kate understands why the restaurant is so popular because both of them _____ _____ _____ _____ the taste of the food and its friendly service. But they _____ _____ _____ _____ and they can't finish their pizza. Since it is very delicious, Kate _____ _____ _____ _____ _____ if she can take it home. In this situation, what would Kate most likely say to the waiter?
Kate Could you pack up these leftovers, please?

01 대화를 듣고, 여자가 구입할 선물을 고르시오.

①
②
③
④
⑤

02 대화를 듣고, 남자가 추천하는 음식점에 관해 언급되지 <u>않은</u> 것을 고르시오.

① 이름   ② 음식의 가격   ③ 메뉴
④ 위치   ⑤ 주차장

03 대화를 듣고, 남자가 전화한 목적으로 가장 적절한 것을 고르시오.

① 주문을 확인하려고
② 제품을 홍보하려고
③ 배송 일정을 변경하려고
④ 배송이 완료되었음을 알리려고
⑤ 부재 시 경비실에 물건을 맡기려고

04 대화를 듣고, 두 사람이 만날 시각을 고르시오.

① 3:00 p.m.   ② 3:30 p.m.   ③ 7:10 p.m.
④ 7:40 p.m.   ⑤ 10:00 p.m.

05 대화를 듣고, 두 사람이 대화하는 장소로 가장 적절한 곳을 고르시오.

① 식당   ② 공항   ③ 극장
④ 서점   ⑤ 백화점

06 다음 그림의 상황에 가장 적절한 대화를 고르시오.

①   ②   ③   ④   ⑤

07 대화를 듣고, 여자가 남자에게 부탁한 일로 가장 적절한 것을 고르시오.

① 우산 고치기   ② 짐 함께 싸기
③ 준비물 구입하기   ④ 일기 예보 확인하기
⑤ 체험 학습 같이 가기

08 다음을 듣고, 학교 자선 행사에 관해 언급되지 <u>않은</u> 것을 고르시오.

① 개최 요일   ② 행사 시간
③ 목표 모금액   ④ 판매 물품 제출 기한
⑤ 수익금 사용 방법

09 다음을 듣고, 무엇에 관한 설명인지 고르시오.

① 하마   ② 기린   ③ 판다
④ 코끼리   ⑤ 코알라

10 다음을 듣고, 두 사람의 대화가 <u>어색한</u> 것을 고르시오.

①   ②   ③   ④   ⑤

11 대화를 듣고, 여자가 할 일로 가장 적절한 것을 고르시오.

① 표 환불하기　　② 영화 예매하기
③ 보고서 작성하기　④ 보고서 제출하기
⑤ 영화 시간 알아보기

12 다음 표를 보면서 대화를 듣고, 여자가 구입할 e-book reader를 고르시오.

	Model	Screen Size	Weight	Price
①	E-220	14×9(cm)	150g	$120
②	E-250	15×10(cm)	160g	$140
③	E-320	16×11(cm)	170g	$180
④	R-115	16×12(cm)	180g	$200
⑤	R-300	18×13(cm)	190g	$230

13 대화를 듣고, 두 사람이 만날 요일을 고르시오.

① 수요일　　② 목요일　　③ 금요일
④ 토요일　　⑤ 일요일

14 대화를 듣고, 남자가 대화 직후에 할 일로 가장 적절한 것을 고르시오.

① 노래 듣기　　② 춤 연습하기
③ 친구 응원하기　④ 음악 작곡하기
⑤ 대회 참가 신청하기

15 다음을 듣고, 방송의 목적으로 가장 적절한 것을 고르시오.

① 연령별 수면 패턴을 조사하려고
② 건강에 좋은 운동을 소개하려고
③ 숙면을 위한 제품을 홍보하려고
④ 수면과 건강의 관계를 알리려고
⑤ 수면의 질을 높이는 방법을 알리려고

16 대화를 듣고, 남자가 지불할 금액을 고르시오.

① $45　　② $46　　③ $50
④ $52　　⑤ $54

17 대화를 듣고, 여자의 마지막 말에 대한 남자의 응답으로 가장 적절한 것을 고르시오.

Man: _____

① You're learning quickly.
② Let me check your order.
③ Okay. We'll send someone then.
④ Sorry. I don't trust you any more.
⑤ Please forgive me. I didn't mean it.

18 대화를 듣고, 남자의 마지막 말에 대한 여자의 응답으로 가장 적절한 것을 고르시오.

Woman: _____

① Sorry, it's all my fault.
② I'm pleased to meet you.
③ Not really. Even I can do it.
④ I have no idea what to do now.
⑤ There's nothing to get angry about.

19 대화를 듣고, 여자의 마지막 말에 대한 남자의 응답으로 가장 적절한 것을 고르시오.

Man: _____

① I can't wait to get a new job.
② All right. I did it all on my own.
③ You had better go back to sleep soon.
④ I recommend that you leave right now.
⑤ I know. I won't let the same thing happen again.

20 다음 상황 설명을 듣고, Jiho가 Lisa에게 할 말로 가장 적절한 것을 고르시오.

Jiho: Lisa, _____

① I'm sorry to hear that.
② don't forget to bring your book.
③ why don't you listen to your friend?
④ can you please turn down the volume?
⑤ if I were you, I would stop complaining.

01 그림 정보 파악

대화를 듣고, 여자가 구입할 선물을 고르시오.

① ② ③
④ ⑤

M Have you decided what to buy for Somi's birthday?
W Not yet. I'm still not sure _____ _____ _____.
M How about this striped cap? She likes this pattern.
W Well, she already has a lot of caps. (한정)
M Umm... what about that T-shirt _____ _____ _____ _____ _____? It looks cute.
W But it's long-sleeved. I think a short-sleeved one will be better 정답 단서
because it's already summer.
M Then you can buy this one with a rabbit on it. 정답 단서
W Good! She likes rabbits. _____ _____ _____ _____.

02 언급되지 않은 것 찾기 🧩

대화를 듣고, 남자가 추천하는 음식점에 관해 언급되지 <u>않은</u> 것을 고르시오.

① 이름 ② 음식의 가격 ③ 메뉴
④ 위치 ⑤ 주차장

W Jaemin, do you know a good Korean restaurant?
M Sure, I know a good place called Korean Garden.
W Oh, _____ _____ _____ _____ there?
M *Bibimbap*, *bulgogi*, *pajeon*, and almost every other Korean dish.
W Sounds delicious. _____ _____ _____ _____ where it is?
M It's across from the police station.
W Is parking available?
M You _____ _____ _____ _____ _____ parking. It has a huge parking lot.

03 목적 파악

대화를 듣고, 남자가 전화한 목적으로 가장 적절한 것을 고르시오.

① 주문을 확인하려고
② 제품을 홍보하려고
③ 배송 일정을 변경하려고
④ 배송이 완료되었음을 알리려고
⑤ 부재 시 경비실에 물건을 맡기려고

Sound Clear ☆ **water**
[t]가 모음 사이에서 약화되어 [워러]로 발음된다.

(Telephone rings.)
M Hello? This is Pure Water Company. Is this Ms. Brown?
W Yes. _____ _____ _____ _____ _____?
M I scheduled my water delivery for tomorrow.
W Is there a problem?
M Yes, I _____ _____ _____ _____ _____. Can I have it delivered the day after tomorrow?
W Sure. That shouldn't be a problem.
M Thank you. Is 5:30 okay?
W _____ _____ _____. I'll be home all day.
M Okay. Your delivery date has been changed. 정답 단서

04 숫자 정보 파악

대화를 듣고, 두 사람이 만날 시각을 고르시오.

① 3:00 p.m.　　② 3:30 p.m.
③ 7:10 p.m.　　④ 7:40 p.m.
⑤ 10:00 p.m.

W　Hey, they're showing *Beyond the Sky* at the MJ Theater.
M　Is that the movie about some explorers traveling through space?
W　Right. _____ _____ _____ _____. Do you want to watch it with me tomorrow?
M　Okay. When do you want to watch it?
W　The movie times are 3:30, 7:40, and 10:00 p.m. _____ _____ _____ _____?
M　Let's take the earliest. I must be home before dinner.
W　Okay. Then why don't we meet there 30 minutes _____ _____ _____ _____?
M　Okay. See you then.

05 장소 추론 🎌

대화를 듣고, 두 사람이 대화하는 장소로 가장 적절한 곳을 고르시오.

① 식당　　② 공항　　③ 극장
④ 서점　　⑤ 백화점

Sound Clear ☆ **flight**
gh가 묵음이라서 [플라잇]으로 발음된다.

M　We've arrived too soon. There's a lot of time left.
W　Yeah, our flight doesn't leave _____ _____ _____ _____.
M　What will we do for two hours?
W　_____ _____ _____ _____ a snack before boarding?
M　No, I'm okay.
W　Then how about doing some duty-free shopping?
M　Good idea. _____ _____ _____ _____ for my family at a duty-free shop. Let's go.

06 그림의 상황에 적절한 대화 찾기

다음 그림의 상황에 가장 적절한 대화를 고르시오.

①　②　③　④　⑤

① W　Whose notebook is this?
　 M　It's my sister's.
② W　Why are you so upset?
　 M　My team _____ _____ _____.
③ W　Do you mind if I close the window?
　 M　No, go ahead. 정답 단서
④ W　Do you know _____ _____ _____ _____ _____?
　 M　I'm not sure, but I think Tom did.
⑤ W　_____ _____ _____ _____, summer or winter?
　 M　I prefer winter.

07 부탁한 일 파악

대화를 듣고, 여자가 남자에게 부탁한 일로 가장 적절한 것을 고르시오.

① 우산 고치기　　② 짐 함께 싸기
③ 준비물 구입하기　　④ 일기 예보 확인하기
⑤ 체험 학습 같이 가기

M　Lily, are you excited about your field trip tomorrow?
W　Of course. _____ _____ _____.
M　Is everything ready now?
W　Yes, Dad. I think I _____ _____ _____ that I need.
M　Did you pack your umbrella, too?
W　Well, I'm not sure if _____ _____ _____ _____. Can you please check the weather forecast?
M　Okay, 정답 단서 _____ _____ _____.

08   언급되지 않은 것 찾기

다음을 듣고, 학교 자선 행사에 관해 언급되지 않은 것을 고르시오.

① 개최 요일   ② 행사 시간
③ 목표 모금액   ④ 판매 물품 제출 기한
⑤ 수익금 사용 방법

W Hello, students. I'd like to tell you about an annual event at our school, the Charity Sale. _____ _____ _____ _____ _____ this coming Friday, from 2 p.m. to 5 p.m. If you _____ _____ _____ _____ and sell your things for charity, please bring them to your homeroom teacher by Wednesday. All the profits from the sale will go to _____ _____ _____ in our town. So let's enjoy the event and help others together!

정답 단서 *정답 단서* *정답 단서*

09   화제 파악

다음을 듣고, 무엇에 관한 설명인지 고르시오.

① 하마   ② 기린   ③ 판다
④ 코끼리   ⑤ 코알라

M This is a cute animal loved by _____ _____ _____ _____ _____. It's a large animal and it has black and white fur. It likes to eat bamboo and climb trees. It also _____ _____ _____ _____ the forest. You can see this animal especially in China, and it's _____ _____ _____ _____ people visit China.

10   어색한 대화 찾기

다음을 듣고, 두 사람의 대화가 어색한 것을 고르시오.

①   ②   ③   ④   ⑤

① **M** What are you going to do tomorrow?
   W I'm going to go fishing.
② **M** _____ _____ _____ _____ your new car?
   W I'm glad you like it.
③ **M** I think _____ _____ _____, _____ _____?
   W Yeah, I met him at your birthday party last year.
④ **M** Can you tell me _____ _____ _____ _____ the train station?
   W Go straight one block and turn left.
⑤ **M** _____ _____ _____! You can do it!
   W Thanks. I'll try again.

11   할 일 파악

대화를 듣고, 여자가 할 일로 가장 적절한 것을 고르시오.

① 표 환불하기   ② 영화 예매하기
③ 보고서 작성하기   ④ 보고서 제출하기
⑤ 영화 시간 알아보기

Sound Clear ☆ **sold out**
앞 단어의 끝 자음과 뒤 단어의 첫 모음이 만나 연음되어 [솔다웃]으로 발음된다.

M Sarah, you look excited today.
W Yeah, _____ _____ _____ _____ _____ Chris Choi's new movie in the theater today.
M Did you already _____ _____ _____?
W Sure, I got it a week ago. Tickets are almost sold out at every theater.
M That's because he has a lot of fans. Are you _____ _____ _____ _____ _____?
W Yes, I'm going to the theater after submitting this report.
M Okay, have fun!

정답 단서

12 도표 정보 파악

다음 표를 보면서 대화를 듣고, 여자가 구입할 e-book reader를 고르시오.

	Model	Screen Size	Weight	Price
①	E-220	14×9(cm)	150g	$120
②	E-250	15×10(cm)	160g	$140
③	E-320	16×11(cm)	170g	$180
④	R-115	16×12(cm)	180g	$200
⑤	R-300	18×13(cm)	190g	$230

Sound Clear ☆ **model**

'모델'은 실제로 [마들]로 발음된다.

W Hi. I'd like to buy an e-book reader.
M Okay, do you have any specific model _____ ?
W Not really, but I'd _____ _____ _____ _____ .
M How about the E-320 model? It's only 170 grams, and the screen is a good size.
W I like it, but it's a little expensive for me. I would like something under $150.
M Then _____ _____ _____ _____ the E-220 model. It's very popular these days.
W I think the screen is _____ _____ . I'll take the next model with a larger screen.

13 특정 정보 파악 ✳

대화를 듣고, 두 사람이 만날 요일을 고르시오.

① 수요일 ② 목요일 ③ 금요일
④ 토요일 ⑤ 일요일

M Excuse me. Did you go to Daehan High School?
W Yes, were you in Mr. Smith's class?
M Yes, it's me, James! _____ _____ , _____ _____ .
W Wow! You haven't changed a bit. Do you have _____ _____ _____ _____ _____ ?
M I'd love to, but I'm busy now. How about meeting next week?
W Sounds great. Any day is fine except Thursday. How about next Saturday?
M I need to _____ _____ _____ _____ that day. What about Friday afternoon?
W Good, let me know your phone number. _____ _____ _____ before then.

14 할 일 파악

대화를 듣고, 남자가 대화 직후에 할 일로 가장 적절한 것을 고르시오.

① 노래 듣기   ② 춤 연습하기
③ 친구 응원하기 ④ 음악 작곡하기
⑤ 대회 참가 신청하기

W Harry, I saw a poster for a contest which is _____ _____ _____ .
M What do you mean by perfect for me?
W It's a singing contest for middle school students. _____ _____ _____ to enter one.
M Really? Tell me more.
W It's going to be held on May 17, and first prize is $100.
M Wow! I should practice harder.
W Oh, and one more thing! You _____ _____ _____ by today.
M Okay, I'll do it right now.

15 목적 파악

다음을 듣고, 방송의 목적으로 가장 적절한 것을 고르시오.

① 연령별 수면 패턴을 조사하려고
② 건강에 좋은 운동을 소개하려고
③ 숙면을 위한 제품을 홍보하려고
④ 수면과 건강의 관계를 알리려고
⑤ 수면의 질을 높이는 방법을 알리려고

W Good morning, everybody. Welcome back to *One-minute Health*. Do you _____ _____ _____ _____ _____ after you wake up? If you want to improve the quality of your sleep, please listen to my suggestions carefully. First, _____ _____ _____ _____ at night. It'll help relax your body and prepare your mind for sleep. Second, _____ _____ _____ _____ _____ you use your smartphone before bed. Try these suggestions tonight. You'll feel much better tomorrow morning.

정답 단서

16 숫자 정보 파악

대화를 듣고, 남자가 지불할 금액을 고르시오.

① $45   ② $46   ③ $50
④ $52   ⑤ $54

Sound Clear ☆ **bottles**
[t]가 [l] 앞에서 약화되어 [바를스]로 발음된다.

W How did you like the food?
M Great. We _____ _____. The steak was especially nice.
W Thanks. The total comes to $54.
M Oh, wait. We ordered 2 bottles of coke, but we didn't open them. Could you please _____ _____ _____ _____ _____?
W Okay. They are $2 each, so that comes to $50.
M Here's my credit card.
W And I'll give you a 10% discount coupon _____ _____ _____ _____.
M Thanks.

함정 ☆
정답 단서

17 마지막 말에 대한 응답 찾기

대화를 듣고, 여자의 마지막 말에 대한 남자의 응답으로 가장 적절한 것을 고르시오.

Man: _____

① You're learning quickly.
② Let me check your order.
③ Okay. We'll send someone then.
④ Sorry. I don't trust you any more.
⑤ Please forgive me. I didn't mean it.

(*Telephone rings.*)
M TM Electronics Store. How can I help you?
W Hi. _____ _____ _____ _____ _____ the home repair service.
M Thanks. _____ _____ _____ _____ the problem?
W My TV screen just went black. I want it fixed as soon as possible.
M _____ _____ _____ _____. May I have your name and address, please?
W Claire Kim at 125 Kings Road.
M Okay, Ms. Kim. Will you be home on Thursday, around noon?
W No, I don't think I will be home at that time. What about 3 p.m.?
M Okay. We'll send someone then.

18 마지막 말에 대한 응답 찾기 ✳

대화를 듣고, 남자의 마지막 말에 대한 여자의 응답으로 가장 적절한 것을 고르시오.

Woman: _____

① Sorry, it's all my fault.
② I'm pleased to meet you.
③ Not really. Even I can do it.
④ I have no idea what to do now.
⑤ There's nothing to get angry about.

W Junsu, you look so tired.
M Yeah, my whole body aches these days.
W How about _____ _____ _____?
M Well, actually I'm thinking of taking a yoga class. But it's a little expensive.
W _____ _____ _____, you can just do yoga at home.
M Really? How can I do that? I don't know any yoga poses.
W You can watch yoga videos online and follow the instructor.
M _____ _____ _____ _____?
W Not really. Even I can do it.

19 마지막 말에 대한 응답 찾기

대화를 듣고, 여자의 마지막 말에 대한 남자의 응답으로 가장 적절한 것을 고르시오.

Man: _____

① I can't wait to get a new job.
② All right. I did it all on my own.
③ You had better go back to sleep soon.
④ I recommend that you leave right now.
⑤ I know. I won't let the same thing happen again.

Sound Clear ☆ **should have**
조동사 다음의 have는 약하게 발음되어 [슈 다브]로 발음된다.

W John, are you still doing your homework? It's already 11 p.m.
M Yes, Mom, but there's a lot to do.
W I told you to _____ _____ _____ _____.
M You're right. I should have followed your advice.
W When do you think _____ _____ _____ _____?
M Unfortunately, I don't know.
W Do you want me to get you a snack?
M That'd be great.
W Okay. But remember you need to _____ _____ _____ _____.
M I know. I won't let the same thing happen again.

20 상황에 적절한 말 찾기

다음 상황 설명을 듣고, Jiho가 Lisa에게 할 말로 가장 적절한 것을 고르시오.

Jiho: Lisa, _____

① I'm sorry to hear that.
② don't forget to bring your book.
③ why don't you listen to your friend?
④ can you please turn down the volume?
⑤ if I were you, I would stop complaining.

M Jiho has an important test tomorrow. He _____ _____ _____ _____ at home, so he decides to go to the library to study. For a little while, he is able to _____ _____ _____ without being interrupted. However, Lisa soon enters the library, and he _____ _____ _____ _____ because he can hear the music that she is listening to. In this situation, what would Jiho say to Lisa?
Jiho Lisa, can you please turn down the volume?

Review Test

Word Check 영어는 우리말로, 우리말은 영어로 써 보기

01 mistake _____

02 celebrate _____

03 information _____

04 apologize _____

05 relax _____

06 enter _____

07 relief _____

08 offer _____

09 participant _____

10 prevent _____

11 take a picture _____

12 chance _____

13 목록, 명단 _____

14 화장실 _____

15 실제의, 진짜의 _____

16 무늬 _____

17 추천하다 _____

18 보호하다 _____

19 인기 많은 _____

20 연구, 조사 _____

21 영수증 _____

22 비슷한 _____

23 ~을 지불하다 _____

24 ~에 만족하다 _____

Expression Check 알맞은 표현을 넣어 문장 완성하기

25 I'm not sleepy _____ _____. 저는 전혀 졸리지 않아요.

26 I guess I _____ _____ _____. 제가 실수한 것 같아요.

27 I _____ _____ _____ on Sundays. 나는 일요일마다 자원봉사 활동을 해.

28 Please _____ _____ the size you need here. 여기에 필요한 사이즈를 써 주세요.

29 Can I _____ _____ your office some time? 언제 한번 제가 교무실에 잠깐 들러도 될까요?

30 You can get one _____ _____ if you buy one. 하나를 사시면 하나를 무료로 받으실 수 있어요.

Word Check
영어는 우리말로, 우리말은 영어로 써 보기

01 deliver _____

02 space _____

03 practice _____

04 perfect _____

05 advice _____

06 ache _____

07 participate _____

08 submit _____

09 available _____

10 parking lot _____

11 take a bath _____

12 distracted _____

13 바꾸다 _____

14 불평하다 _____

15 집중하다 _____

16 용서하다 _____

17 탐험가 _____

18 향상시키다 _____

19 탑승하다 _____

20 할인 _____

21 방해하다 _____

22 일기 예보 _____

23 어려움에 처한 _____

24 모레 _____

Expression Check
알맞은 표현을 넣어 문장 완성하기

25 You need to _____ _____ by today. 넌 오늘까지 등록해야 해.

26 Don't _____ _____! You can do it! 포기하지 마! 넌 할 수 있어!

27 I _____ _____ _____ your advice. 저는 엄마의 충고를 따랐어야 했어요.

28 You _____ _____ _____ worry about parking. 넌 주차에 대해 걱정할 필요 없어.

29 I want it fixed _____ soon _____ _____. 저는 그것이 가능한 한 빨리 수리되길 원해요.

30 He is able to _____ _____ studying without being interrupted.
그는 방해받지 않고 공부에 집중할 수 있다.

1.0배속

1.2배속

01 대화를 듣고, 여자가 구입할 시계를 고르시오.

①
②
③

④
⑤

02 대화를 듣고, 여자가 남자에게 부탁한 일로 가장 적절한 것을 고르시오.

① 요리하기 ② 점심 같이 먹기
③ 도시락 싸 주기 ④ 식당 추천해 주기
⑤ 친구 마중 나가기

03 다음 그림의 상황에 가장 적절한 대화를 고르시오.

① ② ③ ④ ⑤

04 다음을 듣고, 방송의 목적으로 가장 적절한 것을 고르시오.

① 수업 계획을 설명하려고
② 실험 준비물을 공지하려고
③ 실험실 안전 수칙을 설명하려고
④ 실험실 사용 시간을 공지하려고
⑤ 보호 장비 구입 방법을 알리려고

05 대화를 듣고, 모바일 게임에 관해 언급되지 <u>않은</u> 것을 고르시오.

① 이름 ② 규칙 ③ 내용
④ 가격 ⑤ 용량

06 대화를 듣고, 두 사람의 관계로 가장 적절한 것을 고르시오.

① 경찰 – 시민 ② 서점 직원 – 손님
③ 은행 직원 – 고객 ④ 매표소 직원 – 손님
⑤ 시청 공무원 – 민원인

07 다음을 듣고, 두 사람의 대화가 <u>어색한</u> 것을 고르시오.

① ② ③ ④ ⑤

08 대화를 듣고, 여자가 남자에게 부탁한 일로 가장 적절한 것을 고르시오.

① 공부 도와주기 ② 숙제 알려 주기
③ 과제 함께 하기 ④ 공책 보여 주기
⑤ 컴퓨터 빌려주기

09 대화를 듣고, 남자의 마지막 말에 담긴 의도로 가장 적절한 것을 고르시오.

① 감사 ② 요청 ③ 위로
④ 제안 ⑤ 충고

10 대화를 듣고, 남자가 지불할 금액을 고르시오.

① $10 ② $11 ③ $100
④ $110 ⑤ $121

11 대화를 듣고, 여자가 할 일로 가장 적절한 것을 고르시오.

① 선물 사기
② 편지 쓰기
③ 제빵 수업 듣기
④ 케이크 주문하기
⑤ 요리 가르쳐 주기

12 다음을 듣고, 오디션에 관해 언급되지 <u>않은</u> 것을 고르시오.

① 심사 위원
② 참가 자격
③ 개최 요일
④ 개최 장소
⑤ 결과 발표 요일

13 다음 표를 보면서 대화를 듣고, 남자가 주문할 텀블러를 고르시오.

	Material	Capacity	Price	Gift
①	stainless	700ml	₩12,000	○
②	stainless	700ml	₩7,000	×
③	glass	300ml	₩6,000	×
④	stainless	500ml	₩8,000	○
⑤	plastic	500ml	₩9,000	×

14 다음을 듣고, 무엇에 관한 설명인지 고르시오.

① 수영
② 썰매
③ 스키 점프
④ 얼음낚시
⑤ 아이스하키

15 대화를 듣고, 남자가 대화 직후에 할 일로 가장 적절한 것을 고르시오.

① 책 빌려주기
② 도서관에 가기
③ 분리수거하기
④ 숙제 가져오기
⑤ 과학 잡지 읽기

16 대화를 듣고, 남자가 원하는 장래 희망을 고르시오.

① 교사
② 번역가
③ 소설가
④ 상담사
⑤ 작곡가

17 대화를 듣고, 여자의 마지막 말에 대한 남자의 응답으로 가장 적절한 것을 고르시오.

Man: _____

① Well, I don't have a smaller jacket.
② No, I'm not interested in shopping.
③ Okay, I will send it as soon as possible.
④ Many people want to borrow it from me.
⑤ You should think carefully about this problem.

18 대화를 듣고, 남자의 마지막 말에 대한 여자의 응답으로 가장 적절한 것을 고르시오.

Woman: _____

① You can't possibly eat all of them.
② I'm not satisfied with the food here.
③ I'm sorry to keep you waiting so long.
④ That's surprising! How did you do that?
⑤ That's longer than I expected. I'll eat here some other time.

19 대화를 듣고, 여자의 마지막 말에 대한 남자의 응답으로 가장 적절한 것을 고르시오.

Man: _____

① I'd really like to get new ones.
② I'm afraid I can't help you now.
③ If I were you, I wouldn't do that.
④ You ought to be ashamed of yourself.
⑤ You haven't forgotten about your promise.

20 다음 상황 설명을 듣고, Mijoo가 Clark에게 할 말로 가장 적절한 것을 고르시오.

Mijoo: Clark, _____

① will you help me fix it?
② please let me help you.
③ you should try your best.
④ do you mind opening the door?
⑤ can you please turn off the lights?

01 그림 정보 파악 ✽

대화를 듣고, 여자가 구입할 시계를 고르시오.

M Can I help you?

W Yes. I'm looking for a watch.

M What kind of design would you like?

W I want one ＿＿＿＿ ＿＿＿＿ ＿＿＿＿ ＿＿＿＿.

M Then how about this one? It has a dog on the watch face.

W Well, I think that's inconvenient since ＿＿＿＿ ＿＿＿＿ ＿＿＿＿ ＿＿＿＿. Can I see some digital watches?

M How about this one with a cat picture?

W I'd like to buy the one ＿＿＿＿ ＿＿＿＿ ＿＿＿＿ ＿＿＿＿.

02 부탁한 일 파악

대화를 듣고, 여자가 남자에게 부탁한 일로 가장 적절한 것을 고르시오.

① 요리하기　　　② 점심 같이 먹기
③ 도시락 싸 주기　④ 식당 추천해 주기
⑤ 친구 마중 나가기

> **Sound Clear ☆ need to**
> [d]가 [t] 앞에서 거의 발음되지 않고 동화되어 [니투]로 발음된다.

W Henry, can you ＿＿＿＿ ＿＿＿＿ ＿＿＿＿ ＿＿＿＿?

M Sure. What do you need?

W My old friends are coming this weekend, and I need to ＿＿＿＿ ＿＿＿＿ ＿＿＿＿.

M Do you want me to recommend some good places to go?

W Well, I've already decided where to go, but I'm ＿＿＿＿ ＿＿＿＿ ＿＿＿＿ ＿＿＿＿.

M I know some good restaurants.

W Really? Can you recommend some of them?

M No problem.

03 그림의 상황에 적절한 대화 찾기

다음 그림의 상황에 가장 적절한 대화를 고르시오.

① ② ③ ④ ⑤

① **W** What do you think of my new hair color?
　 M I think that color is ＿＿＿＿ ＿＿＿＿ ＿＿＿＿.
② **W** Where can I put this chair?
　 M You can ＿＿＿＿ ＿＿＿＿ ＿＿＿＿ ＿＿＿＿.
③ **W** Do you like your new hairstyle?
　 M Yes, I love it. Thanks.
④ **W** ＿＿＿＿ ＿＿＿＿ ＿＿＿＿ ＿＿＿＿ ＿＿＿＿ your cellphone?
　 M Sure, here it is.
⑤ **W** If I were you, ＿＿＿＿ ＿＿＿＿ ＿＿＿＿.
　 M Okay, I'll follow your advice.

04 목적 파악

다음을 듣고, 방송의 목적으로 가장 적절한 것을 고르시오.

① 수업 계획을 설명하려고
② 실험 준비물을 공지하려고
③ 실험실 안전 수칙을 설명하려고
④ 실험실 사용 시간을 공지하려고
⑤ 보호 장비 구입 방법을 알리려고

M Attention, please. My name is James. For the next 6 months I'll be your lab instructor. I will _____ _____ _____ your experiments, but my most important responsibility is _____ _____ _____ _____.
Please wear safety goggles and gloves at all times _____ _____ _____ _____ _____. Don't smell or taste any unknown substances. At last, you should report all accidents and injuries to me immediately. Thank you.

05 언급되지 않은 것 찾기

대화를 듣고, 모바일 게임에 관해 언급되지 않은 것을 고르시오.

① 이름 　　② 규칙 　　③ 내용
④ 가격 　　⑤ 용량

W I love playing this new mobile game.
M _____ _____ _____ _____ _____ _____?
W It's called *The Legend of Dragons*.
M Tell me more about it.
W It's a game about raising your own dragon.
M Sounds interesting! Is it free to download?
W Sure, _____ _____ _____ _____ from the mobile store. It's only 20 megabytes.
M Great! I'll download and _____ _____ _____ _____.

06 관계 추론

대화를 듣고, 두 사람의 관계로 가장 적절한 것을 고르시오.

① 경찰 – 시민
② 서점 직원 – 손님
③ 은행 직원 – 고객
④ 매표소 직원 – 손님
⑤ 시청 공무원 – 민원인

W I'm sorry to _____ _____ _____ _____. How can I help you?
M I'd like to open a savings account.
W All right. Could I see your ID card?
M Of course, here it is.
W Please read this carefully and _____ _____ _____ _____.
M Okay. (*Pause*) Do I _____ _____ _____ _____?
W Oh, yes. How much do you want to deposit today?
M Fifty dollars.

07 어색한 대화 찾기

다음을 듣고, 두 사람의 대화가 어색한 것을 고르시오.

①　　②　　③　　④　　⑤

① M Can I get your _____ _____ _____?
　 W Of course. What is it?
② M _____ _____ _____ _____ in here.
　 W Sorry. I didn't know that.
③ M I really appreciate _____ _____ _____.
　 W It's my pleasure.
④ M I've been looking forward to summer vacation.
　 W Oh, do you have any special plans?
⑤ M It isn't clear to me _____ _____ _____ _____.
　 W My hobby is taking pictures.

08 부탁한 일 파악

대화를 듣고, 여자가 남자에게 부탁한 일로 가장 적절한 것을 고르시오.

① 공부 도와주기 ② 숙제 알려 주기
③ 과제 함께 하기 ④ 공책 보여 주기
⑤ 컴퓨터 빌려주기

Sound Clear ☆ an hour
h는 묵음이고, 두 단어가 연음되어 [어나워]로 발음된다.

M Mina, why the long face?
W Well, my computer didn't _____ _____ _____
_____ _____.
M What do you mean?
W While I was doing my homework, _____ _____
_____.
M That's too bad. Is there anything that I can help you with?
W _____ _____ _____ _____, can you please lend me
your notebook computer for a while?
M No problem. How long do you need it for?
W I think _____ _____ _____ _____ _____.
M Okay, it's all yours for an hour.

09 의도 파악

대화를 듣고, 남자의 마지막 말에 담긴 의도로 가장 적절한 것을 고르시오.

① 감사 ② 요청 ③ 위로
④ 제안 ⑤ 충고

M Susan, I've been looking for you.
W Minho, what's up? Why are you so excited?
M Guess what! I have _____ _____ _____.
W I'm not sure. What is it?
M I got the full-time job I wanted at Daehan.
W Really? _____ _____ _____ _____? It's a great
company. I'm glad to hear that.
M Yeah, thanks to you, I was able to do it.
W You're welcome, but _____ _____ _____ _____
_____. You did it on your own!
M No way. Without your help, I couldn't have passed the
interview.

10 숫자 정보 파악

대화를 듣고, 남자가 지불할 금액을 고르시오.

① $10 ② $11 ③ $100
④ $110 ⑤ $121

M Hi. I'd like to buy some T-shirts for my school club members.
W _____ _____ _____ _____ these samples and
choose one.
M I want to put a yellow logo on this blue T-shirt. _____
_____ _____ _____ _____?
W A T-shirt is $10. And if you want to add a logo, you'll need to
pay a dollar extra for each one.
M Okay, I'll buy eleven T-shirts.
W Oh wait, _____ _____ _____ _____ _____, you
don't have to pay for each logo.
M Sounds great.

11 할 일 파악

대화를 듣고, 여자가 할 일로 가장 적절한 것을 고르시오.

① 선물 사기   ② 편지 쓰기
③ 제빵 수업 듣기   ④ 케이크 주문하기
⑤ 요리 가르쳐 주기

W Dad's birthday is coming soon. _____ _____ _____ _____ for him?
M I just want to buy him a small gift.
W That's nice, but I'd like to do something special.
M Then _____ _____ _____ a cake for him?
W Great idea, but I don't know how to make a cake.
M There's a baking class for making cakes. Why don't you take it?
W A baking class? Sounds wonderful. I'll take it and learn _____ _____ _____ _____ before his birthday.

12 언급되지 않은 것 찾기

다음을 듣고, 오디션에 관해 언급되지 않은 것을 고르시오.

① 심사 위원   ② 참가 자격   ③ 개최 요일
④ 개최 장소   ⑤ 결과 발표 요일

W Hello, students. Our school music club is looking for members to join and perform _____ _____ _____ _____ _____. Anyone who can play an instrument can _____ _____ _____. If you're interested, come to our club room on the third floor to apply. The audition _____ _____ _____ next Wednesday in the school music room, and the results will be announced on Friday.

13 도표 정보 파악

다음 표를 보면서 대화를 듣고, 남자가 주문할 텀블러를 고르시오.

	Material	Capacity	Price	Gift
①	stainless	700ml	₩12,000	○
②	stainless	700ml	₩7,000	×
③	glass	300ml	₩6,000	×
④	stainless	500ml	₩8,000	○
⑤	plastic	500ml	₩9,000	×

M Narae, can you help me choose a tumbler?
W Yes. _____ _____ _____ _____ do you want?
M First of all, I don't like ones made from plastic.
W Okay. How much do you want it to hold?
M I think 300 milliliters is _____ _____ _____. I want a bigger one.
W How much _____ _____ _____ _____ _____ it?
M I don't want one that is too expensive. I don't want to spend more than 10,000 won.
W Then you have two options left.
M Oh, _____ _____ _____ _____. If I buy it, I can receive an extra gift.

14 화제 파악

다음을 듣고, 무엇에 관한 설명인지 고르시오.

① 수영   ② 썰매   ③ 스키 점프
④ 얼음낚시   ⑤ 아이스하키

M This is something you can use to travel over ice. _____ _____ _____ a framework that slides on two strips of metal or wood. When the river freezes, it's a good time to use this because it can _____ _____ _____ _____. Also, children like to ride in this because they can have a lot of fun on the ice. However, you need to _____ _____ _____ _____ _____ this during spring when the ice starts to melt.

15 할 일 파악

대화를 듣고, 남자가 대화 직후에 할 일로 가장 적절한 것을 고르시오.

① 책 빌려주기　　② 도서관에 가기
③ 분리수거하기　　④ 숙제 가져오기
⑤ 과학 잡지 읽기

M What are you doing? _____ _____ _____.
W I'm doing my science homework for Ms. Park's class.
M Science homework? Did she give us homework?
W Yes, she told us to do research about _____ _____ _____ _____ _____.
M Oh no! I totally forgot about it. What should I do?
W Well, you still have some time. If I were you, I'd go to the library to _____ _____ _____ _____ _____ _____.
M You're right. I think I should go to the library right now.
　　　　　　　　　　　　　　　　　　　정답 단서

16 특정 정보 파악

대화를 듣고, 남자가 원하는 장래 희망을 고르시오.

① 교사　　② 번역가　　③ 소설가
④ 상담사　　⑤ 작곡가

Sound Clear ☆ **matter**
[t]가 모음 사이에서 약화되어 [매러]로 발음된다.

W Jiwoo, what's the matter? You look upset.
M Yes. My mother wants me to become an English teacher _____ _____ _____.
　　　　　　　　　　　　　　　　　한정
W I don't think being a teacher would be a bad idea. And _____ _____ _____ _____.
M But I get so nervous when I speak in front of other people. And I don't want to _____ _____ _____ _____.
W What do you want to be?
M I'd like to translate famous Korean novels into English.
W Sounds good. I know you love reading novels. That would be
　　　　　　　　　　정답 단서
_____ _____ _____ _____ _____.

17 마지막 말에 대한 응답 찾기

대화를 듣고, 여자의 마지막 말에 대한 남자의 응답으로 가장 적절한 것을 고르시오.

Man: _____

① Well, I don't have a smaller jacket.
② No, I'm not interested in shopping.
③ Okay, I will send it as soon as possible.
④ Many people want to borrow it from me.
⑤ You should think carefully about this problem.

(*Telephone rings.*)
M Hi. I've just received the jacket I ordered from your website.
W Is there _____ _____ _____ _____?
M No, it's just a little big. Can I exchange it for a smaller one?
W Sure. Your name please.
M Thomas Lee.
W You ordered a large size. Do you want to exchange it _____ _____ _____ _____?
M Exactly.
W All right, could you please _____ _____ _____ _____ _____? Then we can send you a smaller one.
M Okay, I will send it as soon as possible.

18 마지막 말에 대한 응답 찾기

대화를 듣고, 남자의 마지막 말에 대한 여자의 응답으로 가장 적절한 것을 고르시오.

Woman: ____________________

① You can't possibly eat all of them.
② I'm not satisfied with the food here.
③ I'm sorry to keep you waiting so long.
④ That's surprising! How did you do that?
⑤ That's longer than I expected. I'll eat here some other time.

M Welcome to Brian's BBQ Restaurant.
W Wow, there are ________ ________ ________ ________.
M Yes, on weekends, we usually have more customers than on weekdays. Did you ________ ________ ________?
W No, I didn't.
M Then I'm afraid that you ________ ________ ________ ________ your name on the waiting list and wait.
W How long do you think I'll have to wait?
M ________ ________ ________, but probably 30 minutes or more.
W That's longer than I expected. I'll eat here some other time.

19 마지막 말에 대한 응답 찾기

대화를 듣고, 여자의 마지막 말에 대한 남자의 응답으로 가장 적절한 것을 고르시오.

Man: ____________________

① I'd really like to get new ones.
② I'm afraid I can't help you now.
③ If I were you, I wouldn't do that.
④ You ought to be ashamed of yourself.
⑤ You haven't forgotten about your promise.

Sound Clear☆ new
미국식은 [누]로, 영국식은 [뉴]로 발음된다.

W Welcome to Kim's Eyewear. What can I do for you?
M Hi. I need to get a ☆new pair of glasses.
W When did you get ________ ________ ________ ________?
M About three and a half years ago.
W Oh, that's a long time ago.
M Yes, I think that's why I ________ ________ ________ ________ these days.
W Maybe. Are the frames okay? Do you ________ ________ ________ ________ ________, too?
M I'd really like to get new ones.

20 상황에 적절한 말 찾기

다음 상황 설명을 듣고, Mijoo가 Clark에게 할 말로 가장 적절한 것을 고르시오.

Mijoo: Clark, ____________________

① will you help me fix it?
② please let me help you.
③ you should try your best.
④ do you mind opening the door?
⑤ can you please turn off the lights?

W Mijoo is in the classroom ________ ________ ________ ________ ________. She opens her presentation file on the computer. When she is about to start her presentation, she notices that some students sitting at the back can't see the screen well ________ ________ ________ ________ ________. She sees that her friend Clark is right next to the light switch and wants to ________ ________ ________ ________ (정답 단서). In this situation, what would she say to him?
Mijoo Clark, can you please turn off the lights?

1.0배속   1.2배속

01 대화를 듣고, 여자의 남동생을 고르시오.

 ①    ②   ③

 ④    ⑤

02 대화를 듣고, 여자가 남자에게 전화한 목적으로 가장 적절한 것을 고르시오.

① 대회를 안내하려고
② 해외 발령을 알리려고
③ 경품 당첨을 알리려고
④ 대회 수상 소식을 전하려고
⑤ 여행 상품을 홍보하려고

03 다음 그림의 상황에 가장 적절한 대화를 고르시오.

① ② ③ ④ ⑤

04 대화를 듣고, 남자가 집을 나설 시각을 고르시오.

① 5:00 p.m. ② 6:00 p.m. ③ 6:30 p.m.
④ 7:00 p.m. ⑤ 7:30 p.m.

05 대화를 듣고, 남자가 할 일로 가장 적절한 것을 고르시오.

① 요리하기   ② 산책하기
③ 멜론 사 오기   ④ 방 청소하기
⑤ 여동생 돌보기

06 대화를 듣고, 남자가 여자에게 부탁한 일로 가장 적절한 것을 고르시오.

① 가방 챙기기   ② 수학 도와주기
③ 휴대 전화 찾기   ④ 숙제 가져다주기
⑤ 학교에 데리러 오기

07 다음을 듣고, 두 사람의 대화가 어색한 것을 고르시오.

① ② ③ ④ ⑤

08 다음을 듣고, 아이에 관해 언급되지 않은 것을 고르시오.

① 성별   ② 이름
③ 목격된 장소   ④ 나이
⑤ 옷차림

09 대화를 듣고, 남자의 마지막 말에 담긴 의도로 가장 적절한 것을 고르시오.

① 부탁   ② 사과   ③ 위로
④ 충고   ⑤ 허락

10 대화를 듣고, 남자가 지불할 금액을 고르시오.

① $1   ② $4   ③ $5
④ $6   ⑤ $10

11 대화를 듣고, 두 사람이 대화하는 장소로 가장 적절한 곳을 고르시오.

① 교실　　　② 병원　　　③ 식당
④ 약국　　　⑤ 보건실

12 대화를 듣고, 여자가 남자에게 부탁한 일로 가장 적절한 것을 고르시오.

① 줄 서 있기　　　② 음료수 사 오기
③ 기차표 예매하기　　　④ 도시락 함께 먹기
⑤ 열차 시간 알아보기

13 다음 사무실 배치도를 보면서 대화를 듣고, 두 사람이 사용할 회의실을 고르시오.

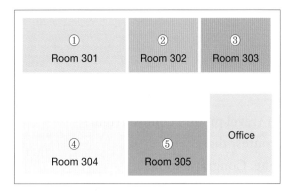

14 다음을 듣고, 무엇에 관한 설명인지 고르시오.

① 군인　　　② 의사　　　③ 비행사
④ 승무원　　　⑤ 엔지니어

15 대화를 듣고, 남자가 대화 직후에 할 일로 가장 적절한 것을 고르시오.

① 제품 비교하기　　　② 외투 교환하기
③ 상품 가격 알아보기　　　④ 할인 쿠폰 사용하기
⑤ 웹 사이트 계정 만들기

16 대화를 듣고, 여자가 새롭게 공부할 언어를 고르시오.

① 영어　　　② 일본어　　　③ 중국어
④ 독일어　　　⑤ 프랑스어

17 다음 상황 설명을 듣고, Emily가 남자에게 할 말로 가장 적절한 것을 고르시오.

Emily: Excuse me. _____

① I think that's amazing.
② I think this is your wallet.
③ I think you'd better hurry.
④ I think I've seen you before.
⑤ I think you picked up the wrong one.

18 대화를 듣고, 남자의 심정으로 가장 적절한 것을 고르시오.

① tired　　　② joyful　　　③ excited
④ worried　　　⑤ disappointed

19 대화를 듣고, 남자의 마지막 말에 대한 여자의 응답으로 가장 적절한 것을 고르시오.

Woman: _____

① Glad to hear that. Have a good time.
② Sure. You can go there without my help.
③ Not really. I don't think it's a good idea.
④ I'm looking forward to my birthday party.
⑤ Okay, just hurry and come home right now.

20 대화를 듣고, 여자의 마지막 말에 대한 남자의 응답으로 가장 적절한 것을 고르시오.

Man: _____

① Of course. I really like my job.
② Yes. Isn't it difficult to get a job?
③ Well, I've thought about it many times.
④ No. Can you tell me when I should meet you?
⑤ I'm not sure. I'll check the map on your website.

01 그림 정보 파악

대화를 듣고, 여자의 남동생을 고르시오.

 ① ② ③
 ④ ⑤

M Who is this man in the picture?

W That's my brother John.

M I like his style. _____ _____ _____ _____. Is he your younger brother?

W No, he's my elder brother. My little brother is _____ _____ _____ _____. He doesn't wear a cap.
정답 단서

M You mean _____ _____ _____ _____ _____?

W No, that's my cousin. My little brother is here.

M I see. He has short hair and is wearing a T-shirt with a bear on it.
정답 단서

W Yes, he likes bears a lot!

02 목적 파악

대화를 듣고, 여자가 남자에게 전화한 목적으로 가장 적절한 것을 고르시오.

① 대회를 안내하려고
② 해외 발령을 알리려고
③ 경품 당첨을 알리려고
④ 대회 수상 소식을 전하려고
⑤ 여행 상품을 홍보하려고

Sound Clear ☆ **grand prize**
자음 세 개가 연속으로 나오면 중간 자음의 발음이 약화되어 [그랜프라이즈]로 발음된다.

(*Cellphone rings.*)

M Hello?

W Hello. This is Hanguk Travel Agency. Is this Paul Lee?

M Yes, it is.

W You entered our travel picture contest, right?

M You mean the contest that _____ _____ _____?

W Yes, that's the one. Congratulations! _____ _____ _____ _____ in the contest.

M Really? I can't believe it!

W Believe it. You won our grand prize of _____ _____ _____ _____ _____ for 3 days.

M Wow, thank you so much!

03 그림의 상황에 적절한 대화 찾기

다음 그림의 상황에 가장 적절한 대화를 고르시오.

① ② ③ ④ ⑤

① M Can you please _____ _____ _____?

   W Okay, no problem.

② M May I take your order?

   W Yes, please. _____ _____ _____ _____ a steak.
   정답 단서

③ M What are you interested in?

   W I'm interested in cooking.

④ M What would you like to eat for lunch?

   W I want to eat sandwiches.

⑤ M Can I _____ _____ _____ _____ being healthy?

   W I think you should eat more vegetables.

04 숫자 정보 파악 ✵

대화를 듣고, 남자가 집을 나설 시각을 고르시오.

① 5:00 p.m.   ② 6:00 p.m.   ③ 6:30 p.m.
④ 7:00 p.m.   ⑤ 7:30 p.m.

W   Did you pack everything _____ _____ _____ _____?
M   Yes, everything is ready.
W   When does the train leave?
M   At 7:30. I think I should leave home at around 6:30. It usually takes about 30 minutes to _____ _____ _____.
W   But it's Friday evening!
M   Oh, you're right. There will be heavy traffic. _____ _____ _____ at 6 o'clock.
W   I think so, too.

05 할 일 파악

대화를 듣고, 남자가 할 일로 가장 적절한 것을 고르시오.

① 요리하기   ② 산책하기
③ 멜론 사 오기   ④ 방 청소하기
⑤ 여동생 돌보기

Sound Clear ☆ **can**

긍정문일 때 발음이 약화되어 [컨] 또는 [큰]으로 발음된다.

W   Kevin. Can you _____ _____ _____ _____?
M   Sure, Mom. What is it?
W   Will you buy some melon for Kate? _____ _____ _____ _____ now.
M   No problem.
W   Why don't you go to the new supermarket? Fruit is cheaper there.
M   Okay, how much money _____ _____ _____?
W   I think a box of melons is about $15, but here's $20 just in case. You can _____ _____ _____.
M   Thank you so much, Mom. Then I can buy my favorite snacks!

06 부탁한 일 파악

대화를 듣고, 남자가 여자에게 부탁한 일로 가장 적절한 것을 고르시오.

① 가방 챙기기   ② 수학 도와주기
③ 휴대 전화 찾기   ④ 숙제 가져다주기
⑤ 학교에 데리러 오기

(*Telephone rings.*)
W   Hello.
M   Mom, it's David.
W   Oh, David. _____ _____ _____ _____ me now? Aren't you in school?
M   My teacher _____ _____ _____ _____ _____ for a moment. Could you please bring my math homework to school?
W   _____ _____ _____ _____ _____? I saw you put it in your bag last night.
M   I did, but after taking it out to check it again, I forgot to _____ _____ _____ _____ again.
W   I see. See you at the main gate in 10 minutes.

07 어색한 대화 찾기

다음을 듣고, 두 사람의 대화가 어색한 것을 고르시오.

① ② ③ ④ ⑤

Sound Clear ☆ **favorite**
1음절에 강세가 있고 2음절의 [ə]가 약화되어 [페이브릿]에 가깝게 발음된다.

① **M** Can you speak more slowly, please?

W Okay, I'll try.

② **M** _____ _____ _____ _____ drink some water?

W Yes, please. I'm so thirsty.

③ **M** May I think about that for a moment?

W Sure, _____ _____ _____.

④ **M** You don't like science, do you?

W No, I don't. Science is my ☆favorite subject.

⑤ **M** What do you think about my new shoes?

W They _____ _____ _____ _____.

W Attention, shoppers. This is an important announcement. We _____ _____ _____ _____ somewhere in the mall. We are looking for a little boy who was last seen _____ *정답 단서* _____ _____ *정답 단서* 30 minutes ago. He is four years old. He is wearing blue jeans, a short-sleeved T-shirt _____ *정답 단서* _____ _____ _____ *정답 단서*, and a bright red cap. If you have seen this child, please notify the nearest security officer right away.

M So you saw a hit-and-run an hour ago?

W Yes. I saw a car _____ _____ _____ _____ a bicycle. It was on Pine Street.

M Did you see the license plate of the car?

W Yeah, but I could only see the first three numbers.

M _____ _____ _____?

W Three, five, and nine.

M _____ _____ _____ _____ _____?

W It was a black, medium-sized car.

M Thank you for your help. If you remember anything else, *정답 단서* please call me.

W How was the food?

M _____ _____ _____ as always.

W Thanks. So you had one spaghetti and a coke, right?

M Yes. How much is it?

W A spaghetti is $5, and a coke is $1, so _____ _____ _____ is $6.

M Oh, I think I have a free drink coupon. Can I use this?

W Sure. Then you just _____ _____ _____ the spaghetti.

M Here you are.

11 장소 추론

대화를 듣고, 두 사람이 대화하는 장소로 가장 적절한 곳을 고르시오.

① 교실   ② 병원   ③ 식당
④ 약국   ⑤ 보건실

Sound Clear ☆ **stomachache**
ch가 [k]로 소리 나서 [스터먹케이크]로 발음된다.

W   Why are you late, Liam?
M   Sorry, Ms. Brown. I have been at the nurse's office.
W   Really?
M   Yes, _____ _____ _____ _____ the school nurse.
W   Oh, you had a stomachache.
M   Yeah, I think I ate lunch too fast.
W   You _____ _____ _____ _____. Do you feel better now?
M   Yes. I took some medicine and rested for an hour.
W   Okay, I hope you won't be sick anymore. Please _____ _____ _____.

12 부탁한 일 파악

대화를 듣고, 여자가 남자에게 부탁한 일로 가장 적절한 것을 고르시오.

① 줄 서 있기   ② 음료수 사 오기
③ 기차표 예매하기   ④ 도시락 함께 먹기
⑤ 열차 시간 알아보기

W   I'm so excited to visit Busan!
M   So am I! Did you _____ _____ _____?
W   Yes, here they are. Our train leaves in 20 minutes.
M   Then we _____ _____ _____ _____.
W   Why don't we go get a drink?
M   That's a good idea. (*Pause*) _____ _____ _____ _____ _____ over there.
W   I think I need to _____ _____ _____ _____. Can you go ahead and get a bottle of coffee for me?

 정답 단서

13 위치 찾기   ❖

다음 사무실 배치도를 보면서 대화를 듣고, 두 사람이 사용할 회의실을 고르시오.

① Room 301	② Room 302	③ Room 303
④ Room 304	⑤ Room 305	Office

M   Which room do you think is good for tomorrow's meeting?
W   Umm... Room 305? _____ _____ _____ our office.
M   Yes, but the air conditioner in that room is _____ _____.
W   Then we can't use that room.
M   What about Room 301? It is a large room, so _____ _____ _____ _____.
W   I think so. (*Pause*) Ah, that room is already reserved.
M   Then how about Room 304? The size is okay, and _____ _____ _____ the air conditioner.
W   Okay, then let's use that room.

M This is a person _____ _____ _____ _____. This person is responsible for keeping passengers safe and getting them to their destinations. Airplanes can't fly without this person, who is _____ _____ _____ _____. Many people would like to do this job even though it's very difficult to do since it takes so much time and effort to learn _____ _____ _____ _____.

15 할 일 파악

대화를 듣고, 남자가 대화 직후에 할 일로 가장 적절한 것을 고르시오.

① 제품 비교하기
② 외투 교환하기
③ 상품 가격 알아보기
④ 할인 쿠폰 사용하기
⑤ 웹 사이트 계정 만들기

Sound Clear ☆ **coupon**
'쿠폰'은 실제로 [쿠판]으로 발음된다.

M Julie, your new coat _____ _____ _____ _____.
W Thanks. I bought it online at a low price.
M Really? It looks so expensive.
W I bought it on a new website called Fashion Up. If you _____ _____ _____, you can get a 50% discount coupon.
M _____ _____ _____ _____! I should create one and get a coupon, too.
W Yeah, but you need to hurry. The special offer will end soon.
M Okay, I'll do it right away.

16 특정 정보 파악

대화를 듣고, 여자가 새롭게 공부할 언어를 고르시오.

① 영어　　② 일본어　　③ 중국어
④ 독일어　　⑤ 프랑스어

M Sumi, do you have any special plans for the summer vacation?
W _____ _____ _____ _____ a foreign language.
M Great idea! Which language?
W Well, actually I haven't decided yet.
M How about Chinese? It's used by more people _____ _____ _____ _____.
W I know, but I think it's _____ _____ _____ _____.
M Then what about Japanese? It's easy to learn because it has a similar word order as Korean.
W Really? Then I'll _____ _____ _____ _____.

17 상황에 적절한 말 찾기

다음 상황 설명을 듣고, Emily가 남자에게 할 말로 가장 적절한 것을 고르시오.

Emily: Excuse me. _____

① I think that's amazing.
② I think this is your wallet.
③ I think you'd better hurry.
④ I think I've seen you before.
⑤ I think you picked up the wrong one.

W Emily is walking on the street. Suddenly, she sees a man _____ _____ _____ _____ drop his wallet. He doesn't notice that _____ _____ _____, and she wants to help him. She picks the wallet up quickly and tries to _____ _____ _____ _____ to give it to him. Finally, she reaches him and is about to give the wallet to him. In this situation, what would Emily say to him?

Emily Excuse me. I think this is your wallet.

18 심정 추론

대화를 듣고, 남자의 심정으로 가장 적절한 것을 고르시오.

① tired ② joyful ③ excited
④ worried ⑤ disappointed

Sound Clear☆ **about it**

[t]가 모음 사이에서 약화되고 뒤 단어의 모음과 연음되어 [어바우릿]으로 발음된다.

M Ava, are you all right? You seem to ________ ________ ________.
W Yeah, actually I just went to see a doctor about it.
M What did he say?
W He said I have some early symptoms of a cold.
M You should be careful so that ________ ________ ________ ________. Why don't you drink some warm lemon tea?
W Lemon tea?
M Yeah, ________ ________ ________ ________ and prevent you from getting a cold.
W Okay, I'll try that.

19 마지막 말에 대한 응답 찾기

대화를 듣고, 남자의 마지막 말에 대한 여자의 응답으로 가장 적절한 것을 고르시오.

Woman: ________________

① Glad to hear that. Have a good time.
② Sure. You can go there without my help.
③ Not really. I don't think it's a good idea.
④ I'm looking forward to my birthday party.
⑤ Okay, just hurry and come home right now.

(*Cellphone rings.*)
M Hello.
W Sam. Where are you now?
M On the school playground. Why?
W ________ ________ ________ ________ ________? It's already 5 p.m.
M Well, I want to play with my friends longer.
W ________ ________ ________ ________ ________ something important. We're supposed to go to your grandma's birthday party at 6 p.m.
M Oh, is it today, not tomorrow? I ________ ________ ________ ________. Sorry, Mom.
W Okay, just hurry and come home right now.

20 마지막 말에 대한 응답 찾기

대화를 듣고, 여자의 마지막 말에 대한 남자의 응답으로 가장 적절한 것을 고르시오.

Man: ________________

① Of course. I really like my job.
② Yes. Isn't it difficult to get a job?
③ Well, I've thought about it many times.
④ No. Can you tell me when I should meet you?
⑤ I'm not sure. I'll check the map on your website.

(*Cellphone rings.*)
M Hello.
W Hello, Mr. Peter Kim. This is Daehan Trading. ________ ________ the initial résumé screening. Congratulations!
M Oh, really? Thank you so much.
W You're welcome. ________ ________ ________ ________ ________ next Friday at 2 p.m. Can you make it then?
M Of course. Where should I ________ ________ ________ ________?
W Please come to our head office in downtown Seoul. Do you know ________ ________ ________?
M I'm not sure. I'll check the map on your website.

Review Test

실전 모의고사 03 회

Word Check
영어는 우리말로, 우리말은 영어로 써 보기

01 injury _____

02 melt _____

03 terrific _____

04 lab _____

05 follow _____

06 immediately _____

07 unknown _____

08 responsibility _____

09 pass _____

10 long face _____

11 fill out _____

12 at all times _____

13 악기 _____

14 주제 _____

15 실험 _____

16 입금하다 _____

17 사고 _____

18 불편한 _____

19 빌려주다 _____

20 금속 _____

21 전설 _____

22 교환하다 _____

23 혼자 힘으로 _____

24 기꺼이 ~하다 _____

Expression Check
알맞은 표현을 넣어 문장 완성하기

25 Did you _____ _____ _____? 예약을 하셨나요?

26 _____ I _____ you, I'd buy another one. 내가 너라면, 나는 다른 걸 살 거야.

27 I'd like to _____ a savings _____. 저는 저축 예금 계좌를 개설하고 싶어요.

28 _____ _____ _____ tumbler do you want? 너는 어떤 종류의 텀블러를 원하니?

29 I'd like to _____ famous Korean novels _____ English.
나는 유명한 한국 소설을 영어로 번역하고 싶어.

30 _____ _____ _____, I couldn't have passed the interview.
네 도움이 없었다면, 난 면접을 통과하지 못했을 거야.

Word Check
영어는 우리말로, 우리말은 영어로 써 보기

01 describe _____

02 ahead _____

03 pack _____

04 somewhere _____

05 hit-and-run _____

06 security _____

07 suit _____

08 downtown _____

09 screen _____

10 aircraft _____

11 take a seat _____

12 just in case _____

13 교통 _____

14 출장 _____

15 언어 _____

16 증상 _____

17 비슷한 _____

18 안경 _____

19 안내 방송 _____

20 노력 _____

21 층 _____

22 취업하다 _____

23 더 이상 ~ 않다 _____

24 따라잡다 _____

Expression Check
알맞은 표현을 넣어 문장 완성하기

25 Can you please _____ _____ _____? 상 좀 차려 주실 수 있어요?

26 You _____ _____ _____ in the contest. 당신은 대회에서 일등을 하셨어요.

27 Your new coat _____ _____ _____ you. 네 새 외투가 너한테 잘 어울려.

28 I _____ some _____ and rested for an hour. 저는 약을 먹고 1시간 동안 쉬었어요.

29 The air conditioner in that room is _____ _____ _____. 그 방의 에어컨은 고장 났어.

30 Can you go ahead and get _____ _____ _____ coffee for me?
네가 먼저 가서 나에게 커피 한 병을 사다 줄 수 있니?

1.0배속

1.2배속

01 대화를 듣고, 여자의 체육 선생님을 고르시오.

① ②

③

④

⑤

02 대화를 듣고, 남자가 여자에게 부탁한 일로 가장 적절한 것을 고르시오.

① 개 돌보기
② 집 청소하기
③ 호텔 예약하기
④ 식물에 물 주기
⑤ 택배 받아 주기

03 대화를 듣고, 여자가 호텔에 체크인할 시각을 고르시오.

① 11:30 a.m.
② 12:00 p.m.
③ 1:00 p.m.
④ 2:00 p.m.
⑤ 3:00 p.m.

04 다음 그림의 상황에 가장 적절한 대화를 고르시오.

① ② ③ ④ ⑤

05 대화를 듣고, 광고 속 제품에 관해 언급되지 않은 것을 고르시오.

① 색상
② 가격
③ 할인 기간
④ 사은품
⑤ 무게

06 대화를 듣고, 두 사람이 대화하는 장소로 가장 적절한 곳을 고르시오.

① 농구장
② 헬스장
③ 보건실
④ 오락실
⑤ 구내식당

07 다음을 듣고, 두 사람의 대화가 어색한 것을 고르시오.

① ② ③ ④ ⑤

08 대화를 듣고, 여자가 남자에게 부탁한 일로 가장 적절한 것을 고르시오.

① 소포 부치기
② 상자 구입하기
③ 용돈 올려 주기
④ 주소 알려 주기
⑤ 책상 수리하기

09 다음을 듣고, 무엇에 관한 안내 방송인지 고르시오.

① 시간표 변경
② 응급 처치 방법
③ 소방 훈련 실시
④ 학교 안전 교육
⑤ 학교 행사 취소

10 대화를 듣고, 여자가 지불할 금액을 고르시오.

① $7
② $10
③ $15
④ $19
⑤ $25

11 대화를 듣고, 남자가 할 일로 가장 적절한 것을 고르시오.

① 낮잠 자기
② 공원 산책하기
③ 병원에 가기
④ 피로 회복제 먹기
⑤ 배구 동아리에 가입하기

12 다음을 듣고, 할인 행사에 관해 언급되지 않은 것을 고르시오.

① 할인 품목
② 할인율
③ 행사 장소
④ 쿠폰 사용 방법
⑤ 행사 마감 시각

13 다음 그림을 보면서 대화를 듣고, 두 사람이 화분을 옮길 위치를 고르시오.

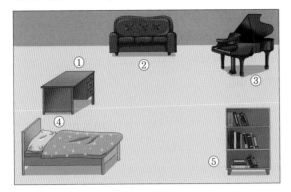

14 다음을 듣고, 무엇에 관한 설명인지 고르시오.

① 풍선　　② 리코더　　③ 헤드폰
④ 호루라기　　⑤ 음주 측정기

15 대화를 듣고, 남자가 어제 한 일로 가장 적절한 것을 고르시오.

① 운동하기　　② 병문안 가기
③ 축구 관람하기　　④ 휴대 전화 수리하기
⑤ 친구에게 전화하기

16 대화를 듣고, 두 사람이 만날 장소를 고르시오.

① 공원 앞　　② 시청 앞　　③ 악기점
④ 지하철역　　⑤ 기타 수리점

17 대화를 듣고, 여자의 마지막 말에 대한 남자의 응답으로 가장 적절한 것을 고르시오.

Man: _____

① You should have studied harder.
② You need to admit that you were wrong.
③ The rider should have reduced his speed.
④ You shouldn't use your phone while crossing the road.
⑤ You must look carefully both ways before you cross the road.

18 대화를 듣고, 남자의 마지막 말에 대한 여자의 응답으로 가장 적절한 것을 고르시오.

Woman: _____

① I was really satisfied with my flight.
② No problem. I'll do that right away.
③ That's a relief. I was worried about it.
④ Yes. Could you please label it 'Handle with care'?
⑤ Don't you know that it's necessary to stay in line?

19 대화를 듣고, 여자의 마지막 말에 대한 남자의 응답으로 가장 적절한 것을 고르시오.

Man: _____

① It's a small world, isn't it?
② Don't worry, just try to relax.
③ Is it okay if I use your phone?
④ I haven't heard about it before.
⑤ I'd like to speak to another person.

20 다음 상황 설명을 듣고, Minsu가 Sarah에게 할 말로 가장 적절한 것을 고르시오.

Minsu: Sarah, _____

① you look really scared.
② everything will be all right.
③ I'm afraid I'm too scared to do it.
④ I'm glad you could come to see me.
⑤ you ought to be ashamed of yourself.

받아쓰기용

01 그림 정보 파악

대화를 듣고, 여자의 체육 선생님을 고르시오.

M Jina! You look so happy.

W Yeah. I have a new P.E. teacher. _____ _____ _____.

M Aha, and you have P.E. class next.

W Yes. He's also very tall.

M I wonder _____ _____ _____ _____.

W Oh! He's right over there. He's playing tennis now.

M Is he _____ _____ _____ _____?

W No. He is wearing a cap, not sunglasses.

02 부탁한 일 파악 ✚

대화를 듣고, 남자가 여자에게 부탁한 일로 가장 적절한 것을 고르시오.

① 개 돌보기　　② 집 청소하기
③ 호텔 예약하기　④ 식물에 물 주기
⑤ 택배 받아 주기

Sound Clear ☆ plants

미국식은 a를 [애]로 발음하여 [플랜츠]로, 영국식은 [아]로 발음하여 [플란츠]로 발음된다.

W John, I heard that you're _____ _____ _____ _____ _____ next week. When are you coming back?

M After two weeks.

W Two weeks? Then what about your dog? Do you want me to 함정 _____ _____ _____?

M That's okay. I'm going to take her to a dog hotel. But I have _____ _____ _____ _____ _____.

W Sure, what is it?

M Can you water the plants ☆ _____ _____ _____? You can just do it every other day. 정답 단서

W No problem. Enjoy your business trip.

03 숫자 정보 파악

대화를 듣고, 여자가 호텔에 체크인할 시각을 고르시오.

① 11:30 a.m.　　② 12:00 p.m.
③ 1:00 p.m.　　④ 2:00 p.m.
⑤ 3:00 p.m.

(*Telephone rings.*)

M Hello. Flower Hotel.

W Hi. I _____ _____ _____ for next Tuesday under the name of Claire Davis.

M Yes, Ms. Davis. What can I help you with?

W I know that the check-in time is 3 p.m. But _____ _____ 함정 _____ _____ have an early check-in?

M What time do you want to check in?

W I think _____ _____ _____ around noon.

M There are not many guests that day, but you will have to wait until 1 p.m. to check in. 정답 단서

W That will be fine. Thank you.

04 그림의 상황에 적절한 대화 찾기

다음 그림의 상황에 가장 적절한 대화를 고르시오.

① ② ③ ④ ⑤

① W Make sure you aren't late.
　 M I'll _____ _____ _____ .
② W Do you want some dessert?
　 M No, thanks. _____ _____ .
③ W What do you want me to call you?
　 M You can call me Dr. Brown.
④ W Please _____ _____ _____ the paintings.
　 M Okay, I'll just enjoy looking at them.
⑤ W Excuse me. _____ _____ _____ _____ take pictures in here.
　 M Sorry, I didn't know that.

05 언급되지 않은 것 찾기 ✽

대화를 듣고, 광고 속 제품에 관해 언급되지 않은 것을 고르시오.

① 색상　② 가격　③ 할인 기간
④ 사은품　⑤ 무게

Sound Clear ☆ **advertisement**

미국식은 [애드버타이즈먼트]로, 영국식은 [어드버티스먼트]로 발음된다.

M Look at this advertisement.
W What's it for?
M It's for a new notebook computer. It comes in two colors: white and black.
W Wow, _____ _____ _____ _____ and only costs $300!
M Yeah, just for this week.
W I think _____ _____ _____ other notebook computers.
M Yeah, and it weighs only 900 grams.
W Let's go to the store and see it.

06 장소 추론

대화를 듣고, 두 사람이 대화하는 장소로 가장 적절한 곳을 고르시오.

① 농구장　② 헬스장　③ 보건실
④ 오락실　⑤ 구내식당

W What's the matter? You don't look so good.
M _____ _____ _____ _____ .
W Why not?
M I _____ _____ _____ _____ _____ because of the pressure of today's game.
W I understand. Do you want to come off the court for a few minutes?
M Can I?
W Sure. _____ _____ _____ , if you feel better, then I will put you in the game again.
M Thanks. I will try to make lots of three-point shots then.
W I believe you will.

다음을 듣고, 두 사람의 대화가 <u>어색한</u> 것을 고르시오.

① ② ③ ④ ⑤

① M Where can I buy some fruit?
  W There's a store _____ _____ _____.
② M I wonder if I could use my credit card.
  W Sorry. _____ _____ _____ _____.
③ M Which kind of movie do you want to see?
  W I want to see a fantasy movie.
④ M _____ _____ _____ _____ bird watching?
  W Yes, I've even tried it before.
⑤ M Do you think I should _____ _____ _____?
  W Yes, I think you should.

08 부탁한 일 파악

대화를 듣고, 여자가 남자에게 부탁한 일로 가장 적절한 것을 고르시오.

① 소포 부치기   ② 상자 구입하기
③ 용돈 올려 주기   ④ 주소 알려 주기
⑤ 책상 수리하기

Sound Clear ☆ **written**
[t]가 모음 사이에서 약화되어 콧소리로 [릅은]으로 발음된다.

(*Cellphone rings.*)
W Dad, it's me, Susan.
M Oh, Susan. What's up?
W _____ _____ _____ _____?
M Not that busy. Do you _____ _____ _____ _____
   _____?
W Yes, please. There's a small box on my desk. Can you mail it
   for me? I have to send it today.   청답 단서
M No problem. Did you _____ _____ _____ on it?
            ☆
W Yeah, it's written on the box. Thanks, Dad.
M You're welcome.

09 주제 파악   ✤

다음을 듣고, 무엇에 관한 안내 방송인지 고르시오.

① 시간표 변경   ② 응급 처치 방법
③ 소방 훈련 실시   ④ 학교 안전 교육
⑤ 학교 행사 취소

M Good morning, students. In fifth period today, a firefighter
   from the 911 rescue center is giving _____ _____
   _____ _____ _____. He's going to talk about things
   that you should do to stay safe at school. Also, you can learn
   about _____ _____ _____ _____ _____ in
   emergency situations. The lecture will _____ _____
   _____ _____ _____. Please come to the lecture hall
   on time before fifth period starts.

10 숫자 정보 파악

대화를 듣고, 여자가 지불할 금액을 고르시오.

① $7   ② $10   ③ $15
④ $19   ⑤ $25

W Hello. _____ _____ _____ _____ some plates.
M You're lucky. All plates are 30% off right now.
W Great. How about these cups? Are they also 30% off?
M Sorry. _____ _____ _____ _____. But if you buy
   one, you can get one free.
W Hmm... I want to buy these two plates and this cup.
M The plate was $10, but _____ _____ _____ _____
   today for only $7. And the cup is $5.
W Here's my credit card.

11 할 일 파악

대화를 듣고, 남자가 할 일로 가장 적절한 것을 고르시오.

① 낮잠 자기　　② 공원 산책하기
③ 병원에 가기　　④ 피로 회복제 먹기
⑤ 배구 동아리에 가입하기

W Peter, you look tired.
M You're right. _____ _____ _____ _____ these days. I don't know why.
W Have you been getting enough sleep?
M I sleep 8 hours a day. I think I need to exercise more.
W Well, why don't you _____ _____ _____ _____ _____ such as walking in the park?
M I think it'd be boring. Can you recommend anything else?
W Then how about joining our volleyball club? We _____ _____ _____ _____.
M Oh, that's a good idea. I'll join your club right away.

12 언급되지 않은 것 찾기

다음을 듣고, 할인 행사에 관해 언급되지 않은 것을 고르시오.

① 할인 품목　　② 할인율
③ 행사 장소　　④ 쿠폰 사용 방법
⑤ 행사 마감 시각

W Hello, everyone. Are you enjoying shopping at Haengbok Mart? Today we are offering our customers _____ _____ _____ _____ _____. All meats including pork, beef, and chicken are 20% off. Shoppers who want to buy some meat, _____ _____ _____ _____ _____ _____ at the back of the store. This deal lasts for only 30 minutes, so it will end at 6:30. It's starting right now. _____ _____ _____ _____ _____!

13 위치 찾기

다음 그림을 보면서 대화를 듣고, 두 사람이 화분을 옮길 위치를 고르시오.

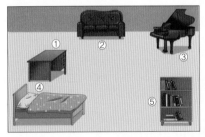

Sound Clear ☆ **little**

[t]가 모음 사이에서 약화되어 [리를]로 발음된다.

W _____ _____ _____ _____ _____ _____ this flowerpot?
M Of course, to where?
W I'm thinking of putting it next to the piano.
M In that case, we should move the piano a little bit.
W _____ _____ _____ _____ _____ _____.
M How about beside the bed?
W I don't think there's enough space. What about placing it next to the bookshelf?
M Oh, we _____ _____ _____ there. That's a great idea.
W Okay. Let's do it now.

14 화제 파악

다음을 듣고, 무엇에 관한 설명인지 고르시오.

① 풍선　　② 리코더　　③ 헤드폰
④ 호루라기　　⑤ 음주 측정기

M This is a thing that you can use to _____ _____ _____ _____ by blowing in it. You can see some people blow this in your everyday life. For example, police officers _____ _____ _____ _____ _____ or for a warning. Also soccer referees use this on the field, especially to begin the game or to stop the game _____ _____ _____.

15 한 일 파악

대화를 듣고, 남자가 어제 한 일로 가장 적절한 것을 고르시오.

① 운동하기
② 병문안 가기
③ 축구 관람하기
④ 휴대 전화 수리하기
⑤ 친구에게 전화하기

W Suho, have you seen Tom these days?
M Don't you know what happened to him?
W No, _____ _____ _____ _____?
M He broke his leg playing soccer a week ago and _____ _____ _____.
W Really? I didn't know that.
M Yeah, that's why he hasn't been at school since last week.
W That's too bad. So is he okay now?
M _____ _____ _____. Actually, I visited him in the hospital yesterday. Why don't you call him?
W Okay, I'll call him right now.

16 특정 정보 파악

대화를 듣고, 두 사람이 만날 장소를 고르시오.

① 공원 앞
② 시청 앞
③ 악기점
④ 지하철역
⑤ 기타 수리점

Sound Clear ☆ **in front of**
앞 단어의 끝 자음과 뒤 단어의 모음이 만나 연음되어 [인프런터브]로 발음된다.

(Cellphone rings.)
W Hi, David. Do you _____ _____ _____ today?
M Not really. Why?
W Well, can you _____ _____ _____ _____ at a music shop?
M Sure, I can help you. Which shop are you going to?
W _____ _____ _____ _____ the music shop near the Greenville subway station.
M _____ _____ _____ _____. I know a better place. What about meeting in front of City Hall in an hour?
W Okay, see you there.

17 마지막 말에 대한 응답 찾기 ✤

대화를 듣고, 여자의 마지막 말에 대한 남자의 응답으로 가장 적절한 것을 고르시오.

Man: _____

① You should have studied harder.
② You need to admit that you were wrong.
③ The rider should have reduced his speed.
④ You shouldn't use your phone while crossing the road.
⑤ You must look carefully both ways before you cross the road.

M Oh, Yubin. What happened to your arm?
W I _____ _____ _____. I must wear this cast for 2 weeks.
M How did it happen?
W I was hit by a bicycle _____ _____ _____ _____ yesterday.
M How did the bike hit you anyway? Did the rider ignore the traffic signal?
W No, the accident was my fault. _____ _____ _____ _____ _____ _____ while I was crossing the road.
M You shouldn't use your phone while crossing the road.

18 마지막 말에 대한 응답 찾기

대화를 듣고, 남자의 마지막 말에 대한 여자의 응답으로 가장 적절한 것을 고르시오.

Woman: _____

① I was really satisfied with my flight.
② No problem. I'll do that right away.
③ That's a relief. I was worried about it.
④ Yes. Could you please label it 'Handle with care'?
⑤ Don't you know that it's necessary to stay in line?

Sound Clear ☆ **check in**
앞 단어의 끝 자음과 뒤 단어의 모음이 만나 연음되어 [체킨]으로 발음된다.

W Hi. I'd like to check in for my flight.
M Could you _____ _____ _____ _____ and e-ticket, please?
W Here they are.
M Are you going to _____ _____ _____ _____?
W Yes, one bag. And I'll _____ _____ _____ _____ _____.
M Okay. Are there any batteries in your bag?
W No, _____ _____ _____ _____.
M Is there anything that can be easily broken in your bag?
W Yes. Could you please label it 'Handle with care'?

19 마지막 말에 대한 응답 찾기

대화를 듣고, 여자의 마지막 말에 대한 남자의 응답으로 가장 적절한 것을 고르시오.

Man: _____

① It's a small world, isn't it?
② Don't worry, just try to relax.
③ Is it okay if I use your phone?
④ I haven't heard about it before.
⑤ I'd like to speak to another person.

(*Cellphone rings.*)
M Congratulations! _____ _____ _____ the *Evening FM Music Show*.
W Am I really on the radio now?
M Yes, you are! _____ _____ _____ _____ _____ _____ every evening?
W Sure, every day before dinner.
M Wow! Thanks. _____ _____ _____ have you called in?
W Hundreds of times. And I finally got through it!
M Great! So _____ _____ _____ _____ answer today's quiz question?
W I'm a little bit nervous right now, but yes!
M Don't worry, just try to relax.

20 상황에 적절한 말 찾기

다음 상황 설명을 듣고, Minsu가 Sarah에게 할 말로 가장 적절한 것을 고르시오.

Minsu: Sarah, _____

① you look really scared.
② everything will be all right.
③ I'm afraid I'm too scared to do it.
④ I'm glad you could come to see me.
⑤ you ought to be ashamed of yourself.

W Minsu is at an amusement park with his classmates _____ _____ _____ _____. He and his best friend Sarah are really _____ _____ _____ _____ there. But Minsu doesn't like riding scary rides because _____ _____ _____ _____ _____. On the other hand, Sarah loves to ride them. So she asks Minsu to ride the roller coaster. In this situation, what would Minsu say to Sarah?
Minsu Sarah, I'm afraid I'm too scared to do it.

01 대화를 듣고, 두 사람이 보고 있는 사진을 고르시오.

①   ②   ③

④   ⑤

02 대화를 듣고, 남자가 여자에게 부탁한 일로 가장 적절한 것을 고르시오.

① 꽃 사 오기
② 공연 녹화하기
③ 연극 표 예매하기
④ 유치원 상담 가기
⑤ 공연에 대신 가 주기

03 다음 그림의 상황에 가장 적절한 대화를 고르시오.

①　　②　　③　　④　　⑤

04 대화를 듣고, 두 사람이 만날 시각을 고르시오.

① 5:30 p.m.　② 6:00 p.m.　③ 6:30 p.m.
④ 6:50 p.m.　⑤ 7:00 p.m.

05 대화를 듣고, 두 사람이 대화하는 장소로 가장 적절한 곳을 고르시오.

① 공항　　② 식당　　③ 우체국
④ 세탁소　⑤ 옷 가게

06 대화를 듣고, 남자가 오늘 전시회에 갈 수 <u>없는</u> 이유를 고르시오.

① 몸이 좋지 않아서
② 친구와 약속이 있어서
③ 시험공부를 해야 해서
④ 수학 숙제를 해야 해서
⑤ 동생의 공부를 도와줘야 해서

07 다음을 듣고, 두 사람의 대화가 <u>어색한</u> 것을 고르시오.

①　　②　　③　　④　　⑤

08 대화를 듣고, 남자의 마지막 말에 담긴 의도로 가장 적절한 것을 고르시오.

① 감사　　② 동의　　③ 요청
④ 위로　　⑤ 충고

09 대화를 듣고, 여자가 할 일로 가장 적절한 것을 고르시오.

① 여권 챙기기
② 날씨 확인하기
③ 여벌 옷 더 넣기
④ 여행 짐 줄이기
⑤ 여행 계획 세우기

10 대화를 듣고, 남자가 지불할 금액을 고르시오.

① $10　　② $18　　③ $20
④ $22　　⑤ $25

11 다음 표를 보면서 대화를 듣고, 여자가 구입할 방향제를 고르시오.

	Scent	Duration	Type
①	mint	1 month	non-liquid
②	mint	2 months	liquid
③	rose	1 month	non-liquid
④	rose	2 months	non-liquid
⑤	strawberry	2 months	liquid

12 다음을 듣고, 요리 경연 대회에 관한 내용과 일치하지 않는 것을 고르시오.

① 다음 달에 개최된다.
② 개인으로 참가해야 한다.
③ 두 시간 이내에 요리를 완성해야 한다.
④ 재료는 각자 준비해야 한다.
⑤ 이번 주 금요일까지 참가 신청을 해야 한다.

13 대화를 듣고, 여자가 남자에게 부탁한 일로 가장 적절한 것을 고르시오.

① 여행 가방 챙겨 주기
② 블로그 링크 보내 주기
③ 여행 안내 책자 빌려주기
④ 독일에 대한 정보 수집하기
⑤ 친구와 방문할 곳 추천해 주기

14 대화를 듣고, 남자가 대화 직후에 할 일로 가장 적절한 것을 고르시오.

① 요리하기
② 설거지하기
③ 음료수 사 오기
④ 저녁 식사하기
⑤ 쓰레기 버리기

15 대화를 듣고, 두 사람의 관계로 가장 적절한 것을 고르시오.

① 교사 – 학생
② 작곡가 – 가수
③ 비행기 승무원 – 탑승객
④ 라디오 디제이 – 청취자
⑤ 콜센터 직원 – 고객

16 대화를 듣고, 두 사람이 수업을 들을 강의실을 고르시오.

① 101
② 105
③ 201
④ 203
⑤ 205

17 다음을 듣고, 방송의 목적으로 가장 적절한 것을 고르시오.

① 학생회 이름을 공모하려고
② 학생회 회의 일정을 알리려고
③ 난방 시설 이용 방법을 알리려고
④ 학생회관 운영 시간을 안내하려고
⑤ 연설 장소가 변경되었음을 알리려고

18 대화를 듣고, 여자의 마지막 말에 대한 남자의 응답으로 가장 적절한 것을 고르시오.

Man: _____

① It's right next to Green Park.
② I jog every morning at Green Park.
③ You should wait about half an hour.
④ Take this medicine three times a day.
⑤ Let's meet at 7 o'clock at the airport.

19 대화를 듣고, 남자의 마지막 말에 대한 여자의 응답으로 가장 적절한 것을 고르시오.

Woman: _____

① Yes. I learned a lot in your class.
② Certainly. I'll go and see a doctor.
③ Great. I think I can fix it right now.
④ Right. I should go home early today.
⑤ Thank you. I'll visit your office after class.

20 다음 상황 설명을 듣고, Amy가 뒷사람에게 할 말로 가장 적절한 것을 고르시오.

Amy: Excuse me. _____

① What makes you like this singer?
② Could you hold my place, please?
③ How long have you been waiting?
④ Do you know how much the ticket is?
⑤ Do you know how many people are waiting here?

01 그림 정보 파악

대화를 듣고, 두 사람이 보고 있는 사진을 고르시오.

①
②
③
④
⑤

M What are you doing, Amy?

W Oh, _____ _____ _____ _____ my old pictures.

M Wow, is this you? So cute! You're wearing a beautiful hat.

W Thanks. I liked this hat _____ _____ _____ _____.

M Who is this boy next to you?

W He's my cousin, David. He's 17 years old now and still wants to be a soccer player.

M I see. That's why _____ _____ _____ _____ _____ _____.

02 부탁한 일 파악 ✖

대화를 듣고, 남자가 여자에게 부탁한 일로 가장 적절한 것을 고르시오.

① 꽃 사 오기
② 공연 녹화하기
③ 연극 표 예매하기
④ 유치원 상담 가기
⑤ 공연에 대신 가 주기

Sound Clear ☆ **record**
동사(기록하다, 녹음하다)는 2음절에 강세를 두어 [뤼컬드]로, 명사(기록, 음반)는 1음절에 강세를 두어 [뤠컬드]로 발음된다.

(*Cellphone rings.*)

W Honey. Where are you? Jenny's kindergarten play starts at six.

M I know, but I'm caught in a bad traffic jam now, so I don't think I can _____ _____ _____ _____.

W Oh, no! Then do you want me to buy flowers?

M _____ _____ _____ _____. I already bought some.

W That's good. How late are you going to be?

M I think I'll be there by 6:10 _____ _____ _____. Can you record the start of the play for me?

W No problem. Actually, I will _____ _____ _____ _____.

03 그림의 상황에 적절한 대화 찾기

다음 그림의 상황에 가장 적절한 대화를 고르시오.

① ② ③ ④ ⑤

① W Hello. Are you ready to order?

   M I haven't decided yet. What's today's special?

② W May I _____ _____ _____ _____, please?

   M Sure. Here it is.

③ W James, what are you _____ _____ _____ _____?

   M I'm reading some Internet news articles.

④ W Is there _____ _____ _____ _____?

   M My leg really hurts and I can barely walk.

⑤ W I need to mail this package to New York.

   M Okay. Let's see _____ _____ _____ _____.

04 숫자 정보 파악

대화를 듣고, 두 사람이 만날 시각을 고르시오.

① 5:30 p.m.　　② 6:00 p.m.
③ 6:30 p.m.　　④ 6:50 p.m.
⑤ 7:00 p.m.

Sound Clear ☆ **how about**
앞 단어의 반모음과 뒤 단어의 첫 모음이 만나 연음되어 [하워바웃]으로 발음된다.

W David, did you _____ _____ _____ _____ the movie we talked about?

M I sure did. It's this evening.

W Thanks, David. Did you get the tickets for 5:30 as we wanted?

M Unfortunately, _____ _____ _____ _____ _____. I got tickets for the 7 o'clock show.

W That's okay. Then _____ _____ _____ _____ _____ _____ _____ at the theater?

M Well, how about 30 minutes before the show? I want to _____ _____ _____ _____ before the movie starts.

W Sounds good. I'll see you at half past six.

05 장소 추론

대화를 듣고, 두 사람이 대화하는 장소로 가장 적절한 곳을 고르시오.

① 공항　　② 식당　　③ 우체국
④ 세탁소　　⑤ 옷 가게

W Hello, Mr. Jordan. Could you _____ _____ _____ _____ this jacket?

M That's quite a big stain. What did you spill on it?

W Some *kimchi* stew splattered on it. Can you remove it?

M No problem.

W When can I get this back? I need to wear it this weekend.

M _____ _____ _____ by tomorrow afternoon.

W That's so fast. Can I also _____ _____ _____ _____ that I dropped off yesterday?

M Yes. You can pick them both up tomorrow afternoon.

06 이유 파악

대화를 듣고, 남자가 오늘 전시회에 갈 수 <u>없는</u> 이유를 고르시오.

① 몸이 좋지 않아서
② 친구와 약속이 있어서
③ 시험공부를 해야 해서
④ 수학 숙제를 해야 해서
⑤ 동생의 공부를 도와줘야 해서

W James, have you heard about the Seoul Trick Art Exhibition?

M No, but that sounds interesting.

W I'm going to see it after school. It's being held at Seoul Art Center. _____ _____ _____ _____?

M I'm sorry, but not this afternoon.

W Why not? I thought _____ _____ _____ _____.

M I'd really love to, but I promised to help my brother study math this afternoon.

W _____ _____ _____ _____ _____ tomorrow?

M That's his exam day, so he needs me today.

07 어색한 대화 찾기

다음을 듣고, 두 사람의 대화가 어색한 것을 고르시오.

①   ②   ③   ④   ⑤

Sound Clear ☆ **Don't worry**

축약된 't는 거의 발음되지 않아 [돈워뤼]로 발음된다.

08 의도 파악

대화를 듣고, 남자의 마지막 말에 담긴 의도로 가장 적절한 것을 고르시오.

① 감사   ② 동의   ③ 요청
④ 위로   ⑤ 충고

09 할 일 파악

대화를 듣고, 여자가 할 일로 가장 적절한 것을 고르시오.

① 여권 챙기기   ② 날씨 확인하기
③ 여벌 옷 더 넣기   ④ 여행 짐 줄이기
⑤ 여행 계획 세우기

10 숫자 정보 파악   🏴

대화를 듣고, 남자가 지불할 금액을 고르시오.

① $10   ② $18   ③ $20
④ $22   ⑤ $25

---

① M   What time _____ _____ _____ _____?

    W   I think I'll be there around 2 p.m.

② M   What are _____ _____ _____ on weekends?

    W   From 9 a.m. to 5 p.m.

③ M   How often do you _____ _____ in a week?

    W   I usually eat out with my roommate.

④ M   Is there a subway station nearby?

    W   Yes, the subway station is just over there.

⑤ M   _____ _____ _____ _____ the dog before going out.

    W   Don't worry. I won't forget.

M   Look at this! This applicant seems very interesting. He worked as an assistant cook for 7 years.

W   Oh, that's a long time. I think he'll _____ _____ _____ _____ to our restaurant.

M   Yeah, and _____ _____ _____ _____.

W   What is it?

M   He _____ _____ _____ _____ _____ for the homeless for 2 years.

W   Wow! What a great guy!

M   I think so, too. He's exactly what we've been looking for.

정답 단서

M   Jane, are you going to pack all these clothes for your trip?

W   Of course. I think I still _____ _____ _____ _____.

M   Do you really think you'll need all of them?

W   Well, _____ _____ _____ it gets too cold or too hot.

M   Oh, come on. You're going on a trip _____ _____ _____ _____ _____!

W   But you never know how the weather might change.

M   Still, _____ _____ _____ _____(한정). It's always better to travel lightly.

W   Okay. I'll take out some clothes, then.

정답 단서

W   I'm finished. How do you like it?

M   I love it. I've never tried this kind of hairstyle before.

W   I think _____ _____ _____ _____.

M   Thank you. How much is it?

W   It's $20 for the haircut.

M   Is there _____ _____ _____?

W   No, I'm sorry. But I'll give you a 10% discount coupon _____ _____ _____ _____. Here you are.

M   That's great. Here's my card.

11 도표 정보 파악

다음 표를 보면서 대화를 듣고, 여자가 구입할 방향제를 고르시오.

	Scent	Duration	Type
①	mint	1 month	non-liquid
②	mint	2 months	liquid
③	rose	1 month	non-liquid
④	rose	2 months	non-liquid
⑤	strawberry	2 months	liquid

Sound Clear ☆ **scent**

c가 묵음이라서 [센트]로 발음된다.

W Honey, I want to _____ _____ _____ _____.
M What kind of scent do you want?
W I had mint last time. Maybe I'll _____ _____ this time.
M Good idea. And why don't you get one that lasts longer than one month?
W I will. I don't want to _____ _____ _____ it too often.
M Exactly. Then you only have two options.
W Yes. Shall I get the liquid type like before?
M Well, since it comes in a bottle, it might _____ _____ _____ _____ _____. Try the other type this time.
W All right. Then I'll buy this one.

12 일치하지 않는 것 찾기

다음을 듣고, 요리 경연 대회에 관한 내용과 일치하지 않는 것을 고르시오.

① 다음 달에 개최된다.
② 개인으로 참가해야 한다.
③ 두 시간 이내에 요리를 완성해야 한다.
④ 재료는 각자 준비해야 한다.
⑤ 이번 주 금요일까지 참가 신청을 해야 한다.

W Good afternoon, students. This is Jennifer from the Student Council. Our school is going to hold its 1st Cooking Competition next month. There are _____ _____ _____ _____ _____ about the competition. First, it's an individual competition. Second, you should complete your dish _____ _____ _____. Third, cooking equipment will be provided, but you should bring your own ingredients. Finally, you _____ _____ _____ _____ the competition by this Thursday. 정답 단서

13 부탁한 일 파악

대화를 듣고, 여자가 남자에게 부탁한 일로 가장 적절한 것을 고르시오.

① 여행 가방 챙겨 주기
② 블로그 링크 보내 주기
③ 여행 안내 책자 빌려주기
④ 독일에 대한 정보 수집하기
⑤ 친구와 방문할 곳 추천해 주기

M Mira, what are you reading?
W I'm reading a tour guidebook of Seoul. My friend from Germany is visiting me next week.
M Oh, I see. _____ _____ _____ where to go?
W I still don't know. This book doesn't seem to 함정 _____ _____ _____.
M Well, I can recommend a good blog about traveling in Seoul.
W Really? Would it be more useful than this book?
M Absolutely. _____ _____ _____ _____ _____ for traveling around Seoul.
W Sounds good. Can you send me the link of the blog? 정답 단서

14 할 일 파악

대화를 듣고, 남자가 대화 직후에 할 일로 가장 적절한 것을 고르시오.

① 요리하기　　　② 설거지하기
③ 음료수 사 오기　　④ 저녁 식사하기
⑤ 쓰레기 버리기

Sound Clear ☆ **Caesar salad**
샐러드의 일종으로 [시절샐러드]로 발음된다.

M　Mom, what are we having for dinner?
W　How about ribeye steak and Caesar salad?
M　Wow, _____ _____. Do you want me to help you cook?
W　No, I'll do it. And after dinner, your dad will _____ _____ _____.
M　Okay. I'm going to buy some cold sodas. Do you need anything else from the store?
W　No, but can you _____ _____ _____ _____ first?
M　Okay. Today is the garbage collection day.
W　Right. _____ _____ _____ _____ _____ soon.

15 관계 추론 ✖

대화를 듣고, 두 사람의 관계로 가장 적절한 것을 고르시오.

① 교사 – 학생
② 작곡가 – 가수
③ 비행기 승무원 – 탑승객
④ 라디오 디제이 – 청취자
⑤ 콜센터 직원 – 고객

M　Good morning. You're on the air. Can you tell us your name and _____ _____ _____ _____ ?
　　정답 단서
W　I'm Suji Park calling from Jeju-do.
M　Hello, Suji. _____ _____ _____ _____. Are you a student?
W　Yes. I'm a third grader in middle school.
M　Oh, I see. So what song _____ _____ _____ _____ ?
W　I'd like to request *Endless Love*. It's for my parents. It's their wedding anniversary today.
　　정답 단서
M　That's so sweet. I'm sure _____ _____ _____.

16 특정 정보 파악

대화를 듣고, 두 사람이 수업을 들을 강의실을 고르시오.

① 101　　② 105　　③ 201
④ 203　　⑤ 205

M　What's the next class, Karen?
W　Social studies.
M　Oh, then we _____ _____ _____. Classroom 101 is in the other building.
W　Haven't you heard that _____ _____ _____ _____ ?
M　Really? To where?
W　Because of the maintenance problem, our class will be in Classroom 203.
　　정답 단서
M　Oh, you mean the room right next to 204?
W　Actually, _____ _____ _____ 204. Classroom 203 is next to 205.
M　I see. Let's go.

17 목적 파악

다음을 듣고, 방송의 목적으로 가장 적절한 것을 고르시오.

① 학생회 이름을 공모하려고
② 학생회 회의 일정을 알리려고
③ 난방 시설 이용 방법을 알리려고
④ 학생회관 운영 시간을 안내하려고
⑤ 연설 장소가 변경되었음을 알리려고

M Attention, students. This is an announcement from the Student Council. _____ _____ _____, the candidates for the president election are giving speeches at 11 tomorrow morning. The event _____ _____ _____ _____ _____ in the auditorium, but the heating system has some problems, so we changed the location. _____ _____ _____ _____ _____ in the student hall located next to the library. See you there at 11 tomorrow.

18 마지막 말에 대한 응답 찾기 ✽

대화를 듣고, 여자의 마지막 말에 대한 남자의 응답으로 가장 적절한 것을 고르시오.

Man: _____

① It's right next to Green Park.
② I jog every morning at Green Park.
③ You should wait about half an hour.
④ Take this medicine three times a day.
⑤ Let's meet at 7 o'clock at the airport.

M Hey, Olivia. What's the matter?
W I fell down and I think I _____ _____ _____.
M That's too bad. Does it hurt a lot?
W Yeah, I think I have to _____ _____ _____ _____.
M I wish I could go with you, but I'm late for class. Do you think _____ _____ _____ _____ _____ ?
W Yes, don't worry. Do you know where the nearest hospital is?
M It's right next to Green Park.

19 마지막 말에 대한 응답 찾기

대화를 듣고, 남자의 마지막 말에 대한 여자의 응답으로 가장 적절한 것을 고르시오.

Woman: _____

① Yes. I learned a lot in your class.
② Certainly. I'll go and see a doctor.
③ Great. I think I can fix it right now.
④ Right. I should go home early today.
⑤ Thank you. I'll visit your office after class.

Sound Clear ☆ **kind of**
앞 단어의 끝 자음과 뒤 단어의 모음이 만나 연음되어 [카인더브]로 발음된다.

W Dr. Jones. Do you have a minute to talk?
M Sure, Lisa. What is it?
W I developed an app over the weekend.
M Really? What kind of app is it?
W It's an app that helps people record their health conditions.
M Wow! It sounds very useful. _____ _____ _____ !
W But it sometimes stops suddenly. I can't _____ _____ _____ what's wrong.
M Maybe we can _____ _____ _____ together. Will you come to my office after class?
W Thank you. I'll visit your office after class.

20 상황에 적절한 말 찾기

다음 상황 설명을 듣고, Amy가 뒷사람에게 할 말로 가장 적절한 것을 고르시오.

Amy: Excuse me. _____

① What makes you like this singer?
② Could you hold my place, please?
③ How long have you been waiting?
④ Do you know how much the ticket is?
⑤ Do you know how many people are waiting here?

W Amy is _____ _____ _____ to buy a ticket for her favorite singer's concert. There are lots of people _____ _____ _____. The line is so long and it is moving very slowly. But suddenly, she needs to go to the restroom, but she doesn't want somebody to _____ _____ _____. In this situation, what would Amy say to the person right behind her?
Amy Excuse me. Could you hold my place, please?

Review Test

Word Check 영어는 우리말로, 우리말은 영어로 써 보기

01 lecture _____

02 include _____

03 guest _____

04 handle _____

05 cost _____

06 bookshelf _____

07 emergency _____

08 ignore _____

09 warning _____

10 referee _____

11 stay in line _____

12 keep in mind _____

13 잘못 _____

14 속도 _____

15 가벼운 _____

16 필요한 _____

17 지루한 _____

18 연결하다 _____

19 후식 _____

20 지속하다, 계속되다 _____

21 인정하다 _____

22 응급 처치 _____

23 교통 신호 _____

24 반면에 _____

Expression Check 알맞은 표현을 넣어 문장 완성하기

25 I wonder what he _____ _____. 난 그가 어떻게 생겼는지 궁금해.

26 Can you recommend _____ _____? 다른 것을 추천해 줄래?

27 Do you want me to _____ _____ her? 너는 내가 그녀를 돌봐 주기를 원하니?

28 Minsu _____ _____ _____ heights. 민수는 고소 공포증이 있다.

29 It's _____ _____ now and only costs $300! 그것은 지금 할인 중이어서 300달러밖에 안 해!

30 _____ _____ _____, we should move the piano a little bit.
그 경우에, 우린 피아노를 약간 옮겨야 해.

Answers p.36

Word Check 영어는 우리말로, 우리말은 영어로 써 보기

01 apply _____

02 ingredient _____

03 candidate _____

04 restroom _____

05 replace _____

06 maintenance _____

07 theater _____

08 exactly _____

09 nearby _____

10 on time _____

11 figure out _____

12 at the latest _____

13 조수, 보조원 _____

14 제거하다 _____

15 요청하다 _____

16 개발하다 _____

17 기사 _____

18 무게가 ~이다 _____

19 개인의 _____

20 강당 _____

21 도구, 장비 _____

22 ~을 신청하다 _____

23 결혼기념일 _____

24 혼자서 _____

Expression Check 알맞은 표현을 넣어 문장 완성하기

25 It might _____ _____ a bigger space. 그것은 더 큰 공간을 차지할지도 몰라요.

26 I _____ _____ and I think I twisted my arm. 나는 넘어졌는데 팔을 삔 것 같아.

27 I'm _____ _____ a bad traffic jam now. 난 지금 심한 교통 체증에 갇혀 있어.

28 Can you _____ _____ the garbage first? 먼저 쓰레기 좀 버려 줄래?

29 Amy is standing _____ _____ to buy a ticket. Amy는 티켓을 사기 위해 줄을 서고 있다.

30 Don't _____ _____ _____ the dog before going out.
외출하기 전에 개에게 먹이 주는 거 잊지 마라.

1.0배속

1.2배속

01 대화를 듣고, 두 사람이 구입할 건조기를 고르시오.

①
SMART 9kg

②
SMART 14kg

③
SMART 14kg

④
NICE 9kg

⑤
NICE 14kg

02 대화를 듣고, 남자가 대화 직후에 할 일로 가장 적절한 것을 고르시오.

① 입사 지원하기　　② 회사 방문하기
③ 이메일 보내기　　④ 회사에 전화하기
⑤ 취업 박람회 참가하기

03 대화를 듣고, 남자의 심정으로 가장 적절한 것을 고르시오.

① calm　　② jealous　　③ pleased
④ excited　　⑤ worried

04 대화를 듣고, 남자가 지불한 금액을 고르시오.

① $10　　② $16　　③ $18
④ $20　　⑤ $26

05 대화를 듣고, 두 사람이 대화하는 장소로 가장 적절한 곳을 고르시오.

① 영화관　　　　② 지하철역
③ 공원 매표소　　④ 버스 정류장
⑤ 고속도로 톨게이트

06 대화를 듣고, 여자가 남자에게 부탁한 일로 가장 적절한 것을 고르시오.

① 택시 예약해 주기
② 룸서비스 해 주기
③ 버스 시간표 알려 주기
④ 아침에 전화로 깨워 주기
⑤ Wonderland 표 예매하기

07 다음을 듣고, 두 사람의 대화가 <u>어색한</u> 것을 고르시오.

①　　②　　③　　④　　⑤

08 대화를 듣고, 남자가 주문할 텀블러의 개수를 고르시오.

① 50개　　② 80개　　③ 100개
④ 130개　　⑤ 150개

09 다음을 듣고, 무엇에 관한 내용인지 고르시오.

① 귀 청소의 중요성
② 청력을 보호하는 방법
③ 수중에서 귀를 보호하는 방법
④ 귀를 다쳤을 때 대처하는 방법
⑤ 청력 검진을 해야 하는 이유

10 대화를 듣고, 남자가 제출한 작품을 다시 가져가려는 이유를 고르시오.

① 부품을 구하기 어려워서
② 더 좋은 아이디어가 떠올라서
③ 제작 비용이 너무 많이 들어서
④ 비현실적이라는 생각이 들어서
⑤ 이미 유사한 작품이 발명되어서

11 대화를 듣고, 남자의 마지막 말에 담긴 의도로 가장 적절한 것을 고르시오.

① 위로　　② 감사　　③ 조언
④ 불평　　⑤ 거절

12 다음을 듣고, 방송의 목적으로 가장 적절한 것을 고르시오.

① 다음 정차 역을 안내하려고
② 열차 안에서의 예절을 알리려고
③ 정차 시간이 길어짐을 알리려고
④ 습득한 물품의 주인을 찾으려고
⑤ 열차 내 편의 시설을 안내하려고

13 다음을 듣고, 포스터 대회에 대해 언급되지 <u>않은</u> 것을 고르시오.

① 참가 자격   ② 주제   ③ 제출일
④ 규격   ⑤ 시상 계획

14 다음 그림의 상황에 가장 적절한 대화를 고르시오.

①   ②   ③   ④   ⑤

15 다음 표를 보면서 대화를 듣고, 두 사람이 선택할 벚꽃 여행을 고르시오.

	Day	Destination	Lunch
①	Saturday	Gyeongju	No
②	Saturday	Jinhae	Yes
③	Sunday	Gyeongju	No
④	Sunday	Gyeongju	Yes
⑤	Sunday	Jinhae	Yes

16 대화를 듣고, 두 사람의 관계로 가장 적절한 것을 고르시오.

① 작가 − 배우   ② 기자 − 작가
③ 기자 − 관람객   ④ 요리사 − TV 연출가
⑤ 영화 제작자 − 감독

17 대화를 듣고, 두 사람이 함께 볼 TV 프로그램으로 가장 적절한 것을 고르시오.

① 퀴즈 쇼   ② 여행 프로그램
③ 요리 프로그램   ④ 뉴스 프로그램
⑤ 과학 다큐멘터리

18 대화를 듣고, 남자의 마지막 말에 대한 여자의 응답으로 가장 적절한 것을 고르시오.

Woman: _____

① Thanks, but I prefer to study alone.
② Can you help me do my homework?
③ Do you know how to get to the library?
④ Sorry, but I don't have much information.
⑤ Are you more comfortable when studying at home?

19 대화를 듣고, 여자의 마지막 말에 대한 남자의 응답으로 가장 적절한 것을 고르시오.

Man: _____

① I'd like to invite some of my friends.
② Sure, I can do that. I'll go right now.
③ Why don't we order a strawberry cake?
④ I can call and ask them what time they are coming.
⑤ Don't forget to pick up the cake on your way back home.

20 다음 상황 설명을 듣고, Helen이 Matthew에게 할 말로 가장 적절한 것을 고르시오.

Helen: Matthew, _____

① have you checked the bus schedule?
② do you know where the bus stop is?
③ can you wake me up in the morning?
④ could you give me some tips for my trip to China?
⑤ can you give me a ride to the airport this Saturday?

받아쓰기용

01 그림 정보 파악

대화를 듣고, 두 사람이 구입할 건조기를 고르시오.

① SMART 9kg
② SMART 14kg
③ SMART 14kg
④ NICE 9kg
⑤ NICE 14kg

M I'm so glad we are finally going to buy a dryer. We needed one last year _____ _____ _____ _____.

W That's true. Our washing machine is from SMART, so I'd prefer to _____ _____ _____ _____.

M Okay. Then what about this 9-kilogram dryer?

W It seems too small. We sometimes need to dry blankets.

M All right. Which color then? The darker-colored one looks good.

W But I think the lighter-colored one would _____ _____ _____ _____ _____.

M Okay. _____ _____ _____ _____ then.

02 할 일 파악

대화를 듣고, 남자가 대화 직후에 할 일로 가장 적절한 것을 고르시오.

① 입사 지원하기   ② 회사 방문하기
③ 이메일 보내기   ④ 회사에 전화하기
⑤ 취업 박람회 참가하기

W Have you heard anything from _____ _____ _____ _____ _____?

M No. I was supposed to hear something yesterday, but they _____ _____ _____ _____ _____ yet.

W I thought you would have heard something by now.

M I know, but _____ _____ _____ _____ _____ for them to examine all the documents. I'm getting worried.

W Hey, why don't you email or call them and ask about it?

M Do you think that would be okay?

W Why not? Just _____ _____ _____ _____.

M Okay, I'll call them. Thank you for your advice.

03 심정 추론 ✕

대화를 듣고, 남자의 심정으로 가장 적절한 것을 고르시오.

① calm   ② jealous   ③ pleased
④ excited   ⑤ worried

Sound Clear ☆ **assignment**
g가 묵음이라서 [어싸인먼트]로 발음된다.

W Dave, what are you looking for on the computer?

M I'm looking for the pictures that I took for my art assignment.

W You mean the assignment _____ _____ _____ in Seoul?

M Yeah. I've checked all the folders, but I can't find them.

W Why don't you just describe the buildings _____ _____?

M I need to _____ _____ _____ three pictures that I took by myself.

W Did you _____ _____ _____ _____ in your camera?

M I deleted all the pictures right after I uploaded them onto the computer.

04 숫자 정보 파악

대화를 듣고, 남자가 지불한 금액을 고르시오.

① $10 ② $16 ③ $18
④ $20 ⑤ $26

W You look really nice today. Is that a new jacket?

M Yes, thanks! I bought it ________ ________ ________ ________ ________ near my office.

W Really? It looks pretty new and fashionable.

M And it was really cheap. They're ________ ________ ________ ________. Everything is 50% off.

W How much was it?

M It was $20 ________ ________ ________.

W Wow! So it was only $10 then?

M Yes. I also bought a pair of shoes. They were originally $16.

W ________ ________ ________ ________! I should go there before the sale ends.

05 장소 추론

대화를 듣고, 두 사람이 대화하는 장소로 가장 적절한 곳을 고르시오.

① 영화관 ② 지하철역
③ 공원 매표소 ④ 버스 정류장
⑤ 고속도로 톨게이트

Sound Clear ☆ **receipt**
p가 묵음이라서 [리씨트]로 발음된다.

M Good afternoon. Here's my ticket.

W That'll be 16,000 won. You've driven ________ ________ ________ ________!

M Yes. Can I pay by credit card?

W Sure. (*Pause*) Here's your card and receipt.

M One question, ma'am. ________ ________ ________ ________ how to get to Park Paradise?

W ________ ________ ________ straight for about two kilometers and take Route 37.

M Take Route 37?

W Right. Sorry, but other cars are ________ ________ ________.

M Oops, I kept you too long. Thanks!

06 부탁한 일 파악

대화를 듣고, 여자가 남자에게 부탁한 일로 가장 적절한 것을 고르시오.

① 택시 예약해 주기
② 룸서비스 해 주기
③ 버스 시간표 알려 주기
④ 아침에 전화로 깨워 주기
⑤ Wonderland 표 예매하기

W Hi, I'm staying in Room 1405. ________ ________ ________ ________ how long it takes from here to Wonderland.

M It takes about 20 minutes by car.

W Are there any buses going there?

M Yes, but there are ________ ________ ________ ________ ________. People usually take a taxi.

W Then can you reserve one for me for tomorrow morning?

M Sure, at what time?

W Well, 8:00 a.m. would be good.

M Okay, I'll call the taxi company now. Please ________ ________ ________ ________ ________ before then.

07 어색한 대화 찾기

다음을 듣고, 두 사람의 대화가 <u>어색한</u> 것을 고르시오.

①   ②   ③   ④   ⑤

① W   I left my bag on the subway.

   M   _____ _____ _____ the lost and found?

② W   What are your plans for this weekend?

   M   Nothing special. What about you?

③ W   How many books can I borrow _____ _____ _____?

   M   You can borrow books for five days.

④ W   Excuse me. Is there a post office nearby?

   M   Sorry, but _____ _____ _____ here myself.

⑤ W   Look at those flowers on Suji's desk.

   M   They're so beautiful. I wonder _____ _____ _____.

08 특정 정보 파악

대화를 듣고, 남자가 주문할 텀블러의 개수를 고르시오.

① 50개   ② 80개   ③ 100개
④ 130개   ⑤ 150개

Sound Clear ☆ **enough**

gh가 [f]로 소리 나서 [이너프]로 발음된다.

W   Sean, are you ready for your restaurant's opening?

M   Almost. I only have to order the free gifts for customers.

W   _____ _____ _____?

M   Tumblers with my restaurant's logo. Do you think 100 tumblers will be enough?

W   I think _____ _____ _____ 50 more tumblers.

M   Isn't 150 too many? For my first restaurant in Cary Town, I ordered 80, and _____ _____ _____.

W   But a lot more people live in this town.

M   You're right. I'll order _____ _____ _____ _____.

09 주제 파악

다음을 듣고, 무엇에 관한 내용인지 고르시오.

① 귀 청소의 중요성
② 청력을 보호하는 방법
③ 수중에서 귀를 보호하는 방법
④ 귀를 다쳤을 때 대처하는 방법
⑤ 청력 검진을 해야 하는 이유

W   Did you know that many people lose their hearing _____ _____ _____ _____? Today, I'm going to tell you some things you should keep in mind to avoid hearing problems. First, keep your music at a low volume. Next, _____ _____ _____ _____ water in your ears when bathing or swimming. Finally, many doctors strongly advise you not to clean your ears at home. _____ _____ _____ _____ _____, see your doctor right away.

10 이유 파악

대화를 듣고, 남자가 제출한 작품을 다시 가져가려는 이유를 고르시오.

① 부품을 구하기 어려워서
② 더 좋은 아이디어가 떠올라서
③ 제작 비용이 너무 많이 들어서
④ 비현실적이라는 생각이 들어서
⑤ 이미 유사한 작품이 발명되어서

M   Hello, Ms. Brandon. Can I take back the sample that _____ _____ _____ _____?

W   Do you mean the one for the student invention contest?

M   Yes. I think I should _____ _____ _____ _____ for the contest.

W   Why? I liked your idea of a chair with a hanger.

M   Yeah, so did I. _____ _____ _____ _____ _____.

W   So what's wrong then?

M   Well, I saw _____ _____ _____ _____ _____ on the Internet. Someone has already invented it.

11 의도 파악

대화를 듣고, 남자의 마지막 말에 담긴 의도로 가장 적절한 것을 고르시오.

① 위로   ② 감사   ③ 조언
④ 불평   ⑤ 거절

Sound Clear ☆ **exactly**

ex 뒤에 모음이 오면 주로 [igz]로 발음되고, [t]는 [l] 앞에서 약화되어 [이그잭-을리]로 발음된다.

M　Monica, you look busy. What's up?

W　I've been _____ _____ _____ my computer all morning.

M　Your new computer? Is there something wrong with it?

W　I don't exactly know. It _____ _____ _____ automatically.

M　It might be _____ _____ _____ _____. Did you visit the service center?

W　I called, but they are closed on weekends.

M　Then _____ _____ _____ _____ an antivirus program? I know a good one.

12 목적 파악

다음을 듣고, 방송의 목적으로 가장 적절한 것을 고르시오.

① 다음 정차 역을 안내하려고
② 열차 안에서의 예절을 알리려고
③ 정차 시간이 길어짐을 알리려고
④ 습득한 물품의 주인을 찾으려고
⑤ 열차 내 편의 시설을 안내하려고

M　Good afternoon, passengers! May I _____ _____ _____, please? We are sorry to inform you that the train will stay at this station _____ _____ _____ _____ because of a technical problem. This is a minor issue and our mechanics are _____ _____ _____. We expect the train will leave in 10 minutes. We're _____ _____ _____ _____. Thank you for your patience.

13 언급되지 않은 것 찾기

다음을 듣고, 포스터 대회에 대해 언급되지 않은 것을 고르시오.

① 참가 자격   ② 주제   ③ 제출일
④ 규격   ⑤ 시상 계획

W　Good morning! Today, I'd like to _____ _____ _____ about this year's Clark County Poster Contest. Any Clark County School student can _____ _____ _____. The topic is "School Safety." The submission dates are from September 10 to September 14. Posters should be no larger than A3 size. All submissions _____ _____ _____ _____ to your art teacher. Good luck to everybody!

14 그림의 상황에 적절한 대화 찾기

다음 그림의 상황에 가장 적절한 대화를 고르시오.

①　②　③　④　⑤

① W　This boy in the picture _____ _____ _____ _____ _____.
　 M　Does he? Actually, he's my twin brother.

② W　Watch out! You almost hit my daughter with your bike.
　 M　Oh, I'm really sorry. Is she okay?

③ W　_____ _____ _____ _____ _____ _____?
　 M　The 8th floor. Thanks a lot.

④ W　You're not allowed to wear shoes in here, sir.
　 M　Oh, I didn't know that. _____ _____ _____ _____.

⑤ W　Excuse me. Could you please be quiet in the reading room?
　 M　I'm sorry. I'll keep my voice down.

15 도표 정보 파악 �

다음 표를 보면서 대화를 듣고, 두 사람이 선택할 벚꽃 여행을 고르시오.

	Day	Destination	Lunch
①	Saturday	Gyeongju	No
②	Saturday	Jinhae	Yes
③	Sunday	Gyeongju	No
④	Sunday	Gyeongju	Yes
⑤	Sunday	Jinhae	Yes

W Chris, _____ _____ _____ _____ any cherry blossom trips?

M Yes. This travel agency is offering several different one-day cherry blossom trips for this weekend.

W Oh, let me see. I need to go to my friend's wedding on Saturday.

M Then let's look at the Sunday trips.

W Gyeongju looks better than Jinhae. Jinhae is _____ _____ _____ _____.
정답 단서

M Okay. Now we have one more option, lunch included or not included.

W I'd prefer the one with the lunch included. _____ _____ _____ _____ _____.
정답 단서

M I agree. Then this one is the best.

16 관계 추론

대화를 듣고, 두 사람의 관계로 가장 적절한 것을 고르시오.

① 작가 – 배우
② 기자 – 작가
③ 기자 – 관람객
④ 요리사 – TV 연출가
⑤ 영화 제작자 – 감독

Sound Clear ☆ **we'd be**
축약된 'd는 거의 발음되지 않아 [위비]로 발음된다.

W Congratulations on winning the year's _____ _____ _____ _____!

M Thank you.

W Have you decided on which company _____ _____ _____ _____ _____ for your next movie?

M Actually, I haven't made the decision yet.

W Well, we'd be pleased to work with you. _____ _____ _____ _____ as one of your potential candidates?

M All right. _____ _____ _____ _____ next week and we can discuss it further.

W Sure. Let me know a convenient time.

17 특정 정보 파악

대화를 듣고, 두 사람이 함께 볼 TV 프로그램으로 가장 적절한 것을 고르시오.

① 퀴즈 쇼   ② 여행 프로그램
③ 요리 프로그램   ④ 뉴스 프로그램
⑤ 과학 다큐멘터리

M _____ _____ _____ Quiz Champion last night?

W No, I didn't. I don't really watch quiz shows.

M What do you usually watch then?

W I mostly watch science documentaries. What about you?

M I like cooking programs. My favorite is the one with _____ _____ _____ _____.
함정

W I've seen that program, too. I like it because he uses _____ _____ _____ _____.

M Actually, it's going to be on tonight. Do you _____ _____ _____ _____ _____?

W Sounds like a good idea.

18 마지막 말에 대한 응답 찾기

대화를 듣고, 남자의 마지막 말에 대한 여자의 응답으로 가장 적절한 것을 고르시오.

Woman: _____

① Thanks, but I prefer to study alone.
② Can you help me do my homework?
③ Do you know how to get to the library?
④ Sorry, but I don't have much information.
⑤ Are you more comfortable when studying at home?

Sound Clear ☆ **totally**

[t]가 모음 사이에서 약화되어 [토럴리]로 발음된다.

M Hey, what's up?
W I'm _____ _____ _____ the library to look up some information.
M For your school assignments?
W Yes. I have so many assignments that I _____ _____ _____ _____ all of them.
M I totally understand. It takes me too much time to _____ _____ _____ _____.
W Right. Sometimes I spend hours doing research in the library.
M Well, I _____ _____ _____ _____ _____, and it has saved me a lot of time. Why don't you join us?
W <u>Thanks, but I prefer to study alone.</u>

---

19 마지막 말에 대한 응답 찾기 ❖

대화를 듣고, 여자의 마지막 말에 대한 남자의 응답으로 가장 적절한 것을 고르시오.

Man: _____

① I'd like to invite some of my friends.
② Sure, I can do that. I'll go right now.
③ Why don't we order a strawberry cake?
④ I can call and ask them what time they are coming.
⑤ Don't forget to pick up the cake on your way back home.

M I'm home. Why are you so busy?
W Don't you remember? Terry and Erica are _____ _____ _____.
M Oh, right! _____ _____ _____ _____ _____?
W At 7.
M Do you want me to help you cook?
W I'm _____ _____ _____.
M Okay. Is there anything I can do for you?
W Well, why don't you _____ _____ _____ _____ that I ordered at Kim's Bakery?
M <u>Sure, I can do that. I'll go right now.</u>

---

20 상황에 적절한 말 찾기

다음 상황 설명을 듣고, Helen이 Matthew에게 할 말로 가장 적절한 것을 고르시오.

Helen: Matthew, _____

① have you checked the bus schedule?
② do you know where the bus stop is?
③ can you wake me up in the morning?
④ could you give me some tips for my trip to China?
⑤ can you give me a ride to the airport this Saturday?

M Helen _____ _____ _____ _____ to China this Saturday. She must arrive at the airport by 7 a.m. _____ _____ _____ _____ _____ _____ _____ at 5 a.m. When she checks the bus schedule though, she finds out that there is no bus before 7 a.m. So Helen _____ _____ _____ _____ _____ Matthew if he can drive her to the airport. In this situation, what would Helen most likely say to Matthew?
Helen Matthew, <u>can you give me a ride to the airport this Saturday?</u>

1.0배속

1.2배속

01 대화를 듣고, 남자가 구입할 USB를 고르시오.

02 대화를 듣고, 여자가 남자에게 전화한 목적으로 가장 적절한 것을 고르시오.

① 지갑을 찾으려고
② 감사의 인사를 하려고
③ 책 반납을 독촉하려고
④ 컴퓨터 수리를 부탁하려고
⑤ 지갑을 주인에게 찾아 주려고

03 다음 그림의 상황에 가장 적절한 대화를 고르시오.

① ② ③ ④ ⑤

04 대화를 듣고, 여자가 방과 후 수업을 시작하는 요일을 고르시오.

① 월요일 ② 화요일 ③ 수요일
④ 목요일 ⑤ 금요일

05 대화를 듣고, 여자의 직업으로 가장 적절한 것을 고르시오.

① nurse ② doctor
③ teacher ④ librarian
⑤ tennis player

06 대화를 듣고, 남자의 심정으로 가장 적절한 것을 고르시오.

① bored ② excited
③ jealous ④ surprised
⑤ disappointed

07 다음을 듣고, 두 사람의 대화가 어색한 것을 고르시오.

① ② ③ ④ ⑤

08 대화를 듣고, 두 사람이 대화 직후에 할 일로 가장 적절한 것을 고르시오.

① 촬영하기 ② 작품 감상하기
③ 동영상 편집하기 ④ 등장인물 구상하기
⑤ 스토리보드 만들기

09 다음을 듣고, 작가에 관해 언급되지 않은 것을 고르시오.

① 이름 ② 취미 ③ 새 책의 제목
④ 어릴 때 꿈 ⑤ 좌우명

10 대화를 듣고, 남자가 지불할 금액을 고르시오.

① $10 ② $12 ③ $17
④ $24 ⑤ $25

11 대화를 듣고, 두 사람이 대화하는 장소로 가장 적절한 곳을 고르시오.

① 교실　　　② 식당　　　③ 미술실
④ 방송실　　⑤ 체육관

12 대화를 듣고, 여자의 마지막 말에 담긴 의도로 가장 적절한 것을 고르시오.

① 격려　　　② 동의　　　③ 부탁
④ 사과　　　⑤ 축하

13 다음 지도를 보면서 대화를 듣고, 여자가 이사할 집을 고르시오.

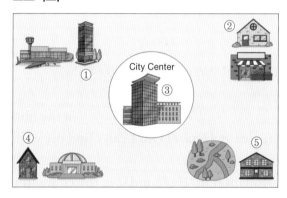

14 다음을 듣고, 무엇에 관한 설명인지 고르시오.

① 선풍기　　② 청소기　　③ 세탁기
④ 식기세척기　⑤ 전자레인지

15 대화를 듣고, 여자가 남자에게 부탁한 일로 가장 적절한 것을 고르시오.

① 문 닫기　　　　　② 전등 끄기
③ 교실 사용 허락하기　④ 춤 가르쳐 주기
⑤ 연습 시간 줄여 주기

16 대화를 듣고, 남자의 택배에 관해 언급되지 <u>않은</u> 것을 고르시오.

① 배송 지역　　　② 빠른 배송 비용
③ 일반 배송 비용　④ 택배 물품의 종류
⑤ 일반 배송 소요 기간

17 다음 상황 설명을 듣고, Ben이 Mina에게 할 말로 가장 적절한 것을 고르시오.

Ben: Mina, _____

① I'm sorry. I made a mistake again.
② you're already late for the show.
③ I don't have any interest in singing.
④ you need to start exercising from today.
⑤ don't give up! I'm sure you'll do a good job.

18 대화를 듣고, 남자가 내일 방과 후에 할 일로 가장 적절한 것을 고르시오.

① 집에 가기　　　② 연기 연습하기
③ 공연 관람하기　④ 드라마 시청하기
⑤ 영어 발음 연습하기

19 대화를 듣고, 남자의 마지막 말에 대한 여자의 응답으로 가장 적절한 것을 고르시오.

Woman: _____

① I like tea more than coffee.
② I'll keep my fingers crossed.
③ Sure. I can help you with that.
④ Oh, that's good for me. Here it is.
⑤ Don't worry. Everything will be okay.

20 대화를 듣고, 여자의 마지막 말에 대한 남자의 응답으로 가장 적절한 것을 고르시오.

Man: _____

① I want to get a refund.
② Can I use my credit card?
③ What's your favorite color?
④ I don't know how to say it.
⑤ That's not what I meant to say.

01 그림 정보 파악

대화를 듣고, 남자가 구입할 USB를 고르시오.

① ② ③
④ ⑤

M Hi. I'm looking for a USB.

W How about this USB stick? _____ _____ _____.

M It looks okay, but I want something different, like those card-shaped ones.

W Those are very popular. Especially this one with a sea painting. _____ _____ _____ _____.

M It looks good, but I like that one _____ _____ _____ _____ _____.

W You mean this one?

M No, the one with a bird _____ _____ _____ _____.

02 목적 파악 ✳

대화를 듣고, 여자가 남자에게 전화한 목적으로 가장 적절한 것을 고르시오.

① 지갑을 찾으려고
② 감사의 인사를 하려고
③ 책 반납을 독촉하려고
④ 컴퓨터 수리를 부탁하려고
⑤ 지갑을 주인에게 찾아 주려고

Sound Clear ☆ **can't find**
영국식은 a를 [아]로 발음하고 축약된 't가 거의 발음되지 않아 [칸–파인드]로 발음된다.

(*Cellphone rings.*)

M Hello.

W Hello. This is Daehan Library. Is this Peter Shin?

M Yes, it is.

W Did you _____ _____ _____ _____ in the library?

M What? Hold on, please. (*Pause*) Oh, I can't find my wallet in my bag.

W Someone just brought it in. He found it in the computer lab _____ _____ _____ _____.

M Right, I was there a while ago. Is there a V-shaped logo _____ _____ _____ _____ _____ _____?

W Yes, there is. I'm calling after finding the contact number inside the wallet. 정답 단서

M Thank you so much! I'll head over shortly to pick it up.

03 그림의 상황에 적절한 대화 찾기

다음 그림의 상황에 가장 적절한 대화를 고르시오.

① ② ③ ④ ⑤

① **W** Excuse me. I think this is my seat.
   M Oh, really? Let me 정답 단서 _____ _____ _____ _____.

② **W** Are you interested in watching movies?
   M Sure, I enjoy watching movies.

③ **W** _____ _____ _____ _____ do you like?
   M Action movies are my favorite.

④ **W** _____ _____ _____ _____ _____?
   M Sorry. It's for my wife.

⑤ **W** _____ _____ _____ do you need?
   M Just one, please.

04 특정 정보 파악

대화를 듣고, 여자가 방과 후 수업을 시작하는 요일을 고르시오.

① 월요일   ② 화요일   ③ 수요일
④ 목요일   ⑤ 금요일

M Hi. How was your history test?

W I didn't _____ _____ _____ _____ again. I don't know what to do.

M Why don't you take Mr. Choi's after-school class? It's on Mondays, Wednesdays, and Fridays.

W _____ _____ _____ _____ _____ ?

M Yes. It is helpful to understand history.

W Really? _____ _____ _____ _____ ?

M Yes. How about starting next Monday?

W I don't think I can _____ _____ _____ _____ _____ because of an assignment. I'll join the class from Wednesday.

M Then let's talk to Mr. Choi.

05 직업 추론

대화를 듣고, 여자의 직업으로 가장 적절한 것을 고르시오.

① nurse   ② doctor
③ teacher   ④ librarian
⑤ tennis player

(*Cellphone rings.*)

M Hello. Ms. Yoon. This is David.

W Oh, David. _____ _____ _____ _____ _____ after school?

M I'm really sorry, but could I talk to you about something?

W Sure, what is it about? I hope _____ _____ _____ _____ .

M Well, I broke my leg playing tennis, so I don't think I can go to school for a few days.

W What? I'm so _____ _____ _____ _____ . Are you okay?

M The doctor said I must stay in the hospital for a week.

W Okay, I'll visit you after class.

06 심정 추론

대화를 듣고, 남자의 심정으로 가장 적절한 것을 고르시오.

① bored   ② excited
③ jealous   ④ surprised
⑤ disappointed

W James, it's raining now. You must be happy.

M Well, you're wrong.

W What? You don't have to play soccer _____ _____ _____ _____ . I know you don't like soccer.

M I didn't because _____ _____ _____ _____ _____ . But I have practiced a lot to get better!

W I see. That's why you've been wearing sportswear so often!

M Yeah. I've been _____ _____ _____ _____ how much I've improved.

W Cheer up! You'll _____ _____ _____ soon.

다음을 듣고, 두 사람의 대화가 어색한 것을 고르시오.

①　　②　　③　　④　　⑤

① **M**　Please _____ _____ _____ _____ Mr. Lee.
　W　Okay, I will.
② **M**　Can you help me find my key?
　W　Sorry, I can't. I'm busy now.
③ **M**　_____ _____! A car is coming!
　W　Oh, thank you so much.
④ **M**　What do you think of his new song?
　W　I don't think it's _____ _____ _____ his first one.
⑤ **M**　I was wondering if I could ask you a favor.
　W　_____ _____ _____ _____ _____.

대화를 듣고, 두 사람이 대화 직후에 할 일로 가장 적절한 것을 고르시오.

① 촬영하기　　② 작품 감상하기
③ 동영상 편집하기　　④ 등장인물 구상하기
⑤ 스토리보드 만들기

Sound Clear ☆ **first step**
자음 세 개가 연속으로 나와 중간 자음의 발음이 약화되어 [퍼스텝]으로 발음된다.

W　What is the social studies homework?
M　It's to _____ _____ _____ about stopping bullying. I saw some other videos online, but no good ideas _____ _____ _____.
W　Why don't we just start shooting?
M　Without any plans? I think we should think of characters first.
W　You're right. That's the first step. Then let's _____ _____ _____ _____ _____.

다음을 듣고, 작가에 관해 언급되지 않은 것을 고르시오.

① 이름　　② 취미　　③ 새 책의 제목
④ 어릴 때 꿈　　⑤ 좌우명

W　Hello, students. I'm Lisa Han. First of all, thank you _____ _____ _____ _____ my new book, *Living in Harmony*. As you know, I was a troublemaker when I was young. _____ _____ _____ when I said that I would be a writer one day. However, now I have written many popular books. I was able to do it _____ _____ _____ _____: "If you sleep now, you will dream. But, if you work toward your dream, you can achieve it."

대화를 듣고, 남자가 지불할 금액을 고르시오.

① $10　　② $12　　③ $17
④ $24　　⑤ $25

W　Welcome to the National Art Museum.
M　Hi. I'd like to buy two adult tickets.
W　They are $10 each. If you're also interested in visiting the National Science Museum, you can buy a combination ticket _____ _____ _____ _____.
M　How much is it?
W　_____ _____ _____ _____ _____, you need to pay $17. But the combination ticket only costs $12.
M　Okay. Then I'll buy two combination tickets.
W　Will you _____ _____ _____ or by credit card?
M　Cash. Here you are.

11 장소 추론

대화를 듣고, 두 사람이 대화하는 장소로 가장 적절한 곳을 고르시오.

① 교실 　② 식당 　③ 미술실
④ 방송실 　⑤ 체육관

W Hi. My name is Lily Park.
M Okay, take a seat. Hmm... you don't _____ _____ _____ _____ _____, right?
W No. But I really want to learn about broadcasting this year.
M _____ _____ _____ _____ _____?
W As I wrote in the application, I want to _____ _____ _____ _____ right here in the school studio.
M What kind of program?
W A program which introduces students' real lives.
M Oh, that sounds interesting.

12 의도 파악 　✽

대화를 듣고, 여자의 마지막 말에 담긴 의도로 가장 적절한 것을 고르시오.

① 격려 　② 동의 　③ 부탁
④ 사과 　⑤ 축하

M Amanda, did you _____ _____ _____?
W Not yet. I couldn't finish it since I was very busy yesterday.
M You always seem busy. Do you have that much to do?
W Not really, but I _____ _____ _____ _____. What do you think is my problem?
M Time management. _____ _____ _____ _____ _____ to manage your time more effectively?
W That's a good idea.
　　　　정답 단서

13 위치 찾기

다음 지도를 보면서 대화를 듣고, 여자가 이사할 집을 고르시오.

M Have you decided where you are going to move to?
W No. I've been _____ _____ _____ _____ for a week.
M How about living in an apartment in the city center?
W _____ _____ _____ _____.
M I see. What about a house near a big supermarket? You can shop easily.
W Yeah, but _____ _____ _____ _____ _____.
M Then what about this house? You can _____ _____ _____ _____ because it's next to a park.
　　　　　　　　　　　　　　　정답 단서
W Is there a park? I didn't see that. I think that's the one!

14 화제 파악

다음을 듣고, 무엇에 관한 설명인지 고르시오.

① 선풍기 　② 청소기 　③ 세탁기
④ 식기세척기 　⑤ 전자레인지

Sound Clear ☆ **automatically**
[t]가 모음 사이에서 약화되어 [어러메리컬리]로 발음된다.

M This is a useful machine in the kitchen. _____ _____ there are many cups and plates to be washed. In this situation, you can _____ _____ _____ _____ _____ by using this machine. Put all the things that need to be washed into this and then _____ _____ _____ _____. In a short time, it'll automatically wash and even dry all the dishes.
　　　　　　　　　　정답 단서

15 부탁한 일 파악

대화를 듣고, 여자가 남자에게 부탁한 일로 가장 적절한 것을 고르시오.

① 문 닫기 ② 전등 끄기
③ 교실 사용 허락하기 ④ 춤 가르쳐 주기
⑤ 연습 시간 줄여 주기

Sound Clear☆ **close**

동사(닫다)는 [클로우즈]로, 형용사(가까운)는 [클로우스]로 발음된다.

W Hello. Mr. Kang.

M Miso, what's up?

W You know ________ ________ ________ ________ ________ for the school talent show.

M Of course. I'm looking forward to seeing it.

W Is it okay to use our classroom for an hour after school? I ________ ________ ________ ________ ________.

정답 단서

M Sure, but don't forget to ☆close the door and ________ ________ ________ ________ ________ ________ ________.

W Okay, Mr. Kang. Thank you so much.

16 언급되지 않은 것 찾기

대화를 듣고, 남자의 택배에 관해 언급되지 않은 것을 고르시오.

① 배송 지역 ② 빠른 배송 비용
③ 일반 배송 비용 ④ 택배 물품의 종류
⑤ 일반 배송 소요 기간

M Good morning. I want to send this box to Busan.

정답 단서

W Okay. ________ ________ ________ ________. (*Pause*) How do you want to send it, by express or regular delivery?

M ________ ________ ________ ________ ________ if I send it by express delivery?

W If you ________ ________ ________ ________ ________, it will get there tomorrow.

M How much will that cost?

W It's 10,000 won.

정답 단서

M That's too expensive. How about regular delivery?

W It's 4,000 won, and it will arrive in about 3 days.

정답 단서 정답 단서

M I'll send it ________ ________ ________ ________.

17 상황에 적절한 말 찾기

다음 상황 설명을 듣고, Ben이 Mina에게 할 말로 가장 적절한 것을 고르시오.

Ben: Mina, ____________________

① I'm sorry. I made a mistake again.
② you're already late for the show.
③ I don't have any interest in singing.
④ you need to start exercising from today.
⑤ don't give up! I'm sure you'll do a good job.

W Ben's friend Mina is going to have an audition to be a singer. She ________ ________ ________ ________ ________ ________ for a long time. She is really ________ ________ ________, and everyone thinks she can be a great singer. However, right before the audition begins, she gets so nervous and seems to lose confidence.

정답 단서

________ ________ ________ ________ ________ ________. In this situation, what would Ben say to her to encourage her?

Ben Mina, don't give up! I'm sure you'll do a good job.

18 할 일 파악

대화를 듣고, 남자가 내일 방과 후에 할 일로 가장 적절한 것을 고르시오.

① 집에 가기　　　② 연기 연습하기
③ 공연 관람하기　　④ 드라마 시청하기
⑤ 영어 발음 연습하기

W　Eddie, do you have any plans for tomorrow?
M　You mean after school? No, _____ _____ _____. Why do you ask?
W　The English drama club _____ _____ _____ _____ at the auditorium.
M　Oh, yes. You're a member of that club so you practiced the performance all summer vacation, didn't you?
W　Yes, I did. _____ _____ _____ we improved our English pronunciation. So would you like to watch the performance?
M　Sure, that would be nice.
W　Great! _____ _____ _____ _____ in the auditorium. Our performance begins at 5 p.m.
M　Okay. I think it will be very interesting.

19 마지막 말에 대한 응답 찾기

대화를 듣고, 남자의 마지막 말에 대한 여자의 응답으로 가장 적절한 것을 고르시오.

Woman: _____

① I like tea more than coffee.
② I'll keep my fingers crossed.
③ Sure. I can help you with that.
④ Oh, that's good for me. Here it is.
⑤ Don't worry. Everything will be okay.

Sound Clear ☆ **sandwiches**
[d]는 약하게 발음되거나 묵음처럼 [샌위치즈]로 발음되기도 한다.

M　Hi. Are you _____ _____ _____?
W　Hmm... do you have any ham sandwiches?
M　Of course. We just made one.
W　Then _____ _____ _____.
M　Do you want anything to drink?
W　_____ _____ _____ _____ _____, please.
M　Do you have a membership card? If you have one, you can have a large _____ _____ _____ _____.
W　Oh, that's good for me. Here it is.

20 마지막 말에 대한 응답 찾기

대화를 듣고, 여자의 마지막 말에 대한 남자의 응답으로 가장 적절한 것을 고르시오.

Man: _____

① I want to get a refund.
② Can I use my credit card?
③ What's your favorite color?
④ I don't know how to say it.
⑤ That's not what I meant to say.

(*Telephone rings.*)
W　Happy Home Shopping Service. How may I help you?
M　Hello. I'd like to buy the bag that's being advertised now.
W　_____ _____! Which color do you want to order?
M　I'd like the red one.
W　I'm sorry, but that color is _____ _____ _____.
M　Already? Then is the blue one available?
W　Yes, you can order a blue one. How would you like to _____ _____ _____ _____?
M　Can I use my credit card?

Word Check
영어는 우리말로, 우리말은 영어로 써 보기

01 mechanic _____

02 award _____

03 recently _____

04 route _____

05 delete _____

06 search _____

07 minor _____

08 originally _____

09 describe _____

10 finally _____

11 give it a try _____

12 at a time _____

13 실용적인 _____

14 잠재적인 _____

15 승객 _____

16 감독 _____

17 논의하다 _____

18 중고의 _____

19 제안하다 _____

20 수집하다 _____

21 감염시키다 _____

22 분실물 보관소 _____

23 제출하다 _____

24 ~을 찾아오다 _____

Expression Check
알맞은 표현을 넣어 문장 완성하기

25 You're not _____ _____ wear shoes in here. 이 안에서는 신발을 신으시면 안 됩니다.

26 My computer _____ _____ _____ automatically. 내 컴퓨터가 계속 자동으로 꺼져.

27 I'm sorry. I'll _____ my voice _____. 죄송해요. 목소리를 낮출게요.

28 I need to include _____ _____ three pictures that I took by myself.
나는 내가 직접 찍은 사진을 최소한 3장 포함시켜야 해.

29 If you _____ _____ hearing, see your doctor right away.
만약 네가 청력에 문제가 있으면, 즉시 진료를 받으렴.

30 I have so many assignments that I can't _____ _____ _____ all of them.
난 숙제가 너무 많아서 그것들 모두를 따라갈 수 없어.

Answers p.47

Word Check 영어는 우리말로, 우리말은 영어로 써 보기

01	pronunciation	_____	13	긴장한	_____
02	encourage	_____	14	자신감	_____
03	manage	_____	15	과제	_____
04	express	_____	16	광고하다	_____
05	choice	_____	17	경험	_____
06	combination	_____	18	참석하다	_____
07	regular	_____	19	가격	_____
08	forest	_____	20	이해하다	_____
09	computer lab	_____	21	심각한	_____
10	character	_____	22	향상되다	_____
11	get a refund	_____	23	생각해 내다	_____
12	give up	_____	24	실수하다	_____

Expression Check 알맞은 표현을 넣어 문장 완성하기

25 I'll _____ _____ shortly to pick it up. 지금 당장 그것을 가지러 갈게요.

26 I didn't _____ _____ _____ _____ again. 난 또 좋은 점수를 받지 못했어.

27 You don't have any experience _____ _____, right? 방송에 경험이 없으시네요, 그렇죠?

28 I'm sorry, but that color is already _____ _____. 죄송하지만, 그 색은 이미 매진되었어요.

29 Don't forget to _____ _____ the lights when you leave. 나갈 때 불 끄는 것을 잊지 마라.

30 Will you pay _____ _____ or by credit card?
현금으로 지불하시나요, 신용 카드로 지불하시나요?

1.0배속

1.2배속

01 대화를 듣고, 남자가 만든 포스터를 고르시오.

① May 7
Sports Club Day

② May 7
Sports Club Day

③ Sports Club Day
May 7

④ Sports Club Day

⑤ Sports Club Day

May 7

02 대화를 듣고, 여자가 남자에게 부탁한 일로 가장 적절한 것을 고르시오.

① 프린터 빌리기　　② 프린터 옮기기
③ 프린터 고르기　　④ 프린터 연결하기
⑤ 프린터 용지 얻기

03 다음 그림의 상황에 가장 적절한 대화를 고르시오.

①　　　②　　　③　　　④　　　⑤

04 대화를 듣고, 남자가 먹을 음식을 고르시오.

① 피자　　② 바나나　　③ 스파게티
④ 샌드위치　　⑤ 카레라이스

05 대화를 듣고, 여자의 가족 여행에 관해 언급되지 <u>않은</u> 것을 고르시오.

① 여행지　　② 음식　　③ 교통수단
④ 날씨　　⑤ 숙박 장소

06 대화를 듣고, 두 사람의 관계로 가장 적절한 것을 고르시오.

① 엄마 – 아들
② 교사 – 학생
③ 여행 가이드 – 관광객
④ 직장 상사 – 부하 직원
⑤ 스포츠 매장 직원 – 손님

07 다음을 듣고, 두 사람의 대화가 <u>어색한</u> 것을 고르시오.

①　　　②　　　③　　　④　　　⑤

08 대화를 듣고, 남자가 시험공부하면서 어려워하는 것을 고르시오.

① 시간 부족　　② 수학 계산
③ 영어 단어 암기　　④ 영어 문법 정리
⑤ 수학 공식 암기

09 다음을 듣고, 방송의 목적으로 가장 적절한 것을 고르시오.

① 동아리 교사를 모집하려고
② 동아리 회원을 모집하려고
③ 새로운 동아리를 소개하려고
④ 동아리 교외 활동을 촉구하려고
⑤ 동아리날 변경 사항을 알리려고

10 대화를 듣고, 남자가 지불할 금액을 고르시오.

① $80　　② $90　　③ $99
④ $100　　⑤ $110

11 대화를 듣고, 여자의 심정으로 가장 적절한 것을 고르시오.

① jealous　　② relieved　　③ pleased
④ surprised　　⑤ ashamed

12 다음을 듣고, 토마토 축제에 관해 언급되지 <u>않은</u> 것을 고르시오.

① 행사 장소　　② 행사 날짜　　③ 준비물
④ 참가 자격　　⑤ 입장료

13 다음 표를 보면서 대화를 듣고, 두 사람이 선택할 수업을 고르시오.

	Class	Course	Day	Fee
①	A	Robot	Monday	$50
②	B	Life Science	Tuesday	$20
③	C	Baseball	Thursday	$25
④	D	Chess	Friday	$20
⑤	E	Tennis	Friday	$25

14 다음을 듣고, 무엇에 관한 설명인지 고르시오.

① 초능력　　② 집중력　　③ 모둠 학습
④ 홈스쿨링　　⑤ 멀티태스킹

15 대화를 듣고, 여자가 대화 직후에 할 일로 가장 적절한 것을 고르시오.

① 일자리 구하기　　② 영어 공부하기
③ 병원 진료 받기　　④ 친구에게 사과하기
⑤ 선생님께 말씀드리기

16 대화를 듣고, 두 사람이 만날 장소를 고르시오.

① 학교 앞　　② 마술 학원　　③ 문화 회관
④ 콘서트홀　　⑤ 여자의 집 앞

17 대화를 듣고, 남자의 마지막 말에 대한 여자의 응답으로 가장 적절한 것을 고르시오.

Woman: _____

① I'll show you how to win.
② They say practice makes perfect.
③ I'd better participate in the contest.
④ If you never give up, nothing is impossible.
⑤ I mean the process is more important than the result.

18 대화를 듣고, 여자의 마지막 말에 대한 남자의 응답으로 가장 적절한 것을 고르시오.

Man: _____

① You must be under a lot of stress.
② That's because you failed the exam.
③ I'm sorry, but I have a lot of work to do.
④ People have different ways of relieving stress.
⑤ Hiking is the most fun I've ever had.

19 대화를 듣고, 남자의 마지막 말에 대한 여자의 응답으로 가장 적절한 것을 고르시오.

Woman: _____

① That's okay. I'm feeling better now.
② The doctor said I need some rest.
③ I'd like to get a professional opinion.
④ She said putting ice on it will be helpful.
⑤ My mom is coming to pick me up.

20 다음 상황 설명을 듣고, Ben이 Jenny에게 할 말로 가장 적절한 것을 고르시오.

Ben: Jenny, _____

① when are they due?
② can you help me? I'm lost.
③ do you mind if I ask you a favor?
④ why don't you read more books?
⑤ how do I get to the public library?

01 그림 정보 파악

대화를 듣고, 남자가 만든 포스터를 고르시오.

Sound Clear ☆ **What about**

[t]가 모음 사이에서 약화되고 뒤 단어의 첫 모음과 연음되어 [와러바웃]으로 발음된다.

M Sumi, could you check the Sports Club Day poster for me?

W Sure, let me see. The title _____ _____ _____ _____ the poster looks good.

M ☆ What about the date _____ _____ _____ _____ under the title?

W It looks very clear. I also like the simple drawings on the left side.

M The art club members _____ _____ _____ _____ and the soccer shoes.

W Nice. I think the other students will like the posters, too.

M I'm _____ _____ _____ _____.

02 부탁한 일 파악

대화를 듣고, 여자가 남자에게 부탁한 일로 가장 적절한 것을 고르시오.

① 프린터 빌리기   ② 프린터 옮기기
③ 프린터 고르기   ④ 프린터 연결하기
⑤ 프린터 용지 얻기

(*Doorbell rings.*)

M Who is it?

W Hello. It's Amy _____ _____.

M Oh, hello. How is it going?

W Fine. I'm having a new printer delivered this afternoon.

M Oh, you _____ _____ _____! Do you need any help carrying it? 함정

W No. That's okay, but do you have some printer paper? 정답 단서 _____ _____ _____ _____ the new printer.

M Sure. Here is some A4 size paper.

W Thank you.

03 그림의 상황에 적절한 대화 찾기

다음 그림의 상황에 가장 적절한 대화를 고르시오.

① ② ③ ④ ⑤

① W Would you give me the menu, please?
   M Wait, please. I will bring you the menu.

② W Can you help me _____ _____ _____?
   M This way, please. They're behind those shelves.

③ W How do you know each other?
   M We're _____ _____ _____ _____ _____.

④ W I'd like a cup of hot chocolate.
   M 정답 단서 _____ _____ _____ _____?

⑤ W What is _____ _____ _____?
   M I like sweet chocolate cake the most.

04 특정 정보 파악 ✳

대화를 듣고, 남자가 먹을 음식을 고르시오.

① 피자   ② 바나나   ③ 스파게티
④ 샌드위치   ⑤ 카레라이스

Sound Clear ☆ **curry**

'카레'는 실제로 [커뤼]로 발음된다.

M I'm home. Mom, I'm so hungry.

W Already? _____ _____ _____ _____ again?

M Right. Today's school lunch was curry and rice.

W Oh, no. You don't like it very much. _____ _____ _____ _____ a sandwich?

M I didn't have enough money.

W Let me make you some seafood spaghetti.

M Wow, that sounds delicious. _____ _____ _____ _____ _____ ?

W About 20 minutes. Do you want a banana _____ _____ _____ ?

M No, thank you.

05 언급되지 않은 것 찾기

대화를 듣고, 여자의 가족 여행에 관해 언급되지 <u>않은</u> 것을 고르시오.

① 여행지   ② 음식   ③ 교통수단
④ 날씨   ⑤ 숙박 장소

M Mina, what did you do last weekend?

W I _____ _____ _____ _____ Jeonju with my family. It only took an hour to get there by train.

M _____ _____ _____ _____ ?

W Wonderful. The weather was warm and _____ _____ _____ _____ .

M Good. Did you visit the Hanok Village there?

W Sure. We stayed at the village overnight and we _____ _____ _____ _____ there.

M That sounds fun. I hope that I can go there soon.

06 관계 추론

대화를 듣고, 두 사람의 관계로 가장 적절한 것을 고르시오.

① 엄마 – 아들
② 교사 – 학생
③ 여행 가이드 – 관광객
④ 직장 상사 – 부하 직원
⑤ 스포츠 매장 직원 – 손님

W Mr. Anderson, I was wondering if I could _____ _____ _____ _____ next week.

M For what?

W I _____ _____ _____ my son's school sports day.

M Of course, I understand. When is it?

W It's next Wednesday.

M No problem. You can _____ _____ _____ _____ then.

W Thank you so much.

M But please _____ _____ _____ _____ _____ for next week's meeting.

W Okay, you don't have to worry about it.

다음을 듣고, 두 사람의 대화가 <u>어색한</u> 것을 고르시오.

① ② ③ ④ ⑤

Sound Clear ☆ **this Saturday**
동일한 발음의 자음이 연이어 나오면 앞 자음 소리가 탈락하여 [디쎄러데이]로 발음된다.

① M How would you like your hair cut?
　 W I'd like _____ _____ _____ _____.
② M What is your favorite kind of music?
　 W I really like music class.
③ M Why don't we go swimming this Saturday?
　 W Sorry. I already _____ _____ _____.
④ M It doesn't look very nice outside today.
　 W You're right. I think _____ _____ _____ _____.
⑤ M I think you look really nice today.
　 W Thank you. _____ _____ _____ _____
　　 a couple of days ago.

08 특정 정보 파악

대화를 듣고, 남자가 시험공부하면서 어려워하는 것을 고르시오.

① 시간 부족　　② 수학 계산
③ 영어 단어 암기　④ 영어 문법 정리
⑤ 수학 공식 암기

W How's your studying going for your final exams?
M Well, I really love to study math, but studying English _____ _____ _____.
W What is the most difficult when you study English? Is it grammar?
M I don't _____ _____ _____ _____ grammar. But I don't know how to memorize new words.
W Listen to the words while memorizing them. _____ _____ _____ _____.
M Okay. I'll try that.

09 목적 파악 ✱

다음을 듣고, 방송의 목적으로 가장 적절한 것을 고르시오.

① 동아리 교사를 모집하려고
② 동아리 회원을 모집하려고
③ 새로운 동아리를 소개하려고
④ 동아리 교외 활동을 촉구하려고
⑤ 동아리날 변경 사항을 알리려고

M Hello, students. This is your student president, Lee Seojin. Our first Club Day is coming this Friday. But there are some _____ _____ _____ _____. The school band and orchestra will start practicing for the festival on schedule. But _____ _____ _____ _____ _____, so please ask your homeroom teachers about this. And all club activities will start at 3 p.m. _____ _____ _____ _____ on Friday. Thank you.

10 숫자 정보 파악

대화를 듣고, 남자가 지불할 금액을 고르시오.

① $80　　② $90　　③ $99
④ $100　⑤ $110

W Siwon, _____ _____ _____ _____ online?
M Yes. I'm ordering new uniforms for my soccer team.
W Wow, they look great. How much are they?
M They're $10 each, and I need to get ten.
W _____ _____ _____? There are eleven people on your team.
M That's because the goalkeeper wears a different jersey.
W Oh, right. How much is _____ _____ _____?
M It's free. And I will get a 10% discount for _____ _____ _____ _____.

11 심정 추론

대화를 듣고, 여자의 심정으로 가장 적절한 것을 고르시오.

① jealous ② relieved
③ pleased ④ surprised
⑤ ashamed

Sound Clear ☆ **talk about it**
[k]와 [t]가 각각 뒤 단어의 모음과 연음되어 [토커바우릿]으로 발음된다.

M Anna, _____ _____ _____ _____?
W Oh, it was the worst. I don't even want to talk about it.
M Come on. _____ _____ _____ _____.
W On my way to school, I slipped on some ice. _____ _____ _____ _____, my ex-boyfriend saw the whole thing and laughed at me.
M Oh, no. Were you hurt?
W No, but just thinking about it makes me want to cry. 정답 단서

12 언급되지 않은 것 찾기

다음을 듣고, 토마토 축제에 관해 언급되지 않은 것을 고르시오.

① 행사 장소 ② 행사 날짜 ③ 준비물
④ 참가 자격 ⑤ 입장료

W Good afternoon, everyone. _____ _____ _____ _____ _____ the 10th Tomato Festival. It will _____ _____ _____ the outdoor plaza in front of City Hall on May 30, from 10 a.m. to 4 p.m. You can _____ _____ _____ _____ _____ at the farmers' market. Since we don't provide any plastic bags, _____ _____ _____ _____ your own shopping bags. The admission price will be $5. To get more information, visit our website. Thank you.

13 도표 정보 파악 ✷

다음 표를 보면서 대화를 듣고, 두 사람이 선택할 수업을 고르시오.

	Class	Course	Day	Fee
①	A	Robot	Monday	$50
②	B	Life Science	Tuesday	$20
③	C	Baseball	Thursday	$25
④	D	Chess	Friday	$20
⑤	E	Tennis	Friday	$25

W Daniel, have you _____ _____ _____ your after-school classes?
M Not yet. Shall we take a class together?
W Okay. _____ _____ _____ the robot class.
M It looks interesting, but the tuition fee is too expensive.
W Then how about the life science class?
M I'd like to take it, but I can't make it _____ _____ _____ _____ _____ on Tuesdays.
W I see. _____ _____ _____ _____ _____?
M Well, not really. I prefer watching to playing.
W Then we only have one choice. Let's sign up for it.

14 화제 파악

다음을 듣고, 무엇에 관한 설명인지 고르시오.

① 초능력 ② 집중력
③ 모둠 학습 ④ 홈스쿨링
⑤ 멀티태스킹

M This is the ability to do two different things at the same time. 정답 단서 For example, _____ _____ _____ while walking, or listening to music or watching TV while studying. You may think _____ _____ _____ when you do more than one thing at the same time. However, the truth is that it might not be as effective. So 정답 단서 _____ _____ _____ _____ _____ two things at once, focus on one thing at a time.

15 할 일 파악

대화를 듣고, 여자가 대화 직후에 할 일로 가장
적절한 것을 고르시오.

① 일자리 구하기   ② 영어 공부하기
③ 병원 진료 받기   ④ 친구에게 사과하기
⑤ 선생님께 말씀드리기

Sound Clear ☆ **part-time**
동일한 발음의 자음이 연이어 나오면 앞 자
음 소리가 탈락하여 [팔타임]으로 발음된다.

W I have _____ _____ _____ _____, Junho.
M What's up? Is it about your new part-time job?
W No. Actually, it is about my friend Jina. I noticed her _____ _____ _____ _____ yesterday.
M Really? So what did you do about it?
W I didn't do anything, but _____ _____ _____ _____ _____.
M Why don't you talk to the teacher about it? I think it could help Jina.
W I think you're right. I'll do it right now.

16 특정 정보 파악

대화를 듣고, 두 사람이 만날 장소를 고르시오.

① 학교 앞   ② 마술 학원   ③ 문화 회관
④ 콘서트홀   ⑤ 여자의 집 앞

W Daniel, do you have any plans this Saturday?
M _____ _____. Why?
W There's a magic show by a famous magician at the cultural center. Why don't we go there?
M A magic show? That sounds very interesting. _____ _____ _____ _____ _____.
W Great. It starts at 7 o'clock. How about meeting at 6:30 at the cultural center?
M Well, it's located near your house. Let's meet _____ _____ _____ _____ _____ and walk there together.
W Okay. See you then.

17 마지막 말에 대한 응답 찾기

대화를 듣고, 남자의 마지막 말에 대한 여자의
응답으로 가장 적절한 것을 고르시오.

Woman: _____

① I'll show you how to win.
② They say practice makes perfect.
③ I'd better participate in the contest.
④ If you never give up, nothing is impossible.
⑤ I mean the process is more important than the result.

M Yena, what are you looking at?
W It's a poster for the school speech contest.
M Are you going to _____ _____ _____ _____?
W Yes. I've been looking forward to it. How about you?
M No, I won't. I don't think I _____ _____ _____ _____ _____.
W But _____ _____ _____ _____ _____ doesn't matter. You can learn a lot while preparing for it.
M I don't understand. What do you mean?
W I mean the process is more important than the result.

18 마지막 말에 대한 응답 찾기 ❋

대화를 듣고, 여자의 마지막 말에 대한 남자의 응답으로 가장 적절한 것을 고르시오.

Man: _____

① You must be under a lot of stress.
② That's because you failed the exam.
③ I'm sorry, but I have a lot of work to do.
④ People have different ways of relieving stress.
⑤ Hiking is the most fun I've ever had.

Sound Clear ☆ **forward to**
[d]가 [t] 앞에서 거의 발음되지 않고 동화되어 [포월투]로 발음된다.

W How was your exam today?
M Not bad. Anyway, I'm so happy _____ _____ _____ _____.
W Same here. I'm looking forward to relaxing in the mountains this weekend.
M Oh, are you going to the mountains?
W Yeah, I've planned a little hike in the woods. _____ _____ _____ _____ _____?
M Nothing special. All I want to do is _____ _____ _____ _____ _____.
W Does it help to relieve your stress? Why don't you do something fun?
M People have different ways of relieving stress.

19 마지막 말에 대한 응답 찾기

대화를 듣고, 남자의 마지막 말에 대한 여자의 응답으로 가장 적절한 것을 고르시오.

Woman: _____

① That's okay. I'm feeling better now.
② The doctor said I need some rest.
③ I'd like to get a professional opinion.
④ She said putting ice on it will be helpful.
⑤ My mom is coming to pick me up.

M Hey, you look like you're really in pain.
W Yes, _____ _____ _____ _____ playing badminton.
M Oh, no! How did it happen?
W Well, after running to smash the shuttlecock _____ _____ _____ _____.
M That's terrible. Did you go see a doctor about it?
W No, but I did _____ _____ _____ _____.
M What did she say?
W She said putting ice on it will be helpful.

20 상황에 적절한 말 찾기

다음 상황 설명을 듣고, Ben이 Jenny에게 할 말로 가장 적절한 것을 고르시오.

Ben: Jenny, _____

① when are they due?
② can you help me? I'm lost.
③ do you mind if I ask you a favor?
④ why don't you read more books?
⑤ how do I get to the public library?

W Ben borrowed some books from the public library. Ben _____ _____ _____ _____ them today. But he is _____ _____ _____ for tomorrow's final exam that he can't go to the library. His cousin Jenny visits his house, and he wants to ask her _____ _____ _____ _____ for him. In this situation, what would Ben most likely say to Jenny?

Ben Jenny, do you mind if I ask you a favor?

1.0배속

1.2배속

01 대화를 듣고, 여자가 구입한 책장을 고르시오.

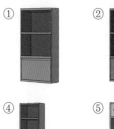
① ②

③

④

⑤

02 대화를 듣고, 여자가 남자에게 부탁한 일로 가장 적절한 것을 고르시오.

① 일찍 퇴근하기　　② 회의 참석하기
③ 정수기 수리하기　　④ 정수기 주문하기
⑤ 서비스 센터에 전화하기

03 대화를 듣고, 남자의 심정으로 가장 적절한 것을 고르시오.

① angry　　② joyful　　③ envious
④ regretful　　⑤ disappointed

04 다음을 듣고, 두 사람의 대화가 <u>어색한</u> 것을 고르시오.

①　　②　　③　　④　　⑤

05 다음을 듣고, 방송의 목적으로 가장 적절한 것을 고르시오.

① 회의의 개회를 선언하려고
② 다음 회의 장소를 안내하려고
③ 오늘의 메인 뉴스를 전달하려고
④ 환경 오염의 심각성을 보여 주려고
⑤ 소식지 전달 방식 변경을 알리려고

06 대화를 듣고, 두 사람이 대화하는 장소로 가장 적절한 곳을 고르시오.

① 극장　　② 식당　　③ 가구점
④ 헬스장　　⑤ 사진관

07 대화를 듣고, 두 사람의 관계로 가장 적절한 것을 고르시오.

① 비행기 승무원 − 탑승객
② 식당 종업원 − 손님
③ 매표소 직원 − 관람객
④ 우체국 직원 − 손님
⑤ 옷 가게 직원 − 손님

08 대화를 듣고, 남자가 대화 직후에 할 일로 가장 적절한 것을 고르시오.

① 점심 식사하기　　② 준비 운동 하기
③ 안전 요원 부르기　　④ 입장권 구입하기
⑤ 수영모 구입하기

09 다음을 듣고, 무엇에 관한 내용인지 고르시오.

① 지구 온난화의 문제점
② 올바른 쓰레기 처리 방법
③ 음식 섭취를 줄이는 방법
④ 음식물 쓰레기를 줄이는 방법
⑤ 음식물 쓰레기가 증가하는 이유

10 대화를 듣고, 두 사람이 만날 시각을 고르시오.

① 6:00 p.m.　　② 7:00 p.m.　　③ 8:40 p.m.
④ 8:50 p.m.　　⑤ 9:00 p.m.

11 다음 표를 보면서 대화를 듣고, 내용과 일치하지 <u>않는</u> 것을 고르시오.

	Package Tour	
①	Trip	Five-day trip
②	Total Price	$1,400
③	Room	A double room
④	Meal	Breakfast only
⑤	Ticket	Round-trip tickets

12 대화를 듣고, 두 사람이 지불할 주차 요금을 고르시오.

① 1,000원　　② 2,000원　　③ 3,000원
④ 10,000원　　⑤ 30,000원

13 대화를 듣고, 남자가 여자에게 부탁한 일로 가장 적절한 것을 고르시오.

① 메뉴 추가하기
② 후식 주문하기
③ 소스 가져다주기
④ 인원수 변경하기
⑤ 에어컨 끄기

14 대화를 듣고, 여자가 오늘 점심 식사를 같이 못하는 이유를 고르시오.

① 다이어트 중이어서
② 업무가 너무 많아서
③ 다른 약속이 있어서
④ 건강 검진을 받아야 해서
⑤ 해산물 알레르기가 있어서

15 다음 표를 보면서 대화를 듣고, 여자가 등록할 수업의 강사를 고르시오.

	Morning	Evening
Mon.	Listening (Jenny)	Reading (Steve)
Tues.	Reading (Brad)	Listening (Steve)
Wed.	Listening (Diana)	Reading (Matt)
Thur.	Reading (Jenny)	Listening (Brad)
Fri.	Grammar (Matt)	Grammar (Diana)

① Jenny
② Brad
③ Matt
④ Steve
⑤ Diana

16 다음 그림의 상황에 가장 적절한 대화를 고르시오.

① ② ③ ④ ⑤

17 다음을 듣고, Firefly Tour에 관해 언급되지 않은 것을 고르시오.

① 소요 시간
② 제공되는 것
③ 투어 비용
④ 주의 사항
⑤ 화장실의 위치

18 대화를 듣고, 남자의 마지막 말에 대한 여자의 응답으로 가장 적절한 것을 고르시오.

Woman: _____

① I'll keep my eyes on your bike.
② I'd better get a new bike soon.
③ Shall we go to the bookstore together?
④ Too bad. You should have been more careful.
⑤ I don't think you're allowed to park your bike here.

19 대화를 듣고, 여자의 마지막 말에 대한 남자의 응답으로 가장 적절한 것을 고르시오.

Man: _____

① Why don't you play the piano?
② They must have enjoyed your singing.
③ It was a good idea to do volunteer work.
④ Doing volunteer work at the hospital is worthless.
⑤ Don't be disappointed. I'm sure you will do better the next time.

20 다음 상황 설명을 듣고, Monica가 Brian에게 할 말로 가장 적절한 것을 고르시오.

Monica: Brian, _____

① are you fond of cooking?
② have you tasted the seafood pasta?
③ did you make all the food yourself?
④ I'll make another one for you the next time.
⑤ can you tell me the recipe for this pasta?

Dictation 10 회

01 그림 정보 파악

대화를 듣고, 여자가 구입한 책장을 고르시오.

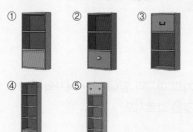

① ② ③ ④ ⑤

Sound Clear ☆ **bottom**

미국식은 모음 사이의 [t]를 약하게 발음하여 [바럼]으로, 영국식은 [t]를 정확히 발음하여 [바텀]으로 발음된다.

M Your new bookcase is really nice. Where did you get it?
W I ordered it online.
M I see. I like that it has three shelves. _____ _____ _____ _____ and not too short.
W Yeah. At first, I was _____ _____ _____ _____ with five shelves, but I thought it would be too tall.
M It _____ _____ _____ _____ _____. What is the drawer at the bottom for?
W That is for keeping my stuff in.
M The handle on the drawer is a good idea, too.
W Yes. That _____ _____ _____ _____ to use.

02 부탁한 일 파악

대화를 듣고, 여자가 남자에게 부탁한 일로 가장 적절한 것을 고르시오.

① 일찍 퇴근하기 ② 회의 참석하기
③ 정수기 수리하기 ④ 정수기 주문하기
⑤ 서비스 센터에 전화하기

W Honey, can you get home by 6 o'clock this evening?
M Why?
W _____ _____ _____ _____ our water purifier. We didn't have any hot water yesterday.
M Did you _____ _____ _____ _____ ?
W Yes, I did. The repairman will come around 6 o'clock. But I can't _____ _____ _____ _____ _____.
M Oh, you said you _____ _____ _____ _____ today.
W Yes, so can you leave the office early?
M Sure. Don't worry. 정답 단서

03 심정 추론

대화를 듣고, 남자의 심정으로 가장 적절한 것을 고르시오.

① angry ② joyful ③ envious
④ regretful ⑤ disappointed

M Look outside! It's raining.
W Yeah, the weather forecaster said that _____ _____ _____ in the afternoon.
M Really? That's why my mom _____ _____ _____ an umbrella with me this morning.
W Mine, too.
M So did you _____ _____ _____ _____ _____ ?
W Of course. Why? Didn't you bring yours?
M No, I didn't. _____ _____ _____ a nice day this morning, so I didn't think we would have rain this afternoon.
W Oh, dear. You're going to _____ _____.
M I know. It's my fault. I should have listened to Mom. 정답 단서

04 어색한 대화 찾기

다음을 듣고, 두 사람의 대화가 <u>어색한</u> 것을 고르시오.

①   ②   ③   ④   ⑤

Sound Clear ☆ **give you**

[v]가 뒤의 반모음 [j]를 만나 연음되어 [기뷰]로 발음된다.

① W You are late for school again.
  M I'm sorry. I got up late and _____ _____ _____ .
② W Excuse me. Do you know how to get to the National Museum?
  M Take line 4 for three stops and get off at National Museum Station.
③ W How often do you have your hair cut?
  M _____ _____ _____ _____ .
④ W You look very busy today. Can I ☆give you a hand?
  M Oh, yes. I really need _____ _____ _____ _____ .
⑤ W Would you like to go see a movie tonight?
  M You can say that again. _____ _____ _____ _____ .

05 목적 파악

다음을 듣고, 방송의 목적으로 가장 적절한 것을 고르시오.

① 회의의 개회를 선언하려고
② 다음 회의 장소를 안내하려고
③ 오늘의 메인 뉴스를 전달하려고
④ 환경 오염의 심각성을 보여 주려고
⑤ 소식지 전달 방식 변경을 알리려고

W Good afternoon, ladies and gentlemen. I _____ _____ _____ _____ before we wrap up our conference. To date, you've been receiving our monthly newsletters in the mail. However, we're _____ _____ _____ _____ _____ _____ . This will avoid late delivery and lost mail. Also, it will help us protect the environment. You will be able to read your first newsletter online _____ _____ _____ . Thank you.

06 장소 추론 �֍

대화를 듣고, 두 사람이 대화하는 장소로 가장 적절한 곳을 고르시오.

① 극장   ② 식당   ③ 가구점
④ 헬스장   ⑤ 사진관

W Hi. I came here to have my picture taken.
M Okay. _____ 정답 단서 _____ _____ _____ ?
W It's for issuing a driver's license. _____ _____ _____ _____ _____ to develop the picture?
M It shouldn't take more than 5 minutes.
W So quick! Do you have a mirror?
M Sure. It's on the wall. When you're ready, please _____ _____ _____ over there.

07 관계 추론

대화를 듣고, 두 사람의 관계로 가장 적절한 것을 고르시오.

① 비행기 승무원 – 탑승객
② 식당 종업원 – 손님
③ 매표소 직원 – 관람객
④ 우체국 직원 – 손님
⑤ 옷 가게 직원 – 손님

W Excuse me. How long will it be until we land?
M _____ _____ _____ arrive in Incheon at 4:30.
W Then we still have one more hour left before landing.
M Right. _____ _____ _____ _____ ?
W Actually, my son's begging me for something to drink. Can he get some orange juice, please?
M Of course. 정답 단서 _____ _____ _____ _____ for him.
W Thank you.

08 할 일 파악

대화를 듣고, 남자가 대화 직후에 할 일로 가장 적절한 것을 고르시오.

① 점심 식사하기　② 준비 운동 하기
③ 안전 요원 부르기　④ 입장권 구입하기
⑤ 수영모 구입하기

W Are you ready, Tom?
M Absolutely. _____ _____ _____ _____ jump into the swimming pool. Let's go.
W Wait! Why aren't you wearing your swimming cap?
M My swimming cap? _____ _____ _____ _____ _____, so I don't think I need it.
W No way! It says here that everyone must wear a swimming cap in the water.
M Really? But I didn't bring it today.
W You can buy one at the shop _____ _____ _____ _____.
M Okay. I'll go get one right now.

09 주제 파악 ✣

다음을 듣고, 무엇에 관한 내용인지 고르시오.

① 지구 온난화의 문제점
② 올바른 쓰레기 처리 방법
③ 음식 섭취를 줄이는 방법
④ 음식물 쓰레기를 줄이는 방법
⑤ 음식물 쓰레기가 증가하는 이유

Sound Clear ☆ **amount of food**
amount의 [t]가 of의 모음과 연음되고, of의 [v]와 food의 [f]가 유사하여 [어마운 토푸드]로 발음된다.

M Our Earth suffers because of food waste. Here are three good tips that will help you reduce your food waste. First, _____ _____ _____ _정답 단서_ what you need before going grocery shopping. Second, _____ _____ _____ what you throw away and try not to buy too much of it the next time. Finally, prepare only the amount your family will eat that day. If you _____ _____ _____, you can _____ _____ _____ the amount of food you throw away.

10 숫자 정보 파악

대화를 듣고, 두 사람이 만날 시각을 고르시오.

① 6:00 p.m.　② 7:00 p.m.　③ 8:40 p.m.
④ 8:50 p.m.　⑤ 9:00 p.m.

W Dad, I'm going to see a musical with Erin tonight.
M When and where is the musical playing?
W _____ _____ _____ 7 o'clock and ends around 8:40 at the Central Theater.
M Oh, the theater is very close to my office. Do you want me to pick you up _____ _____ _____ _____?
W Can you do that? But you usually leave your office at 6 o'clock.
M Well, I can work _____ _____ _____ _____. Did you say it ends at 8:40?
W Yes. Where do you want us to _____ _____ _____?
M Let's meet in front of the theater at 8:50. _정답 단서_
W All right. Thanks, Dad.

11 도표 정보 파악

다음 표를 보면서 대화를 듣고, 내용과 일치하지 <u>않는</u> 것을 고르시오.

	Package Tour	
①	Trip	Five-day trip
②	Total Price	$1,400
③	Room	A double room
④	Meal	Breakfast only
⑤	Ticket	Round-trip tickets

M Have you decided where you would like to go?

W No, but I want to _____ _____ _____ _____ with my friend.

M What is your budget?

W We can afford about $700 each. We need _____ _____ _____ _____ .

M In that case, our package to Thailand is perfect for you. For two people, the total cost is $1,400.

W _____ _____ _____ _____ _____ _____ ?

M It includes a double room, breakfast and dinner, plus round-trip plane tickets. 정답 단서

W That sounds great! We'll take it.

12 숫자 정보 파악

대화를 듣고, 두 사람이 지불할 주차 요금을 고르시오.

① 1,000원 ② 2,000원 ③ 3,000원
④ 10,000원 ⑤ 30,000원

M Do you remember where _____ _____ _____ _____ ?

W It's in section B201.

M Oh, good. How much do we need to _____ _____ _____ ?

W Check the parking ticket. All the information is there.

M Right. Hmm... it's 1,000 won for every hour. _____ 정답 단서 _____ _____ _____ _____ ?

W Three hours.

M 정답 단서 Wait! We get one hour of free parking _____ _____ 정답 단서 _____ _____ more than 30,000 won. We spent more than 30,000 won here today.

W That's great.

13 부탁한 일 파악

대화를 듣고, 남자가 여자에게 부탁한 일로 가장 적절한 것을 고르시오.

① 메뉴 추가하기 ② 후식 주문하기
③ 소스 가져다주기 ④ 인원수 변경하기
⑤ 에어컨 끄기

Sound Clear ☆ **Could you**
[d]가 뒤의 반모음 [j]를 만나 동화되어 [쿠 쥬]로 발음된다.

W Are you ready to order?

M Yes. I'd like a Caesar salad and the beef steak.

W _____ _____ _____ _____ your steak?

M Medium, please.

W Okay. Do you need _____ _____ _____ ?

M Just water, please. By the way, may I ask you a favor?

W Sure. What is it?

M ☆ Could you please _____ _____ _____ _____ _____ ? It's very cold in here.

W No problem. I'll do it right away.

14 이유 파악

대화를 듣고, 여자가 오늘 점심 식사를 같이 못 하는 이유를 고르시오.

① 다이어트 중이어서
② 업무가 너무 많아서
③ 다른 약속이 있어서
④ 건강 검진을 받아야 해서
⑤ 해산물 알레르기가 있어서

Sound Clear ☆ **Have you**

[v]가 뒤의 반모음 [j]를 만나 동화되어 [해뷰]로 발음된다.

M Have you been to the new Italian restaurant near our office?
W No, but I heard their cream spaghetti tastes pretty good.
M Really? It's _____ _____ _____ _____.
W I love cream spaghetti as well. _____ _____ _____ _____ _____ _____ sometime?
M Okay. How about lunch today?
W Sorry. I have to skip lunch today. I have a medical checkup this afternoon. 정답 단서
M I see. _____ _____ _____ _____ ?
W Sounds great.

15 도표 정보 파악

다음 표를 보면서 대화를 듣고, 여자가 등록할 수업의 강사를 고르시오.

	Morning	Evening
Mon.	Listening (Jenny)	Reading (Steve)
Tues.	Reading (Brad)	Listening (Steve)
Wed.	Listening (Diana)	Reading (Matt)
Thur.	Reading (Jenny)	Listening (Brad)
Fri.	Grammar (Matt)	Grammar (Diana)

① Jenny   ② Brad   ③ Matt
④ Steve   ⑤ Diana

M Hello. English Assistance Center.
W Hi. I heard you have excellent tutors available.
M Yes, we do. What _____ _____ _____ _____ with?
W I need help with reading. Do you _____ _____ _____ _____ on Mondays?
M Yes, we have an evening class on Mondays. But _____ _____ _____ _____. How about Tuesday mornings?
W I _____ _____ _____ _____ every morning.
M Then there is only one class left for you.
W Okay. I'll sign up for it.

16 그림의 상황에 적절한 대화 찾기

다음 그림의 상황에 가장 적절한 대화를 고르시오.

① ② ③ ④ ⑤

① W How may I help you?
   M I'd like to _____ _____ _____ _____ _____.
② W You're supposed to slow down around this area. 정답 단서
   M Oh, I'm sorry. I didn't see the sign.
③ W I'd like to check in now.
   M Okay. Do you _____ _____ _____ ?
④ W What happened to your leg?
   M I hurt it while I was playing basketball.
⑤ W _____ _____ _____ _____ today.
   M It is. There must be an accident up ahead.

17 언급되지 않은 것 찾기

다음을 듣고, Firefly Tour에 관해 언급되지 않은 것을 고르시오.

① 소요 시간   ② 제공되는 것
③ 투어 비용   ④ 주의 사항
⑤ 화장실의 위치

W Welcome to our Firefly Tour. I'm going to guide you on a fascinating journey on our beautiful boat. We _____ _____ _____ _____ for about two hours, and you can eat snacks and drinks on the deck freely. Be sure to _____ _____ _____ _____ _____ and don't scare away the fireflies with the flash of your cameras. Please note that the restrooms are _____ _____ _____ _____. Thank you.

18 마지막 말에 대한 응답 찾기

대화를 듣고, 남자의 마지막 말에 대한 여자의 응답으로 가장 적절한 것을 고르시오.

Woman: ______________________

① I'll keep my eyes on your bike.
② I'd better get a new bike soon.
③ Shall we go to the bookstore together?
④ Too bad. You should have been more careful.
⑤ I don't think you're allowed to park your bike here.

Sound Clear ☆ **Don't you**

[t]가 뒤의 반모음 [j]를 만나 동화되어 [돈츄]로 발음된다.

W Hey, Sam. What's up? You look ________ ________ ________.
M Yeah. I ran to school today.
W ☆Don't you usually ride your bike to school?
M Yes, but it was stolen ________ ________ ________. I parked it in front of the bookstore, and somebody took it.
W Didn't you ________ ________ ________ ________ ________?
M No. I thought it would be okay.
W Too bad. You should have been more careful.

19 마지막 말에 대한 응답 찾기

대화를 듣고, 여자의 마지막 말에 대한 남자의 응답으로 가장 적절한 것을 고르시오.

Man: ______________________

① Why don't you play the piano?
② They must have enjoyed your singing.
③ It was a good idea to do volunteer work.
④ Doing volunteer work at the hospital is worthless.
⑤ Don't be disappointed. I'm sure you will do better the next time.

W Good afternoon, Jimmy.
M Hello, Maria. ________ ________ ________ ________ ________ on the weekend?
W Oh, you remembered that I played the piano for children in the hospital.
M Yes. You were really excited.
W I was, but my first time volunteering wasn't very successful.
M ________ ________ ________ ________?
W The music that I chose was boring for them. Most of the children ________ ________ ________.
M Don't be disappointed. I'm sure you will do better the next time.

20 상황에 적절한 말 찾기

다음 상황 설명을 듣고, Monica가 Brian에게 할 말로 가장 적절한 것을 고르시오.

Monica: Brian, ______________________

① are you fond of cooking?
② have you tasted the seafood pasta?
③ did you make all the food yourself?
④ I'll make another one for you the next time.
⑤ can you tell me the recipe for this pasta?

M Monica's friend Brian invited her to his house. Brian prepared ________ ________ ________ ________ food for her. Monica is ________ ________ ________ that everything is so delicious, especially the seafood pasta. Even though Brian is not a professional chef, Monica thinks that it is the best pasta she ________ ________ ________. Monica wonders how Brian made it. In this situation, what do you think Monica probably asks Brian?

정답 단서

Monica Brian, can you tell me the recipe for this pasta?

Review Test

Word Check 영어는 우리말로, 우리말은 영어로 써 보기

01 magician _____

02 outdoor _____

03 return _____

04 matter _____

05 tourist _____

06 due _____

07 admission _____

08 tuition fee _____

09 slip _____

10 at once _____

11 on schedule _____

12 day off _____

13 의견 _____

14 불가능한 _____

15 능력 _____

16 암기하다 _____

17 준비하다 _____

18 운동회 _____

19 전문적인 _____

20 없애 주다, 덜다 _____

21 공공 도서관 _____

22 배송비 _____

23 넘어지다 _____

24 설상가상으로 _____

Expression Check 알맞은 표현을 넣어 문장 완성하기

25 All I want to do is _____ _____ _____ my sleep. 내가 원하는 건 밀린 잠을 자는 거야.

26 Studying English _____ me _____. 영어 공부가 저를 미치게 해요.

27 You look like you're really _____ _____. 너 정말 아파 보여.

28 _____ you win _____ _____ doesn't matter. 네가 우승을 할지 못할지는 중요하지 않아.

29 I noticed her _____ _____ an English exam. 난 그녀가 영어 시험에서 부정행위하는 걸 봤어.

30 The title _____ _____ _____ _____ the poster looks good.
포스터 맨 위에 있는 제목이 좋아 보이네.

Answers p.59

Word Check 영어는 우리말로, 우리말은 영어로 써 보기

01 avoid _____

02 issue _____

03 assistance _____

04 envious _____

05 budget _____

06 inexpensive _____

07 suffer _____

08 conference _____

09 regretful _____

10 journey _____

11 keep track of _____

12 cut down on _____

13 성공적인 _____

14 훔치다 _____

15 실망한 _____

16 쓸모없는 _____

17 조리법 _____

18 맨 아래 _____

19 (필름을) 현상하다 _____

20 전달, 배달 _____

21 환경 _____

22 운전면허증 _____

23 주차권 _____

24 숨이 찬 _____

Expression Check 알맞은 표현을 넣어 문장 완성하기

25 Don't _____ _____ the fireflies with the flash of your cameras.
카메라 플래시 빛으로 반딧불이를 쫓아 버리지 않도록 하세요.

26 How often do you _____ your hair _____? 너는 얼마나 자주 머리를 자르니?

27 There's _____ _____ _____ our water purifier. 우리 정수기에 문제가 있어요.

28 Most of the children didn't _____ _____. 대부분의 아이들은 주의를 기울이지 않았어.

29 You're supposed to _____ _____ around this area. 이 부근에서는 속도를 줄이셔야 합니다.

30 _____ _____ _____ the amount of food you throw away. 당신이 버리는 음식의 양을 줄이세요.

1.0배속

1.2배속

01 대화를 듣고, 여자가 구입할 옷을 고르시오.

02 대화를 듣고, 남자가 지불할 금액을 고르시오.

① $5 　　② $9 　　③ $10
④ $11 　　⑤ $12

03 대화를 듣고, 남자가 여자에게 전화한 목적으로 가장 적절한 것을 고르시오.

① 예약하기 위해서
② 불평하기 위해서
③ 예약을 확인하기 위해서
④ 친절한 서비스에 감사하기 위해서
⑤ 호텔에 가는 방법을 확인하기 위해서

04 다음 그림의 상황에 가장 적절한 대화를 고르시오.

① 　　② 　　③ 　　④ 　　⑤

05 대화를 듣고, 남자가 대화 직후에 할 일로 가장 적절한 것을 고르시오.

① 와인 사 오기 　　② 피자 만들기
③ 샐러드 만들기 　　④ 케이크 찾아오기
⑤ 점심 식사 주문하기

06 다음을 듣고, 두 사람의 대화가 어색한 것을 고르시오.

① 　　② 　　③ 　　④ 　　⑤

07 대화를 듣고, 남자의 현재 몸무게를 고르시오.

① 70kg 　　② 75kg 　　③ 80kg
④ 85kg 　　⑤ 87kg

08 대화를 듣고, 여자에 관한 내용과 일치하지 않는 것을 고르시오.

① 한국에 오기 전에 호주에서 지내고 있었다.
② 지난주에 한국에 도착했다.
③ 현재 여름 방학 기간이다.
④ 한국에 한 달 동안 머무를 예정이다.
⑤ 제주도로 이사할 예정이다.

09 다음을 듣고, 무엇에 관한 안내 방송인지 고르시오.

① 주차 안내 　　② 미아 찾기
③ 폐점 안내 　　④ 편의 시설 안내
⑤ 놀이공원 홍보

10 대화를 듣고, 여자가 남자에게 부탁한 일로 가장 적절한 것을 고르시오.

① 회의 취소하기 　　② 회의 주제 바꾸기
③ 회의 자료 나눠 주기 　④ 회의 시간 변경하기
⑤ 회의 참석자 명단 확인하기

11 대화를 듣고, 여자의 심정으로 가장 적절한 것을 고르시오.

① angry 　　② happy 　　③ lonely
④ nervous 　　⑤ proud

12 다음을 듣고, The World of Tradition에 관한 내용으로 언급되지 <u>않은</u> 것을 고르시오.

① 목적   ② 하는 일   ③ 기간
④ 입장료   ⑤ 예약 방법

13 다음 게시판을 보면서 대화를 듣고, 내용과 일치하지 <u>않는</u> 것을 고르시오.

Natural History Museum

Hours

Monday ~ Friday: ① 9 a.m. ~ ② 5 p.m.
Saturday: ③ 10 a.m. ~ ④ 2 p.m.

Tickets

Adults: $5
8~12 years: $3
⑤ 7 and under: free

---

14 대화를 듣고, 여자가 책을 빌릴 수 <u>없는</u> 이유를 고르시오.

① 책이 훼손되어서
② 다른 학교 학생이어서
③ 도서관 카드가 없어서
④ 책을 반납하지 않아서
⑤ 대출 가능 시간이 지나서

15 다음을 듣고, 무엇에 관한 설문 조사 결과인지 고르시오.

① 좋아하는 스포츠
② 여행하고 싶은 나라
③ 방학 동안 하고 싶은 것
④ 방학 동안 배우고 싶은 것
⑤ 인기 있는 여가 활동

16 대화를 듣고, 여자의 평소 등교 시각을 고르시오.

① 7:00 a.m.   ② 7:15 a.m.   ③ 7:30 a.m.
④ 8:30 a.m.   ⑤ 8:45 a.m.

17 대화를 듣고, 남자의 마지막 말에 대한 여자의 응답으로 가장 적절한 것을 고르시오.

Woman: _____

① I'm sorry to hear that.
② Okay. Let me help you.
③ All right. I'll do it right now.
④ Okay. Let's meet at the bus stop.
⑤ How long have you been abroad?

18 대화를 듣고, 여자의 마지막 말에 대한 남자의 응답으로 가장 적절한 것을 고르시오.

Man: _____

① Well, that's too expensive.
② Would you like some dessert?
③ Sorry. I don't like Chinese food.
④ Please get me something to drink.
⑤ Can you reserve a table by the window for us?

19 대화를 듣고, 남자의 마지막 말에 대한 여자의 응답으로 가장 적절한 것을 고르시오.

Woman: _____

① There is a bakery next to the bank.
② My mother taught me how to cook.
③ I'm thinking of learning how to bake.
④ My grandmother is good at baking cookies.
⑤ Thanks. I want to open my own bakery someday.

20 다음 상황 설명을 듣고, Jisu가 Jimmy에게 할 말로 가장 적절한 것을 고르시오.

Jisu: Jimmy, _____

① I don't like watching movies.
② could we meet around 4 p.m.?
③ I want to watch a musical with you.
④ my grandmother is visiting my family.
⑤ let's have dinner and talk about the project.

01 그림 정보 파악

대화를 듣고, 여자가 구입할 옷을 고르시오.

① ② ③

④ ⑤

M Can I help you?

W Yes, please. I'm looking for _____ _____ _____ _____ _____ _____.

M How old is she?

W _____ _____ _____ _____.

M Then how about this sweater _____ _____ _____ _____? It's very popular.

W I don't know. It looks a little old-fashioned. How much is the cardigan over there?

M Do you mean the one with a tie belt? Oh, _____ _____ _____. It's $40.

W That's great. I will take it.

02 숫자 정보 파악 ✳

대화를 듣고, 남자가 지불할 금액을 고르시오.

① $5 ② $9 ③ $10
④ $11 ⑤ $12

W Hello. What _____ _____ _____ _____ _____?

M I would like five chicken nuggets and a cheese sandwich.

W The nuggets are $1 each and the cheese sandwich is $5.

M I'm going to have the nuggets here, but I _____ _____ _____ _____ _____.

W If you pay $1 extra, you can also _____ _____ _____ _____ _____.

M No, thank you. Can I use this 10% coupon?

W Oh, sure. _____ _____ _____ _____ _____.

M Thanks. Here's my credit card.

03 목적 파악

대화를 듣고, 남자가 여자에게 전화한 목적으로 가장 적절한 것을 고르시오.

① 예약하기 위해서
② 불평하기 위해서
③ 예약을 확인하기 위해서
④ 친절한 서비스에 감사하기 위해서
⑤ 호텔에 가는 방법을 확인하기 위해서

Sound Clear ☆ **suite**

suite(스위트룸)와 sweet(달콤한)는 [스윗]으로 발음이 같으므로 맥락을 통해 의미를 파악해야 한다.

(*Telephone rings.*)

W City Hotel. How can I help you?

M Hi. I'd like to confirm my reservation at your hotel.

W Sure. Can you tell me your name and _____ _____ _____ _____ _____?

M My name is Adam Smith and I'm going to arrive at your hotel on January 13.

W Thanks. You _____ _____ _____ _____ _____ _____ in one of our junior suite rooms.

M That's correct. Thank you.

W No problem. We're _____ _____ _____ _____ you soon.

04 그림의 상황에 적절한 대화 찾기

다음 그림의 상황에 가장 적절한 대화를 고르시오.

① ② ③ ④ ⑤

① W Where can I take you?
   M The airport. Please get me there _____ _____ _____ _____.
② W How long will it take to get to City Hall by car?
   M It'll _____ _____ _____ _____.
③ W What are you going to do after you graduate?
   M I'll go to Canada to _____ _____ _____ _____.
④ W Excuse me. Is this bus headed to the Canadian Embassy?
   M We've just passed it. 정답 단서 _____ _____ _____ _____ _____ and walk back.
⑤ W I'm sorry, but could you show me something else?
   M If you don't like this one, how about that one?

05 할 일 파악

대화를 듣고, 남자가 대화 직후에 할 일로 가장 적절한 것을 고르시오.

① 와인 사 오기   ② 피자 만들기
③ 샐러드 만들기   ④ 케이크 찾아오기
⑤ 점심 식사 주문하기

W Oh, it's already 11 o'clock. We have to hurry.
M Relax. We've got plenty of _____ _____ _____.
W Okay. Steve, did you put the pizza in the oven?
M Yes, I did. _____ _____ _____ _____?
W I cut the vegetables yesterday and _____ _____ _____ _____ _____. I'll make it now. Where is the wine?
M The wine is on the table. Where is the cake?
W Oh, I forgot to pick up the cake from the bakery. We 정답 단서 _____ _____ _____ _____.
M Okay. I'll go.

06 어색한 대화 찾기 ✽

다음을 듣고, 두 사람의 대화가 <u>어색한</u> 것을 고르시오.

① ② ③ ④ ⑤

Sound Clear ☆ **How would you**
How의 끝 모음과 would의 끝 자음이 각각 뒤의 반모음 [w], [j]와 만나 [하우쥬]로 발음된다.

① M How would you like your steak?
   W Thank you for saying so.
② M Will you go for a walk with me?
   W Sorry, I can't. I _____ _____ _____ _____ _____ now.
③ M What's the matter? You look tired.
   W I _____ _____ _____ _____ because of the noise from upstairs.
④ M Are you _____ _____ _____?
   W Yes. I'll have the meatball spaghetti with a lemonade.
⑤ M _____ _____ _____ _____ I open the window? It's so hot in here.
   W Of course not. Go ahead.

07 특정 정보 파악

대화를 듣고, 남자의 현재 몸무게를 고르시오.

① 70kg ② 75kg ③ 80kg
④ 85kg ⑤ 87kg

Sound Clear ☆ **weighed**

gh가 묵음이라서 [웨이드]로 발음된다.

W Hi, James. You look different!
M Really? I've been exercising hard these days.
W You look great! How long _____ _____ _____ _____ _____ ?
M It's been almost six months now.
W _____ _____ ! Why did you start exercising?
M I weighed 70 kilograms a year ago. But after I started having late night snack, I gained 15 kilograms.
W Late night snacks _____ _____ _____ _____ _____ .
M Yes, so I decided to lose some weight and become healthy again. I _____ _____ _____ _____ in six months.

---

08 일치하지 않는 것 찾기

대화를 듣고, 여자에 관한 내용과 일치하지 <u>않</u>는 것을 고르시오.

① 한국에 오기 전에 호주에서 지내고 있었다.
② 지난주에 한국에 도착했다.
③ 현재 여름 방학 기간이다.
④ 한국에 한 달 동안 머무를 예정이다.
⑤ 제주도로 이사할 예정이다.

M Hi, Amy. _____ _____ _____ _____ !
W Hi, Brian. How have you been?
M Good. When did you _____ _____ _____ _____ ?
W I came back last week. It's summer vacation there.
M _____ _____ _____ _____ _____ in Korea?
W For a month. But I'm planning to travel in Jeju-do with my mom for a week.
M That's good. Have a great time there.

---

09 주제 파악

다음을 듣고, 무엇에 관한 안내 방송인지 고르시오.

① 주차 안내   ② 미아 찾기
③ 폐점 안내   ④ 편의 시설 안내
⑤ 놀이공원 홍보

M Thank you for visiting Fun World. We are looking for a four-year-old boy named Brian. The boy _____ _____ _____ _____ of the parking lot. _____ _____ _____ _____ and a yellow T-shirt. He's also wearing a red cap and blue sneakers. _____ _____ _____ _____ _____ or can see him now, please call the customer service center right away. Thank you very much.

---

10 부탁한 일 파악

대화를 듣고, 여자가 남자에게 부탁한 일로 가장 적절한 것을 고르시오.

① 회의 취소하기
② 회의 주제 바꾸기
③ 회의 자료 나눠 주기
④ 회의 시간 변경하기
⑤ 회의 참석자 명단 확인하기

(*Cellphone rings.*)
W Hey, Sam. Are you busy now?
M No. What's up?
W I need a favor. I came to Tim's school to meet his teacher, and _____ _____ _____ _____ _____ .
M Oh, so are you going to be _____ _____ _____ _____ ?
W Yes. I think I can get there by 4:20. Can you give everyone the materials to look over until I get there?
M Sure, no problem. _____ _____ _____ _____ ?
W They are on my desk. Thank you so much.

11 심정 추론

대화를 듣고, 여자의 심정으로 가장 적절한 것을 고르시오.

① angry ② happy ③ lonely
④ nervous ⑤ proud

M Sally, you're the next speaker. Are you ready?
W No. My hands are shaking.
M _____ _____ *정답 단서*. You did your best to prepare for this speech contest.
W I don't know. The others _____ _____ _____ _____, and they look so confident. What if I forget _____ _____ _____?
M I'm sure you will do great, too.

12 언급되지 않은 것 찾기

다음을 듣고, The World of Tradition에 관한 내용으로 언급되지 않은 것을 고르시오.

① 목적 ② 하는 일 ③ 기간
④ 입장료 ⑤ 예약 방법

Sound Clear ☆ **Tradition**
[t]와 [r]이 연달아 나와 [츄레디션]으로 발음된다.

W Please come to the National Museum and _____ _____ _____ _____, The World of Tradition. This exhibition will give visitors an opportunity to _____ _____ _____ _____ from all over the world. You can watch traditional music and dance performances and _____ _____ _____ of many countries. From February 22 to February 28, the exhibition opens at 9 a.m. and lasts for 9 hours every day. _____ _____ _____, please visit our website. Thank you.

13 도표 정보 파악

다음 게시판을 보면서 대화를 듣고, 내용과 일치하지 않는 것을 고르시오.

Natural History Museum
Hours
Monday ~ Friday: ① 9 a.m. ~ ② 5 p.m.
Saturday: ③ 10 a.m. ~ ④ 2 p.m.

Tickets
Adults: $5
8~12 years: $3
⑤ 7 and under: free

(*Telephone rings.*)
W Natural History Museum. How can I help you?
M Can you tell me _____ _____ _____ _____?
W Sure. We open at 9 a.m., Monday through Saturday.
M And when do you close? *정답 단서*
W We _____ _____ _____ _____ _____ _____ and 2 p.m. on Saturdays.
M And how much is a ticket for a 4-year-old child?
W _____ _____ _____ _____ 7 and under.
M That's great. Thank you for your help.

14 이유 파악

대화를 듣고, 여자가 책을 빌릴 수 없는 이유를 고르시오.

① 책이 훼손되어서
② 다른 학교 학생이어서
③ 도서관 카드가 없어서
④ 책을 반납하지 않아서
⑤ 대출 가능 시간이 지나서

W Excuse me. How many books can I borrow?
M _____ _____ _____ _____.
W That's great. I want to borrow these books.
M Do you _____ _____ _____ _____?
W Yes, here it is.
M Wait a minute. Oh, you _____ _____ _____ _____ yet. You can't borrow any more books.
W Really? Can you tell me the name of _____ _____ _____ _____ _____?
M Sure. Let me check.

15 주제 파악

다음을 듣고, 무엇에 관한 설문 조사 결과인지 고르시오.

① 좋아하는 스포츠
② 여행하고 싶은 나라
③ 방학 동안 하고 싶은 것
④ 방학 동안 배우고 싶은 것
⑤ 인기 있는 여가 활동

Sound Clear ☆ **want to**
동일한 발음의 자음이 연이어 나오면 앞 자음 소리가 탈락하여 [원투]로 발음된다.

M Good afternoon, everyone. I _____ _____ _____ about what our classmates want to do during vacation. The largest number of students, 12, said they want to _____ _____ _____ _____. Four students want to go camping. The number of students who want to _____ _____ _____ was larger than the number of students who want to go camping. _____ _____ _____ came from only 2 students who want to play sports during vacation.

16 숫자 정보 파악

대화를 듣고, 여자의 평소 등교 시각을 고르시오.

① 7:00 a.m. ② 7:15 a.m. ③ 7:30 a.m.
④ 8:30 a.m. ⑤ 8:45 a.m.

W Dad, I'm late for school! Can you _____ _____ _____ _____, please?
M Isn't it too early to go to school? What time do you have to be at school?
W I usually go to school by 8:30, but _____ _____ _____ _____ _____ today.
M I see. What time is the meeting?
W It's at 7:30.
M It's 7:15 now, so _____ _____ _____ _____. Let me get my keys.
W Thank you, Dad.

17 마지막 말에 대한 응답 찾기

대화를 듣고, 남자의 마지막 말에 대한 여자의 응답으로 가장 적절한 것을 고르시오.

Woman: _____

① I'm sorry to hear that.
② Okay. Let me help you.
③ All right. I'll do it right now.
④ Okay. Let's meet at the bus stop.
⑤ How long have you been abroad?

W Look at this mess! David, I told you to _____ _____ _____ an hour ago.
M Sorry, Mom. But I was busy.
W Busy? You've been playing computer games _____ _____!
M Yeah, but....
W David, you _____ _____ _____ _____ _____ less than one hour every day.
M Sorry, Mom. _____ _____ _____ _____ and start cleaning right now.
W Okay. Let me help you.

18 마지막 말에 대한 응답 찾기 ✽

대화를 듣고, 여자의 마지막 말에 대한 남자의
응답으로 가장 적절한 것을 고르시오.

Man: _____

① Well, that's too expensive.

② Would you like some dessert?

③ Sorry. I don't like Chinese food.

④ Please get me something to drink.

⑤ Can you reserve a table by the
window for us?

(*Telephone rings.*)

W Mr. Choi's Chinese Restaurant. How can I help you?

M _____ _____ _____ _____ _____ _____ .

W Can I have your name, please?

M Paul Lee.

W _____ _____ _____ _____ would you like to make
a reservation?

M June 30, this coming Tuesday at 6 p.m.

W How many people are there _____ _____ _____ ?

M _____ _____ _____ _____ .

W Okay, your reservation is confirmed. Do you _____
_____ _____ ?

M Can you reserve a table by the window for us?

---

19 마지막 말에 대한 응답 찾기

대화를 듣고, 남자의 마지막 말에 대한 여자의
응답으로 가장 적절한 것을 고르시오.

Woman: _____

① There is a bakery next to the bank.

② My mother taught me how to cook.

③ I'm thinking of learning how to bake.

④ My grandmother is good at baking
cookies.

⑤ Thanks. I want to open my own
bakery someday.

Sound Clear ☆ **right away**
앞 단어의 끝 자음과 뒤 단어의 모음이 만나
연음되어 [롸이러웨이]로 발음된다.

M I love this cheesecake! _____ _____ _____ _____
_____ right away!

W I'm so glad you like it.

M Yeah, where did you buy it?

W Believe it or not, _____ _____ _____ _____ .

M I can't believe it! This is the best cheesecake I've ever tasted!

W I've been _____ _____ _____ these days. Baking is
really fun.

M You should _____ _____ _____ _____ . You're really
talented!

W Thanks. I want to open my own bakery someday.

---

20 상황에 적절한 말 찾기

다음 상황 설명을 듣고, Jisu가 Jimmy에게 할
말로 가장 적절한 것을 고르시오.

Jisu: Jimmy, _____

① I don't like watching movies.

② could we meet around 4 p.m.?

③ I want to watch a musical with you.

④ my grandmother is visiting my family.

⑤ let's have dinner and talk about the
projoot.

M Jisu and her friend Jimmy planned to _____ _____
_____ _____ this afternoon. They promised to meet
_____ _____ _____ _____ _____ _____ at
3 o'clock. But Jisu's mom called from work and asked Jisu
to look after her sister _____ _____ _____ _____
_____ _____ . Jisu's mom will get home around 3:30, so
Jisu can't meet Jimmy until 4. What should Jisu tell Jimmy?

Jisu Jimmy, could we meet around 4 p.m.?

1.0배속

1.2배속

01 대화를 듣고, 남자가 구입할 안경을 고르시오.

02 대화를 듣고, 여자가 남자에게 부탁한 일로 가장 적절한 것을 고르시오.

① 약 사 오기   ② 진료 예약해 주기
③ 주스 사 오기   ④ 요리해 주기
⑤ 병원에 같이 가기

03 다음 그림의 상황에 가장 적절한 대화를 고르시오.

①   ②   ③   ④   ⑤

04 대화를 듣고, 남자가 할 일로 가장 적절한 것을 고르시오.

① 여행 가기   ② 생일 선물 사기
③ 동아리 활동하기   ④ 생일 파티에 가기
⑤ 아버지 마중 나가기

05 대화를 듣고, International Rock Festival에 관해 언급되지 않은 것을 고르시오.

① 때   ② 장소   ③ 출연진
④ 입장료   ⑤ 준비물

06 대화를 듣고, 여자가 늦은 이유로 가장 적절한 것을 고르시오.

① 버스를 놓쳐서
② 교통 체증 때문에
③ 교통사고가 나서
④ 아이 돌보미가 늦게 와서
⑤ 택시가 잘못된 주소로 가서

07 다음을 듣고, 두 사람의 대화가 어색한 것을 고르시오.

①   ②   ③   ④   ⑤

08 대화를 듣고, 여자가 파티에 가져가기로 한 것을 고르시오.

① 주스   ② 풍선   ③ 샐러드
④ 케이크   ⑤ 닭 요리

09 다음을 듣고, 방송의 목적으로 가장 적절한 것을 고르시오.

① 열차 시간표 변경을 공지하려고
② 폭설로 인한 열차 지연을 알리려고
③ 열차에 짐을 싣는 방법을 설명하려고
④ 궂은 날씨로 인한 교통 체증을 알리려고
⑤ 캐나다 왕복 열차표 이용 방법을 안내하려고

10 대화를 듣고, 남자가 지불할 금액을 고르시오.

① $10   ② $15   ③ $20
④ $50   ⑤ $60

11 대화를 듣고, 두 사람이 대화하는 장소로 가장 적절한 곳을 고르시오.

① 약국   ② 병원   ③ 독서실
④ 자동차 안   ⑤ 비행기 안

12 다음을 듣고, 영어 말하기 대회에 관해 언급되지 <u>않은</u> 것을 고르시오.

① 대회 장소 ② 참가 인원 ③ 연설 주제
④ 심사 위원 ⑤ 우승자 발표일

13 다음 표를 보면서 대화를 듣고, 두 사람이 볼 영화를 고르시오.

	Movie	Time	Day
①	Titanic	8:30 a.m.	Saturday
②	Titanic	10:30 a.m.	Saturday
③	Avatar	1:00 p.m.	Saturday
④	Avatar	4:00 p.m.	Sunday
⑤	Jaws	7:30 p.m.	Sunday

14 다음을 듣고, 무엇에 관한 설명인지 고르시오.

① 파이 ② 피자 ③ 볶음밥
④ 오믈렛 ⑤ 파스타

15 대화를 듣고, 남자가 대화 직후에 할 일로 가장 적절한 것을 고르시오.

① 짐 싸기 ② 택시 부르기
③ 꽃병 포장하기 ④ 가스 밸브 잠그기
⑤ 화분에 물 주기

16 대화를 듣고, 남자가 집에 올 때 들러야 할 장소를 고르시오.

① 매표소 ② 세탁소 ③ 영화관
④ 옷 가게 ⑤ 도서관

17 대화를 듣고, 여자의 마지막 말에 대한 남자의 응답으로 가장 적절한 것을 고르시오.

Man: _____

① I can lend my cellphone to you.
② I have to carry a portable battery.
③ I will visit there right after school.
④ You can exchange it for a new one if you want.
⑤ Please connect me to the customer service center.

18 대화를 듣고, 남자의 마지막 말에 대한 여자의 응답으로 가장 적절한 것을 고르시오.

Woman: _____

① We can go to school by bicycle.
② I just made it out of my old jeans.
③ You can help me solve this problem.
④ I'm sure all your hard work will be rewarded.
⑤ We can't stop global environmental pollution.

19 대화를 듣고, 여자의 마지막 말에 대한 남자의 응답으로 가장 적절한 것을 고르시오.

Man: _____

① Let me check lost and found.
② What time do you want to meet?
③ Here is the schedule for the trains today.
④ Okay. I'll check the security camera first.
⑤ Why don't you take a taxi? It's more convenient.

20 다음 상황 설명을 듣고, Sandra가 Sally에게 할 말로 가장 적절한 것을 고르시오.

Sandra: Sally, _____

① if I were you, I wouldn't say that.
② you don't have to apologize.
③ let's stop fighting and be friends again.
④ why don't you text her and say you're sorry?
⑤ give me an honest apology and I'll forgive you.

받아쓰기용

01 그림 정보 파악

대화를 듣고, 남자가 구입할 안경을 고르시오.

W Can I help you?

M Yes, please. I'm looking for glasses.

W What kind of glasses _____ _____ _____ _____ _____ ?

M I want to try rimless glasses.

W I think rimless glasses would _____ _____ _____ 정답 단서 _____. What shape of lenses do you want?

M So far, I've always worn round glasses. I want to _____ _____ _____.

W How about this pair with square-shaped lenses? Why don't you try them on? 정답 단서

M Oh, I think they _____ _____ _____. I'll take them.

02 부탁한 일 파악

대화를 듣고, 여자가 남자에게 부탁한 일로 가장 적절한 것을 고르시오.

① 약 사 오기　　② 진료 예약해 주기
③ 주스 사 오기　　④ 요리해 주기
⑤ 병원에 같이 가기

Sound Clear ☆ coughing

cough(기침하다)의 gh가 [f]로 소리 나서 [커핑]으로 발음된다.

(*Cellphone rings.*)

M Honey, I'll be a little late coming home.

W Okay, but I hope you _____ _____ _____ _____.

M Don't worry. How do you feel now? You were coughing ☆ a lot this morning.

W _____ _____ _____ _____ _____. I'll cook some chicken soup to soothe my throat.

M That's a good idea. Do you want me to get some medicine on 함정 my way home?

W No, _____ _____ _____ _____ _____. But can you pick up some juice? 정답 단서

M Sure. I'll get some for you.

03 그림의 상황에 적절한 대화 찾기

다음 그림의 상황에 가장 적절한 대화를 고르시오.

① ② ③ ④ ⑤

① M Let's _____ _____ _____ _____ _____ _____.

W Okay. Why don't you wear more comfortable shoes?

② M You seem to _____ _____ _____. What happened?

W My new shoes scraped the skin off my heels.

③ M Can you explain what I should do?

W Remove your shoes before stepping on the scale, please.

④ M I'm sorry that I _____ _____ _____.

W That's all right.

⑤ M Are you looking for high heels or low heels?

W I'm _____ _____ _____ _____.

04 할 일 파악 ❖

대화를 듣고, 남자가 할 일로 가장 적절한 것을 고르시오.

① 여행 가기　　② 생일 선물 사기
③ 동아리 활동하기　　④ 생일 파티에 가기
⑤ 아버지 마중 나가기

(*Telephone rings.*)

W Hello, John. This is Sandy.
M Hi, Sandy. What's up?
W Today is Julie's birthday. Can you _____ _____ _____ ? 함정
M I'm afraid I can't.
W Why not? Is it because of your sports club activity? 함정
M No. I have to go to the airport. My dad's coming back from his business trip, and _____ _____ _____ _____ . I need to help him.
W Oh, I see. You _____ _____ _____ to see him again.

05 언급되지 않은 것 찾기

대화를 듣고, International Rock Festival에 관해 언급되지 않은 것을 고르시오.

① 때　　② 장소　　③ 출연진
④ 입장료　　⑤ 준비물

W Do you know _____ _____ _____ _____ next month?
M You mean the International Rock Festival. When is it?
W It's on the first weekend of June. Do you want to go to it with me?
M Sure. _____ _____ _____ _____ _____ ?
W On Songdo Island in Incheon. The admission is 50,000 won.
M Well, it's not cheap, but I think _____ _____ _____ _____ _____ .
W I think so, too. Oh, we need to _____ _____ _____ _____ .
M Okay. I can do that.

06 이유 파악

대화를 듣고, 여자가 늦은 이유로 가장 적절한 것을 고르시오.

① 버스를 놓쳐서
② 교통 체증 때문에
③ 교통사고가 나서
④ 아이 돌보미가 늦게 와서
⑤ 택시가 잘못된 주소로 가서

W I'm so sorry that I am late.
M That's okay. I _____ _____ _____ _____ .
W I took a taxi, but it took longer than I expected.
M _____ _____ _____ _____ ?
W It was not that bad. The problem was that I wasn't able to _____ _____ _____ _____ .
M Oh, was something wrong?
W My babysitter was late because she missed the bus.
M You _____ _____ _____ _____ . 함정 Anyway, let's start the meeting now.
정답 단서

07 어색한 대화 찾기

다음을 듣고, 두 사람의 대화가 어색한 것을 고르시오.

① ② ③ ④ ⑤

Sound Clear ☆ headache

ch가 [k]로 소리 나서 [헤데이크]로 발음된다.

① M Do you have plans today?
  W Yes. I'm going to see a movie with Paul.
② M _____ _____ _____ _____ your textbook?
  W I'm afraid I can't because I don't have it right now.
③ M Is it okay if _____ _____ _____ _____ ?
  W Sure. Go ahead.
④ M Hello. What seems to be the problem?
  W _____ _____ _____ a terrible headache.
⑤ M When do you usually _____ _____ _____ ?
  W When I'm stressed, I eat something sweet.

08 특정 정보 파악

대화를 듣고, 여자가 파티에 가져가기로 한 것을 고르시오.

① 주스   ② 풍선   ③ 샐러드
④ 케이크   ⑤ 닭 요리

W Good afternoon. Where are you going?
M I'm _____ _____ _____ _____ _____. I need to buy some juice for Anna's party.
W Oh, I totally _____ _____ _____ _____ ! I was supposed to bring a salad!
M What? How could you forget? Do you need my help?
W Yes. Can you buy me a bottle of Italian salad dressing at the store? I will _____ _____ _____ _____ _____.
M Sure, I can do that.
W Thanks.

09 목적 파악

다음을 듣고, 방송의 목적으로 가장 적절한 것을 고르시오.

① 열차 시간표 변경을 공지하려고
② 폭설로 인한 열차 지연을 알리려고
③ 열차에 짐을 싣는 방법을 설명하려고
④ 굻은 날씨로 인한 교통 체증을 알리려고
⑤ 캐나다 왕복 열차표 이용 방법을 안내하려고

M Attention, passengers. _____ _____ _____ _____ _____, Train 2322 to Whistler Village will be delayed. If you _____ _____ _____ _____ on the train, please remove all items and get off the train now. If the delay _____ _____ _____ _____ _____, we will offer you a free round-trip ticket to anywhere Via Rail travels in Canada. We will keep you informed of any updates _____ _____ _____ _____ _____. Thank you.

10 숫자 정보 파악

대화를 듣고, 남자가 지불할 금액을 고르시오.

① $10   ② $15   ③ $20
④ $50   ⑤ $60

W Welcome to Marine Wonder Aquarium. How can I help you?
M I'd like to _____ _____ _____. How much are they?
W A ticket for adults is $20 and one for children is $10.
M _____ _____ _____ _____ _____, please.
W Okay. Is either of your children under 36 months? _____ _____ _____ _____ _____.
M Yes. One of them is 15 months old.
W All right. Then two adult tickets and one child ticket.
M Great. _____ _____ _____.

11 장소 추론

대화를 듣고, 두 사람이 대화하는 장소로 가장 적절한 곳을 고르시오.

① 약국
② 병원
③ 독서실
④ 자동차 안
⑤ 비행기 안

M Oh, please help me. My leg really hurts.
W What's wrong? Do you _____ _____ _____ _____ ?
M Yes. Maybe it's just that I've been sitting for several hours.
W Can you get up and _____ _____ _____ _____ _____ _____ ?
M But the seat belt sign is still on.
W You're right. We still _____ _____ _____ _____ _____ to go before landing.
M Oh, I _____ _____ _____ _____ anymore.
W I'll ask the flight attendant for some help.

정답 단서

12 언급되지 않은 것 찾기

다음을 듣고, 영어 말하기 대회에 관해 언급되지 않은 것을 고르시오.

① 대회 장소
② 참가 인원
③ 연설 주제
④ 심사 위원
⑤ 우승자 발표일

W Hello, students! The English Speech Contest _____ _____ _____ today in our school auditorium. Fifty students _____ _____ _____ _____ this year. The judges are three English teachers from our school including Mr. Johnson, the native English teacher. _____ _____ _____ _____ _____ on April 24, and this year's winner will receive a computer. The contest will start at 5 o'clock. Please _____ _____ _____ .

13 도표 정보 파악

다음 표를 보면서 대화를 듣고, 두 사람이 볼 영화를 고르시오.

	Movie	Time	Day
①	Titanic	8:30 a.m.	Saturday
②	Titanic	10:30 a.m.	Saturday
③	Avatar	1:00 p.m.	Saturday
④	Avatar	4:00 p.m.	Sunday
⑤	Jaws	7:30 p.m.	Sunday

M Some famous old movies are _____ _____ _____ _____ again.
W Wow! I really want to see some of my favorite old movies again. Why don't we watch one together?
M Sounds good. _____ _____ _____ _____ _____ _____ ? I'm free this weekend.
W Well, I _____ _____ _____ on Saturday.
M Then there are only two movies that we can see.
W Yes. How about seeing the one that starts earlier?
M Okay, then _____ _____ _____ _____ .

14 화제 파악

다음을 듣고, 무엇에 관한 설명인지 고르시오.

① 파이
② 피자
③ 볶음밥
④ 오믈렛
⑤ 파스타

Sound Clear ☆ **dough**
gh가 묵음이라서 [도우]로 발음된다.

M This is _____ _____ _____ _____ _____ . Now it has become one of _____ _____ _____ ☆ _____ in the world. It is usually a round, flat wheat dough _____ _____ _____ , cheese, olives and various other ingredients and baked in an oven. In formal restaurants it is eaten with a knife and fork, but in casual settings it is _____ _____ _____ to be eaten while held in the hand.

15 할 일 파악

대화를 듣고, 남자가 대화 직후에 할 일로 가장 적절한 것을 고르시오.

① 짐 싸기
② 택시 부르기
③ 꽃병 포장하기
④ 가스 밸브 잠그기
⑤ 화분에 물 주기

Sound Clear ☆ **vase**

미국식은 [베이스]로, 영국식은 [바스]로 발음된다.

W Jack, are you finished packing?
M _____ _____ _____. Mom, did you buy something for grandmother?
W Yes. I bought a beautiful flower vase for her.
M A vase? Isn't it too fragile _____ _____ _____ _____ _____?
W Don't worry. I _____ _____ _____ well. Hey, did you water the plants?
M Yes, I did. Mom, did you _____ _____ _____ _____ _____?
W Oh, I forgot to do that.
M Mom, you'd better call a taxi. I'll turn off the valve.

16 특정 정보 파악

대화를 듣고, 남자가 집에 올 때 들러야 할 장소를 고르시오.

① 매표소
② 세탁소
③ 영화관
④ 옷 가게
⑤ 도서관

(*Cellphone rings.*)
W Chris, where are you now?
M I'm in front of the theater. _____ _____ _____ _____ a movie with my friends.
W When _____ _____ _____ _____ _____?
M In about two hours.
W Then when you come home, can you drop by the dry cleaner's?
M To _____ _____ _____ _____?
W Yes. Our clothes are already dry cleaned. Please pick them up _____ _____ _____ _____.
M Okay, leave it to me.

17 마지막 말에 대한 응답 찾기

대화를 듣고, 여자의 마지막 말에 대한 남자의 응답으로 가장 적절한 것을 고르시오.

Man: _____

① I can lend my cellphone to you.
② I have to carry a portable battery.
③ I will visit there right after school.
④ You can exchange it for a new one if you want.
⑤ Please connect me to the customer service center.

W Why do you _____ _____ _____ _____ _____?
M My smartphone is not working.
W You bought the smartphone _____ _____ _____ _____, didn't you?
M Yes. It's only been two weeks, but it has already _____ _____ _____ _____ _____.
W What's the problem?
M At first, it _____ _____ _____ _____. And now it won't turn on.
W You must be very upset. Why don't you visit the customer service center?
M I will visit there right after school.

18 마지막 말에 대한 응답 찾기

대화를 듣고, 남자의 마지막 말에 대한 여자의 응답으로 가장 적절한 것을 고르시오.

Woman: ______________________

① We can go to school by bicycle.
② I just made it out of my old jeans.
③ You can help me solve this problem.
④ I'm sure all your hard work will be rewarded.
⑤ We can't stop global environmental pollution.

Sound Clear ☆ **ought to**

동일한 발음의 자음이 연이어 나오면 앞 자음 소리가 탈락하여 [오웃투]로 발음된다.

M Hey, I love your bag. It's really cool.
W Thanks. Actually, I ________ ________ ________ ________.
M No kidding! Where did you get the idea?
W I watched a famous video clip. They showed ________ ________ ________ ________.
M What an interesting idea! You know, there are ________ ________ ________ ________ ________ ________.
W That's right. I think we ☆ought to make every effort to ________ ________ ________.
M Then what can we do to help the earth?
W We can go to school by bicycle.

19 마지막 말에 대한 응답 찾기

대화를 듣고, 여자의 마지막 말에 대한 남자의 응답으로 가장 적절한 것을 고르시오.

Man: ______________________

① Let me check lost and found.
② What time do you want to meet?
③ Here is the schedule for the trains today.
④ Okay. I'll check the security camera first.
⑤ Why don't you take a taxi? It's more convenient.

M How can I help you?
W Hi. I want to ________ ________ ________.
M Yes, what is it?
W Last night, when I ________ ________ ________ ________ ________, I found one of my windows was broken.
M Oh, and everything was fine when you left in the morning?
W Yes, I ________ ________ ________ ________ in the morning. Can you find out who did this?
M Okay, I'll check the security camera first.

20 상황에 적절한 말 찾기

다음 상황 설명을 듣고, Sandra가 Sally에게 할 말로 가장 적절한 것을 고르시오.

Sandra: Sally, ______________________

① if I were you, I wouldn't say that.
② you don't have to apologize.
③ let's stop fighting and be friends again.
④ why don't you text her and say you're sorry?
⑤ give me an honest apology and I'll forgive you.

W Sally and Sandra are sisters. A few days ago, Sally ________ ________ ________ ________ her best friend. Sally got so angry and said things that she shouldn't have. Sally feels so bad about this situation, and she's ________ ________ ________ at night. Sandra thinks that ________ ________ ________ ________, the worse the situation will get. So Sandra wants to advise Sally to apologize ________ ________ ________ ________. In this situation, what would Sandra most likely say to Sally?
Sandra Sally, why don't you text her and say you're sorry?

Review Test

Word Check 영어는 우리말로, 우리말은 영어로 써 보기

01 opportunity _____

02 borrow _____

03 section _____

04 correct _____

05 culture _____

06 plenty of _____

07 graduate _____

08 confirm _____

09 old-fashioned _____

10 work out _____

11 at most _____

12 look over _____

13 대사관 _____

14 자신감 있는 _____

15 주중, 평일 _____

16 다양한 _____

17 냉장고 _____

18 전시회 _____

19 사라지다 _____

20 (설문) 조사 _____

21 떨리다, 흔들리다 _____

22 전통 _____

23 체중을 줄이다 _____

24 전 세계의 _____

Expression Check 알맞은 표현을 넣어 문장 완성하기

25 _____ _____ at the next stop. 다음 정거장에서 내리세요.

26 Late night snacks _____ _____ _____ your health. 야식은 네 건강에 좋지 않아.

27 It's free for children _____ _____ _____. 7세 이하의 어린이는 무료입니다.

28 When did you _____ _____ _____ Australia? 넌 언제 호주에서 돌아왔니?

29 My mom is _____ _____. 저희 어머니는 (이제) 50세가 되십니다.

30 Jisu's mom asked Jisu to _____ _____ her sister.
지수의 엄마는 지수에게 그녀의 여동생을 돌봐 달라고 말했다.

Word Check
영어는 우리말로, 우리말은 영어로 써 보기

01 pain _____

02 frustrated _____

03 broken _____

04 soothe _____

05 landing _____

06 textbook _____

07 wheat _____

08 forgive _____

09 pollution _____

10 admission ticket _____

11 make an effort _____

12 rimless _____

13 보상하다 _____

14 충전하다 _____

15 싣다 _____

16 깨지기 쉬운 _____

17 휴대용의 _____

18 국제의 _____

19 두통 _____

20 기원, 유래 _____

21 지연시키다; 지연 _____

22 안전벨트 _____

23 지금까지 _____

24 쥐가 나다 _____

Expression Check
알맞은 표현을 넣어 문장 완성하기

25 I'm _____ _____ watch a movie with my friend. 저는 지금 막 친구들과 영화를 보려던 참이에요.

26 The cough is _____ _____. 기침이 더 심해지고 있어요.

27 Can you get up and walk _____ _____ _____ the aisle?
일어나셔서 통로를 왔다갔다 걸으실 수 있나요?

28 I'm sorry that I _____ _____ your foot. 당신의 발을 밟아서 죄송합니다.

29 I'm _____ _____ a terrible headache. 저는 끔찍한 두통에 시달리고 있어요.

30 Sally _____ _____ _____ with her best friend. Sally는 가장 친한 친구와 다퉜다.

1.0배속

1.2배속

01 대화를 듣고, 내일의 날씨로 가장 적절한 것을 고르시오.

①
②
③
④
⑤

02 대화를 듣고, 여자가 남자에게 부탁한 일로 가장 적절한 것을 고르시오.

① 생일 선물 구입하기
② 생일 파티 준비하기
③ 생일 케이크 찾아오기
④ 공항에서 아버지 모셔오기
⑤ 파티에 가고 있다고 아버지께 알리기

03 대화를 듣고, 두 사람이 대화하는 장소로 가장 적절한 곳을 고르시오.

① 공항   ② 서점   ③ 식당
④ 기차역   ④ 백화점

04 다음 그림의 상황에 가장 적절한 대화를 고르시오.

①   ②   ③   ④   ⑤

05 대화를 듣고, 남자가 환불을 받을 수 없는 이유를 고르시오.

① 물건을 사용해서   ② 영수증이 없어서
③ 가격표를 분실해서   ④ 환불 기간이 지나서
⑤ 물건에 흠집이 생겨서

06 다음 표를 보면서 대화를 듣고, 내용과 일치하지 않는 것을 고르시오.

No. 214
Name: ① Minho Park
Phone Number: ② 010-1234-5678
Preference: ③ helping the elderly

Place	Day
④ Little Angel Orphanage	⑤ Friday

07 다음을 듣고, 두 사람의 대화가 어색한 것을 고르시오.

①   ②   ③   ④   ⑤

08 대화를 듣고, 남자가 여자에게 부탁한 일로 가장 적절한 것을 고르시오.

① 컴퓨터 골라 주기
② 컴퓨터 수리해 주기
③ 문서 출력 방법 알려 주기
④ 이메일 계정 만들어 주기
⑤ 이메일에 파일 첨부 방법 알려 주기

09 다음을 듣고, 무엇에 관한 안내 방송인지 고르시오.

① 수영장 안전 수칙
② 수영장 이용 안내
③ 요가 수업 주의 사항
④ 피트니스 센터 이용 안내
⑤ 피트니스 센터 등록 방법

10 대화를 듣고, 남자가 지불할 금액을 고르시오.

① $22   ② $25   ③ $32   ④ $35   ⑤ $38

11 대화를 듣고, 여자가 대화 직후에 할 일로 가장 적절한 것을 고르시오.

① 프린터 청소하기
② 프린터에 토너 넣기
③ 회사 웹 사이트에 가입하기
④ 프린터를 무선 인터넷에 연결하기
⑤ 프린터 드라이버 프로그램 설치하기

12 다음을 듣고, 여자가 메시지를 남긴 목적으로 가장 적절한 것을 고르시오.

① 파티에 초대하려고
② 파티를 취소하려고
③ 파티 준비물을 알리려고
④ 파티 일정 변경을 알리려고
⑤ 파티에 참석하지 못함을 알리려고

13 대화를 듣고, 남자의 장래 희망을 고르시오.

① 작가   ② 교사   ③ 의사
④ 비행사   ⑤ 상담가

14 다음을 듣고, 무엇에 관한 광고인지 고르시오.

① 이어폰   ② 컴퓨터   ③ 카메라
④ 복사기   ⑤ 스마트폰

15 대화를 듣고, 남자가 방학 동안 할 일로 가장 적절한 것을 고르시오.

① 여행하기   ② 로봇 수업 듣기
③ 중국어 배우기   ④ 컴퓨터 배우기
⑤ 수영 수업 듣기

16 대화를 듣고, 팟캐스트에 관해 언급되지 <u>않은</u> 것을 고르시오.

① 진행자   ② 방송 내용   ③ 업로드 요일
④ 업로드 시각 ⑤ 특별 코너

17 대화를 듣고, 남자의 마지막 말에 대한 여자의 응답으로 가장 적절한 것을 고르시오.

Woman: _____

① Your room has a great view.
② Thank you for staying with us.
③ You can have breakfast and dinner.
④ The restroom is at the end of the hall.
⑤ In the Garden Restaurant. It's next to the lobby.

18 대화를 듣고, 여자의 마지막 말에 대한 남자의 응답으로 가장 적절한 것을 고르시오.

Man: _____

① Okay. I'll wait until you're done.
② Yes. I like ham sandwiches the best.
③ Sure. I can finish them in 10 minutes.
④ No. I don't have to go to school early today.
⑤ Sorry. I don't like drinking milk in the morning.

19 대화를 듣고, 남자의 마지막 말에 대한 여자의 응답으로 가장 적절한 것을 고르시오.

Woman: _____

① You should not wake her up.
② I don't like hot and humid weather.
③ You should bring your laptop to work.
④ It's bad for your health to work all day.
⑤ There are lots of quiet and beautiful beaches in Phuket.

20 다음 상황 설명을 듣고, Jessica가 남자에게 할 말로 가장 적절한 것을 고르시오.

Jessica: _____

① Haven't we met before?
② Do you like musicals, too?
③ Can I see your ID card, please?
④ Excuse me. May I sit next to you?
⑤ Sorry, but I think you're sitting in my seat.

01 특정 정보 파악

대화를 듣고, 내일의 날씨로 가장 적절한 것을 고르시오.

① ② ③

④ ⑤

W Dad, what are you doing?

M _____ _____. I'm going to go camping tomorrow with your uncle.

W That's great! But did you check the weather for tomorrow? Look at the sky. I think it's going to rain!

M I already _____ _____ _____ _____. It says it's going to rain tonight, but it's going to be sunny tomorrow.

W That sounds great! Can I go with you?

M Sure. But _____ _____ _____ _____ _____ early tonight. We will leave at 6 a.m. tomorrow.

W Okay. Thanks, Dad.

02 부탁한 일 파악

대화를 듣고, 여자가 남자에게 부탁한 일로 가장 적절한 것을 고르시오.

① 생일 선물 구입하기
② 생일 파티 준비하기
③ 생일 케이크 찾아오기
④ 공항에서 아버지 모셔오기
⑤ 파티에 가고 있다고 아버지께 알리기

(Cellphone rings.)

M Kate, where are you? _____ _____ _____ _____ _____ _____?

W I'm still at the office. I had a meeting, and _____ _____ _____ _____ now.

M Then you will be late for Dad's birthday party.

W Yeah, I think so. Can you tell Dad that _____ _____ _____?

M Sure. I'll tell him.

W I think _____ _____ _____ about 40 minutes to get home. I'll hurry.

03 장소 추론

대화를 듣고, 두 사람이 대화하는 장소로 가장 적절한 곳을 고르시오.

① 공항   ② 서점   ③ 식당
④ 기차역   ④ 백화점

Sound Clear ☆ help us

앞 단어의 끝 자음과 뒤 단어의 모음이 만나 연음되어 [헬퍼스]로 발음된다.

W Excuse me. Can you help us?

M Sure. What can I do for you?

W We want to _____ _____ _____ _____ _____. But I'm not sure we're on the right platform.

M _____ _____ _____ _____ _____. (Pause) Oh, you should go to platform 4.

W Platform 4? How can we get there quickly?

M It's easy. Just _____ _____ _____ _____ and turn left.

W Thank you so much.

04 그림의 상황에 적절한 대화 찾기

다음 그림의 상황에 가장 적절한 대화를 고르시오.

① ② ③ ④ ⑤

Sound Clear ☆ **lift them**

자음 세 개가 연속으로 나와 중간 자음의 발음이 약화되어 [리프템]으로 발음된다.

① M Watch out! _____ _____ _____ _____.

   W Oh, thank you.

② M Can you help me _____ _____ _____?

   W Sure. Let's lift them together.

③ M What's wrong? You look sick.

   W I _____ _____ _____ and runny nose.

④ M How can I help you?

   W Can I reserve a table for two for dinner tonight?

⑤ M What seems to be the problem?

   W I think Roger has a stomachache. It _____ _____ _____ yesterday.

05 이유 파악

대화를 듣고, 남자가 환불을 받을 수 없는 이유를 고르시오.

① 물건을 사용해서
② 영수증이 없어서
③ 가격표를 분실해서
④ 환불 기간이 지나서
⑤ 물건에 흠집이 생겨서

W May I help you?

M Yes, please. Can I get a refund for this T-shirt?

W Let me see. _____ _____ _____ _____ _____?

M Sure. Here it is.

W I'm sorry, but you bought this T-shirt over a month ago. In that case, we can't _____ _____ _____ _____.

M Why not? I didn't wear it and _____ _____ _____ _____ _____ _____ _____.

W I'm so sorry. But you must bring the item back within 15 days to get a refund. It's _____ _____ _____, and we inform all of our customers about it.

M Oh, I must have forgotten it.

06 도표 정보 파악 ✽

다음 표를 보면서 대화를 듣고, 내용과 일치하지 않는 것을 고르시오.

No. 214
Name: ① Minho Park
Phone Number: ② 010-1234-5678
Preference: ③ helping the elderly

Place	Day
④ Little Angel Orphanage	⑤ Friday

(*Telephone rings.*)

W For a Better World Volunteer Center. How may I help you?

M Hello. I'd like to _____ _____ _____.

W Great. Can you tell me your name and phone number?

M I'm Minho Park, and my phone number is 010-1234-5678.

W Thank you. What kind of volunteer work _____ _____ _____ _____?

M I'd like to _____ _____ _____.

W Okay. Can you volunteer this Friday afternoon at Little Angel Orphanage?

M Yes. _____ _____ _____ _____.

다음을 듣고, 두 사람의 대화가 <u>어색한</u> 것을 고르시오.

①   ②   ③   ④   ⑤

08 부탁한 일 파악 ✳

대화를 듣고, 남자가 여자에게 부탁한 일로 가장 적절한 것을 고르시오.

① 컴퓨터 골라 주기
② 컴퓨터 수리해 주기
③ 문서 출력 방법 알려 주기
④ 이메일 계정 만들어 주기
⑤ 이메일에 파일 첨부 방법 알려 주기

Sound Clear ☆ button

미국식은 [번은]으로, 영국식은 [t]를 정확히 발음하여 [버튼]으로 발음된다.

09 주제 파악

다음을 듣고, 무엇에 관한 안내 방송인지 고르시오.

① 수영장 안전 수칙
② 수영장 이용 안내
③ 요가 수업 주의 사항
④ 피트니스 센터 이용 안내
⑤ 피트니스 센터 등록 방법

10 숫자 정보 파악

대화를 듣고, 남자가 지불할 금액을 고르시오.

① $22   ② $25   ③ $32
④ $35   ⑤ $38

---

① W   Is it okay if I _____ _____ _____?

   M   Okay. How long do you need it for?

② W   Do you think I _____ _____ _____?

   M   Yes, I think you should.

③ W   Can you do me a favor?

   M   Sure, I really _____ _____ _____.

④ W   Long time, no see. How have you been?

   M   Good. How about you?

⑤ W   _____ _____ _____ _____ _____?

   M   How about at 7 o'clock?

M   I want to _____ _____ _____ _____ _____ _____, but I don't know how to do it. Can you help me?

W   Sure. That's easy. Did you _____ _____ _____ _____ _____?

M   Yes. And I've finished the email.

W   Just click the "attach files" button and then double-click on the file you _____ _____ _____. 정답 단서

M   (*Click sound*) Oh, I did it!

W   Yes. Then click the "send" button, and that's it.

M   Thank you so much.

M   Welcome to Good Health Fitness Center. Our center offers _____ _____ _____ _____ _____. On the first floor, there is a weight room so you can _____ _____ _____ with trainers. On the second floor, you can take yoga classes every hour. _____ _____ _____ _____, you can enjoy our swimming pool. If you want to take swimming lessons, please talk to the manager. Thank you so much for choosing our center.

M   I'd like to buy some flowers for my wife.

W   What kind of flowers do you _____ _____ _____?

M   I don't know. How much are the red roses?

W   They are $2 each. How about the pink tulips? They _____ _____ _____ _____ _____.

M   I like them. How much are they?

W   They are $3 each, but _____ _____ _____ _____, you can get them for $12.

M   Then I will take five red roses and five pink tulips. _____ _____ _____ _____?

W   Sure. Wait a minute.

11 할 일 파악

대화를 듣고, 여자가 대화 직후에 할 일로 가장 적절한 것을 고르시오.

① 프린터 청소하기
② 프린터에 토너 넣기
③ 회사 웹 사이트에 가입하기
④ 프린터를 무선 인터넷에 연결하기
⑤ 프린터 드라이버 프로그램 설치하기

(Telephone rings.)

M AP Service Center. How can I help you?

W Hello. I bought one of your company's printers, but I think ________ ________ ________ ________.

M Oh, what's the problem?

W I ________ ________ ________ ________ ________ ________, but nothing happened.

M Oh, I see. Did you ________ ________ ________ ________ ________ on your computer?

W No. How can I ________ ________ ________?

M Open our company's website and download the program and install it. 정답 단서

W Oh, I see. I'll do that now.

12 목적 파악

다음을 듣고, 여자가 메시지를 남긴 목적으로 가장 적절한 것을 고르시오.

① 파티에 초대하려고
② 파티를 취소하려고
③ 파티 준비물을 알리려고
④ 파티 일정 변경을 알리려고
⑤ 파티에 참석하지 못함을 알리려고

W Hello. This is Suzie. Do you remember that we made plans to ________ ________ ________ ________ for Irene this Saturday? But I heard that Irene ________ ________ ________ in town until Sunday as she is spending three days with her family in Busan. So ________ ________ ________ ________ and will throw the party on Monday at her house. Call me back when you get this message. Bye.

13 특정 정보 파악

대화를 듣고, 남자의 장래 희망을 고르시오.

① 작가 ② 교사 ③ 의사
④ 비행사 ⑤ 상담가

W What are you doing?

M ________ ________ ________ ________ for tomorrow's English writing class.

W Oh, what's it about?

M ________ ________ ________ ________ ________.

W I know you've always wanted to help others.

M Right. I want to ________ ________ ________ ________ and do volunteer work in foreign countries.

W Then are you going to be a volunteer?

M No, I'm planning to be a doctor and ________ ________ ________ ________ ________ in need. 정답 단서

14 화제 파악

다음을 듣고, 무엇에 관한 광고인지 고르시오.

① 이어폰 ② 컴퓨터 ③ 카메라
④ 복사기 ⑤ 스마트폰

Sound Clear☆ battery

[t]가 모음 사이에서 약화되어 [배러뤼]로 발음된다.

M Let me introduce our latest model HC120 to you. The screen is ________ ________ ________ for watching movies. And the battery☆ ________ ________ ________ ________. When you make calls with this new model, it will sound as if the person is right next to you! It has an amazing camera, so you can take pictures you'll ________ ________ ________ ________. You can get a 10% discount if you buy one this week.

15 할 일 파악 🏴

대화를 듣고, 남자가 방학 동안 할 일로 가장 적절한 것을 고르시오.

① 여행하기　　② 로봇 수업 듣기
③ 중국어 배우기　④ 컴퓨터 배우기
⑤ 수영 수업 듣기

W Hi, John. What are you doing?
M Hey, Jessy. I'm looking at the school website. _____ _____ _____ _____ _____ for this summer vacation?
W Actually, I want to learn Chinese this summer vacation.
M Oh, there is a Chinese class _____ _____ _____ _____ _____ _____ ! And there are several other classes.
W Oh, really? Which classes are you going to take?
M I will take the robot class.
W That sounds interesting! Do you think I can _____ _____ _____ ?
M Perhaps. Let's check the schedule.

16 언급되지 않은 것 찾기

대화를 듣고, 팟캐스트에 관해 언급되지 <u>않은</u> 것을 고르시오.

① 진행자　　　② 방송 내용
③ 업로드 요일　④ 업로드 시각
⑤ 특별 코너

Sound Clear ☆ find out about
[d]와 [t]가 각각 뒤 단어의 모음과 연음되어 [파인다우러바웃]으로 발음된다.

W What were you doing?
M I was listening to Jenny's podcast. It's about new books.
W Sounds interesting. Do you usually listen to it?
M Yes. She _____ _____ _____ _____ every Monday.
W What do you like about the podcast?
M I can find out about new books. Also, I really _____ _____ _____ _____ .
W The special segments? What are they about?
M A guest speaker reads a book, and _____ _____ _____ _____ _____ _____ !
W That's interesting! I'll have to download the podcasts.

17 마지막 말에 대한 응답 찾기

대화를 듣고, 남자의 마지막 말에 대한 여자의 응답으로 가장 적절한 것을 고르시오.

Woman: _____

① Your room has a great view.
② Thank you for staying with us.
③ You can have breakfast and dinner.
④ The restroom is at the end of the hall.
⑤ In the Garden Restaurant. It's next to the lobby.

M Hi. _____ _____ _____ _____ _____ _____ .
W Okay. Can you tell me your name, please?
M My name is Dan Brown.
W Thank you. You're _____ _____ _____ _____ in a deluxe room with a king bed.
M That's correct.
W Here is your key. _____ _____ _____ _____ _____ ?
M Where can I have breakfast?
W In the Garden Restaurant. It's next to the lobby.

18 마지막 말에 대한 응답 찾기

대화를 듣고, 여자의 마지막 말에 대한 남자의 응답으로 가장 적절한 것을 고르시오.

Man: _____

① Okay. I'll wait until you're done.
② Yes. I like ham sandwiches the best.
③ Sure. I can finish them in 10 minutes.
④ No. I don't have to go to school early today.
⑤ Sorry. I don't like drinking milk in the morning.

M Mom, _____ _____ _____ _____ in a minute.
W This early? What about your breakfast? I'm making egg sandwiches.
M I have no time. I have to _____ _____ _____ _____ with my group members before class.
W They're almost ready. It wouldn't take long to have one.
M Yeah, but _____ _____ _____ _____. A glass of milk will be enough.
W Then take the sandwiches to school.
M Okay. I can _____ _____ _____ _____ _____.
W Good idea. Just give me a minute to pack them.
M Okay. I'll wait until you're done.

19 마지막 말에 대한 응답 찾기

대화를 듣고, 남자의 마지막 말에 대한 여자의 응답으로 가장 적절한 것을 고르시오.

Woman: _____

① You should not wake her up.
② I don't like hot and humid weather.
③ You should bring your laptop to work.
④ It's bad for your health to work all day.
⑤ There are lots of quiet and beautiful beaches in Phuket.

Sound Clear ☆ brochure
ch가 [ʃ]로 소리 나서 [브로슈어]로 발음된다.

W Hi, David. What are you looking at?
M Oh, sorry. _____ _____ _____ _____. I'm looking at a brochure about Thailand.
W Are you planning to go on a vacation? I'm so jealous of you!
M I'm just thinking about taking a break for a while. I _____ _____ _____ _____ _____ these days.
W I think you need to be refreshed. _____ _____ _____ _____ in the sunshine would be good for you.
M Do you know any good places to rest _____ _____ _____?
W There are lots of quiet and beautiful beaches in Phuket.

20 상황에 적절한 말 찾기

다음 상황 설명을 듣고, Jessica가 남자에게 할 말로 가장 적절한 것을 고르시오.

Jessica: _____

① Haven't we met before?
② Do you like musicals, too?
③ Can I see your ID card, please?
④ Excuse me. May I sit next to you?
⑤ Sorry, but I think you're sitting in my seat.

W Jessica is at the theater to watch a musical. When she _____ _____ _____ _____, most people are already in their seats. She goes to her seat, but finds that it's already taken by a man. She _____ _____ _____ _____ again and confirms that she is not wrong. The musical _____ _____ _____. In this situation, what would Jessica most likely say to the man?
Jessica Sorry, but I think you're sitting in my seat.

1.0배속
 1.2배속

01 대화를 듣고, 남자가 구입할 가방을 고르시오.

02 대화를 듣고, 두 사람이 내일 만날 시각을 고르시오.
① 12:00 p.m. ② 2:00 p.m. ③ 4:00 p.m.
④ 5:00 p.m. ⑤ 5:30 p.m.

03 다음 그림의 상황에 가장 적절한 대화를 고르시오.

① ② ③ ④ ⑤

04 대화를 듣고, 남자가 지불할 금액을 고르시오.
① $30 ② $50 ③ $170
④ $180 ⑤ $360

05 대화를 듣고, Creamy에 관해 언급되지 <u>않은</u> 것을 고르시오.
① 품종 ② 색깔 ③ 먹는 양
④ 몸무게 ⑤ 나이

06 대화를 듣고, 여자의 심정으로 가장 적절한 것을 고르시오.
① excited ② hopeful ③ nervous
④ satisfied ⑤ disappointed

07 다음을 듣고, 두 사람의 대화가 <u>어색한</u> 것을 고르시오.
① ② ③ ④ ⑤

08 대화를 듣고, 여자가 남자에게 부탁한 일로 가장 적절한 것을 고르시오.
① 집 청소하기 ② 이메일 확인하기
③ 열차표 예매하기 ④ 할머니 마중 나가기
⑤ 열차 도착 시각 알아보기

09 다음을 듣고, 무엇에 관한 설문 조사 결과인지 고르시오.
① 장래 희망 ② 여가 시간 활동
③ 좋아하는 스포츠 ④ 좋아하는 영화 장르
⑤ 게임 중독 극복 방법

10 대화를 듣고, 남자가 어제 한 일로 가장 적절한 것을 고르시오.
① 병원 가기 ② 수영장 가기
③ 만화책 읽기 ④ 배드민턴 치기
⑤ 뮤지컬 관람하기

11 대화를 듣고, 두 사람이 대화하고 있는 장소로 가장 적절한 곳을 고르시오.
① 은행 ② 호텔 ③ 학교
④ 미용실 ⑤ 영화관

12 다음을 듣고, Fresh Farm Festival에 관해 언급되지 <u>않은</u> 것을 고르시오.
① 개최 장소 ② 개최 일시 ③ 준비물
④ 입장료 ⑤ 예매 방법

13 다음 성적표를 보면서 대화를 듣고, 내용과 일치하지 <u>않는</u> 것을 고르시오.

Report Card	
Name of student: Judy Clinton	
Subject	Grade
① Korean	95
② English	75
③ Math	85
④ Science	85
⑤ History	97

14 다음을 듣고, 무엇에 관한 설명인지 고르시오.

① 콜라　　　② 커피　　　③ 녹차
④ 코코아　　⑤ 에너지 음료

15 대화를 듣고, 남자가 대화 직후에 할 일로 가장 적절한 것을 고르시오.

① 가방 확인하기　　② 경찰에 신고하기
③ 자판기 이용하기　　④ 엄마에게 전화하기
⑤ 분실물 보관소 확인하기

16 대화를 듣고, 남자의 마지막 말에 담긴 의도로 가장 적절한 것을 고르시오.

① 격려　　② 허락　　③ 축하
④ 사과　　⑤ 조언

17 대화를 듣고, 여자의 마지막 말에 대한 남자의 응답으로 가장 적절한 것을 고르시오.

Man: _____

① Never mind. It's not your fault.
② Thank you for postponing the test.
③ I wish I had studied harder for the test.
④ I think sending text messages would be better.
⑤ Sorry, but there's not enough time to cover all the subjects.

18 대화를 듣고, 남자의 마지막 말에 대한 여자의 응답으로 가장 적절한 것을 고르시오.

Woman: _____

① I'm afraid she won't go with you.
② Forget about sports as a profession.
③ She's not the girl you're looking for.
④ I said I'm a big fan of Michael Jordan.
⑤ I think the two of you have much in common.

19 대화를 듣고, 여자의 마지막 말에 대한 남자의 응답으로 가장 적절한 것을 고르시오.

Man: _____

① We can be best friends again!
② You should keep your promise.
③ You can't be rude to your friends.
④ Don't mention it. What are friends for?
⑤ Don't judge people by their appearances.

20 다음 상황 설명을 듣고, David가 Mark에게 할 말로 가장 적절한 것을 고르시오.

David: Mark, _____

① how do I change my major?
② I believe you'll be a great scientist.
③ I think it'll be good for you to give it up.
④ why don't you read science fiction books?
⑤ I didn't know that you were interested in science.

01 그림 정보 파악

대화를 듣고, 남자가 구입할 가방을 고르시오.

① 　② 　③

④ 　⑤

Sound Clear ☆ **pattern**

미국식은 모음 사이의 [t]를 약하게 발음하여 [패런]으로, 영국식은 [t]를 정확히 발음하여 [패튼]으로 발음된다.

W　Jake, you need a new bag _____ _____ _____ _____ next month?

M　Yes, I do. My bag is _____ _____.

W　There are many kinds of bags here. How about a striped bag or a check bag?

M　I don't want any pattern. And I want to buy one with a shoulder strap.

W　Then how about that bag with pockets _____ _____ _____?

M　Hmm... it looks good, but I don't like the round bag.

W　Oh, I found one. Look at _____ _____ _____ _____ _____ on the front.

M　It's perfect. Let's get it.

02 숫자 정보 파악

대화를 듣고, 두 사람이 내일 만날 시각을 고르시오.

① 12:00 p.m.　② 2:00 p.m.
③ 4:00 p.m.　④ 5:00 p.m.
⑤ 5:30 p.m.

(*Telephone rings.*)

M　Hello, Janet. This is Brian.

W　Oh, hi. What's up?

M　Are you busy tomorrow afternoon? I really need _____ _____ _____ _____.

W　Hmm... how about meeting around 4:00? _____ _____ _____ _____ _____ at 2:00, so we can meet after that.

M　I have a class at 4 o'clock. Are you busy at 5:30?

W　I have a badminton lesson at 5. Then how about _____ _____ _____?

M　That sounds good. Then let's meet at Joe's Café at noon.

W　Great. See you tomorrow.

03 그림의 상황에 적절한 대화 찾기

다음 그림의 상황에 가장 적절한 대화를 고르시오.

①　②　③　④　⑤

① W　Where can I _____ _____ _____ _____?
　 M　They're right over there, in section two.

② W　What's the matter with your puppy?
　 M　_____ _____ _____ _____ since yesterday.

③ W　How often do you exercise here?
　 M　I work out here _____ _____ _____ _____.

④ W　When are the books due?
　 M　_____ _____ _____ _____ by next Thursday.

⑤ W　Hi. Would you like to order?
　 M　Yes, please. I'd like one cheeseburger and a coke.

04 숫자 정보 파악

대화를 듣고, 남자가 지불할 금액을 고르시오.

① $30 ② $50 ③ $170
④ $180 ⑤ $360

Sound Clear ☆ **sign up**

sign의 g는 묵음이고, 두 단어가 연음되어 [싸이넙]으로 발음된다.

W Good morning, Happy Fitness Center. How can I help you?

M Hi. I'd like to ________ ________ ________ ________. I heard your center has good facilities.

W You've ________ ________ ________ ________.

M How much is the membership fee?

W It's $30 a month. But if you ________ ________ ________ ________, it's just $170.

M Wow! The annual fee is less than the fee for 6 months.

W Yes. And if you get an annual membership, it also ________ ________ ________ ________ ________ once a week.

M Sounds perfect. I will ☆sign up for an annual membership.

05 언급되지 않은 것 찾기

대화를 듣고, Creamy에 관해 언급되지 않은 것을 고르시오.

① 품종 ② 색깔 ③ 먹는 양
④ 몸무게 ⑤ 나이

M Hi, Susan. Is this your dog?

W Yes, he's a dachshund, a German dog.

M Dachshunds are ________ ________ ________ but your dog is a light cream color.

W ________ ________ ________ ________ ________ Creamy.

M Oh, I see. Does he eat a lot?

W Yes, ________ ________ ________. He eats almost 3 kilograms of dog food a week.

M Wow. How old is he?

W He is three years old. Do you ________ ________ ________ ________?

M Yes. He's so cute. I'd like to have a pet, too.

06 심정 추론

대화를 듣고, 여자의 심정으로 가장 적절한 것을 고르시오.

① excited ② hopeful ③ nervous
④ satisfied ⑤ disappointed

M What did you think of the movie?

W Well, I thought it was not bad, but I think I ________ ________ ________.

M What do you mean? I thought it ________ ________ ________ ________ and great music.

W Well, the concert scene was kind of exciting. But there were some unrealistic scenes.

M Oh, I really ________ ________ ________ ________ ________.

W And some special effects in the movie were not very impressive.

M Yeah, I know what you mean.

다음을 듣고, 두 사람의 대화가 <u>어색한</u> 것을 고르시오.

① ② ③ ④ ⑤

Sound Clear ☆ **not at all**
각 [t]가 뒤 단어의 모음과 연음되어 [나래럴]로 발음된다.

① M May I _____ _____ _____ to check your visa?
　 W Okay. Here you are.
② M Have you ever _____ _____ _____ _____?
　 W Yes. I went bungee jumping last summer.
③ M Are we allowed to take pictures in here?
　 W Thank you so much for _____ _____ _____.
④ M Where do you want to spend the coming vacation?
　 W Well, I would like to go anywhere cooler than here.
⑤ M Do you mind _____ _____ _____ _____?
　 W No, not at all. Here you are.

08 부탁한 일 파악

대화를 듣고, 여자가 남자에게 부탁한 일로 가장 적절한 것을 고르시오.

① 집 청소하기　　　② 이메일 확인하기
③ 열차표 예매하기　④ 할머니 마중 나가기
⑤ 열차 도착 시각 알아보기

W Mark, if you're not busy, can you help me?
M Why not? What do you _____ _____ _____ _____?
W Do you remember that your grandma is coming to visit tomorrow?
M Sure. So do you want me to _____ _____ _____?
W No, I'll do that. I'm wondering what time the first train from Busan gets in tomorrow. 정답 단서
M Is she taking the first train? I'll _____ _____ _____ _____ _____ on the computer.
W Thanks. That's all I need you to do.

09 주제 파악

다음을 듣고, 무엇에 관한 설문 조사 결과인지 고르시오.

① 장래 희망　　　② 여가 시간 활동
③ 좋아하는 스포츠　④ 좋아하는 영화 장르
⑤ 게임 중독 극복 방법

M Last week, we surveyed _____ _____ _____ on the activities they enjoy doing in their spare time. Among the 180 students, _____ _____ _____ 정답 단서 that they spend most of their spare time playing computer games. 45 students said they watch TV or go to the movies, and 23 students read books in their spare time. And _____ _____ _____ _____ _____ said they spend time outside exercising such as playing soccer or basketball.

10 한 일 파악

대화를 듣고, 남자가 어제 한 일로 가장 적절한 것을 고르시오.

① 병원 가기　　　② 수영장 가기
③ 만화책 읽기　　④ 배드민턴 치기
⑤ 뮤지컬 관람하기

W Do you have any special plans this weekend?
M No. I might just stay at home and _____ _____ _____.
W Hey, why don't we go swimming? 함정
M Sorry, I can't. I _____ _____ _____ while playing badminton yesterday. 정답 단서
W Did you go to see a doctor? 함정
M No, I just _____ _____ _____ on the area. 함정
W Oh, I see. Then how about watching a musical? 함정
M That's a good idea. Then I'll _____ _____ _____ _____ _____ online and book tickets.

11 장소 추론

대화를 듣고, 두 사람이 대화하고 있는 장소로 가장 적절한 곳을 고르시오.

① 은행　　② 호텔　　③ 학교
④ 미용실　　⑤ 영화관

M Hi, Ms. Kim.

W Hi, John. What's up?

M Well, could you please ＿＿＿＿ ＿＿＿＿ ＿＿＿＿ ＿＿＿＿?

W Sure, what is it?

M I heard that it will rain this afternoon, but I ＿＿＿＿ ＿＿＿＿ ＿＿＿＿ ＿＿＿＿ ＿＿＿＿.

W Aha, so you want me to lend you one, right?

M Exactly. Can I borrow an umbrella later?

W No problem. ＿＿＿＿ ＿＿＿＿ ＿＿＿＿ ＿＿＿＿ again after *정답 단서* school.

M Thank you so much.

12 언급되지 않은 것 찾기 ✹

다음을 듣고, Fresh Farm Festival에 관해 언급되지 않은 것을 고르시오.

① 개최 장소　　② 개최 일시　　③ 준비물
④ 입장료　　⑤ 예매 방법

W Good afternoon, everyone. Let me tell you about our annual Fresh Farm Festival. It will ＿＿＿＿ ＿＿＿＿ ＿＿＿＿ Seoul Square from 10 a.m. to 6 p.m. this Saturday. You can buy fresh fruit and vegetables from all over the country. You should ＿＿＿＿ ＿＿＿＿ ＿＿＿＿ ＿＿＿＿ ＿＿＿＿ and cups. The admission will be $3, and children under 5 ＿＿＿＿ ＿＿＿＿ ＿＿＿＿ ＿＿＿＿. Thank you.

13 도표 정보 파악

다음 성적표를 보면서 대화를 듣고, 내용과 일치하지 않는 것을 고르시오.

Report Card	
Name of student: Judy Clinton	
Subject	Grade
① Korean	95
② English	75
③ Math	85
④ Science	85
⑤ History	97

Sound Clear ☆ **really**

'리얼리'라고 명확하게 발음되지 않고 [륄리]에 가깝게 발음된다.

M Why the long face, Judy?

W I'm ＿＿＿＿ ＿＿＿＿ ＿＿＿＿ ＿＿＿＿ in English. I got 75. How about you, John?

M I got 85. How about Korean? You're very good at it.

W I got 93. I ＿＿＿＿ ＿＿＿＿ ＿＿＿＿ that I would get at least 95. *정답 단서*

M Well, it's a high grade. What about your other grades? You always ＿＿＿＿ ＿＿＿＿ ＿＿＿＿ ＿＿＿＿ ＿＿＿＿.

W I have no problem with an 85 in math and science. I think ＿＿＿＿ ＿＿＿＿ ＿＿＿＿ ＿＿＿＿.

M Then did you get over 90 only in Korean?

W No. I got a 97 in history. I studied history ☆ really hard.

14 화제 파악

다음을 듣고, 무엇에 관한 설명인지 고르시오.

① 콜라　　② 커피　　③ 녹차
④ 코코아　　⑤ 에너지 음료

M This is one of the most popular drinks in the world. Its color is very dark, and it tastes ＿＿＿＿ ＿＿＿＿ ＿＿＿＿ ＿＿＿＿. This can prevent you from ＿＿＿＿ ＿＿＿＿ ＿＿＿＿ due to its caffeine content. But it can also help you feel less tired and ＿＿＿＿ ＿＿＿＿ ＿＿＿＿ ＿＿＿＿. Roasting its beans is a very important process because that has a big influence on ＿＿＿＿ ＿＿＿＿ ＿＿＿＿.

15 할 일 파악

대화를 듣고, 남자가 대화 직후에 할 일로 가장 적절한 것을 고르시오.

① 가방 확인하기
② 경찰에 신고하기
③ 자판기 이용하기
④ 엄마에게 전화하기
⑤ 분실물 보관소 확인하기

M My wallet is gone. It's not inside my bag.

W You _____ _____ _____ _____ _____ at home. Why don't you call your mom and check?

M I had it with me in the morning. I remember taking it out to buy a Sprite from the vending machine before _____ _____ _____ _____.

W Have you checked the places you went earlier?

M I have, but I couldn't find it. _____ _____ _____ _____ now?

W Why don't you check with lost and found?

M Okay. I hope somebody has _____ _____ _____ and taken it there.

16 의도 파악

대화를 듣고, 남자의 마지막 말에 담긴 의도로 가장 적절한 것을 고르시오.

① 격려   ② 허락   ③ 축하
④ 사과   ⑤ 조언

Sound Clear ☆ **must have**

앞 단어의 [t]와 뒤 단어의 [h]가 만나 연음 되어 [머슷테브]로 발음된다.

M Hi, Jessy. I want to _____ _____ _____.

W Hey, Tim. I was surprised that you left in the middle of the performance, but I heard your mom _____ _____ _____! What happened?

M My mom _____ _____ _____ _____ _____ and broke her leg.

W You must have been really upset yesterday. Is she okay?

M Yes, she's better. She was treated at a hospital yesterday, and she's resting at home now.

W _____ _____ _____! I hope your mom will get better soon.

M Thank you. Once again, I'm really sorry for leaving the theater without saying anything.

17 마지막 말에 대한 응답 찾기

대화를 듣고, 여자의 마지막 말에 대한 남자의 응답으로 가장 적절한 것을 고르시오.

Man: _____

① Never mind. It's not your fault.
② Thank you for postponing the test.
③ I wish I had studied harder for the test.
④ I think sending text messages would be better.
⑤ Sorry, but there's not enough time to cover all the subjects.

W Steve, can I ask you something?

M Yes. What is that?

W I think I told the students to _____ _____ _____ _____ for the vocabulary test.

M I _____ _____ _____. Just a second. You said the test covers lesson 5.

W It's actually lesson 6. I _____ _____ _____.

M Oh, no. Then we should tell the students right away.

W Can you help me _____ _____ _____ _____ _____?

M I think sending text messages would be better.

18 마지막 말에 대한 응답 찾기

대화를 듣고, 남자의 마지막 말에 대한 여자의 응답으로 가장 적절한 것을 고르시오.

Woman: _____

① I'm afraid she won't go with you.
② Forget about sports as a profession.
③ She's not the girl you're looking for.
④ I said I'm a big fan of Michael Jordan.
⑤ I think the two of you have much in common.

M Tell me more about the girl you want to _____ _____ _____.
W Okay. She's my best friend from elementary school.
M _____ _____ _____ _____ to do?
W She likes dancing. She was _____ _____ _____ _____ _____ in middle school.
M I see. I hope she likes sports, too.
W Yeah. She _____ _____ _____. Her favorite sport is basketball.
M Cool. Then we can go to watch basketball games together.
W I think the two of you have much in common.

19 마지막 말에 대한 응답 찾기 ✽

대화를 듣고, 여자의 마지막 말에 대한 남자의 응답으로 가장 적절한 것을 고르시오.

Man: _____

① We can be best friends again!
② You should keep your promise.
③ You can't be rude to your friends.
④ Don't mention it. What are friends for?
⑤ Don't judge people by their appearances.

Sound Clear ☆ **Actually**
1음절에 강세가 있고, 2음절의 [t]가 약화되어 [액츄얼리] 또는 [액슈얼리]로 발음된다.

W Jerry is angry with me. I don't know _____ _____ _____ _____.
M Oh, did anything happen between you?
W ☆ Actually, _____ _____ _____ _____ about his dark skin.
M That wasn't very thoughtful of you.
W But I _____ _____ _____ _____ _____.
M Hey, what's funny to some _____ _____ _____ _____ _____ _____.
W I thought it was okay because we are best friends.
M You can't be rude to your friends.

20 상황에 적절한 말 찾기

다음 상황 설명을 듣고, David가 Mark에게 할 말로 가장 적절한 것을 고르시오.

David: Mark, _____

① how do I change my major?
② I believe you'll be a great scientist.
③ I think it'll be good for you to give it up.
④ why don't you read science fiction books?
⑤ I didn't know that you were interested in science.

W Mark and David _____ _____ _____. Mark tells David that he doesn't _____ _____ _____ very well, but he wants to understand it better. David knows that Mark likes reading. So David thinks that once Mark enjoys reading stories related to science, science itself _____ _____ _____ _____. In this situation, what would David most likely say to Mark?

David Mark, why don't you read science fiction books?

Review Test

Word Check 영어는 우리말로, 우리말은 영어로 써 보기

01 company _____

02 refund _____

03 share _____

04 volunteer _____

05 inform _____

06 reserve _____

07 latest _____

08 forever _____

09 stairs _____

10 view _____

11 have in mind _____

12 strengthen _____

13 근육 _____

14 고아원 _____

15 고객, 손님 _____

16 토하다 _____

17 첨부하다 _____

18 방침, 정책 _____

19 토론하다 _____

20 가격표 _____

21 질투하는 _____

22 설치하다 _____

23 지하 _____

24 의학의 _____

Expression Check 알맞은 표현을 넣어 문장 완성하기

25 Are you _____ your _____ _____? 너 집에 오고 있는 중이니?

26 I feel so _____ _____ working these days. 나는 요즘 일하는 게 너무 지겨워.

27 They _____ _____ _____ red roses. 그것들은 빨간색 장미와 잘 어울려요.

28 I want to help people _____ _____. 나는 어려움에 처한 사람들을 돕고 싶어.

29 We made plans to _____ _____ surprise _____ for Irene.
우리는 Irene을 위한 깜짝파티를 열기로 계획했다.

30 I _____ the printer _____ my computer, but nothing happened.
저는 프린터를 제 컴퓨터에 연결했는데 아무 반응이 없었어요.

Answers p.82

Word Check
영어는 우리말로, 우리말은 영어로 써 보기

01	outdoor		13	치료하다
02	sour		14	여권
03	profession		15	내용물, 함유량
04	postpone		16	영향
05	unrealistic		17	무례한
06	impressive		18	매년의, 연례의
07	ointment		19	게시판
08	judge		20	제공하다
09	strap		21	외모
10	special effect		22	볶다, 굽다
11	front		23	잠깐 들르다
12	dairy product		24	시설

Expression Check
알맞은 표현을 넣어 문장 완성하기

25 I think the two of you _____ much ____ __ _____. 내 생각에 너희 둘은 공통점이 많은 것 같아.

26 My mom _____ _____ at the station. 우리 엄마가 역에서 넘어지셨어.

27 I'm _____ _____ my grade in English. 나는 내 영어 점수에 실망했어.

28 _____ _____ _____ tried any extreme sports? 당신은 익스트림 스포츠를 해 본 적이 있나요?

29 This can _____ you _____ getting a good sleep due to its caffeine content.
이것은 카페인 성분 때문에 당신이 숙면을 취하는 것을 방해할 수 있습니다.

30 The festival will _____ _____ in Seoul Square this Saturday.
축제는 이번 주 토요일에 서울 광장에서 개최됩니다.

01 대화를 듣고, 여자가 구입할 컴퓨터를 고르시오.

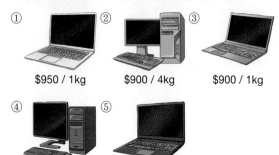

① $950 / 1kg   ② $900 / 4kg   ③ $900 / 1kg

④ $950 / 5kg   ⑤ $950 / 1.2kg

02 대화를 듣고, 두 사람이 대화하는 장소로 가장 적절한 곳을 고르시오.

① 학교   ② 식당   ③ 스키장
④ 체육관   ⑤ 스케이트장

03 대화를 듣고, 두 사람이 만날 시각을 고르시오.

① 5:00 p.m.   ② 5:30 p.m.   ③ 6:00 p.m.
④ 6:30 p.m.   ⑤ 7:00 p.m.

04 대화를 듣고, 두 사람이 대화 직후에 할 일로 가장 적절한 것을 고르시오.

① 학교에 가기   ② 지하철 타기
③ 식당 예약하기   ④ 점심 식사하기
⑤ 요리 학원 가기

05 대화를 듣고, 여자가 환불받으려는 이유를 고르시오.

① 냄새가 나서   ② 손상된 곳이 있어서
③ 질감이 좋지 않아서   ④ 사이즈가 맞지 않아서
⑤ 색이 마음에 들지 않아서

06 다음을 듣고, 두 사람의 대화가 <u>어색한</u> 것을 고르시오.

①   ②   ③   ④   ⑤

07 다음 그림의 상황에 가장 적절한 대화를 고르시오.

①   ②   ③   ④   ⑤

08 대화를 듣고, 여자가 남자에게 부탁한 일로 가장 적절한 것을 고르시오.

① 탁자 고치기
② 쇼핑 목록 불러 주기
③ 시장에 데리러 오기
④ 쇼핑 목록에 있는 물건 사 오기
⑤ 쇼핑 목록 사진 찍어서 보내 주기

09 다음을 듣고, 무엇에 관한 안내 방송인지 고르시오.

① 자선 단체 기부 독려
② 자원봉사 동아리 회원 모집
③ 자원봉사자 지원 자격
④ 자원봉사자 교육 프로그램
⑤ 자원봉사자 교육 강사 모집

10 대화를 듣고, 포스터에서 고쳐야 할 부분을 고르시오.

① 동아리 사진   ② 동아리방 위치
③ 동아리 이름   ④ 동아리 연락처
⑤ 동아리 면접 날짜

11 대화를 듣고, 여자가 남자에게 부탁한 일로 가장 적절한 것을 고르시오.

① 옷 포장하기   ② 뜨개질 함께 배우기
③ 스웨터 입어 보기   ④ 깜짝파티 준비하기
⑤ 여자의 오빠 위로하기

12 대화를 듣고, 지도에서 여자가 가려는 장소를 고르시오.

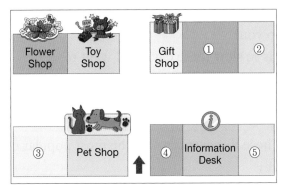

13 대화를 듣고, 남자가 지불할 금액을 고르시오.

① $12　　② $14　　③ $16
④ $18　　⑤ $20

14 다음을 듣고, 무엇에 관한 설명인지 고르시오.

① 야구　　② 농구　　③ 탁구
④ 축구　　⑤ 핸드볼

15 다음 표를 보면서 대화를 듣고, 내용과 일치하지 <u>않는</u> 것을 고르시오.

The Most Popular Christmas Present		
①	Toys	12
②	Accessaries	7
③	Smartphones	5
④	Bicycles	4
⑤	Books	2

16 대화를 듣고, 남자의 직업으로 가장 적절한 것을 고르시오.

① doctor　　　　② firefighter
③ salesperson　　④ taxi driver
⑤ police officer

17 대화를 듣고, 여자의 마지막 말에 대한 남자의 응답으로 가장 적절한 것을 고르시오.

Man: _____

① I want to be a police officer.
② I visited my grandma last week.
③ You must not park your car here.
④ The fine for a traffic signal violation is $70.
⑤ You should rent a car when you visit the city.

18 대화를 듣고, 남자의 마지막 말에 대한 여자의 응답으로 가장 적절한 것을 고르시오.

Woman: _____

① Where are you going to stay?
② I'll take them. How much are they?
③ I will have a pizza. What about you?
④ Would you like some hot tea instead?
⑤ Okay, you win. Let's eat something else.

19 대화를 듣고, 여자의 마지막 말에 대한 남자의 응답으로 가장 적절한 것을 고르시오.

Man: _____

① I hope you will get better soon.
② You should tell her how you feel.
③ You'd better not tell her the truth.
④ Why don't you buy a new camera?
⑤ I think you should tell her the truth.

20 다음 상황 설명을 듣고, Steve가 웨이터에게 할 말로 가장 적절한 것을 고르시오.

Steve: _____

① Can you get my coat?
② Can you wrap the food to go?
③ Where is the restaurant located?
④ The meal was very disappointing.
⑤ Can you give us separate bills, please?

Dictation **15** 회

01 그림 정보 파악

대화를 듣고, 여자가 구입할 컴퓨터를 고르시오.

①
$950 / 1kg

②
$900 / 4kg

③
$900 / 1kg

④
$950 / 5kg

⑤
$950 / 1.2kg

M How can I help you?

W My computer is so slow these days, so I want to _____ _____ _____ _____.

M Do you want to buy a desktop computer?

W No, I want to _____ _____ _____ _____ _____.

M That's right. These three laptops are the most popular ones.

W I want one that is _____ _____ _____ _____.

M Then how about this one? It weighs only 1 kilogram and it costs $900. [정답 단서] _____ _____ _____ _____.

W It looks great. I'll take it.

02 장소 추론

대화를 듣고, 두 사람이 대화하는 장소로 가장 적절한 곳을 고르시오.

① 학교　　② 식당　　③ 스키장
④ 체육관　　⑤ 스케이트장

W Look at the girl _____ _____ _____ _____ and blue jacket! She's really fast!

M Yeah, I think she's _____ _____ _____ _____ _____ here.

W I want to be fast like her. But I don't think I am improving.

M Come on, you only started skating _____ _____ _____.

W I know. But it's really difficult for me to keep practicing.

M _____ _____ _____. I'm sure you will improve quickly.

W Thanks.

03 숫자 정보 파악

대화를 듣고, 두 사람이 만날 시각을 고르시오.

① 5:00 p.m. ② 5:30 p.m. ③ 6:00 p.m.
④ 6:30 p.m. ⑤ 7:00 p.m.

Sound Clear ☆ **Definitely**
[t]가 [l] 앞에서 약화되어 [데피닛리]로 발음된다.

M Hi. Are you free this Saturday?

W Well, _____ _____ _____. Why do you ask?

M I have tickets to see the Berlin Philharmonic Orchestra at the Art Center. Do you want to go?

W ☆ Definitely! What time is it?

M Let me see. It starts at 7:00 p.m. Let's meet [정답 단서] _____ _____ _____.

W Why don't we _____ _____ _____ before that?

M Good idea. Then how about 6:00 p.m.? [함정]

W Oh, _____ _____ _____ _____ _____ to the concert. Let's meet two hours before the concert. [정답 단서]

M Okay. See you then.

04 할 일 파악 🏴󠁧󠁢󠁥󠁮󠁧󠁿

대화를 듣고, 두 사람이 대화 직후에 할 일로
가장 적절한 것을 고르시오.

① 학교에 가기　　② 지하철 타기
③ 식당 예약하기　④ 점심 식사하기
⑤ 요리 학원 가기

Sound Clear ☆ **Vietnamese**

Vietnam(베트남)은 실제로 [뷔엣남]으로 발음되며, Vietnamese(베트남의)는 [뷔엣나미즈]로 발음된다.

W　Hey, Jason. Long time, no see.
M　Hi, Katie. _____ _____ _____ _____ you again. How are you?
W　I'm good. _____ _____ _____ _____?
M　Actually, I'm going to a new restaurant to eat lunch.
W　Oh, really? _____ _____ _____ _____ there?
M　No, I'm alone. Do you want to have lunch with me? _{정답 단서}
W　Why not? _____ _____ _____ is it?
M　It's a Vietnamese restaurant. I heard their rice noodles are delicious.
W　I love Vietnamese food! Let's go!

05 이유 파악

대화를 듣고, 여자가 환불받으려는 이유를 고르시오.

① 냄새가 나서
② 손상된 곳이 있어서
③ 질감이 좋지 않아서
④ 사이즈가 맞지 않아서
⑤ 색이 마음에 들지 않아서

M　How can I help you?
W　I want to _____ _____ _____ _____ this sweater.
M　I can help you with that. Can I ask you the reason why _____ _____ _____ _____ _____?
W　I ordered this online, but the color is different from what I saw _____ _____ _____. _{정답 단서}
M　Oh, we're really sorry about the problem. Actually, this sweater comes in six different colors, so why don't you _____ _____ _____ _____ _____ and consider an exchange first?
W　Okay, I can do that.
M　Good. This way, please.

06 어색한 대화 찾기

다음을 듣고, 두 사람의 대화가 어색한 것을 고르시오.

①　②　③　④　⑤

① W　Let me _____ _____ _____ for you.
　 M　Thank you so much.
② W　Do you think I should eat less to _____ _____?
　 M　I think you should exercise more.
③ W　What did you do during summer vacation?
　 M　_____ _____ _____ _____ my grandmother.
④ W　What time do you go to bed?
　 M　Normally around 11 p.m.
⑤ W　What would you like to do in the future?
　 M　I want to become a photographer and _____ _____ _____ _____.

07 그림의 상황에 적절한 대화 찾기

다음 그림의 상황에 가장 적절한 대화를 고르시오.

① ② ③ ④ ⑤

Sound Clear ☆ exhausted

ex가 [igz]로 소리 나고 h는 묵음이라서 [이그저스티드]로 발음된다.

① W　Excuse me. Can you tell me where the subway station is?
　 M　No problem. Go straight and turn left. _____ _____ _____ _____.

② W　Are we there yet? I'm exhausted!
　 M　We are almost there. You can do it!

③ W　We're late. I think _____ _____ _____ _____ _____.
　 M　No, I don't think so. We should take the subway.

④ W　The flowers are so beautiful. I want to take some home.
　 M　You should not _____ _____ _____.

⑤ W　Why don't you go hiking this afternoon?
　 M　I'd love to, but I can't. I _____ _____ _____.

08 부탁한 일 파악

대화를 듣고, 여자가 남자에게 부탁한 일로 가장 적절한 것을 고르시오.

① 탁자 고치기
② 쇼핑 목록 불러 주기
③ 시장에 데리러 오기
④ 쇼핑 목록에 있는 물건 사 오기
⑤ 쇼핑 목록 사진 찍어서 보내 주기

(*Cellphone rings.*)
W　Hey, Jim. It's me.
M　What's up, Kate? Did you _____ _____ _____ _____?
W　Yes, I did. But I think I left my shopping list on the table at home.
M　Do you _____ _____ _____ _____ every time you go to the market?
W　Yes. Can you look on the table and _____ _____ _____ _____?
M　Sure. Let me see. (*Pause*) Oh, I found it. It says tomatoes, cheese, _____ _____, _____ _____ _____.
W　Can you take a picture of the list and send it to me?
M　Sure. I will send it to you right away.

09 주제 파악

다음을 듣고, 무엇에 관한 안내 방송인지 고르시오.

① 자선 단체 기부 독려
② 자원봉사 동아리 회원 모집
③ 자원봉사자 지원 자격
④ 자원봉사자 교육 프로그램
⑤ 자원봉사자 교육 강사 모집

M　Welcome to our volunteer training program. _____ _____ _____ _____ three days, and each day you have to take five hours of classes. After you finish the program, you will get a certificate and can _____ _____ _____ _____ _____ organized by Good Will Foundation. If you have any questions, _____ _____ _____ _____ one of our staff members. Now, let me introduce our first lecturer.

10 특정 정보 파악

대화를 듣고, 포스터에서 고쳐야 할 부분을 고르시오.

① 동아리 사진　　② 동아리방 위치
③ 동아리 이름　　④ 동아리 연락처
⑤ 동아리 면접 날짜

M　Hey, Kate. What are you doing?

W　I'm _____ _____ _____ _____ for our club.

M　Oh, can I see it?

W　Sure. _____ _____ _____ of us working together on the poster.

M　I like them. And I like the way you highlighted the name of our club.

W　Thanks. _____ _____ _____ _____ or anything that should be corrected?

M　Let me see. (*Pause*) Oh, you should change the interview date to January 15. 정답 단서

W　Okay. What about the contact number?

M　_____ _____ _____. Nice work.

11 부탁한 일 파악

대화를 듣고, 여자가 남자에게 부탁한 일로 가장 적절한 것을 고르시오.

① 옷 포장하기　　② 뜨개질 함께 배우기
③ 스웨터 입어 보기　　④ 깜짝파티 준비하기
⑤ 여자의 오빠 위로하기

Sound Clear ☆ **knitting**
k가 묵음이라서 [니팅]으로 발음된다.

M　What are you doing?

W　I'm knitting a sweater. _____ _____ _____.

M　Oh, I can't imagine you knitting something. Is this your new hobby?

W　No, you know I'm not really good _____ _____ _____.

M　Then what made you decide to knit a sweater?

W　My brother _____ _____ _____ his girlfriend recently. I want to give him a present to cheer him up.

M　Wow, great. It's a kind of surprise present then.

W　Can you try it on for me? 함정

M　정답 단서 No problem. Your brother and I _____ _____ _____ _____.

12 위치 찾기

대화를 듣고, 지도에서 여자가 가려는 장소를 고르시오.

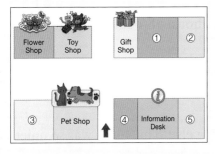

W　Excuse me. I'm looking for the food court. Do you know _____ _____ _____?

M　Sure. It's near the bakery.

W　Where is the bakery?

M　Turn right at the first corner and go straight until you _____ _____ _____ _____.

W　And then?

M　Across from the information desk, you will see the bakery. The food court is _____ _____ _____ _____.

W　Thank you so much.

13 숫자 정보 파악

대화를 듣고, 남자가 지불할 금액을 고르시오.

① $12   ② $14   ③ $16
④ $18   ⑤ $20

W How can I help you?
M I'd like to _____ _____ _____ _____.
W Let me see. You have two shirts and a coat.
M Yes, right. _____ _____ _____ _____?
W It's $3 for each shirt and $10 for the coat.
M I _____ _____ _____ _____. Can I use this?
W Sure, you can get $2 off with this coupon.
M Thanks.

14 화제 파악

다음을 듣고, 무엇에 관한 설명인지 고르시오.

① 야구   ② 농구   ③ 탁구
④ 축구   ⑤ 핸드볼

W This sport is played by two teams. Each team has 9 players. The offensive team hits the ball with a bat and _____ _____ _____ _____. On the other hand, the defensive team tries to _____ _____ _____ _____ _____ the bases by catching the ball and throwing it to the bases. When a batter advances around four bases and reaches the last base, or home plate, _____ _____ _____.

15 도표 정보 파악

다음 표를 보면서 대화를 듣고, 내용과 일치하지 않는 것을 고르시오.

The Most Popular Christmas Present		
①	Toys	12
②	Accessaries	7
③	Smartphones	5
④	Bicycles	4
⑤	Books	2

W Did you see the poll in the school newspaper?
M No, I didn't. _____ _____ _____?
W It's about the most popular Christmas presents.
M Oh, what was _____ _____ _____ _____?
W It was toys. Twelve students chose toys. What do you want to get _____ _____ _____ _____?
M I want to get a bicycle.
W Four students chose bicycles, and eight students chose accessories.
M That's interesting.
W Five students chose smartphones, and _____ _____ _____ _____ students chose books.

16 직업 추론

대화를 듣고, 남자의 직업으로 가장 적절한 것을 고르시오.

① doctor   ② firefighter
③ salesperson   ④ taxi driver
⑤ police officer

Sound Clear ☆ **quiet**

[콰이엇]으로 발음된다. [콰잇]으로 발음되는 quite(꽤, 상당히)과 구분하여 알아 둔다.

M Can you tell me what you saw that night?
W I was _____ _____ _____ _____ _____, and I saw someone leaving Mr. Bell's house through the window.
M Can you remember _____ _____ _____ _____?
W He was wearing a black baseball cap and blue jacket. He looked tall and skinny.
M Did you see anyone get hurt or _____ _____ _____?
W No, I didn't see or hear anything else. The house was so quiet.
M I see. Thank you for your time.

17 마지막 말에 대한 응답 찾기

대화를 듣고, 여자의 마지막 말에 대한 남자의 응답으로 가장 적절한 것을 고르시오.

Man: _____

① I want to be a police officer.
② I visited my grandma last week.
③ You must not park your car here.
④ The fine for a traffic signal violation is $70.
⑤ You should rent a car when you visit the city.

M Good afternoon. Show me your driver's license, please.
W Did I _____ _____ _____, officer?
M Yes, I'm afraid you _____ _____ _____ _____. You're not supposed to turn right while the light is red.
W Oh, I didn't know that. I'm sorry. Here is my license.
M I will have to _____ _____ _____ _____.
W How much is the fine?
M The fine for a traffic signal violation is $70.

18 마지막 말에 대한 응답 찾기

대화를 듣고, 남자의 마지막 말에 대한 여자의 응답으로 가장 적절한 것을 고르시오.

Woman: _____

① Where are you going to stay?
② I'll take them. How much are they?
③ I will have a pizza. What about you?
④ Would you like some hot tea instead?
⑤ Okay, you win. Let's eat something else.

Sound Clear ☆ **nutritious**
[t]와 [r]이 연달아 나와 [뉴츄리셔스]로 발음된다.

W I'm hungry. _____ _____ _____.
M Okay. What do you want to eat?
W I want to _____ _____ _____ _____ _____.
M Again? You ate a cheeseburger yesterday! Eating fast food like hamburgers every day is not _____ _____ _____ _____.
W But I love hamburgers! Why can't I have them every day?
M As teens, we need to _____ _____ _____ to grow, but fast food is not nutritious!
W Okay, you win. Let's eat something else.

19 마지막 말에 대한 응답 찾기

대화를 듣고, 여자의 마지막 말에 대한 남자의 응답으로 가장 적절한 것을 고르시오.

Man: _____

① I hope you will get better soon.
② You should tell her how you feel.
③ You'd better not tell her the truth.
④ Why don't you buy a new camera?
⑤ I think you should tell her the truth.

M What's the matter? You look upset!
W _____ _____ _____ my sister.
M Why?
W Yesterday, she wore my skirt without telling me and _____ _____ _____ _____ on it.
M Oh, that's terrible.
W And today, she told me she lost my camera! _____ _____ _____ _____ using my things without my permission!
M You should tell her how you feel.

20 상황에 적절한 말 찾기

다음 상황 설명을 듣고, Steve가 웨이터에게 할 말로 가장 적절한 것을 고르시오.

Steve: _____

① Can you get my coat?
② Can you wrap the food to go?
③ Where is the restaurant located?
④ The meal was very disappointing.
⑤ Can you give us separate bills, please?

M Steve and Kate _____ _____ _____ _____ at a fancy restaurant. The food was very good, and they _____ _____ _____ together. As the price of the meal was a little expensive, they agree to go Dutch. They _____ _____ _____ the restaurant, and they want to _____ _____ _____. What will Steve say to the waiter?
Steve Can you give us separate bills, please?

1.0배속   1.2배속

01 대화를 듣고, 남자가 구입할 카드를 고르시오.

①   ②   ③

④    ⑤

02 대화를 듣고, 여자가 남자에게 부탁한 일로 가장 적절한 것을 고르시오.

① 자전거 빌려주기   ② 버스 시간 알려 주기
③ 하이킹 함께 가기   ④ 아침에 일찍 깨워 주기
⑤ 자전거로 함께 등교하기

03 다음 표를 보면서 대화를 듣고, 내용과 일치하지 <u>않는</u> 것을 고르시오.

Reservation Card
① Name: Tony Brown
② Contact Number: 010-234-5678
③ Number of People: 4 adults and 2 kids
④ Time & Date: October 30, at 7 p.m.
⑤ Order: 2 Servings of Smoked Duck, 4 Servings of Bacon Fried Rice

04 다음을 듣고, 방송의 목적으로 가장 적절한 것을 고르시오.

① 강의가 취소되었음을 알리려고
② 강의 장소가 변경되었음을 알리려고
③ 강의에 참석할 학생들을 모집하려고
④ 일정 취소에 대한 환불을 공지하려고
⑤ 멸종 위기의 동물 보호 캠페인을 홍보하려고

05 대화를 듣고, 여자가 지불한 금액을 고르시오.

① $15   ② $20   ③ $35
④ $40   ⑤ $50

06 대화를 듣고, 두 사람의 관계로 가장 적절한 것을 고르시오.

① 경찰 – 운전자   ② 가방 가게 직원 – 손님
③ 우체국 직원 – 고객   ④ 트레이너 – 운동선수
⑤ 항공사 직원 – 승객

07 다음을 듣고, 두 사람의 대화가 <u>어색한</u> 것을 고르시오.

①   ②   ③   ④   ⑤

08 대화를 듣고, 여자가 대화 직후에 할 일로 가장 적절한 것을 고르시오.

① 학교에 가기   ② 병원에 가기
③ 회의 취소하기   ④ 남편에게 전화하기
⑤ 선생님께 전화하기

09 대화를 듣고, 남자의 새 집에 관해 언급되지 <u>않은</u> 것을 고르시오.

① 전망   ② 층수   ③ 이웃
④ 관리비   ⑤ 통학 소요 시간

10 다음을 듣고, 수업에 관해 언급되지 <u>않은</u> 것을 고르시오.

① 강사 이름   ② 수업 시간
③ 감점 요인   ④ 조별 과제 주제
⑤ 시험 계획

11 대화를 듣고, 여자의 할머니가 젊어 보이는 이유를 고르시오.

① 집안 내력이므로
② 건강식만 드셔서
③ 규칙적인 운동을 하셔서
④ 아침에 일찍 일어나셔서
⑤ 매사를 긍정적으로 생각하셔서

12 다음을 듣고, 공연 안내의 내용과 일치하지 <u>않는</u> 것을 고르시오.

① 공연 시간은 약 세 시간이다.
② 휴식 시간은 20분이다.
③ 매점은 3층 엘리베이터 옆에 있다.
④ 공연 중에는 사진 촬영이 금지된다.
⑤ 휴대 전화를 꺼야 한다.

13 다음 표를 보면서 대화를 듣고, 두 사람이 보게 될 영화를 고르시오.

	Movie	Time	Review
①	The Grinch	5:40 ~ 7:20 p.m.	★★★★★
②	Free Solo	7:30 ~ 9:20 p.m.	★★★★
③	Spider-Man	5:30 ~ 7:30 p.m.	★★★★★
④	Cold War	6:20 ~ 8:30 p.m.	★★★★★
⑤	The Moon	6:00 ~ 7:50 p.m.	★★★★

14 다음을 듣고, 무엇에 관한 설명인지 고르시오.

① 약국   ② 응급실   ③ 수술실
④ 경찰서   ⑤ 소방서

15 대화를 듣고, 남자가 여자에게 부탁한 일로 가장 적절한 것을 고르시오.

① 식당 예약하기   ② 가방 가져다주기
③ 음식 포장해 오기   ④ 식당 위치 알려 주기
⑤ 식당에서 기다리기

16 대화를 듣고, 남자가 내일 아침에 일어날 시각을 고르시오.

① 5:00 a.m.   ② 5:30 a.m.   ③ 6:00 a.m.
④ 6:30 a.m.   ⑤ 7:00 a.m.

17 대화를 듣고, 여자의 마지막 말에 대한 남자의 응답으로 가장 적절한 것을 고르시오.

Man: _____

① Finally, I was shown a red card.
② You didn't see an exciting game.
③ Yes, I was. But he apologized to me.
④ No. I don't think it's my fault this time.
⑤ Right. I don't want to stay in the hospital for another week.

18 대화를 듣고, 남자의 마지막 말에 대한 여자의 응답으로 가장 적절한 것을 고르시오.

Woman: _____

① Cheer up. You are recovering fast.
② You'd better do as your father says.
③ I think you should go to her funeral.
④ It was stupid of you to miss the exam.
⑤ Cheer up. It will take some time for him to accept her death.

19 대화를 듣고, 여자의 마지막 말에 대한 남자의 응답으로 가장 적절한 것을 고르시오.

Man: _____

① Do you think I need more practice?
② I was the vocalist in the school band.
③ I'm not into anything related to music.
④ But I can't sing in front of many people.
⑤ I am! That's exactly the club I'm looking for.

20 다음 상황 설명을 듣고, Minho가 Sandra에게 할 말로 가장 적절한 것을 고르시오.

Minho: Sandra, _____

① there's no school on Saturday.
② I like Seoul better than Jeju-do.
③ Why not? Let's meet at 3 o'clock.
④ I'll take you wherever you want to go.
⑤ I'd love to, but I can't. We're taking a family trip that day.

01 그림 정보 파악

대화를 듣고, 남자가 구입할 카드를 고르시오.

 ① ② ③

④ ⑤

M I'm looking for a card for my younger brother.

W How about this one? This superhero character is _____

_____ _____ _____.

M Well, he loves robots and cars, not superheroes.

W Sure. What about this one with three small cars?

M Oh, can I see that car-shaped one _____?
정답 단서

W Okay. You can get that card _____ _____ _____

_____ in it. One is "Happy Birthday," and the other is "I Love You."

M I'll buy the one that says "Happy Birthday."
정답 단서

02 부탁한 일 파악

대화를 듣고, 여자가 남자에게 부탁한 일로 가장 적절한 것을 고르시오.

① 자전거 빌려주기
② 버스 시간 알려 주기
③ 하이킹 함께 가기
④ 아침에 일찍 깨워 주기
⑤ 자전거로 함께 등교하기

Sound Clear ☆ apart**ment**

자음 세 개가 연속으로 나오면 중간 자음의 발음이 약화되어 [아팔먼트]로 발음된다.

M You were late for school again today. Did you oversleep?

W No, I got up early and _____ _____ _____ _____

_____, but there was heavy traffic.

M I used to have that problem, too. So I decided to just bike to school.

W _____ _____ _____ _____ _____ you to get here?

M Only fifteen minutes. Why don't you do _____ _____?

W But I'm not sure if I can _____ _____ _____ _____

_____ by myself. Can I ride with you?
정답 단서

M No problem. Let's meet at 8:20 in front of the apartment bike rack tomorrow morning. ☆

03 도표 정보 파악

다음 표를 보면서 대화를 듣고, 내용과 일치하지 않는 것을 고르시오.

Reservation Card
① Name: Tony Brown
② Contact Number: 010-234-5678
③ Number of People: 4 adults and 2 kids
④ Time & Date: October 30, at 7 p.m.
⑤ Order: 2 Servings of Smoked Duck,
4 Servings of Bacon Fried Rice

M I'd like to make a reservation.

W When would you like to make a reservation for?

M This Friday, at seven in the evening.

W That will be on October 30 at 7 p.m. _____ _____

_____ _____ _____ in your party?

M Six people. Four adults and two kids.

W All right. Are there any specific dishes you would like us to

_____ _____ _____?

M Well, we would like 4 servings of smoked duck for the adults and 2 servings of bacon fried rice for the kids.

W Sure. Could you _____ _____ _____ _____ and contact number, please?

M My name is Tony Brown, and my number is 010-234-5678.

04 목적 파악

다음을 듣고, 방송의 목적으로 가장 적절한 것을 고르시오.

① 강의가 취소되었음을 알리려고
② 강의 장소가 변경되었음을 알리려고
③ 강의에 참석할 학생들을 모집하려고
④ 일정 취소에 대한 환불을 공지하려고
⑤ 멸종 위기의 동물 보호 캠페인을 홍보하려고

M Attention, students. This is an announcement from the science department. Dr. Bruce Phillips' speech _____ _____ _____ was supposed to be at 5 p.m. today. But I'm sorry to announce that today's speech has been canceled _____ _____ _____ _____ _____. Instead, there will be a documentary movie titled *Saving Polar Bears*. Again, we're very sorry _____ _____ _____ _____ _____.

05 숫자 정보 파악

대화를 듣고, 여자가 지불한 금액을 고르시오.

① $15   ② $20   ③ $35
④ $40   ⑤ $50

M Suji, your shoes look very nice.
W Do they? I bought this pair at Claire's Choice. They're _____ _____ _____ _____ right now.
M Really? How much did you pay for them?
W The original price was $40, but _____ _____ _____ _____ _____ at 50% off.
M Fifty percent? Then you got them for just $20, right?
W Actually, I _____ _____ _____ _____ than that.
M Even more? How?
W Well, I used a five-dollar discount coupon I _____ _____ _____ _____.

06 관계 추론

대화를 듣고, 두 사람의 관계로 가장 적절한 것을 고르시오.

① 경찰 – 운전자
② 가방 가게 직원 – 손님
③ 우체국 직원 – 고객
④ 트레이너 – 운동선수
⑤ 항공사 직원 – 승객

W Do you have any baggage to check in?
M _____ _____ _____.
W Please place your bag _____ _____ _____.
M Okay. One bag is free, right?
W Yes. The free checked baggage allowance is one bag, but it must not exceed 20 kilograms _____ _____.
M I didn't know that regulation.
W Sorry, but _____ _____ _____ _____ your bag is $50.

07 어색한 대화 찾기

다음을 듣고, 두 사람의 대화가 어색한 것을 고르시오.

①   ②   ③   ④   ⑤

Sound Clear ☆ **present**
명사(선물)는 [프레즌트]로, 동사(주다)는 [프리젠트]로 발음된다.

① M Did you finish _____ _____ _____?
   W Yes, I finished it yesterday.
② M Why didn't you _____ _____ _____ _____?
   W Okay. Let's make it at five.
③ M Do you have any seat preference?
   W Please let me _____ _____ _____ _____.
④ M Did you buy a present for her?
   W Not yet. I'm just _____ _____ _____.
⑤ M Can you tell me the way to the post office?
   W Go straight two blocks. It's on your left.

08 할 일 파악

대화를 듣고, 여자가 대화 직후에 할 일로 가장 적절한 것을 고르시오.

① 학교에 가기　　② 병원에 가기
③ 회의 취소하기　④ 남편에게 전화하기
⑤ 선생님께 전화하기

(*Cellphone rings.*)

M Hello, Mom. It's me.

W Steve, what's up?

M I'm _____ _____ _____ _____ _____, so I have to leave school early.

W Oh, no! Your voice sounds bad. Did you _____ _____ from your teacher?

M Yes. And the school nurse told me to _____ _____ _____ right away. So could you come to the school and take me to the doctor's?

W I really want to, but I _____ _____ _____ _____. Instead, I'll call your dad and ask him if he can pick you up now. ← 정답 단서

M Okay. I'll be in the nurse's office.

09 언급되지 않은 것 찾기

대화를 듣고, 남자의 새 집에 관해 언급되지 않은 것을 고르시오.

① 전망　　② 층수　　③ 이웃
④ 관리비　⑤ 통학 소요 시간

Sound Clear ☆ **neighborhood**
gh가 묵음이라서 [네이버후드]로 발음된다.

M Hi, Jenny. My family moved to a new apartment.

W Oh, _____ _____ _____ _____?

M The place is not that large but the view is great. My house is on the 27th floor. ← 정답 단서

W Wow, you _____ _____ _____ _____ _____. ← 정답 단서 How's your neighborhood?

M People are very kind. But one disadvantage is that _____ _____ _____ _____. ← 정답 단서

W How far?

M Well, it used to take about fifteen minutes to go to school, but now it takes double the time. ← 정답 단서

W Oh, _____ _____ _____ _____ in the morning.

10 언급되지 않은 것 찾기

다음을 듣고, 수업에 관해 언급되지 않은 것을 고르시오.

① 강사 이름　　② 수업 시간
③ 감점 요인　　④ 조별 과제 주제
⑤ 시험 계획

W Hello. My name is Joan Brown. I'm going to teach English Literature to you _____ _____. We are going to meet every Thursday from 10 a.m. to 12 p.m. If you're late for the class, I will _____ _____ _____ _____. You will have two reports to write: one is an individual report, and the other is _____ _____ _____. Plus, you will _____ _____ _____ _____ at the end of the semester. Are there any questions?

11 이유 파악

대화를 듣고, 여자의 할머니가 젊어 보이는 이유를 고르시오.

① 집안 내력이므로
② 건강식만 드셔서
③ 규칙적인 운동을 하셔서
④ 아침에 일찍 일어나셔서
⑤ 매사를 긍정적으로 생각하셔서

M Is she your grandmother? Wow! She looks so young.

W Yes, many people say that. She really _____ _____ _____ _____ _____.

M Do you know what her secret is? Does she eat only healthy food? 한정

W I don't think so. _____ _____ _____ _____.

M Oh, does she?

W Yeah, she _____ _____ _____ _____ at 6 a.m. every morning.

M Now I see. Regular exercise is her secret. 정답 단서

W Yeah, I think so.

12 일치하지 않는 것 찾기

다음을 듣고, 공연 안내의 내용과 일치하지 않는 것을 고르시오.

① 공연 시간은 약 세 시간이다.
② 휴식 시간은 20분이다.
③ 매점은 3층 엘리베이터 옆에 있다.
④ 공연 중에는 사진 촬영이 금지된다.
⑤ 휴대 전화를 꺼야 한다.

M Welcome to this season's first performance at Wilson Youth Theater. The play will _____ _____ _____ _____ and we'll have a fifteen-minute break after one and a half hours. A snack shop is _____ _____ _____ _____, 정답 단서 next to the elevator. We'd also like to remind you that both photography and recording are forbidden. Now, please _____ _____ _____ _____. We shall begin shortly.

13 도표 정보 파악

다음 표를 보면서 대화를 듣고, 두 사람이 보게 될 영화를 고르시오.

	Movie	Time	Review
①	The Grinch	5:40 ~ 7:20 p.m.	★★★★★
②	Free Solo	7:30 ~ 9:20 p.m.	★★★★
③	Spider-Man	5:30 ~ 7:30 p.m.	★★★★★
④	Cold War	6:20 ~ 8:30 p.m.	★★★★★
⑤	The Moon	6:00 ~ 7:50 p.m.	★★★★

W Which movie do you want to see?

M What about *Spider-Man*?

W Sorry, I've already seen it with my brother. _____ _____ _____ _____.

M Then what about *Free Solo*?

W Don't you think it _____ _____ _____? I have to be home by 9 o'clock.

M So the movie should finish before 8. Then there are _____ _____ _____ _____ we can see.

W How about this one that got five stars from the critics?

M Okay. I don't think _____ _____ _____.

14 화제 파악

다음을 듣고, 무엇에 관한 설명인지 고르시오.

① 약국 ② 응급실 ③ 수술실
④ 경찰서 ⑤ 소방서

Sound Clear ☆ urgent treatment
동일한 [t] 발음이 연이어 나오고, [t]와 [r]이 연달아 나와 [얼전츄릿먼트]로 발음된다.

W This is a department in a hospital, and it operates 24 hours a day. People who have _____ _____ _____ _____ _____ are taken there for urgent treatment. It is not necessary _____ _____ _____ _____ first. If you need to get there really fast, _____ _____ _____ 119 for an ambulance. We often call it ER, which is the short form for this.

15 부탁한 일 파악

대화를 듣고, 남자가 여자에게 부탁한 일로 가장 적절한 것을 고르시오.

① 식당 예약하기   ② 가방 가져다주기
③ 음식 포장해 오기   ④ 식당 위치 알려 주기
⑤ 식당에서 기다리기

(*Cellphone rings.*)

M Hello, Sally. It's Eric.
W Hi, Eric! What's up?
M _____ _____ _____ at the cafeteria?
W Yes, but I am just about to leave.
M Whew, that's good. Then _____ _____ _____ _____ my bag is still there?
W Your bag? _____ _____ _____ _____ _____ ?
M It's a small blue bag with two short handles on the top.
W Let me check. (*Pause*) Oh, here it is! _____ _____ _____ _____ _____ .
M Yes! Could you bring it back to the dorm? Call me when you get back, and I'll go and get it.

16 숫자 정보 파악

대화를 듣고, 남자가 내일 아침에 일어날 시각을 고르시오.

① 5:00 a.m. ② 5:30 a.m. ③ 6:00 a.m.
④ 6:30 a.m. ⑤ 7:00 a.m.

Sound Clear ☆ **You'd better**
축약된 'd는 거의 발음되지 않아 [유베러]로 발음된다.

W Jason, it's already 11 o'clock. You should go to bed.
M I know, Mom. But I've not finished my report yet. I have to _____ _____ _____ _____ tomorrow.
W Why don't you get up early tomorrow and finish it? You look so tired.
M Okay. I'm so tired. _____ _____ _____ _____ _____ an hour before I usually leave for school?
W Sure. _____ _____ _____ _____ at 8, so I will wake you up at 7.
M _____ _____ I think about it, that's too late. You'd better wake me up at 6.
W Okay, I will.

17 마지막 말에 대한 응답 찾기

대화를 듣고, 여자의 마지막 말에 대한 남자의 응답으로 가장 적절한 것을 고르시오.

Man: _____

① Finally, I was shown a red card.
② You didn't see an exciting game.
③ Yes, I was. But he apologized to me.
④ No. I don't think it's my fault this time.
⑤ Right. I don't want to stay in the hospital for another week.

W Hi, Brian! How's your leg?
M Hi, Jenny. It hurts a lot. But thanks for coming here.
W How can't I come _____ _____ _____ ? When will you leave here?
M I'll be out of here tomorrow. I can use crutches to move around.
W That sounds good. Anyway, _____ _____ _____ _____ _____ _____ ?
M I broke it while playing soccer last Friday.
W You _____ _____ _____ _____ hard by an opponent.
M Yes, I was. But he apologized to me.

18 마지막 말에 대한 응답 찾기

대화를 듣고, 남자의 마지막 말에 대한 여자의 응답으로 가장 적절한 것을 고르시오.

Woman: ______________________

① Cheer up. You are recovering fast.
② You'd better do as your father says.
③ I think you should go to her funeral.
④ It was stupid of you to miss the exam.
⑤ Cheer up. It will take some time for him to accept her death.

W Hi, Seho. You ________ ________ ________ ________ last week. Why?
M My grandmother suddenly ________ ________ ________ ________. I was at her funeral.
W Oh, I'm really sorry to hear that.
M Thanks. I am worried about my father. He is ________ ________ ________ ________.
W Her sudden death ________ ________ ________ your father.
M It is hard for me to watch him feel sad and depressed.
W Cheer up. It will take some time for him to accept her death.

19 마지막 말에 대한 응답 찾기

대화를 듣고, 여자의 마지막 말에 대한 남자의 응답으로 가장 적절한 것을 고르시오.

Man: ______________________

① Do you think I need more practice?
② I was the vocalist in the school band.
③ I'm not into anything related to music.
④ But I can't sing in front of many people.
⑤ I am! That's exactly the club I'm looking for.

Sound Clear ☆ **join it**

앞 단어의 끝 자음과 뒤 단어의 모음이 만나 연음되어 [조이닛]으로 발음된다.

W Why the long face, Mark?
M I ________ ________ ________ ________ for the school band.
W That's too bad. The club is very popular.
M I really wanted to join it, so I practiced hard for a few days.
W I'm sorry to hear that. Well, how about ________ ________ ________ ________ ________ ________?
M Is there a musical club in our school?
W Sure. I believe you're interested in ________ ________ ________ ________ ________.
M I am! That's exactly the club I'm looking for.

20 상황에 적절한 말 찾기

다음 상황 설명을 듣고, Minho가 Sandra에게 할 말로 가장 적절한 것을 고르시오.

Minho: Sandra, ______________________

① there's no school on Saturday.
② I like Seoul better than Jeju-do.
③ Why not? Let's meet at 3 o'clock.
④ I'll take you wherever you want to go.
⑤ I'd love to, but I can't. We're taking a family trip that day.

M Minho is going to ________ ________ ________ to Jeju-do with his family this Saturday. On Wednesday afternoon, Minho is having lunch with Sandra, ________ ________ ________ ________ ________. Sandra asks him to show her around Seoul this Saturday. Minho would ________ ________ ________ ________ ________, but he has to refuse because of his plan to take a trip to Jeju-do that day. In this situation, what would Minho most likely say to Sandra?
Minho Sandra, I'd love to, but I can't. We're taking a family trip that day.

Review Test

Word Check
영어는 우리말로, 우리말은 영어로 써 보기

01 defensive _____

02 luggage _____

03 certificate _____

04 exhausted _____

05 located _____

06 organize _____

07 advance _____

08 bill _____

09 fancy _____

10 agree to _____

11 lose weight _____

12 get better _____

13 진실, 사실 _____

14 위반하다 _____

15 영양가 있는 _____

16 강사 _____

17 분리된 _____

18 여론 조사 _____

19 허락 _____

20 선택하다 _____

21 강조하다 _____

22 교통 규칙 _____

23 비쩍 마른 _____

24 비용을 각자 부담하다 _____

Expression Check
알맞은 표현을 넣어 문장 완성하기

25 Did you see anything _____ _____? 당신은 무언가 불이 난 것을 보셨나요?

26 They are _____ _____ leave the restaurant. 그들은 식당을 막 떠나려고 하고 있다.

27 You can _____ _____ any volunteer work. 넌 어떤 자원봉사 활동에도 참여할 수 있어.

28 My brother _____ _____ _____ his girlfriend recently.
나의 오빠가 최근에 여자 친구와 헤어졌어.

29 She wore my skirt without telling me and _____ _____ leaving a stain on it.
그녀는 나에게 말도 하지 않고 내 치마를 입더니 결국 치마에 얼룩을 남겼어.

30 Do you make a shopping list _____ _____ you go to the market?
당신은 시장에 갈 때마다 쇼핑 목록을 작성하나요?

Answers p.93

Word Check 영어는 우리말로, 우리말은 영어로 써 보기

01 forbid _____

02 opponent _____

03 specific _____

04 operate _____

05 recover _____

06 critic _____

07 endangered _____

08 overweight _____

09 deduct _____

10 due to _____

11 exceed _____

12 used to _____

13 거절하다 _____

14 무게 _____

15 치료 _____

16 긴급한 _____

17 우울한 _____

18 불리한 점, 약점 _____

19 부서 _____

20 규정 _____

21 문학 _____

22 장례식 _____

23 고층의 _____

24 전학생 _____

Expression Check 알맞은 표현을 넣어 문장 완성하기

25 Do you have any baggage to _____ _____? 부치실 짐이 있으십니까?

26 I have to _____ _____ this report tomorrow. 저는 내일 이 리포트를 제출해야 해요.

27 My grandmother _____ _____ last week. 우리 할머니는 지난주에 돌아가셨어.

28 I believe you're interested in acting _____ _____ _____ singing.
너는 노래뿐만 아니라 연기에도 관심 있잖아.

29 You'll take a final exam _____ _____ _____ _____ the semester.
여러분은 학기말에 기말고사를 보게 될 것입니다.

30 _____ is "Happy Birthday," and _____ _____ is "I Love You."
하나는 'Happy Birthday'이고, 다른 하나는 'I Love You'예요.

01 대화를 듣고, 사진 속에서 Elsie를 고르시오.

02 대화를 듣고, 여자가 크리스마스에 할 일로 가장 적절한 것을 고르시오.

① 집 청소하기
② 식당 예약하기
③ 선물 구입하기
④ 음식 준비하기
⑤ 크리스마스트리 장식하기

03 다음 그림의 상황에 가장 적절한 대화를 고르시오.

① ② ③ ④ ⑤

04 대화를 듣고, 남자가 책을 가져오기로 한 요일을 고르시오.

① Tuesday
② Wednesday
③ Thursday
④ Friday
⑤ Saturday

05 대화를 듣고, 남자가 여자에게 전화한 목적으로 가장 적절한 것을 고르시오.

① 치킨을 주문하려고
② 주소를 확인하려고
③ 주문을 변경하려고
④ 학교 이름을 물어보려고
⑤ 배송 시간을 알려 주려고

06 대화를 듣고, 두 사람이 대화하는 장소로 가장 적절한 곳을 고르시오.

① 카페   ② 서점   ③ 식당
④ 미용실   ⑤ 옷 가게

07 다음을 듣고, 두 사람의 대화가 어색한 것을 고르시오.

①   ②   ③   ④   ⑤

08 대화를 듣고, 남자가 여자에게 부탁한 일로 가장 적절한 것을 고르시오.

① 장보기   ② 약 사 오기
③ 저녁 차리기   ④ 병원 예약하기
⑤ 엄마 마중 나가기

09 대화를 듣고, 여자가 할 시간제 일자리에 관해 언급되지 않은 것을 고르시오.

① 기간   ② 급여   ③ 근무 장소
④ 근무 시간   ⑤ 통근 시간

10 대화를 듣고, 남자가 지불할 금액을 고르시오.

① $2   ② $3   ③ $4   ④ $5   ⑤ $6

11 다음을 듣고, 안데르센에 관해 언급되지 않은 것을 고르시오.

① 출생지   ② 형제자매   ③ 부모의 직업
④ 집필 장르   ⑤ 대표작

12 대화를 듣고, 두 사람이 내일 오전에 할 일로 가장 적절한 것을 고르시오.

① 쇼핑하기　　　　② 바다낚시 하기
③ 호텔에서 쉬기　　④ 수족관 구경하기
⑤ 해산물 요리 먹기

13 다음을 듣고, 무엇에 관한 안내 방송인지 고르시오.

① 관람객 주의 사항
② 동물원 안전 수칙
③ 사파리 동물 관람 수칙
④ 열대 지방 여행 프로그램
⑤ 동물원 일일 캠프 프로그램

14 다음을 듣고, 무엇에 관한 설명인지 고르시오.

① 간호사　　　② 체육 교사　　　③ 수영 선수
④ 소방대원　　⑤ 인명 구조 요원

15 다음 표를 보면서 대화를 듣고, 여자가 신청할 수업을 고르시오.

	Class	Day	Time
①	Aerobic	Mon. Fri.	5 ~ 6 p.m.
②	Dance	Wed. Fri.	5 ~ 6 p.m.
③	Badminton	Tues. Thur.	6 ~ 7 p.m.
④	Tennis	Mon. Wed.	6 ~ 7 p.m.
⑤	Yoga	Tues. Fri.	7 ~ 8 p.m.

16 대화를 듣고, 남자가 도착할 시각을 고르시오.

① 5:10 p.m.　② 5:30 p.m.　③ 5:40 p.m.
④ 6:10 p.m.　⑤ 6:30 p.m.

17 대화를 듣고, 남자의 마지막 말에 대한 여자의 응답으로 가장 적절한 것을 고르시오.

Woman: _____

① We have different tastes in music.
② You should listen to your teacher.
③ Can you bring me those earphones?
④ Listen to fast music when you study.
⑤ Music can help you relax, but it makes it more difficult to focus.

18 대화를 듣고, 여자의 마지막 말에 대한 남자의 응답으로 가장 적절한 것을 고르시오.

Man: _____

① It only takes one business day.
② It's much cheaper to buy them online.
③ Hurry up! We don't have enough time.
④ There are lots of books available online.
⑤ You'd better visit the bookstore in the morning.

19 대화를 듣고, 남자의 마지막 말에 대한 여자의 응답으로 가장 적절한 것을 고르시오.

Woman: _____

① I don't know why she likes them.
② Sorry. I can't tell you. It's a secret.
③ What do you want for your birthday?
④ I think her roommate might know about that.
⑤ I wonder if she would like to go to the concert.

20 다음 상황 설명을 듣고, Jisu가 Philip 선생님에게 할 말로 가장 적절한 것을 고르시오.

Jisu: Mr. Philip, _____

① would you lead our volunteer club?
② can you tell me why you volunteer?
③ tell me how to improve my English skills.
④ could you translate this book into English?
⑤ why don't you take part in something more meaningful?

01 그림 정보 파악

대화를 듣고, 사진 속에서 Elsie를 고르시오.

Sound Clear ☆ **must be**

자음 세 개가 연속으로 나와 중간 자음의 발음이 약화되어 [머슷비]로 발음된다.

M Is that a class picture _____ _____ _____ _____?
Who's your best friend?

W It's Elsie. _____ _____ _____ _____.

M Umm... is she the tall girl standing next to your teacher?

W No, she isn't _____ _____ _____. She is wearing glasses. 정답 단서

M Then is she next to the boy wearing a baseball cap?

W No, she is near that boy. Elsie always _____ _____ _____ _____.

M Oh, I found her. She ☆ must be the girl wearing big headphones.

W Yes, exactly. That's my best friend Elsie. 정답 단서

02 할 일 파악

대화를 듣고, 여자가 크리스마스에 할 일로 가장 적절한 것을 고르시오.

① 집 청소하기
② 식당 예약하기
③ 선물 구입하기
④ 음식 준비하기
⑤ 크리스마스트리 장식하기

M What do you want to do this coming Christmas?

W Well, why don't we just stay home?

M Really? You _____ _____ _____ _____ _____?

W There were so many people everywhere last year. So _____ _____ _____ _____ at home.

M Okay, then I'm going to _____ _____ _____ _____ _____.

W Thanks. Then I'll decorate the Christmas tree with lights and a big star on top. 정답 단서

M I'm sure the tree will _____ _____!

03 그림의 상황에 적절한 대화 찾기

다음 그림의 상황에 가장 적절한 대화를 고르시오.

① ② ③ ④ ⑤

① W May I pet the puppy?
M Sure. She _____ _____ _____.

② W Can I bring my dog with me in here?
M No. _____ _____ _____ of your pet, no animals are allowed. 정답 단서

③ W Did you take the dog out for a walk today?
M Not yet. I usually walk the dog in the evening.

④ W I wonder _____ _____ _____ _____ _____.
M It has black hair and short legs.

⑤ W _____ _____ _____ _____ would you like to have?
M A dog. Dogs are my favorite pets.

04 특정 정보 파악

대화를 듣고, 남자가 책을 가져오기로 한 요일을 고르시오.

① Tuesday   ② Wednesday
③ Thursday   ④ Friday
⑤ Saturday

W   Did you _____ _____ _____ on the Space Race?
M   No, I'm reading a book on the development of space rockets for the report.
W   It sounds interesting. I'd like to read it.
M   Okay. _____ _____ _____ _____ _____ after I'm finished.
W   Thanks. When is the report deadline?
M   I have to _____ _____ _____ _____ by Wednesday.
W   Then can you bring it to the writing club meeting on Saturday?
M   No problem.

05 목적 파악

대화를 듣고, 남자가 여자에게 전화한 목적으로 가장 적절한 것을 고르시오.

① 치킨을 주문하려고
② 주소를 확인하려고
③ 주문을 변경하려고
④ 학교 이름을 물어보려고
⑤ 배송 시간을 알려 주려고

Sound Clear ☆ **used to**
'~하곤 했다'의 의미인 경우 [유즈드투]가 아니라 [유스투]로 발음된다.

(*Telephone rings.*)
M   Hello. This is Chicken Heaven. Is this Ms. Park?
W   Yes. Is there a problem?
M   Yes. We're not _____ _____ _____ _____ to deliver the chicken to. Your school isn't on the map.
W   Oh, our school _____ _____ _____ _____. We used to be Seowon Middle School.
M   All right. We'll be there in a few minutes.
W   Oh, _____ _____ _____ a 1.5-liter bottle of coke, too?
M   No problem. We'll add that to your order of two fried chickens.

06 장소 추론

대화를 듣고, 두 사람이 대화하는 장소로 가장 적절한 곳을 고르시오.

① 카페   ② 서점   ③ 식당
④ 미용실   ⑤ 옷 가게

W   Hi. I'm here for an appointment at 3 o'clock.
M   Let me see. Oh, Ms. Jessica Anderson. Please _____ _____ _____ _____.
W   Thank you. I'd like my hair dyed light brown.
M   Okay, and I think a wavy perm might _____ _____ _____ _____.
W   No, I don't like perms. How long do you think it will take to dye my hair?
M   Probably two hours. Do you want to grab anything _____ _____ _____ _____?
W   Yes. I think I'll _____ _____ _____ _____ and some magazines.

07 어색한 대화 찾기

다음을 듣고, 두 사람의 대화가 어색한 것을 고르시오.

① ② ③ ④ ⑤

Sound Clear☆ last night
자음 세 개가 연속으로 나오면 중간 자음의 발음이 약화되어 [라스나잇]으로 발음된다.

① **M** Can I talk to Mr. Brown, please?
W I'm sorry, but he's ________ ________ ________ ________ now.
② **M** Did you watch *Christmas in Paris* last night?
W I wanted to, but I couldn't. It was the best movie ever.
③ **M** I was late for school this morning.
W Really? ________ ________ ________ ________ home earlier.
④ **M** Do you mind if I close the window?
W Not at all. I ________ ________ ________ ________, too.
⑤ **M** Can you help me do my math homework today?
W I'm afraid I can't. ________ ________ ________ ________.

08 부탁한 일 파악

대화를 듣고, 남자가 여자에게 부탁한 일로 가장 적절한 것을 고르시오.

① 장보기 ② 약 사 오기
③ 저녁 차리기 ④ 병원 예약하기
⑤ 엄마 마중 나가기

M Where are you going, Jenny?
W I'm ________ ________ ________ ________ ________.
M Are you going to the store on Main Street?
W Yes. Mom will be late today, so ________ ________ ________ ________ ________ for dinner.
M Good. Could you get some digestive medicine for me?
W Oh, Dad, do you still ________ ________ ________? Shouldn't you see a doctor?
M No, ________ ________ ________.
W All right. I'll get it for you.

09 언급되지 않은 것 찾기

대화를 듣고, 여자가 할 시간제 일자리에 관해 언급되지 않은 것을 고르시오.

① 기간 ② 급여 ③ 근무 장소
④ 근무 시간 ⑤ 통근 시간

W I got a part-time job for this winter vacation.
M ________ ________ ________! What kind of work will you do?
W I'm going to work in my uncle's bakery.
M So are you going to work ________ ________ ________?
W No. I'll work just four hours a day. From eight to noon.
M You'll have to get up early in the morning.
W I don't think so. The bakery is only five minutes on foot ________ ________ ________.

10 숫자 정보 파악

대화를 듣고, 남자가 지불할 금액을 고르시오.

① $2 ② $3 ③ $4
④ $5 ⑤ $6

M I need to return these two books.
W Oh, it appears these books are ________ ________ ________.
M I forgot they were overdue. Sorry.
W You know you ________ ________ ________ ________ ________, right? The late fee is 25 cents a day.
M So I have to pay 25 cents for each day for each book? That's a lot.
W And what happened to this one?
M I ________ ________ ________ ________, and the cover tore off.
W Hmm... you have to pay $2 ________ ________ ________.

11 언급되지 않은 것 찾기

다음을 듣고, 안데르센에 관해 언급되지 <u>않은</u> 것을 고르시오.

① 출생지   ② 형제자매
③ 부모의 직업   ④ 집필 장르
⑤ 대표작

W Today, I'll tell you about _____ _____ Hans Christian Andersen. He was born on April 2, 1805, in Odense, Denmark. _____ _____ _____ _____ _____ and his mother a washerwoman. Although Andersen wrote novels, poems, plays, and travelogues, he is best remembered for his fairy tales. Some of _____ _____ _____ _____ _____ include *The Little Mermaid*, *The Nightingale*, and *The Ugly Duckling*.

12 할 일 파악

대화를 듣고, 두 사람이 내일 오전에 할 일로 가장 적절한 것을 고르시오.

① 쇼핑하기   ② 바다낚시 하기
③ 호텔에서 쉬기   ④ 수족관 구경하기
⑤ 해산물 요리 먹기

W _____ _____ _____ the air is different in Jeju-do.
M I agree. Mom, what are we going to do tomorrow morning?
W The weather forecast says we will have a strong wind tomorrow morning, so _____ _____ _____ _____.
M Ah, it's too bad I can't go sea fishing.
W Come on. Let's _____ _____ _____ _____ _____ in the guidebook. How about the aquarium?
M Um... I think it's too far from the hotel. Why don't we go shopping nearby the hotel instead?
W Good idea. Let's _____ _____ _____ _____ now.
M Okay. I'd like to have some seafood dishes.

13 주제 파악

다음을 듣고, 무엇에 관한 안내 방송인지 고르시오.

① 관람객 주의 사항
② 동물원 안전 수칙
③ 사파리 동물 관람 수칙
④ 열대 지방 여행 프로그램
⑤ 동물원 일일 캠프 프로그램

M Central Park Zoo has a special program designed to _____ _____ _____ _____. Please join us for our one-day zoo camp experience. During this one-day camp, you'll explore the Tropic Zone and _____ _____ _____ _____ in the tropics. Campers will also enjoy a jungle safari. _____ _____ _____ hands-on investigations and up-close animal encounters. The camp requires pre-registration. _____ _____ _____ _____. Thank you.

14 화제 파악

다음을 듣고, 무엇에 관한 설명인지 고르시오.

① 간호사   ② 체육 교사
③ 수영 선수   ④ 소방대원
⑤ 인명 구조 요원

Sound Clear ☆ **whistle**
t가 묵음이라서 [위슬]로 발음된다.

W These people _____ _____ _____ _____ or at a swimming pool. They supervise the safety of swimmers, surfers, and people _____ _____ _____ _____ _____. They are excellent swimmers, and they are trained in a variety of life-saving skills _____ _____ _____. They always wear a whistle around their necks and have important rescue or communication equipment _____ _____ _____.

15 도표 정보 파악

다음 표를 보면서 대화를 듣고, 여자가 신청할 수업을 고르시오.

	Class	Day	Time
①	Aerobic	Mon. Fri.	5~6 p.m.
②	Dance	Wed. Fri.	5~6 p.m.
③	Badminton	Tues. Thur.	6~7 p.m.
④	Tennis	Mon. Wed.	6~7 p.m.
⑤	Yoga	Tues. Fri.	7~8 p.m.

Sound Clear ☆ **aerobics**

'에어로빅'은 실제로 [애로우빅스]로 발음된다.

M Look at this notice. The community center provides free exercise classes for residents.

W Oh, there are many good classes. Dad, I'd really like to _____ _____ _____ _____ _____.

M But I think the class is too late. You should _____ _____ _____ _____ _____ _____.

W Oh, that's too bad.

M How about aerobics? The classes are from 5:00 to 6:00 in the afternoon.

W Dad, I usually come home at 5:30. And every Monday I don't _____ _____ _____ _____.

M Then you have only one option left. Would you like to take it?

W Sure. I have to do something to _____ _____ _____.

16 숫자 정보 파악 ✳

대화를 듣고, 남자가 도착할 시각을 고르시오.

① 5:10 p.m. ② 5:30 p.m. ③ 5:40 p.m.
④ 6:10 p.m. ⑤ 6:30 p.m.

(*Cellphone rings.*)

M Hello? Shelly, are you there already?

W Yeah, I'm _____ _____ _____ _____ _____.
Where are you?

M Sorry. I'm on my way. I _____ _____ _____, and I had to wait for twenty minutes to get the next one.

W Oh, my. The movie starts at 6:00 and it's already 5:40.

M I'm really sorry. I think it will take half an hour for me to get there. 정답 단서

W Then _____ _____ _____ _____ to a later movie. 정답 단서

M Sounds perfect. A movie starting after 6:20 should be okay.

W All right. See you soon.

17 마지막 말에 대한 응답 찾기

대화를 듣고, 남자의 마지막 말에 대한 여자의 응답으로 가장 적절한 것을 고르시오.

Woman: _____

① We have different tastes in music.
② You should listen to your teacher.
③ Can you bring me those earphones?
④ Listen to fast music when you study.
⑤ Music can help you relax, but it makes it more difficult to focus.

W Mike, didn't you hear me?

M Oh, Mom. I'm sorry. I _____ _____ _____.

W What were you doing? I called you several times.

M I was studying _____ _____ _____ _____ on my earphones.

W I told you before that it's not helpful for you to study while listening to music.

M Yes, I know. But some good music _____ _____ _____ _____ when I study.

W Music can help you relax, but it makes it more difficult to focus.

18 마지막 말에 대한 응답 찾기

대화를 듣고, 여자의 마지막 말에 대한 남자의 응답으로 가장 적절한 것을 고르시오.

Man: _____

① It only takes one business day.
② It's much cheaper to buy them online.
③ Hurry up! We don't have enough time.
④ There are lots of books available online.
⑤ You'd better visit the bookstore in the morning.

Sound Clear ☆ **textbook**
자음 세 개가 연속으로 나오면 중간 자음의 발음이 약화되어 [텍스북]으로 발음된다.

W Jack, did you buy a textbook?
M A textbook? _____ _____ _____ _____ _____?
W We need to buy a new science textbook for Thursday's class.
M Oh, I totally _____ _____ _____.
W Then let's go to the bookstore together.
M Well, why don't we just _____ _____ _____ _____?
     They are delivered very quickly these days.
W Really? How long does it take?
M It only takes one business day.

19 마지막 말에 대한 응답 찾기

대화를 듣고, 남자의 마지막 말에 대한 여자의 응답으로 가장 적절한 것을 고르시오.

Woman: _____

① I don't know why she likes them.
② Sorry. I can't tell you. It's a secret.
③ What do you want for your birthday?
④ I think her roommate might know about that.
⑤ I wonder if she would like to go to the concert.

M What are you thinking about?
W Yena's birthday is _____ _____ _____. But I have no idea what to buy for her.
M Me neither! We need to think about _____ _____ _____ _____.
W You're right. What are her interests?
M _____ _____ _____ _____, she likes music, swimming, and reading.
W Maybe we could get her _____ _____ _____.
M Good idea. Who would know her favorite groups?
W I think her roommate might know about that.

20 상황에 적절한 말 찾기

다음 상황 설명을 듣고, Jisu가 Philip 선생님에게 할 말로 가장 적절한 것을 고르시오.

Jisu: Mr. Philip, _____

① would you lead our volunteer club?
② can you tell me why you volunteer?
③ tell me how to improve my English skills.
④ could you translate this book into English?
⑤ why don't you take part in something more meaningful?

M Jisu is interested in volunteer work. Recently, she decided to _____ _____ _____ _____ _____. The volunteer work in the club is to _____ _____ _____ _____ into English for African children. But she learns that every club needs a teacher to _____ _____ _____ _____ _____. So Jisu wants to ask her English teacher Mr. Philip to take that role. In this situation, what would Jisu most likely say to Mr. Philip?
Jisu Mr. Philip, would you lead our volunteer club?

1.0배속

1.2배속

01 다음 그림의 상황에 가장 적절한 대화를 고르시오.

Size 8

① ② ③ ④ ⑤

02 대화를 듣고, 두 사람이 대화하는 장소로 가장 적절한 곳을 고르시오.

① 식당 ② 교실 ③ 서점
④ 도서관 ⑤ 옷 가게

03 대화를 듣고, 남자가 여자에게 부탁한 일로 가장 적절한 것을 고르시오.

① 간식 사 오기 ② 책 가져오기
③ 책 반납해 주기 ④ 병문안 같이 가기
⑤ 여벌 옷 가져오기

04 다음을 듣고, 방송의 목적으로 가장 적절한 것을 고르시오.

① 가게 이전을 알리려고
② 새로운 제품을 홍보하려고
③ 주차장 이용을 안내하려고
④ 할인 행사를 알리려고
⑤ 적립금과 쿠폰 사용 방법을 설명하려고

05 대화를 듣고, 여자가 영화관에서 사용한 금액을 고르시오.

① $11 ② $15 ③ $18
④ $21 ⑤ $23

06 다음을 듣고, 두 사람의 대화가 어색한 것을 고르시오.

① ② ③ ④ ⑤

07 다음 표를 보면서 대화를 듣고, 내용과 일치하지 않는 것을 고르시오.

The BEST AIR	① ECONOMY
Name: John Spencer	To: ② Tokyo
Flight: BJ459	Gate: 7
Departure Time: ③ 6:30 a.m.	
Date: ④ AUG 12, THU	
Seat: 32A ⑤ (Window seat)	

08 대화를 듣고, 여자가 남자에게 부탁한 일로 가장 적절한 것을 고르시오.

① 뮤지컬 관람하기 ② 오디션 알아봐 주기
③ 상대역 연기해 주기 ④ 감독에게 전화해 주기
⑤ 연습 장면 녹화해 주기

09 대화를 듣고, 남자가 여자에게 전화한 목적으로 가장 적절한 것을 고르시오.

① 분실물을 찾기 위해
② 꽃다발을 주문하기 위해
③ 꽃의 품질에 대해 항의하기 위해
④ 화분 관리 방법을 문의하기 위해
⑤ 카드 결제가 가능한지 묻기 위해

10 대화를 듣고, 식당에 관해 언급되지 않은 것을 고르시오.

① 음식의 맛 ② 서비스 ③ 음식의 가격
④ 실내 장식 ⑤ 집과의 거리

11 대화를 듣고, 여자가 최고의 휴가를 보내지 못한 이유로 가장 적절한 것을 고르시오.

① 시간이 부족해서　　② 식중독에 걸려서
③ 전화기를 잃어버려서　④ 관광 명소가 부족해서
⑤ 사람들이 불친절해서

12 대화를 듣고, 여자가 남자에게 충고한 내용으로 가장 적절한 것을 고르시오.

① 병원 진료 받기
② 규칙적으로 운동하기
③ 실내 환기 자주 하기
④ 황사 전용 마스크 구입하기
⑤ 공기 질이 안 좋을 때 밖에서 운동하지 않기

13 대화를 듣고, 두 사람이 대화 직후에 할 일로 가장 적절한 것을 고르시오.

① 지갑 사러 가기　　② 기차표 예매하기
③ 케이크 찾아오기　④ 할머니 모시러 가기
⑤ 경찰서에 지갑 가져다주기

14 대화를 듣고, 남자의 결혼기념일을 고르시오.

① 5월 7일　　② 5월 10일　　③ 5월 12일
④ 5월 14일　　⑤ 5월 15일

15 대화를 듣고, 두 사람이 만나기로 한 시각을 고르시오.

① 4:20 p.m.　② 4:30 p.m.　③ 4:50 p.m.
④ 5:00 p.m.　⑤ 5:10 p.m.

16 대화를 듣고, 여자가 학생회장 출마를 위해 가장 먼저 할 일을 고르시오.

① 자기소개서 쓰기　　② 후보 연설문 쓰기
③ 후보 연설 연습하기　④ 부모님께 허락 받기
⑤ 선거 운동원 모집하기

17 대화를 듣고, 여자의 마지막 말에 대한 남자의 응답으로 가장 적절한 것을 고르시오.

Man: _____

① I went to the movies last night.
② I once met them at a restaurant.
③ I've watched the drama many times.
④ All of the characters are great. I like them all.
⑤ I hope I can travel around the world like the main character.

18 대화를 듣고, 남자의 마지막 말에 대한 여자의 응답으로 가장 적절한 것을 고르시오.

Woman: _____

① The bridge is under construction.
② How can I get to the bus station?
③ It's a long distance for them to walk.
④ I'm afraid not. It's the same for children.
⑤ Are there any seats available on the bus?

19 대화를 듣고, 여자의 마지막 말에 대한 남자의 응답으로 가장 적절한 것을 고르시오.

Man: _____

① The total is $50.
② I like cheese pizza more.
③ Yes, I want the pizza to go.
④ Extra toppings are free today.
⑤ It will take about half an hour.

20 다음 상황 설명을 듣고, Cindy가 Sam에게 할 말로 가장 적절한 것을 고르시오.

Cindy: Sam, _____

① when did you get your cellphone?
② do you want me to take a picture?
③ this is the best show I've ever seen.
④ we're not supposed to use cellphones during the show.
⑤ can I send a text message using your phone?

받아쓰기용

01 그림 정보 파악

다음 그림의 상황에 가장 적절한 대화를 고르시오.

① ② ③ ④ ⑤

Sound Clear ☆ **aisle**

s가 묵음이라서 [아일]로 발음된다.

① W What's the matter? You look upset.

   M I can't find my book. I think I _____ _____ _____ _____ _____.

② W Can you show me these sandals in a size 8?

   M Sorry. *정답 단서* _____ _____ _____ _____.

③ W Excuse me, but where can I find the diapers?

   M They're in aisle ☆ 7.

④ W Are you going to drink your coffee _____ _____ _____ _____ _____?

   M I'll take it out.

⑤ W I will have the seafood spaghetti.

   M Okay, do you want _____ _____ _____?

02 장소 추론 🏴

대화를 듣고, 두 사람이 대화하는 장소로 가장 적절한 곳을 고르시오.

① 식당   ② 교실   ③ 서점
④ 도서관   ⑤ 옷 가게

W May I help you?

M Yes, please. I'm looking for _____ _____ _____ of Charles Brown's novel, *A New Life*.

W Okay, let me check. (*Pause*) It's in section E, next to the foreign language section. Do you want me to _____ _____ _____ _____?

M Oh, thank you so much.

W Here is your book.

M _____ _____ _____ _____ _____?

W Sure, you can get a 10% discount with this coupon.

03 부탁한 일 파악

대화를 듣고, 남자가 여자에게 부탁한 일로 가장 적절한 것을 고르시오.

① 간식 사 오기   ② 책 가져오기
③ 책 반납해 주기   ④ 병문안 같이 가기
⑤ 여벌 옷 가져오기

(*Cellphone rings.*)

W Hi, Patrick. This is Lisa.

M Oh, hi, Lisa.

W I heard you're _____ _____ _____. What happened?

M I fell down the stairs and _____ _____ _____ last week. But I'm doing better now.

W Well, Jerry and I are _____ _____ _____ _____ this afternoon. Would you like your favorite snack?

M No, thanks. But can you bring me some books to read? I'm so bored in here. *한정* *정답 단서*

W No problem. We'll bring you _____ _____ _____ and magazines.

04 목적 파악

다음을 듣고, 방송의 목적으로 가장 적절한 것을 고르시오.

① 가게 이전을 알리려고
② 새로운 제품을 홍보하려고
③ 주차장 이용을 안내하려고
④ 할인 행사를 알리려고
⑤ 적립금과 쿠폰 사용 방법을 설명하려고

W Welcome to Magic Shoes. It has been 5 years _____ _____ _____ _____, and we want to show our gratitude to all of our customers. We are having a BUY ONE PAIR, GET ONE FREE sale from today until next Tuesday. _____ _____ _____ _____ _____, you can use your store points or any coupons you have to _____ _____ _____. Thank you again for shopping here.

05 숫자 정보 파악

대화를 듣고, 여자가 영화관에서 사용한 금액을 고르시오.

① $11   ② $15   ③ $18
④ $21   ⑤ $23

W There are a lot of movies playing. What do you want to see?
M How about *Flying Man*? It's _____ _____ _____.
W Good. How much is a ticket?
M It's $8 a ticket for the 2D movie, and $15 for the 4D movie.
W Let's see it in 4D! _____ _____ _____ _____!
M Okay. Do you want to have popcorn?
W _____ _____ _____ and share it.
M Okay. It's $6 for a bucket, so here's $3. While you're buying the popcorn, I will buy the tickets.
W Okay, I'll _____ _____ _____ _____ for my ticket.

06 어색한 대화 찾기

다음을 듣고, 두 사람의 대화가 어색한 것을 고르시오.

①   ②   ③   ④   ⑤

① **W** Did you _____ _____ _____ _____ last night?
   M Yes, I'm really upset. The team I like lost again.
② **W** I would like to open a new account.
   M Okay, can you _____ _____ _____ _____?
③ **W** You're from Busan, right?
   M Yes, I have lived there for 18 years.
④ **W** Are there _____ _____ _____?
   M Yes, two seats in the front row are available now.
⑤ **W** _____ _____ _____ _____ _____?
   M I'm afraid not. I don't have time.

07 도표 정보 파악

다음 표를 보면서 대화를 듣고, 내용과 일치하지 <u>않는</u> 것을 고르시오.

The BEST AIR	① ECONOMY
Name: John Spencer	To: ② Tokyo
Flight: BJ459	Gate: 7
Departure Time: ③ 6:30 a.m.	
Date: ④ AUG 12, THU	
Seat: 32A ⑤ (Window seat)	

Sound Clear ☆ **August**

미국식은 [어거스트]로, 영국식은 [오거스트]로 발음된다.

M I would like to _____ _____ _____ to Tokyo on Friday, August 13.
W We only have a six-thirty flight on Friday morning.
M Oh, really? _____ _____ _____. How about on Thursday, August 12?
W We only have a 2 o'clock flight on Thursday afternoon.
M That's better. I'll take it.
W _____ _____ _____ _____ _____?
M Economy class, please. And can I get a window seat?
W Sure.

08 부탁한 일 파악

대화를 듣고, 여자가 남자에게 부탁한 일로 가장 적절한 것을 고르시오.

① 뮤지컬 관람하기
② 오디션 알아봐 주기
③ 상대역 연기해 주기
④ 감독에게 전화해 주기
⑤ 연습 장면 녹화해 주기

W Dad, I've _____ _____ _____ _____.
M Tell me. What is it?
W Do you remember the musical that I auditioned for last month?
M Yeah. Unfortunately, you _____ _____ _____.
W Right. But I got a phone call from the director and he _____ _____ _____ _____ _____.
M Congratulations! _____ _____ _____ I can help you with?
W Actually, there is. It would be really great if you could record me practicing.   정답 단서
M No problem.

09 목적 파악

대화를 듣고, 남자가 여자에게 전화한 목적으로 가장 적절한 것을 고르시오.

① 분실물을 찾기 위해
② 꽃다발을 주문하기 위해
③ 꽃의 품질에 대해 항의하기 위해
④ 화분 관리 방법을 문의하기 위해
⑤ 카드 결제가 가능한지 묻기 위해

Sound Clear ☆ **dropped it**
앞 단어의 끝 자음과 뒤 단어의 모음이 만나 연음되어 [드랍딧]으로 발음된다.

(*Telephone rings.*)
W Jamie's Flower Shop. May I help you?
M Hi. I bought _____ _____ _____ this morning at your store. Do you remember me?
W Sure. Is there any problem?
M No. But I think I accidently dropped _____ _____ _____ _____ _____ at your store.
W Oh, really? Where do you think you dropped it? ☆
M _____ _____ _____ _____ the front door near the stack of flowerpots? It's blue with my name, Jonathan White on it.
W Yes, I found it.
M Thank you so much. _____ _____ _____ this evening to get it.

10 언급되지 않은 것 찾기 �֎

대화를 듣고, 식당에 관해 언급되지 않은 것을 고르시오.

① 음식의 맛   ② 서비스   ③ 음식의 가격
④ 실내 장식   ⑤ 집과의 거리

W Sam, how was your pasta?
M Great. All the food was really good. How about your dish, Mom?
W _____ _____ _____, and I think the service is great, too.
M That's true. I like the quiet atmosphere and the simple interior.
W Yeah, the white walls and _____ _____ _____.
M I'd like to come back again soon. It's extremely _____ _____ _____ _____.
W Yeah, it's just a five-minute walk from the house.

11 이유 파악

대화를 듣고, 여자가 최고의 휴가를 보내지 못한 이유로 가장 적절한 것을 고르시오.

① 시간이 부족해서
② 식중독에 걸려서
③ 전화기를 잃어버려서
④ 관광 명소가 부족해서
⑤ 사람들이 불친절해서

W Hi, Brian. You look great!
M Thanks. _____ _____ _____? You went to Europe, right?
W Yeah, it was good. But I didn't have _____ _____ _____ there.
M Why not? Didn't you like the cities in Europe?
W I liked them. I _____ _____ _____ _____ and interesting markets. And the people were kind there.
M Then what was the problem?
W _____ _____ _____ _____ and had to go to the emergency room because of that.
M Oh, I'm sorry to hear that.

12 특정 정보 파악

대화를 듣고, 여자가 남자에게 충고한 내용으로 가장 적절한 것을 고르시오.

① 병원 진료 받기
② 규칙적으로 운동하기
③ 실내 환기 자주 하기
④ 황사 전용 마스크 구입하기
⑤ 공기 질이 안 좋을 때 밖에서 운동하지 않기

Sound Clear ☆ **hardly**
미국식은 [r]을 정확히 발음하여 [할들리]로. 영국식은 [r]을 거의 발음하지 않아서 [하-들리]로 발음된다.

M It feels like the yellow dust season is _____ _____ _____ _____ _____.
W I agree. We hardly have any days with clear skies.
M I _____ _____ _____ _____ and itchy eyes all the time.
W That's too bad. Do you wear a mask when you go out?
M Yes. I _____ _____ _____ _____ when I go out.
W And you should not exercise outside when the air quality is bad. 정답 단서
M I know, but I really enjoy playing soccer with my friends in my free time.
W But it's really _____ _____ _____ _____.

13 할 일 파악

대화를 듣고, 두 사람이 대화 직후에 할 일로 가장 적절한 것을 고르시오.

① 지갑 사러 가기
② 기차표 예매하기
③ 케이크 찾아오기
④ 할머니 모시러 가기
⑤ 경찰서에 지갑 가져다주기

W Look! There's something on the street.
M _____ _____ _____. Somebody must have lost it.
W We should take this to the police station.
M Do you know 함정 _____ _____ _____ _____ _____?
W Yes, there is one next to Seoul Station.
M Then _____ _____ _____ _____ first at the station, and then take the wallet to the police station.
W That's a good idea. Grandma _____ _____ _____ _____ us.
M We should hurry. Let's go.

14 특정 정보 파악

대화를 듣고, 남자의 결혼기념일을 고르시오.

① 5월 7일　② 5월 10일　③ 5월 12일
④ 5월 14일　⑤ 5월 15일

W There are ＿＿＿＿ ＿＿＿＿ ＿＿＿＿ on your calendar!
M Yes, right. There are a lot of family events in May.
W I know it's Children's Day on May 5. ＿＿＿＿ ＿＿＿＿ ＿＿＿＿ a week after that?
M That's my mother's birthday.
W I see. You've also got the date circled ＿＿＿＿ ＿＿＿＿ ＿＿＿＿ ＿＿＿＿.
M That's my wedding anniversary!
W You do have ＿＿＿＿ ＿＿＿＿ ＿＿＿＿ ＿＿＿＿ ＿＿＿＿ in May!
M Yeah, it's a really busy month for me.

15 숫자 정보 파악 ✳

대화를 듣고, 두 사람이 만나기로 한 시각을 고르시오.

① 4:20 p.m.　　② 4:30 p.m.
③ 4:50 p.m.　　④ 5:00 p.m.
⑤ 5:10 p.m.

(*Cellphone rings.*)
M Hi, Jennifer. What's up?
W I just called to ＿＿＿＿ ＿＿＿＿ ＿＿＿＿ ＿＿＿＿ ＿＿＿＿. It's our church's Christmas party.
M That sounds great. When is it?
W It's this Friday. ＿＿＿＿ ＿＿＿＿ ＿＿＿＿ ＿＿＿＿ at 5:00. 한정
Can you come?
M Sure, I'd love to. All our classes are finished at 4:30. Let's meet 20 minutes ＿＿＿＿ ＿＿＿＿ ＿＿＿＿ ＿＿＿＿. 한정
W Then let's make it ten to five in front of the church.
M Okay. See you then. 정답 단서

16 할 일 파악

대화를 듣고, 여자가 학생회장 출마를 위해 가장 먼저 할 일을 고르시오.

① 자기소개서 쓰기
② 후보 연설문 쓰기
③ 후보 연설 연습하기
④ 부모님께 허락 받기
⑤ 선거 운동원 모집하기

Sound Clear ☆ **campaign**
g가 묵음이라서 [캠페인]으로 발음된다.

W Hello, Mr. Smith. Can I ask you something?
M Sure, Jane. What is it?
W I'm thinking about ＿＿＿＿ ＿＿＿＿ ＿＿＿＿ ＿＿＿＿, but I don't know what I should do.
M Oh, that's great! Why do you want to be student president?
W I want to help the students ＿＿＿＿ ＿＿＿＿ ＿＿＿＿ ＿＿＿＿.
M Well, think about how you can really listen to them, and ＿＿＿＿ ＿＿＿＿ ＿＿＿＿ ＿＿＿＿ to help them.
W I got it. That could be my ☆ campaign speech.
M That's right. But ＿＿＿＿ ＿＿＿＿ ＿＿＿＿, you must submit a letter of self-introduction. 정답 단서
W Oh, then ＿＿＿＿ ＿＿＿＿ ＿＿＿＿ ＿＿＿＿ that first. Thank you so much.

17 마지막 말에 대한 응답 찾기

대화를 듣고, 여자의 마지막 말에 대한 남자의 응답으로 가장 적절한 것을 고르시오.

Man: _____

① I went to the movies last night.
② I once met them at a restaurant.
③ I've watched the drama many times.
④ All of the characters are great. I like them all.
⑤ I hope I can travel around the world like the main character.

M Are you _____ _____ _____, *Summer Story*?
W Yes, the story is really interesting, isn't it?
M I agree with you. I've heard that the drama is _____ _____ _____ _____ _____.
W Really? That's why the drama is _____ _____. I can't wait to see the next episode.
M _____ _____ _____ that drama.
W You're right. What do you think about the actors and actresses?
M <u>All of the characters are great. I like them all.</u>

---

18 마지막 말에 대한 응답 찾기

대화를 듣고, 남자의 마지막 말에 대한 여자의 응답으로 가장 적절한 것을 고르시오.

Woman: _____

① The bridge is under construction.
② How can I get to the bus station?
③ It's a long distance for them to walk.
④ I'm afraid not. It's the same for children.
⑤ Are there any seats available on the bus?

W Welcome to Safari World. Can I help you?
M Yes, please. I'd like to buy tickets. _____ _____ _____ _____ _____.
W How old are your children?
M One is 7 years old, and _____ _____ is 5 years old.
W It's $10 for an adult and $5 for children under 12.
M And how much is the tour bus?
W It's $4 _____ _____ _____.
M Can I _____ _____ _____ for the children?
W <u>I'm afraid not. It's the same for children.</u>

---

19 마지막 말에 대한 응답 찾기

대화를 듣고, 여자의 마지막 말에 대한 남자의 응답으로 가장 적절한 것을 고르시오.

Man: _____

① The total is $50.
② I like cheese pizza more.
③ Yes, I want the pizza to go.
④ Extra toppings are free today.
⑤ It will take about half an hour.

M John's Pizza Delivery. How may I help you?
W Hi. I want a large pepperoni pizza and a meatball spaghetti.
M Okay. Do you _____ _____ _____?
W Yes, I want extra cheese and olives.
M I got it. _____ _____ _____?
W A bottle of coke, please. How long will it take?
M <u>It will take about half an hour.</u>

---

20 상황에 적절한 말 찾기

다음 상황 설명을 듣고, Cindy가 Sam에게 할 말로 가장 적절한 것을 고르시오.

Cindy: Sam, _____

① when did you get your cellphone?
② do you want me to take a picture?
③ this is the best show I've ever seen.
④ we're not supposed to use cellphones during the show.
⑤ can I send a text message using your phone?

M Cindy and Sam are sitting in the theater to watch a musical. As the musical starts, _____ _____ _____ _____ _____ and the curtains open. In the middle of the show, Cindy notices that Sam _____ _____ _____ _____ _____ to send text messages. Cindy knows that they're not allowed to use cellphones during the performance. She thinks that she should tell him to _____ _____ _____ _____. In this situation, what would Cindy most likely say to him?
Cindy <u>Sam, we're not supposed to use cellphones during the show.</u>

Review Test

Word Check 영어는 우리말로, 우리말은 영어로 써 보기

01 explore _____

02 translate _____

03 supervise _____

04 fantastic _____

05 overdue _____

06 damage _____

07 encounter _____

08 investigation _____

09 digestive medicine _____

10 tropic zone _____

11 close at hand _____

12 take part in _____

13 구조 _____

14 자연 _____

15 동화 _____

16 장식하다 _____

17 염색하다 _____

18 의미 있는 _____

19 기한, 마감 일자 _____

20 필요하다, 요구하다 _____

21 주민, 거주자 _____

22 연체료 _____

23 취향 _____

24 역할 _____

Expression Check 알맞은 표현을 넣어 문장 완성하기

25 I dropped it _____ _____. 제가 실수로 그것을 떨어뜨렸어요.

26 You _____ _____ _____ home earlier. 넌 좀 더 일찍 집을 나섰어야 했어.

27 I have to do something to get _____ _____. 저는 몸매를 유지하기 위해서 뭔가를 해야 해요.

28 He _____ _____ on April 2, 1805, in Odense, Denmark.
그는 1805년 4월 2일에 덴마크의 오덴세에서 태어났습니다.

29 They are trained in _____ _____ _____ life-saving skills including first aid.
그들은 응급 처치를 포함한 다양한 인명 구조 기술 훈련을 받습니다.

30 Every club needs a teacher to be _____ _____ _____ it.
모든 동아리에는 동아리를 담당할 교사가 필요하다.

Answers p.105

Word Check 영어는 우리말로, 우리말은 영어로 써 보기

01	distance		13	통로
02	realistic		14	실수로, 잘못하여
03	atmosphere		15	실내 장식
04	be into		16	주인공
05	gorgeous		17	열두 개의
06	itchy		18	공연
07	row		19	자기소개
08	gratitude		20	초대하다
09	food poisoning		21	창가석
10	occasion		22	응급실
11	sore		23	~을 (차에) 태우러 가다
12	be in trouble		24	공사 중인

Expression Check 알맞은 표현을 넣어 문장 완성하기

25 I'll _____ _____ this evening to get it. 제가 오늘 저녁에 그것을 가지러 들를게요.

26 Can you _____ _____ this form? 이 양식을 작성해 주시겠어요?

27 Let's make it _____ to _____ in front of the church. 교회 앞에서 5시 10분 전에 만나자.

28 The drama _____ _____ _____ a real story. 그 드라마는 실제 이야기를 바탕으로 한다.

29 I'm thinking about _____ _____ student president.
저는 학생회장에 출마하는 것에 대해 생각 중이에요.

30 _____ _____ _____ this sale, you can use any coupons you have.
이 할인 행사 이외에도, 여러분이 가지고 계신 어떤 쿠폰도 사용하실 수 있습니다.

PART

3

고난도
모의고사
19-20회

1.0배속

1.2배속

01 대화를 듣고, 남자가 완성한 표지를 고르시오.

①
②
③

④
⑤

02 대화를 듣고, 여자가 남자에게 부탁한 일로 가장 적절한 것을 고르시오.

① 책 반납하기　　② 사진 인화하기
③ 음악 담당하기　　④ 소장품 빌려주기
⑤ 전시품 배치하기

03 다음 그림의 상황에 가장 적절한 대화를 고르시오.

①　　②　　③　　④　　⑤

04 대화를 듣고, 남자가 식당을 예약한 요일과 시각을 고르시오.

① Saturday, 6 p.m.　　② Saturday, 8 p.m.
③ Sunday, 6 p.m.　　④ Sunday, 7 p.m.
⑤ Sunday, 8 p.m.

05 대화를 듣고, 축제에 관해 언급되지 않은 것을 고르시오.

① 축제 내용　　② 개최 날짜　　③ 개최 장소
④ 주최 기관　　⑤ 할인 여부

06 대화를 듣고, 여자가 남자에게 부탁한 일로 가장 적절한 것을 고르시오.

① 함께 쇼핑하기
② 친구 마중 나가기
③ 고궁 안내해 주기
④ 식당 위치 알려 주기
⑤ 불고기 조리법 알려 주기

07 다음을 듣고, 두 사람의 대화가 어색한 것을 고르시오.

①　　　②　　　③　　　④　　　⑤

08 다음을 듣고, 지구를 위해 할 수 있는 일로 언급되지 않은 것을 고르시오.

① 나무 심기
② 자전거 타기
③ 종이컵 사용하지 않기
④ 장바구니 가지고 다니기
⑤ 버려지는 물의 양 줄이기

09 다음을 듣고, 방송의 목적으로 가장 적절한 것을 고르시오.

① 소방 훈련 일정을 공지하려고
② 벼룩시장 개최 소식을 알리려고
③ 체육 대회가 연기되었음을 알리려고
④ 체육 대회 종목을 공지하려고
⑤ 미세 먼지의 유해성을 설명하려고

10 대화를 듣고, 남자가 지불할 금액을 고르시오.

① $1　② $2　③ $27　④ $28　⑤ $29

11 대화를 듣고, 남자가 할 일로 가장 적절한 것을 고르시오.

① 악기 배우기　　　② 오디션 연습하기
③ 엄마에게 전화하기　④ 밴드 신청서 제출하기
⑤ 공부 계획서 작성하기

12 대화를 듣고, 두 사람이 대화하고 있는 장소로 가장 적절한 곳을 고르시오.

① 교회   ② 서점   ③ 분실물 보관소
④ 미술관   ⑤ 관광 안내소

13 다음 표를 보면서 대화를 듣고, 두 사람이 선택할 수업을 고르시오.

	Course	Time	Level	Instructor
①	5-week	1 hour	Advanced	Chinese
②	5-week	3 hours	Intermediate	Korean
③	5-week	3 hours	Advanced	Korean
④	10-week	1 hour	Intermediate	Chinese
⑤	10-week	3 hours	Advanced	Chinese

14 다음을 듣고, 무엇에 관한 설명인지 고르시오.

① 부츠   ② 비옷   ③ 우산
④ 고글   ⑤ 목도리

15 대화를 듣고, 여자가 대화 직후에 할 일로 가장 적절한 것을 고르시오.

① 외국인 인터뷰하기
② 한국에 관한 책 쓰기
③ 자신의 경험 이야기하기
④ 인터넷으로 자료 수집하기
⑤ 친구에게 남자의 전화번호 주기

16 대화를 듣고, 남자가 공항에 도착해야 할 시각을 고르시오.

① 7:00 a.m.   ② 7:30 a.m.   ③ 8:15 a.m.
④ 8:30 a.m.   ⑤ 10:40 a.m.

17 대화를 듣고, 남자의 마지막 말에 대한 여자의 응답으로 가장 적절한 것을 고르시오.

Woman: _____

① Tell me the purpose of your visit.
② I once left my bag in a museum.
③ It will be on your left. You can't miss it.
④ You should have brought a different kind of map.
⑤ It'll be so much fun to visit the Modern Art Museum.

18 대화를 듣고, 여자의 마지막 말에 대한 남자의 응답으로 가장 적절한 것을 고르시오.

Man: _____

① Ask your teachers for help.
② Make sure that it's not your fault.
③ Yes. You can expect a better result than last year.
④ Of course. Whatever you decide, I'm always with you.
⑤ Sure. Try to think "I can and will do better than this."

19 대화를 듣고, 남자의 마지막 말에 대한 여자의 응답으로 가장 적절한 것을 고르시오.

Woman: _____

① Great! Let's take a short break.
② That's a relief. Thank you so much.
③ It's more expensive than I expected.
④ You'd better book the tickets online.
⑤ Hurry up! We don't have enough time.

20 다음 상황 설명을 듣고, Suji가 판매 직원에게 할 말로 가장 적절한 것을 고르시오.

Suji: Excuse me. _____

① Where is the fitting room?
② Can I get a discount on this dress?
③ Do you have this dress in a bigger size?
④ Does this dress come in different colors?
⑤ Can you recommend shoes that will go well with this dress?

받아쓰기용

01 그림 정보 파악

대화를 듣고, 남자가 완성한 표지를 고르시오.

① School News
② School News
③ School News
④ School News
⑤ School News

M Sally, I need your help with the cover design of the school magazine.

W Why don't you put our school logo _____ _____ _____ _____ _____ _____ ?

M But I'm afraid it might look too simple.

W Then you can put students' photo in the middle.

M That sounds like a great idea.

W Then you'd better _____ _____ _____ _____ to the top right-hand corner.

M You're right. Where should I put the title?

W I think _____ _____ _____ _____ _____ .

M I agree. Thank you for your help.

02 부탁한 일 파악

대화를 듣고, 여자가 남자에게 부탁한 일로 가장 적절한 것을 고르시오.

① 책 반납하기
② 사진 인화하기
③ 음악 담당하기
④ 소장품 빌려주기
⑤ 전시품 배치하기

Sound Clear ☆ exhibition
h가 묵음이라서 [엑시비션]으로 발음된다.

W Hi, Daniel. Are you going to be busy later today?

M I don't _____ _____ _____ _____ today. Why do you ask?

W I need your help. Do you know about our club's photo ☆exhibition?

M Yes. Do you need help in _____ _____ _____ ?

W Actually, Jina is already going to help with that. What I need help with is the music.

M Music? Oh, _____ _____ _____ _____ to choose from. You can borrow whatever you need.

W I have a bigger favor than that. Can you be in charge of the music during the exhibition? 정답 단서

M Sure. I just need to return these books to the library then _____ _____ _____ _____ . 한정

W Thank you so much.

03 그림의 상황에 적절한 대화 찾기

다음 그림의 상황에 가장 적절한 대화를 고르시오.

① ② ③ ④ ⑤

04 숫자 정보 파악

대화를 듣고, 남자가 식당을 예약한 요일과 시각을 고르시오.

① Saturday, 6 p.m. ② Saturday, 8 p.m.
③ Sunday, 6 p.m. ④ Sunday, 7 p.m.
⑤ Sunday, 8 p.m.

05 언급되지 않은 것 찾기

대화를 듣고, 축제에 관해 언급되지 <u>않은</u> 것을 고르시오.

① 축제 내용 ② 개최 날짜 ③ 개최 장소
④ 주최 기관 ⑤ 할인 여부

---

① W How much is this swimming cap?

M It's for rent, _____ _____ _____. It's $3 for the day.

② W What's your secret to _____ _____ _____?

M I swim every day so that I can stay healthy.

③ W What if I _____ _____ _____ _____ _____?

M Don't worry. A lifeguard will rescue you.

④ W The life vest will _____ _____ _____.

M Oh, no. _____ _____ _____ _____ _____.

⑤ W Sorry. You can't go in the pool unless you are wearing a cap.

M Oh, I didn't know that.

(*Telephone rings.*)

W Shogun Restaurant. May I help you?

M Hi. I'd like to make a reservation for this Saturday evening.

W I'm sorry, sir, but _____ _____ _____ _____ _____ _____ on Saturday evening.

M Oh, really? What about on Sunday?

W On Sunday, we _____ _____ _____ _____ _____ at 6 p.m. and at 8 p.m.

M Then I'll book a table at 6 p.m.

W Okay. How many people is the reservation for?

M There will be _____ _____ _____.

W All right. May I _____ _____ _____, please?

M My name is Jason Foster.

W John, what are you looking at?

M Hi, Amy. _____ _____ _____ _____ _____ for the World Food Festival.

W The World Food Festival? Is there really food from around the world?

M Yes, visitors can taste over _____ _____ _____ _____ _____ _____ from all around the world.

W Wow, that sounds very interesting! When is it?

M It's May 28 at the World Culture Center.

W _____ _____ _____ _____?

M Of course. Since we are students, we can get a 40% discount.

W That's cool. I'd like to _____ _____ _____.

06 부탁한 일 파악

대화를 듣고, 여자가 남자에게 부탁한 일로 가장 적절한 것을 고르시오.

① 함께 쇼핑하기
② 친구 마중 나가기
③ 고궁 안내해 주기
④ 식당 위치 알려 주기
⑤ 불고기 조리법 알려 주기

W Sejin, I need your help.
M What is it?
W My friend Julia is coming to Korea next week. Can you _____ _____ _____ _____ where I can take her?
M Is there anything about Korea that she is particularly interested in?
W She did say that she likes Korean royal palaces.
M Why don't you take her to Changdeokgung? It's _____ _____ _____ _____ in Korea.
W Sounds good. Umm, are there any Korean restaurants near the palace that serve *bulgogi*?
M Yeah, there's one _____ _____ _____ _____.
W Wow. Please let me know the location of the restaurant.
M Okay. _____ _____ _____ _____ in a text message.

07 어색한 대화 찾기

다음을 듣고, 두 사람의 대화가 <u>어색한</u> 것을 고르시오.

①   ②   ③   ④   ⑤

① M Do you know how long it takes to get there?
  W Well, _____ _____ _____ how you go there.
② M Why don't we go shopping this Saturday?
  W Sorry. I _____ _____ _____ _____.
③ M Do you have any special plans for this coming holiday?
  W Yeah, I'm planning to go camping with friends.
④ M When did you come back from your trip to Europe?
  W Last Friday. I'm sorry. I _____ _____ _____ _____ _____ I was back.
⑤ M The printer is broken again. How will I print the report?
  W _____ _____ _____ _____ _____ what kind of paper you print the report on.

08 언급되지 않은 것 찾기

다음을 듣고, 지구를 위해 할 수 있는 일로 언급되지 <u>않은</u> 것을 고르시오.

① 나무 심기
② 자전거 타기
③ 종이컵 사용하지 않기
④ 장바구니 가지고 다니기
⑤ 버려지는 물의 양 줄이기

> **Sound Clear** ☆ **instead of**
> 앞 단어의 끝 자음과 뒤 단어의 모음이 만나 연음되어 [인스테더브]로 발음된다.

W What is special about April 22? It is Earth Day. Our Earth is _____ _____ _____, but many people don't care enough about the environment. Here are several things we can do to _____ _____ _____. First, we can ride a bike or walk to school instead of taking a car. We can also stop using paper cups and use something reusable instead. When we go shopping, we can _____ _____ _____ _____ _____. Finally, by using less water, we can _____ _____.

09 목적 파악 ✜

다음을 듣고, 방송의 목적으로 가장 적절한 것을 고르시오.

① 소방 훈련 일정을 공지하려고
② 벼룩시장 개최 소식을 알리려고
③ 체육 대회가 연기되었음을 알리려고
④ 체육 대회 종목을 공지하려고
⑤ 미세 먼지의 유해성을 설명하려고

M Good afternoon, everyone. This is an announcement _____ _____ _____ _____ _____. This year's sports day was going to be held this Friday, but there is a change in the schedule. Because of concern about the amount of fine dust _____ _____ _____, we have decided to reschedule the event for your health. We are expecting the air quality _____ _____ _____ next week, so we will inform you of the rescheduled date as soon as possible. Please be _____ _____ _____ _____ _____ this Friday. Thank you.

10 숫자 정보 파악

대화를 듣고, 남자가 지불할 금액을 고르시오.

① $1　　② $2　　③ $27
④ $28　　⑤ $29

W Good afternoon. May I help you?
M I bought these pants here last week. _____ _____ _____ _____ _____ for a bigger pair.
W Sorry, but I can't seem to find a bigger size in the same style.
M Then can I _____ _____ _____?
W Sure. You can get a full refund of $27. 한정
M Hmm... do you have _____ _____ _____ _____ in a size 28?
W Sure. How about this pair? I think they will _____ _____ _____ _____.
M They are the right size. I'll take them.
W They are $29 and the pants you are returning are $27. You just 한정 need to _____ _____ _____.

11 할 일 파악

대화를 듣고, 남자가 할 일로 가장 적절한 것을 고르시오.

① 악기 배우기
② 오디션 연습하기
③ 엄마에게 전화하기
④ 밴드 신청서 제출하기
⑤ 공부 계획서 작성하기

W James, you look so down. What's wrong?
M Well, my mom _____ _____ _____ _____ _____ the music band.
W Really? That's too bad.
M Yeah. You know how much I want to join it.
W Of course. _____ _____ _____ _____ _____?
M She keeps saying that I _____ _____ _____ _____ _____ in the band and study at the same time.
W Then why don't you make a study plan and show it to her? That would _____ _____ _____ _____. 정답 단서
M That's a good idea! I'll make one right away.

12 장소 추론

대화를 듣고, 두 사람이 대화하고 있는 장소로 가장 적절한 곳을 고르시오.

① 교회
② 서점
③ 분실물 보관소
④ 미술관
⑤ 관광 안내소

W   Excuse me. Can I _____ _____ _____ _____ _____ _____ ?

M   Sure. Which language would like to have?

W   Korean, please.

M   Here you are. _____ _____ _____ _____ _____ ?

W   Can you recommend some places to visit around here?

M   Sure. _____ _____ _____ _____ the Modern Art Museum. Let me show you on the map. It's right here next to this church.

W   Great! That looks easy to get to.

M   _____ _____ _____ _____ _____ for this area, just call this center.

W   Thank you so much.

13 도표 정보 파악

다음 표를 보면서 대화를 듣고, 두 사람이 선택할 수업을 고르시오.

	Course	Time	Level	Instructor
①	5-week	1 hour	Advanced	Chinese
②	5-week	3 hours	Intermediate	Korean
③	5-week	3 hours	Advanced	Korean
④	10-week	1 hour	Intermediate	Chinese
⑤	10-week	3 hours	Advanced	Chinese

Sound Clear ☆ **this summer**
동일한 발음의 자음이 연이어 나오면 앞 자음 소리가 탈락하여 [디써머]로 발음된다.

M   Jimin, _____ _____ _____ _____ a Chinese course for this summer?

W   No, not yet. Let's take one together. Which one do you think we should take?

M   Well, we _____ _____ _____ : a 5-week course or a 10-week course.

W   I prefer the shorter one. I don't want to _____ _____ 정답 단서 _____ _____ _____ .

M   Okay. But then let's take the course that is 3 hours a day. One hour _____ _____ _____ . 정답 단서

W   I agree. It's an intermediate level like last winter's course, right? 정답 단서

M   Yes. And the class will be delivered by a Korean instructor. 정답 단서

W   Good. Do you know _____ _____ _____ ?

M   From next Monday.

14 화제 파악

다음을 듣고, 무엇에 관한 설명인지 고르시오.

① 부츠   ② 비옷   ③ 우산
④ 고글   ⑤ 목도리

M This is something you carry in your hand or in your bag. You need this _____ _____ _____ _____ because it keeps your hair and clothes from getting wet. You probably carry this on a cloudy day as well _____ _____ _____ _____ _____. But even on a very bright day, you can also use this to _____ _____ _____ _____ _____ _____. You shouldn't open this indoors. In Western culture, there is a superstition that says opening this indoors _____ _____ _____ _____.

15 할 일 파악

대화를 듣고, 여자가 대화 직후에 할 일로 가장 적절한 것을 고르시오.

① 외국인 인터뷰하기
② 한국에 관한 책 쓰기
③ 자신의 경험 이야기하기
④ 인터넷으로 자료 수집하기
⑤ 친구에게 남자의 전화번호 주기

W Hey, Mike. Do you have a minute?
M Of course. What's up, Soyoung?
W One of my friends is writing a book about Korea. She's looking for some foreigners _____ _____ _____ _____ _____ in Korea.
M Really? That's interesting.
W I think _____ _____ _____ _____ _____ for it. Can you tell her about your experiences?
M Well, I don't know _____ _____ _____ _____ _____ _____.
W Oh, you don't have to worry about anything. All you need to do is just to tell her about your everyday life in Korea.
M Okay, _____ _____ _____ _____.
W Thank you. I'll give her your phone number.

정답 단서

16 숫자 정보 파악

대화를 듣고, 남자가 공항에 도착해야 할 시각을 고르시오.

① 7:00 a.m.   ② 7:30 a.m.
③ 8:15 a.m.   ④ 8:30 a.m.
⑤ 10:40 a.m.

(*Telephone rings.*)
M Good morning. I'd like to book a flight to Chicago.
W _____ _____ _____ _____ _____, please?
M I would like to travel on May 15 in the morning.
W Yes, sir. I'll check the flight schedule for you. _____ _____ _____, please?
M Sure.
W _____ _____ _____ _____ _____ leaving Incheon at 10:40 a.m.
M What time does it arrive in Chicago?
W It arrives at 8:30 a.m. _____ _____.
M That sounds good. What time should I _____ _____ _____ _____?
W You have to be at the terminal by 7:00 a.m. at the latest.

정답 단서

17 마지막 말에 대한 응답 찾기

대화를 듣고, 남자의 마지막 말에 대한 여자의 응답으로 가장 적절한 것을 고르시오.

Woman: ______________________

① Tell me the purpose of your visit.
② I once left my bag in a museum.
③ It will be on your left. You can't miss it.
④ You should have brought a different kind of map.
⑤ It'll be so much fun to visit the Modern Art Museum.

W Excuse me. Do you need any help? You look like you're lost.
M Yes. ________ ________ ________ ________ ________ for half an hour, but I still can't find the museum.
W Really? What museum do you want to go to?
M The History Museum. It says it's on Redwood Street ________ ________ ________.
W Oh, that one is the Modern Art Museum. The History Museum is on Oak Street.
M Then do you know ________ ________ ________ ________ ________?
W Go straight up Pine Street for two blocks and then ________ ________ ________ ________ ________.
M Okay. Is it on my left or right?
W It will be on your left. You can't miss it.

18 마지막 말에 대한 응답 찾기

대화를 듣고, 여자의 마지막 말에 대한 남자의 응답으로 가장 적절한 것을 고르시오.

Man: ______________________

① Ask your teachers for help.
② Make sure that it's not your fault.
③ Yes. You can expect a better result than last year.
④ Of course. Whatever you decide, I'm always with you.
⑤ Sure. Try to think "I can and will do better than this."

Sound Clear☆ **exam**
ex 뒤에 모음이 오면 주로 [igz]로 소리 나서 [이그잼]으로 발음된다.

M Jina, how was your exam☆ today?
W It was ________ ________ ________ ________.
M Do you think you will ________ ________ ________ ________?
W Dad, I think I tried hard. But the result will not be good.
M Oh, that's too bad. But ________ ________ ________ ________ ________ than the result.
W But ________ ________ ________ ________ ________ to study because I really tried hard this time.
M Come on. Hang in there. You just need to ________ ________ ________ ________.
W Can I do well?
M Sure. Try to think "I can and will do better than this."

19 마지막 말에 대한 응답 찾기

대화를 듣고, 남자의 마지막 말에 대한 여자의 응답으로 가장 적절한 것을 고르시오.

Woman: _____

① Great! Let's take a short break.
② That's a relief. Thank you so much.
③ It's more expensive than I expected.
④ You'd better book the tickets online.
⑤ Hurry up! We don't have enough time.

Sound Clear ☆ **next train**
동일한 [t] 발음이 연이어 나오고 [t]와 [r]이 연달아 나와서 [넥스츄레인]로 발음된다.

W Excuse me. Could you help me?
M Sure, what can I do for you?
W I have just _____ _____ _____ back to London Station. I don't know what to do.
M I'm sorry to hear that. Could you _____ _____ _____ _____ _____?
W Here you are.
M The next train to London Station will arrive in 30 minutes and you can _____ _____ _____.
W That's great. Do I need to _____ _____ _____?
M No. You are allowed to _____ _____ _____ to any later train leaving within 2 hours.
W That's a relief. Thank you so much.

20 상황에 적절한 말 찾기

다음 상황 설명을 듣고, Suji가 판매 직원에게 할 말로 가장 적절한 것을 고르시오.

Suji: Excuse me. _____

① Where is the fitting room?
② Can I get a discount on this dress?
③ Do you have this dress in a bigger size?
④ Does this dress come in different colors?
⑤ Can you recommend shoes that will go well with this dress?

W Suji is _____ _____ _____ _____ _____ at a department store. She finally finds a cute pink dress she likes. She likes its style because it is not too long and not too short. She can also save money _____ _____ _____ _____. But when she tries it on in the fitting room, she finds that the dress is _____ _____ _____. She wants to try on another size, but _____ _____ _____ 정답 단서. In this situation, what would Suji say to the salesperson?
Suji Excuse me. Do you have this dress in a bigger size?

01 대화를 듣고, 남자의 과학 보고서가 있는 곳을 고르시오.

02 대화를 듣고, 남자가 Lisa에게 전화하려는 이유를 고르시오.

① 메뉴를 정하려고
② 영화를 정하려고
③ 영화표를 예매하려고
④ 약속 시간을 확인하려고
⑤ 약속 장소를 확인하려고

03 다음 그림의 상황에 가장 적절한 대화를 고르시오.

①   ②   ③   ④   ⑤

04 대화를 듣고, 여자가 남자에게 전화한 목적으로 가장 적절한 것을 고르시오.

① 신간을 홍보하려고
② 대출 기간을 연장하려고
③ 도서관에 관해 불평하려고
④ 도서관 프로그램을 문의하려고
⑤ 도서 대출 가능 여부를 물어보려고

05 다음을 듣고, 모아이 상에 관해 언급되지 않은 것을 고르시오.

① 위치
② 제작 이유
③ 조각상의 수
④ 머리와 몸통의 비율
⑤ 평균 높이

06 다음을 듣고, 방송의 내용과 일치하지 않는 것을 고르시오.

① 가방은 두 가지 색상으로 나온다.
② 가방에는 방수 기능이 있다.
③ 가방 안쪽에는 주머니가 두 개 있다.
④ 평소 가격보다 30달러 저렴하게 판매한다.
⑤ 앱으로 주문하면 추가 할인을 받을 수 있다.

07 다음을 듣고, 두 사람의 대화가 어색한 것을 고르시오.

①   ②   ③   ④   ⑤

08 대화를 듣고, 남자가 여자에게 부탁한 일로 가장 적절한 것을 고르시오.

① 데이트하기
② 식당 예약하기
③ 경찰에 신고하기
④ 식당 전화번호 알려 주기
⑤ 꽃 박람회 가는 방법 알려 주기

09 대화를 듣고, 두 사람이 대화하는 장소로 가장 적절한 곳을 고르시오.

① 세관
② 호텔
③ 여행사
④ 비행기 안
⑤ 입국 심사대

10 대화를 듣고, 남자가 채용되면 주급으로 받을 금액을 고르시오.

① $200
② $240
③ $250
④ $280
⑤ $300

11 다음 표를 보면서 대화를 듣고, 여자가 신청할 수업을 고르시오.

	Class	Instructor	Day / Time
①	Tennis	Jonathan	Sat. (2 hours)
②	Tennis	Natalia	Sun. (2 hours)
③	Tennis	Natalia	Fri. (1 hour)
④	Swimming	Natalia	Sat. (2 hours)
⑤	Swimming	Jonathan	Fri. (1 hour)

12 대화를 듣고, ST Ski Resort에 관해 언급되지 <u>않은</u> 것을 고르시오.

① 서울에서 리조트까지의 소요 시간
② 슬로프 개수
③ 평균 대기 시간
④ 스키 강습 유무
⑤ 방문객 수 제한 범위

13 대화를 듣고, 여자가 할 일로 가장 적절한 것을 고르시오.

① 식당 예약하기　　　② 선물 포장하기
③ 케이크 주문하기　　④ 생일 카드 구입하기
⑤ 조부모님께 연락하기

14 다음을 듣고, 무엇에 관한 설명인지 고르시오.

① 논문　　　② 사진집　　　③ 교과서
④ 영어 사전　　⑤ 백과사전

15 대화를 듣고, 여자가 대화 직후에 할 일로 가장 적절한 것을 고르시오.

① 채소 씻기　　　② 음식 주문하기
③ 감자 사러 가기　④ 식당 예약하기
⑤ 조리법 찾아보기

16 대화를 듣고, 남자가 신발을 사러 갈 날짜를 고르시오.

① July 5　　② July 6　　③ July 7
④ July 9　　⑤ July 10

17 대화를 듣고, 여자의 마지막 말에 대한 남자의 응답으로 가장 적절한 것을 고르시오.

Man: _____

① You had better lose some weight.
② I'm really worried about my health.
③ You should get a physical checkup.
④ Then what about eating healthier foods?
⑤ You shouldn't eat anything prior to the checkup.

18 대화를 듣고, 남자의 마지막 말에 대한 여자의 응답으로 가장 적절한 것을 고르시오.

Woman: _____

① You must have read it several times.
② It's kind of you to lend me the book.
③ Did you get any messages while I was out?
④ You should. I think this book is her best work ever.
⑤ Sure. First, you should think of why we should read books.

19 대화를 듣고, 여자의 마지막 말에 대한 남자의 응답으로 가장 적절한 것을 고르시오.

Man: _____

① Get some sleep and you'll feel better.
② Exercising is better than taking a nap.
③ You should stay up late at night to study.
④ Try not to use your phone in bed at night.
⑤ You are not allowed to use your phone in class.

20 다음 상황 설명을 듣고, Jennifer가 Jiyoon에게 할 말로 가장 적절한 것을 고르시오.

Jennifer: Jiyoon, _____

① this food doesn't suit my taste.
② it's much better than I expected.
③ I'll treat you to lunch the next time.
④ I've always wanted to try this food.
⑤ I don't have any preference where we go.

Dictation **20**회

01 그림 정보 파악

대화를 듣고, 남자의 과학 보고서가 있는 곳을 고르시오.

M Mom, have you seen my science report? _____ _____ _____ _____ in my room.

W Well, have you checked on the tea table? I think I saw _____ _____ _____ _____ on it.

M Really? No, this paper is just a computer company's advertisement. Would you check the kitchen, Mom?

W I _____ _____ _____ _____, and it wasn't there.

M I checked on the couch and piano. But I still can't find it.

W Why don't you check under the couch? Maybe you _____ _____ after you read it.

M Okay. Let me see. You're right. I found it.

W That's good. Please _____ _____ _____ where you put your things the next time.

02 이유 파악

대화를 듣고, 남자가 Lisa에게 전화하려는 이유를 고르시오.

① 메뉴를 정하려고
② 영화를 정하려고
③ 영화표를 예매하려고
④ 약속 시간을 확인하려고
⑤ 약속 장소를 확인하려고

W Mike, shouldn't you be leaving for your lunch date with Lisa?

M _____ _____ _____ _____, Mom.

W Where are you going for lunch?

M We're meeting at Thai Table. It's just a ten-minute walk.

W Thai Table is a chain restaurant. Are you meeting at the one in our neighborhood?

M What? _____ _____ _____ Thai Table?

W Yeah, I heard there's a new Thai Table next to the theater downtown.

M Oh my! We are going to a movie after lunch. She might think that we are meeting at the restaurant _____ _____ _____.

W I'm afraid so. I think you'd better check with her.

M You're right. I'll _____ _____ _____ _____ now.

03 그림의 상황에 적절한 대화 찾기

다음 그림의 상황에 가장 적절한 대화를 고르시오.

① ② ③ ④ ⑤

① W The light bulb in my room just _____ _____.
   M I'll check if we have an extra light bulb in the closet.
② W Hold the chair tightly while I _____ _____ _____.
   M Don't worry. I'm holding it firmly.
③ W Would you put away those dangerous items?
   M Sure. Just sit down and relax _____ _____ _____ _____ _____.
④ W _____ _____ _____ _____ of this restaurant.
   M Yes. The classical music and the colorful lighting are good.
⑤ W Did you see the lightning last night?
   M Yes, _____ _____ _____ _____ _____.

04 목적 파악

대화를 듣고, 여자가 남자에게 전화한 목적으로 가장 적절한 것을 고르시오.

① 신간을 홍보하려고
② 대출 기간을 연장하려고
③ 도서관에 관해 불평하려고
④ 도서관 프로그램을 문의하려고
⑤ 도서 대출 가능 여부를 물어보려고

(*Telephone rings.*)
M Hello. Daehan Library.
W Hi. I want to know _____ _____ _____ _____.
M Okay, which book?
W Kevin Lee's new book.
M You mean *The Red Cup's Secret* _____ _____ _____ _____ _____?
W Yes, I've been looking forward to reading it.
M Well, I'm sorry, but it has already been checked out.
W That's too bad. Then can I _____ _____ _____ _____ _____?
M Sure. I'll contact you when the book is returned. May I have your name and number?
W It's Julie Jang. My number is 010-123-4567.

05 언급되지 않은 것 찾기

다음을 듣고, 모아이 상에 관해 언급되지 <u>않은</u> 것을 고르시오.

① 위치   ② 제작 이유
③ 조각상의 수   ④ 머리와 몸통의 비율
⑤ 평균 높이

Sound Clear ☆ **the island**

모음 앞의 the는 [디]로 발음되고, island의 s는 묵음이라서 [디아일랜드]로 발음된다.

W The Moai Statues are located in Easter Island. There are more than 900 statues throughout the island. They are _____ _____ _____ _____ _____ and almost all of them have overly large heads. The ratio _____ _____ _____ _____ _____ is three-to-five. _____ _____ _____ the moai statues is about four meters. They are one of the most mysterious statues in the world. It is _____ _____ _____ _____ _____ _____ they were created. In 1995, UNESCO named Easter Island a World Heritage Site.

06 일치하지 않는 것 찾기

다음을 듣고, 방송의 내용과 일치하지 <u>않는</u> 것을 고르시오.

① 가방은 두 가지 색상으로 나온다.
② 가방에는 방수 기능이 있다.
③ 가방 안쪽에는 주머니가 두 개 있다.
④ 평소 가격보다 30달러 저렴하게 판매한다.
⑤ 앱으로 주문하면 추가 할인을 받을 수 있다.

M Welcome back, viewers! The first item that I'm going to show you is _____ _____ _____. It comes in blue and red. It's waterproof so you _____ _____ _____ _____ your bag in the rain. It also has two inner pockets that _____ _____ _____ for you to carry many small things. It usually sells for $50, but just for today we're offering it for only $30. _____ _____ _____ _____ _정답 단서_
if you download our app on your smartphone and order it there. Don't miss this great opportunity!

07 어색한 대화 찾기

다음을 듣고, 두 사람의 대화가 <u>어색한</u> 것을 고르시오.

①   ②   ③   ④   ⑤

① **M** Excuse me. Could you help me find a book?
  W Me, too. I have already read the book.
② **M** _____ _____ _____ _____ how I can get to J Art Center?
  W It is near here. You can walk there.
③ **M** How about having some tea _____ _____ _____?
  W Absolutely. I'd love a cup.
④ **M** _____ _____ _____ _____ _____, white or black?
  W I prefer white to black.
⑤ **M** Did you find it hard to accept your illness?
  W No, it wasn't _____ _____ _____ _____.

08 부탁한 일 파악

대화를 듣고, 남자가 여자에게 부탁한 일로 가장 적절한 것을 고르시오.

① 데이트하기
② 식당 예약하기
③ 경찰에 신고하기
④ 식당 전화번호 알려 주기
⑤ 꽃 박람회 가는 방법 알려 주기

Sound Clear ☆ **police station**
동일한 발음의 자음이 연이어 나오면 앞 자음 소리가 탈락하여 [폴리스테이션]으로 발음된다.

W James, you seem to be happy today. What's up?
M Molly finally _____ _____ _____ _____ with me.
W Good for you. What are your plans for the date?
M I'm not sure yet, but _____ _____ _____ _____ _____ to a flower exhibition and then dinner.
W Sounds good. What restaurant do you have in mind?
M That's the problem. I _____ _____ _____ _____ _____.
W Have you ever been to Orga Garden next to the ☆police station downtown? I'm sure Molly would love it.
M Oh, then please let me know the phone number.
W Sure. _____ _____ _____ _정답 단서_ and make a reservation.
_함정_

09 장소 추론

대화를 듣고, 두 사람이 대화하는 장소로 가장 적절한 곳을 고르시오.

① 세관　　② 호텔　　③ 여행사
④ 비행기 안　⑤ 입국 심사대

Sound Clear ☆ **passport**

미국식은 a를 [애]로 발음하여 [패스포트]로, 영국식은 [아]로 발음하여 [파스포트]로 발음된다.

M Good morning. _____ _____ _____ a good vacation package?

W Certainly. When would you like to leave?

M At the beginning of the lunar New Year's holiday.

W Well, _____ _____ _____ soon. Air tickets and hotel rooms at that time are _____ _____ _____.

M Really? Are there any package tours left to a warm place?

W Yes, look at this brochure. _____ _____ _____ 정답 단서 _____? It's a five-day package tour to Thailand.

M Oh, it looks good. I'd like to book it.

W Good. Then I need your passport number for the reservation.

M Okay. Here you are.

10 숫자 정보 파악

대화를 듣고, 남자가 채용되면 주급으로 받을 금액을 고르시오.

① $200　　② $240　　③ $250
④ $280　　⑤ $300

(*Telephone rings.*)

W Hello.

M Hello. _____ _____ _____ _____ _____ for a library assistant. Is the job still available?

W Yes. Are you a student?

M Yes, I am. I'm looking for a part-time job during the winter vacation.

W Okay. Do you know _____ _____ _____?

M _____ _____ _____ _____ _____, the working hours are from one to five, and it's $10 per hour.

W Right. You're supposed to work _____ _____ _____ _____, but if you want, you can work on Saturdays, too.

M Sorry. I don't want to work on weekends.

W Okay. I don't think _____ 정답 단서 _____. You'll hear from us pretty soon.

11 도표 정보 파악

다음 표를 보면서 대화를 듣고, 여자가 신청할 수업을 고르시오.

	Class	Instructor	Day / Time
①	Tennis	Jonathan	Sat. (2 hours)
②	Tennis	Natalia	Sun. (2 hours)
③	Tennis	Natalia	Fri. (1 hour)
④	Swimming	Natalia	Sat. (2 hours)
⑤	Swimming	Jonathan	Fri. (1 hour)

Sound Clear ☆ **Take a look at**
각 [k]가 뒤 단어의 모음과 연음되어 [테이커루껫]으로 발음된다.

W ☆ Take a look at this. There are some interesting sports classes at Central Sports Center.

M I _____ _____ _____ _____ _____ there, and they were all good. I especially liked the tennis and swimming classes.

W Did you? I'm interested in _____ _____ _____.

M Then why don't you take a tennis class?

W I will. _____ _____ _____ _____ _____, 정답 단서
Jonathan or Natalia?

M Natalia. She's excellent.

W Okay. I'll take her class. But why is the Friday class shorter than the others? 정답 단서

M The Friday one doesn't _____ _____ _____ _____
_____. There's only a lesson.

W I see. I'll choose the longer one. I want to practice with my partners, too. 정답 단서

12 언급되지 않은 것 찾기 ❋

대화를 듣고, ST Ski Resort에 관해 언급되지 않은 것을 고르시오.

① 서울에서 리조트까지의 소요 시간
② 슬로프 개수
③ 평균 대기 시간
④ 스키 강습 유무
⑤ 방문객 수 제한 범위

W Jason, you've been to ST Ski Resort before, right?

M Yes, several times. It usually _____ _____ _____
_____ from Seoul.

W Do you know _____ _____ _____ there are?

M Over 20. If you are a beginner, the green slopes are the best choice.

W Thanks. Are there any ski lessons for beginners?

M Sure, the ski school _____ _____ _____ _____
_____. When are you thinking of going?

W I'm going with some friends this weekend. It _____
_____ _____ _____, right?

M I don't think so. The resort only admits 7,000 skiers every day.

W Wow, I didn't know _____ _____ _____ _____ on the number of visitors. Thank you so much.

13 할 일 파악

대화를 듣고, 여자가 할 일로 가장 적절한 것을 고르시오.

① 식당 예약하기　② 선물 포장하기
③ 케이크 주문하기　④ 생일 카드 구입하기
⑤ 조부모님께 연락하기

W You remember this Saturday is Mom's birthday, right?
M Sure. Have you decided _____ _____ _____ _____?
W Yeah. I called Shelly's Restaurant and made a reservation for a big family room.
M Good. Our grandparents _____ _____ _____ _____, too. Did you order a birthday cake?
W Yes. I ordered a cake and a flower basket. _____ _____ _____ _____ _____.
M Great. Is there anything else that we have to do?
W We should wrap her present and buy a birthday card.
M I'm _____ _____ _____ _____ _____. 한정 I'll buy a beautiful card.
W Okay. I'll take care of the wrapping. 정답 단서

14 화제 파악

다음을 듣고, 무엇에 관한 설명인지 고르시오.

① 논문　② 사진집　③ 교과서
④ 영어 사전　⑤ 백과사전

W This is a reference book. This has a lot of information _____ _____ _____. The information is usually arranged in alphabetical order and sometimes _____ _____ _____. This has _____ _____ _____ that you can find this book in libraries, schools and other educational institutions. This is not limited to simple definitions of a word or topic. This _____ _____ _____ _____ _____. This also often includes many maps and illustrations.

15 할 일 파악

대화를 듣고, 여자가 대화 직후에 할 일로 가장 적절한 것을 고르시오.

① 채소 씻기　② 음식 주문하기
③ 감자 사러 가기　④ 식당 예약하기
⑤ 조리법 찾아보기

Sound Clear ☆ **out of**
앞 단어의 끝 자음과 뒤 단어의 모음이 만나 연음되어 [아우러브]로 발음된다.

M What do you _____ _____ _____ for dinner?
W I don't know. I want to try something new.
M Okay. Let's _____ _____ _____ _____ on the Internet.
W Good idea. Let's see what we can find.
M Oh, how about this chicken curry? We both like chicken and curry.
W _____ _____ _____ and it doesn't look too hard to make.
M Yeah. Do we _____ _____ _____ _____?
W We're out of potatoes. Can you wash all the vegetables? I'll go get some potatoes. 한정
정답 단서

16 특정 정보 파악

대화를 듣고, 남자가 신발을 사러 갈 날짜를 고르시오.

① July 5 ② July 6 ③ July 7
④ July 9 ⑤ July 10

W What are you doing on the computer?
M I'm looking for running shoes on the Internet. But I don't think I can _____ _____ _____ _____ _____.
W When do you leave?
M Next Friday, July 10.
W Today is already July 5. _____ _____ _____ _____ _____ Mary's Shoes on Main Street?
M I think that store is too expensive.
W I heard that Mary's Shoes is having a sale until tomorrow.
M Then _____ _____ _____ right now.
W But the store closes at 7 p.m. and it's already 8. Let's go tomorrow.
M Okay. _____ _____ _____ _____.

17 마지막 말에 대한 응답 찾기 ✥

대화를 듣고, 여자의 마지막 말에 대한 남자의 응답으로 가장 적절한 것을 고르시오.

Man: _____

① You had better lose some weight.
② I'm really worried about my health.
③ You should get a physical checkup.
④ Then what about eating healthier foods?
⑤ You shouldn't eat anything prior to the checkup.

> **Sound Clear** ☆ **weight**
> gh가 묵음이라서 [웨이트]로 발음된다.

M Hi, Ella. What's up?
W Well, _____ _____ _____ _____ _____ _____.
M Oh, how was it? Is everything okay?
W Not so good. The doctor said I _____ _____ _____ _____, and it can cause other diseases.
M Oh, no. What should you do to _____ _____ _____?
W The doctor advised me to lose some weight.
M Then you need to exercise regularly.
W Yeah, but I've been swimming every morning _____ _____ _____ now.
M Then what about eating healthier foods?

18 마지막 말에 대한 응답 찾기

대화를 듣고, 남자의 마지막 말에 대한 여자의 응답으로 가장 적절한 것을 고르시오.

Woman: _____

① You must have read it several times.
② It's kind of you to lend me the book.
③ Did you get any messages while I was out?
④ You should. I think this book is her best work ever.
⑤ Sure. First, you should think of why we should read books.

W Have you read Janet Jones' new book?
M _____ _____ _____ _____ of *Magic Castle*?
W Yes. Her new book *Silent Village*, _____ _____ _____. I've already read it.
M What's the story about?
W It's about an orphaned boy who has to _____ _____ _____ _____ to save his village.
M Sounds interesting. What do you think of it?
W It's just fascinating. He travels all over the world and _____ _____ _____.
M It must be thrilling. I think I should read it myself.
W You should. I think this book is her best work ever.

19 마지막 말에 대한 응답 찾기

대화를 듣고, 여자의 마지막 말에 대한 남자의 응답으로 가장 적절한 것을 고르시오.

Man: _____

① Get some sleep and you'll feel better.
② Exercising is better than taking a nap.
③ You should stay up late at night to study.
④ Try not to use your phone in bed at night.
⑤ You are not allowed to use your phone in class.

M Kate, are you tired?

W No, Mr. Benson. Why do you think so?

M You cannot concentrate on the lesson, and _____ _____ _____ _____ during the class.

W Oh, I'm sorry. I'm not _____ _____ _____ these days.

M What time do you usually go to bed?

W I usually go to bed before midnight, but _____ _____ _____ until 3 o'clock last night.

M Are you _____ _____ _____ ?

W No. I was just surfing the Internet on my smartphone and didn't realize _____ _____ _____ _____ .

M Try not to use your phone in bed at night.

20 상황에 적절한 말 찾기

다음 상황 설명을 듣고, Jennifer가 Jiyoon에게 할 말로 가장 적절한 것을 고르시오.

Jennifer: Jiyoon, _____

① this food doesn't suit my taste.
② it's much better than I expected.
③ I'll treat you to lunch the next time.
④ I've always wanted to try this food.
⑤ I don't have any preference where we go.

M Jennifer is a student from England _____ _____ _____ . Today, her Korean friend, Jiyoon, takes her to a Korean restaurant for lunch. The restaurant specializes in *cheonggukjang*, and Jennifer _____ _____ _____ _____ . Jiyoon explains that it is made from soybean and healthy food. Jennifer thinks _____ _____ _____ _____ _____ . But after having some, Jennifer is surprised to find it's delicious. Jiyoon asks Jennifer _____ _____ _____ . In this situation, what would Jennifer most likely say to Jiyoon?

Jennifer Jiyoon, it's much better than I expected.

Review Test

Word Check
영어는 우리말로, 우리말은 영어로 써 보기

01	reduce	13	태도
02	concern	14	중급의
03	option	15	현대의
04	previous	16	긍정적인
05	reschedule	17	목적
06	right-hand	18	배열하다, 정돈하다
07	location	19	절약하다
08	float	20	미신
09	fitting room	21	재사용할 수 있는
10	look good on	22	미세 먼지
11	as well	23	현지 시각
12	take a break	24	동시에

Expression Check
알맞은 표현을 넣어 문장 완성하기

25 _____ _____ I fall into the deep water? 제가 만약 깊은 물에 빠지면 어떻게 하죠?

26 Our Earth is _____ _____ pollution. 우리 지구는 오염으로 고통받고 있습니다.

27 It _____ your hair and cloths _____ getting wet. 그것은 당신의 머리와 옷이 젖는 것을 막아 줍니다.

28 You have to be in here by 7:00 _____ _____ _____. 늦어도 7시까지는 이곳에 오셔야 해요.

29 We can walk to school _____ _____ taking a car.
우리는 학교에 차를 타고 가는 대신에 걸어갈 수 있어.

30 Changdeokgung is _____ _____ the most famous _____ in Korea.
창덕궁은 한국에서 가장 유명한 궁전들 중 하나이다.

Answers p.119

Word Check   영어는 우리말로, 우리말은 영어로 써 보기

01	evil		13	전문으로 하다
02	institution		14	조각하다
03	orphaned		15	섬
04	scared		16	명명하다, 지정하다
05	advertisement		17	조각상
06	classify		18	붐비는
07	release		19	비율
08	reliable		20	주제
09	definition		21	질병
10	burn out		22	졸다
11	to death		23	낮잠을 자다
12	author		24	참고, 참조

Expression Check   알맞은 표현을 넣어 문장 완성하기

25 We're _____ _____ potatoes. 우리는 감자가 떨어졌어요.

26 What do you _____ _____ having for dinner? 저녁으로 무엇을 먹고 싶니?

27 What restaurant do you _____ _____ _____ ? 너는 어느 식당을 생각하고 있니?

28 Molly finally agreed to _____ _____ _____ _____ with me.
Molly가 마침내 나와 데이트하는 데 동의했어.

29 You cannot _____ _____ the lesson and you are dozing off during the class.
너는 수업에 집중을 못하고 수업 시간에 졸더구나.

30 _____ _____ _____ I know, the working hours are from one to five.
제가 알기로는, 근무 시간은 1시부터 5시까지예요.

Word List

실전 모의고사 03 회

☐ inconvenient	불편한
☐ be worried about	～에 대해 걱정하다
☐ lab	실험실
☐ experiment	실험
☐ safety	안전
☐ at all times	항상
☐ injury	부상
☐ immediately	즉시
☐ legend	전설
☐ raise	기르다
☐ savings account	저축 예금 계좌
☐ fill out	작성하다
☐ deposit	입금하다
☐ look forward to	～을 기대하다
☐ shut down	(기계가) 멈추다
☐ guess	알아맞히다
☐ terrific	아주 좋은
☐ thanks to	～ 덕분에
☐ interview	면접
☐ special	특별한
☐ perform	공연하다
☐ instrument	악기
☐ apply	지원하다
☐ announce	발표하다
☐ first of all	무엇보다도
☐ option	선택(권)
☐ extra	추가의
☐ consist of	～로 구성되다
☐ framework	뼈대, 골조
☐ slide	미끄러지다
☐ freeze	얼다
☐ topic	주제
☐ translate	번역하다
☐ receive	받다
☐ exchange	교환하다
☐ reservation	예약
☐ write down	기록하다, 적다
☐ that's why	그래서 ～하다
☐ be ashamed of	～을 부끄러워하다
☐ presentation	발표

실전 모의고사 04 회

☐ suit	어울리다
☐ agency	대행사
☐ win first prize	1등을 하다
☐ set the table	상을 차리다
☐ healthy	건강한
☐ pack	(짐을) 싸다
☐ traffic	교통
☐ had better	～하는 게 낫다
☐ just in case	만약을 위해서
☐ look good on	～에게 잘 어울리다
☐ short-sleeved	반소매의, 짧은 소매의
☐ notify	알리다
☐ hit-and-run	뺑소니 사고
☐ security	안전
☐ license plate	(자동차) 번호판
☐ describe	묘사하다
☐ stomachache	복통
☐ medicine	약
☐ not ~ anymore	더 이상 ～ 않다
☐ convenience store	편의점
☐ ahead	미리
☐ out of order	고장 난
☐ comfortably	편안하게
☐ responsible	책임이 있는
☐ passenger	승객
☐ destination	목적지
☐ aircraft	항공기
☐ effort	노력
☐ create	만들다
☐ account	계정
☐ special offer	특가 판매
☐ order	순서
☐ give it a try	한번 해 보다
☐ catch up with	따라잡다
☐ amazing	놀라운
☐ symptom	증상
☐ prevent A from B	A가 B하지 못하게 막다
☐ be supposed to	～하기로 되어 있다
☐ company	회사
☐ screen	가려내다, 조사하다

Word List

실전 모의고사 05 회

☐	wonder	궁금해하다
☐	look after	~을 돌보다
☐	every other day	이틀마다
☐	possible	가능한
☐	check in	체크인하다
☐	keep in mind	명심하다
☐	touch	만지다
☐	advertisement	광고
☐	cost	가격이 ~이다
☐	pressure	압박, 압박감
☐	mail	(우편으로) 부치다
☐	period	수업 시간
☐	rescue	구조
☐	lecture	강의
☐	first aid	응급 처치
☐	emergency	비상 (사태)
☐	situation	상황
☐	plate	접시
☐	meat	육류
☐	include	포함하다
☐	chance	기회
☐	in that case	그런 경우에
☐	space	공간
☐	blow	(입으로) 불다
☐	control	통제
☐	warning	경고
☐	referee	심판
☐	cast	깁스
☐	hit	치다
☐	on one's way to	~에 가는 도중에
☐	ignore	무시하다
☐	text message	문자 메시지
☐	admit	인정하다
☐	passport	여권
☐	relief	안심, 안도
☐	handle	다루다
☐	with care	주의 깊게, 신중히
☐	necessary	필요한
☐	height	높이; (주로 복수로) 높은 곳
☐	on the other hand	반면에

실전 모의고사 06 회

☐	traffic jam	교통 체증
☐	at the latest	늦어도
☐	entire	전체의
☐	boarding pass	탑승권
☐	article	기사
☐	barely	거의 ~ 못하는
☐	weigh	무게가 ~이다
☐	unfortunately	불행히도, 유감스럽게도
☐	stain	얼룩
☐	spill	쏟다
☐	splatter	튀다
☐	remove	제거하다
☐	exhibition	전시회
☐	nearby	근처에
☐	applicant	지원자
☐	assistant	조수, 보조원
☐	take out	꺼내다
☐	air freshener	방향제
☐	scent	향
☐	replace	교체하다
☐	liquid	액체
☐	take up	차지하다
☐	duration	(지속되는) 기간
☐	competition	경연 대회
☐	individual	개인의
☐	equipment	도구, 장비
☐	ingredient	재료
☐	apply for	~을 신청하다
☐	throw away	버리다
☐	garbage	쓰레기
☐	on the air	방송 중인
☐	request	요청하다
☐	maintenance	유지, 보수 관리
☐	candidate	후보자
☐	election	선거
☐	location	위치
☐	twist	삐다
☐	condition	상태
☐	impressed	인상 깊은, 감동 받은
☐	figure out	이해하다

실전 모의고사 07 회

□ rainy season	장마철
□ match	어울리다
□ apply to	~에 지원하다
□ inform	알리다, 통지하다
□ examine	검토하다
□ document	서류
□ assignment	과제, 숙제
□ unique	독특한
□ at least	최소한, 적어도
□ secondhand	중고의
□ fashionable	유행하는
□ originally	원래
□ distance	거리
□ lost and found	분실물 보관소
□ at a time	한 번에
□ due to	~ 때문에
□ preventable	예방 가능한
□ cause	원인
□ bathe	목욕하다
□ have trouble ~ing	~하는 데 어려움을 겪다
□ invention	발명, 발명품
□ practical	실용적인
□ turn off	~을 끄다
□ automatically	자동으로
□ infect	감염시키다
□ technical	기술적인
□ minor	사소한
□ mechanic	기술자
□ patience	인내
□ submission	제출(물)
□ hand in	제출하다
□ watch out	조심하다
□ take off	(옷·신발·모자 등을) 벗다
□ director	감독
□ award	상
□ make a decision	결정하다
□ potential	잠재적인
□ candidate	후보자, 지원자
□ look up	검색하다, 찾아보다
□ keep up with	(뒤처지지 않도록) 따라가다

실전 모의고사 08 회

□ reasonably	적정하게
□ forest	숲
□ wallet	지갑
□ contact number	연락처 전화번호
□ head over	가다, 향하다
□ pick up	~을 찾아오다
□ helpful	도움이 되는
□ anytime	언제든지
□ attend	참석하다
□ serious	심각한
□ don't have to	~할 필요가 없다
□ be good at	~을 잘하다
□ improve	향상되다, 나아지다
□ regards	안부 (인사)
□ social studies	(과목) 사회
□ bullying	약자 괴롭히기
□ come to mind	생각이 떠오르다
□ come up with	생각해 내다
□ one day	언젠가
□ however	그러나
□ achieve	이루다, 성취하다
□ combination	결합
□ separately	따로따로, 별도로
□ cash	현금
□ experience	경험
□ broadcasting	방송
□ application	지원서
□ management	관리, 경영
□ effectively	효과적으로
□ afford	~할 여유가 있다
□ area	지역, 구역
□ machine	기계
□ imagine	상상하다
□ express	신속한, 급행의
□ regular	보통의
□ confidence	자신감
□ quit	그만두다
□ pronunciation	발음
□ membership	회원 자격(신분)
□ get a refund	환불받다

Word List

실전 모의고사 09 회

☐ upstairs	위층
☐ shelf	선반, 책꽂이
☐ each other	서로
☐ seafood	해산물
☐ overnight	하룻밤 동안
☐ day off	쉬는 날
☐ a couple of	몇 개의, 두서너 개의
☐ drive ~ crazy	~을 미치게 하다
☐ grammar	문법
☐ memorize	암기하다
☐ effective	효과적인
☐ orchestra	오케스트라, 관현악단
☐ on schedule	예정대로
☐ activity	활동
☐ uniform	유니폼, 제복
☐ shipping charge	배송비
☐ slip	미끄러지다
☐ to make matters worse	설상가상으로
☐ whole	전체의
☐ laugh at	~을 비웃다
☐ take place	개최되다
☐ quality	품질
☐ admission	입장
☐ tuition fee	수업료
☐ ability	능력
☐ at the same time	동시에
☐ truth	사실, 진실
☐ at once	동시에, 한꺼번에
☐ cheat	부정행위를 하다
☐ magician	마술사
☐ locate	위치하다
☐ participate in	~에 참가하다
☐ chance	가능성
☐ matter	중요하다
☐ process	과정
☐ relieve	없애 주다, 덜다
☐ in pain	아픈
☐ professional	전문적인
☐ opinion	의견
☐ due	만기가 된

실전 모의고사 10 회

☐ at first	처음에
☐ drawer	서랍
☐ bottom	맨 아래
☐ water purifier	정수기
☐ weather forecaster	기상 캐스터
☐ get wet	젖다
☐ envious	부러운
☐ regretful	후회하는
☐ get off	(차에서) 내리다
☐ terrific	훌륭한, 아주 좋은
☐ wrap up	끝내다
☐ conference	회의
☐ switch	바꾸다
☐ environment	환경
☐ issue	발급하다
☐ develop	(필름을) 현상하다
☐ land	착륙하다
☐ beg	간청하다, 애원하다
☐ suffer	고통받다
☐ waste	쓰레기
☐ keep track of	~을 기록하다, 추적하다
☐ cut down on	~을 줄이다
☐ budget	예산
☐ round-trip	왕복의
☐ purchase	구입하다, 사다
☐ by the way	그런데
☐ skip	거르다, 건너뛰다
☐ medical checkup	건강 검진
☐ assistance	도움, 지원
☐ tutor	강사, 지도 교사
☐ slow down	속도를 줄이다
☐ horrible	끔찍한
☐ fascinating	환상적인
☐ on board	선상에
☐ deck	갑판
☐ out of breath	숨이 찬
☐ volunteer work	자원봉사 활동
☐ pay attention	주의를 기울이다
☐ worthless	쓸모없는
☐ be fond of	~을 좋아하다

실전 모의고사 11 회

☐ turn	(나이가) ~가 되다
☐ old-fashioned	구식의, 유행이 지난
☐ confirm	확인하다
☐ correct	옳은
☐ as soon as possible	가능한 한 빨리
☐ graduate	졸업하다
☐ head	향하다
☐ embassy	대사관
☐ plenty of	많은
☐ refrigerator	냉장고
☐ go for a walk	산책하러 가다
☐ noise	소음
☐ work out	운동하다
☐ be good for	~에 좋다
☐ lose weight	살을 빼다
☐ pleasant	기쁜
☐ have a great time	즐거운 시간을 보내다
☐ named	~라고 하는, ~라는 이름의
☐ disappear	사라지다
☐ parking lot	주차장
☐ customer service center	고객 서비스 센터
☐ right away	지금 바로
☐ material	자료
☐ look over	살펴보다
☐ shake	떨리다, 흔들리다
☐ confident	자신감 있는
☐ tradition	전통
☐ opportunity	기회
☐ various	다양한
☐ natural	자연의
☐ weekday	주중, 평일
☐ at most	최대한으로
☐ survey	(설문) 조사
☐ give ~ a ride	~을 태워다 주다
☐ response	응답, 대답
☐ mess	엉망진창
☐ abroad	해외에
☐ melt	녹다
☐ talented	재능이 있는
☐ someday	언젠가

실전 모의고사 12 회

☐ rimless	테가 없는
☐ so far	지금까지
☐ square-shaped	사각형 모양의
☐ match	어울리다
☐ cough	기침하다
☐ soothe	진정시키다
☐ scrape	까지다, 찰과상을 내다
☐ remove	벗다, 제거하다
☐ step on	~을 밟다
☐ scale	저울
☐ international	국제의
☐ island	섬
☐ worth	~할 가치가 있는
☐ frustrated	좌절감을 느끼는
☐ suffer from	~로 고통받다
☐ get stressed out	스트레스를 받다
☐ delay	지연시키다; 지연
☐ load	싣다
☐ departure	출발
☐ admission	입장, 입장료
☐ have a cramp	쥐가 나다
☐ aisle	통로
☐ stand	견디다
☐ flight attendant	승무원
☐ auditorium	강당
☐ register	신청하다, 등록하다
☐ judge	심사위원
☐ appointment	약속
☐ origin	기원, 유래
☐ flat	평평한
☐ formal	격식의
☐ cut into slices	조각으로 자르다
☐ fragile	깨지기 쉬운
☐ wrap	포장하다
☐ be over	끝나다
☐ charge	충전하다
☐ portable	휴대용의
☐ reward	보상하다
☐ pollution	오염
☐ have an argument	말다툼을 하다

Word List

☐ forecast	예보, 예측
☐ platform	플랫폼, 승강장
☐ stairs	계단
☐ wet	젖은
☐ fever	열
☐ runny nose	콧물이 흐르는
☐ vomit	토하다
☐ price tag	가격표
☐ policy	방침, 정책
☐ orphanage	고아원
☐ laptop	노트북 컴퓨터
☐ attach	첨부하다
☐ account	계정
☐ a variety of	다양한
☐ strengthen	강화하다
☐ muscle	근육
☐ ground floor	지하
☐ go well with	~와 잘 어울리다
☐ connect	연결되다
☐ install	설치하다
☐ throw a party	파티를 열다
☐ spend	(시간을) 보내다
☐ essay	(짧은 논문식) 과제물
☐ foreign	외국의
☐ medical	의학의
☐ latest	최신의
☐ forever	영원히
☐ several	몇 개의
☐ both	둘 다
☐ upload	업로드하다
☐ segment	부분
☐ celebrity	유명 인사
☐ view	전망
☐ discuss	토론하다
☐ in a hurry	서둘러, 급히
☐ brochure	(안내) 책자
☐ disturb	방해하다
☐ humid	습한
☐ confirm	확인하다, 확증하다
☐ ID card	신분증

☐ semester	학기
☐ strap	끈
☐ front	앞
☐ dairy product	유제품
☐ facility	시설
☐ fee	요금
☐ annual	매년의, 연례의
☐ session	수업
☐ sign up for	~을 신청하다(가입하다)
☐ pet	쓰다듬다; 애완동물
☐ dramatic	극적인
☐ scene	장면
☐ unrealistic	비현실적인
☐ special effect	특수 효과
☐ impressive	인상적인
☐ passport	여권
☐ anywhere	어디든지
☐ survey	설문 조사하다
☐ respond	응답하다
☐ least	가장 적은
☐ skin	까지다
☐ ointment	연고
☐ take place	개최하다, 일어나다
☐ be disappointed with	~에 실망하다
☐ at least	최소한, 적어도
☐ struggle	힘겹게 하다, 고군분투하다
☐ bitter	맛이 쓴
☐ slightly	약간
☐ content	내용물, 함유량
☐ increase	증가시키다
☐ roast	볶다, 굽다
☐ vending machine	자동판매기
☐ treat	치료하다
☐ vocabulary	어휘
☐ cover	다루다, 포함시키다
☐ postpone	연기하다
☐ profession	직업
☐ thoughtful	사려 깊은
☐ related to	~와 관련 있는
☐ major	전공

실전 모의고사 15 회

☐ definitely	분명히, 틀림없이
☐ alone	혼자의
☐ reason	이유
☐ consider	고려하다
☐ exchange	교환; 교환하다
☐ normally	보통
☐ photographer	사진작가
☐ exhausted	지친
☐ every time	~할 때마다
☐ dish soap	주방용 세제
☐ certificate	수료증
☐ organize	조직하다, 편성하다
☐ foundation	재단
☐ feel free to	자유롭게 ~하다
☐ staff	직원
☐ highlight	강조하다
☐ miss	놓치다
☐ knit	뜨다, 짜다
☐ break up with	~와 헤어지다
☐ cheer up	힘내다
☐ build	체격
☐ across from	~ 건너편에
☐ offensive	공격하는
☐ defensive	수비의
☐ advance	전진하다
☐ score	득점하다
☐ poll	여론 조사
☐ skinny	비쩍 마른
☐ get hurt	다치다
☐ violate	위반하다
☐ traffic rule	교통 규칙
☐ fine	벌금
☐ nutritious	영양가 있는
☐ instead	대신에
☐ end up ~ing	결국 ~하게 되다
☐ stain	얼룩
☐ permission	허락
☐ fancy	고급의, 일류의
☐ go Dutch	비용을 각자 부담하다
☐ separate	분리된

실전 모의고사 16 회

☐ the other	(둘 또는 여럿 중) 나머지 하나
☐ oversleep	늦잠 자다
☐ do the same	똑같이 하다
☐ bike rack	자전거 보관대
☐ party	일행
☐ serving	(음식의) 1인분
☐ department	부서
☐ endangered	멸종 위기에 처한
☐ species	종(種)
☐ cancel	취소하다
☐ flyer	전단지
☐ baggage	짐, 수하물
☐ scale	저울
☐ allowance	허용(량)
☐ exceed	초과하다
☐ regulation	규정
☐ charge	요금
☐ preference	선호
☐ permission	허락
☐ nurse's office	보건실
☐ high-rise	고층의
☐ disadvantage	불리한 점, 약점
☐ literature	문학
☐ deduct	공제하다, 감하다
☐ individual	개인의
☐ assignment	과제
☐ regularly	규칙적으로
☐ remind	상기시키다
☐ photography	사진 촬영
☐ forbid	금지하다
☐ critic	평론가, 비평가
☐ operate	운영하다
☐ injury	부상
☐ urgent	긴급한
☐ dorm(= dormitory)	기숙사
☐ crutch	목발
☐ pass away	돌아가시다
☐ funeral	장례식
☐ try out for	~에 지원하다
☐ transfer student	전학생

Word List

□ everywhere	모든 곳에
□ decorate	장식하다
□ fantastic	환상적인
□ bite	물다
□ development	발전
□ deadline	기한, 마감 일자
□ exact	정확한
□ add	추가하다, 더하다
□ dye	염색하다
□ be on the other line	통화 중이다
□ chilly	쌀쌀한
□ digestive medicine	소화제
□ serious	심각한
□ part-time	시간제의, 파트타임의
□ all day long	하루 종일
□ overdue	기한이 지난
□ late fee	연체료
□ drop	떨어뜨리다
□ tear off	찢어내다
□ damage	손상
□ travelogue	여행기
□ fairy tale	동화
□ aquarium	수족관
□ designed	계획된, 고안된
□ explore	탐험하다
□ tropic zone	열대 지역
□ investigation	조사, 연구
□ encounter	만남, 조우
□ pre-registration	사전 등록
□ supervise	관리하다, 감독하다
□ a variety of	여러 가지의
□ whistle	호루라기
□ equipment	장비
□ close at hand	쉽게 손닿는 곳에
□ resident	주민, 거주자
□ get in shape	좋은 몸 상태(몸매)를 유지하다
□ business day	영업일, 평일
□ form	만들다, 구성하다
□ in charge of	~을 담당해서, ~을 맡아서
□ meaningful	의미 있는

□ edition	판, 호
□ foreign language	외국어
□ fiction	소설
□ gratitude	감사
□ in addition to	~ 이외에, ~에 덧붙여
□ share	공유하다, 나누다
□ match	경기
□ row	줄, 열
□ economy class	일반석
□ dozen	열두 개의
□ accidently	실수로, 잘못하여
□ stack	더미
□ flowerpot	화분
□ atmosphere	분위기
□ interior	인테리어, 실내 장식
□ neat	깔끔한
□ extremely	매우, 극도로
□ gorgeous	멋진
□ food poisoning	식중독
□ yellow dust	황사
□ hardly	거의 ~ 않다(없다)
□ sore	아픈, 쓰린
□ itchy	간지러운
□ occasion	때, 행사
□ run for	~에 출마하다
□ student president	학생회장
□ be in trouble	어려움에 처하다
□ specific	구체적인
□ campaign speech	선거 연설
□ self-introduction	자기소개
□ be based on	~을 기반으로 하다
□ realistic	현실적인
□ episode	1회 방송분
□ be into	~에 열광하다
□ main character	주인공
□ under construction	공사 중인
□ distance	거리
□ extra	추가의
□ notice	알아차리다
□ take out	꺼내다

고난도 모의고사 19 회

☐ right-hand	오른쪽의
☐ arrange	배열하다, 정돈하다
☐ display	전시물
☐ collection	모음, 소장품
☐ rent	대여
☐ lifeguard	안전 요원, 인명 구조 요원
☐ rescue	구조하다
☐ life vest	구명조끼
☐ float	뜨다
☐ culture	문화
☐ particularly	특별히
☐ royal	왕의
☐ location	위치
☐ depend on	~에 달려 있다
☐ previous	앞의, 사전의
☐ broken	고장 난, 부서진
☐ care	신경 쓰다
☐ reusable	재사용할 수 있는
☐ wastewater	폐수
☐ concern	염려
☐ fine dust	미세 먼지
☐ reschedule	일정을 변경하다
☐ regular class	정규 수업
☐ difference	차이
☐ change one's mind	~의 마음을 바꾸다
☐ modern	현대의
☐ intermediate	중급의
☐ registration	등록
☐ just in case	만약을 위해서, 혹시나 해서
☐ superstition	미신
☐ direct	직항의
☐ local time	현지 시각
☐ be lost	길을 잃다
☐ purpose	목적
☐ process	과정
☐ desire	의욕, 욕구
☐ positive	긍정적인
☐ attitude	태도
☐ switch	변경하다, 바꾸다
☐ fitting room	탈의실

고난도 모의고사 20 회

☐ downtown	시내에
☐ (light) bulb	전구
☐ burn out	(전구가) 나가다, 꺼지다
☐ firmly	단단히
☐ atmosphere	분위기
☐ to death	극도로
☐ publish	출판하다
☐ put a hold on	(도서관 책을) 예약하다
☐ statue	조각상
☐ figure	형상
☐ carve	깎아서 만들다, 조각하다
☐ overly	몹시, 지나치게
☐ ratio	비율
☐ mysterious	신비한
☐ waterproof	방수의
☐ opportunity	기회
☐ absolutely	전적으로, 틀림없이
☐ condition	조건
☐ as far as	~하는 한
☐ session	시간, 시기
☐ crowded	붐비는
☐ admit	허용하다
☐ take care of	(일·책임 등을) 맡다
☐ reference	참고, 참조
☐ classify	분류하다
☐ reliable	믿을 만한
☐ definition	정의
☐ illustration	삽화
☐ knowledge	지식
☐ ingredient	재료
☐ be out of	~이 떨어지다(바닥나다)
☐ have no choice	선택의 여지가 없다
☐ (physical) checkup	건강 검진
☐ high blood pressure	고혈압
☐ prior to	~하기 전에
☐ release	발표하다, 공개하다
☐ doze off	졸다
☐ take a nap	낮잠을 자다
☐ stay up late at night	밤늦게까지 깨어 있다
☐ specialize	전문으로 하다

동아출판 영어 교재 가이드

영역	브랜드	초1~2	초3~4	초5~6	중1	중2	중3	고1	고2	고3
문법	[초·중등] 개념서 **그래머 클리어 스타터 중학 영문법 클리어**		Grammar CLEAR Starter 1	Grammar CLEAR Starter 2	중학 영문법 클리어 1	중학 영문법 클리어 2	중학 영문법 클리어 3			
	[중등] 문법 문제서 **그래머 클라우드 3000제**				그래머 클라우드 3000제 LEVEL 1	그래머 클라우드 3000제 LEVEL 2	그래머 클라우드 3000제 LEVEL 3			
	[중등] 실전 문제서 **빠르게 통하는 영문법 핵심 1200제**				빠르게 통하는 영문법 1200 1	빠르게 통하는 영문법 1200 2	빠르게 통하는 영문법 1200 3			
	[중등] 서술형 영문법 **서술형에 더 강해지는 중학 영문법**				서술형에 더 강해지는 중학 영문법 1	서술형에 더 강해지는 중학 영문법 2	서술형에 더 강해지는 중학 영문법 3			
	[고등] 시험 영문법 **시험에 더 강해지는 고등 영문법**							시험에 더 강해지는 고등영문법		
	[고등] 개념서 **Supreme 고등 영문법**							Supreme 고등영문법		
어법	[고등] 기본서 **Supreme 수능 어법** 기본 실전							Supreme 수능 어법 / Supreme 수능 어법		
쓰기	[중등] 영작 집중 훈련서 **중학 문법+쓰기 클리어**				중학 문법+쓰기 클리어 1	중학 문법+쓰기 클리어 2	중학 문법+쓰기 클리어 3			

LISTENING CLEAR))

중학영어듣기 모의고사 20회

ANSWERS

3

동아출판)

LISTENING CLEAR

중학영어듣기 모의고사 20회

3

01 ②	02 ⑤	03 ⑤	04 ②	05 ③
06 ⑤	07 ①	08 ③	09 ④	10 ④
11 ②	12 ④	13 ③	14 ②	15 ③
16 ③	17 ⑤	18 ④	19 ③	20 ④

01 ②

M Hi. How can I help you?

W Hi. I'm looking for curtains for my daughter's room.

M Okay. Well, how about these curtains with a lot of stars?

W They look nice, but her last curtains had stars, too. I want something different.

M I see. Then I recommend these with stripes or these with flowers.

W I prefer simple patterns. I'll take the curtains with stripes.

M Good choice. Please write down the size you need here.

남 안녕하세요. 무엇을 도와드릴까요?

여 안녕하세요. 제 딸의 방에 달아 줄 커튼을 찾고 있어요.

남 네. 음, 별이 많이 그려진 이 커튼은 어떠세요?

여 좋아 보이지만, 그 애의 이전 커튼에도 별이 있었거든요. 전 다른 것을 원해요.

남 알겠습니다. 그러시면, 이 줄무늬 커튼이나 꽃무늬 커튼을 추천 드립니다.

여 저는 단순한 무늬를 선호해요. 줄무늬가 있는 커튼으로 할게요.

남 잘 고르셨어요. 여기에 필요하신 사이즈를 써 주세요.

해설 여자는 단순한 무늬를 선호한다며 줄무늬 커튼을 사겠다고 했다.

어휘 look for ~을 찾다 curtain 커튼 last 가장 최근의, 바로 앞의 recommend 추천하다 stripe 줄무늬 pattern 무늬 choice 선택

02 ⑤

W Have you heard about the new TV program starting soon on channel KNT?

M Oh, you mean the program hosted by Ken Kim, right?

W That's right. It's a program about the real lives of K-pop stars in their homes.

M Sounds very interesting. When is it going to start?

W Next Wednesday. I can't wait for it.

M Same here. I'm sure many teenagers will love this program.

W I guess you're right.

여 KNT 채널에서 곧 시작하는 새로운 TV 프로그램에 대해 들어 봤니?

남 오, Ken Kim이 진행하는 프로그램 말하는 거지, 그렇지?

여 맞아. 그건 케이 팝 스타들의 집에서의 실제 생활에 관한 프로 그램이야.

남 아주 흥미로운데. 언제 시작하니?

여 다음 주 수요일이야. 너무 기다려져.

남 나도 그래. 난 많은 십 대들이 이 프로그램을 아주 좋아할 거라고 확신해.

여 네 말이 맞는 것 같아.

해설 방송 시간대는 언급되지 않았다.

어휘 channel 채널 host 진행하다 real 실제의, 진짜의 can't wait 몹시 바라다, 어서 ~하고 싶다 teenager 십 대

03 ⑤

(Telephone rings.)

M Smart Learning Center. How can I help you?

W Hi. I sent an entry for the math contest last week, but I couldn't find my name on the list of participants.

M Oh, really? Can I have your name?

W Anna Choi.

M Okay. (Pause) Your name is on the list that we have.

W Whew, that's a relief. I guess I made a mistake.

M Yes, I think so.

W Sorry for the inconvenience.

(전화벨이 울린다.)

남 Smart Learning Center입니다. 무엇을 도와드릴까요?

여 안녕하세요. 지난주에 수학 경시대회 참가 신청을 했는데, 참가 자 명단에서 제 이름을 찾을 수가 없어서요.

남 오, 정말요? 이름이 어떻게 되시나요?

여 Anna Choi입니다.

남 알겠습니다. (잠시 후) 저희가 갖고 있는 명단에는 이름이 있네요.

여 휴, 다행이네요. 제가 실수한 것 같아요.

남 네, 그러신 것 같습니다.

여 불편을 끼쳐 드려서 죄송합니다.

해설 여자는 수학 경시대회 참가 신청 여부를 확인하려고 전화했다.

어휘 send an entry 참가 신청을 하다 list 목록, 명단 participant 참가자 relief 안도 mistake 실수 inconvenience 불편

04 ②

(Cellphone rings.)

M Hello, Mina. It's me, Sam.

W Oh, hi, Sam. What's up?

M I'm going to the hip-hop concert this Saturday. Do you want to go there together?

W That would be great. What time and where should we meet?

M The concert starts at 8. How about meeting at 7:30 near the ticket office?

W Well, why don't we meet earlier and eat dinner together before the concert?

M Sounds good. Then what about at 6:30?

W Okay, see you then.

(휴대 전화가 울린다.)

남 여보세요, 미나야. 나야, Sam.

여 오, 안녕, Sam. 무슨 일이야?

남 나는 이번 주 토요일에 힙합 콘서트에 갈 거야. 그곳에 함께 갈래?

여 그거 좋겠다. 몇 시에 어디에서 만날까?

남 콘서트는 8시에 시작해. 매표소 근처에서 7시 30분에 만나는 게 어때?

여 음, 좀 더 일찍 만나서 콘서트 전에 같이 저녁을 먹는 게 어때?

남 좋아. 그러면 6시 30분 어떠니?

여 알았어, 그때 봐.

해설 콘서트는 8시에 시작하는데 두 사람은 6시 30분에 만나서 함께 저녁을 먹기로 했다.

어휘 near ~에서 가까이 ticket office 매표소

05 ③

M Claire, why are you so late? You've missed <u>almost half of the game</u>.

W Sorry. I <u>missed the bus</u>. What's the score?

M Three to one. Our team is winning now. Player number four is batting extremely well.

W Great! I hope our team will win today's game.

M Me, too. <u>I was so upset</u> when our team lost yesterday.

W Don't worry. Our pitcher is the best.

M Right. He throws the fastest ball in the world.

W Look! He just <u>struck out the batter</u>!

남 Claire, 왜 이렇게 늦었어? 넌 경기를 거의 절반이나 놓쳤잖아.

여 미안해. 버스를 놓쳤지 뭐야. 점수가 어떻게 되니?

남 3대 1이야. 우리 팀이 지금 이기고 있어. 4번 선수가 아주 잘 치고 있어.

여 잘됐다! 나는 우리 팀이 오늘 경기를 이겼으면 좋겠어.

남 나도 그래. 어제 우리 팀이 졌을 때 정말 속상했어.

여 걱정하지 마. 우리 투수는 최고거든.

남 맞아. 그는 세계에서 가장 빠른 공을 던져.

여 봐! 그가 방금 타자를 삼진 시켰어.

해설 야구 경기를 직접 관람하고 있는 상황이므로 대화가 이루어지는 장소는 야구장이다.

어휘 miss 놓치다 score 점수 bat 공을 치다 extremely 매우, 극도로 pitcher 투수 strike out 삼진 시키다 batter 타자

06 ⑤

① W Are you <u>satisfied with your job</u>?

　 M Of course, I love it.

② W Do you like <u>playing the piano</u>?

　 M Yes, I'm interested in playing it.

③ W Excuse me. Where is the bathroom?

　 M It's <u>right over there</u>.

④ W Can I send my luggage to Incheon?

　 M Okay, let me help you with that.

⑤ W Where can I <u>take a bus</u> to the city center?

　 M There's a bus stop in front of gate number 7.

① 여 너는 네 일에 만족하니?

　 남 물론이지, 난 내 일을 정말 좋아해.

② 여 너는 피아노 연주하는 것을 좋아하니?

　 남 응, 나는 피아노 연주에 흥미가 있어.

③ 여 실례합니다. 화장실이 어디에 있나요?

　 남 바로 저쪽에 있어요.

④ 여 제 짐을 인천으로 보낼 수 있나요?

　 남 네, 제가 도와드릴게요.

⑤ 여 시내로 가는 버스를 어디에서 탈 수 있나요?

　 남 7번 게이트 앞에 버스 정류장이 있어요.

해설 공항 안내 센터에서 버스 정류장이 어디에 있는지 묻고 답하는 상황이다.

어휘 be satisfied with ~에 만족하다 be interested in ~에 관심 있다 bathroom 화장실 luggage 짐, 수하물 in front of ~ 앞에

07 ①

W Peter, what are you looking for?

M I'm looking for my cellphone. I don't know <u>where it is</u>.

W Don't you remember where you put it?

M I thought I <u>put it on the table</u> after calling Jiho, but it's not there.

W Did you look anywhere else?

M Sure. Well, can you call me? Then I think I can hear it ring.

W No problem. <u>Wait a second</u>.

여 Peter, 너 무엇을 찾고 있니?

남 내 휴대 전화를 찾고 있어. 그게 어디에 있는지 모르겠어.

여 그것을 어디에 두었는지 기억나지 않니?

남 지호한테 전화하고 나서 탁자 위에 둔 것 같은데 거기에 없네.

여 다른 곳도 봤어?

남 물론이지. 음, 나한테 전화 좀 해 줄래? 그러면 휴대 전화가 울리는 소리를 들을 수 있을 것 같아.

여 그래. 잠깐 기다려.

해설 남자는 휴대 전화를 찾기 위해 여자에게 전화를 걸어 달라고 부탁했다.

어휘 remember 기억하다 call 전화하다 ring 울리다 wait a second 잠깐 기다리다

08 ③

M Hello, everyone. This year, the city of Busan is celebrating its 12th Sea Festival at Haeundae Beach! This festival <u>will be held</u> from July 19 to 30. You can buy tickets online at www.sfestival.org. There will be <u>many interesting events</u> such as a jazz concert, a dance contest, and a fishing trip. Come and enjoy the summer at the Sea Festival!

남 여러분, 안녕하세요. 올해, 부산시가 해운대 해변에서 제12회 바다 축제를 열 예정입니다! 이번 축제는 7월 19일부터 30일까지 개최됩니다. 입장권은 www.sfestival.org에서 온라인으로 구입하실 수 있습니다. 재즈 콘서트, 댄스 경연 대회, 그리고 낚시 여행과 같은 많은 흥미로운 행사들이 있을 것입니다. 바다 축제에 오셔서 여름을 즐겨 보세요!

해설 입장권 가격은 언급되지 않았다.

어휘 celebrate 기념하다, 축하하다   festival 축제   hold 열다, 개최하다   event 행사   such as ~와 같은

09 ④

W This is a useful thing when you have a bad cold. As you know, in order to get better, you need to be careful not to breathe in cold air. This can help you get well because it keeps cold air from reaching your throat. Therefore, you can protect your throat even though you are outside. Also, this can be helpful in preventing the cold from spreading to others.

여 이것은 당신이 심한 감기에 걸렸을 때 유용한 것이다. 알다시피, 몸이 낫기 위해서는 차가운 공기를 마시지 않도록 주의해야 한다. 이것은 차가운 공기가 목구멍에 닿는 것을 막아 주기 때문에 당신이 회복하는 것을 도와줄 수 있다. 그러므로 당신은 밖에 있더라도 당신의 목을 보호할 수 있다. 또한, 이것은 다른 사람들에게 감기를 옮기지 않도록 하는 데 도움이 될 수 있다.

해설 차가운 공기가 목구멍에 닿지 않도록 막아 주며, 감기가 전염되는 것을 막아 주는 데 도움이 되는 것은 마스크이다.

어휘 useful 유용한   cold 감기   in order to ~하기 위해서   breathe 숨을 쉬다   keep A from ~ing A가 ~하지 못하게 막다   protect 보호하다   prevent 막다, 예방하다   spread 퍼지게 하다

10 ④

① M Can you do me a favor?
　W I'm sorry, but I'm very busy.
② M What's your plan for this year?
　W I'm thinking of studying Chinese.
③ M Do you mind if I take this chair?
　W Not at all. Go ahead.
④ M I'm afraid you can't take pictures in here.
　W I really appreciate your help.
⑤ M I have an important test tomorrow.
　W I'll keep my fingers crossed for you.

① 남 나 좀 도와줄 수 있니?
　여 미안하지만, 내가 아주 바빠.
② 남 올해 너의 계획은 무엇이니?
　여 중국어를 공부할 생각이야.
③ 남 제가 이 의자를 가져가도 되나요?
　여 네, 그렇게 하세요.
④ 남 죄송하지만 여기서는 사진을 찍으시면 안 돼요.

여 도와주셔서 정말 감사합니다.
⑤ 남 나는 내일 중요한 시험이 있어.
　여 너를 위해 행운을 빌어줄게.

해설 ④ 사진 촬영이 불가능하다는 말에 도와줘서 고맙다고 답하는 것은 어색하다.

어휘 do ~ a favor ~의 부탁을 들어주다   take a picture 사진을 찍다   appreciate 감사하다   keep one's fingers crossed 행운을 빌다

11 ②

M Somi, are the preparations for your trip going well?
W Well, everything is fine except one thing.
M Oh, what's the problem?
W I'm going to rent a car for the trip, but I'm not sure if the hotel offers free parking or not.
M Did you check the website?
W I did, but there was no information about it.
M Then why don't you send an email to the hotel?
W That's a great idea. I'll send an email right now.

남 소미야, 여행 준비는 잘 되고 있니?
여 음, 하나 빼고는 다 괜찮아.
남 오, 뭐가 문제인데?
여 나는 여행하는 동안 차를 빌리려고 하는데, 호텔이 무료 주차를 제공하는지 어떤지 모르겠어.
남 웹 사이트를 확인해 봤어?
여 확인했어. 그런데 그것에 관한 정보는 없었어.
남 그러면 호텔에 이메일을 보내는 건 어때?
여 그거 좋은 생각이다. 지금 당장 이메일을 보내야겠어.

해설 여자는 호텔이 무료 주차를 제공하는지 아닌지를 알아보기 위해 지금 당장 이메일을 보내겠다고 했다.

어휘 preparation 준비   except ~을 제외하고   rent 빌리다   offer 제공하다   park 주차하다   information 정보   send an email 이메일을 보내다

12 ④

M Jisu, I have the schedule for swimming lessons at our city community center.
W Really? Let's look at it together.
M Which do you prefer, a morning or an afternoon lesson?
W A morning lesson is better, but there are only advanced-level lessons in the morning.
M Then we can choose an afternoon lesson for beginners.
W Yeah, I think so. Which day is better for you, Saturday or Sunday?
M As for me, Saturday is better. How about you?
W Me, too. I do volunteer work on Sundays.

남 지수야, 내가 우리 지역 문화 센터에서 하는 수영 수업 시간표를 가지고 있어.
여 정말? 같이 한번 보자.

남 너는 오전 수업과 오후 수업 중 어느 것이 더 좋니?
여 오전 수업이 더 좋아. 하지만 오전엔 상급 수준 수업밖에 없네.
남 그러면 우리는 초급자를 위한 오후 수업을 선택할 수 있어.
여 응, 내 생각도 그래. 너는 토요일과 일요일 중에서 어느 요일이 더 좋니?
남 나는 토요일이 더 좋아. 너는 어때?
여 나도 그래. 난 일요일에는 자원봉사를 하거든.

해설 두 사람은 초급 수준의 오후 수업을 토요일에 들을 것이다.

어휘 prefer 더 좋아하다, 선호하다 advanced 상급의 choose 선택하다 beginner 초보자 do volunteer work 자원봉사를 하다

13 ③

W Hi, Woojin. I have to apologize to you.
M Why?
W Well, I'm so sorry that I forgot your birthday.
M What do you mean?
W Yesterday was your birthday, but I missed it.
M What are you talking about? My birthday hasn't come yet.
W Really? Then whose birthday is on July 8?
M I'm not sure. But mine is tomorrow.
W Oh, sorry. I thought it was yesterday.

여 안녕, 우진아. 나 너에게 사과해야 해.
남 왜?
여 음, 네 생일을 잊어버려서 정말 미안해.
남 그게 무슨 말이야?
여 어제가 네 생일이었는데, 내가 지나쳐 버렸어.
남 무슨 말을 하는 거야? 내 생일은 아직 안 왔어.
여 정말? 그러면 7월 8일은 누구의 생일이지?
남 잘 모르겠어. 하지만 내 생일은 내일이야.
여 오, 미안해. 난 어제인 줄 알았어.

해설 남자의 생일은 어제인 7월 8일이 아니라 내일이라고 했으므로 7월 10일이다.

어휘 apologize 사과하다 forget 잊다 mean 의미하다 miss 놓치다, 지나치다

14 ②

W Jacob, it's already 11 p.m. Aren't you going to bed?
M I'm not sleepy at all.
W Did you drink some coffee?
M No, you know I don't like coffee.
W Well, how about taking a warm shower? It'll make you relax.
M I already took one.
W Then why don't you drink some hot milk? I've heard that it's helpful to fall asleep.
M Okay, I'll try that right now.

여 Jacob, 벌써 11시야. 안 잘 거니?
남 진혀 즐리지 않아요.
여 커피 마셨니?

남 아니요, 저 커피 안 좋아하는 거 아시잖아요.
여 음, 따뜻한 물로 샤워를 해 보는 게 어때? 너를 편안하게 해 줄 거야.
남 이미 했어요.
여 그러면 따뜻한 우유를 좀 마셔보는 게 어떠니? 그게 잠드는 데 도움이 된다고 들었거든.
남 알았어요. 지금 당장 해 볼게요.

해설 여자가 남자에게 샤워를 해 보라고 권하자 남자는 이미 했다고 말했다.

어휘 not ~ at all 전혀 ~하지 않은 take a shower 샤워하다 relax 편하게 하다 helpful 도움이 되는 fall asleep 잠이 들다

15 ③

M Hello, book lovers. One of the world's most beloved writers Andrew Lee will visit our bookstore next Tuesday, at 3 p.m. This is an event to celebrate his latest novel, A Peaceful Mind. First, he will be signing copies of the book. After that, he will read his favorite parts of the book to visitors who registered on our website in advance. Thank you.

남 안녕하세요, 책을 사랑하는 여러분. 세계에서 가장 인기 있는 작가들 중 한 명인 Andrew Lee가 다음 주 화요일 오후 3시에 저희 서점을 방문할 것입니다. 그의 최근 소설 〈A Peaceful Mind〉를 기념하기 위한 행사입니다. 먼저, 그는 책에 사인을 해 드릴 것입니다. 그 후에, 웹 사이트에서 미리 등록한 사람들에게 그가 가장 좋아하는 책의 일부분을 읽어 드릴 것입니다. 감사합니다.

해설 Andrew Lee라는 작가를 초청하는 행사를 알리기 위한 안내 방송이다.

어휘 beloved 인기 많은, 사랑받는 celebrate 기념하다 latest 최근의 copy (책의) 한 부 register 등록하다 in advance 미리

16 ③

M I'd like to buy a stuffed animal for my 5-year-old niece.
W How about this stuffed giraffe? It's very popular among that age group and it's only $10.
M It's cute, but she already has a similar one.
W Then what about this elephant? You can get one for free if you buy one.
M Oh, it's cute, too. How much is it?
W It's $15.
M It's cheaper than I expected. I'll buy two.
W Well, remember you only need to pay for one.
M Oh, that's right. Thanks.

남 다섯 살짜리 조카를 위한 봉제 인형을 사고 싶어요.
여 이 기린 인형은 어떠세요? 그 나이대에서 아주 인기 있고 가격도 10달러밖에 안 해요.
남 귀엽지만, 그녀는 이미 비슷한 것을 갖고 있어요.

여 그러시면 이 코끼리 인형은 어떠세요? 하나를 사시면 하나를 공짜로 받으실 수 있어요.
남 오, 그것도 귀엽네요. 얼마예요?
여 15달러예요.
남 제가 예상했던 것보다 더 싸네요. 두 개를 살게요.
여 그러시면, 손님께서는 한 개 값만 지불하시면 된다는 걸 기억하세요.
남 오, 맞아요. 감사합니다.

해설 남자는 1+1 행사를 하는 15달러짜리 코끼리 인형을 두 개 사겠다고 했으므로 15달러만 지불하면 된다.

어휘 stuffed animal 봉제 인형 niece (여자) 조카 popular 인기 있는 similar 비슷한 for free 무료로 expect 예상하다, 기대하다 pay for ~을 지불하다

17 ⑤

W Noah, you didn't keep your promise.
M Mom, what do you mean?
W Don't you remember? You promised to hang your jacket in the closet instead of leaving it on the floor.
M Oh, I totally forgot about it. I'm so sorry.
W It's too late. As I warned you, I'm not going to give you any allowance for two weeks.
M Mom, please let it go just this once.
W (Sighs) Okay, but remember this will be the last time.
M Thank you for giving me another chance.

여 Noah, 너 약속 안 지켰구나.
남 엄마, 무슨 말씀이세요?
여 기억 안 나니? 네 재킷을 바닥에 던져두는 대신 옷장 안에 걸어 두겠다고 약속했잖니.
남 오, 완전히 잊고 있었어요. 정말 죄송해요.
여 너무 늦었어. 너한테 경고한 대로, 2주 동안 용돈을 주지 않을 거야.
남 엄마, 제발 이번 한 번만 봐 주세요.
여 (한숨을 쉬며) 알았어, 하지만 이번이 마지막이란 걸 기억하렴.
남 기회를 한 번 더 주셔서 감사합니다.

해설 이번이 마지막이라는 말에 기회를 한 번 더 주셔서 감사하다고 응답하는 것이 자연스럽다.
① 물론이에요. 나중에 말씀 드릴게요.
② 그렇게 하지 않으셨어야 해요.
③ 제가 어떻게 해낼지 말씀해 주세요.
④ 행운이 있기를 바랄게요.

어휘 keep one's promise 약속을 지키다 promise 약속하다 hang 걸다 closet 옷장 instead of ~ 대신에 totally 완전히 warn 경고하다 allowance 용돈 let it go 봐주다, 내버려두다 chance 기회

18 ④

M Minji, I've been looking for you!
W Me? For what?
M You know there will be a science fair, right?

W Yes, at the end of the month.
M Will you enter the fair with me?
W Yes, of course. I'd love to. Do you have a project topic yet?
M Actually, I haven't decided yet. Why don't we go to the library and do some research together now?
W I have no time now. How about after school tomorrow?

남 민지야, 너를 계속 찾고 있었어!
여 나를? 무엇 때문에?
남 너 과학 박람회가 있다는 거 알지, 그렇지?
여 응. 이번 달 말에.
남 나랑 같이 박람회에 참가할래?
여 응, 물론이지. 참가하고 싶어. 넌 이미 프로젝트 주제를 정했니?
남 사실, 아직 결정하지 못했어. 지금 도서관에 가서 함께 조사해 보는 게 어때?
여 지금은 시간이 없어. 내일 방과 후는 어떠니?

해설 도서관에 가자고 제안하는 말에 대한 동의 또는 거절의 응답이 와야 한다.
① 널 만나서 정말 기뻐.
② 주제를 바꾸는 것이 가능하니?
③ 기운 내! 너는 다음에 더 잘할 거야.
⑤ 내일까지 책 다 읽는 거 잊지 마.

어휘 fair 박람회 enter 참가하다 topic 주제 decide 결정하다 research 연구, 조사 pleasure 기쁨 possible 가능한 change 바꾸다

19 ③

(Cellphone rings.)
M Hello?
W Hello, Mr. Jones. This is Rachel, your student from last year. Do you remember me?
M Of course! Is there anything wrong, Rachel?
W No, I was just looking at some pictures of my middle school days, and they reminded me of you.
M I see. So how's everything going? Are you doing well in high school?
W Pretty well. If you don't mind, can I drop by your office some time? I would like to say hi.
M Why not? You're welcome any time.

(휴대 전화가 울린다.)
남 여보세요?
여 안녕하세요, Jones 선생님. 저는 작년에 선생님 반 학생이었던 Rachel이에요. 저를 기억하세요?
남 물론이지! 무슨 일이 있니, Rachel?
여 아니요, 그냥 중학교 시절의 사진들을 좀 보고 있었는데, 선생님이 생각났어요.
남 그랬구나. 그래서 잘 지내니? 고등학교에서 잘 하고 있지?
여 아주 잘 지내고 있어요. 괜찮으시다면, 언제 한번 제가 교무실에 잠깐 들러도 될까요? 인사 드리고 싶어요.
남 왜 안 되겠니? 언제든 환영이란다.

해설 옛 제자가 자신을 만나러 오고 싶다고 했으므로 그에 대한 응답으로 언제든지 환영한다고 말하는 것이 자연스럽다.
① 기운 내! 너는 더 잘할 수 있어.
② 여기에서 크게 말하는 것은 잘못된 일이야.
④ 반드시 항상 최선을 다하도록 하렴.
⑤ 네가 나를 만나러 와서 놀랐단다.

어휘 wrong 잘못된   look at ~을 보다   remind A of B A에게 B를 상기시키다   drop by 잠깐 들르다   loudly 크게, 큰소리로   make sure 반드시 ~ 하다

20 ④

W Kate and her friend are having dinner at a popular Italian restaurant. Now Kate understands why the restaurant is so popular because both of them are very satisfied with the taste of the food and its friendly service. But they ordered too much food and they can't finish their pizza. Since it is very delicious, Kate wants to ask the waiter if she can take it home. In this situation, what would Kate most likely say to the waiter?

Kate Could you pack up these leftovers, please?

여 Kate와 그녀의 친구가 인기 있는 이탈리아 식당에서 저녁 식사를 하고 있다. 이제 Kate는 왜 이 식당이 그렇게 인기가 많은지 이해할 수 있었는데 그들 둘 다 음식 맛과 친절한 서비스에 아주 만족하기 때문이다. 하지만 그들은 너무 많은 음식을 주문해서 피자를 다 먹을 수 없다. 그것이 너무 맛있으므로, Kate는 그것을 집으로 가져갈 수 있는지 식당 종업원에게 물어보고 싶어 한다. 이 상황에서, Kate는 종업원에게 무엇이라고 말할 것 같은가?

Kate 남은 음식을 포장해 주실 수 있나요?

해설 남은 음식을 포장해 줄 수 있는지 물어보고 싶은 상황이다.
① 신용 카드로 지불해도 되나요?
② 영수증을 주시겠어요?
③ 오늘 밤 4명 테이블을 예약할 수 있나요?
⑤ 이 피자를 환불받을 수 있나요?

어휘 understand 이해하다   both of ~ 둘 다   be satisfied with ~에 만족하다   taste 맛   friendly 친절한   order 주문하다   receipt 영수증   pack up 포장하다   leftover 남은 음식   get a refund 환불받다

01 ⑤	02 ②	03 ③	04 ①	05 ②
06 ③	07 ④	08 ③	09 ③	10 ②
11 ④	12 ②	13 ③	14 ⑤	15 ⑤
16 ③	17 ③	18 ③	19 ⑤	20 ④

01 ⑤

M Have you decided what to buy for Somi's birthday?
W Not yet. I'm still not sure what she would like.
M How about this striped cap? She likes this pattern.
W Well, she already has a lot of caps.
M Umm... what about that T-shirt with a bear on it? It looks cute.
W But it's long-sleeved. I think a short-sleeved one will be better because it's already summer.
M Then you can buy this one with a rabbit on it.
W Good! She likes rabbits. I'll get that one.

남 소미 생일을 위해 무엇을 살지 결정했니?
여 아직 못했어. 그녀가 무엇을 좋아할지 아직 모르겠어.
남 이 줄무늬 모자는 어때? 그녀는 이 무늬를 좋아하잖아.
여 음, 그녀는 이미 많은 모자를 가지고 있는 걸.
남 음… 곰이 그려진 저 티셔츠는 어때? 귀여워 보이는데.
여 그렇지만 긴소매잖아. 벌써 여름이니까 반소매가 더 좋을 것 같아.
남 그러면 토끼가 그려진 이걸 사면 되겠다.
여 좋은 걸! 그녀는 토끼를 좋아하거든. 그걸로 살게.

해설 여자는 토끼가 그려진 반소매 티셔츠를 사겠다고 했다.

어휘 decide 결정하다   sure 확신하는   striped 줄무늬의   pattern 무늬   long-sleeved 긴소매의   short-sleeved 반소매의, 짧은 소매의

02 ②

W Jaemin, do you know a good Korean restaurant?
M Sure, I know a good place called Korean Garden.
W Oh, what do they serve there?
M Bibimbap, bulgogi, pajeon, and almost every other Korean dish.
W Sounds delicious. Can you tell me where it is?
M It's across from the police station.
W Is parking available?
M You don't have to worry about parking. It has a huge parking lot.

여 재민아, 너 괜찮은 한국 음식점을 아니?
남 물론이지, Korean Garden이라는 좋은 곳을 알아.
여 오, 거기에서 무엇을 파는데?
남 비빔밥, 불고기, 파전, 그리고 거의 모든 한국 요리가 있어.
여 맛있겠다. 그것이 어디에 있는지 말해 줄래?
남 경찰서 맞은편에 있어.

여 주차가 가능할까?
남 주차에 대해서는 걱정할 필요 없어. 굉장히 큰 주차장이 있거든.

해설 음식의 가격은 언급되지 않았다.

어휘 place 장소　delicious 맛있는　across from ～ 맞은편에　available 이용할 수 있는　worry about ～에 대해 걱정하다　huge 매우 큰　parking lot 주차장

03 ③

(Telephone rings.)
M Hello? This is Pure Water Company. Is this Ms. Brown?
W Yes. What are you calling about?
M I scheduled my water delivery for tomorrow.
W Is there a problem?
M Yes, I would like to reschedule it. Can I have it delivered the day after tomorrow?
W Sure. That shouldn't be a problem.
M Thank you. Is 5:30 okay?
W Anytime is okay. I'll be home all day.
M Okay. Your delivery date has been changed.

(전화벨이 울린다.)
남 여보세요? Pure Water Company입니다. Brown 씨이신가요?
여 네. 무슨 일로 전화하시는 거죠?
남 제가 내일 생수를 배달하기로 했죠.
여 문제가 있나요?
남 네, 일정을 변경하고 싶어서요. 제가 모레 배달해 드려도 될까요?
여 물론이죠. 그건 문제가 안돼요.
남 감사합니다. 5시 30분 괜찮으세요?
여 언제든 괜찮아요. 하루 종일 집에 있을 거예요.
남 알겠습니다. 배송 일정이 변경되었습니다.

해설 남자는 내일로 예정되어 있던 생수 배달 일정을 모레로 변경하기 위해 전화했다.

어휘 schedule 예정하다, 일정을 잡다　delivery 배달　reschedule 일정을 변경하다　deliver 배달하다　the day after tomorrow 모레　anytime 언제든지　change 변경하다

04 ①

W Hey, they're showing Beyond the Sky at the MJ Theater.
M Is that the movie about some explorers traveling through space?
W Right. I heard it's good. Do you want to watch it with me tomorrow?
M Okay. When do you want to watch it?
W The movie times are 3:30, 7:40, and 10:00 p.m. Which one do you prefer?
M Let's take the earliest. I must be home before dinner.
W Okay. Then why don't we meet there 30 minutes

before the movie starts?
M Okay. See you then.

여 야, MJ 극장에서 〈Beyond the Sky〉가 상영 중이야.
남 그거 우주를 여행하는 몇몇 탐험가들에 관한 영화지?
여 맞아. 좋다고 하더라. 내일 나랑 그 영화 볼래?
남 좋아. 언제 보고 싶은데?
여 상영 시간이 오후 3시 30분, 7시 40분, 그리고 10시야. 너는 어떤 게 더 좋니?
남 가장 빠른 걸로 보자. 저녁 식사 전에 집에 들어가야 해.
여 좋아. 그럼 영화 시작하기 30분 전에 거기서 만나는 게 어때?
남 좋아. 그때 보자.

해설 가장 빠른 시간인 3시 30분 영화를 보기로 했고 영화 시작 30분 전에 만나기로 했으므로, 두 사람이 만날 시각은 오후 3시이다.

어휘 beyond ～을 넘어서　explorer 탐험가　travel 여행하다　space 우주

05 ②

M We've arrived too soon. There's a lot of time left.
W Yeah, our flight doesn't leave for another two hours.
M What will we do for two hours?
W Do you feel like a snack before boarding?
M No, I'm okay.
W Then how about doing some duty-free shopping?
M Good idea. I'll buy some gifts for my family at a duty-free shop. Let's go.

남 우리 너무 일찍 도착했어. 시간이 많이 남아.
여 그래, 우리 비행기는 두 시간 후에 출발해.
남 두 시간 동안 뭐하지?
여 탑승하기 전에 간식을 좀 먹고 싶니?
남 아니, 난 괜찮아.
여 그럼 면세점에서 쇼핑하는 건 어때?
남 좋은 생각이야. 면세점에서 가족들 선물을 좀 사야겠어. 가자.

해설 비행기 탑승 전에 면세점에서 쇼핑을 하기로 했으므로 대화가 이루어지는 장소는 공항이다.

어휘 flight 항공편　leave 출발하다, 떠나다　snack 간식　board 탑승하다　gift 선물　duty-free shop 면세점

06 ③

① W Whose notebook is this?
　 M It's my sister's.
② W Why are you so upset?
　 M My team lost the game.
③ W Do you mind if I close the window?
　 M No, go ahead.
④ W Do you know who broke the window?
　 M I'm not sure, but I think Tom did.
⑤ W Which do you prefer, summer or winter?
　 M I prefer winter.

① 여 이것은 누구 공책이니?
　 남 내 여동생 거야.

② **여** 너 왜 그렇게 기분이 안 좋니?
　남 우리 팀이 경기에서 졌어.
③ **여** 내가 창문을 닫아도 될까?
　남 응, 닫아.
④ **여** 너는 누가 창문을 깼는지 아니?
　남 확실하지는 않지만, Tom이 그런 것 같아.
⑤ **여** 너는 여름과 겨울 중에서 어느 것을 더 좋아하니?
　남 난 겨울을 더 좋아해.

해설 여자가 추워하면서 남자에게 창문을 닫아도 되는지 묻는 상황이다.

어휘 upset 속상한, 화가 난　lose (경기를) 지다　Do you mind if ~? ~해도 괜찮겠습니까?　break 깨뜨리다

07 ④

M Lily, are you excited about your field trip tomorrow?
W Of course. I can't wait.
M Is everything ready now?
W Yes, Dad. I think I packed almost everything that I need.
M Did you pack your umbrella, too?
W Well, I'm not sure if it will rain or not. Can you please check the weather forecast?
M Okay, wait a second.

남 Lily, 내일 체험 학습이 기대되니?
여 물론이죠. 너무 기다려져요.
남 이제 다 준비되었니?
여 네, 아빠. 제가 필요한 거의 모든 것을 싼 것 같아요.
남 우산도 챙겼니?
여 음, 비가 올지 안 올지 모르겠어요. 일기 예보를 확인해 주실래요?
남 알았어, 잠깐만 기다리렴.

해설 여자는 남자에게 일기 예보를 확인해 달라고 부탁했다.

어휘 field trip 체험 학습　ready 준비된　pack 싸다　weather forecast 일기 예보

08 ③

W Hello, students. I'd like to tell you about an annual event at our school, the Charity Sale. It's going to be held this coming Friday, from 2 p.m. to 5 p.m. If you would like to participate and sell your things for charity, please bring them to your homeroom teacher by Wednesday. All the profits from the sale will go to people in need in our town. So let's enjoy the event and help others together!

여 학생 여러분, 안녕하세요. 우리 학교의 연례행사인 Charity Sale에 대해 말씀드리려고 합니다. 그것은 다가오는 금요일 오후 2시부터 5시까지 열릴 것입니다. 참가하여 자선을 위해 물건들을 판매하고 싶으면, 담임 선생님께 수요일까지 가져다 드리세요. 모든 판매 수익은 우리 마을의 어려운 사람들에게 전달될 것입니다. 그러니 함께 행사를 즐기고 다른 사람들을 도와줍시다!

해설 목표 모금액은 언급되지 않았다.

어휘 annual 매년의, 연례의　charity 자선　hold 열다, 개최하다　participate 참가하다　profit 수익　in need 궁핍한, 어려움에 처한

09 ③

M This is a cute animal loved by many people around the world. It's a large animal and it has black and white fur. It likes to eat bamboo and climb trees. It also likes to walk around the forest. You can see this animal especially in China, and it's one of the reasons people visit China.

남 이것은 전 세계의 많은 사람들에게 사랑받는 귀여운 동물입니다. 그것은 큰 동물이고, 검은색과 흰색 털을 가지고 있습니다. 그것은 대나무를 먹는 것과 나무에 오르는 것을 좋아합니다. 그것은 또한 숲을 걸어다니는 것을 좋아합니다. 여러분은 특히 중국에서 이 동물을 볼 수 있으며, 그것이 사람들이 중국을 방문하는 이유들 중 하나입니다.

해설 검은색과 흰색 털을 가지고 있으며 대나무 먹는 것을 좋아하는 동물은 판다이다.

어휘 around the world 전 세계의　fur 털　bamboo 대나무　forest 숲　especially 특히　reason 이유

10 ②

① **M** What are you going to do tomorrow?
　W I'm going to go fishing.
② **M** Are you satisfied with your new car?
　W I'm glad you like it.
③ **M** I think you know him, don't you?
　W Yeah, I met him at your birthday party last year.
④ **M** Can you tell me how to get to the train station?
　W Go straight one block and turn left.
⑤ **M** Don't give up! You can do it!
　W Thanks. I'll try again.

① **남** 내일 뭐 할 거야?
　여 나는 낚시하러 갈 거야.
② **남** 새로 산 차에 만족하니?
　여 네가 그것을 좋아해서 기뻐.
③ **남** 네가 그를 아는 것 같아, 그렇지 않니?
　여 맞아, 작년 네 생일 파티에서 그를 만났어.
④ **남** 기차역에 어떻게 가는지 말씀해 주시겠어요?
　여 한 블록 직진해서 왼쪽으로 도세요.
⑤ **남** 포기하지 마! 넌 할 수 있어!
　여 고마워. 다시 해 볼게.

해설 ② 새로 산 차에 대해 만족하는지 묻는 말에 상대방이 그걸 좋아해서 기쁘다고 답하는 것은 어색하다.

어휘 go fishing 낚시하러 가다　be satisfied with ~에 만족하다　how to ~하는 방법　turn left 좌회전하다　give up 포기하다

11 ④

M Sarah, you look excited today.
W Yeah, I'm finally going to see Chris Choi's new movie in the theater today.
M Did you already buy a ticket?
W Sure, I got it a week ago. Tickets are almost sold out at every theater.
M That's because he has a lot of fans. Are you going to the theater soon?
W Yes, I'm going to the theater after submitting this report.
M Okay, have fun!

남 Sarah, 너 오늘 신나 보인다.
여 응, 오늘 드디어 Chris Choi의 새 영화를 극장에서 보거든.
남 표는 벌써 샀니?
여 물론, 일주일 전에 샀어. 표가 극장마다 거의 매진이야.
남 그가 팬이 많아서 그래. 곧 극장에 갈 거니?
여 응, 이 보고서를 제출하고 나서 극장에 갈 거야.
남 알았어, 즐거운 시간 보내!

해설 여자는 극장에 가기 전에 보고서를 제출할 것이라고 했다.

어휘 excited 신이 난   theater 극장   sold out 다 팔린, 매진된   fan 팬   submit 제출하다

12 ②

W Hi. I'd like to buy an e-book reader.
M Okay, do you have any specific model in mind?
W Not really, but I'd prefer a lighter one.
M How about the E-320 model? It's only 170 grams, and the screen is a good size.
W I like it, but it's a little expensive for me. I would like something under $150.
M Then take a look at the E-220 model. It's very popular these days.
W I think the screen is too small. I'll take the next model with a larger screen.

여 안녕하세요. 저는 전자책 단말기를 사고 싶어요.
남 네, 마음에 두고 있는 특정 모델이 있으세요?
여 아니요, 하지만 저는 보다 가벼운 걸 선호해요.
남 E-320 모델은 어때요? 170g밖에 안 나가고 화면 사이즈가 괜찮아요.
여 마음에 들지만, 저에게는 약간 비싸네요. 150달러 미만이 좋겠어요.
남 그러시면 E-220 모델을 한번 보세요. 요즘 아주 인기 있어요.
여 화면이 너무 작은 것 같아요. 저는 화면이 좀 더 큰 다음 모델을 살게요.

해설 여자는 150달러가 넘지 않으면서 E-220 모델보다 화면이 더 큰 다음 모델을 사겠다고 했다.

어휘 e-book reader 전자책 단말기   specific 특정한   light 가벼운   screen 화면   a little 약간   take a look at 한번 보다   popular 인기 있는

13 ③

M Excuse me. Did you go to Daehan High School?
W Yes, were you in Mr. Smith's class?
M Yes, it's me, James! Long time, no see.
W Wow! You haven't changed a bit. Do you have time to grab a coffee?
M I'd love to, but I'm busy now. How about meeting next week?
W Sounds great. Any day is fine except Thursday. How about next Saturday?
M I need to go to the dentist that day. What about Friday afternoon?
W Good, let me know your phone number. I'll call you before then.

남 실례합니다. 대한 고등학교에 다니셨나요?
여 네, Smith 선생님 반이셨어요?
남 응, 나야, James! 오랜만이야.
여 와! 너는 하나도 안 변했구나. 커피 한 잔 마실 시간 있어?
남 그러고 싶지만, 지금은 바빠. 다음 주에 만나는 게 어때?
여 좋아. 목요일 외에는 언제든 괜찮아. 다음 주 토요일은 어때?
남 그날에는 치과에 가야 해. 금요일 오후는 어떠니?
여 좋아, 네 전화번호를 알려 줘. 그 전에 전화할게.

해설 두 사람은 다음 주 금요일 오후에 만나기로 했다.

어휘 high school 고등학교   change 변하다   grab 잡다, 잠깐 ~하다   except ~을 제외하고   dentist 치과의사

14 ⑤

W Harry, I saw a poster for a contest which is perfect for you.
M What do you mean by perfect for me?
W It's a singing contest for middle school students. You've always wanted to enter one.
M Really? Tell me more.
W It's going to be held on May 17, and first prize is $100.
M Wow! I should practice harder.
W Oh, and one more thing! You need to sign up by today.
M Okay, I'll do it right now.

여 Harry, 내가 너에게 딱 맞는 경연 대회 포스터를 봤어.
남 나에게 딱 맞는다는 게 무슨 말이야?
여 중학생들을 위한 노래 경연 대회야. 넌 항상 참가하고 싶어 했잖아.
남 정말? 더 말해 줘.
여 그건 5월 17일에 열리는데, 1등 상금이 100달러야.
남 와! 난 더 열심히 연습해야겠다.
여 오, 그리고 한 가지 더 있어! 오늘까지 신청해야 해.
남 알았어, 지금 당장 할게.

해설 남자는 지금 당장 노래 경연 대회에 참가 신청을 하겠다고 했다.

어휘 poster 포스터   perfect 적합한, 완벽한   prize 상, 상금   practice 연습하다   sign up 신청하다, 등록하다

어휘 especially 특히   total 합계, 총액   order 주문하다
bottle 병   take ~ off (표시된 금액 등에서) ~을 빼다   bill
계산서   discount 할인

15 ⑤

W Good morning, everybody. Welcome back to *One-minute Health*. Do you feel refreshed or still tired after you wake up? If you want to improve the quality of your sleep, please listen to my suggestions carefully. First, take a warm bath at night. It'll help relax your body and prepare your mind for sleep. Second, reduce the amount of time you use your smartphone before bed. Try these suggestions tonight. You'll feel much better tomorrow morning.

여 안녕하세요, 여러분. '1분 건강' 시간입니다. 잠에서 깨고 나면 상쾌하신가요, 아니면 여전히 피곤하신가요? 수면의 질을 향상 시키고 싶으시면, 제가 제안하는 것들을 잘 들어보세요. 먼저, 밤에 따뜻한 목욕을 하세요. 그것은 당신의 몸의 긴장을 풀어주 고 마음을 잠들기 위한 상태로 준비하도록 도와줄 것입니다. 둘 째, 잠들기 전에 스마트폰 사용 시간을 줄이세요. 오늘 밤에 이 제안들을 시도해 보세요. 당신은 내일 아침에 훨씬 더 나아진 것을 느낄 것입니다.

해설 잠들기 전 목욕하기, 스마트폰 사용 시간 줄이기와 같은 수면 의 질을 향상시키는 방법을 알려 주고 있다.

어휘 refreshed 상쾌한   wake up 깨다   improve 향상시키다
quality 질, 우수함   suggestion 제안   take a bath 목욕하다
relax 긴장을 풀다   prepare 준비하다   reduce 줄이다
amount 양

16 ③

W How did you like the food?
M Great. We enjoyed everything. The steak was especially nice.
W Thanks. The total comes to $54.
M Oh, wait. We ordered 2 bottles of coke, but we didn't open them. Could you please take them off the bill?
W Okay. They are $2 each, so that comes to $50.
M Here's my credit card.
W And I'll give you a 10% discount coupon for your next visit.
M Thanks.

여 음식은 어땠나요?
남 훌륭했어요. 우리는 모든 것을 즐겼어요. 스테이크가 특히 좋았 어요.
여 감사합니다. 총 54달러입니다.
남 오, 잠깐만요. 우리는 콜라 두 병을 주문했는데, 개봉하지 않았 어요. 그것들을 계산서에서 제외시켜 주시겠어요?
여 네. 각 병은 2달러니까, 50달러입니다.
남 여기 제 신용 카드 드릴게요.
여 그리고 다음 방문 시에 사용하실 수 있는 10퍼센트 할인 쿠폰 을 드릴게요.
남 고맙습니다.

해설 남자는 총 54달러에서 개봉하지 않은 2달러짜리 콜라 두 병 을 제외하고 50달러를 지불하면 된다.

17 ③

(*Telephone rings.*)
M TM Electronics Store. How can I help you?
W Hi. I'd like to ask for the home repair service.
M Thanks. What seems to be the problem?
W My TV screen just went black. I want it fixed as soon as possible.
M Sorry for the inconvenience. May I have your name and address, please?
W Claire Kim at 125 Kings Road.
M Okay, Ms. Kim. Will you be home on Thursday, around noon?
W No, I don't think I will be home at that time. What about 3 p.m.?
M Okay. We'll send someone then.

(*전화벨이 울린다.*)
남 TM Electronics Store입니다. 무엇을 도와드릴까요?
여 안녕하세요. 홈 수리 서비스를 신청하고 싶어서요.
남 감사합니다. 뭐가 문제죠?
여 TV 화면이 까맣게 변했어요. 가능한 한 빨리 수리되길 원해요.
남 불편을 끼쳐 드려서 죄송합니다. 이름과 주소를 말씀해 주시겠 어요?
여 Kings 가 125번지에 사는 Claire Kim입니다.
남 알겠습니다. Kim 선생님. 목요일 정오경에 집에 계신가요?
여 아니요. 그때는 집에 없을 것 같아요. 오후 3시는 어떠세요?
남 네. 그때 기사를 보내 드리겠습니다.

해설 여자가 수리 서비스를 받을 시각으로 오후 3시는 어떤지 되 물었으므로, 이를 수락하며 그때 기사를 보내 주겠다고 답하는 것 이 자연스럽다.
① 빨리 배우시네요.
② 주문을 확인하겠습니다.
④ 죄송합니다. 저는 당신을 더 이상 믿지 않아요.
⑤ 용서해 주세요. 그럴 의도는 아니었어요.

어휘 repair 수리; 수리하다   problem 문제   fix 수리하다   as
soon as possible 가능한 한 빨리   inconvenience 불편
trust 믿다, 신뢰하다   forgive 용서하다

18 ③

W Junsu, you look so tired.
M Yeah, my whole body aches these days.
W How about getting some exercise?
M Well, actually I'm thinking of taking a yoga class. But it's a little expensive.
W In that case, you can just do yoga at home.
M Really? How can I do that? I don't know any yoga poses.
W You can watch yoga videos online and follow the instructor.

M Wouldn't it be difficult?
W Not really. Even I can do it.

여 준수야, 너 정말 피곤해 보여.
남 응, 요즘 온몸이 아파.
여 운동을 좀 하는 게 어때?
남 음, 사실 나는 요가 수업을 들을까 생각 중이야. 그런데 좀 비싸네.
여 그런 경우라면, 집에서 그냥 요가를 할 수 있어.
남 정말? 어떻게 그것을 할 수 있니? 나는 요가 자세를 전혀 모르는데.
여 온라인으로 요가 동영상을 보고 강사를 따라 하면 돼.
남 어렵지 않을까?
여 그렇지 않아. 나도 그걸 할 수 있는걸.

해설 요가 동영상을 보고 따라 하는 게 어렵지 않을지 묻는 말에 대한 긍정 또는 부정의 응답이 와야 한다.
① 미안해, 모두 내 잘못이야.
② 널 만나서 기뻐.
④ 지금 무엇을 해야 할지 모르겠어.
⑤ 화낼 거 없어.

어휘 ache 아프다   these days 요즈음   actually 사실, 실제로   yoga 요가   pose 자세   online 온라인으로   follow 따르다, 따라 하다   instructor 강사   fault 잘못

19   ⑤

W John, are you still doing your homework? It's already 11 p.m.
M Yes, Mom, but there's a lot to do.
W I told you to start working on it earlier.
M You're right. I should have followed your advice.
W When do you think you can finish it?
M Unfortunately, I don't know.
W Do you want me to get you a snack?
M That'd be great.
W Okay. But remember you need to manage your time better.
M I know. I won't let the same thing happen again.

여 John, 아직 숙제하는 중이니? 벌써 밤 11시야.
남 네, 엄마, 그렇지만 해야 할 게 많아요.
여 더 일찍 시작하라고 내가 말했잖니.
남 맞아요. 엄마의 충고를 따랐어야 했어요.
여 언제 그걸 끝낼 수 있을 것 같니?
남 불행하게도, 모르겠어요.
여 내가 간식을 좀 갖다 줄까?
남 그러면 좋겠어요.
여 그래. 하지만 넌 시간 관리를 더 잘해야 한다는 것을 기억하렴.
남 알겠어요. 다시는 똑같은 일이 일어나지 않도록 할게요.

해설 시간 관리를 더 잘해야 한다는 여자의 조언에 다시는 똑같은 일이 일어나지 않도록 하겠다고 답하는 것이 자연스럽다.
① 새로운 직장을 구하는 걸 기다릴 수 없어요.
② 네. 제가 모든 걸 했어요.
③ 곧 다시 주무시는 게 좋겠어요.
④ 지금 바로 출발하실 것을 추천해요.

어휘 should have p.p. ~했어야 했다   follow 따르다   advice 충고, 조언   unfortunately 유감스럽게도, 불행하게도   manage 관리하다   on one's own 혼자, 혼자 힘으로   recommend 추천하다

20   ④

M Jiho has an important test tomorrow. He can't concentrate on studying at home, so he decides to go to the library to study. For a little while, he is able to focus on studying without being interrupted. However, Lisa soon enters the library, and he gets distracted by her because he can hear the music that she is listening to. In this situation, what would Jiho say to Lisa?
Jiho Lisa, can you please turn down the volume?

남 지호는 내일 중요한 시험이 있다. 그는 집에서 공부에 집중할 수가 없어서 공부하기 위해 도서관에 가기로 결심한다. 잠시 동안, 그는 방해받지 않고 공부에 집중할 수 있다. 하지만, Lisa가 곧 도서관에 들어오고, 그는 그녀가 듣고 있는 음악 소리가 들리기 때문에 그녀로 인해 산만해진다. 이러한 상황에서, 지호는 Lisa에게 뭐라고 말하겠는가?
지호 Lisa, 소리 좀 줄여 줄래?

해설 도서관에서 음악 소리 때문에 집중할 수 없어서 소리를 줄여 달라고 요청하려는 상황이다.
① 그런 말을 들어서 유감이야.
② 네 책 가져오는 걸 잊지 마.
③ 네 친구 말을 듣는 게 어때?
⑤ 내가 너라면, 나는 불평을 그만 하겠어.

어휘 concentrate 집중하다   decide 결심하다   focus on ~에 집중하다   interrupt 방해하다   enter 들어가다, 들어오다   distracted 산만해진   turn down (소리 등을) 줄이다   complain 불평하다

Word Check 01회

01 실수	**02** 기념하다, 축하하다
03 정보	**04** 사과하다
05 편하게 하다	**06** ~에 참가하다
07 안도	**08** 제공하다
09 참가자	**10** 막다, 예방하다
11 사진을 찍다	**12** 기회
13 list	**14** bathroom
15 real	**16** pattern
17 recommend	**18** protect
19 beloved	**20** research
21 receipt	**22** similar
23 pay for	**24** be satisfied with

Expression Check

25 at all	**26** made a mistake
27 do volunteer work	**28** write down
29 drop by	**30** for free

Word Check 02회

01 배달하다	**02** 우주
03 연습하다	**04** 적합한, 완벽한
05 충고, 조언	**06** 아프다
07 참가하다	**08** 제출하다
09 이용할 수 있는	**10** 주차장
11 목욕하다	**12** 산만해진
13 change	**14** complain
15 concentrate	**16** forgive
17 explorer	**18** improve
19 board	**20** discount
21 interrupt	**22** weather forecast
23 in need	**24** the day after tomorrow

Expression Check

25 sign up	**26** give up
27 should have followed	**28** don't have to
29 as, as possible	**30** focus on

01 ⑤	02 ④	03 ③	04 ③	05 ②
06 ③	07 ⑤	08 ⑤	09 ①	10 ④
11 ③	12 ①	13 ④	14 ②	15 ②
16 ②	17 ③	18 ⑤	19 ①	20 ⑤

01 ⑤

M Can I help you?
W Yes. I'm looking for a watch.
M What kind of design would you like?
W I want one with an animal picture.
M Then how about this one? It has a dog on the watch face.
W Well, I think that's inconvenient since it has no numbers. Can I see some digital watches?
M How about this one with a cat picture?
W I'd like to buy the one with two sitting cats.

남 도와드릴까요?
여 네. 전 시계를 찾고 있어요.
남 어떤 종류의 디자인을 원하시나요?
여 동물 그림이 있는 시계를 원해요.
남 그러면 이건 어떠세요? 시계 숫자판에 개가 그려져 있어요.
여 음, 그것은 숫자가 없어서 불편한 것 같아요. 디지털 시계를 볼 수 있을까요?
남 이 고양이 그림이 있는 시계는 어떠세요?
여 저는 고양이 두 마리가 앉아 있는 그림의 시계를 사고 싶어요.

해설 여자는 고양이 두 마리가 앉아 있는 그림이 그려진 디지털 시계를 사겠다고 했다.

어휘 look for ~을 찾다 design 디자인 watch face 시계 숫자판 inconvenient 불편한 digital 디지털의

02 ④

W Henry, can you give me a hand?
M Sure. What do you need?
W My old friends are coming this weekend, and I need to make a plan.
M Do you want me to recommend some good places to go?
W Well, I've already decided where to go, but I'm worried about what to eat.
M I know some good restaurants.
W Really? Can you recommend some of them?
M No problem.

여 Henry, 나 좀 도와줄 수 있어?
남 물론이지. 뭐가 필요하니?
여 내 옛 친구들이 이번 주말에 오거든. 그래서 계획을 세워야 해.
남 갈 만한 좋은 장소를 추천해 줄까?
여 음, 난 이미 갈 곳은 정했는데, 무엇을 먹어야 할지가 걱정이야.

남 내가 몇몇 좋은 식당들을 알고 있어.
여 정말? 그것들 중 몇 곳을 추천해 줄 수 있니?
남 문제없지.

해설 여자는 자신의 옛 친구들과 식사할 좋은 식당을 추천해 달라고 부탁했다.

어휘 give ~ a hand ~을 도와주다 make a plan 계획하다 recommend 추천하다 decide 결정하다 be worried about ~에 대해 걱정하다

03 ③

① W What do you think of my new hair color?
　M I think that color is good for you.
② W Where can I put this chair?
　M You can put it over there.
③ W Do you like your new hairstyle?
　M Yes, I love it. Thanks.
④ W Is it okay to use your cellphone?
　M Sure, here it is.
⑤ W If I were you, I'd buy another one.
　M Okay, I'll follow your advice.

① 여 제 새로운 머리 색에 대해 어떻게 생각하세요?
　남 색이 당신에게 잘 어울리는 것 같아요.
② 여 이 의자를 어디에 놓을까요?
　남 저쪽에 놓으시면 됩니다.
③ 여 새로운 헤어스타일이 마음에 드시나요?
　남 네, 좋아요. 고마워요.
④ 여 당신의 휴대 전화를 써도 될까요?
　남 물론이죠, 여기 있어요.
⑤ 여 제가 당신이라면, 다른 걸 살 거예요.
　남 알았어요, 당신의 충고를 따를게요.

해설 여자 미용사와 남자 손님이 머리 모양에 대해 대화를 나누는 상황이다.

어휘 over there 저쪽에 hairstyle 머리 모양 follow 따르다 advice 조언, 충고

04 ③

M Attention, please. My name is James. For the next 6 months I'll be your lab instructor. I will help you set up your experiments, but my most important responsibility is to keep you safe. Please wear safety goggles and gloves at all times while you're in the lab. Don't smell or taste any unknown substances. At last, you should report all accidents and injuries to me immediately. Thank you.

남 주목해 주세요. 제 이름은 James입니다. 저는 앞으로 6개월 동안 여러분과 함께 할 실험실 강사입니다. 저는 여러분의 실험 준비를 도와드리겠지만, 저의 가장 중요한 책임은 여러분을 안전하게 지키는 것입니다. 실험실에 있는 동안에는 항상 보호 안경과 장갑을 착용해 주십시오. 알 수 없는 물질은 냄새를 맡거나 맛을 보지 마십시오. 마지막으로, 모든 사고와 부상은 즉시 저에게 알려 주시기 바랍니다. 감사합니다.

해설 실험실 강사가 실험실에서 학생들의 안전을 지키기 위한 수칙을 설명하고 있다.

어휘 lab 실험실 instructor 강사 set up 준비하다 experiment 실험 responsibility 책임 safety 안전 at all times 항상 unknown 알 수 없는 substance 물질 accident 사고 injury 부상 immediately 즉시

05 ②

W I love playing this new mobile game.
M What's the name of it?
W It's called *The Legend of Dragons*.
M Tell me more about it.
W It's a game about raising your own dragon.
M Sounds interesting! Is it free to download?
W Sure, you can download it from the mobile store. It's only 20 megabytes.
M Great! I'll download and play it right now.

여 나는 이 새로운 모바일 게임 하는 게 정말 좋아.
남 이름이 뭔데?
여 〈The Legend of Dragons〉야.
남 더 자세히 얘기해 봐.
여 그건 너 자신의 용을 키우는 것에 관한 게임이야.
남 흥미로운 걸! 다운로드는 무료니?
여 물론이지. 모바일 상점에서 다운로드할 수 있어. 그것은 단지 20메가바이트야.
남 좋은데! 지금 바로 다운로드해 봐야지.

해설 게임 규칙은 언급되지 않았다.

어휘 mobile 이동하는; 휴대 전화 legend 전설 dragon 용 raise 기르다 free 무료의 download 다운로드하다

06 ③

W I'm sorry to have kept you waiting. How can I help you?
M I'd like to open a savings account.
W All right. Could I see your ID card?
M Of course, here it is.
W Please read this carefully and fill out the form.
M Okay. (*Pause*) Do I have to sign here?
W Oh, yes. How much do you want to deposit today?
M Fifty dollars.

여 기다리시게 해서 죄송합니다. 무엇을 도와드릴까요?
남 저축 예금 계좌를 개설하고 싶어서요.
여 네, 신분증을 볼 수 있을까요?
남 물론이죠, 여기 있어요.
여 이것을 신중히 읽어 보시고 서식을 작성해 주세요.
남 알겠습니다. (잠시 후) 여기에 서명을 해야 하나요?
여 오, 맞습니다. 오늘은 얼마를 입금하시길 원하세요?
남 50달러요.

해설 통장을 개설하려는 고객과 은행 직원 사이의 대화이다.

어휘 savings account 저축 예금 계좌 ID card 신분증 carefully 주의 깊게 fill out 작성하다, 기입하다 form 서식,

양식 sign 서명하다 deposit 입금하다

07 ⑤

① **M** Can I get your advice on something?
  W Of course. What is it?
② **M** Drinks are not allowed in here.
  W Sorry. I didn't know that.
③ **M** I really appreciate what you've done.
  W It's my pleasure.
④ **M** I've been looking forward to summer vacation.
  W Oh, do you have any special plans?
⑤ **M** It isn't clear to me what this picture means.
  W My hobby is taking pictures.

① 남 조언을 구할 수 있을까요?
  여 물론이죠. 뭔데요?
② 남 이곳은 음료수가 금지되어 있습니다.
  여 죄송합니다. 몰랐어요.
③ 남 당신이 해 주신 것에 대해 정말 감사드려요.
  여 천만에요.
④ 남 저는 여름 방학을 기대해 왔어요.
  여 오, 특별한 계획이 있나요?
⑤ 남 이 사진이 무엇을 의미하는지 잘 모르겠어요.
  여 제 취미는 사진을 찍는 것입니다.

해설 ⑤ 사진의 의미를 잘 이해할 수 없다는 말에 자신의 취미가 사진 촬영이라고 답하는 것은 어색하다.

어휘 advice 조언, 충고 allow 허락하다 appreciate 감사하다 look forward to ~을 기대하다

08 ⑤

M Mina, why the long face?
W Well, my computer didn't let me finish my homework.
M What do you mean?
W While I was doing my homework, it just shut down.
M That's too bad. Is there anything that I can help you with?
W If you don't mind, can you please lend me your notebook computer for a while?
M No problem. How long do you need it for?
W I think an hour will be enough.
M Okay, it's all yours for an hour.

남 미나야, 왜 그렇게 시무룩하니?
여 음, 컴퓨터 때문에 숙제를 끝내지 못했어.
남 무슨 말이야?
여 내가 숙제를 하고 있는데, 컴퓨터가 멈췄어.
남 정말 안됐구나. 내가 도와줄 수 있는 게 있니?
여 괜찮다면, 네 노트북 컴퓨터 좀 잠시 빌려줄래?
남 문제없지. 얼마 동안 필요하니?
여 한 시간이면 충분할 것 같아.
남 알았어, 한 시간 동안 마음대로 써.

해설 여자는 남자에게 노트북 컴퓨터를 빌려 달라고 부탁했다.

어휘 long face 시무룩한 얼굴 shut down (기계가) 멈추다 lend 빌려주다 for a while 잠시 동안 enough 충분한

09 ①

M Susan, I've been looking for you.
W Minho, what's up? Why are you so excited?
M Guess what! I have some terrific news.
W I'm not sure. What is it?
M I got the full-time job I wanted at Daehan.
W Really? You got the job? It's a great company. I'm glad to hear that.
M Yeah, thanks to you, I was able to do it.
W You're welcome, but I didn't really do anything. You did it on your own!
M No way. Without your help, I couldn't have passed the interview.

남 Susan, 난 너를 찾고 있었어.
여 민호야, 무슨 일이야? 왜 그렇게 신났어?
남 알아맞혀 봐! 아주 좋은 소식이 있어.
여 잘 모르겠어. 무슨 일이니?
남 대한에서 내가 원했던 정규직 일자리를 구했어.
여 정말? 너 취직했다고? 그곳은 큰 회사잖아. 그 말을 들으니 기쁘다.
남 응, 네 덕분에 해낼 수 있었어.
여 천만에, 하지만 난 정말 아무것도 안 했는걸. 네가 스스로 해 낸 거야!
남 말도 안 돼. 네 도움이 없었다면, 난 면접을 통과하지 못했을 거야.

해설 남자는 여자의 도움이 없었다면 취직을 하지 못했을 것이라고 말하며 여자에게 감사를 표현하고 있다.

어휘 guess 알아맞히다 terrific 아주 좋은 full-time job 정규직 thanks to ~ 덕분에 on one's own 혼자 힘으로 without ~ 없이 pass 합격하다, 통과하다 interview 면접

10 ④

M Hi. I'd like to buy some T-shirts for my school club members.
W Take a look at these samples and choose one.
M I want to put a yellow logo on this blue T-shirt. How much will it be?
W A T-shirt is $10. And if you want to add a logo, you'll need to pay a dollar extra for each one.
M Okay, I'll buy eleven T-shirts.
W Oh wait, if you order over ten, you don't have to pay for each logo.
M Sounds great.

남 안녕하세요. 저는 학교 동아리 회원들이 입을 티셔츠 좀 사고 싶어요.
여 이 샘플들을 보시고 하나 골라 보세요.
남 이 파란색 티셔츠에 노란색 로고를 넣고 싶어요. 얼마인가요?
여 티셔츠는 10달러입니다. 그리고 로고를 추가하고 싶으시면, 각각 1달러를 더 내셔야 해요.

남 네, 티셔츠 11장 살게요.

여 오, 잠깐만요. 10장 넘게 주문하시면, 로고 비용은 안 내셔도 됩니다.

남 잘됐네요.

해설 남자는 로고($1)를 넣은 티셔츠($10)를 11장 주문했는데 티셔츠를 10장 넘게 주문하면 로고 비용이 무료라고 했으므로 티셔츠 가격만 지불하면 된다.

어휘 member 회원   sample 샘플, 견본품   choose 고르다

11 ③

W Dad's birthday is coming soon. What can we do for him?

M I just want to buy him a small gift.

W That's nice, but I'd like to do something special.

M Then how about making a cake for him?

W Great idea, but I don't know how to make a cake.

M There's a baking class for making cakes. Why don't you take it?

W A baking class? Sounds wonderful. I'll take it and learn how to make a cake before his birthday.

여 아빠 생신이 얼마 안 남았어. 아빠를 위해 우리가 무엇을 할 수 있을까?

남 난 그냥 작은 선물을 사 드리고 싶어.

여 그것도 좋지만, 난 뭔가 특별한 걸 하고 싶어.

남 그러면 아빠를 위해 케이크를 만드는 게 어때?

여 좋은 생각이지만, 나는 케이크 만드는 방법을 몰라.

남 케이크를 만드는 제빵 수업이 있어. 그 수업을 듣는 게 어때?

여 제빵 수업? 좋은 걸. 난 그 수업을 들어서 아빠 생신 전에 케이크 만드는 방법을 배울 거야.

해설 여자는 케이크 만드는 방법을 배우기 위해 제빵 수업을 들을 것이다.

어휘 special 특별한   baking 제빵

12 ①

W Hello, students. Our school music club is looking for members to join and perform in our concert this summer. Anyone who can play an instrument can have an audition. If you're interested, come to our club room on the third floor to apply. The audition will be held next Wednesday in the school music room, and the results will be announced on Friday.

여 학생 여러분, 안녕하세요. 우리 학교 음악 동아리가 이번 여름에 콘서트에 참여해서 공연할 멤버를 찾고 있습니다. 악기를 연주할 수 있는 사람은 누구나 오디션을 볼 수 있습니다. 관심이 있으시면, 3층에 있는 우리 동아리실로 지원하러 오세요. 오디션은 다음 주 수요일에 학교 음악실에서 열리고, 결과는 금요일에 발표될 것입니다.

해설 심사 위원에 관해서는 언급되지 않았다.

어휘 perform 공연하다   instrument 악기   audition 오디션   floor 층   apply 지원하다   hold 열다, 개최하다   result 결과

announce 발표하다

13 ④

M Narae, can you help me choose a tumbler?

W Yes. What kind of tumbler do you want?

M First of all, I don't like ones made from plastic.

W Okay. How much do you want it to hold?

M I think 300 milliliters is too small for me. I want a bigger one.

W How much are you willing to pay for it?

M I don't want one that is too expensive. I don't want to spend more than 10,000 won.

W Then you have two options left.

M Oh, I'll order this one. If I buy it, I can receive an extra gift.

남 나래야, 내가 텀블러 선택하는 것 좀 도와줄 수 있니?

여 그래. 너는 어떤 종류의 텀블러를 원하니?

남 무엇보다도, 나는 플라스틱으로 만들어진 것은 싫어.

여 좋아. 얼마나 많은 용량을 원하니?

남 300밀리리터는 나한테 너무 적은 것 같아. 나는 더 큰 것을 원해.

여 너는 얼마를 지불할 의향이 있니?

남 너무 비싸지 않은 걸 원해. 10,000원 넘게 쓰고 싶지 않아.

여 그러면 두 가지 선택이 남았네.

남 오, 나 이걸로 주문할래. 만약 이걸 사면, 추가 선물을 받을 수 있어.

해설 남자는 플라스틱이 아니고 300ml보다 크며 10,000원을 넘지 않고, 선물을 받을 수 있는 텀블러를 주문할 것이다.

어휘 choose 선택하다   first of all 무엇보다도   hold 담다   be willing to 기꺼이 ~하다   pay for ~을 지불하다   spend 소비하다, 쓰다   option 선택(권)   order 주문하다   extra 추가의

14 ②

M This is something you can use to travel over ice. This consists of a framework that slides on two strips of metal or wood. When the river freezes, it's a good time to use this because it can make you move faster. Also, children like to ride in this because they can have a lot of fun on the ice. However, you need to be careful not to use this during spring when the ice starts to melt.

남 이것은 얼음 위를 다닐 때 사용할 수 있는 것이다. 이것은 가늘고 긴 두 조각의 금속 또는 나무 위에 미끄러지는 뼈대로 구성되어 있다. 강이 얼면, 이것을 사용하기에 좋은 시기인데, 왜냐하면 이것은 여러분을 더 빨리 움직일 수 있게 해 주기 때문이다. 또한, 아이들은 얼음 위에서 아주 즐거운 시간을 보낼 수 있기 때문에 이것을 타는 것을 좋아한다. 하지만, 얼음이 녹기 시작하는 봄에는 이것을 사용하지 않도록 조심해야 한다.

해설 얼음 위에서 이동할 때 사용할 수 있으며 아이들이 얼음 위에서 타는 것을 좋아하는 것은 썰매이다.

어휘 consist of ~로 구성되다   framework 뼈대, 골조
slide 미끄러지다   strip (천·널빤지 등의) 가늘고 긴 조각
metal 금속   freeze 얼다   careful 조심하는   melt 녹다

해설 남자는 한국 소설을 영어로 번역하는 일을 하고 싶어 한다.

어휘 nervous 긴장하는   give up 포기하다   dream 꿈
translate 번역하다   famous 유명한   novel 소설

15 ②

M What are you doing? You look busy.
W I'm doing my science homework for Ms. Park's class.
M Science homework? Did she give us homework?
W Yes, she told us to do research about how to protect the earth.
M Oh no! I totally forgot about it. What should I do?
W Well, you still have some time. If I were you, I'd go to the library to find some books about the topic.
M You're right. I think I should go to the library right now.

남 뭐 하고 있니? 바빠 보여.
여 박 선생님 수업을 위해 과학 숙제를 하고 있어.
남 과학 숙제? 선생님께서 우리에게 숙제를 내 주셨니?
여 응, 선생님께서 우리에게 지구를 보호하는 방법에 대해 조사하라고 말씀하셨어.
남 맙소사! 나는 그걸 완전히 잊고 있었어. 어떻게 해야 하지?
여 음, 아직 시간이 좀 있어. 내가 너라면, 그 주제에 관한 책들을 찾으러 도서관에 가겠어.
남 네 말이 맞아. 지금 당장 도서관에 가야겠어.

해설 남자는 잊고 있던 과학 숙제를 하기 위해 지금 당장 도서관에 가겠다고 했다.

어휘 research 조사, 연구   protect 보호하다   totally 완전히
library 도서관   topic 주제

16 ②

W Jiwoo, what's the matter? You look upset.
M Yes. My mother wants me to become an English teacher just like her.
W I don't think being a teacher would be a bad idea. And you're good at English.
M But I get so nervous when I speak in front of other people. And I don't want to give up my dream.
W What do you want to be?
M I'd like to translate famous Korean novels into English.
W Sounds good. I know you love reading novels. That would be the perfect job for you.

여 지우야, 무슨 일이니? 너 속상해 보여.
남 맞아. 우리 엄마는 내가 엄마처럼 영어 선생님이 되길 바라서.
여 선생님 되는 것이 나쁜 건 아닐 것 같은데. 그리고 넌 영어를 잘하잖아.
남 하지만 난 다른 사람들 앞에서 말할 때 너무 긴장이 돼. 그리고 난 내 꿈을 포기하고 싶지 않아.
여 넌 뭐가 되고 싶어?
남 나는 유명한 한국 소설을 영어로 번역하고 싶어.
여 좋은 것 같아. 난 네가 소설 읽기를 좋아한다는 걸 알아. 그것은 너에게 딱 맞는 직업이 될 거야.

17 ③

(Telephone rings.)
M Hi. I've just received the jacket I ordered from your website.
W Is there anything wrong with it?
M No, it's just a little big. Can I exchange it for a smaller one?
W Sure. Your name please.
M Thomas Lee.
W You ordered a large size. Do you want to exchange it for a medium one?
M Exactly.
W All right, could you please send it back to us? Then we can send you a smaller one.
M Okay, I will send it as soon as possible.

(전화벨이 울린다.)
남 안녕하세요. 저는 귀사의 웹 사이트에서 주문한 재킷을 방금 받았는데요.
여 제품에 무슨 문제가 있나요?
남 아니요, 그냥 조금 커서요. 더 작은 것으로 교환할 수 있을까요?
여 물론이죠. 이름을 알려 주세요.
남 Thomas Lee입니다.
여 큰 사이즈를 주문하셨군요. 중간 사이즈로 교환하기를 원하시나요?
남 맞아요.
여 알겠습니다. 저희에게 그것을 다시 보내 주시겠어요? 그러면 더 작은 것을 보내 드릴게요.
남 네, 가능한 한 빨리 보내 드리겠습니다.

해설 교환을 원하는 제품을 보내 달라는 말에 가능한 한 빨리 보내겠다고 답하는 것이 자연스럽다.
① 음, 저는 더 작은 재킷을 갖고 있지 않아요.
② 아니에요, 저는 쇼핑하는 데 관심 없어요.
④ 많은 사람들이 저에게 그것을 빌리고 싶어 해요.
⑤ 이 문제에 대해서 곰곰이 생각하셔야 합니다.

어휘 receive 받다   exchange 교환하다   medium 중간의
be interested in ~에 관심이 있다   as soon as possible
가능한 한 빨리   borrow 빌리다   problem 문제

18 ⑤

M Welcome to Brian's BBQ Restaurant.
W Wow, there are so many people waiting.
M Yes, on weekends, we usually have more customers than on weekdays. Did you make a reservation?
W No, I didn't.
M Then I'm afraid that you need to write down your name on the waiting list and wait.
W How long do you think I'll have to wait?

M I'm not sure, but probably 30 minutes or more.

W That's longer than I expected. I'll eat here some other time.

남 Brian's BBQ Restaurant에 오신 것을 환영합니다.

여 와, 기다리는 사람들이 정말 많네요.

남 네, 주말에는 평일보다 대개 손님들이 더 많아요. 예약하셨나요?

여 아니요, 안 했어요.

남 그러시면 유감스럽지만 이름을 대기 명단에 쓰시고 기다리셔야 합니다.

여 얼마나 오래 기다려야 할 것 같나요?

남 확실하지는 않지만 아마 30분 이상일 거예요.

여 예상했던 것보다 더 기네요. 다음에 이곳에서 식사할게요.

해설 음식을 먹으려면 30분 이상 기다려야 한다고 했으므로 예상했던 것보다 오래 걸린다며 다음에 오겠다고 답하는 것이 자연스럽다.

① 그것들 모두를 드실 수는 없을 거예요.
② 저는 이곳 음식이 만족스럽지 않아요.
③ 너무 오래 기다리시게 해서 죄송합니다.
④ 놀라워요! 그것을 어떻게 하셨나요?

어휘 customer 손님 weekday 평일, 주중 reservation 예약 write down 기록하다, 적다 list 명단 be satisfied with ~에 만족하다 surprising 놀라운 expect 기대하다

19 ①

W Welcome to Kim's Eyewear. What can I do for you?

M Hi. I need to get a new pair of glasses.

W When did you get the ones you're wearing?

M About three and a half years ago.

W Oh, that's a long time ago.

M Yes, I think that's why I can't see things clearly these days.

W Maybe. Are the frames okay? Do you need to buy new frames, too?

M I'd really like to get new ones.

여 Kim's Eyewear에 오신 것을 환영합니다. 무엇을 도와드릴까요?

남 안녕하세요. 저는 새 안경이 필요해요.

여 쓰고 계신 안경은 언제 사셨나요?

남 3년 반 전에요.

여 오, 오래 전이군요.

남 네, 그래서 제가 요즘 사물을 또렷하게 못 보는 것 같아요.

여 그러실 것 같아요. 안경테는 괜찮으세요? 안경테도 새로 사실 건가요?

남 저는 정말 새것을 사고 싶어요.

해설 안경테를 새로 살 것인지 물었으므로 새것을 사고 싶다고 답하는 것이 자연스럽다.
② 지금 도와드릴 수 없어서 죄송합니다.
③ 제가 당신이라면 그렇게 하지 않을 텐데요.
④ 스스로를 부끄러워해야 할 거예요.
⑤ 약속을 잊지 않으셨군요.

어휘 eyewear 안경류 glasses 안경 that's why 그래서 ~하다 clearly 또렷하게, 분명히 these days 요즈음 frame (주로 복수로) 안경테 be ashamed of ~을 부끄러워하다 promise 약속

20 ⑤

W Mijoo is in the classroom preparing to give a presentation. She opens her presentation file on the computer. When she is about to start her presentation, she notices that some students sitting at the back can't see the screen well because the lights are on. She sees that her friend Clark is right next to the light switch and wants to ask for his help. In this situation, what would she say to him?

Mijoo Clark, can you please turn off the lights?

여 미주는 교실에서 발표를 준비하고 있다. 그녀는 발표 파일을 컴퓨터에서 연다. 막 발표를 시작하려고 할 때, 그녀는 뒤에 앉아 있는 몇몇 학생들이 전등이 켜져 있어서 화면을 잘 볼 수 없다는 것을 알아차린다. 그녀는 그녀의 친구인 Clark가 전등 스위치 바로 옆에 있는 것을 보고 그의 도움을 요청하기를 원한다. 이러한 상황에서, 그녀는 그에게 뭐라고 말할까?

미주 Clark, 전등 좀 꺼 줄 수 있니?

해설 전등 스위치 바로 옆에 있는 Clark에게 전등을 꺼 달라고 부탁하려는 상황이다.
① 내가 그것을 고치는 걸 도와줄래?
② 내가 너를 도와줄게.
③ 너는 최선을 다해야 해.
④ 문을 열어도 되겠니?

어휘 prepare 준비하다 presentation 발표 be about to 막 ~하려고 하다 notice 알아차리다 screen 화면 light 전등 switch 스위치 fix 수리하다 try one's best 최선을 다하다 turn off ~을 끄다

01 ③		**02** ④		**03** ②		**04** ②		**05** ③	
06 ④		**07** ④		**08** ②		**09** ①		**10** ③	
11 ①		**12** ②		**13** ④		**14** ③		**15** ⑤	
16 ②		**17** ②		**18** ④		**19** ⑤		**20** ⑤	

01 ③

M Who is this man in the picture?
W That's my brother John.
M I like his style. His cap suits him. Is he your younger brother?
W No, he's my elder brother. My little brother is standing next to him. He doesn't wear a cap.
M You mean the one with the glasses?
W No, that's my cousin. My little brother is here.
M I see. He has short hair and is wearing a T-shirt with a bear on it.
W Yes, he likes bears a lot!

남 사진 속 이 남자는 누구니?
여 내 남자형제 John이야.
남 난 그의 스타일이 마음에 들어. 모자가 그와 잘 어울려. 네 남동생이니?
여 아니, 그는 나의 오빠야. 내 남동생은 그의 옆에 서 있어. 그는 모자를 쓰고 있지 않아.
남 안경 쓴 아이 말이니?
여 아니, 그 애는 내 사촌이야. 내 남동생은 여기 있어.
남 알겠다. 그는 머리가 짧고 곰이 그려진 티셔츠를 입고 있네.
여 맞아, 그는 곰을 매우 좋아해!

해설 여자의 남동생은 모자를 쓰지 않았으며 머리가 짧고, 곰이 그려진 티셔츠를 입고 있다고 했다.

어휘 suit 어울리다 elder brother 오빠, 형 glasses 안경 cousin 사촌

02 ④

(Cellphone rings.)
M Hello?
W Hello. This is Hanguk Travel Agency. Is this Paul Lee?
M Yes, it is.
W You entered our travel picture contest, right?
M You mean the contest that closed last month?
W Yes, that's the one. Congratulations! You won first prize in the contest.
M Really? I can't believe it!
W Believe it. You won our grand prize of a free trip to Japan for 3 days.
M Wow, thank you so much!

(휴대 전화가 울린다.)

남 여보세요?
여 여보세요. Hanguk Travel Agency입니다. Paul Lee 씨 맞나요?
남 네, 맞아요.
여 저희 여행 사진 대회에 참가하셨죠, 그렇죠?
남 지난달에 끝난 대회 말씀이신가요?
여 네, 그거예요. 축하합니다! 대회에서 일등을 하셨어요.
남 정말요? 믿을 수가 없어요!
여 사실이에요. 당신은 3일 동안의 일본 무료 여행권의 최우수상을 수상하셨어요.
남 와, 정말 고마워요!

해설 여자는 남자가 여행 사진 대회에서 수상한 사실을 전하려고 전화했다.

어휘 agency 대행사 enter 참가하다, 응모하다 contest 대회, 경연 win first prize 1등을 하다 believe 믿다 free 무료의 grand prize 최우수상

03 ②

① M Can you please set the table?
 W Okay, no problem.
② M May I take your order?
 W Yes, please. I'd like to order a steak.
③ M What are you interested in?
 W I'm interested in cooking.
④ M What would you like to eat for lunch?
 W I want to eat sandwiches.
⑤ M Can I get your advice on being healthy?
 W I think you should eat more vegetables.

① 남 상 좀 차려 주실 수 있어요?
 여 네, 문제없어요.
② 남 주문하시겠어요?
 여 네. 저는 스테이크를 주문하고 싶어요.
③ 남 당신은 무엇에 관심이 있나요?
 여 저는 요리에 관심이 있어요.
④ 남 점심으로 뭐 먹고 싶어요?
 여 저는 샌드위치를 먹고 싶어요.
⑤ 남 건강해지는 것에 대한 당신의 조언을 얻을 수 있을까요?
 여 당신은 더 많은 채소를 먹어야 할 것 같아요.

해설 식당에서 손님이 종업원에게 스테이크를 주문하는 상황이다.

어휘 set the table 상을 차리다 order 주문; 주문하다 be interested in ~에 관심이 있다 advice 조언, 충고 healthy 건강한

04 ②

W Did you pack everything for your business trip?
M Yes, everything is ready.
W When does the train leave?
M At 7:30. I think I should leave home at around 6:30. It usually takes about 30 minutes to get to the station.
W But it's Friday evening!
M Oh, you're right. There will be heavy traffic. I'd

better leave at 6 o'clock.

W I think so, too.

여 출장을 위한 짐은 다 쌌어요?
남 네, 모든 게 준비됐어요.
여 기차는 언제 출발해요?
남 7시 30분이에요. 6시 30분쯤에 집에서 나가야 할 것 같아요. 보통 기차역까지는 30분 정도 걸리거든요.
여 하지만 금요일 저녁이잖아요!
남 오, 당신 말이 맞아요. 교통 체증이 있을 거예요. 6시에 나서는 게 좋겠네요.
여 저도 그렇게 생각해요.

해설 남자는 교통 체증 때문에 6시에 집을 나서는 게 좋겠다고 말했다.

어휘 pack (짐을) 싸다 business trip 출장 ready 준비된 traffic 교통 had better ~하는 것이 좋겠다

05 ③

W Kevin. Can you do me a favor?
M Sure, Mom. What is it?
W Will you buy some melon for Kate? She wants to have one now.
M No problem.
W Why don't you go to the new supermarket? Fruit is cheaper there.
M Okay, how much money should I take?
W I think a box of melons is about $15, but here's $20 just in case. You can spend the change.
M Thank you so much, Mom. Then I can buy my favorite snacks!

여 Kevin, 나 좀 도와줄 수 있니?
남 물론이죠, 엄마. 뭔데요?
여 Kate를 위해 멜론 좀 사다 줄래? 그 애가 지금 그걸 먹고 싶어 하는구나.
남 문제없어요.
여 새로 문을 연 슈퍼마켓에 가는 게 어떠니? 그곳이 과일이 좀 더 싸거든.
남 알겠어요. 돈을 얼마나 가져가야 하나요?
여 멜론 한 상자에 15달러 정도인데 만약을 위해서 여기 20달러 가져가렴. 잔돈은 네가 써도 된단다.
남 정말 고마워요, 엄마. 그러면 전 제가 좋아하는 간식을 살 수 있어요!

해설 여자가 남자에게 Kate를 위해 멜론을 사다 달라고 부탁하자 남자는 그러겠다고 했다.

어휘 do ~ a favor ~의 부탁을 들어주다 just in case 만약을 위해서 change 잔돈 snack 간식

06 ④

(Telephone rings.)
W Hello.
M Mom, it's David.

W Oh, David. Why are you calling me now? Aren't you in school?
M My teacher let me use my phone for a moment. Could you please bring my math homework to school?
W You didn't take it with you? I saw you put it in your bag last night.
M I did, but after taking it out to check it again, I forgot to put it back in again.
W I see. See you at the main gate in 10 minutes.

(전화벨이 울린다.)
여 여보세요.
남 엄마, 저 David예요.
여 오, David. 왜 지금 전화하는 거니? 너 학교에 있지 않니?
남 선생님께서 잠시 전화를 쓰도록 허락해 주셨어요. 제 수학 숙제를 학교로 가져다주실 수 있으세요?
여 너 그것을 가지고 가지 않았니? 난 네가 어젯밤에 그걸 가방에 넣는 걸 봤는데.
남 그랬지만, 다시 확인하려고 꺼낸 후에 다시 넣는 걸 잊어버렸어요.
여 알겠다. 10분 후에 정문에서 보자.

해설 남자는 여자에게 집에 두고 온 수학 숙제를 학교로 가져다 달라고 부탁했다.

어휘 use 사용하다 for a moment 잠시 동안 bring 가져오다 forget 잊다 main gate 정문

07 ④

① M Can you speak more slowly, please?
　 W Okay, I'll try.
② M Would you like to drink some water?
　 W Yes, please. I'm so thirsty.
③ M May I think about that for a moment?
　 W Sure, take your time.
④ M You don't like science, do you?
　 W No, I don't. Science is my favorite subject.
⑤ M What do you think about my new shoes?
　 W They look good on you.

① 남 조금 더 천천히 말씀해 주실래요?
　 여 네, 그럴게요.
② 남 물 좀 마실래요?
　 여 네, 주세요. 목이 너무 말라요.
③ 남 제가 그것에 대해 잠시만 생각해 봐도 될까요?
　 여 물론이죠, 천천히 하세요.
④ 남 너는 과학을 좋아하지 않지, 그렇지?
　 여 응, 안 좋아해. 과학은 내가 가장 좋아하는 과목이야.
⑤ 남 내 새 신발에 대해 어떻게 생각하니?
　 여 너한테 잘 어울려.

해설 ④ 과학을 좋아하지 않는지 묻는 말에 안 좋아한다고 답한 후 과학을 가장 좋아한다고 이어서 말하는 것은 어색하다.

어휘 slowly 천천히 thirsty 목이 마른 subject 과목 look good on ~에게 잘 어울리다

08 ②

W Attention, shoppers. This is an important announcement. We have a lost child somewhere in the mall. We are looking for a little boy who was last seen on the second floor 30 minutes ago. He is four years old. He is wearing blue jeans, a short-sleeved T-shirt with a rainbow on it, and a bright red cap. If you have seen this child, please notify the nearest security officer right away.

여 고객 여러분, 주목해 주세요. 중요한 안내 방송입니다. 쇼핑 몰 안 어딘가에 길을 잃은 아이가 있습니다. 2층에서 30분 전에 마지막으로 목격된 어린 남자 아이를 찾는 중입니다. 그는 네 살입니다. 그는 청바지와 무지개가 그려진 반소매 티셔츠를 입고 있으며, 밝은 빨간색 모자를 쓰고 있습니다. 이 아이를 보셨으면, 가장 가까운 안전 요원에게 즉시 알려 주세요.

해설 네 살짜리 남자 아이를 찾는 안내 방송으로, 아이의 이름은 언급되지 않았다.

어휘 announcement 공지, 알림   somewhere 어딘가에   last 마지막으로   floor 층   short-sleeved 반소매의, 짧은 소매의   rainbow 무지개   notify 알리다   security 안전

09 ①

M So you saw a hit-and-run an hour ago?
W Yes. I saw a car hit a man on a bicycle. It was on Pine Street.
M Did you see the license plate of the car?
W Yeah, but I could only see the first three numbers.
M What were they?
W Three, five, and nine.
M Can you describe the car?
W It was a black, medium-sized car.
M Thank you for your help. If you remember anything else, please call me.

남 그래서 1시간 전에 뺑소니 사고를 보셨다고요?
여 네. 자동차가 자전거를 탄 남자를 치는 것을 봤어요. Pine 가에서 있었어요.
남 그 자동차의 번호판을 보셨나요?
여 네, 그렇지만 처음 세 숫자만 볼 수 있었어요.
남 그것들이 뭐죠?
여 3, 5, 그리고 9예요.
남 차를 묘사하실 수 있나요?
여 검은색의 중간 크기의 차였어요.
남 도와주셔서 감사합니다. 그 밖에 다른 것이 기억나시면, 전화 주세요.

해설 남자는 마지막에 뺑소니 사고와 관련하여 기억나는 것이 있으면 전화해 달라고 부탁했다.

어휘 hit-and-run 뺑소니 사고   license plate (자동차) 번호판   describe 묘사하다   medium-sized 중간 크기의   else 또 다른, 그 밖의

10 ③

W How was the food?
M It was great as always.
W Thanks. So you had one spaghetti and a coke, right?
M Yes. How much is it?
W A spaghetti is $5, and a coke is $1, so the total price is $6.
M Oh, I think I have a free drink coupon. Can I use this?
W Sure. Then you just need to pay for the spaghetti.
M Here you are.

여 음식은 어땠나요?
남 항상 그렇듯 훌륭했어요.
여 고맙습니다. 그러면 스파게티 하나와 콜라 하나를 드셨네요, 그렇죠?
남 네. 얼마예요?
여 스파게티는 5달러이고 콜라는 1달러니까, 총 가격은 6달러입니다.
남 오, 저는 무료 음료 쿠폰이 있는 것 같아요. 이것을 써도 되나요?
여 물론이죠. 그러시면 스파게티만 계산하시면 됩니다.
남 여기 있어요.

해설 남자는 스파게티와 콜라를 먹었지만 무료 음료 쿠폰을 사용할 수 있으므로 스파게티 가격인 5달러만 지불하면 된다.

어휘 total 총, 전체의   price 가격   coupon 쿠폰   pay for ~을 지불하다

11 ①

W Why are you late, Liam?
M Sorry, Ms. Brown. I have been at the nurse's office.
W Really?
M Yes, here's the note from the school nurse.
W Oh, you had a stomachache.
M Yeah, I think I ate lunch too fast.
W You should have eaten slowly. Do you feel better now?
M Yes. I took some medicine and rested for an hour.
W Okay, I hope you won't be sick anymore. Please take your seat.

여 Liam, 왜 늦었니?
남 죄송해요, Brown 선생님. 저는 보건실에 있었어요.
여 정말?
남 네, 여기 보건 선생님의 메모가 있어요.
여 오, 배가 아팠구나.
남 네, 점심을 너무 빨리 먹은 것 같아요.
여 천천히 먹었어야지. 지금은 괜찮니?
남 네. 약 좀 먹고 한 시간 동안 쉬었어요.
여 좋아, 네가 더 이상 안 아프길 바란다. 자리에 앉으렴.

해설 배가 아파서 보건실에 있다가 늦게 온 학생과 교사가 교실에서 나누는 대화이다.

12 ②

W I'm so excited to visit Busan!
M So am I! Did you get our tickets?
W Yes, here they are. Our train leaves in 20 minutes.
M Then we have some time left.
W Why don't we go get a drink?
M That's a good idea. (*Pause*) Let's go to the convenience store over there.
W I think I need to go to the bathroom. Can you go ahead and get a bottle of coffee for me?

여 난 부산을 방문하게 돼서 정말 신이 나!
남 나도 그래! 우리 표는 받았어?
여 응, 여기 있어. 우리 기차는 20분 후에 출발해.
남 그러면 시간이 좀 남았네.
여 마실 것 좀 사러 가는 게 어때?
남 그거 좋은 생각이야. (잠시 후) 저쪽에 있는 편의점에 가자.
여 나는 화장실을 가야 할 것 같아. 네가 먼저 가서 내게 커피 한 병을 사다 줄 수 있니?

해설 여자는 남자에게 편의점에서 커피 한 병을 사다 달라고 부탁했다.

어휘 leave 떠나다, 출발하다 convenience store 편의점 bathroom 화장실 ahead 미리 bottle 병

13 ④

M Which room do you think is good for tomorrow's meeting?
W Umm... Room 305? It's close to our office.
M Yes, but the air conditioner in that room is out of order.
W Then we can't use that room.
M What about Room 301? It is a large room, so we can talk comfortably.
W I think so. (*Pause*) Ah, that room is already reserved.
M Then how about Room 304? The size is okay, and there's no problem with the air conditioner.
W Okay, then let's use that room.

남 내일 회의를 위해 어느 방이 좋다고 생각해?
여 음… 305호실? 우리 사무실과 가깝잖아.
남 맞아, 하지만 그 방은 에어컨이 고장이야.
여 그러면 우리는 그 방을 쓸 수 없겠네.
남 301호실은 어때? 넓은 방이어서 편안하게 이야기할 수 있어.
여 나도 그렇게 생각해. (잠시 후) 아, 그 방은 이미 예약되어 있네.
남 그럼 304호실은 어때? 크기도 괜찮고 에어컨에 문제도 없어.
여 좋아, 그러면 그 방을 사용하자.

해설 두 사람은 크기도 괜찮고 에어컨도 문제가 없는 304호실을 회의실로 사용하기로 했다.

14 ③

M This is a person who works in airplanes. This person is responsible for keeping passengers safe and getting them to their destinations. Airplanes can't fly without this person, who is trained to fly aircraft. Many people would like to do this job even though it's very difficult to do since it takes so much time and effort to learn how to fly an airplane.

남 이 사람은 비행기 안에서 일하는 사람입니다. 이 사람은 승객들을 안전하게 보호하고 그들을 목적지까지 데려다주는 책임을 지고 있습니다. 비행기는 항공기를 조종하는 훈련을 받은 이 사람 없이는 비행할 수 없습니다. 비행기를 조종하는 방법을 배우는 데는 아주 많은 시간과 노력이 들기 때문에 이 일을 하는 것은 매우 어려움에도 불구하고 많은 사람들은 이 일을 하고 싶어 합니다.

해설 비행기를 조종하는 일을 하는 사람은 비행사이다.

어휘 responsible 책임이 있는 passenger 승객 safe 안전한 destination 목적지 train 훈련시키다 aircraft 항공기 even though 비록 ~이지만 effort 노력

15 ⑤

M Julie, your new coat looks good on you.
W Thanks. I bought it online at a low price.
M Really? It looks so expensive.
W I bought it on a new website called Fashion Up. If you create an account, you can get a 50% discount coupon.
M What a good deal! I should create one and get a coupon, too.
W Yeah, but you need to hurry. The special offer will end soon.
M Okay, I'll do it right away.

남 Julie, 네 새 외투가 너한테 잘 어울린다.
여 고마워. 온라인에서 싼 가격으로 샀어.
남 정말? 아주 비싸 보이는데.
여 Fashion Up이라고 하는 새로운 웹 사이트에서 샀어. 계정을 만들면, 50퍼센트 할인 쿠폰을 받을 수 있어.
남 정말 좋은 거래네! 나도 하나 만들어서 쿠폰을 받아야겠어.
여 응, 하지만 넌 서둘러야 해. 특가 판매가 곧 종료되거든.
남 알았어, 지금 당장 할게.

해설 남자는 지금 당장 새로 생긴 온라인 쇼핑몰의 계정을 만들겠다고 했다.

어휘 at a low price 싼 가격으로 create 만들다 account 계정 discount 할인 hurry 서두르다 special offer 특가 판매 end 끝나다

16   ②

M Sumi, do you have any special plans for the summer vacation?

W I'm planning to study a foreign language.

M Great idea! Which language?

W Well, actually I haven't decided yet.

M How about Chinese? It's used by more people than any other language.

W I know, but I think it's too difficult to learn.

M Then what about Japanese? It's easy to learn because it has a similar word order as Korean.

W Really? Then I'll give it a try.

남 수미야, 여름 방학을 위한 특별한 계획 있니?

여 나는 외국어를 공부할 계획이야.

남 좋은 생각이야! 어떤 언어?

여 음, 사실 아직 결정하지 못했어.

남 중국어는 어때? 그건 어떤 다른 언어보다 더 많은 사람들에 의해서 사용되잖아.

여 나도 알아, 하지만 그건 배우기 너무 어려운 것 같아.

남 그러면 일본어는 어때? 한국어와 어순이 비슷해서 배우기 쉬워.

여 정말? 그러면 한번 해 볼게.

해설 남자가 여자에게 한국어와 어순이 비슷해서 배우기 쉬운 일본어를 배워 보라고 권하자 여자가 한번 해 보겠다고 했다.

어휘 special 특별한   be planning to ~할 계획이다   foreign 외국의   language 언어   actually 실제로   decide 결정하다   similar 비슷한   order 순서   give it a try 한번 해 보다

17   ②

W Emily is walking on the street. Suddenly, she sees a man in front of her drop his wallet. He doesn't notice that he dropped something, and she wants to help him. She picks the wallet up quickly and tries to catch up with the man to give it to him. Finally, she reaches him and is about to give the wallet to him. In this situation, what would Emily say to him?

Emily Excuse me. I think this is your wallet.

여 Emily는 길을 걸어가고 있다. 갑자기, 그녀는 그녀 앞의 남자가 그의 지갑을 떨어뜨리는 것을 본다. 그는 그가 뭔가를 떨어뜨렸다는 것을 알아채지 못하고, 그녀는 그를 돕기를 원한다. 그녀는 지갑을 재빨리 주워서 그 남자에게 그것을 주기 위해 그를 따라잡으려고 한다. 마침내, 그녀는 그를 따라잡고 그에게 막 지갑을 전해 주려 한다. 이 상황에서, Emily는 그에게 뭐라고 말할 것인가?

Emily 실례합니다. 이것이 당신의 지갑인 것 같아요.

해설 지갑을 떨어뜨린 남자에게 지갑을 전해 주려는 상황이다.

① 놀라운 것 같아요.

③ 서두르시는 게 좋을 것 같아요.

④ 전에 당신을 본 적이 있는 것 같아요.

⑤ 당신은 잘못 가져가신 것 같아요.

18   ④

M Ava, are you all right? You seem to have a cold.

W Yeah, actually I just went to see a doctor about it.

M What did he say?

W He said I have some early symptoms of a cold.

M You should be careful so that it doesn't get worse. Why don't you drink some warm lemon tea?

W Lemon tea?

M Yeah, it'll keep you warm and prevent you from getting a cold.

W Okay, I'll try that.

남 Ava, 너 괜찮아? 감기 걸린 것 같은데.

여 응, 사실 그것 때문에 방금 병원에 다녀왔어.

남 의사 선생님이 뭐라고 하셨니?

여 감기 초기 증상이 있다고 하셨어.

남 넌 더 나빠지지 않도록 조심해야 해. 따뜻한 레몬차 좀 마시는 게 어때?

여 레몬차?

남 응. 그건 너를 따뜻하게 해 주고 감기에 걸리지 않도록 해 줄 거야.

여 알았어, 마셔 볼게.

해설 남자는 여자가 감기에 걸려 병원에 다녀왔다고 했으므로 걱정스러울 것이다.

어휘 have a cold 감기에 걸리다   symptom 증상   careful 조심하는   get worse 악화되다   prevent A from B A가 B하지 못하게 막다

19   ⑤

(Cellphone rings.)

M Hello.

W Sam. Where are you now?

M On the school playground. Why?

W Are you coming home now? It's already 5 p.m.

M Well, I want to play with my friends longer.

W You seem to be forgetting something important. We're supposed to go to your grandma's birthday party at 6 p.m.

M Oh, is it today, not tomorrow? I totally forgot about it. Sorry, Mom.

W Okay, just hurry and come home right now.

(휴대 전화가 울린다.)

남 여보세요.

여 Sam. 너 지금 어디니?

남 학교 운동장이에요. 왜요?

여 너 지금 집에 올 거지? 벌써 오후 5시야.

남 저, 친구들과 더 놀고 싶어요.

여 너 중요한 것을 잊은 것 같구나. 오후 6시에 할머니 생신 잔치에 가기로 했잖니.

남 오, 그게 내일이 아니라 오늘이에요? 완전히 잊고 있었어요. 죄송해요, 엄마.

여 알았어, 지금 바로 서둘러서 집에 오렴.

해설 남자가 할머니 생신 잔치에 가는 것을 잊어버려서 죄송하다고 말했으므로 이에 대해 여자는 괜찮으니 서둘러 집에 오라고 말하는 것이 가장 적절하다.

① 그 말을 들으니 기쁘구나. 좋은 시간 보내라.
② 물론이야. 너는 내 도움 없이 그곳에 갈 수 있어.
③ 아니야. 그건 좋은 생각이 아닌 것 같구나.
④ 내 생일 파티가 기대되는구나.

어휘 playground 운동장 already 이미, 벌써 be supposed to ~하기로 되어 있다 have a good time 즐거운 시간을 보내다 look forward to ~을 기대하다 hurry 서두르다

20 ⑤

(*Cellphone rings.*)

M Hello.

W Hello, Mr. Peter Kim. This is Daehan Trading. You've passed the initial résumé screening. Congratulations!

M Oh, really? Thank you so much.

W You're welcome. We'd like to interview you next Friday at 2 p.m. Can you make it then?

M Of course. Where should I go for the interview?

W Please come to our head office in downtown Seoul. Do you know where it is?

M I'm not sure. I'll check the map on your website.

(휴대 전화가 울린다.)

남 여보세요.

여 여보세요, Peter Kim 씨. 대한 무역입니다. 첫 번째 이력서 심사에 합격하셨습니다. 축하드립니다!

남 오, 정말요? 정말 감사합니다.

여 천만에요. 다음 주 금요일 오후 2시에 면접을 보고 싶은데요. 그때 괜찮으신가요?

남 물론이죠. 제가 면접을 보러 어디로 가야 하나요?

여 서울 시내에 있는 저희 본사로 오시면 됩니다. 어딘지 아시나요?

남 잘 모르겠어요. 웹 사이트에서 지도를 확인하겠습니다.

해설 여자가 남자에게 본사가 어디인지 아는지 물었으므로 이에 대한 긍정 또는 부정의 응답이 와야 한다.

① 물론이에요. 저는 제 일을 정말 좋아합니다.
② 네. 취업하기가 어렵지 않으나요?
③ 음, 그것에 대해 여러 번 생각해 봤어요.
④ 아니요. 제가 언제 당신을 만나 뵐지 알려 주시겠어요?

어휘 trading 무역 résumé 이력서 screen 가려내다, 조사하다 interview 면접하다; 면접 head office 본사 downtown 시내 get a job 취업하다 map 지도

Review Test
pp.60~61

Word Check
03회

01 부상
02 녹다
03 아주 좋은
04 실험실
05 따르다
06 즉시
07 알 수 없는
08 책임
09 합격하다, 통과하다
10 시무룩한 얼굴
11 작성하다
12 항상
13 instrument
14 topic
15 experiment
16 deposit
17 accident
18 inconvenient
19 lend
20 metal
21 legend
22 exchange
23 on one's own
24 be willing to

Expression Check

25 make a reservation
26 If, were
27 open, account
28 What kind of
29 translate, into
30 Without your help

Word Check
04회

01 묘사하다
02 미리
03 (짐을) 싸다
04 어딘가에
05 뺑소니 사고
06 안전
07 어울리다
08 시내
09 가려내다, 조사하다
10 항공기
11 자리에 앉다
12 만약을 위해서
13 traffic
14 business trip
15 language
16 symptom
17 similar
18 glasses
19 announcement
20 effort
21 floor
22 get a job
23 not ~ anymore
24 catch up with

Expression Check

25 set the table
26 won first prize
27 looks good on
28 took, medicine
29 out of order
30 a bottle of

01 ③	02 ④	03 ③	04 ⑤	05 ④
06 ①	07 ②	08 ①	09 ④	10 ④
11 ⑤	12 ④	13 ⑤	14 ④	15 ②
16 ②	17 ④	18 ④	19 ②	20 ③

01 ③

M Jina! You look so happy.
W Yeah. I have a new P.E. teacher. He's really handsome.
M Aha, and you have P.E. class next.
W Yes. He's also very tall.
M I wonder what he looks like.
W Oh! He's right over there. He's playing tennis now.
M Is he the one with sunglasses?
W No. He is wearing a cap, not sunglasses.

남 지나야! 너 기분이 정말 좋아 보인다.
여 응. 체육 선생님이 새로 오셨거든. 정말 잘생기셨어.
남 아하, 그리고 넌 다음 시간이 체육 시간이구나.
여 응. 선생님은 키도 엄청 크셔.
남 선생님이 어떻게 생기셨는지 궁금하네.
여 오! 선생님이 바로 저기에 계셔. 지금 테니스를 치고 계셔.
남 선글라스 쓰신 분이니?
여 아니. 선글라스가 아니라 모자를 쓰고 계셔.

해설 여자의 체육 선생님은 테니스를 치고 있고 모자를 쓰고 있다고 했다.

어휘 P.E. 체육 handsome 잘생긴 wonder 궁금해하다 look like ~처럼 보이다

02 ④

W John, I heard that you're going on a business trip next week. When are you coming back?
M After two weeks.
W Two weeks? Then what about your dog? Do you want me to look after her?
M That's okay. I'm going to take her to a dog hotel. But I have another favor to ask you.
W Sure, what is it?
M Can you water the plants while I'm away? You can just do it every other day.
W No problem. Enjoy your business trip.

여 John, 나는 네가 다음 주에 출장 간다고 들었어. 언제 돌아오니?
남 2주 후에.
여 2주라고? 그럼 네 개는 어떻게 해? 내가 그녀를 돌봐 줄까?
남 괜찮아. 애견 호텔에 맡길 거야. 하지만 너에게 다른 걸 부탁하려고 해.
여 물론이지, 그게 뭔데?

남 내가 떠나 있는 동안 식물에 물 좀 줄래? 이틀에 한 번이면 돼.
여 문제없어. 출장 잘 다녀와.

해설 남자는 여자에게 자신이 출장 가 있는 동안 식물에 물을 줄 것을 부탁했다.

어휘 business trip 출장 look after ~을 돌보다 favor 부탁 every other day 이틀마다

03 ③

(Telephone rings.)
M Hello. Flower Hotel.
W Hi. I made a reservation for next Tuesday under the name of Claire Davis.
M Yes, Ms. Davis. What can I help you with?
W I know that the check-in time is 3 p.m. But is it possible to have an early check-in?
M What time do you want to check in?
W I think I'll be there around noon.
M There are not many guests that day, but you will have to wait until 1 p.m. to check in.
W That will be fine. Thank you.

(전화벨이 울린다.)
남 안녕하세요. Flower Hotel입니다.
여 안녕하세요. 저는 Claire Davis라는 이름으로 다음 주 화요일에 예약했어요.
남 네, Davis 씨. 무엇을 도와드릴까요?
여 체크인 시간이 오후 3시라고 알고 있어요. 그런데 빨리 체크인하는 것이 가능할까요?
남 몇 시에 체크인하기를 원하시나요?
여 저는 정오쯤에 거기에 도착할 것 같아요.
남 그날 투숙객이 많지는 않지만, 체크인하시려면 오후 1시까지는 기다리셔야 할 거예요.
여 괜찮아요. 감사합니다.

해설 체크인하려면 오후 1시까지는 기다려야 한다고 하자 여자는 1시도 괜찮다고 답했다.

어휘 reservation 예약 possible 가능한 check in 체크인하다 guest 손님

04 ⑤

① W Make sure you aren't late.
　 M I'll keep that in mind.
② W Do you want some dessert?
　 M No, thanks. I'm already full.
③ W What do you want me to call you?
　 M You can call me Dr. Brown.
④ W Please do not touch the paintings.
　 M Okay, I'll just enjoy looking at them.
⑤ W Excuse me. You're not allowed to take pictures in here.
　 M Sorry, I didn't know that.

① 여 늦지 않도록 하세요.
　 남 명심할게요.

② 여 후식 좀 먹을래요?
　남 고맙지만 괜찮아요. 이미 배가 불러요.
③ 여 제가 당신을 뭐라고 부를까요?
　남 Dr. Brown이라고 부르시면 됩니다.
④ 여 그림을 만지지 마세요.
　남 알았어요, 그냥 그것들을 보기만 할게요.
⑤ 여 실례합니다. 여기서 사진을 찍으시면 안 됩니다.
　남 죄송합니다, 몰랐어요.

[해설] 미술관에서 사진 촬영을 금지하는 상황이다.

[어휘] keep in mind 명심하다   dessert 후식   full 배부른
touch 만지다   allow 허용하다   take a picture 사진을 찍다

05 ④

M Look at this advertisement.
W What's it for?
M It's for a new notebook computer. It comes in two colors: white and black.
W Wow, it's on sale now and only costs $300!
M Yeah, just for this week.
W I think it's much cheaper than other notebook computers.
M Yeah, and it weighs only 900 grams.
W Let's go to the store and see it.

남 이 광고 좀 봐.
여 무엇에 관한 거야?
남 새로운 노트북 컴퓨터에 관한 광고야. 노트북 컴퓨터가 흰색과 검은색 두 가지 색상으로 나오네.
여 우와, 지금 할인 중이어서 300달러밖에 안 해!
남 응, 이번 주 동안만이야.
여 다른 노트북 컴퓨터들보다 훨씬 더 싼 것 같아.
남 응, 그리고 무게가 겨우 900그램이야.
여 가게에 가서 그것을 보자.

[해설] 사은품은 언급되지 않았다.

[어휘] advertisement 광고   on sale 할인 중인   cost 가격이
~이다   cheap (가격이) 싼   weigh 무게가 ~이다

06 ①

W What's the matter? You don't look so good.
M I'm not feeling well.
W Why not?
M I couldn't sleep well last night because of the pressure of today's game.
W I understand. Do you want to come off the court for a few minutes?
M Can I?
W Sure. After a break, if you feel better, then I will put you in the game again.
M Thanks. I will try to make lots of three-point shots then.
W I believe you will.

여 무슨 일이니? 너 정말 안 좋아 보이는구나.

남 몸 상태가 안 좋아요.
여 왜 안 좋니?
남 오늘 경기에 대한 압박감 때문에 어젯밤에 잠을 잘 못 잤거든요.
여 그랬구나. 잠시 코트에서 나가 있고 싶니?
남 그래도 돼요?
여 물론이지. 쉬고 나서 네가 괜찮아지면 너를 다시 경기에 넣어줄게.
남 감사합니다. 그때는 3점 슛을 많이 넣도록 노력할게요.
여 난 네가 그럴 거라고 믿어.

[해설] 여자는 몸 상태가 안 좋은 남자에게 코트 밖으로 나가서 쉬어도 된다고 했고, 남자는 휴식 후에 3점 슛을 많이 넣겠다고 했으므로 농구장에서 이루어지는 대화이다.

[어휘] pressure 압박, 압박감   court 코트, 경기장   for a few minutes 잠시 동안   break 휴식   believe 믿다

07 ②

① M Where can I buy some fruit?
　W There's a store on the corner.
② M I wonder if I could use my credit card.
　W Sorry. It's not on sale.
③ M Which kind of movie do you want to see?
　W I want to see a fantasy movie.
④ M Have you heard about bird watching?
　W Yes, I've even tried it before.
⑤ M Do you think I should apologize to him?
　W Yes, I think you should.

① 남 과일을 어디에서 살 수 있을까요?
　여 모퉁이에 가게가 있어요.
② 남 제가 신용 카드를 사용할 수 있는지 궁금해요.
　여 죄송합니다. 그건 할인 중이 아니에요.
③ 남 너는 어떤 종류의 영화를 보고 싶니?
　여 나는 판타지 영화를 보고 싶어.
④ 남 새 관찰하기에 대해 들어 본 적 있니?
　여 응, 나는 전에 해 본 적이 있어.
⑤ 남 너는 내가 그에게 사과를 해야 한다고 생각하니?
　여 응, 네가 그래야 할 것 같아.

[해설] ② 신용 카드를 사용해도 되는지 묻는 말에 할인 중이 아니라고 답하는 것은 어색하다.

[어휘] credit card 신용 카드   on sale 할인 중인   fantasy movie 판타지 영화   apologize 사과하다

08 ①

(Cellphone rings.)
W Dad, it's me, Susan.
M Oh, Susan. What's up?
W Are you busy now?
M Not that busy. Do you want me to do something?
W Yes, please. There's a small box on my desk. Can you mail it for me? I have to send it today.
M No problem. Did you write the address on it?
W Yeah, it's written on the box. Thanks, Dad.

M You're welcome.

(휴대 전화가 울린다.)

여 아빠, 저예요, Susan.

남 오, Susan. 무슨 일이니?

여 지금 바쁘세요?

남 별로 바쁘지 않아. 내가 무언가를 해 주기를 원하니?

여 네. 제 책상 위에 작은 상자가 있는데요. 저를 위해 그것을 부쳐 주실 수 있으세요? 오늘 그것을 부쳐야 해서요.

남 그래. 상자에 주소는 써 놨니?

여 네, 상자 위에 적혀 있어요. 고마워요, 아빠.

남 천만에.

해설 여자는 남자에게 자신의 책상 위에 있는 소포를 부쳐 달라고 부탁했다.

어휘 mail (우편으로) 부치다   write 쓰다   address 주소

09 ④

M Good morning, students. In fifth period today, a firefighter from the 911 rescue center is giving <u>a lecture about school safety</u>. He's going to talk about things that you should do to stay safe at school. Also, you can learn about <u>how to give first aid</u> in emergency situations. The lecture will <u>last for about an hour</u>. Please come to the lecture hall on time before fifth period starts.

남 안녕하세요, 학생 여러분. 오늘 5교시에, 911 구조 센터의 소방관 한 분이 오셔서 학교 안전에 대해 강의하실 것입니다. 그분은 여러분이 학교에서 안전하게 지내기 위해 해야 할 일들에 대해 이야기해 주실 것입니다. 또한, 여러분은 비상 상황에서 응급 처치를 하는 방법에 대해서도 배울 수 있습니다. 강의는 약 한 시간 동안 지속될 거예요. 5교시가 시작하기 전에, 강당으로 제때 오세요.

해설 소방관이 학교에 방문하여 학교 안전에 대해 강의할 것임을 알리는 안내 방송이다.

어휘 period 수업 시간   firefighter 소방관   rescue 구조   lecture 강의   safety 안전   first aid 응급 처치   emergency 비상 (사태)   situation 상황   last 지속하다, 계속되다

10 ④

W Hello. <u>I'd like to buy</u> some plates.

M You're lucky. All plates are 30% off right now.

W Great. How about these cups? Are they also 30% off?

M Sorry. <u>They're not on sale</u>. But if you buy one, you can get one free.

W Hmm... I want to buy these two plates and this cup.

M The plate was $10, but <u>you can get it</u> today for only $7. And the cup is $5.

W Here's my credit card.

여 안녕하세요. 접시를 좀 사고 싶어요.

남 운이 좋으시네요. 지금 모든 접시들이 30퍼센트 할인 중입니다.

여 잘됐네요. 이 컵들은 어때요? 이것들도 30퍼센트 할인되나요?

남 죄송합니다. 그것들은 할인이 안 됩니다. 하지만 하나를 사시면, 하나를 공짜로 받으실 수 있어요.

여 음… 저는 이 접시 두 개와 이 컵을 사고 싶어요.

남 접시는 10달러였지만, 오늘은 단 7달러에 사실 수 있어요. 그리고 컵은 5달러입니다.

여 여기 제 신용 카드 있어요.

해설 여자는 7달러짜리 접시 두 개와 5달러짜리 컵 하나를 사겠다고 했으므로 지불할 금액은 19달러이다.

어휘 would like to ~하고 싶다   plate 접시   free 무료로

11 ⑤

W Peter, you look tired.

M You're right. <u>I'm not feeling good</u> these days. I don't know why.

W Have you been getting enough sleep?

M I sleep 8 hours a day. I think I need to exercise more.

W Well, why don't you <u>start with a light exercise</u> such as walking in the park?

M I think it'd be boring. Can you recommend anything else?

W Then how about joining our volleyball club? We <u>practice twice a week</u>.

M Oh, that's a good idea. I'll join your club right away.

여 Peter, 너 피곤해 보여.

남 네 말이 맞아. 나 요즘 몸 상태가 안 좋아. 왜 그런지 모르겠어.

여 잠을 충분히 자고 있니?

남 나는 하루에 8시간 자. 난 운동을 더 해야 할 것 같아.

여 음, 공원에서 걷는 것과 같은 가벼운 운동으로 시작하는 게 어때?

남 그건 지루할 것 같아. 그 밖에 다른 것을 추천해 줄래?

여 그러면 우리 배구 동아리에 가입하는 게 어때? 우리는 일 주일에 두 번 연습해.

남 오, 그거 좋은 생각이다. 당장 너희 동아리에 가입할게.

해설 남자는 여자의 배구 동아리에 당장 가입하겠다고 했다.

어휘 tired 피곤한   these days 요즘   exercise 운동하다   light 가벼운   boring 지루한   recommend 추천하다   join 가입하다   practice 연습하다

12 ④

W Hello, everyone. Are you enjoying shopping at Haengbok Mart? Today we are offering our customers <u>a great discount on meat</u>. All meats including pork, beef, and chicken are 20% off. Shoppers who want to buy some meat, <u>please hurry to the meat department</u> at the back of the store. This deal lasts for only 30 minutes, so it will end at 6:30. It's starting right now. <u>Don't miss this great chance!</u>

여 여러분, 안녕하세요. Haengbok Mart에서 쇼핑을 즐기고 계

신가요? 저희는 오늘 손님 여러분께 육류를 크게 할인해 드릴 것입니다. 돼지고기, 소고기, 그리고 닭고기를 포함한 모든 육류가 20퍼센트 할인됩니다. 육류를 사고 싶으신 손님께서는 서둘러 가게 뒤편에 있는 육류 코너로 오세요. 이 행사는 단지 30분만 지속되어 6시 30분에 끝납니다. 지금 바로 시작합니다. 좋은 기회를 놓치지 마세요!

해설 쿠폰 사용 방법은 언급되지 않았다.

어휘 offer 제공하다   customer 손님   discount 할인 meat 육류   include 포함하다   pork 돼지고기   beef 소고기 hurry 서두르다   last 지속되다   miss 놓치다   chance 기회

13 ⑤

W Can you help me move this flowerpot?
M Of course, to where?
W I'm thinking of putting it next to the piano.
M In that case, we should move the piano a little bit.
W It's hard to move it.
M How about beside the bed?
W I don't think there's enough space. What about placing it next to the bookshelf?
M Oh, we have enough space there. That's a great idea.
W Okay. Let's do it now.

여 이 화분 옮기는 것 좀 도와줄래?
남 물론이지, 어디로?
여 난 그것을 피아노 옆에 둘까 생각 중이야.
남 그 경우에는, 우리가 피아노를 약간 옮겨야 해.
여 피아노를 옮기기는 어려워.
남 침대 옆은 어때?
여 충분한 공간이 없는 것 같아. 책장 옆에 두는 건 어때?
남 오, 거기에는 충분한 공간이 있어. 좋은 생각이야.
여 좋아. 지금 그걸 하자.

해설 책장 옆에 충분한 공간이 있어서 두 사람은 책장 옆으로 화분을 옮기기로 했다.

어휘 move 옮기다   flowerpot 화분   in that case 그런 경우에   a little bit 약간   beside ~ 옆에   space 공간 bookshelf 책장

14 ④

M This is a thing that you can use to make a high sound by blowing in it. You can see some people blow this in your everyday life. For example, police officers use this for traffic control or for a warning. Also soccer referees use this on the field, especially to begin the game or to stop the game for a while.

남 이것은 높은 소리를 내기 위해 불어서 사용하는 것입니다. 당신은 일상생활 속에서 몇몇 사람들이 이것을 부는 것을 볼 수 있습니다. 예를 들어, 경찰관들은 교통 통제나 경고를 하기 위해 이것을 사용합니다. 또한 축구 심판들은 경기장에서 이것을 사용하는데, 특히 경기를 시작하거나 경기를 잠시 중단시키기 위해 사용합니다.

해설 입으로 불면 높은 소리가 나고 경찰관이나 축구 심판이 사용하는 것은 호루라기이다.

어휘 sound 소리   blow (입으로) 불다   everyday 일상의, 매일의   for example 예를 들어   traffic 교통   control 통제 warning 경고   referee 심판   especially 특히   for a while 잠시 동안

15 ②

W Suho, have you seen Tom these days?
M Don't you know what happened to him?
W No, what do you mean?
M He broke his leg playing soccer a week ago and he's in the hospital.
W Really? I didn't know that.
M Yeah, that's why he hasn't been at school since last week.
W That's too bad. So is he okay now?
M He's getting better. Actually, I visited him in the hospital yesterday. Why don't you call him?
W Okay, I'll call him right now.

여 수호야, 요즘 Tom 봤니?
남 너 그에게 무슨 일이 일어났는지 모르니?
여 응, 무슨 뜻이야?
남 그는 일주일 전에 축구를 하다가 다리가 부러져서 병원에 있어.
여 정말? 난 몰랐어.
남 응. 그래서 그가 지난주부터 학교에 못 나왔던 거야.
여 그것 참 안됐다. 그래서 지금은 괜찮대?
남 좋아지고 있대. 사실, 난 어제 그를 병문안 갔었어. 그에게 전화해 보는 게 어때?
여 알았어, 지금 당장 전화해 볼게.

해설 남자는 어제 Tom의 병문안을 갔었다고 했다.

어휘 happen (일이) 일어나다   mean 의미하다   break 부러지다   hospital 병원   that's why 그래서 ~하다 actually 사실   call 전화하다

16 ②

(Cellphone rings.)
W Hi, David. Do you have any plans today?
M Not really. Why?
W Well, can you help me buy a guitar at a music shop?
M Sure, I can help you. Which shop are you going to?
W I'm thinking of visiting the music shop near the Greenville subway station.
M That's an expensive store. I know a better place. What about meeting in front of City Hall in an hour?
W Okay, see you there.

(휴대 전화가 울린다.)
여 안녕, David. 오늘 무슨 계획 있니?
남 아니. 왜?
여 음, 악기점에서 내가 기타 사는 것 좀 도와줄 수 있니?
남 물론, 도와줄 수 있지. 어느 가게에 갈 거니?

여 Greenville 지하철역 근처에 있는 악기점에 갈 생각이야.

남 거긴 비싼 가게야. 내가 더 좋은 곳을 알아. 1시간 후에 시청 앞에서 만나는 게 어때?

여 좋아, 거기서 봐.

해설 두 사람은 시청 앞에서 만나기로 했다.

어휘 plan 계획 music shop 악기점 I'm thinking of ~할 생각이다 near ~ 근처에 subway station 지하철역 place 장소 in front of ~ 앞에 City Hall 시청

17 ④

M Oh, Yubin. What happened to your arm?

W I broke my arm. I must wear this cast for 2 weeks.

M How did it happen?

W I was hit by a bicycle on my way to school yesterday.

M How did the bike hit you anyway? Did the rider ignore the traffic signal?

W No, the accident was my fault. I was sending a text message while I was crossing the road.

M You shouldn't use your phone while crossing the road.

남 아, 유빈아. 네 팔에 무슨 일이니?

여 팔이 부러졌어. 2주 동안 깁스를 해야 해.

남 어쩌다가 그랬어?

여 어제 학교에 가다가 자전거에 치였어.

남 어떻게 하다가 자전거가 너를 친 거니? 자전거 탄 사람이 교통 신호를 무시했니?

여 아니야, 사고는 내 잘못이었어. 내가 길을 건너면서 문자 메시지를 보내고 있었어.

남 너는 길을 건너면서 휴대 전화를 사용하지 말아야 해.

해설 여자가 길을 건너면서 휴대 전화를 사용하다가 자전거에 치였다고 했으므로, 길에서 휴대 전화를 사용하지 말라는 말이 이어지는 것이 가장 적절하다.

① 너는 더 열심히 공부했어야 해.

② 너는 네가 틀렸음을 인정할 필요가 있어.

③ 그 자전거를 탄 사람이 속도를 줄였어야 해.

⑤ 너는 길을 건너기 전에 양쪽을 주의 깊게 살펴봐야 해.

어휘 arm 팔 cast 깁스 hit 치다 on one's way to ~에 가는 도중에 ignore 무시하다 traffic signal 교통 신호 accident 사고 fault 잘못 text message 문자 메시지 admit 인정하다 reduce 줄이다 speed 속도 both ways 양쪽 방향, 좌우

18 ④

W Hi. I'd like to check in for my flight.

M Could you show me your passport and e-ticket, please?

W Here they are.

M Are you going to check in any luggage?

W Yes, one bag. And I'll carry this one with me.

M Okay. Are there any batteries in your bag?

W No, I took them out.

M Is there anything that can be easily broken in your bag?

W Yes. Could you please label it 'Handle with care'?

여 안녕하세요. 비행기 탑승 수속을 하려고 합니다.

남 여권과 전자 항공권을 보여 주시겠어요?

여 여기 있어요.

남 부치실 짐이 있으신가요?

여 네, 가방이 하나 있어요. 그리고 이것은 제가 가지고 갈 거예요.

남 알겠습니다. 가방 안에 배터리가 있나요?

여 아니요, 빼 놨어요.

남 가방 안에 쉽게 깨지는 게 있나요?

여 네. 그것에 '취급 주의'라는 라벨을 붙여 주시겠어요?

해설 남자가 여자의 가방 안에 쉽게 깨지는 것이 있는지 물었으므로 이에 대한 긍정 또는 부정의 응답이 와야 한다.

① 저는 제 비행편에 정말 만족했어요.

② 물론이에요. 지금 바로 그렇게 할게요.

③ 다행이네요. 그것에 대해 걱정했거든요.

⑤ 줄을 서야 한다는 거 모르세요?

어휘 flight 항공편 passport 여권 luggage 짐, 수하물 battery 배터리 be satisfied with ~에 만족하다 relief 안심, 안도 be worried about ~에 대해 걱정하다 label 라벨을 붙이다 handle 다루다 with care 주의 깊게, 신중히 necessary 필요한 stay in line 줄을 서다

19 ②

(Cellphone rings.)

M Congratulations! You're connected to the *Evening FM Music Show*.

W Am I really on the radio now?

M Yes, you are! Do you listen to my show every evening?

W Sure, every day before dinner.

M Wow! Thanks. How many times have you called in?

W Hundreds of times. And I finally got through it!

M Great! So are you ready to answer today's quiz question?

W I'm a little bit nervous right now, but yes!

M Don't worry, just try to relax.

(휴대 전화가 울린다.)

남 축하합니다! Evening FM Music Show에 연결되셨어요.

여 제가 지금 정말 라디오에 나오나요?

남 네, 그렇습니다! 저희 쇼를 매일 저녁에 들으시나요?

여 물론이죠, 매일 저녁 식사 전에요.

남 와! 감사합니다. 몇 번이나 전화하셨어요?

여 수백 번이요. 그리고 마침내 제가 해냈네요!

남 굉장하시네요! 그러시면 오늘의 퀴즈 문제에 답할 준비가 되셨나요?

여 지금 약간 긴장되지만, 준비됐습니다!

남 걱정하지 마시고, 긴장을 푸세요.

해설 여자가 약간 긴장된다고 했으므로 걱정하지 말고 긴장을 풀라는 말이 이어지는 것이 가장 적절하다.

① 세상 정말 좁죠, 그렇지 않나요?

③ 당신 전화 좀 사용해도 되나요?

④ 전에 그것에 대해 들어 본 적이 없어요.

⑤ 저는 다른 사람과 이야기하고 싶어요.

어휘 Congratulations! 축하해! connect 연결하다 be ready to ~할 준비가 되다 a little bit 약간 nervous 긴장한

20 ③

W Minsu is at an amusement park with his classmates on a school trip. He and his best friend Sarah are really happy to spend time there. But Minsu doesn't like riding scary rides because he is afraid of heights. On the other hand, Sarah loves to ride them. So she asks Minsu to ride the roller coaster. In this situation, what would Minsu say to Sarah?

Minsu Sarah, I'm afraid I'm too scared to do it.

여 민수는 그의 반 친구들과 함께 수학여행으로 놀이공원에 와 있다. 그와 그의 가장 친한 친구인 Sarah는 그곳에서 정말 즐거운 시간을 보내고 있다. 하지만 민수는 고소 공포증이 있기 때문에 무서운 놀이 기구 타는 것을 좋아하지 않는다. 반면에, Sarah는 그것들을 타는 것을 아주 좋아한다. 그래서 그녀는 민수에게 롤러코스터를 타자고 말한다. 이런 상황에서, 민수는 Sarah에게 뭐라고 말할 것인가?

민수 Sarah, 나는 너무 무서워서 그것을 탈 수 없을 것 같아.

해설 민수는 고소 공포증이 있으므로 롤러코스터를 타자는 Sarah에게 거절의 말을 하는 것이 가장 적절하다.

① 너 정말 겁에 질린 것 같아.

② 모든 게 잘 될 거야.

④ 네가 나를 보러 올 수 있다니 기뻐.

⑤ 너는 자신을 부끄러워해야 해.

어휘 amusement park 놀이공원 classmate 학급 친구 spend (시간을) 보내다 ride 타다; 놀이 기구 scary 무서운 be afraid of ~을 무서워하다 height 높이; (주로 복수로) 높은 곳 on the other hand 반면에 roller coaster 롤러코스터 be ashamed of ~을 부끄러워하다

01 ③	02 ②	03 ⑤	04 ③	05 ④
06 ⑤	07 ③	08 ②	09 ④	10 ③
11 ④	12 ⑤	13 ②	14 ⑤	15 ④
16 ④	17 ⑤	18 ①	19 ⑤	20 ②

01 ③

M What are you doing, Amy?

W Oh, I'm just looking at my old pictures.

M Wow, is this you? So cute! You're wearing a beautiful hat.

W Thanks. I liked this hat when I was young.

M Who is this boy next to you?

W He's my cousin, David. He's 17 years old now and still wants to be a soccer player.

M I see. That's why he was holding a soccer ball.

남 Amy, 뭐 하고 있니?

여 오, 그냥 내 오래된 사진들을 보고 있어.

남 와, 이거 너야? 정말 귀엽다! 너 예쁜 모자를 쓰고 있구나.

여 고마워. 난 어렸을 때 이 모자를 좋아했거든.

남 네 옆에 있는 이 소년은 누구니?

여 그는 내 사촌 David야. 지금 17살인데 여전히 축구 선수가 되기를 원해.

남 알겠다. 그래서 그가 축구공을 들고 있었구나.

해설 두 사람은 모자를 쓴 소녀와 축구공을 들고 있는 소년이 함께 있는 사진을 보고 있다.

어휘 picture 사진, 그림 cute 귀여운 cousin 사촌 still 여전히 hold 들고 있다

02 ②

(Cellphone rings.)

W Honey. Where are you? Jenny's kindergarten play starts at six.

M I know, but I'm caught in a bad traffic jam now, so I don't think I can make it on time.

W Oh, no! Then do you want me to buy flowers?

M You don't have to. I already bought some.

W That's good. How late are you going to be?

M I think I'll be there by 6:10 at the latest. Can you record the start of the play for me?

W No problem. Actually, I will record the entire performance.

(전화벨이 울린다.)

여 여보. 어디에 있어요? Jenny의 유치원 연극이 6시에 시작하잖아요.

남 알아요, 하지만 내가 지금 심한 교통 체증에 갇혀 있어요. 그래서 제시간에 도착하지 못할 것 같아요.

여 오, 안 돼요! 그러면 제가 꽃을 살까요?

남 그럴 필요 없어요. 내가 이미 샀어요.

여 잘됐네요. 얼마나 늦을까요?

남 늦어도 6시 10분까지는 도착할 것 같아요. 나를 위해 연극 시작 부분을 녹화해 줄 수 있어요?

여 그럼요. 사실, 나는 공연 전체를 녹화할 거예요.

해설 남자는 공연에 늦을 것 같다고 말하며 여자에게 공연 시작 부분을 녹화해 달라고 부탁했다.

어휘 kindergarten 유치원 traffic jam 교통 체증 on time 제시간에 don't have to ~할 필요 없다 already 이미, 벌써 at the latest 늦어도 record 녹화하다 entire 전체의 performance 공연

03 ⑤

① W Hello. Are you ready to order?
　 M I haven't decided yet. What's today's special?
② W May I see your boarding pass, please?
　 M Sure. Here it is.
③ W James, what are you doing on the computer?
　 M I'm reading some Internet news articles.
④ W Is there something wrong with you?
　 M My leg really hurts and I can barely walk.
⑤ W I need to mail this package to New York.
　 M Okay. Let's see how much it weighs.

① 여 안녕하세요. 주문하시겠어요?
　 남 아직 결정 못했어요. 오늘의 스페셜 메뉴가 뭔가요?
② 여 탑승권 좀 볼 수 있을까요?
　 남 그럼요. 여기 있어요.
③ 여 James, 컴퓨터로 뭐 하고 있니?
　 남 나는 인터넷 뉴스 기사를 읽고 있어.
④ 여 어디가 아프신가요?
　 남 다리가 너무 아파서 거의 걷지를 못해요.
⑤ 여 이 소포를 뉴욕으로 부치려고 합니다.
　 남 네. 무게가 얼마나 나가는지 봅시다.

해설 우체국에서 소포를 부치려는 여자와 남자 직원이 대화를 나누는 상황이다.

어휘 be ready to ~할 준비가 되다 boarding pass 탑승권 article 기사 hurt 아프다, 다치게 하다 barely 거의 ~ 못하는 package 소포 weigh 무게가 ~이다

04 ③

W David, did you book the tickets for the movie we talked about?

M I sure did. It's this evening.

W Thanks, David. Did you get the tickets for 5:30 as we wanted?

M Unfortunately, those were all sold out. I got tickets for the 7 o'clock show.

W That's okay. Then shall we meet at ten to seven at the theater?

M Well, how about 30 minutes before the show? I want to have something to drink before the movie starts.

W Sounds good. I'll see you at half past six.

여 David, 우리가 얘기한 영화표 예매했니?

남 당연히 했지. 오늘 저녁이야.

여 고마워, David. 우리가 원하던 대로 5시 30분 표를 산 거야?

남 아쉽지만, 그 표는 모두 매진됐어. 7시 표를 샀어.

여 괜찮아. 그러면 7시 10분 전에 극장에서 만날까?

남 음, 상영 30분 전에 만나면 어때? 영화 시작 전에 뭐 좀 마시고 싶어.

여 좋아. 6시 반에 만나자.

해설 영화는 7시에 시작인데 두 사람은 영화가 시작하기 30분 전인 6시 30분에 만나기로 했다.

어휘 book 예약하다 unfortunately 불행히도, 유감스럽게도 sold out 다 팔린, 매진된 theater 극장

05 ④

W Hello, Mr. Jordan. Could you take a look at this jacket?

M That's quite a big stain. What did you spill on it?

W Some *kimchi* stew splattered on it. Can you remove it?

M No problem.

W When can I get this back? I need to wear it this weekend.

M It'll be ready by tomorrow afternoon.

W That's so fast. Can I also pick up the coat that I dropped off yesterday?

M Yes. You can pick them both up tomorrow afternoon.

여 안녕하세요, Jordan 씨. 이 재킷 좀 봐 주실래요?

남 꽤 큰 얼룩이네요. 그것에 무엇을 쏟으셨어요?

여 김치찌개가 여기에 튀었어요. 그것을 지워주실 수 있나요?

남 문제없어요.

여 이것을 언제 찾을 수 있을까요? 이번 주말에 입어야 하거든요.

남 내일 오후까지는 준비될 겁니다.

여 아주 빠르네요. 제가 어제 맡긴 코트도 찾을 수 있을까요?

남 그럼요. 내일 오후에 둘 다 찾아가실 수 있습니다.

해설 여자가 남자에게 얼룩이 묻은 옷을 맡기면서 찾으러 오는 날짜를 확인하고 있으므로 대화가 이루어지는 장소는 세탁소이다.

어휘 take a look at ~을 보다 stain 얼룩 spill 쏟다 stew 찌개 splatter 튀다 remove 제거하다 get ~ back ~을 되찾다 drop off 맡기다 pick up ~을 찾아오다

06 ⑤

W James, have you heard about the Seoul Trick Art Exhibition?

M No, but that sounds interesting.

W I'm going to see it after school. It's being held at Seoul Art Center. Will you join me?

M I'm sorry, but not this afternoon.

W Why not? I thought you'd want to go.

M I'd really love to, but I promised to help my brother study math this afternoon.

W Why don't you do that tomorrow?

M That's his exam day, so he needs me today.

여 James, Seoul Trick Art Exhibition에 대해 들어 봤니?

남 아니, 하지만 흥미로운 것 같아.

여 나는 방과 후에 그것을 보러 갈 거야. 그것은 Seoul Art Center에서 열리고 있어. 너도 같이 갈래?

남 미안하지만, 오늘 오후에는 안 돼.

여 왜 안 돼? 네가 가고 싶어 할 줄 알았는데.

남 정말 가고 싶은데, 오늘 오후에 내 남동생이 수학 공부하는 걸 도와주기로 약속했어.

여 내일 하는 게 어때?

남 내일이 그의 시험이야. 그래서 그는 오늘 내가 필요해.

해설 남자는 오늘 동생의 수학 공부를 도와줘야 해서 전시회에 갈 수 없다고 했다.

어휘 exhibition 전시회 hold 열다, 개최하다 promise 약속하다 math 수학

07 ③

① **M** What time will you get there?
　W I think I'll be there around 2 p.m.
② **M** What are the opening hours on weekends?
　W From 9 a.m. to 5 p.m.
③ **M** How often do you eat out in a week?
　W I usually eat out with my roommate.
④ **M** Is there a subway station nearby?
　W Yes, the subway station is just over there.
⑤ **M** Don't forget to feed the dog before going out.
　W Don't worry. I won't forget.

① **남** 너는 몇 시에 거기에 도착하니?
　여 오후 2시쯤에 도착할 것 같아.
② **남** 주말 영업시간이 어떻게 되나요?
　여 오전 9시부터 오후 5시까지입니다.
③ **남** 너는 일주일에 얼마나 자주 외식을 하니?
　여 나는 보통 룸메이트와 함께 외식을 해.
④ **남** 근처에 지하철역이 있나요?
　여 네, 지하철역이 바로 저기에 있어요.
⑤ **남** 나가기 전에 개에게 먹이 주는 거 잊지 마라.
　여 걱정 마세요. 잊어버리지 않을게요.

해설 ③ 얼마나 자주 외식을 하는지 묻는 말에 보통 룸메이트와 함께 외식을 한다고 답하는 것은 어색하다.

어휘 opening hours 영업시간 eat out 외식하다 roommate 룸메이트 nearby 근처에 feed 먹이를 주다

08 ②

M Look at this! This applicant seems very interesting. He worked as an assistant cook for 7 years.

W Oh, that's a long time. I think he'll be a great help to our restaurant.

M Yeah, and here's one more thing.

W What is it?

M He ran a free meal service for the homeless for 2 years.

W Wow! What a great guy!

M I think so, too. He's exactly what we've been looking for.

남 이것 좀 봐! 이 지원자는 매우 흥미로워 보여. 그는 7년 동안 보조 요리사로 일했어.

여 오, 그건 긴 시간이야. 그는 우리 식당에 큰 도움이 될 것 같아.

남 응, 그리고 하나 더 있어.

여 뭔데?

남 그는 노숙자들을 위해서 2년 동안 무료 급식 서비스를 운영했어.

여 와! 정말 훌륭한 사람인 걸!

남 나도 그렇게 생각해. 그는 바로 우리가 찾고 있던 사람이야.

해설 I think so, too.는 상대방의 말에 동의하는 표현이다.

어휘 applicant 지원자 assistant 조수, 보조원 meal 식사 homeless 노숙자의 exactly 정확히

09 ④

M Jane, are you going to pack all these clothes for your trip?

W Of course. I think I still need some more clothes.

M Do you really think you'll need all of them?

W Well, just in case it gets too cold or too hot.

M Oh, come on. You're going on a trip for only a few days!

W But you never know how the weather might change.

M Still, don't take too much. It's always better to travel lightly.

W Okay. I'll take out some clothes, then.

남 Jane, 여행하는 데 이 옷들을 모두 가져갈 거니?

여 당연하지. 아직도 옷이 좀 더 필요한 것 같아.

남 정말 그 옷들이 모두 필요할 거라고 생각하니?

여 음, 너무 추워지거나 너무 더워질 때를 대비하는 거지.

남 오, 잠깐만. 넌 겨우 며칠 여행하는 거잖아!

여 하지만 날씨가 어떻게 변할지는 결코 모를 일이지.

남 그래도, 너무 많이 가져가지 마. 가볍게 여행을 하는 게 항상 더 좋아.

여 알았어. 그러면 옷을 좀 꺼낼게.

해설 여행에 옷을 너무 많이 가져가지 말라는 남자의 조언에 따라 여자는 옷을 좀 꺼내기로 했다.

어휘 just in case 만약의 경우에 change 변하다 still 그런데도, 그럼에도 불구하고 travel 여행하다 lightly 가볍게 take out 꺼내다

10 ③

W I'm finished. How do you like it?

M I love it. I've never tried this kind of hairstyle before.

W I think it really suits you.

M Thank you. How much is it?

W It's $20 for the haircut.

M Is there any discount available?

W No, I'm sorry. But I'll give you a 10% discount

coupon for your next visit. Here you are.

M That's great. Here's my card.

여 다 되셨습니다. 마음에 드세요?

남 아주 마음에 들어요. 저는 전에 이런 헤어스타일을 해 본 적이 없어요.

여 손님께 정말 잘 어울리시는 것 같아요.

남 감사합니다. 얼마예요?

여 커트는 20달러입니다.

남 할인 가능한 것이 있나요?

여 아니요, 죄송합니다. 하지만 다음 방문 때 사용하실 10퍼센트 할인 쿠폰을 드리겠습니다. 여기 있습니다.

남 잘됐네요. 카드 여기 있습니다.

해설 여자는 남자의 커트 비용이 20달러라고 했고 할인은 안 된다고 했다.

어휘 suit ~에 어울리다   discount 할인   available 이용할 수 있는

11 ④

W Honey, I want to buy an air freshener.

M What kind of scent do you want?

W I had mint last time. Maybe I'll try something different this time.

M Good idea. And why don't you get one that lasts longer than one month?

W I will. I don't want to worry about replacing it too often.

M Exactly. Then you only have two options.

W Yes. Shall I get the liquid type like before?

M Well, since it comes in a bottle, it might take up a bigger space. Try the other type this time.

W All right. Then I'll buy this one.

여 여보, 나 방향제 하나 사고 싶어요.

남 어떤 종류의 향을 원해요?

여 지난번에는 민트 향이었어요. 이번에는 좀 다른 것을 써 볼까 해요.

남 좋은 생각이에요. 그리고 한 달 넘게 지속되는 것을 사는 게 어때요?

여 그럴 거예요. 너무 자주 교체할 걱정을 하고 싶지 않아요.

남 맞아요. 그러면 이제 두 개의 선택밖에 안 남네요.

여 네. 지난번처럼 액체형으로 할까요?

남 음, 그것은 병으로 나오니까 공간을 더 많이 차지할 거예요. 이번에는 다른 종류로 써 봐요.

여 알겠어요. 그럼 이것으로 살게요.

해설 여자는 민트 향이 아니면서 한 달 넘게 지속되고 액체형이 아닌 것을 구입하기로 했다.

어휘 air freshener 방향제   scent 향   last 지속되다 replace 교체하다   liquid 액체   bottle 병   take up 차지하다 space 공간, 자리   type 종류   duration (지속되는) 기간

12 ⑤

W Good afternoon, students. This is Jennifer from the Student Council. Our school is going to hold its 1st Cooking Competition next month. There are several things you should know about the competition. First, it's an individual competition. Second, you should complete your dish within two hours. Third, cooking equipment will be provided, but you should bring your own ingredients. Finally, you need to apply for the competition by this Thursday.

여 학생 여러분, 안녕하세요. 저는 학생회의 Jennifer입니다. 우리 학교는 다음 달에 제1회 요리 경연 대회를 개최할 예정입니다. 대회에 관해 알고 있어야 할 사항들이 몇 가지 있습니다. 먼저, 이것은 개인 대회입니다. 둘째, 2시간 이내에 요리를 완성해야 합니다. 셋째, 요리 도구는 제공되지만, 여러분들이 자신의 재료를 가지고 오셔야 합니다. 마지막으로, 이번 주 목요일까지 대회 참가 신청을 해야 합니다.

해설 이번 주 목요일까지 참가 신청을 해야 한다고 했다.

어휘 hold 개최하다   competition 경연 대회   several 몇몇의 individual 개인의   complete 완성하다   dish 음식, 요리 equipment 도구, 장비   provide 제공하다   ingredient 재료 apply for ~을 신청하다

13 ②

M Mira, what are you reading?

W I'm reading a tour guidebook of Seoul. My friend from Germany is visiting me next week.

M Oh, I see. Have you decided where to go?

W I still don't know. This book doesn't seem to have much information.

M Well, I can recommend a good blog about traveling in Seoul.

W Really? Would it be more useful than this book?

M Absolutely. It's the most popular blog for traveling around Seoul.

W Sounds good. Can you send me the link of the blog?

남 미라야, 무엇을 읽고 있니?

여 서울 여행 안내 책자를 읽고 있어. 다음 주에 독일에서 내 친구가 오거든.

남 오, 그렇구나. 어디에 갈지 결정했어?

여 아직 잘 모르겠어. 이 책에는 많은 정보가 없는 것 같아.

남 그럼, 내가 서울 여행에 관한 괜찮은 블로그를 추천해 줄 수 있어.

여 정말? 이 책보다 더 유용할까?

남 물론이지. 서울 여행에 관해서는 가장 인기 있는 블로그야.

여 잘됐다. 나한테 그 블로그 링크를 보내줄래?

해설 여자는 남자에게 서울 여행에 관한 블로그 링크를 보내 달라고 부탁했다.

어휘 guidebook 안내서   Germany 독일   information 정보   recommend 추천하다   blog 블로그   useful 유용한 popular 인기 있는

14 ⑤

M Mom, what are we having for dinner?
W How about ribeye steak and Caesar salad?
M Wow, sounds perfect. Do you want me to help you cook?
W No, I'll do it. And after dinner, your dad will wash the dishes.
M Okay. I'm going to buy some cold sodas. Do you need anything else from the store?
W No, but can you throw away the garbage first?
M Okay. Today is the garbage collection day.
W Right. The truck will be here soon.

남 엄마, 저녁에 우리 뭐 먹어요?
여 립아이 스테이크와 시저 샐러드 어떠니?
남 와, 완벽해요. 요리하시는 거 도와드릴까요?
여 아니, 내가 할게. 그리고 식사 후에는 아버지가 설거지하실 거야.
남 알겠어요. 저 시원한 탄산음료를 사러 갈 거예요. 가게에서 다른 필요한 거 있으세요?
여 아니, 하지만 먼저 쓰레기 좀 버려 줄래?
남 네. 오늘이 쓰레기 수거하는 날이잖아요.
여 맞아. 트럭이 곧 올 거야.

해설 여자가 가게에 가려는 남자에게 먼저 쓰레기를 버려 달라고 부탁하자 남자는 그러겠다고 했다.

어휘 perfect 완벽한   wash the dishes 설거지하다   throw away 버리다   garbage 쓰레기   collection 수집, 수거

15 ④

M Good morning. You're on the air. Can you tell us your name and where you're calling from?
W I'm Suji Park calling from Jeju-do.
M Hello, Suji. You sound quite young. Are you a student?
W Yes. I'm a third grader in middle school.
M Oh, I see. So what song would you like to request?
W I'd like to request *Endless Love*. It's for my parents. It's their wedding anniversary today.
M That's so sweet. I'm sure they'll love it.

남 안녕하세요. 방송에 연결되셨습니다. 본인의 이름과 어디서 전화하시는지 말씀해 주시겠어요?
여 저는 박수지이고 제주도에서 전화하고 있습니다.
남 안녕하세요, 수지 씨. 목소리가 꽤 어리게 들리는데요. 학생이신가요?
여 네. 중학교 3학년입니다.
남 오, 그렇군요. 자, 무슨 노래를 신청하시겠어요?
여 〈Endless Love〉를 신청하고 싶습니다. 저희 부모님을 위해서요. 오늘이 부모님 결혼기념일이거든요.
남 정말 좋네요. 부모님께서 좋아하실 거라고 확신해요.

해설 부모님의 결혼기념일을 위해 노래를 신청하는 청취자와 라디오 디제이가 나누는 대화이다.

어휘 on the air 방송 중인   grader 학년생   request 요청하다   parents 부모   wedding anniversary 결혼기념일

16 ④

M What's the next class, Karen?
W Social studies.
M Oh, then we need to hurry. Classroom 101 is in the other building.
W Haven't you heard that the classroom was changed?
M Really? To where?
W Because of the maintenance problem, our class will be in Classroom 203.
M Oh, you mean the room right next to 204?
W Actually, it's across from 204. Classroom 203 is next to 205.
M I see. Let's go.

남 다음 수업이 뭐니, Karen?
여 사회야.
남 오, 그러면 우리 서둘러야겠다. 101호 강의실은 다른 건물에 있잖아.
여 너 강의실이 변경되었다는 소식 못 들었니?
남 정말? 어디로?
여 보수 문제 때문에 우리 수업은 203호 강의실에서 있을 거야.
남 오, 204호 바로 옆에 있는 강의실 말하는 거지?
여 사실, 그것은 204호 건너편에 있어. 203호 강의실은 205호 옆에 있어.
남 알겠어. 가자.

해설 두 사람이 들을 사회 수업의 강의실이 101호에서 203호로 변경되었다고 했다.

어휘 social studies (과목) 사회   hurry 서두르다   change 바꾸다   maintenance 유지, 보수 관리   problem 문제

17 ⑤

M Attention, students. This is an announcement from the Student Council. As you know, the candidates for the president election are giving speeches at 11 tomorrow morning. The event was going to be held in the auditorium, but the heating system has some problems, so we changed the location. The speeches will be delivered in the student hall located next to the library. See you there at 11 tomorrow.

남 학생 여러분, 주목해 주세요. 학생회에서 안내 방송 드립니다. 여러분이 알고 있는 것처럼, 내일 오전 11시에 학생회장 선거 후보자들이 연설을 할 것입니다. 행사는 강당에서 열릴 예정이었지만, 난방 시스템에 문제가 있어서 장소를 변경했습니다. 연설은 도서관 옆에 위치한 학생회관에서 진행될 것입니다. 내일 11시에 그곳에서 뵙겠습니다.

해설 학생회장 선거 후보자들의 연설 장소가 강당에서 학생회관으로 변경되었음을 알리는 안내 방송이다.

어휘 announcement 공지, 알림   candidate 후보자   presidnet 회장   election 선거   auditorium 강당   heating 난방   location 위치   deliver (연설 등을) 하다   located ~에 위치한

18 ①

M Hey, Olivia. What's the matter?
W I fell down and I think I twisted my arm.
M That's too bad. Does it hurt a lot?
W Yeah, I think I have to go to the hospital.
M I wish I could go with you, but I'm late for class. Do you think you can go by yourself?
W Yes, don't worry. Do you know where the nearest hospital is?
M It's right next to Green Park.

남 Olivia, 안녕. 무슨 일 있니?
여 넘어졌는데 팔을 삔 것 같아.
남 참 안됐구나. 많이 아프니?
여 응, 나 병원에 가야 할 것 같아.
남 내가 같이 갈 수 있으면 좋을 텐데, 수업에 늦었어. 너 혼자 갈 수 있겠니?
여 응, 걱정하지 마. 가장 가까운 병원이 어디에 있는지 아니?
남 그것은 Green Park 바로 옆에 있어.

해설 가장 가까운 병원이 어디에 있는지 물었으므로 병원의 위치를 알려 주는 응답이 적절하다.
② 나는 Green Park에서 매일 아침 조깅을 해.
③ 너는 약 30분을 기다려야 해.
④ 이 약을 하루에 세 번 드세요.
⑤ 공항에서 7시에 만나자.

어휘 fall down 넘어지다 twist 삐다 arm 팔 by oneself 혼자서 medicine 약 airport 공항

19 ⑤

W Dr. Jones. Do you have a minute to talk?
M Sure, Lisa. What is it?
W I developed an app over the weekend.
M Really? What kind of app is it?
W It's an app that helps people record their health conditions.
M Wow! It sounds very useful. I'm so impressed!
W But it sometimes stops suddenly. I can't figure out exactly what's wrong.
M Maybe we can check it out together. Will you come to my office after class?
W Thank you. I'll visit your office after class.

여 Jones 선생님. 잠깐 얘기할 시간 있으세요?
남 물론이지, Lisa. 그게 뭐니?
여 제가 주말 동안 앱을 하나 개발했어요.
남 정말? 어떤 종류의 앱이니?
여 사람들이 자신의 건강 상태를 기록하는 것을 도와주는 앱이에요.
남 와! 아주 유용할 것 같구나. 정말 멋진데!
여 그런데 그것이 가끔 갑자기 멈춰요. 뭐가 문제인지 정확히 모르겠어요.
남 우리가 함께 점검해 볼 수 있을 거야. 수업 끝나고 내 연구실로 올래?
여 감사합니다. 수입 끝나고 선생님 연구실로 가겠습니다.

해설 남자는 여자가 만든 앱의 문제점을 함께 점검해 보자고 하면서 자신의 연구실로 오라고 했으므로, 이에 대한 감사의 말과 함께 수업 끝나고 가겠다고 응답하는 것이 자연스럽다.
① 네. 저는 선생님 수업에서 많은 것을 배웠어요.
② 물론이에요. 병원 진료를 받겠습니다.
③ 굉장해요. 지금 당장 고칠 수 있을 것 같아요.
④ 맞아요. 저는 오늘 일찍 집에 가야 해요.

어휘 develop 개발하다 record 기록하다 health 건강 condition 상태 useful 유용한 impressed 인상 깊은, 감동받은 suddenly 갑자기 figure out 이해하다 fix 수리하다

20 ②

W Amy is standing in line to buy a ticket for her favorite singer's concert. There are lots of people ahead of her. The line is so long and it is moving very slowly. But suddenly, she needs to go to the restroom, but she doesn't want somebody to take her place. In this situation, what would Amy say to the person right behind her?
Amy Excuse me. Could you hold my place, please?

여 Amy는 자신이 가장 좋아하는 가수의 콘서트 표를 사기 위해 줄을 서고 있다. 그녀의 앞에는 많은 사람들이 있다. 줄은 너무 길고 아주 천천히 움직이고 있다. 그러나 갑자기, 그녀는 화장실에 가야 하지만 누군가가 자신의 자리를 차지하기를 원하지 않는다. 이 상황에서, Amy는 바로 뒤에 있는 사람에게 무엇이라고 말하겠는가?
Amy 실례합니다. 제 자리 좀 맡아 주시겠어요?

해설 표를 사기 위해 줄을 서 있다가 화장실에 가야 하는 상황이므로 뒷사람에게 자리를 맡아 달라고 부탁하는 것이 자연스럽다.
① 왜 이 가수를 좋아하시나요?
③ 얼마나 오래 기다리고 계신가요?
④ 표가 얼마인지 아시나요?
⑤ 여기에서 몇 명이 기다리고 있는지 아시나요?

어휘 in line 줄을 서서 ahead of ~의 앞에 restroom 화장실 right 바로 behind ~ 뒤에

Word Check
05회

01 강의	**02** 포함하다
03 손님	**04** 다루다
05 가격이 ~이다	**06** 책장
07 비상 (사태)	**08** 무시하다
09 경고	**10** 심판
11 줄을 서다	**12** 명심하다
13 fault	**14** speed
15 light	**16** necessary
17 boring	**18** connect
19 dessert	**20** last
21 admit	**22** first aid
23 traffic signal	**24** on the other hand

Expression Check

25 looks like	**26** anything else
27 look after	**28** is afraid of
29 on sale	**30** In that case

Word Check
06회

01 적용하다	**02** 재료
03 후보자	**04** 화장실
05 교체하다	**06** 유지, 보수 관리
07 극장	**08** 정확히
09 근처에	**10** 제시간에
11 이해하다	**12** 늦어도
13 assistant	**14** remove
15 request	**16** develop
17 article	**18** weigh
19 individual	**20** auditorium
21 equipment	**22** apply for
23 wedding anniversary	**24** by oneself

Expression Check

25 take up	**26** fell down
27 caught in	**28** throw away
29 in line	**30** forget to feed

01 ②	02 ④	03 ⑤	04 ③	05 ⑤
06 ①	07 ③	08 ⑤	09 ②	10 ⑤
11 ③	12 ③	13 ⑤	14 ③	15 ④
16 ⑤	17 ③	18 ①	19 ②	20 ⑤

01 ②

M I'm so glad we are finally going to buy a dryer. We needed one last year <u>during the rainy season</u>.

W That's true. Our washing machine is from SMART, so I'd prefer to <u>get the same brand</u>.

M Okay. Then what about this 9-kilogram dryer?

W It seems too small. We sometimes need to dry blankets.

M All right. Which color then? The darker-colored one looks good.

W But I think the lighter-colored one would <u>match with our washing machine</u>.

M Okay. <u>Let's get that one</u> then.

남 드디어 우리가 건조기를 사게 되다니 너무 좋아요. 작년 장마철에 건조기가 필요했잖아요.

여 맞아요. 우리 세탁기가 SMART에서 나온 거니까, 나는 같은 브랜드를 사고 싶어요.

남 좋아요. 그럼 이 9킬로그램짜리 건조기는 어때요?

여 그건 너무 작아 보여요. 우리는 때때로 이불도 건조시켜야 하거든요.

남 맞아요. 그럼 무슨 색으로요? 진한 색이 보기가 좋은데요.

여 하지만 난 밝은 색이 우리 세탁기와 어울릴 것 같아요.

남 좋아요. 그러면 그걸로 삽시다.

해설 두 사람은 SMART 브랜드이면서 9킬로그램보다 용량이 크고 밝은 색의 건조기를 사기로 했다.

어휘 finally 드디어   dryer 건조기   rainy season 장마철   washing machine 세탁기   blanket 이불, 담요   match 어울리다

02 ④

W Have you heard anything from <u>the company you applied to</u>?

M No. I was supposed to hear something yesterday, but they <u>haven't informed me of anything</u> yet.

W I thought you would have heard something by now.

M I know, but <u>it takes a long time</u> for them to examine all the documents. I'm getting worried.

W Hey, why don't you email or call them and ask about it?

M Do you think that would be okay?

W Why not? Just <u>give it a try</u>.

M Okay, I'll call them. Thank you for your advice.

여 네가 지원한 회사에서 어떤 소식이라도 들었니?

남 아니. 어제 소식을 듣기로 되어 있었는데, 아직 나에게 아무것도 알려 주지 않았어.

여 지금쯤이면 네가 무슨 소식을 들었을 줄 알았는데.

남 맞아, 그런데 그들이 모든 서류를 검토하는 데 시간이 오래 걸리네. 점점 걱정이 되고 있어.

여 저런, 그들에게 이메일을 보내거나 전화해서 물어보는 게 어때?

남 그래도 될까?

여 왜 안 되겠어? 한번 해 봐.

남 그래, 그들에게 전화해 봐야겠어. 조언해 줘서 고마워.

해설 남자는 입사 지원한 회사에서 아무런 연락이 없어서 회사에 전화해 보겠다고 했다.

어휘 company 회사   apply to ～에 지원하다   be supposed to ～하기로 되어 있다   inform 알리다, 통지하다   examine 검토하다   document 서류   give it a try 한번 해 보다   advice 조언, 충고

03 ⑤

W Dave, what are you looking for on the computer?

M I'm looking for the pictures that I took for my art assignment.

W You mean the assignment about unique buildings in Seoul?

M Yeah. I've checked all the folders, but I can't find them.

W Why don't you just describe the buildings without the pictures?

M I need to include at least three pictures that I took by myself.

W Did you check the memory card in your camera?

M I deleted all the pictures right after I uploaded them onto the computer.

여 Dave, 컴퓨터로 무엇을 찾고 있니?

남 미술 숙제로 찍은 사진들을 찾고 있어.

여 서울의 독특한 건물들에 대한 숙제 말하는 거야?

남 응. 모든 폴더를 확인해 봤지만, 그것들을 못 찾겠어.

여 사진 없이 그냥 건물들을 묘사하면 어때?

남 내가 직접 찍은 사진을 최소한 3장 포함시켜야 해.

여 카메라의 메모리 카드를 확인해 봤어?

남 컴퓨터에 사진을 업로드한 후에 바로 모두 삭제했어.

해설 남자는 미술 숙제를 위해 찍은 사진을 찾지 못하고 있으므로 걱정스러울 것이다.

어휘 assignment 과제, 숙제   unique 독특한   folder 폴더   describe 묘사하다   include 포함하다   at least 최소한, 적어도   delete 지우다, 삭제하다   upload 업로드하다

04 ③

W You look really nice today. Is that a new jacket?

M Yes, thanks! I bought it at the secondhand clothing store near my office.

W Really? It looks pretty new and fashionable.

M And it was really cheap. They're having a big sale. Everything is 50% off.

W How much was it?

M It was $20 before the sale.

W Wow! So it was only $10 then?

M Yes. I also bought a pair of shoes. They were originally $16.

W That's a great deal! I should go there before the sale ends.

여 너 오늘 정말 멋져 보인다. 새 재킷이니?

남 응, 고마워! 회사 근처에 있는 중고 옷가게에서 샀어.

여 정말? 아주 새것처럼 보이고 멋져.

남 게다가 정말 저렴했어. 세일을 크게 하고 있거든. 모든 것이 50퍼센트 할인이야.

여 얼마였는데?

남 세일 전에는 20달러였어.

여 와! 그럼 10달러밖에 안 한 거야?

남 응. 신발도 한 켤레 샀어. 원래는 16달러였지.

여 정말 잘 샀구나! 나도 세일 끝나기 전에 가봐야겠다.

해설 남자는 20달러였던 재킷과 16달러였던 신발을 모두 50퍼센트 할인된 가격에 샀다고 했다.

어휘 secondhand 중고의   fashionable 유행하는   everything 모든 것   originally 원래

05 ⑤

M Good afternoon. Here's my ticket.

W That'll be 16,000 won. You've driven quite a long distance!

M Yes. Can I pay by credit card?

W Sure. (Pause) Here's your card and receipt.

M One question, ma'am. Could you tell me how to get to Park Paradise?

W Just keep driving straight for about two kilometers and take Route 37.

M Take Route 37?

W Right. Sorry, but other cars are waiting behind you.

M Oops, I kept you too long. Thanks!

남 안녕하세요. 표 여기 있습니다.

여 16,000원입니다. 꽤 장거리를 운전해 오셨네요!

남 네. 신용 카드로 지불해도 되나요?

여 그럼요. (잠시 후) 여기 카드와 영수증 있습니다.

남 한 가지 여쭤볼게요. Park Paradise로 가는 길을 알려 주실 수 있나요?

여 2킬로미터 정도 계속 직진하시다가 37번 국도를 타세요.

남 37번 국도를 타라고요?

여 맞아요. 죄송하지만 다른 차들이 고객님 뒤에서 기다리고 있습니다.

남 이런, 제가 너무 오래 붙잡고 있었네요. 감사합니다!

해설 고속도로 톨게이트에서 요금을 지불하면서 나누는 대화이다.

어휘 distance 거리   receipt 영수증   Route (국도) ～번(호선)   behind ～ 뒤에

06 ①

W Hi, I'm staying in Room 1405. I'd like to ask how long it takes from here to Wonderland.
M It takes about 20 minutes by car.
W Are there any buses going there?
M Yes, but there are many stops on the route. People usually take a taxi.
W Then can you reserve one for me for tomorrow morning?
M Sure, at what time?
W Well, 8:00 a.m. would be good.
M Okay, I'll call the taxi company now. Please come to the front desk before then.

여 안녕하세요. 저는 1405호에 투숙하고 있는데요. 여기서 Wonderland까지 얼마나 걸리는지 여쭤보려고요.
남 자동차로 20분 정도 걸립니다.
여 거기로 가는 버스가 있나요?
남 네, 하지만 그 노선에 정류장이 많이 있습니다. 사람들은 보통 택시를 타요.
여 그럼 내일 아침에 택시를 예약해 주실 수 있나요?
남 그럼요. 몇 시에요?
여 음, 아침 8시가 좋겠어요.
남 알겠습니다. 제가 지금 택시 회사에 전화해 둘게요. 그 전에 프런트 데스크로 오세요.

해설 여자는 Wonderland에 가기 위해 남자에게 택시를 예약해 달라고 부탁했다.

어휘 stay 머무르다   stop 정류장   route 노선   take a taxi 택시를 타다   reserve 예약하다   company 회사

07 ③

① W I left my bag on the subway.
  M Have you checked the lost and found?
② W What are your plans for this weekend?
  M Nothing special. What about you?
③ W How many books can I borrow at a time?
  M You can borrow books for five days.
④ W Excuse me. Is there a post office nearby?
  M Sorry, but I'm a stranger here myself.
⑤ W Look at those flowers on Suji's desk.
  M They're so beautiful. I wonder who sent them.

① 여 지하철에 가방을 두고 내렸어.
  남 분실물 보관소를 확인해 봤니?
② 여 이번 주말 계획이 뭐야?
  남 특별한 건 없어. 너는 어때?
③ 여 제가 한 번에 몇 권의 책을 빌릴 수 있나요?
  남 책을 5일간 빌리실 수 있어요.
④ 여 실례합니다. 근처에 우체국이 있나요?
  남 죄송하지만, 저도 여기가 처음이에요.
⑤ 여 수지의 책상 위에 있는 저 꽃 좀 봐.
  남 정말 아름답다. 누가 보냈는지 궁금하네.

해설 ③ 한 번에 몇 권의 책을 빌릴 수 있는지 묻는 말에 대출 기간을 답하는 것은 어색하다.

어휘 lost and found 분실물 보관소   special 특별한   borrow 빌리다   at a time 한 번에   nearby 근처에   wonder 궁금하다

08 ⑤

W Sean, are you ready for your restaurant's opening?
M Almost. I only have to order the free gifts for customers.
W What's the gift?
M Tumblers with my restaurant's logo. Do you think 100 tumblers will be enough?
W I think you'd better order 50 more tumblers.
M Isn't 150 too many? For my first restaurant in Cary Town, I ordered 80, and it was enough.
W But a lot more people live in this town.
M You're right. I'll order the number you suggested.

여 Sean, 식당 개업 준비는 됐니?
남 거의. 손님들에게 무료로 줄 선물만 주문하면 돼.
여 선물이 뭔데?
남 식당 로고가 새겨진 텀블러야. 100개면 충분하겠지?
여 50개는 더 주문하는 게 좋을 것 같은데.
남 150개는 너무 많지 않아? Cary Town에서의 첫 번째 식당에서는 80개 주문했는데 충분했어.
여 하지만 이 마을에는 훨씬 더 많은 사람들이 살잖아.
남 네 말이 맞아. 네가 제안한 개수를 주문할게.

해설 남자는 처음에 100개를 주문하려고 했으나 여자가 50개를 더 주문하라고 권하자 여자의 제안대로 주문하겠다고 했다.

어휘 be ready for ~할 준비가 되다   order 주문하다   customer 손님, 고객   tumbler 텀블러   enough 충분한   suggest 제안하다

09 ②

W Did you know that many people lose their hearing due to preventable causes? Today, I'm going to tell you some things you should keep in mind to avoid hearing problems. First, keep your music at a low volume. Next, try not to get water in your ears when bathing or swimming. Finally, many doctors strongly advise you not to clean your ears at home. If you have trouble hearing, see your doctor right away.

여 많은 사람들이 예방 가능한 이유들로 인해 청력을 잃는다는 것을 아셨나요? 오늘은, 청력 문제를 피하기 위해 기억하셔야 할 몇 가지 것들에 대해 말씀드리려고 합니다. 먼저, 음악 볼륨을 낮게 유지하세요. 다음으로, 목욕이나 수영할 때 귀에 물이 들어가지 않도록 하세요. 마지막으로, 많은 의사들이 집에서는 귀를 청소하지 말 것을 강력하게 충고하고 있습니다. 청력에 문제가 있으시면, 즉시 의사의 진료를 받으세요.

해설 음악 볼륨 낮추기, 귀에 물이 들어가지 않게 하기, 집에서 귀 청소하지 않기 등 청력을 보호하는 방법에 대한 내용이다.

어휘 lose 잃다   hearing 청력   due to ~ 때문에   preventable 예방 가능한   cause 원인   keep in mind

명심하다 bathe 목욕하다 strongly 강하게 advise 조언하다 have trouble ~ing ~하는 데 어려움을 겪다

10 ⑤

M Hello, Ms. Brandon. Can I take back the sample that I submitted to you?
W Do you mean the one for the student invention contest?
M Yes. I think I should find a new item for the contest.
W Why? I liked your idea of a chair with a hanger.
M Yeah, so did I. I thought it was practical.
W So what's wrong then?
M Well, I saw a similar kind of chair on the Internet. Someone has already invented it.

남 안녕하세요, Brandon 선생님. 제가 제출한 샘플을 다시 가져가도 될까요?
여 학생 발명 대회를 위해 제출한 것 말이니?
남 네. 대회를 위한 새로운 아이템을 찾아봐야 할 것 같아요.
여 왜? 옷걸이가 달린 의자 아이디어 좋았는데.
남 네, 저도 그랬어요. 저는 그것이 실용적이라고 생각했어요.
여 그런데 무슨 문제가 있니?
남 음, 제가 인터넷에서 비슷한 종류의 의자를 봤어요. 누군가 이미 그것을 발명했더라고요.

해설 남자는 자신이 제출한 발명품과 유사한 종류의 의자를 인터넷에서 발견해서 제출한 작품을 다시 가져가겠다고 했다.

어휘 take back 되찾다 sample 샘플 submit 제출하다 invention 발명, 발명품 hanger 옷걸이 practical 실용적인 similar 비슷한, 유사한

11 ③

M Monica, you look busy. What's up?
W I've been trying to fix my computer all morning.
M Your new computer? Is there something wrong with it?
W I don't exactly know. It keeps turning off automatically.
M It might be infected by a virus. Did you visit the service center?
W I called, but they are closed on weekends.
M Then why don't you download an antivirus program? I know a good one.

남 Monica, 바빠 보이네. 무슨 일이야?
여 아침 내내 컴퓨터를 고쳐 보려고 노력 중이야.
남 네 새 컴퓨터? 무슨 문제라도 있어?
여 정확히는 모르겠어. 컴퓨터가 계속 자동으로 꺼져.
남 바이러스에 감염됐을 수도 있어. 서비스 센터에 가 봤니?
여 전화했는데, 주말에는 닫는대.
남 그럼 바이러스 퇴치 프로그램을 다운로드해 보는 게 어때? 내가 좋은 것을 알고 있어.

해설 남자는 여자에게 바이러스 퇴치 프로그램을 다운로드해 보라고 조언했다.

어휘 fix 고치다 exactly 정확히 keep ~ing 계속 ~하다 turn off ~을 끄다 automatically 자동으로 infect 감염시키다 antivirus 바이러스 퇴치용인

12 ③

M Good afternoon, passengers! May I have your attention, please? We are sorry to inform you that the train will stay at this station a little longer than scheduled because of a technical problem. This is a minor issue and our mechanics are working on it right now. We expect the train will leave in 10 minutes. We're sorry for the inconvenience. Thank you for your patience.

남 승객 여러분, 안녕하십니까! 잠깐 주목해 주시겠어요? 기술상의 문제 때문에 열차가 이번 역에서 예정보다 조금 더 오래 머무를 것임을 알려 드리게 되어 유감입니다. 이것은 사소한 문제이며 저희 기술자들이 지금 바로 작업하고 있습니다. 열차는 10분 내로 출발할 것으로 예상됩니다. 불편을 드려 죄송합니다. 기다려 주셔서 감사합니다.

해설 기술상의 문제 때문에 열차가 예정보다 오래 정차할 것임을 알리는 안내 방송이다.

어휘 passenger 승객 inform 알리다 scheduled 예정된 technical 기술적인 minor 사소한 mechanic 기술자 expect 예상하다 inconvenience 불편 patience 인내

13 ⑤

W Good morning! Today, I'd like to make an announcement about this year's Clark County Poster Contest. Any Clark County School student can enter this contest. The topic is "School Safety." The submission dates are from September 10 to September 14. Posters should be no larger than A3 size. All submissions should be handed in to your art teacher. Good luck to everybody!

여 안녕하세요! 오늘, 저는 올해의 Clark County 포스터 대회에 관해 알려 드리려고 합니다. Clark County School 학생이라면 누구나 이 대회에 참여할 수 있습니다. 주제는 '학교 안전'입니다. 제출일은 9월 10일부터 9월 14일까지입니다. 포스터는 A3 사이즈를 넘지 않아야 합니다. 모든 제출 작품은 여러분의 미술 선생님께 제출해야 합니다. 모두에게 행운을 빌어요!

해설 포스터 대회의 시상 계획은 언급되지 않았다.

어휘 announcement 공지, 알림 enter 참가하다 safety 안전 submission 제출(물) hand in 제출하다

14 ③

① **W** This boy in the picture looks just like you.
  M Does he? Actually, he's my twin brother.
② **W** Watch out! You almost hit my daughter with your bike.
  M Oh, I'm really sorry. Is she okay?

③ **W** Which floor are you going to?
　M The 8th floor. Thanks a lot.
④ **W** You're not allowed to wear shoes in here, sir.
　M Oh, I didn't know that. I'll take them off.
⑤ **W** Excuse me. Could you please be quiet in the reading room?
　M I'm sorry. I'll keep my voice down.

① 여 사진 속 이 남자아이가 꼭 너를 닮았어.
　남 그래 보이니? 사실, 나의 쌍둥이 형제야.
② 여 조심하세요! 당신이 자전거로 제 딸을 거의 칠 뻔했어요.
　남 오, 정말 죄송합니다. 따님은 괜찮은가요?
③ 여 몇 층으로 가세요?
　남 8층입니다. 정말 감사합니다.
④ 여 이 안에서는 신발을 신으시면 안 됩니다, 손님.
　남 오, 몰랐어요. 벗을게요.
⑤ 여 실례합니다. 독서실에서 좀 조용히 해 주실래요?
　남 죄송해요. 목소리를 낮출게요.

해설 엘리베이터 안에서 무거운 가방을 들고 있는 남자를 위해 여자가 버튼을 대신 눌러 주려는 상황이다.

어휘 watch out 조심하다　hit 치다　floor 층　be allowed to ~하는 것이 허용되다　take off (옷·신발·모자 등을) 벗다

15 ④

W Chris, have you searched for any cherry blossom trips?
M Yes. This travel agency is offering several different one-day cherry blossom trips for this weekend.
W Oh, let me see. I need to go to my friend's wedding on Saturday.
M Then let's look at the Sunday trips.
W Gyeongju looks better than Jinhae. Jinhae is too far from here.
M Okay. Now we have one more option, lunch included or not included.
W I'd prefer the one with the lunch included. It would be more convenient.
M I agree. Then this one is the best.

여 Chris, 벚꽃 여행 찾아봤니?
남 응. 이 여행사는 이번 주말에 몇몇 다양한 1일 벚꽃 여행을 제공하고 있어.
여 오, 어디 보자. 난 토요일에는 친구 결혼식에 가야 해.
남 그럼 일요일 여행을 보자.
여 경주가 진해보다 더 좋아 보여. 진해는 여기서 너무 멀어.
남 좋아. 이제 점심을 포함할지 포함하지 않을지에 대한 한 가지 선택 사항이 더 있네.
여 나는 점심을 포함한 게 더 좋겠어. 더 편할 거야.
남 나도 동의해. 그럼 이게 최선이네.

해설 두 사람은 일요일에 경주에 가기로 했고, 점심이 포함된 옵션을 선택할 것이다.

어휘 search 찾다　travel agency 여행사　offer 제공하다
far 먼　option 선택 사항　include 포함하다　convenient
편리한　destination 목적지

16 ⑤

W Congratulations on winning the year's best movie director award!
M Thank you.
W Have you decided on which company you'd like to work with for your next movie?
M Actually, I haven't made the decision yet.
W Well, we'd be pleased to work with you. Could you include us as one of your potential candidates?
M All right. Give me a call next week and we can discuss it further.
W Sure. Let me know a convenient time.

여 올해의 최고 영화 감독상 수상을 축하드립니다!
남 감사합니다.
여 다음 영화는 어느 회사와 작업하실지 결정하셨나요?
남 사실은 아직 결정하지 못했습니다.
여 그럼, 저희가 감독님과 작업해 보고 싶습니다. 고려해 볼 후보자들 중 하나에 저희를 포함시켜 주시겠어요?
남 좋습니다. 다음 주에 전화 주시면 더 많이 논의해 보죠.
여 그럼요. 편하신 시간 알려 주세요.

해설 최고의 영화 감독상을 받은 감독과 영화 제작사 관계자가 나누는 대화이다.

어휘 director 감독　award 상　make a decision 결정하다
potential 잠재적인　candidate 후보자, 지원자　discuss
논의하다　convenient 편리한

17 ③

M Did you watch *Quiz Champion* last night?
W No, I didn't. I don't really watch quiz shows.
M What do you usually watch then?
W I mostly watch science documentaries. What about you?
M I like cooking programs. My favorite is the one with the chef from England.
W I've seen that program, too. I like it because he uses unique ways to cook.
M Actually, it's going to be on tonight. Do you want to watch it together?
W Sounds like a good idea.

남 어젯밤에 〈Quiz Champion〉 봤니?
여 아니, 안 봤어. 난 정말로 퀴즈 쇼는 안 봐.
남 그럼 넌 보통 뭘 보니?
여 나는 대개 과학 다큐멘터리를 봐. 너는 어때?
남 나는 요리 프로그램을 좋아해. 내가 가장 좋아하는 것은 영국 출신의 요리사가 나오는 거야.
여 나도 그 프로그램을 본 적 있어. 그 사람이 요리하는 데 독특한 방식을 사용해서 좋아.
남 사실, 오늘밤에 방송해. 같이 볼래?
여 좋은 생각이야.

해설 두 사람은 영국인 요리사가 나오는 요리 프로그램을 함께 보기로 했다.

어휘 mostly 대개 documentary 다큐멘터리 chef 요리사 unique 독특한 tonight 오늘밤

18 ①

M Hey, what's up?

W I'm on my way to the library to look up some information.

M For your school assignments?

W Yes. I have so many assignments that I can't keep up with all of them.

M I totally understand. It takes me too much time to collect all the information.

W Right. Sometimes I spend hours doing research in the library.

M Well, I recently joined a study group, and it has saved me a lot of time. Why don't you join us?

W Thanks, but I prefer to study alone.

남 안녕, 뭐하니?

여 정보 좀 찾으러 도서관에 가는 중이야.

남 학교 숙제 때문에?

여 응. 숙제가 너무 많아서 전부 다 따라갈 수가 없어.

남 전적으로 이해해. 내가 모든 정보를 수집하기에는 시간이 너무 오래 걸려.

여 맞아. 가끔은 도서관에서 조사하느라 몇 시간씩 보내기도 해.

남 음, 나는 최근에 스터디 그룹에 들어갔는데, 시간이 많이 절약 돼. 너도 같이 할래?

여 고맙지만, 나는 혼자 공부하는 걸 더 좋아해.

해설 남자가 여자에게 자신이 속한 스터디 그룹에 들어오라고 제 안했으므로 이에 대한 수락 또는 거절의 응답이 와야 한다.

② 내가 숙제하는 것 좀 도와줄래?

③ 도서관에 어떻게 가는지 아니?

④ 미안하지만, 나는 많은 정보가 없어.

⑤ 너는 집에서 공부할 때 더 편하니?

어휘 on one's way to ~에 가는 도중에 look up 검색하다, 찾아보다 information 정보 assignment 과제, 숙제 keep up with (뒤쳐지지 않도록) 따라가다 totally 전적으로 collect 수집하다 research 조사, 연구 recently 최근에 save 절약하다 alone 혼자 comfortable 편안한

19 ②

M I'm home. Why are you so busy?

W Don't you remember? Terry and Erica are coming this evening.

M Oh, right! What time are they coming?

W At 7.

M Do you want me to help you cook?

W I'm almost finished cooking.

M Okay. Is there anything I can do for you?

W Well, why don't you pick up the cake that I ordered at Kim's Bakery?

M Sure, I can do that. I'll go right now.

남 나 집에 왔어요. 왜 그렇게 바빠요?

여 기억 안 나요? Terry와 Erica가 오늘 저녁에 오잖아요.

남 아, 맞아요! 그들이 몇 시에 오나요?

여 7시요.

남 요리하는 거 도와줄까요?

여 요리는 거의 끝났어요.

남 좋아요. 내가 당신을 위해 할 일이 있어요?

여 음, 내가 Kim's Bakery에 주문해 둔 케이크 좀 찾아와 줄래 요?

남 그럼요, 할 수 있어요. 지금 당장 갈게요.

해설 여자가 자신이 주문해 둔 케이크를 찾아와 달라고 했으므로 그것을 찾아오겠다고 응답하는 것이 자연스럽다.

① 제 친구 몇 명을 초대하고 싶어요.

③ 딸기 케이크를 주문하는 게 어때요?

④ 그들에게 전화해서 몇 시에 올지 물어볼 수 있어요.

⑤ 집에 돌아오는 길에 케이크 찾아오는 거 잊지 마세요.

어휘 remember 기억하다 almost 거의 pick up ~을 찾아오다 order 주문하다 invite 초대하다

20 ⑤

M Helen has a business trip to China this Saturday. She must arrive at the airport by 7 a.m. She's planning to take the bus at 5 a.m. When she checks the bus schedule though, she finds out that there is no bus before 7 a.m. So Helen wants to ask her friend Matthew if he can drive her to the airport. In this situation, what would Helen most likely say to Matthew?

Helen Matthew, can you give me a ride to the airport this Saturday?

남 Helen은 이번 주 토요일에 중국으로 출장을 간다. 그녀는 오전 7시까지 공항에 도착해야 한다. 그녀는 오전 5시에 버스를 탈 계획이다. 하지만 버스 시간표를 확인했을 때, 그녀는 오전 7시 전에는 버스가 없다는 것을 알게 된다. 그래서 Helen은 친구인 Matthew에게 자신을 공항까지 태워다 줄 수 있는지 물어보고 싶어 한다. 이 상황에서, Helen은 Matthew에게 무엇이라고 말할 것 같은가?

Helen Matthew, 이번 주 토요일에 나를 공항에 태워다 줄 수 있니?

해설 이른 시간에 공항 버스가 없어서 자신을 공항까지 태워다 달라고 부탁해야 하는 상황이다.

① 버스 시간표를 확인했니?

② 버스 정류장이 어디에 있는지 아니?

③ 아침에 나 좀 깨워 줄 수 있니?

④ 중국 여행을 위한 조언을 좀 해 줄 수 있니?

어휘 business trip 출장 airport 공항 bus schedule 버스 시간표 find out 알아내다 give ~ a ride ~을 태워주다

01 ①	**02** ⑤	**03** ①	**04** ③	**05** ③
06 ⑤	**07** ⑤	**08** ④	**09** ②	**10** ④
11 ④	**12** ②	**13** ⑤	**14** ④	**15** ③
16 ④	**17** ⑤	**18** ③	**19** ④	**20** ②

01 ①

M Hi. I'm looking for a USB.

W How about this USB stick? It's reasonably priced.

M It looks okay, but I want something different, like those card-shaped ones.

W Those are very popular. Especially this one with a sea painting. It's the most popular.

M It looks good, but I like that one with the painting of the forest.

W You mean this one?

M No, the one with a bird flying over the forest.

남 안녕하세요. 저는 USB를 찾고 있어요.

여 이 막대 모양 USB는 어떠세요? 가격이 적당해요.

남 좋아 보이지만, 저는 저 카드 모양 USB처럼 뭔가 다른 것을 원해요.

여 저것들은 아주 인기 있어요. 특히 이 바다 그림이 그려진 것이 요. 그게 가장 인기 있어요.

남 좋아 보이지만, 저는 숲이 그려진 저것이 마음에 들어요.

여 이것 말씀이신가요?

남 아뇨, 새 한 마리가 숲 위를 날고 있는 것이요.

해설 남자는 새 한 마리가 숲 위를 날고 있는 카드 모양의 USB를 골랐다.

어휘 look for ~을 찾다   stick 막대   price 가격을 매기다 reasonably 적정하게   card-shaped 카드 모양의   popular 인기 있는   especially 특히   forest 숲

02 ⑤

(Cellphone rings.)

M Hello.

W Hello. This is Daehan Library. Is this Peter Shin?

M Yes, it is.

W Did you lose a yellow wallet in the library?

M What? Hold on, please. (Pause) Oh, I can't find my wallet in my bag.

W Someone just brought it in. He found it in the computer lab on the third floor.

M Right, I was there a while ago. Is there a V-shaped logo on the outside of the wallet?

W Yes, there is. I'm calling after finding the contact number inside the wallet.

M Thank you so much! I'll head over shortly to pick it up.

(휴대 전화가 울린다.)

남 여보세요.

여 여보세요. Daehan Library입니다. Peter Shin 씨 맞나요?

남 네, 접니다.

여 도서관에서 노란색 지갑을 잃어버리셨나요?

남 뭐라고요? 잠깐만요. (잠시 후) 오, 가방 안에 지갑이 안 보이네 요.

여 어떤 분이 방금 그걸 가져다 주셨어요. 그는 지갑을 3층 컴퓨터 실에서 발견하셨대요.

남 맞아요, 아까 거기에 있었어요. 지갑 바깥쪽에 V 모양의 로고가 있나요?

여 네, 있어요. 지갑 안에서 연락처를 찾아 전화를 드리는 거예요.

남 정말 고마워요! 지금 당장 가지러 갈게요.

해설 여자는 지갑의 주인인 남자에게 지갑을 찾아 주기 위해 전화 했다.

어휘 wallet 지갑   computer lab 컴퓨터실   floor 층 outside 외부, 바깥 부분   contact number 연락처 전화번호 head over 가다, 향하다   shortly 바로, 곧   pick up ~을 찾아오다

03 ①

① W Excuse me. I think this is my seat.

   M Oh, really? Let me check my seat number.

② W Are you interested in watching movies?

   M Sure, I enjoy watching movies.

③ W What kind of movies do you like?

   M Action movies are my favorite.

④ W Is this seat taken?

   M Sorry. It's for my wife.

⑤ W How many tickets do you need?

   M Just one, please.

① 여 실례합니다. 이곳은 제 자리인 것 같아요.

   남 오, 정말요? 제 좌석 번호를 확인해 볼게요.

② 여 너는 영화를 보는 것에 관심이 있니?

   남 물론이지, 나는 영화 보는 것을 즐겨.

③ 여 너는 어떤 종류의 영화를 좋아하니?

   남 액션 영화가 내가 가장 좋아하는 영화야.

④ 여 이 자리에 사람 있나요?

   남 죄송합니다. 제 아내 자리입니다.

⑤ 여 표가 몇 장 필요하신가요?

   남 한 장만요.

해설 극장에서 자리를 확인하는 상황이다.

어휘 seat number 좌석 번호   be interested in ~에 관심이 있다   wife 아내   need 필요로 하다

04 ③

M Hi. How was your history test?

W I didn't get a good grade again. I don't know what to do.

M Why don't you take Mr. Choi's after-school class? It's on Mondays, Wednesdays, and Fridays.

W Do you take that class?

M Yes. It is helpful to understand history.

W Really? Can I start anytime?

M Yes. How about starting next Monday?

W I don't think I can attend the class on Monday because of an assignment. I'll join the class from Wednesday.

M Then let's talk to Mr. Choi.

남 안녕. 역사 시험은 어땠어?

여 또 좋은 점수를 받지 못했어. 나는 어떻게 해야 할지 모르겠어.

남 최 선생님의 방과 후 수업을 들어 보는 게 어때? 월요일, 수요일, 금요일에 수업이 있어.

여 너는 그 수업을 듣니?

남 응. 그것은 역사를 이해하는 데 도움이 돼.

여 정말? 아무 때나 시작해도 돼?

남 응. 다음 주 월요일에 시작하는 게 어때?

여 나는 과제 때문에 월요일 수업에는 참석하지 못할 것 같아. 수요일부터 수업에 참여하게.

남 그럼 최 선생님께 말씀드리자.

해설 여자는 과제 때문에 월요일 수업에는 참석하지 못하고 수요일부터 참석하겠다고 했다.

어휘 history 역사 grade 점수 helpful 도움이 되는 understand 이해하다 anytime 언제든지 attend 참석하다 because of ~ 때문에 assignment 과제

05 ③

(Cellphone rings.)

M Hello. Ms. Yoon. This is David.

W Oh, David. Why are you calling me after school?

M I'm really sorry, but could I talk to you about something?

W Sure, what is it about? I hope it's not anything serious.

M Well, I broke my leg playing tennis, so I don't think I can go to school for a few days.

W What? I'm so sorry to hear that. Are you okay?

M The doctor said I must stay in the hospital for a week.

W Okay, I'll visit you after class.

(휴대 전화가 울린다.)

남 안녕하세요. 윤 선생님. 저 David예요.

여 오, David. 방과 후에 무슨 일로 전화했니?

남 정말 죄송하지만, 뭘 좀 말씀드려도 될까요?

여 물론이지, 무엇에 관한 거니? 심각한 게 아니면 좋겠구나.

남 저, 제가 테니스를 치다가 다리가 부러져서 며칠 동안 학교에 못 갈 것 같아요.

여 뭐라고? 정말 안됐구나. 괜찮은 거니?

남 의사 선생님께서 1주일 동안 병원에 입원해 있어야 한다고 말씀하셨어요.

여 알았다. 방과 후에 병문안 갈게.

해설 남자는 다리를 다쳐서 학교에 며칠 동안 못 갈 것 같다고 여자에게 알렸고, 여자는 방과 후에 병문안을 가겠다고 했으므로 여자의 직업은 선생님임을 알 수 있다.

어휘 serious 심각한 break 부러뜨리다 leg 다리 for a few days 며칠 동안

06 ⑤

W James, it's raining now. You must be happy.

M Well, you're wrong.

W What? You don't have to play soccer because of the rain. I know you don't like soccer.

M I didn't because I wasn't good at it. But I have practiced a lot to get better!

W I see. That's why you've been wearing sportswear so often!

M Yeah. I've been looking forward to showing how much I've improved.

W Cheer up! You'll get another chance soon.

여 James, 지금 비가 오고 있어. 너 기분 좋겠다.

남 음, 네가 틀렸어.

여 뭐라고? 너는 비 때문에 축구를 안 해도 되잖아. 난 네가 축구를 안 좋아하는 걸로 아는데.

남 내가 축구를 잘하지 못해서 그랬지. 하지만 난 더 잘 하려고 연습을 많이 했어!

여 알겠다. 그래서 네가 그렇게 자주 운동복을 입고 있었구나!

남 응. 난 내가 얼마나 많이 향상됐는지를 보여 주길 기대해 왔거든.

여 기운 내! 곧 다른 기회가 올 거야.

해설 남자는 자신의 축구 실력이 향상된 모습을 보여 주려고 했는데 비 때문에 축구를 못 하게 되어 실망했을 것이다.

어휘 must be ~임에 틀림없다 don't have to ~할 필요가 없다 be good at ~을 잘하다 practice 연습하다 sportswear 운동복 look forward to ~을 기대하다 improve 향상되다, 나아지다 chance 기회

07 ⑤

① **M** Please give my regards to Mr. Lee.

　W Okay, I will.

② **M** Can you help me find my key?

　W Sorry, I can't. I'm busy now.

③ **M** Watch out! A car is coming!

　W Oh, thank you so much.

④ **M** What do you think of his new song?

　W I don't think it's as good as his first one.

⑤ **M** I was wondering if I could ask you a favor.

　W Please give me a hand.

① 남 이 선생님께 안부 전해 주세요.

　여 네, 그럴게요.

② 남 내 열쇠 찾는 것 좀 도와줄래?

　여 미안하지만, 안 돼. 난 지금 바쁘거든.

③ 남 조심하세요! 차가 오고 있어요!

　여 오, 정말 고마워요.

④ 남 그의 새 노래에 대해 어떻게 생각해?

　여 나는 그의 첫 번째 노래만큼 좋지는 않은 것 같아.

⑤ 남 부탁 하나 드려도 될지 모르겠네요.

　여 저 좀 도와주세요.

해설 ⑤ 도움을 요청하는 상대방의 말에는 응답하지 않고 오히려 자신을 도와 달라고 말하는 것은 어색하다.

어휘 regards 안부 (인사) favor 호의 give ~ a hand ~을 도와주다

08 ④

W What is the social studies homework?

M It's to make a video about stopping bullying. I saw some other videos online, but no good ideas came to mind.

W Why don't we just start shooting?

M Without any plans? I think we should think of characters first.

W You're right. That's the first step. Then let's come up with some characters.

여 사회 숙제가 뭐지?

남 따돌림 금지에 관한 동영상을 만드는 거야. 나는 온라인으로 몇몇 다른 동영상들을 봤는데, 좋은 생각이 안 떠올랐어.

여 그냥 촬영을 시작해 보면 어때?

남 계획도 없이? 먼저 등장인물들에 대해 생각해 봐야 할 것 같아.

여 네 말이 맞아. 그게 첫 번째 단계지. 그럼 등장인물을 먼저 생각해 내자.

해설 두 사람은 동영상을 찍기 전에 먼저 등장인물을 구상하기로 고 했다.

어휘 social studies (과목) 사회 bullying 약자 괴롭히기 come to mind 생각이 떠오르다 shoot 촬영하다 character 등장인물 come up with 생각해 내다

09 ②

W Hello, students. I'm Lisa Han. First of all, thank you for your interest in my new book, *Living in Harmony*. As you know, I was a troublemaker when I was young. Nobody believed me when I said that I would be a writer one day. However, now I have written many popular books. I was able to do it thanks to my motto: "If you sleep now, you will dream. But, if you work toward your dream, you can achieve it."

여 학생 여러분, 안녕하세요. 저는 Lisa Han이에요. 우선, 저의 새 책 〈Living in Harmony〉에 관심 가져 주셔서 감사드립니다. 여러분도 아시다시피, 저는 어릴 때 문제아였습니다. 제가 언젠가 작가가 되겠다고 말했을 때 아무도 믿지 않았어요. 하지만, 저는 지금 많은 인기 있는 책들을 썼습니다. 저는 저의 좌우명 덕분에 그것을 해낼 수 있었어요. "지금 잠을 자면 꿈을 꿀 것이다. 하지만, 꿈을 향하여 노력한다면, 그것을 이룰 수 있다."

해설 작가의 취미는 언급되지 않았다.

어휘 troublemaker 말썽꾸러기 believe 믿다 writer 작가 one day 언젠가 however 그러나 popular 인기 있는 thanks to ~ 덕분에 motto 좌우명 sleep 잠을 자다 dream 꿈을 꾸다; 꿈 achieve 이루다, 성취하다

10 ④

W Welcome to the National Art Museum.

M Hi. I'd like to buy two adult tickets.

W They are $10 each. If you're also interested in visiting the National Science Museum, you can buy a combination ticket at a reduced price.

M How much is it?

W If you visit them separately, you need to pay $17. But the combination ticket only costs $12.

M Okay. Then I'll buy two combination tickets.

W Will you pay in cash or by credit card?

M Cash. Here you are.

여 National Art Museum에 오신 것을 환영합니다.

남 안녕하세요. 성인 표 두 장을 사고 싶어요.

여 각각 10달러입니다. 만약 National Science Museum 방문에도 관심이 있으시면, 통합권을 할인된 가격으로 구입하실 수 있습니다.

남 그건 얼마죠?

여 그곳들을 따로따로 가시면 17달러를 내셔야 합니다. 하지만 통합권은 12달러밖에 안 해요.

남 좋아요. 그러면 통합권 두 장 살게요.

여 현금으로 지불하시나요, 신용카드로 지불하시나요?

남 현금이요. 여기 있어요.

해설 남자는 12달러짜리 통합권을 두 장 사겠다고 했다.

어휘 adult 성인 combination 결합 reduced 할인된 price 가격 separately 따로따로, 별도로 cost 가격이 ~이다 cash 현금

11 ④

W Hi. My name is Lily Park.

M Okay, take a seat. Hmm... you don't have any experience in broadcasting, right?

W No. But I really want to learn about broadcasting this year.

M Can you tell me why?

W As I wrote in the application, I want to make a special program right here in the school studio.

M What kind of program?

W A program which introduces students' real lives.

M Oh, that sounds interesting.

여 안녕하세요. 제 이름은 Lily Park입니다.

남 좋아요, 앉으세요. 음… 방송 경험이 전혀 없네요, 그렇죠?

여 네. 하지만 저는 올해 방송에 대해서 정말 배우고 싶어요.

남 이유를 말해 줄래요?

여 지원서에 썼듯이, 저는 바로 이곳 학교 방송실에서 특별한 프로그램을 만들고 싶어요.

남 어떤 종류의 프로그램이죠?

여 학생들의 실제 생활을 소개하는 프로그램이요.

남 오, 흥미롭군요.

해설 학교 방송실에서 방송부원을 뽑기 위해 면접을 실시하고 있는 상황이다.

어휘 experience 경험 broadcasting 방송 application

지원서 special 특별한 studio 방송실 introduce 소개하다
real 실제의 life 생활

apartment 아파트 city center 도심 afford ～할 여유가
있다 near ～ 가까이에, 근처에 area 지역, 구역 take a
walk 산책하다

12 ②

M Amanda, did you <u>finish your homework</u>?
W Not yet. I couldn't finish it since I was very busy yesterday.
M You always seem busy. Do you have that much to do?
W Not really, but I <u>never have enough time</u>. What do you think is my problem?
M Time management. <u>How about creating a schedule</u> to manage your time more effectively?
W That's a good idea.

남 Amanda, 숙제 다 했니?
여 아니, 아직. 어제 너무 바빠서 끝내지 못했어.
남 너는 항상 바빠 보여. 할 일이 그렇게 많니?
여 그건 아닌데, 난 결코 시간이 충분하지 않아. 내 문제가 뭐라고 생각하니?
남 시간 관리. 네 시간을 더 효과적으로 관리하기 위해 일정표를 만들어 보는 건 어때?
여 좋은 생각이야.

해설 여자는 시간을 효과적으로 관리하기 위해 일정표를 만들어 보라는 남자의 제안에 동의했다.

어휘 enough 충분한 management 관리, 경영 create 만들다, 창조하다 manage 관리하다 effectively 효과적으로

13 ⑤

M Have you decided where you are going to move to?
W No. I've been <u>looking at this map</u> for a week.
M How about living in an apartment in the city center?
W <u>I can't afford it</u>.
M I see. What about a house near a big supermarket? You can shop easily.
W Yeah, but <u>those areas are too busy</u>.
M Then what about this house? You can <u>take a walk every day</u> because it's next to a park.
W Is there a park? I didn't see that. I think that's the one!

남 너 어디로 이사할지 결정했니?
여 아니. 난 일주일 동안 이 지도를 보고 있는 중이야.
남 도심에 있는 아파트에서 사는 건 어때?
여 난 그럴 여유가 없어.
남 알겠어. 큰 슈퍼 근처의 집은 어때? 쉽게 쇼핑할 수 있잖아.
여 응, 그렇지만 그런 지역들은 너무 번잡해.
남 그러면 이 집은 어때? 그건 공원 옆에 있어서 매일 산책을 할 수 있어.
여 공원이 있어? 그걸 못 봤네. 그곳이 적합한 것 같아!

해설 여자는 공원 옆에 있어서 매일 산책할 수 있는 집으로 이사하기로 했다.

어휘 decide 결정하다 move 이사하다 map 지도

14 ④

M This is a useful machine in the kitchen. <u>Imagine that</u> there are many cups and plates to be washed. In this situation, you can <u>save your energy and time</u> by using this machine. Put all the things that need to be washed into this and then <u>turn on the switch</u>. In a short time, it'll automatically wash and even dry all the dishes.

남 이것은 부엌에 있는 유용한 기계입니다. 씻어야 할 많은 컵들과 접시들이 있다고 상상해 보세요. 이러한 상황에서, 이 기계를 사용함으로써 당신은 당신의 에너지와 시간을 절약할 수 있습니다. 씻어야 하는 모든 것들을 이 안에 넣고 스위치를 켜세요. 얼마 후에, 그것은 자동적으로 모든 그릇들을 씻어 주고 심지어 건조시킬 것입니다.

해설 그릇들을 자동으로 씻어 주고 건조시키는 기계는 식기세척기이다.

어휘 useful 유용한 machine 기계 imagine 상상하다
plate 접시 wash 씻다 turn on 켜다 switch 스위치
automatically 자동적으로 even 심지어 dry 말리다,
건조시키다 dish 그릇

15 ③

W Hello. Mr. Kang.
M Miso, what's up?
W You know <u>I've been practicing my dancing</u> for the school talent show.
M Of course. I'm looking forward to seeing it.
W Is it okay to use our classroom for an hour after school? <u>I need a place to practice</u>.
M Sure, but don't forget to close the door and <u>turn off the lights when you leave</u>.
W Okay, Mr. Kang. Thank you so much.

여 안녕하세요. 강 선생님.
남 미소야, 무슨 일이니?
여 아시는 것처럼 저는 학교 장기 자랑을 위해 춤을 연습하고 있어요.
남 물론이지. 나는 그걸 보는 게 정말 기대가 된단다.
여 방과 후에 한 시간 동안 우리 교실을 사용해도 될까요? 연습할 장소가 필요해요.
남 물론이지, 하지만 나갈 때 문을 닫고 불을 끄는 것을 잊지 마라.
여 네, 강 선생님. 정말 감사합니다.

해설 여자는 남자에게 춤 연습을 위해 방과 후에 교실을 사용하게 해 달라고 부탁했다.

어휘 practice 연습하다 talent show 장기 자랑 place 장소
close 닫다 turn off ～을 끄다 light 전등

16 ④

M Good morning. I want to send this box to Busan.
W Okay. <u>Let me weigh it</u>. (*Pause*) How do you want to send it, by express or regular delivery?
M <u>How long will it take</u> if I send it by express delivery?
W If you <u>send it by express delivery</u>, it will get there tomorrow.
M How much will that cost?
W It's 10,000 won.
M That's too expensive. How about regular delivery?
W It's 4,000 won, and it will arrive in about 3 days.
M I'll send it <u>by regular delivery service</u>.

남 안녕하세요. 이 상자를 부산에 보내고 싶어요.
여 네. 무게를 재 보겠습니다. (잠시/ 후) 빠른 배송과 일반 배송 중에서 어떻게 보내실 건가요?
남 빠른 배송으로 보내면 얼마나 걸릴까요?
여 빠른 배송으로 보내시면 내일 도착합니다.
남 얼마인가요?
여 10,000원입니다.
남 너무 비싸네요. 일반 배송은 어떤가요?
여 그것은 4,000원이고, 약 3일 후에 도착합니다.
남 일반 배송 서비스로 보내겠습니다.

[해설] 택배 물품의 종류는 언급되지 않았다.

[어휘] send 보내다   express 신속한, 급행의   regular 보통의   delivery 배송   arrive 도착하다

17 ⑤

W Ben's friend Mina is going to have an audition to be a singer. She <u>has been waiting for this chance</u> for a long time. She is really <u>good at singing</u>, and everyone thinks she can be a great singer. However, right before the audition begins, she gets so nervous and seems to lose confidence. <u>She is even about to quit</u>. In this situation, what would Ben say to her to encourage her?
Ben Mina, <u>don't give up! I'm sure you'll do a good job.</u>

여 Ben의 친구 미나는 가수가 되기 위해 오디션을 보려고 한다. 그녀는 이번 기회를 오랫동안 기다려 왔다. 그녀는 노래를 정말 잘하고 모두가 그녀는 훌륭한 가수가 될 수 있다고 생각한다. 하지만, 오디션이 시작되기 바로 전에, 그녀는 너무 긴장되어 자신감을 잃은 것 같다. 그녀는 심지어 그만두려고 한다. 이런 상황에서, Ben은 그녀의 용기를 북돋아 주기 위하여 뭐라고 말할까?
Ben 미나야, 포기하지 마! 넌 틀림없이 잘할 거야.

[해설] 미나가 오디션 직전에 자신감을 잃어 그만두려고 하는 상황이므로 용기를 북돋아 주는 말을 하는 것이 적절하다.
① 미안해. 내가 또 실수했어.
② 넌 이미 그 프로그램에 늦었어.
③ 나는 노래하는 것에 전혀 관심 없어.
④ 넌 오늘부터 운동을 시작해야 해.

[어휘] audition 오디션   wait for ~을 기다리다   chance 기회   be good at ~을 잘하다   nervous 긴장한   confidence 자신감   quit 그만두다   encourage 용기를 북돋우다   make a mistake 실수하다   give up 포기하다   do a good job 잘하다

18 ③

W Eddie, do you have any plans for tomorrow?
M You mean after school? No, <u>I'm going straight home</u>. Why do you ask?
W The English drama club <u>is giving a performance</u> at the auditorium.
M Oh, yes. You're a member of that club so you practiced the performance all summer vacation, didn't you?
W Yes, I did. <u>Thanks to you</u> we improved our English pronunciation. So would you like to watch the performance?
M Sure, that would be nice.
W Great! <u>I'll look for you</u> in the auditorium. Our performance begins at 5 p.m.
M Okay. I think it will be very interesting.

여 Eddie, 내일 어떤 계획이 있니?
남 방과 후에 말이니? 아니, 나는 집에 곧장 갈 거야. 왜 물어보니?
여 영어 연극 동아리가 강당에서 공연을 하거든.
남 아, 맞다. 너 그 동아리 회원이어서 여름 방학 내내 공연 연습했잖아, 그렇지 않니?
여 그래, 맞아. 네 덕분에 우리 영어 발음도 향상됐지. 그래서 말인데 너 공연 보러 올래?
남 당연하지, 멋질 거야.
여 잘됐다! 내가 강당에서 너를 찾을게. 우리 공연은 오후 5시에 시작해.
남 알았어. 아주 재미있을 것 같아.

[해설] 남자는 내일 방과 후에 여자의 영어 연극 동아리 공연을 관람할 것이다.

[어휘] plan 계획   mean 의미하다   performance 공연   auditorium 강당   practice 연습하다   improve 향상시키다   pronunciation 발음

19 ④

M Hi. Are you <u>ready to order</u>?
W Hmm... do you have any ham sandwiches?
M Of course. We just made one.
W Then <u>I'll have one</u>.
M Do you want anything to drink?
W <u>A regular size iced coffee</u>, please.
M Do you have a membership card? If you have one, you can have a large <u>for the same price</u>.
W Oh, that's good for me. Here it is.

남 안녕하세요, 주문하시겠어요?
여 음… 햄샌드위치 있나요?

남 물론이죠. 방금 하나 만들었어요.
여 그러면 그걸로 할게요.
남 마실 것도 원하시나요?
여 보통 사이즈의 아이스커피 하나 주세요.
남 회원 카드가 있으신가요? 가지고 계시다면, 같은 가격으로 큰 사이즈를 드실 수 있어요.
여 오, 잘됐네요. 여기 있어요.

해설 남자가 회원 카드가 있으면 같은 가격으로 큰 사이즈의 음료를 마실 수 있다고 했으므로, 회원 카드의 소지 여부와 관련된 응답이 와야 한다.
① 저는 커피보다 차를 더 좋아해요.
② 행운을 빌게요.
③ 물론이에요. 제가 그것을 도와드릴 수 있어요.
⑤ 걱정하지 마세요. 모든 게 잘될 거예요.

어휘 order 주문하다　regular 보통의　membership 회원 자격(신분)　price 가격　keep one's fingers crossed 행운을 빌다

20 ②

(Telephone rings.)
W Happy Home Shopping Service. How may I help you?
M Hello. I'd like to buy the bag that's being advertised now.
W Good choice! Which color do you want to order?
M I'd like the red one.
W I'm sorry, but that color is already sold out.
M Already? Then is the blue one available?
W Yes, you can order a blue one. How would you like to pay for your bag?
M Can I use my credit card?

(전화벨이 울린다.)
여 Happy Home Shopping Service입니다. 무엇을 도와드릴까요?
남 안녕하세요. 저는 지금 광고되고 있는 가방을 사고 싶어요.
여 훌륭한 선택이십니다! 어떤 색을 주문하고 싶으세요?
남 빨간색이 좋아요.
여 죄송하지만, 그 색은 이미 매진되었어요.
남 벌써요? 그러면 파란색은 가능한가요?
여 네, 파란색은 주문 가능합니다. 가방 값을 어떻게 지불하실 건가요?
남 신용 카드를 사용해도 되나요?

해설 여자가 지불 방법을 물었으므로 신용 카드를 사용해도 되는지 묻는 말이 적절하다.
① 환불받고 싶어요.
③ 가장 좋아하는 색이 무엇인가요?
④ 그것을 어떻게 말해야 할지 모르겠어요.
⑤ 제가 말하려 했던 것은 그게 아니에요.

어휘 advertise 광고하다　choice 선택　sold out 다 팔린, 매진된　available 이용할 수 있는　pay for ~을 지불하다 get a refund 환불받다

Review Test　pp.96~97

07회

Word Check

01 기술자　02 상
03 최근에　04 노선
05 지우다, 삭제하다　06 찾다
07 사소한　08 원래
09 묘사하다　10 드디어
11 한번 해 보다　12 한 번에
13 practical　14 potential
15 passenger　16 director
17 discuss　18 secondhand
19 suggest　20 collect
21 infect　22 lost and found
23 hand in　24 pick up

Expression Check

25 allowed to　26 keeps turning off
27 keep, down　28 at least
29 have trouble　30 keep up with

08회

Word Check

01 발음　02 용기를 북돋우다
03 관리하다　04 신속한, 급행의
05 선택　06 결합
07 보통의　08 숲
09 컴퓨터실　10 등장인물
11 환불받다　12 포기하다
13 nervous　14 confidence
15 assignment　16 advertise
17 experience　18 attend
19 price　20 understand
21 serious　22 improve
23 come up with　24 make a mistake

Expression Check

25 head over　26 get a good grade
27 in broadcasting　28 sold out
29 turn off　30 in cash

01 ③	**02** ⑤	**03** ④	**04** ③	**05** ②
06 ④	**07** ②	**08** ③	**09** ⑤	**10** ②
11 ⑤	**12** ④	**13** ④	**14** ⑤	**15** ⑤
16 ⑤	**17** ⑤	**18** ④	**19** ④	**20** ③

01 ③

M Sumi, could you check the Sports Club Day poster for me?

W Sure, let me see. The title at the top of the poster looks good.

M What about the date on the right side under the title?

W It looks very clear. I also like the simple drawings on the left side.

M The art club members helped draw the basketball and the soccer shoes.

W Nice. I think the other students will like the posters, too.

M I'm glad to hear that.

남 수미야, 스포츠 동아리의 날 포스터 좀 확인해 줄래?
여 물론이지, 어디 보자. 포스터 맨 위에 있는 제목이 보기 좋네.
남 제목 아래 오른쪽에 있는 날짜는 어떠니?
여 아주 또렷하게 보여. 나는 왼쪽에 있는 간단한 그림들도 마음에 들어.
남 미술부 회원들이 농구공과 축구화 그리는 걸 도와줬어.
여 좋은데. 다른 학생들도 포스터를 좋아할 것 같아.
남 그 말을 들으니 기뻐.

해설 남자는 제목이 맨 위에 있고, 제목 아래의 오른쪽에 날짜가 있으며, 왼쪽에는 농구공과 축구화 그림이 있는 포스터를 만들었다.

어휘 title 제목   at the top of ~의 맨 위에   on the right (left) side 오른쪽(왼쪽)에   simple 단순한   drawing 그림

02 ⑤

(*Doorbell rings.*)

M Who is it?

W Hello. It's Amy from upstairs.

M Oh, hello. How is it going?

W Fine. I'm having a new printer delivered this afternoon.

M Oh, you finally bought one! Do you need any help carrying it?

W No. That's okay, but do you have some printer paper? I'd like to test the new printer.

M Sure. (*Pause*) Here is some A4 size paper.

W Thank you.

(초인종이 울린다.)
남 누구세요?

여 안녕. 위층에 사는 Amy야.
남 오, 안녕. 어떻게 지내니?
여 잘 지내. 오늘 오후에 새 프린터가 배달될 예정이야.
남 오, 드디어 샀구나! 옮기는 것 좀 도와줄까?
여 아니, 괜찮아. 그런데 프린터 용지를 좀 가지고 있니? 새 프린터를 시험해 보고 싶거든.
남 물론이지. (잠시 후) A4 용지 여기 있어.
여 고마워.

해설 여자는 새 프린터를 테스트하기 위해 남자에게 프린터 용지를 얻으려고 한다.

어휘 upstairs 위층   deliver 배달하다   finally 드디어   carry 나르다   printer 프린터

03 ④

① **W** Would you give me the menu, please?
  M Wait, please. I will bring you the menu.
② **W** Can you help me find the cookbooks?
  M This way, please. They're behind those shelves.
③ **W** How do you know each other?
  M We're in the same cooking class.
④ **W** I'd like a cup of hot chocolate.
  M For here or to go?
⑤ **W** What is your favorite dessert?
  M I like sweet chocolate cake the most.

① 여 메뉴 좀 주시겠어요?
  남 잠시만 기다려 주세요. 메뉴를 가져다 드릴게요.
② 여 요리책 찾는 것 좀 도와주시겠어요?
  남 이쪽입니다. 저 책꽂이 뒤에 있어요.
③ 여 너희들은 서로 어떻게 아는 사이니?
  남 우리는 같은 요리 수업을 들어.
④ 여 핫초코 한 잔 주세요.
  남 여기서 드실 건가요, 가져가실 건가요?
⑤ 여 가장 좋아하는 디저트가 뭐예요?
  남 저는 달콤한 초콜릿 케이크를 가장 좋아해요.

해설 패스트푸드점에서 손님이 음료를 주문하는 상황이다.

어휘 behind ~ 뒤에   shelf 선반, 책꽂이   each other 서로   favorite 가장 좋아하는   dessert 후식

04 ③

M I'm home. Mom, I'm so hungry.

W Already? Didn't you have lunch again?

M Right. Today's school lunch was curry and rice.

W Oh, no. You don't like it very much. Why didn't you buy a sandwich?

M I didn't have enough money.

W Let me make you some seafood spaghetti.

M Wow, that sounds delicious. How long will it take?

W About 20 minutes. Do you want a banana while you're waiting?

M No, thank you.

남 저 왔어요. 엄마, 저 너무 배고파요.

여 벌써? 너 또 점심 안 먹었니?

남 네. 오늘 학교 점심이 카레라이스였어요.

여 오, 저런. 너 그거 별로 안 좋아하잖아. 샌드위치를 사 먹지 그랬니?

남 돈이 충분하지 않았어요.

여 내가 해산물 스파게티를 만들어 줄게.

남 와, 맛있을 것 같아요. 얼마나 걸려요?

여 20분 정도 걸려. 기다리는 동안 바나나를 먹을래?

남 아뇨, 괜찮아요.

해설 남자는 엄마가 만들어 주는 해산물 스파게티를 먹기로 했다.

어휘 already 이미, 벌써   enough 충분한   seafood 해산물   delicious 맛있는

05 ②

M Mina, what did you do last weekend?

W I took a trip to Jeonju with my family. It only took an hour to get there by train.

M How was the trip?

W Wonderful. The weather was warm and the sky was clear.

M Good. Did you visit the Hanok Village there?

W Sure. We stayed at the village overnight and we met some foreign tourists there.

M That sounds fun. I hope that I can go there soon.

남 미나야, 지난 주말에 뭐했니?

여 가족들과 전주로 여행 다녀왔어. 기차로 겨우 한 시간밖에 안 걸렸어.

남 여행은 어땠니?

여 굉장했지. 날씨도 따뜻하고 하늘도 맑았어.

남 좋았겠다. 거기에서 Hanok Village도 방문했니?

여 물론이지. 우리는 그 마을에서 하룻밤 잤는데. 거기에서 외국인 여행객 몇 명을 만났어.

남 재밌었겠다. 나도 곧 그곳에 갈 수 있으면 좋겠어.

해설 가족 여행 중에 먹었던 음식은 언급되지 않았다.

어휘 take a trip 여행을 가다   village 마을   stay 머무르다   overnight 하룻밤 동안   foreign 외국의   tourist 관광객

06 ④

W Mr. Anderson, I was wondering if I could get a day off next week.

M For what?

W I want to attend my son's school sports day.

M Of course, I understand. When is it?

W It's next Wednesday.

M No problem. You can have the day off then.

W Thank you so much.

M But please don't forget to finish your work for next week's meeting.

W Okay, you don't have to worry about it.

여 Anderson 부장님, 제가 다음 주에 하루 휴가를 쓸 수 있을지 궁금합니다.

남 무엇 때문이죠?

여 제 아들의 학교 운동회에 참석하고 싶어서요.

남 물론이죠, 알겠어요. 그게 언제죠?

여 다음 주 수요일이에요.

남 문제없어요. 그때는 쉬도록 하세요.

여 정말 감사합니다.

남 하지만 다음 주 회의를 위한 업무를 끝내는 걸 잊지 마세요.

여 네, 그것에 대해서는 걱정하지 않으셔도 돼요.

해설 휴가 신청과 마쳐야 하는 업무에 대해 이야기하고 있으므로 직장 상사와 부하 직원 사이의 대화임을 알 수 있다.

어휘 I was wondering if ~일지 궁금하다   day off 쉬는 날   attend 참석하다   sports day 운동회   finish 끝마치다   worry about ~에 대해 걱정하다

07 ②

① M How would you like your hair cut?
   W I'd like my hair cut short.
② M What is your favorite kind of music?
   W I really like music class.
③ M Why don't we go swimming this Saturday?
   W Sorry. I already have other plans.
④ M It doesn't look very nice outside today.
   W You're right. I think it's going to rain.
⑤ M I think you look really nice today.
   W Thank you. I just bought this jacket a couple of days ago.

① 남 머리카락을 어떻게 잘라 드릴까요?
   여 짧게 잘라 주세요.
② 남 너는 어떤 종류의 음악을 가장 좋아하니?
   여 나는 음악 수업을 정말 좋아해.
③ 남 이번 주 토요일에 수영하러 가는 게 어때?
   여 미안해, 이미 다른 계획이 있어.
④ 남 오늘 바깥 날씨가 별로 좋아 보이지 않아.
   여 네 말이 맞아. 비가 올 것 같아.
⑤ 남 너 오늘 정말 멋져 보이는 것 같아.
   여 고마워. 이 재킷 며칠 전에 샀어.

해설 ② 가장 좋아하는 음악의 종류를 묻는 말에 음악 수업을 좋아한다고 답하는 것은 어색하다.

어휘 already 이미, 벌써   plan 계획   a couple of 몇 개의, 두서너 개의

08 ③

W How's your studying going for your final exams?

M Well, I really love to study math, but studying English drives me crazy.

W What is the most difficult when you study English? Is it grammar?

M I don't have any problem with grammar. But I don't know how to memorize new words.

W Listen to the words while memorizing them. It'd be more effective.

M Okay. I'll try that.

여 기말고사 공부는 잘 되어 가니?

남 저, 수학 공부하는 건 정말 좋은데요, 영어 공부하는 게 너무 힘들어요.

여 영어 공부할 때 뭐가 가장 힘드니? 문법이니?

남 문법은 별 문제가 없어요. 그런데 새로운 단어를 어떻게 외워야 할지 모르겠어요.

여 외우면서 단어를 들어보렴. 그게 더 효과적일 거야.

남 좋아요. 그렇게 해 볼게요.

해설 남자는 영어 공부가 힘들다고 말하면서 새로운 영어 단어를 어떻게 외워야 할지 모르겠다고 했다.

어휘 final exam 기말고사　drive ~ crazy ~를 미치게 하다　grammar 문법　problem 문제　memorize 암기하다　effective 효과적인

09 ⑤

M Hello, students. This is your student president, Lee Seojin. Our first Club Day is coming this Friday. But there are some <u>changes in the plans</u>. The school band and orchestra will start practicing for the festival on schedule. But <u>their practice rooms were changed</u>, so please ask your homeroom teachers about this. And all club activities will start at 3 p.m. <u>instead of at 2</u> on Friday. Thank you.

남 안녕하세요, 학생 여러분. 저는 학생회장 이서진입니다. 우리의 첫 번째 동아리날이 이번 주 금요일입니다. 하지만 계획에 일부 변경 사항이 있습니다. 학교 밴드와 오케스트라는 예정대로 축제 연습을 시작합니다. 하지만 연습실이 변경되었으니 이것에 대해 담임 선생님들께 여쭤보시기 바랍니다. 또한, 모든 동아리 활동이 금요일 2시가 아니라 3시에 시작됩니다. 감사합니다.

해설 동아리날에 관해 일부 변경 사항이 있음을 알리는 안내 방송이다.

어휘 student president 학생회장　change 바꾸다, 변경하다　orchestra 오케스트라, 관현악단　practice 연습하다　on schedule 예정대로　activity 활동　instead of ~ 대신에

10 ②

W Siwon, <u>are you buying something</u> online?

M Yes. I'm ordering new uniforms for my soccer team.

W Wow, they look great. How much are they?

M They're $10 each, and I need to get ten.

W <u>Why only ten</u>? There are eleven people on your team.

M That's because the goalkeeper wears a different jersey.

W Oh, right. How much is <u>the shipping charge</u>?

M It's free. And I will get a 10% discount for <u>buying more than five</u>.

여 시원아, 너 온라인으로 뭐 사고 있니?

남 응. 우리 축구팀을 위해 새 유니폼을 주문하는 중이야.

여 와, 멋져 보여. 그것들은 얼마니?

남 한 벌에 10달러인데, 10벌을 사야 해.

여 왜 10벌만 사니? 너희 팀은 11명이잖아.

남 골키퍼는 다른 옷을 입기 때문이지.

여 아, 그렇구나. 배송비는 얼마니?

남 무료야. 그리고 5벌보다 더 많이 사면 10퍼센트 할인도 받을 수 있어.

해설 남자는 10달러짜리 축구 유니폼을 10벌 주문하고 있다. 배송비는 무료이며 10퍼센트 할인을 받을 수 있으므로 남자가 지불할 금액은 90달러이다.

어휘 online 온라인으로　uniform 유니폼, 제복　each 각각　jersey (운동 경기용) 셔츠　shipping charge 배송비　free 무료의　discount 할인

11 ⑤

M Anna, <u>how was your day</u>?

W Oh, it was the worst. I don't even want to talk about it.

M Come on. <u>Tell me what happened</u>.

W On my way to school, I slipped on some ice. <u>To make matters worse</u>, my ex-boyfriend saw the whole thing and laughed at me.

M Oh, no. Were you hurt?

W No, but just thinking about it makes me want to cry.

남 Anna, 오늘 어땠니?

여 아, 최악이었어. 말도 하고 싶지 않아.

남 저런. 무슨 일이 있었는지 말해 봐.

여 학교 가는 길에, 빙판 길에서 미끄러졌어. 설상가상으로, 내 전 남자친구가 모든 것을 목격했고 날 비웃었어.

남 오, 저런. 너 다쳤니?

여 아니, 하지만 그것에 대해 생각만 해도 울고 싶어.

해설 여자는 빙판 길에서 넘어진 모습을 옛 남자 친구가 봤다고 말하며 그것을 생각하는 것만으로도 울고 싶다고 했으므로 창피한 심정일 것이다.

어휘 happen 일어나다　on one's way to ~에 가는 길에　slip 미끄러지다　to make matters worse 설상가상으로　ex-boyfriend 전 남자친구　whole 전체의　laugh at ~을 비웃다

12 ④

W Good afternoon, everyone. <u>Let me tell you about</u> the 10th Tomato Festival. It will <u>take place in</u> the outdoor plaza in front of City Hall on May 30, from 10 a.m. to 4 p.m. You can <u>buy high quality fresh tomatoes</u> at the farmers' market. Since we don't provide any plastic bags, <u>don't forget to bring</u> your own shopping bags. The admission price will be $5. To get more information, visit our website. Thank you.

여 안녕하세요, 여러분. 제10회 토마토 축제에 대해 말씀 드리겠습니다. 축제는 5월 30일 오전 10시부터 오후 4시까지 시청 앞 야외 광장에서 개최됩니다. 여러분은 고품질의 신선한 토마토를 농산물 직판장에서 구입하실 수 있습니다. 비닐봉투를 전

혀 제공하지 않으므로, 여러분의 장바구니 가져오시는 걸 잊지 마세요. 입장료는 5달러입니다. 더 많은 정보를 얻고 싶으시면, 저희 웹 사이트를 방문해 주세요. 감사합니다.

해설 축제에 참가할 수 있는 자격은 언급되지 않았다.

어휘 take place 개최되다   outdoor 야외의   quality 품질   plastic bag 비닐봉투   admission 입장   information 정보

13   ④

W Daniel, have you signed up for your after-school classes?
M Not yet. Shall we take a class together?
W Okay. I'm thinking of the robot class.
M It looks interesting, but the tuition fee is too expensive.
W Then how about the life science class?
M I'd like to take it, but I can't make it because of my volunteer work on Tuesdays.
W I see. Are you interested in sports?
M Well, not really. I prefer watching to playing.
W Then we only have one choice. Let's sign up for it.

여 Daniel, 방과 후 수업 신청했니?
남 아직. 우리 수업 같이 들을까?
여 좋아. 난 로봇 수업을 들을 생각이야.
남 재미있어 보이지만 수업료가 너무 비싸.
여 그럼 생명과학은 어때?
남 그러고 싶지만, 난 화요일에 자원봉사 활동 때문에 안 돼.
여 알겠어. 너 스포츠에 관심 있니?
남 글쎄. 아닌 것 같아. 나는 하는 것보다는 보는 걸 더 좋아해.
여 그러면 한 가지 선택만 남아 있네. 그 수업에 등록하자.

해설 두 사람은 수업료가 비싼 로봇 수업을 제외했고, 화요일 수업이 아니면서 스포츠가 아닌 수업을 등록하기로 했다.

어휘 sign up for ~을 신청하다   tuition fee 수업료   life science 생명과학   volunteer work 자원봉사 활동   prefer A to B B보다 A를 더 좋아하다

14   ⑤

M This is the ability to do two different things at the same time. For example, sending text messages while walking, or listening to music or watching TV while studying. You may think it's more efficient when you do more than one thing at the same time. However, the truth is that it might not be as effective. So instead of trying to do two things at once, focus on one thing at a time.

남 이것은 동시에 두 가지 다른 일을 하는 능력입니다. 예를 들면, 걸어가면서 문자 메시지를 보낸다거나, 공부하면서 음악을 듣거나 TV를 보는 것입니다. 여러분은 동시에 한 가지보다 더 많은 일을 하면 그것이 더 효율적이라고 생각할지도 모릅니다. 하지만, 사실은 효과적이지 않을 수도 있습니다. 그러므로 한 번에 두 가지 일을 하려고 하는 것 대신에, 한 번에 하나에만 집중하세요.

해설 동시에 두 가지 일을 하는 것, 즉 멀티태스킹에 관한 설명이다.

어휘 ability 능력   at the same time 동시에   send a text message 문자 메시지를 보내다   efficient 효과적인   truth 사실, 진실   instead of ~ 대신에   at once 동시에, 한꺼번에   focus on ~에 집중하다

15   ⑤

W I have something to tell you, Junho.
M What's up? Is it about your new part-time job?
W No. Actually, it is about my friend Jina. I noticed her cheating on an English exam yesterday.
M Really? So what did you do about it?
W I didn't do anything, but I'm not comfortable with it.
M Why don't you talk to the teacher about it? I think it could help Jina.
W I think you're right. I'll do it right now.

여 너에게 할 말이 있어, 준호야.
남 무슨 일이야? 너의 새로운 아르바이트에 관한 거니?
여 아니. 사실은, 내 친구 지나에 관한 거야. 내가 어제 영어 시험 볼 때 그녀가 부정행위를 하는 것을 목격했어.
남 정말? 그래서 넌 어떻게 했니?
여 아무 것도 안했지만 그것 때문에 마음이 편하지 않아.
남 그것에 대해 선생님께 말씀드리는 게 어때? 그게 지나에게 도움이 될 수 있을 것 같아.
여 네 말이 맞는 것 같아. 지금 당장 그렇게 할게.

해설 여자는 시험에서 부정행위를 한 친구에 대해 선생님께 말씀드리겠다고 했다.

어휘 part-time job 시간제 근무, 아르바이트   actually 사실   notice ~을 알아차리다   cheat 부정행위를 하다   comfortable 편안한   right now 지금 당장

16   ⑤

W Daniel, do you have any plans this Saturday?
M Nothing special. Why?
W There's a magic show by a famous magician at the cultural center. Why don't we go there?
M A magic show? That sounds very interesting. I'd like to watch it.
W Great. It starts at 7 o'clock. How about meeting at 6:30 at the cultural center?
M Well, it's located near your house. Let's meet in front of your house and walk there together.
W Okay. See you then.

여 Daniel, 이번 토요일에 무슨 계획 있니?
남 특별한 것 없는데. 왜?
여 문화 회관에서 유명한 마술사의 마술 쇼가 있어. 거기에 가 보는 게 어때?
남 마술 쇼? 아주 재미있겠는 걸. 그거 보고 싶다.
여 좋아. 그건 7시에 시작해. 문화 회관에서 6시 30분에 만나는 게 어때?

남 음, 그건 너희 집 근처에 있잖아. 너희 집 앞에서 만나서 같이 걸어가자.

여 좋아. 그때 보자.

해설 두 사람은 여자의 집 앞에서 만나서 문화 회관까지 같이 걸어가기로 했다.

어휘 magic 마술   famous 유명한   magician 마술사
cultural center 문화 회관   be located 위치하다

---

17 ⑤

M Yena, what are you looking at?

W It's a poster for the school speech contest.

M Are you going to participate in the contest?

W Yes. I've been looking forward to it. How about you?

M No, I won't. I don't think I have any chance to win.

W But whether you win or not doesn't matter. You can learn a lot while preparing for it.

M I don't understand. What do you mean?

W I mean the process is more important than the result.

남 예나야, 뭘 보고 있니?

여 학교 말하기 대회 포스터야.

남 너 대회에 참가할 거니?

여 응. 난 그것을 기대하고 있었어. 넌 어때?

남 아니, 난 안 할 거야. 나는 우승할 가능성이 전혀 없는 것 같아.

여 하지만 네가 우승을 하든 못하든 중요하지 않아. 넌 그것을 준비하면서 많이 배울 수 있어.

남 이해가 안 돼. 그게 무슨 뜻이야?

여 과정이 결과보다 더 중요하다는 의미야.

해설 여자가 대회를 준비하면서 많은 것을 배울 수 있다고 하자 남자가 그 말의 의미를 물었으므로, 과정이 결과보다 중요하다는 응답이 적절하다.
① 내가 우승하는 방법을 너에게 보여 줄게.
② 연습하면 완벽해진다고들 말하잖아.
③ 나는 대회에 참가하는 게 낫겠어.
④ 네가 포기하지 않는다면, 불가능이란 없어.

어휘 participate in ~에 참가하다   look forward to ~을 기대하다   chance 가능성   whether ~인지 아닌지   matter 중요하다   prepare 준비하다   give up 포기하다   impossible 불가능한   process 과정   result 결과

---

18 ④

W How was your exam today?

M Not bad. Anyway, I'm so happy final exams are finished.

W Same here. I'm looking forward to relaxing in the mountains this weekend.

M Oh, are you going to the mountains?

W Yeah, I've planned a little hike in the woods. Do you have any plans?

M Nothing special. All I want to do is catch up on my sleep.

W Does it help to relieve your stress? Why don't you do something fun?

M People have different ways of relieving stress.

여 오늘 시험 어땠어?

남 나쁘지 않았어. 어쨌든, 기말고사가 끝나서 너무 행복해.

여 나도 그래. 난 이번 주말에 산에서 휴식을 취할 것이 기대돼.

남 오, 너 산에 갈 거야?

여 응, 숲에서 하이킹을 좀 할 계획이야. 너는 어떤 계획이 있니?

남 특별한 건 없어. 내가 원하는 건 밀린 잠을 자는 거야.

여 그게 스트레스 해소에 도움이 되니? 재미있는 것을 하는 게 어떠니?

남 사람마다 스트레스를 푸는 방법이 달라.

해설 남자가 스트레스 해소를 위해 그냥 잠을 자고 싶다고 하자 여자는 뭔가 재미있는 일을 해 보라고 권했으므로, 각자 다른 방식으로 스트레스를 푼다는 말을 하는 것이 가장 적절하다.
① 넌 엄청난 스트레스를 받고 있구나.
② 그건 네가 시험에 떨어졌기 때문이야.
③ 미안하지만, 난 해야 할 일이 많아.
⑤ 하이킹은 내가 지금껏 했던 것 중 가장 재미있는 거야.

어휘 anyway 어쨌든   final exam 기말고사   Same here. 나도 마찬가지이다.   catch up on ~을 만회하다, 따라잡다   relieve 없애 주다, 덜다   stress 스트레스   fail 실패하다

---

19 ④

M Hey, you look like you're really in pain.

W Yes, I hurt my ankle playing badminton.

M Oh, no! How did it happen?

W Well, after running to smash the shuttlecock I fell down.

M That's terrible. Did you go see a doctor about it?

W No, but I did see the school nurse.

M What did she say?

W She said putting ice on it will be helpful.

남 야, 너 정말 아파 보여.

여 응, 배드민턴 치다가 발목을 다쳤어.

남 오, 저런! 어떻게 된 일이니?

여 그냥, 셔틀콕을 세게 내리치려고 달려가다가 넘어졌어.

남 끔찍해라. 병원에는 갔었니?

여 아니, 하지만 보건실에 다녀왔어.

남 보건 선생님께서 뭐라고 하셨니?

여 얼음찜질이 도움이 될 거라고 말씀하셨어.

해설 남자가 발목을 다친 여자에게 보건 선생님이 뭐라고 하셨는지 물었으므로 그와 관련된 응답이 와야 한다.
① 괜찮아. 나는 이제 나아지고 있어.
② 의사 선생님이 내가 휴식이 필요하다고 하셨어.
③ 나는 전문가의 의견을 받고 싶어.
⑤ 엄마가 나를 데리러 오실 거야.

어휘 in pain 아픈   ankle 발목   smash 세게 내리치다   shuttlecock 셔틀콕   fall down 넘어지다   school nurse 보건 선생님   rest 휴식   professional 전문적인   opinion 의견   helpful 도움이 되는

20 ③

W Ben borrowed some books from the public library. Ben is supposed to return them today. But he is so busy studying for tomorrow's final exam that he can't go to the library. His cousin Jenny visits his house, and he wants to ask her to return the books for him. In this situation, what would Ben most likely say to Jenny?

Ben Jenny, do you mind if I ask you a favor?

여 Ben은 공공 도서관에서 책을 몇 권 빌렸다. Ben은 오늘 그것들을 반납하기로 되어 있다. 하지만 내일 있을 기말고사 공부를 하느라 너무 바빠서 도서관에 갈 수가 없다. 그의 사촌 Jenny가 그의 집에 왔고, 그는 Jenny에게 그를 위해서 책들을 반납해 줄 것을 부탁하고 싶어 한다. 이런 상황에서, Ben은 Jenny에게 뭐라고 말할 것 같은가?

Ben Jenny, 부탁 하나 들어 줄 수 있니?

해설 책을 대신 반납해 줄 것을 부탁하려는 상황이므로 도움을 요청하는 말을 해야 자연스럽다.
① 언제가 만기일이니?
② 나 좀 도와줄래? 난 길을 잃었어.
④ 더 많은 책을 읽는 게 어떠니?
⑤ 공공 도서관에 어떻게 가니?

어휘 borrow 빌리다 public library 공공 도서관 be supposed to ~하기로 되어 있다 return 반납하다 be busy ~ing ~하느라 바쁘다 due 만기가 된

01 ②	02 ①	03 ④	04 ⑤	05 ⑤
06 ⑤	07 ①	08 ⑤	09 ④	10 ④
11 ④	12 ②	13 ⑤	14 ④	15 ③
16 ②	17 ③	18 ④	19 ⑤	20 ⑤

01 ②

M Your new bookcase is really nice. Where did you get it?
W I ordered it online.
M I see. I like that it has three shelves. It's not too tall and not too short.
W Yeah. At first, I was thinking of ordering one with five shelves, but I thought it would be too tall.
M It looks good in your bedroom. What is the drawer at the bottom for?
W That is for keeping my stuff in.
M The handle on the drawer is a good idea, too.
W Yes. That makes it more convenient to use.

남 너의 새 책장이 정말 멋지다. 그것을 어디에서 샀니?
여 온라인으로 주문했어.
남 그렇구나. 3단이라 좋네. 너무 높지도 않고 너무 낮지도 않아.
여 응. 처음에, 5단 책장을 주문하려고 했는데, 너무 높을 것 같더라고.
남 네 침실에 잘 어울린다. 하단 서랍은 무엇을 위한 거야?
여 내 물건을 넣어두려고.
남 서랍에 손잡이가 있는 것도 좋은 생각이네.
여 응. 사용하기 더 편리해.

해설 여자가 구입한 책장은 3단이고, 하단에 손잡이가 달린 서랍이 있다고 했다.

어휘 bookcase 책장 order 주문하다 shelf 선반 at first 처음에 drawer 서랍 bottom 맨 아래 stuff 물건 convenient 편리한 use 사용하다

02 ①

W Honey, can you get home by 6 o'clock this evening?
M Why?
W There's a problem with our water purifier. We didn't have any hot water yesterday.
M Did you call the service center?
W Yes, I did. The repairman will come around 6 o'clock. But I can't get home by that time.
M Oh, you said you have an important meeting today.
W Yes, so can you leave the office early?
M Sure. Don't worry.

여 여보, 오늘 저녁에 6시까지 집에 갈 수 있어요?
남 왜요?

여 우리 정수기에 문제가 있어서요. 어제 온수가 안 나왔잖아요.

남 서비스 센터에 전화했어요?

여 네, 했어요. 수리 기사가 6시쯤에 올 거예요. 그런데 내가 그때까지는 집에 못 가서요.

남 아, 오늘 중요한 회의가 있다고 했죠.

여 네, 그래서 당신이 일찍 퇴근할 수 있어요?

남 물론이죠. 걱정하지 말아요.

해설 여자는 정수기 수리 기사가 올 때까지 자신은 집에 갈 수 없으므로 남자에게 일찍 퇴근해 달라고 부탁했다.

어휘 water purifier 정수기   service center 서비스 센터
repairman 수리 기사   important 중요한   meeting 회의
leave the office 퇴근하다

03 ④

M Look outside! It's raining.

W Yeah, the weather forecaster said that it would rain in the afternoon.

M Really? That's why my mom told me to carry an umbrella with me this morning.

W Mine, too.

M So did you bring your umbrella with you?

W Of course. Why? Didn't you bring yours?

M No, I didn't. It looked like a nice day this morning, so I didn't think we would have rain this afternoon.

W Oh, dear. You're going to get wet.

M I know. It's my fault. I should have listened to Mom.

남 밖을 좀 봐! 비가 오네.

여 응, 기상 캐스터가 오후에 비가 올 거라고 했어.

남 정말? 그래서 엄마가 오늘 아침에 우산을 가져가라고 하셨구나.

여 나도 그래.

남 그래서 넌 우산 가지고 왔니?

여 물론이지. 왜? 너는 안 가지고 왔어?

남 응, 안 가지고 왔어. 오늘 아침에는 날씨가 좋은 것 같아서, 오늘 오후에 비가 올 거라는 생각을 못했어.

여 오, 저런. 넌 비를 맞겠구나.

남 맞아. 내 잘못이야. 엄마 말씀을 들었어야 했어.

해설 남자는 우산을 가지고 가라는 엄마의 말을 듣지 않은 것에 대해 후회하고 있다.

어휘 weather forecaster 기상 캐스터   That's why ~ 그래서
~하다   get wet 젖다   fault 잘못   should have p.p.
~했어야 했다   joyful 즐거운   envious 부러운   regretful
후회하는   disappointed 실망한

04 ⑤

① W You are late for school again.

　 M I'm sorry. I got up late and missed the bus.

② W Excuse me. Do you know how to get to the National Museum?

　 M Take line 4 for three stops and get off at National Museum Station.

③ W How often do you have your hair cut?

M About once a month.

④ W You look very busy today. Can I give you a hand?

　 M Oh, yes. I really need someone to help me.

⑤ W Would you like to go see a movie tonight?

　 M You can say that again. The movie was terrific.

① 여 너 또 학교에 늦었구나.

　 남 죄송합니다. 늦잠을 자서 버스를 놓쳤어요.

② 여 실례합니다. 국립박물관에 어떻게 가는지 아시나요?

　 남 4호선을 타고 세 정거장을 가신 후 국립박물관역에서 내리세요.

③ 여 너는 얼마나 자주 머리를 자르니?

　 남 한 달에 한 번 정도.

④ 여 너 오늘 정말 바빠 보여. 내가 도와줄까?

　 남 오, 그래. 난 도와줄 누군가가 정말 필요해.

⑤ 여 오늘 밤에 영화 보러 갈래?

　 남 물론이지. 그 영화 대단했어.

해설 ⑤ 영화를 보러 가자는 제안에 동의한 후 이미 본 것처럼 이어서 말하는 것은 어색하다.

어휘 be late for ~에 늦다   miss 놓치다   get off (차에서)
내리다   have one's hair cut 머리를 자르다   give ~ a hand
~를 도와주다   terrific 훌륭한, 아주 좋은

05 ⑤

W Good afternoon, ladies and gentlemen. I have a short announcement before we wrap up our conference. To date, you've been receiving our monthly newsletters in the mail. However, we're switching the newsletter delivery to email. This will avoid late delivery and lost mail. Also, it will help us protect the environment. You will be able to read your first newsletter online from next month. Thank you.

여 신사숙녀 여러분, 안녕하세요. 회의를 마치기 전에, 간단하게 공지할 사항이 있습니다. 지금까지, 여러분은 매달 우편으로 소식지를 받아오고 계셨습니다. 하지만, 저희는 소식지 전달을 이메일로 바꾸려고 합니다. 이렇게 하면 배달이 늦거나 우편물이 분실되는 일을 피하게 될 것입니다. 또한, 이것은 우리가 환경을 보호하는 데 도움이 될 것입니다. 여러분은 다음 달부터 온라인으로 첫 번째 소식지를 읽으실 수 있을 것입니다. 감사합니다.

해설 우편으로 전달하던 소식지의 전달 방식을 바꾸어 이메일로 보낼 것임을 알리는 방송이다.

어휘 announcement 공지, 알림   wrap up 마무리하다
conference 회의   to date 지금까지   receive 받다
newsletter 소식지   switch 바꾸다   delivery 전달, 배달
avoid 피하다   lost 분실된   protect 보호하다   environment
환경

06 ⑤

W Hi. I came here to have my picture taken.

M Okay. What do you need it for?

W It's for issuing a driver's license. How long will it take to develop the picture?

M It shouldn't take more than 5 minutes.

W So quick! Do you have a mirror?

M Sure. It's on the wall. When you're ready, please take a seat over there.

여 안녕하세요. 사진을 찍으려고 왔는데요.

남 네. 어떤 용도로 필요하신가요?

여 운전면허증 발급용이에요. 사진을 현상하는 데 얼마나 걸리나요?

남 5분 이상 걸리지 않을 겁니다.

여 아주 빠르네요! 거울이 있나요?

남 그럼요. 벽에 있습니다. 준비되시면, 저기에 앉으세요.

해설 운전면허증 발급용 사진 촬영과 인화에 대한 대화가 이루어지는 장소는 사진관이다.

어휘 have one's picture taken (사진관에서) 사진을 찍다 issue 발급하다　driver's license 운전면허증　develop (필름을) 현상하다　mirror 거울　take a seat 앉다

07 ①

W Excuse me. How long will it be until we land?

M We're expected to arrive in Incheon at 4:30.

W Then we still have one more hour left before landing.

M Right. Do you need anything?

W Actually, my son's begging me for something to drink. Can he get some orange juice, please?

M Of course. Let me get some for him.

W Thank you.

여 실례합니다. 착륙할 때까지 얼마나 걸리나요?

남 4시 30분에 인천에 도착 예정입니다.

여 그러면 아직 착륙까지 1시간 더 남은 거군요.

남 맞습니다. 뭐 필요하신 거 있으세요?

여 사실은, 제 아들이 마실 것을 달라고 해서요. 오렌지 주스 좀 가져다주시겠어요?

남 그럼요. 아드님께 주스를 가져다 드릴게요.

여 고맙습니다.

해설 착륙 시간에 대해 묻고 답하고 여자가 남자에게 음료를 요청한 것으로 보아 비행기 승무원과 탑승객이 나누는 대화임을 알 수 있다.

어휘 land 착륙하다 (↔ take off 이륙하다)　expect 예상하다 beg 간청하다, 애원하다

08 ⑤

W Are you ready, Tom?

M Absolutely. I can't wait to jump into the swimming pool. Let's go.

W Wait! Why aren't you wearing your swimming cap?

M My swimming cap? My hair is quite short, so I don't think I need it.

W No way! It says here that everyone must wear a swimming cap in the water.

M Really? But I didn't bring it today.

W You can buy one at the shop on the first floor.

M Okay. I'll go get one right now.

여 준비됐니, Tom?

남 당연하지. 난 수영장에 얼른 뛰어들고 싶어. 가자.

여 기다려! 너 수영모는 왜 안 썼니?

남 수영모? 내 머리는 아주 짧아서 수영모가 필요 없을 것 같아.

여 안 돼! 물속에서는 모든 사람들이 수영모를 써야 한다고 여기 써 있잖아.

남 정말? 하지만 난 오늘 안 가지고 왔는데.

여 1층에 있는 가게에서 수영모를 살 수 있어.

남 알겠어. 지금 바로 가서 하나 사 올게.

해설 수영모를 준비하지 않은 남자는 수영장에 들어가기 전에 수영모를 사 오겠다고 했다.

어휘 can't wait to 매우 ~하고 싶다　quite 꽤

09 ④

M Our Earth suffers because of food waste. Here are three good tips that will help you reduce your food waste. First, make a list of what you need before going grocery shopping. Second, keep track of what you throw away and try not to buy too much of it the next time. Finally, prepare only the amount your family will eat that day. If you follow these tips, you can cut down on the amount of food you throw away.

남 우리의 지구가 음식물 쓰레기 때문에 고통받고 있습니다. 여기에 음식물 쓰레기를 줄이는 데 도움이 되는 세 가지 좋은 조언들이 있습니다. 첫째, 식료품 쇼핑을 하러 가기 전에 필요한 것에 관한 목록을 작성하세요. 둘째, 버리는 것을 추적해 보고 다음에는 그것을 너무 많이 사지 않도록 노력하세요. 마지막으로, 여러분 가족이 그날 먹을 양만 준비하세요. 여러분이 이 조언들을 따르면, 버리는 음식의 양을 줄일 수 있습니다.

해설 지구를 위해 음식물 쓰레기를 줄이는 방법을 소개하고 있다.

어휘 suffer 고통받다　waste 쓰레기　reduce 줄이다 grocery 식료품　keep track of ~을 기록하다, 추적하다 throw away 버리다　prepare 준비하다　amount 양 follow 따르다　cut down on ~을 줄이다

10 ④

W Dad, I'm going to see a musical with Erin tonight.

M When and where is the musical playing?

W It starts at 7 o'clock and ends around 8:40 at the Central Theater.

M Oh, the theater is very close to my office. Do you want me to pick you up on my way home?

W Can you do that? But you usually leave your office at 6 o'clock.

M Well, I can work until the show ends. Did you say it ends at 8:40?

W Yes. Where do you want us to wait for you?

M Let's meet in front of the theater at 8:50.
W All right. Thanks, Dad.

여 아빠, 오늘밤에 Erin이랑 뮤지컬 보러 갈 거예요.
남 뮤지컬은 언제 어디서 공연하니?
여 Central Theater에서 7시에 시작해서 8시 40분쯤에 끝나요.
남 오, 극장이 우리 회사와 아주 가깝구나. 내가 집에 가는 길에 널 데리러 갈까?
여 그러실 수 있으세요? 하지만 아빠는 보통 6시에 퇴근하시잖아요.
남 음, 공연이 끝날 때까지 일할 수 있단다. 8시 40분에 끝난다고 했지?
여 네. 저희가 어디서 기다릴까요?
남 8시 50분에 극장 앞에서 만나자.
여 네. 감사합니다, 아빠.

해설 공연이 8시 40분에 끝나므로 두 사람은 극장 앞에서 8시 50분에 만나기로 했다.

어휘 tonight 오늘밤에   end 끝나다   theater 극장   pick up ~을 (차에) 태우러 가다   on one's way 도중에, 가는 길에   until ~할 때까지   wait for ~을 기다리다   in front of ~ 앞에

11 ④

M Have you decided where you would like to go?
W No, but I want to take a five-day trip with my friend.
M What is your budget?
W We can afford about $700 each. We need an inexpensive package tour.
M In that case, our package to Thailand is perfect for you. For two people, the total cost is $1,400.
W What's included in the package?
M It includes a double room, breakfast and dinner, plus round-trip plane tickets.
W That sounds great! We'll take it.

남 어디로 가실지 결정하셨나요?
여 아니요, 하지만 친구와 함께 5일짜리 여행을 가고 싶어요.
남 예산은 어떻게 되시나요?
여 1인당 700달러 정도면 좋겠어요. 저렴한 패키지여행이 필요해요.
남 그런 경우라면, 저희의 태국 패키지 상품이 안성맞춤입니다. 2인 총액이 1,400달러입니다.
여 패키지에 무엇이 포함되어 있나요?
남 2인실, 아침 식사와 저녁 식사, 그리고 왕복 항공권이 포함됩니다.
여 그거 좋네요! 그걸로 할게요.

해설 아침 식사와 저녁 식사가 모두 포함된다고 했다.

어휘 budget 예산   afford 감당할 수 있는   inexpensive 저렴한   perfect 완벽한   include 포함하다   round-trip 왕복의

12 ②

M Do you remember where we parked our car?
W It's in section B201.

M Oh, good. How much do we need to pay for parking?
W Check the parking ticket. All the information is there.
M Right. Hmm... it's 1,000 won for every hour. How long were we here for?
W Three hours.
M Wait! We get one hour of free parking with a purchase of more than 30,000 won. We spent more than 30,000 won here today.
W That's great.

남 우리 차 어디에 주차했는지 기억하니?
여 B201 구역에 있어.
남 오, 다행이다. 주차 요금으로 얼마를 내야 하지?
여 주차권 확인해 봐. 모든 정보가 거기에 있어.
남 그러네. 음… 시간당 1,000원이네. 우리가 여기에 얼마나 있었지?
여 세 시간.
남 잠깐만! 3만 원 이상 구입하면 1시간 무료 주차야. 우리는 오늘 여기에서 3만 원 넘게 썼잖아.
여 잘됐다.

해설 주차 시간은 세 시간이지만 30,000원 이상 구매했을 경우 한 시간은 무료이다. 주차 요금은 시간당 1,000원이므로 두 시간에 해당하는 요금인 2,000원을 내면 된다.

어휘 park 주차하다   pay for ~을 지불하다   parking ticket 주차권   information 정보   purchase 구입하다, 사다   spend (돈을) 쓰다, 소비하다

13 ⑤

W Are you ready to order?
M Yes. I'd like a Caesar salad and the beef steak.
W How would you like your steak?
M Medium, please.
W Okay. Do you need anything to drink?
M Just water, please. By the way, may I ask you a favor?
W Sure. What is it?
M Could you please turn off the air conditioner? It's very cold in here.
W No problem. I'll do it right away.

여 주문하시겠어요?
남 네, 시저샐러드와 소고기 스테이크 주세요.
여 스테이크는 어떻게 해 드릴까요?
남 중간으로 구워주세요.
여 알겠습니다. 마실 것이 필요하신가요?
남 그냥 물 주세요. 그런데, 부탁 좀 드려도 될까요?
여 그럼요. 무엇인가요?
남 에어컨을 꺼 주시겠어요? 이 안이 너무 춥네요.
여 알겠습니다. 바로 그렇게 하겠습니다.

해설 남자는 식당 안이 너무 춥다며 에어컨을 꺼 달라고 부탁했다.

어휘 be ready to ~할 준비가 되다   by the way 그런데   ask ~ a favor ~에게 부탁하다   turn off ~을 끄다

14 ④

M Have you been to the new Italian restaurant near our office?

W No, but I heard their cream spaghetti tastes pretty good.

M Really? It's one of my favorite dishes.

W I love cream spaghetti as well. Shall we go and try it sometime?

M Okay. How about lunch today?

W Sorry. I have to skip lunch today. I have a medical checkup this afternoon.

M I see. What about lunch tomorrow then?

W Sounds great.

남 우리 사무실 근처에 새로 생긴 이태리 식당에 가 봤어?

여 아니, 하지만 그곳의 크림 스파게티가 아주 맛있다는 얘기는 들었어.

남 그래? 그게 내가 가장 좋아하는 음식 중 하나인데.

여 나도 크림 스파게티 좋아해. 언제 같이 가서 먹어 볼까?

남 좋아. 오늘 점심은 어때?

여 미안해. 오늘은 점심 못 먹어. 오늘 오후에 건강 검진이 있거든.

남 그렇구나. 그러면 내일 점심은 어때?

여 좋지.

[해설] 여자는 오늘 오후에 건강 검진을 받아야 해서 점심을 같이 먹을 수 없다고 했다.

[어휘] taste ~ 맛이 나다   dish 요리   as well 또한   sometime 언젠가   skip 거르다, 건너뛰다   medical checkup 건강 검진

15 ③

M Hello. English Assistance Center.

W Hi. I heard you have excellent tutors available.

M Yes, we do. What do you need help with?

W I need help with reading. Do you have a reading class on Mondays?

M Yes, we have an evening class on Mondays. But it's already fully booked. How about Tuesday mornings?

W I have a piano lesson every morning.

M Then there is only one class left for you.

W Okay. I'll sign up for it.

남 안녕하세요. English Assistance Center입니다.

여 안녕하세요. 이곳에 훌륭한 선생님들이 계시다고 들었어요.

남 네, 맞습니다. 어떤 도움이 필요하신가요?

여 독해 부분의 도움이 필요해요. 월요일에 독해 수업이 있나요?

남 네, 월요일 저녁 수업이 있습니다. 하지만 이미 예약이 꽉 찼습니다. 화요일 오전은 어떠세요?

여 제가 매일 아침 피아노 수업이 있어서요.

남 그러면 딱 한 수업만 남게 되네요.

여 알겠어요. 그 수업에 등록할게요.

[해설] 여자는 독해 수업을 들을 예정이고 오후 수업만 가능한데, 월요일 오후는 예약이 다 차서 수요일 오후 Matt의 수업을 들을 것이다.

[어휘] assistance 도움, 지원   excellent 훌륭한   tutor 강사, 지도 교사   available 이용할 수 있는   book 예약하다   sign up for ~에 등록하다

16 ②

① W How may I help you?
　M I'd like to open a new bank account.

② W You're supposed to slow down around this area.
　M Oh, I'm sorry. I didn't see the sign.

③ W I'd like to check in now.
　M Okay. Do you have a reservation?

④ W What happened to your leg?
　M I hurt it while I was playing basketball.

⑤ W The traffic is horrible today.
　M It is. There must be an accident up ahead.

① 여 무엇을 도와드릴까요?
　남 새 은행 계좌를 개설하려고요.

② 여 이 부근에서는 속도를 줄이셔야 합니다.
　남 오, 죄송합니다. 표지판을 못 봤어요.

③ 여 지금 체크인 하려고 합니다.
　남 알겠습니다. 예약하셨나요?

④ 여 다리가 어떻게 된 거니?
　남 농구하다가 다쳤어.

⑤ 여 오늘 교통 상태가 끔찍하네.
　남 맞아. 앞쪽에서 사고가 난 게 틀림없어.

[해설] 자동차의 운행 속도가 제한된 스쿨 존에서 경찰관이 운전자에게 주의를 주는 상황이다.

[어휘] open a bank account 은행 계좌를 개설하다   be supposed to ~하기로 되어 있다   slow down 속도를 줄이다   sign 표지판   check in 체크인하다   reservation 예약   hurt 다치다   traffic 교통   horrible 끔찍한   accident 사고   up ahead 그 앞쪽에

17 ③

W Welcome to our Firefly Tour. I'm going to guide you on a fascinating journey on our beautiful boat. We will be on board for about two hours, and you can eat snacks and drinks on the deck freely. Be sure to keep your life jackets on and don't scare away the fireflies with the flash of your cameras. Please note that the restrooms are on the lower deck. Thank you.

여 Firefly Tour에 오신 것을 환영합니다. 저는 아름다운 배 위에서의 환상적인 여정을 여러분께 안내할 것입니다. 우리는 약 두 시간 동안 항해를 할 것이고, 여러분은 갑판 위의 간식과 음료를 마음껏 드실 수 있습니다. 반드시 구명조끼를 입으시고 카메라의 플래시 빛으로 반딧불이를 쫓아 버리지 않도록 하세요. 화장실은 아래쪽 갑판에 있습니다. 감사합니다.

[해설] 투어의 비용은 언급되지 않았다.

[어휘] firefly 반딧불이   fascinating 환상적인   journey 여정, 여행   on board 선상에   deck 갑판   freely 마음껏,

자유롭게 scare away (겁을 주어) 쫓아 버리다 flash 플래시
restroom 화장실

18 ④

W Hey, Sam. What's up? You look out of breath.
M Yeah. I ran to school today.
W Don't you usually ride your bike to school?
M Yes, but it was stolen several days ago. I parked it in front of the bookstore, and somebody took it.
W Didn't you have a lock on it?
M No. I thought it would be okay.
W Too bad. You should have been more careful.

여 안녕, Sam. 무슨 일이니? 숨차 보이네.
남 응. 오늘 학교에 뛰어왔어.
여 너는 보통 학교에 자전거를 타고 오지 않니?
남 응, 하지만 며칠 전에 자전거를 도난당했어. 서점 앞에 세워 두었는데 누군가 그것을 가져갔어.
여 자물쇠를 채우지 않니?
남 응. 괜찮을 줄 알았거든.
여 너무 안됐다. 너는 좀 더 조심했어야 해.

해설 자물쇠를 채우지 않아서 자전거를 도난당한 남자에게 안됐다고 하며 좀 더 조심했어야 한다는 충고의 말을 하는 것이 자연스럽다.
① 내가 네 자전거에서 눈을 떼지 않고 (지키고) 있을게.
② 나는 곧 새 자전거를 사는 게 좋겠어.
③ 우리 함께 서점에 갈까?
⑤ 여기에 네 자전거를 세워 두면 안 될 것 같아.

어휘 out of breath 숨이 찬 steal 훔치다 park 주차하다
lock 자물쇠 keep one's eyes on ~에서 눈을 떼지 않다
careful 주의하는 be allowed to ~하는 것이 허용되다

19 ⑤

W Good afternoon, Jimmy.
M Hello, Maria. How was your volunteer work on the weekend?
W Oh, you remembered that I played the piano for children in the hospital.
M Yes. You were really excited.
W I was, but my first time volunteering wasn't very successful.
M What do you mean?
W The music that I chose was boring for them. Most of the children didn't pay attention.
M Don't be disappointed. I'm sure you will do better the next time.

여 Jimmy, 안녕.
남 안녕, Maria. 주말에 자원봉사 활동 어땠니?
여 오, 내가 병원에서 아이들한테 피아노 연주해 준다는 거 기억하는구나.
남 응. 넌 정말 신났었잖아.
여 그랬는데, 내 첫 번째 자원봉사 활동은 별로 성공적이지 못했어.

남 그게 무슨 말이니?
여 내가 선택한 음악이 아이들에게 지루했나 봐. 대부분의 아이들이 주의를 기울이지 않더라고.
남 실망하지 마. 다음에는 틀림없이 더 잘할 거야.

해설 여자가 자원봉사 활동이 성공적이지 못했다고 의기소침해 있으므로 격려의 말을 하는 것이 적절하다.
① 피아노를 연주하는 게 어때?
② 그들은 네 노래를 틀림없이 즐겼을 거야.
③ 자원봉사를 하는 것은 좋은 생각이었어.
④ 병원에서 자원봉사를 하는 것은 쓸모없어.

어휘 volunteer work 자원봉사 활동 excited 신난
successful 성공적인 choose 선택하다 boring 지루한
most of 대부분의 pay attention 주의를 기울이다
worthless 쓸모없는 disappointed 실망한

20 ⑤

M Monica's friend Brian invited her to his house. Brian prepared many different kinds of food for her. Monica is even more surprised that everything is so delicious, especially the seafood pasta. Even though Brian is not a professional chef, Monica thinks that it is the best pasta she has ever tasted. Monica wonders how Brian made it. In this situation, what do you think Monica probably asks Brian?
Monica Brian, can you tell me the recipe for this pasta?

남 Monica의 친구 Brian은 그녀를 그의 집에 초대했다. Brian은 그녀를 위해 많은 다양한 종류의 음식을 준비했다. Monica는 모든 것이 너무 맛있어서 훨씬 더 놀랐는데, 특히 해산물 파스타가 맛있다. 비록 Brian이 전문 요리사는 아니지만, Monica는 그녀가 지금껏 맛 본 것 중 최고의 파스타라고 생각한다. Monica는 Brian이 어떻게 그것을 만들었는지 궁금해한다. 이 상황에서, Monica는 Brian에게 무엇이라고 물어볼 것 같은가?
Monica Brian, 이 파스타의 조리법을 나에게 말해 줄 수 있니?

해설 Brian이 만든 파스타가 맛있어서 그것을 어떻게 만들었는지 궁금해하는 상황이다.
① 너는 요리하는 것을 좋아하니?
② 너는 해산물 파스타를 맛본 적 있니?
③ 네가 모든 음식을 직접 만들었니?
④ 다음에 너에게 또 하나 만들어 줄게.

어휘 invite 초대하다 prepare 준비하다 even 훨씬
surprised 놀란 delicious 맛있는 especially 특히 even
though 비록 ~이지만 professional 전문적인 chef 요리사
be fond of ~을 좋아하다 recipe 조리법

Review Test

pp.114~115

Word Check
09회

01 마술사	**02** 야외의
03 반납하다	**04** 중요하다
05 관광객	**06** 만기가 된
07 입장	**08** 수업료
09 미끄러지다	**10** 동시에
11 예정대로	**12** 쉬는 날
13 opinion	**14** impossible
15 ability	**16** memorize
17 prepare	**18** sports day
19 professional	**20** relieve
21 public library	**22** shipping charge
23 fall down	**24** to make matters worse

Expression Check

25 catch up on	**26** drives, crazy
27 in pain	**28** Whether, or not
29 cheating on	**30** at the top of

Word Check
10회

01 피하다	**02** 발급하다
03 도움, 지원	**04** 부러운
05 예산	**06** 저렴한
07 고통받다	**08** 회의
09 후회하는	**10** 여정, 여행
11 ~을 기록하다, 추적하다	**12** ~을 줄이다
13 successful	**14** steal
15 disappointed	**16** worthless
17 recipe	**18** bottom
19 develop	**20** delivery
21 environment	**22** driver's license
23 parking ticket	**24** out of breath

Expression Check

25 scare away	**26** have, cut
27 a problem with	**28** pay attention
29 slow down	**30** Cut down on

실전 모의고사 **11**회

pp.116~123

01 ②	02 ②	03 ③	04 ④	05 ④
06 ①	07 ②	08 ⑤	09 ②	10 ③
11 ④	12 ④	13 ③	14 ④	15 ③
16 ④	17 ②	18 ⑤	19 ⑤	20 ②

01 ②

M Can I help you?
W Yes, please. I'm looking for a birthday gift for my mom.
M How old is she?
W She is turning 50.
M Then how about this sweater with a flower pattern? It's very popular.
W I don't know. It looks a little old-fashioned. How much is the cardigan over there?
M Do you mean the one with a tie belt? Oh, it's on sale. It's $40.
W That's great. I will take it.

남 도와드릴까요?
여 네. 저는 어머니를 위한 생신 선물을 찾고 있어요.
남 어머니 연세가 어떻게 되시죠?
여 50세가 되십니다.
남 그러면 이 꽃무늬가 있는 스웨터는 어떠신가요? 아주 인기 있어요.
여 모르겠어요. 약간 유행이 지나 보여요. 저쪽에 있는 카디건은 얼마인가요?
남 끈이 있는 카디건 말씀이신가요? 오. 그것은 할인 중입니다. 40달러예요.
여 좋네요. 그걸로 살게요.

해설 여자는 끈이 있는 카디건을 사겠다고 했다.

어휘 turn (나이가) ~가 되다　pattern 무늬　popular 인기 있는　old-fashioned 구식의, 유행이 지난　cardigan 카디건(앞이 트인 스웨터)　on sale 할인 중인

02 ②

W Hello. What would you like to order?
M I would like five chicken nuggets and a cheese sandwich.
W The nuggets are $1 each and the cheese sandwich is $5.
M I'm going to have the nuggets here, but I want the sandwich to go.
W If you pay $1 extra, you can also have a glass of lemonade.
M No, thank you. Can I use this 10% coupon?
W Oh, sure. You can get 10% off.
M Thanks. Here's my credit card.

여 안녕하세요. 무엇을 주문하시겠어요?
남 치킨너겟 다섯 개와 치즈샌드위치 하나 주세요.
여 너겟은 하나에 1달러이고 치즈샌드위치는 5달러입니다.
남 너겟은 여기에서 먹지만 샌드위치는 가져갈 거예요.
여 1달러를 추가하시면 레몬에이드도 한 잔 드실 수 있습니다.
남 아니요, 괜찮아요. 이 10퍼센트 쿠폰을 사용할 수 있나요?
여 오, 물론입니다. 10퍼센트 할인 받으실 수 있어요.
남 감사합니다. 여기 카드 있어요.

해설 남자는 치킨너겟($1) 다섯 개와 치즈샌드위치($5) 한 개를 주문한 후 10퍼센트 쿠폰을 사용했으므로 9달러를 지불하면 된다.

어휘 order 주문하다 pay 지불하다 extra 추가 요금 use 사용하다 off 할인하여

03 ③

(Telephone rings.)
W City Hotel. How can I help you?
M Hi. I'd like to confirm my reservation at your hotel.
W Sure. Can you tell me your name and the date of your stay?
M My name is Adam Smith and I'm going to arrive at your hotel on January 13.
W Thanks. You made a reservation for two nights in one of our junior suite rooms.
M That's correct. Thank you.
W No problem. We're looking forward to seeing you soon.

(전화벨이 울린다.)
여 City Hotel입니다. 무엇을 도와드릴까요?
남 안녕하세요. 호텔 예약을 확인하고 싶습니다.
여 네. 이름과 머무시는 날짜를 말씀해 주시겠어요?
남 제 이름은 Adam Smith이고 1월 13일에 호텔에 도착할 예정입니다.
여 감사합니다. 주니어 스위트룸으로 2박을 예약하셨군요.
남 맞습니다. 감사합니다.
여 천만에요. 곧 만나 뵙기를 바랍니다.

해설 남자는 호텔에 예약한 내용을 확인하기 위해 전화했다.

어휘 confirm 확인하다 reservation 예약 stay 방문, 머무름 arrive 도착하다 look forward to ~을 기대하다

04 ④

① W Where can I take you?
  M The airport. Please get me there as soon as possible.
② W How long will it take to get to City Hall by car?
  M It'll take about thirty minutes.
③ W What are you going to do after you graduate?
  M I'll go to Canada to study for two years.
④ W Excuse me. Is this bus headed to the Canadian Embassy?
  M We've just passed it. Get off at the next stop and walk back.

⑤ W I'm sorry, but could you show me something else?
  M If you don't like this one, how about that one?

① 여 어디로 모실까요?
  남 공항이요. 가능한 한 빨리 가 주세요.
② 여 시청까지 자동차로 얼마나 걸릴까요?
  남 30분 정도 걸릴 거예요.
③ 여 넌 졸업 후에 뭐 할 거니?
  남 2년 동안 캐나다로 유학 갈 거야.
④ 여 실례합니다. 이 버스가 캐나다 대사관으로 가나요?
  남 방금 지나쳤어요. 다음 정류장에서 내리셔서 되돌아 걸어가세요.
⑤ 여 미안하지만 다른 걸 보여주시겠어요?
  남 이게 마음에 안 드시면, 저건 어떠세요?

해설 버스 안에서 승객과 기사가 대화를 나누는 상황이므로 버스가 서는 정류장에 대해 묻고 답하는 대화가 적절하다.

어휘 airport 공항 as soon as possible 가능한 한 빨리 graduate 졸업하다 head 향하다 embassy 대사관 get off 내리다 stop 정류장 else 또 다른, 그 밖의

05 ④

W Oh, it's already 11 o'clock. We have to hurry.
M Relax. We've got plenty of time to prepare lunch.
W Okay. Steve, did you put the pizza in the oven?
M Yes, I did. What about the salad?
W I cut the vegetables yesterday and put them in the refrigerator. I'll make it now. Where is the wine?
M The wine is on the table. Where is the cake?
W Oh, I forgot to pick up the cake from the bakery. We have to go get it.
M Okay. I'll go.

여 오, 벌써 11시예요. 서둘러야 해요.
남 진정해요. 우리는 점심 준비할 시간이 충분해요.
여 알았어요. Steve, 피자를 오븐에 넣었나요?
남 네, 넣었어요. 샐러드는 어때요?
여 어제 채소를 잘라서 냉장고에 넣어 두었어요. 지금 만들 거예요. 와인은 어디에 있나요?
남 와인은 테이블 위에 있어요. 케이크는 어디에 있죠?
여 오, 제과점에서 케이크 찾아오는 것을 깜빡했어요. 우리는 가서 가져와야 해요.
남 좋아요. 내가 갈게요.

해설 여자가 제과점에서 케이크를 찾아와야 한다고 말하자 남자가 가겠다고 했다.

어휘 hurry 서두르다 plenty of 많은 prepare 준비하다 vegetable 채소 refrigerator 냉장고 forget to ~할 것을 잊다 pick up ~을 찾아오다

06 ①

① M How would you like your steak?
  W Thank you for saying so.
② M Will you go for a walk with me?

W Sorry, I can't. I have to finish this work now.

③ M What's the matter? You look tired.

W I couldn't sleep last night because of the noise from upstairs.

④ M Are you ready to order?

W Yes. I'll have the meatball spaghetti with a lemonade.

⑤ M Do you mind if I open the window? It's so hot in here.

W Of course not. Go ahead.

① 남 스테이크를 어떻게 구워 드릴까요?
여 그렇게 말씀해 주셔서 감사합니다.
② 남 나랑 같이 산책하러 갈래?
여 미안하지만 안 돼. 나는 지금 이 일을 끝내야 해.
③ 남 무슨 일이야? 너 피곤해 보여.
여 어젯밤에 위층 소음 때문에 잠을 잘 수 없었어.
④ 남 주문하시겠습니까?
여 네. 저는 레몬에이드와 함께 미트볼 스파게티를 먹겠습니다.
⑤ 남 제가 창문을 열어도 될까요? 여기가 너무 더워서요.
여 물론이죠. 어서 여세요.

해설 ① 스테이크를 어떻게 구워 줄지 묻는 말에 고맙다고 답하는 것은 어색하다.

어휘 go for a walk 산책하러 가다   finish 끝내다   because of ～ 때문에   noise 소음   upstairs 위층

07 ②

W Hi, James. You look different!

M Really? I've been exercising hard these days.

W You look great! How long have you been working out?

M It's been almost six months now.

W That's amazing! Why did you start exercising?

M I weighed 70 kilograms a year ago. But after I started having late night snack, I gained 15 kilograms.

W Late night snacks aren't good for your health.

M Yes, so I decided to lose some weight and become healthy again. I have lost 10 kilograms in six months.

여 안녕, James. 너 달라 보여!
남 정말? 나 요즘 열심히 운동하고 있어.
여 멋져 보이네! 얼마나 오랫동안 운동을 했니?
남 이제 거의 6개월이 다 돼가.
여 놀랍다! 넌 왜 운동을 시작했니?
남 나는 1년 전에 70킬로그램이었어. 그런데 밤늦게 간식을 먹기 시작한 후에, 15킬로그램이 쪘어.
여 야식은 네 건강에 좋지 않아.
남 맞아, 그래서 나는 살을 빼고 다시 건강해지기로 결심했어. 나는 6개월 내에 10킬로그램을 뺐어.

해설 남자는 1년 전에 70킬로그램이었으나 야식 때문에 15킬로그램이 쪄서 운동으로 10킬로그램을 뺐다고 했으므로 현재 몸무게는 75킬로그램이다.

어휘 different 다른   exercise 운동하다   these days 요즘   work out 운동하다   weigh 무게가 ～이다   gain (무게가) 늘다, 얻다   be good for ～에 좋다   lose weight 체중을 줄이다   healthy 건강한

08 ⑤

M Hi, Amy. What a pleasant surprise!

W Hi, Brian. How have you been?

M Good. When did you come back from Australia?

W I came back last week. It's summer vacation there.

M How long are you staying in Korea?

W For a month. But I'm planning to travel in Jeju-do with my mom for a week.

M That's good. Have a great time there.

남 안녕, Amy. 정말 반가워!
여 안녕, Brian. 어떻게 지냈니?
남 잘 지냈어. 호주에서 언제 돌아왔니?
여 지난주에 돌아왔어. 그곳은 여름 방학이거든.
남 한국에는 얼마나 머물 예정이니?
여 한 달 동안. 하지만 나는 일주일 동안 엄마와 제주도를 여행할 계획이야.
남 좋겠다. 그곳에서 즐거운 시간 보내.

해설 여자는 제주도로 이사하는 것이 아니라 여행을 할 예정이라고 했다.

어휘 pleasant 기쁜   come back 돌아오다   vacation 방학   stay 머무르다   plan 계획하다   travel 여행하다   have a great time 즐거운 시간을 보내다

09 ②

M Thank you for visiting Fun World. We are looking for a four-year-old boy named Brian. The boy disappeared near section C of the parking lot. He is wearing blue jeans and a yellow T-shirt. He's also wearing a red cap and blue sneakers. If you have seen the boy or can see him now, please call the customer service center right away. Thank you very much.

남 Fun World를 찾아 주셔서 감사합니다. 저희는 Brian이라는 이름의 네 살짜리 남자 아이를 찾고 있습니다. 그 남자 아이는 주차장 C 구역 근처에서 사라졌습니다. 그는 청바지와 노란색 티셔츠를 입고 있습니다. 그는 또한 빨간색 모자를 쓰고 파란색 운동화를 신고 있습니다. 이 남자 아이를 보셨거나 지금 보고 계시면, 지금 바로 고객 서비스 센터로 전화해 주시기 바랍니다. 대단히 감사합니다.

해설 놀이공원에서 길을 잃은 남자 아이를 찾는 안내 방송이다.

어휘 look for ～을 찾다   named ～라고 하는, ～라는 이름의   disappear 사라지다   section 구역   parking lot 주차장   jeans 청바지   sneakers 운동화   customer service center 고객 서비스 센터   right away 지금 바로

10 ③

(Cellphone rings.)
W Hey, Sam. Are you busy now?
M No. What's up?
W I need a favor. I came to Tim's school to meet his teacher, and it took longer than I expected.
M Oh, so are you going to be late for the meeting?
W Yes. I think I can get there by 4:20. Can you give everyone the materials to look over until I get there?
M Sure, no problem. Where are the materials?
W They are on my desk. Thank you so much.

(휴대 전화가 울린다.)
여 안녕하세요, Sam. 지금 바쁘세요?
남 아니요. 무슨 일이세요?
여 부탁이 있어요. 제가 지금 Tim의 학교에 선생님을 만나러 왔는데, 예상보다 더 오래 걸렸어요.
남 아, 그러면 회의에 늦으시나요?
여 네. 4시 20분까지는 도착할 수 있을 것 같아요. 제가 도착할 때까지 모든 사람들에게 검토할 자료를 나누어 주시겠어요?
남 물론, 문제없어요. 자료는 어디에 있나요?
여 제 책상 위에 있어요. 정말 감사합니다.

해설 여자는 회의에 늦을 것 같다고 말하면서 남자에게 회의 자료를 미리 나누어 줄 것을 부탁했다.

어휘 favor 도움, 호의   expect 예상하다, 기대하다   meeting 회의   material 자료   look over 살펴보다

11 ④

M Sally, you're the next speaker. Are you ready?
W No. My hands are shaking.
M Don't worry. You did your best to prepare for this speech contest.
W I don't know. The others are giving great speeches, and they look so confident. What if I forget what to say?
M I'm sure you will do great, too.

남 Sally, 네가 다음 발표자야. 준비됐니?
여 아니요. 제 손이 떨리고 있어요.
남 걱정하지 마! 너는 이번 말하기 대회 준비를 위해 최선을 다했잖아.
여 모르겠어요. 다른 사람들은 연설을 아주 잘하고 아주 자신 있어 보여요. 제가 말할 내용을 잊어버리면 어쩌죠?
남 나는 너도 잘할 거라고 확신해.

해설 말하기 대회에 참가하는 여자는 손이 떨린다고 하며 말할 내용을 잊어버릴까 봐 초조해하고 있다.

어휘 shake 떨다, 흔들리다   worry 걱정하다   prepare 준비하다   speech 말하기, 연설   confident 자신감 있는   forget 잊어버리다

12 ④

W Please come to the National Museum and enjoy our special exhibition, The World of Tradition.

This exhibition will give visitors an opportunity to experience various traditional cultures from all over the world. You can watch traditional music and dance performances and taste traditional foods of many countries. From February 22 to February 28, the exhibition opens at 9 a.m. and lasts for 9 hours every day. For online reservations, please visit our website. Thank you.

여 국립박물관에 오셔서 저희의 특별 전시회 The World of Tradition을 즐기세요. 이 전시회는 방문객들에게 전 세계의 다양한 전통 문화를 경험해 볼 기회를 줄 것입니다. 전통 음악과 춤 공연을 관람하고 많은 국가들의 전통 음식을 맛보실 수 있습니다. 2월 22일부터 2월 28일까지, 전시회는 매일 오전 9시에 개장하여 9시간 동안 진행됩니다. 온라인 예약을 하시려면, 저희 웹사이트를 방문해 주세요. 감사합니다.

해설 전시회의 입장료는 언급되지 않았다.

어휘 exhibition 전시회   tradition 전통   opportunity 기회   various 다양한   culture 문화   all over the world 전 세계의   performance 공연   reservation 예약

13 ③

(Telephone rings.)
W Natural History Museum. How can I help you?
M Can you tell me when the museum opens?
W Sure. We open at 9 a.m., Monday through Saturday.
M And when do you close?
W We close at 5 p.m. on weekdays and 2 p.m. on Saturdays.
M And how much is a ticket for a 4-year-old child?
W It's free for children 7 and under.
M That's great. Thank you for your help.

(전화벨이 울린다.)
여 Natural History Museum입니다. 무엇을 도와드릴까요?
남 박물관의 개장 시간을 말씀해 주시겠습니까?
여 네. 저희는 월요일부터 토요일까지 오전 9시에 문을 엽니다.
남 그러면 언제 문을 닫나요?
여 주중에는 오후 5시, 토요일에는 오후 2시에 문을 닫습니다.
남 그리고 4세 어린이는 입장권이 얼마인가요?
여 7세 이하의 어린이는 무료입니다.
남 좋군요. 도와주셔서 감사합니다.

해설 월요일부터 토요일까지 오전 9시에 문을 연다고 했다.

어휘 natural 자연의   history 역사   close 닫다   weekday 주중, 평일   ticket 입장권   free 무료의   under ~ 미만의

14 ④

W Excuse me. How many books can I borrow?
M Three books at most.
W That's great. I want to borrow these books.
M Do you have a library card?
W Yes, here it is.
M Wait a minute. Oh, you haven't returned a book yet.

You can't borrow any more books.

W Really? Can you tell me the name of <u>the book I haven't returned</u>?

M Sure. Let me check.

여 실례합니다. 제가 몇 권의 책을 빌릴 수 있죠?

남 최대한 세 권입니다.

여 잘됐군요. 이 책들을 빌리고 싶습니다.

남 도서관 카드를 가지고 있나요?

여 네, 여기 있어요.

남 잠깐만요. 아, 아직 책 한 권을 반납하지 않으셨네요. 책을 더 빌리실 수 없습니다.

여 정말요? 제가 반납하지 않은 책의 이름을 말씀해 주시겠어요?

남 네. 확인해 보겠습니다.

해설 남자는 여자가 반납하지 않은 책이 있어서 책을 더 빌릴 수 없다고 말했다.

어휘 borrow 빌리다   at most 최대한으로   return 반납하다   check 확인하다

15 ③

M Good afternoon, everyone. I <u>did a survey</u> about what our classmates want to do during vacation. The largest number of students, 12, said they want to <u>travel to foreign countries</u>. Four students want to go camping. The number of students who want to <u>relax at home</u> was larger than the number of students who want to go camping. <u>The smallest response</u> came from only 2 students who want to play sports during vacation.

남 여러분. 안녕하세요. 저는 우리 반 친구들이 방학 동안 하고 싶은 것에 대해 설문 조사를 했습니다. 가장 많은 수의 학생인 12명이 해외 여행을 하고 싶다고 말했습니다. 4명의 학생은 캠핑을 가고 싶어 합니다. 집에서 쉬고 싶어 하는 학생들의 수가 캠핑을 가고 싶어 하는 학생들보다 많았습니다. 가장 적은 수의 응답은 방학 동안 운동을 하고 싶어 하는 2명의 학생들뿐이었습니다.

해설 방학 동안 하고 싶은 것에 대한 설문 조사 결과이다.

어휘 survey (설문) 조사   classmate 반 친구   vacation 방학   foreign 외국의   relax 휴식을 취하다   response 응답, 대답

16 ④

W Dad, I'm late for school! Can you <u>give me a ride</u>, please?

M Isn't it too early to go to school? What time do you have to be at school?

W I usually go to school by 8:30, but <u>I have a group meeting</u> today.

M I see. What time is the meeting?

W It's at 7:30.

M It's 7:15 now, so <u>we've got to hurry</u>. Let me get my keys.

W Thank you, Dad.

여 아빠, 저 학교에 늦었어요! 저 좀 태워다 주시겠어요?

남 학교에 가기에는 너무 이르지 않니? 몇 시에 학교에 가야 하니?

여 보통 학교에 8시 30분까지 가지만, 오늘은 조 모임이 있어요.

남 그렇구나. 모임은 몇 시니?

여 7시 30분에 있어요.

남 지금 7시 15분이니까, 서둘러야겠구나. 내가 열쇠를 가져오마.

여 고맙습니다. 아빠.

해설 여자의 평소 등교 시각은 8시 30분이지만 오늘은 조 모임 때문에 7시 30분까지 가야 한다고 했다.

어휘 be late for ~에 늦다   give ~ a ride ~을 태워다 주다   usually 보통, 대개   hurry 서두르다

17 ②

W Look at this mess! David, I told you to <u>clean your room</u> an hour ago.

M Sorry, Mom. But I was busy.

W Busy? You've been playing computer games <u>for hours</u>!

M Yeah, but....

W David, you <u>promised to play computer games</u> less than one hour every day.

M Sorry, Mom. <u>I'll stop playing games</u> and start cleaning right now.

W Okay, let me help you.

여 이 난장판 좀 보렴! David, 네 방을 치우라고 1시간 전에 말했잖니.

남 죄송해요, 엄마. 하지만 전 바빴어요.

여 바빴다고? 넌 몇 시간째 컴퓨터 게임을 하고 있잖아!

남 맞아요, 하지만….

여 David, 넌 컴퓨터 게임을 매일 1시간 이내 하기로 약속했잖니.

남 죄송해요, 엄마. 게임 그만하고 지금 바로 청소를 시작할게요.

여 그래. 내가 도와줄게.

해설 남자가 게임을 그만하고 청소를 하겠다고 했으므로 여자는 그에 대한 긍정의 응답을 하는 것이 적절하다.

① 그 말을 들으니 안됐구나.

③ 알았어. 지금 바로 할게.

④ 그래. 버스 정류장에서 만나자.

⑤ 넌 얼마나 오랫동안 외국에 있었니?

어휘 mess 엉망진창   clean 청소하다   promise 약속하다   bus stop 버스 정류장   abroad 해외에

18 ⑤

(Telephone rings.)

W Mr. Choi's Chinese Restaurant. How can I help you?

M <u>I'd like to book a table</u>.

W Can I have your name, please?

M Paul Lee.

W <u>What day and time</u> would you like to make a reservation?

M June 30, this coming Tuesday at 6 p.m.

W How many people are there in your party?

M Five people including me.

W Okay, your reservation is confirmed. Do you need anything else?

M Can you reserve a table by the window for us?

(전화벨이 울린다.)

여 Mr. Choi's Chinese Restaurant입니다. 무엇을 도와드릴까요?

남 테이블을 예약하고 싶습니다.

여 이름을 말씀해 주시겠어요?

남 Paul Lee입니다.

여 무슨 요일 몇 시에 예약하기를 원하시나요?

남 다가오는 화요일인 6월 30일 오후 6시입니다.

여 모두 몇 명이신가요?

남 저를 포함해서 5명입니다.

여 네, 예약이 확정되었습니다. 다른 필요하신 것은 없으신가요?

남 창가 자리를 예약해 주실 수 있나요?

해설 예약을 확정한 후 다른 필요한 것이 있는지 물었으므로 요청 사항을 말하는 응답이 가장 적절하다.

① 음, 그건 너무 비싸네요.

② 후식을 드릴까요?

③ 죄송합니다. 저는 중국 음식을 좋아하지 않아요.

④ 마실 것 좀 가져다주세요.

어휘 book 예약하다 (= reserve)　reservation 예약 include 포함하다　confirm 확정하다　dessert 후식

19 ⑤

M I love this cheesecake! It melts in my mouth right away!

W I'm so glad you like it.

M Yeah, where did you buy it?

W Believe it or not, I baked it myself.

M I can't believe it! This is the best cheesecake I've ever tasted!

W I've been taking baking classes these days. Baking is really fun.

M You should open your own bakery. You're really talented!

W Thanks. I want to open my own bakery someday.

남 이 치즈케이크 정말 좋아요! 입에서 바로 녹아 버려요.

여 마음에 드신다니 정말 기쁩니다.

남 네, 어디에서 사셨나요?

여 믿으실지 모르겠지만, 제가 직접 구웠어요.

남 믿을 수 없군요! 이것은 제가 지금껏 맛본 치즈케이크 중 최고예요.

여 제가 요즘 제빵 수업을 듣고 있거든요. 제빵은 정말 재미있어요.

남 제과점을 하셔야겠어요. 정말 재능이 있으시네요!

여 고맙습니다. 저도 언젠가 제과점을 열고 싶어요.

해설 남자가 여자에게 제빵에 재능이 있다고 칭찬했으므로 그에 대한 감사의 응답을 하는 것이 적절하다.

① 은행 옆에 제과점이 하나 있어요.

② 어머니께서 요리하는 법을 가르쳐 주셨어요.

③ 저는 제빵을 배울 생각이에요.

④ 할머니께서는 쿠키를 잘 구우세요.

어휘 melt 녹다　believe it or not 믿거나 말거나　bake 굽다 taste 맛보다　take a class 수업을 듣다　talented 재능이 있는　be good at ~을 잘하다　someday 언젠가

20 ②

M Jisu and her friend Jimmy planned to go see a movie this afternoon. They promised to meet in front of the ticket office at 3 o'clock. But Jisu's mom called from work and asked Jisu to look after her sister until she gets home from work. Jisu's mom will get home around 3:30, so Jisu can't meet Jimmy until 4. What should Jisu tell Jimmy?

Jisu Jimmy, could we meet around 4 p.m.?

남 지수와 그녀의 친구 Jimmy는 오늘 오후에 영화를 보러 가기로 계획했다. 그들은 매표소 앞에서 3시에 만나기로 약속했다. 하지만 지수의 엄마가 직장에서 전화를 해서 지수에게 그녀가 퇴근해서 집에 올 때까지 그녀의 여동생을 돌봐달라고 말했다. 지수의 엄마는 약 3시 30분에 집에 올 것이고, 그래서 지수는 Jimmy를 4시까지는 만날 수 없다. 지수는 Jimmy에게 뭐라고 말해야 할까?

지수 Jimmy야, 우리 4시쯤에 만나도 될까?

해설 지수는 Jimmy와 3시에 만나기로 약속했지만 여동생을 돌봐야 해서 4시까지는 만날 수 없는 상황이다.

① 나는 영화를 보고 싶지 않아.

③ 나는 너와 뮤지컬을 보고 싶어.

④ 우리 할머니가 우리 가족을 방문하신대.

⑤ 저녁을 먹고 과제에 대해 이야기해 보자.

어휘 plan 계획하다　promise 약속하다　ticket office 매표소 look after 돌보다　until ~할 때까지　project 과제, 프로젝트

01 ④	02 ③	03 ②	04 ⑤	05 ③
06 ④	07 ⑤	08 ③	09 ②	10 ④
11 ⑤	12 ③	13 ④	14 ②	15 ④
16 ②	17 ③	18 ①	19 ④	20 ④

01 ④

W Can I help you?

M Yes, please. I'm looking for glasses.

W What kind of glasses would you like to buy?

M I want to try rimless glasses.

W I think rimless glasses would look good on you. What shape of lenses do you want?

M So far, I've always worn round glasses. I want to try something different.

W How about this pair with square-shaped lenses? Why don't you try them on?

M Oh, I think they match my face. I'll take them.

여 도와드릴까요?

남 네. 안경을 찾고 있어요.

여 어떤 종류의 안경을 사고 싶으신가요?

남 테가 없는 안경을 써 보고 싶어요.

여 테가 없는 안경이 손님께 잘 어울리실 것 같네요. 어떤 모양의 렌즈를 원하세요?

남 지금까지, 저는 항상 둥근 안경을 써 왔거든요. 다른 것을 써 보고 싶어요.

여 사각형 모양 렌즈가 있는 이 안경은 어떠세요? 한번 써 보시겠어요?

남 아, 제 얼굴에 어울리는 것 같아요. 이걸로 할게요.

해설 남자는 테가 없는 사각형 모양의 안경을 사겠다고 했다.

어휘 glasses 안경   kind 종류   rimless 테가 없는   look good on ~와 잘 어울리다   shape 모양   so far 지금까지   square-shaped 사각형 모양의   match 어울리다

02 ③

(Cellphone rings.)

M Honey, I'll be a little late coming home.

W Okay, but I hope you won't be too late.

M Don't worry. How do you feel now? You were coughing a lot this morning.

W The cough is getting worse. I'll cook some chicken soup to soothe my throat.

M That's a good idea. Do you want me to get some medicine on my way home?

W No, I've already taken some medicine. But can you pick up some juice?

M Sure. I'll get some for you.

(휴대 선화가 울린다.)

남 여보, 집에 좀 늦게 들어갈 것 같아요.

여 네, 하지만 너무 늦지 않으면 좋겠어요.

남 걱정 말아요. 지금 몸은 좀 어때요? 오늘 아침에 기침을 많이 하던데요.

여 기침이 더 심해지고 있어요. 그래서 목을 좀 진정시켜 줄 치킨 수프를 만들려고 해요.

남 좋은 생각이에요. 집에 가는 길에 약을 좀 사다 줄까요?

여 아니에요, 약은 이미 먹었어요. 그런데 주스 좀 사다 줄래요?

남 물론이죠. 사 가지고 갈게요.

해설 여자는 남자에게 주스를 사다 줄 것을 부탁했다.

어휘 a little 약간   cough 기침하다   soothe 진정시키다   throat 목(구멍)   medicine 약   on one's way home 집에 오는 길에   already 이미, 벌써   pick up ~을 사다

03 ②

① M Let's go out for a walk.

W Okay. Why don't you wear more comfortable shoes?

② M You seem to have trouble walking. What happened?

W My new shoes scraped the skin off my heels.

③ M Can you explain what I should do?

W Remove your shoes before stepping on the scale, please.

④ M I'm sorry that I stepped on your foot.

W That's all right.

⑤ M Are you looking for high heels or low heels?

W I'm looking for flat shoes.

① 남 산책하러 갑시다.

여 좋아요. 더 편한 신발을 신는 게 어때요?

② 남 걷기 힘들어 보여요. 무슨 문제가 있나요?

여 새 신발 때문에 발뒤꿈치가 까졌어요.

③ 남 제가 어떻게 해야 할지 설명해 주시겠어요?

여 신발을 벗고 체중계에 올라가 주세요.

④ 남 발을 밟아서 죄송합니다.

여 괜찮습니다.

⑤ 남 높은 굽을 찾으시나요, 낮은 굽을 찾으시나요?

여 전 평평한 신발을 찾고 있어요.

해설 발뒤꿈치를 아파하며 잘 걷지 못하는 여자에게 무슨 문제가 있는지 물어보는 내용의 대화가 적절하다.

어휘 comfortable 편안한   have trouble ~ing ~하는 데 어려움이 있다   scrape 까지다, 찰과상을 내다   skin 피부   heel 뒤꿈치   remove 벗다, 제거하다   step on ~을 밟다   scale 체중계   flat 평평한, 납작한

04 ⑤

(Telephone rings.)

W Hello, John. This is Sandy.

M Hi, Sandy. What's up?

W Today is Julie's birthday. Can you come to her party?

M I'm afraid I can't.

W Why not? Is it because of your sports club activity?

M No. I have to go to the airport. My dad's coming back from his business trip, and he's got lots of luggage. I need to help him.

W Oh, I see. You must be excited to see him again.

(전화벨이 울린다.)

여 여보세요, John. 나 Sandy야.

남 안녕, Sandy. 무슨 일이야?

여 오늘이 Julie 생일이야. 그녀의 파티에 가지 않을래?

남 난 못 갈 것 같아.

여 왜? 스포츠 동아리 활동 때문이니?

남 아니. 공항에 가야 해. 아버지께서 출장에서 돌아오시는데 짐이 많으시대. 내가 도와드려야 해.

여 오, 알았어. 아버지를 다시 만나서 신나겠구나.

[해설] 남자는 출장에서 돌아오시는 아버지를 마중 나갈 것이라고 했다.

[어휘] because of ~ 때문에   activity 활동   airport 공항 business trip 출장   luggage 짐, 수하물

05 ③

W Do you know there is a rock festival next month?

M You mean the International Rock Festival. When is it?

W It's on the first weekend of June. Do you want to go to it with me?

M Sure. Where will it be held?

W On Songdo Island in Incheon. The admission is 50,000 won.

M Well, it's not cheap, but I think it will be worth it.

W I think so, too. Oh, we need to bring a mat and parasol.

M Okay. I can do that.

여 다음 달에 록 페스티벌이 있는 거 알아?

남 International Rock Festival 말하는구나. 언제니?

여 6월 첫 번째 주말이야. 나와 함께 갈래?

남 물론이지. 어디서 열리니?

여 인천에 있는 송도에서. 입장료는 50,000원이야.

남 음, 싸진 않지만, 그만한 가치가 있을 거라고 생각해.

여 나도 그렇게 생각해. 아, 우리는 돗자리와 양산을 가져가야 해.

남 알았어. 그럴 수 있어.

[해설] 출연진이 누구인지는 언급되지 않았다.

[어휘] international 국제의   hold 열다, 개최하다   island 섬 admission 입장(료)   worth ~할 가치가 있는   mat 돗자리 parasol 양산

06 ④

W I'm so sorry that I am late.

M That's okay. I got your text message.

W I took a taxi, but it took longer than I expected.

M Was there a traffic jam?

W It was not that bad. The problem was that I wasn't

able to leave the house on time.

M Oh, was something wrong?

W My babysitter was late because she missed the bus.

M You must have been frustrated. Anyway, let's start the meeting now.

여 늦어서 죄송합니다.

남 괜찮습니다. 문자 메시지를 받았어요.

여 택시를 탔는데 예상보다 더 오래 걸렸어요.

남 교통 체증이 있었나요?

여 그렇게 나쁘진 않았어요. 제가 집에서 제시간에 출발할 수 없었다는 게 문제였죠.

남 아, 뭐가 잘못됐나요?

여 아이 돌봐 주시는 분께서 버스를 놓쳐서 늦게 오셨어요.

남 당혹스러우셨겠네요. 어쨌든, 이제 회의를 시작합시다.

[해설] 여자는 아이를 돌봐 주는 사람이 늦게 오는 바람에 집에서 제시간에 출발할 수 없어서 회의에 늦었다고 했다.

[어휘] take a taxi 택시를 타다   expect 기대하다   traffic jam 교통 체증   problem 문제   on time 제시간에   babysitter 아이 돌보미   miss 놓치다   frustrated 좌절감을 느끼는

07 ⑤

① M Do you have plans today?

W Yes. I'm going to see a movie with Paul.

② M Can you lend me your textbook?

W I'm afraid I can't because I don't have it right now.

③ M Is it okay if I close the window?

W Sure. Go ahead.

④ M Hello. What seems to be the problem?

W I'm suffering from a terrible headache.

⑤ M When do you usually get stressed out?

W When I'm stressed, I eat something sweet.

① 남 오늘 계획 있니?

여 응. Paul과 영화 보러 갈 거야.

② 남 네 교과서 좀 빌려줄래?

여 미안하지만 지금 내게 없어서 안 되겠어.

③ 남 창문을 좀 닫아도 될까?

여 당연하지. 그렇게 해.

④ 남 안녕하세요. 무슨 문제가 있으신가요?

여 끔찍한 두통에 시달리고 있어요.

⑤ 남 너는 보통 언제 스트레스를 받니?

여 나는 스트레스를 받을 때, 단것을 먹어.

[해설] ⑤ 언제 스트레스를 받는지 묻는 말에 스트레스 받을 때 단것을 먹는다고 답하는 것은 어색하다.

[어휘] lend 빌려주다   textbook 교과서   suffer from ~로 고통받다   terrible 끔찍한   headache 두통   get stressed out 스트레스를 받다

08 ③

W Good afternoon. Where are you going?

M I'm going to the grocery store. I need to buy some juice for Anna's party.

W Oh, I totally forgot about the party! I was supposed to bring a salad!

M What? How could you forget? Do you need my help?

W Yes. Can you buy me a bottle of Italian salad dressing at the store? I will go and make the salad.

M Sure, I can do that.

W Thanks.

여 안녕. 어디에 가는 중이니?

남 식료품점에 가고 있어. 나는 Anna의 파티에 가져갈 주스를 사야 해.

여 아, 그 파티에 대해 완전히 잊고 있었어! 나는 샐러드를 가져가기로 했는데!

남 뭐라고? 그것을 어떻게 잊을 수가 있니? 내 도움이 필요하니?

여 응. 가게에서 이태리 샐러드 드레싱 한 병을 사다 줄 수 있니? 나는 가서 샐러드를 만들게.

남 물론, 할 수 있지.

여 고마워.

해설 남자는 파티에 주스를, 여자는 샐러드를 가져가기로 했다.

어휘 grocery store 식료품점   totally 완전히   forget 잊다   be supposed to ~하기로 되어 있다   a bottle of ~ 한 병

---

09 ②

M Attention, passengers. Due to the heavy snowfall, Train 2322 to Whistler Village will be delayed. If you have loaded your luggage on the train, please remove all items and get off the train now. If the delay lasts more than 12 hours, we will offer you a free round-trip ticket to anywhere Via Rail travels in Canada. We will keep you informed of any updates about the new departure time. Thank you.

남 승객 여러분께 알려 드립니다. 폭설로 인하여, Whistler Village행 2322 열차가 지연될 것입니다. 짐을 열차에 실어 놓으신 승객 여러분은 모든 물품을 치워 주시고 지금 기차에서 하차해 주시기 바랍니다. 12시간 이상 지연된다면, 여러분께 캐나다에서 Via Rail이 운행하는 곳은 어디든지 갈 수 있는 무료 왕복표를 제공할 것입니다. 새로운 출발 시간에 대한 소식을 계속 알려 드리겠습니다. 감사합니다.

해설 폭설로 인해 열차 출발이 지연됨을 알리는 안내 방송이다.

어휘 passenger 승객   snowfall 강설(량)   delay 지연시키다; 지연   load 싣다   luggage 짐   remove 치우다, 내보내다   get off 내리다   offer 제공하다   round-trip 왕복 여행의   inform 알리다   update 업데이트하다   departure 출발

---

10 ④

W Welcome to Marine Wonder Aquarium. How can I help you?

M I'd like to buy admission tickets. How much are they?

W A ticket for adults is $20 and one for children is $10.

M Two adults and two children, please.

W Okay. Is either of your children under 36 months? Admission is free for them.

M Yes. One of them is 15 months old.

W All right. Then two adult tickets and one child ticket.

M Great. Here's the money.

여 Marine Wonder Aquarium에 오신 것을 환영합니다. 무엇을 도와드릴까요?

남 입장권을 사려고 합니다. 얼마인가요?

여 성인 입장권은 20달러이고, 어린이는 10달러입니다.

남 성인 두 장, 어린이 두 장 주세요.

여 알겠습니다. 36개월 미만 아이가 있나요? 그 아이들은 입장료가 무료입니다.

남 네. 한 명은 15개월이에요.

여 알겠습니다. 그럼 어른 두 장과 어린이 한 장이군요.

남 네. 돈은 여기 있습니다.

해설 어린이 한 명은 무료 입장이므로 성인 입장권 두 장(각 20달러)과 어린이 입장권 한 장(10달러) 가격을 합하여 총 50달러를 지불해야 한다.

어휘 admission ticket 입장권   adult 성인, 어른   under ~ 미만인   admission 입장, 입장료   free 무료인

---

11 ⑤

M Oh, please help me. My leg really hurts.

W What's wrong? Do you have a cramp in your leg?

M Yes. Maybe it's just that I've been sitting for several hours.

W Can you get up and walk up and down the aisle?

M But the seat belt sign is still on.

W You're right. We still have another two hours to go before landing.

M Oh, I can't stand the pain anymore.

W I'll ask the flight attendant for some help.

남 아, 도와주세요. 다리가 너무 아파요.

여 무슨 일이죠? 다리에 쥐가 났나요?

남 네. 몇 시간 동안 앉아만 있어서 그런가 봐요.

여 일어나셔서 통로를 왔다갔다 걸으실 수 있나요?

남 하지만 안전벨트 표시등이 아직 켜 있어요.

여 맞아요. 착륙하기까지 아직도 두 시간을 더 가야 해요.

남 아, 더 이상 고통을 못 참겠어요.

여 제가 승무원에게 도움을 요청해 볼게요.

해설 착륙하기까지 두 시간을 더 가야 하며 승무원에게 도움을 요청하겠다는 여자의 말을 통해 비행기 안에서 이루어지는 대화임을 알 수 있다.

어휘 have a cramp 쥐가 나다   up and down 이리저리 〔왔다갔다〕   aisle 통로   seat belt 안전벨트   landing 착륙   stand 견디다   pain 통증   not ~ anymore 더 이상 ~ 않다   flight attendant 비행기 승무원

12 ③

W Hello, students! The English Speech Contest will be held today in our school auditorium. Fifty students registered for the contest this year. The judges are three English teachers from our school including Mr. Johnson, the native English teacher. The winner will be announced on April 24, and this year's winner will receive a computer. The contest will start at 5 o'clock. Please don't miss it.

여 안녕하세요, 학생 여러분! 오늘 영어 말하기 대회가 우리 학교 강당에서 열립니다. 올해는 50명의 학생들이 대회에 참가 신청을 했습니다. 심사 위원은 원어민 영어 선생님이신 Johnson 선생님을 포함하여 우리 학교 영어 선생님 세 분입니다. 우승자는 4월 24일에 발표되며, 올해 우승자는 컴퓨터를 받게 됩니다. 대회는 5시에 시작합니다. 놓치지 마십시오.

해설 연설 주제는 언급되지 않았다.

어휘 auditorium 강당 register 신청하다, 등록하다 judge 심사 위원 include 포함하다 native 원어민의 winner 우승자 announce 알리다 receive 받다 miss 놓치다

13 ④

M Some famous old movies are playing in the theater again.
W Wow! I really want to see some of my favorite old movies again. Why don't we watch one together?
M Sounds good. When is good for you? I'm free this weekend.
W Well, I have an appointment on Saturday.
M Then there are only two movies that we can see.
W Yes. How about seeing the one that starts earlier?
M Okay, then I'll book the tickets.

남 몇몇 유명한 오래된 영화들이 극장에서 다시 상영 중이야.
여 우와! 난 내가 가장 좋아하는 오래된 영화들을 다시 보고 싶어. 하나 같이 보는 게 어때?
남 좋지. 넌 언제가 좋니? 난 이번 주말에는 한가해.
여 음, 난 토요일에는 약속이 있어.
남 그러면 우리가 볼 수 있는 영화가 두 개밖에 없네.
여 맞아. 더 일찍 시작하는 걸 보는 게 어때?
남 알았어, 그럼 내가 표를 예매할게.

해설 두 사람은 일요일에 상영하는 영화 중 일찍 시작하는 영화를 보기로 했다.

어휘 famous 유명한 theater 극장 free 한가한 appointment 약속 book 예약하다

14 ②

M This is a dish of Italian origin. Now it has become one of the most popular foods in the world. It is usually a round, flat wheat dough topped with tomatoes, cheese, olives and various other ingredients and baked in an oven. In formal restaurants it is eaten with a knife and fork, but in casual settings it is cut into slices to be eaten while held in the hand.

남 이것은 이탈리아에서 유래한 음식이다. 지금은 세계에서 가장 인기 있는 음식들 중 하나가 되었다. 이것은 보통 둥글고 평평한 밀가루 반죽으로 위에 토마토, 치즈, 올리브, 이외에도 다양한 재료들이 올려지고 오븐에서 구워진다. 격식 있는 식당에서는 나이프와 포크로 먹지만, 격식을 차리지 않는 곳에서는 조각으로 잘라 손으로 들고 먹는다.

해설 이탈리아에서 유래한 음식이며 둥글고 평평한 밀가루 반죽 위에 토핑을 올려 오븐에 구워 먹는 것은 피자이다.

어휘 dish 요리 origin 기원, 유래 round 둥근 flat 평평한 wheat 밀 dough 반죽 top 올리다 ingredient 재료 formal 격식의 casual 격식을 차리지 않는 setting 장소, 환경 cut into slices 조각으로 자르다

15 ④

W Jack, are you finished packing?
M I'm almost finished. Mom, did you buy something for grandmother?
W Yes. I bought a beautiful flower vase for her.
M A vase? Isn't it too fragile to take on the plane?
W Don't worry. I wrapped it up well. Hey, did you water the plants?
M Yes, I did. Mom, did you turn off the gas valve?
W Oh, I forgot to do that.
M Mom, you'd better call a taxi. I'll turn off the valve.

여 Jack, 짐을 다 쌌니?
남 거의 마쳤어요. 엄마, 할머니께 드릴 건 사셨어요?
여 응. 할머니를 위한 예쁜 꽃병을 샀단다.
남 꽃병이요? 그건 너무 부서지기 쉬워서 비행기로 가져갈 수 없지 않을까요?
여 걱정하지 마. 내가 잘 포장했어. 얘, 화분에 물 줬니?
남 네, 주었어요. 엄마, 가스 밸브는 잠그셨어요?
여 오, 그걸 잊어버렸네.
남 엄마, 엄마는 택시를 부르시는 게 좋겠어요. 제가 밸브를 잠글게요.

해설 남자는 엄마에게 택시를 부르라고 말하며 자신이 가스 밸브를 잠그겠다고 했다.

어휘 pack 짐을 싸다 vase 꽃병 fragile 깨지기 쉬운 wrap 포장하다 water 물을 주다 turn off ~을 잠그다, 끄다 had better ~하는 것이 좋겠다

16 ②

(Cellphone rings.)
W Chris, where are you now?
M I'm in front of the theater. I'm about to watch a movie with my friends.
W When will the movie be over?
M In about two hours.
W Then when you come home, can you drop by the dry cleaner's?

M To pick up some clothes?

W Yes. Our clothes are already dry cleaned. Please pick them up on your way home.

M Okay, leave it to me.

(휴대 전화가 울린다.)

여 Chris, 지금 어디니?

남 극장 앞에 있어요. 지금 막 친구들과 영화를 보려던 참이에요.

여 영화가 언제 끝나니?

남 약 2시간 후에요.

여 그러면 집에 올 때, 세탁소에 좀 들를 수 있니?

남 옷 찾으려요?

여 그래. 우리 옷들이 벌써 드라이클리닝이 다 되었대. 집에 오는 길에 그것 좀 찾아오렴.

남 네, 제게 맡기세요.

해설 여자가 남자에게 집에 오는 길에 세탁소에 들러 옷을 찾아오라고 하자 남자는 그러겠다고 했다.

어휘 be about to 막 ~하려던 참이다   be over 끝나다 drop by ~에 들르다   dry cleaner's 세탁소   pick up ~을 찾아오다   on one's way ~하는 도중에   leave it to ~에게 맡기다

17 ③

W Why do you have such a long face?

M My smartphone is not working.

W You bought the smartphone just two weeks ago, didn't you?

M Yes. It's only been two weeks, but it has already stopped working a few times.

W What's the problem?

M At first, it had a charging problem. And now it won't turn on.

W You must be very upset. Why don't you visit the customer service center?

M I will visit there right after school.

여 너 왜 그렇게 우울하니?

남 내 스마트폰이 작동이 안 돼.

여 너 스마트폰을 겨우 2주 전에 샀잖아, 안 그래?

남 맞아. 겨우 2주 됐는데, 벌써 여러 번 작동이 멈췄어.

여 뭐가 문제니?

남 처음에는 충전 문제가 있었어. 그리고 지금은 켜지지 않아.

여 너 정말 화나겠구나. 고객 서비스 센터에 가 보는 게 어때?

남 방과 후에 바로 그곳에 갈 거야.

해설 여자가 서비스 센터에 가 보라고 제안했으므로 방과 후에 그 곳에 갈 거라고 응답하는 것이 가장 적절하다.

① 내가 너한테 내 휴대 전화를 빌려줄 수 있어.

② 난 휴대용 배터리를 가지고 다녀야 해.

④ 원하신다면 그것을 새것으로 교환하실 수 있습니다.

⑤ 고객 서비스 센터로 연결해 주시기 바랍니다.

어휘 work 작동하다   a few times 여러 번   charge 충전하다 turn on 켜지다, 켜다   customer 고객   portable 휴대용의 lend 빌려주다   exchange 교환하다   connect 연결하다

18 ①

M Hey, I love your bag. It's really cool.

W Thanks. Actually, I made this bag myself.

M No kidding! Where did you get the idea?

W I watched a famous video clip. They showed how to make eco-bags.

M What an interesting idea! You know, there are various ways to save the earth.

W That's right. I think we ought to make every effort to protect the environment.

M Then what can we do to help the earth?

W We can go to school by bicycle.

남 야, 네 가방이 마음에 든다. 정말 멋진데.

여 고마워. 사실, 내가 이 가방을 직접 만들었어.

남 정말 대단해! 그런 아이디어가 어디에서 나왔니?

여 유명한 동영상을 하나 봤어. 거기에서 에코백 만드는 방법을 보여줬어.

남 정말 재미있는 아이디어네! 너도 알다시피, 지구를 구하는 방법이 다양하잖아.

여 맞아. 우리는 환경을 보호하기 위해 모든 노력을 해야 한다고 생각해.

남 그러면 우리가 지구를 돕기 위해 뭘 할 수 있을까?

여 우리는 자전거를 타고 학교에 갈 수 있어.

해설 지구를 돕기 위해 무엇을 할 수 있을지 물었으므로 환경 보호와 관련된 응답이 와야 한다.

② 난 그냥 오래된 청바지로 그걸 만들었어.

③ 너는 내가 이 문제 푸는 걸 도와줄 수 있어.

④ 난 너의 모든 노력이 보상받을 거라고 확신해.

⑤ 우리는 세계의 환경 오염을 막을 수 없어.

어휘 various 다양한   save 구하다   ought to ~해야 한다 make an effort 노력하다   protect 보호하다   environment 환경   problem 문제   reward 보상하다   global 세계의 pollution 오염

19 ④

M How can I help you?

W Hi. I want to ask you something.

M Yes, what is it?

W Last night, when I came back home from work, I found one of my windows was broken.

M Oh, and everything was fine when you left in the morning?

W Yes, I didn't notice anything wrong in the morning. Can you find out who did this?

M Okay, I'll check the security camera first.

남 무엇을 도와드릴까요?

여 안녕하세요. 여쭤 볼 게 있어서요.

남 네, 그게 뭔가요?

여 어젯밤에 제가 퇴근해서 집으로 돌아왔을 때, 저희 창문 중 하나가 깨진 것을 발견했어요.

남 아, 그런데 아침에 출발하실 때는 모든 것이 괜찮았나요?

여 네, 저는 아침에는 잘못된 것을 발견하지 못했어요. 누가 그랬는지 좀 알아봐 주실 수 있나요?

남 네. 먼저 방범 카메라를 확인해 볼게요.

[해설] 누가 창문을 깼는지 알아봐 달라고 했으므로 그것을 확인할 수 있는 방법과 관련된 응답이 와야 한다.
① 분실물 보관소를 확인해 볼게요.
② 몇 시에 만나기를 원하시나요?
③ 여기에 오늘 기차 시간표가 있습니다.
⑤ 택시를 타는 것이 어떠신가요? 그것이 더 편리해요.

[어휘] broken 깨진   notice 알아차리다   wrong 잘못된   find out 알아내다   lost and found 분실물 보관소   security camera 방범(감시) 카메라   convenient 편리한

20 ④

W   Sally and Sandra are sisters. A few days ago, Sally <u>had</u> <u>an</u> <u>argument</u> <u>with</u> her best friend. Sally got so angry and said things that she shouldn't have. Sally feels so bad about this situation, and she's <u>having</u> <u>trouble</u> <u>sleeping</u> at night. Sandra thinks that <u>the</u> <u>longer</u> <u>she</u> <u>waits</u>, the worse the situation will get. So Sandra wants to advise Sally to apologize <u>as</u> <u>soon</u> <u>as</u> <u>possible</u>. In this situation, what would Sandra most likely say to Sally?

Sandra   Sally, why don't you text her and say you're sorry?

여   Sally와 Sandra는 자매이다. 며칠 전에, Sally는 가장 친한 친구와 다퉜다. Sally는 너무 화가 나서 하지 말아야 할 말을 해 버렸다. Sally는 이 상황이 너무 신경 쓰여서 밤에 잠을 잘 못 잔다. Sandra는 그녀가 오래 기다릴수록 상황이 더 나빠질 거라고 생각한다. 그래서 Sandra는 Sally에게 가능한 한 빨리 사과하라고 조언하고 싶어 한다. 이런 상황에서, Sandra는 Sally에게 뭐라고 말할 것 같은가?

Sandra   Sally, 그녀에게 문자 메시지를 보내서 미안하다고 말하는 게 어떠니?

[해설] Sally가 친구와 다툰 것에 대해 신경 쓰는 것을 보고 가능한 한 빨리 친구에게 사과하라고 조언하려는 상황이다.
① 내가 너라면, 그렇게 말하지 않을 거야.
② 네가 사과할 필요 없어.
③ 우리 그만 싸우고 다시 친구가 되자.
⑤ 네가 진심으로 사과하면 내가 널 용서해 줄게.

[어휘] have an argument 말다툼을 하다   situation 상황   have trouble ~ing ~하는 데 어려움을 겪다   advise 조언하다   apologize 사과하다   as soon as possible 가능한 한 빨리   honest 정직한   apology 사과   forgive 용서하다

Review Test
pp.132~133

Word Check [11회]

01 기회	02 빌리다
03 구역	04 옳은
05 문화	06 많은
07 졸업하다	08 확정하다
09 구식의, 유행이 지난	10 운동하다
11 최대한으로	12 살펴보다
13 embassy	14 confident
15 weekday	16 various
17 refrigerator	18 exhibition
19 disappear	20 survey
21 shake	22 tradition
23 lose weight	24 all over the world

Expression Check

25 Get off	26 aren't good for
27 seven and under	28 come back from
29 turning fifty	30 look after

Word Check [12회]

01 통증	02 당황한
03 깨진	04 진정시키다
05 착륙	06 교과서
07 밀	08 용서하다
09 오염	10 입장권
11 노력하다	12 테가 없는
13 reward	14 charge
15 load	16 fragile
17 portable	18 international
19 headache	20 origin
21 delay	22 seat belt
23 so far	24 have a cramp

Expression Check

25 about to	26 getting worse
27 up and down	28 stepped on
29 suffering from	30 had an argument

01 ②	02 ⑤	03 ④	04 ⑤	05 ④
06 ③	07 ③	08 ⑤	09 ④	10 ①
11 ⑤	12 ④	13 ③	14 ⑤	15 ②
16 ④	17 ⑤	18 ①	19 ⑤	20 ⑤

01 ②

W Dad, what are you doing?

M I'm packing. I'm going to go camping tomorrow with your uncle.

W That's great! But did you check the weather for tomorrow? Look at the sky. I think it's going to rain!

M I already checked the weather forecast. It says it's going to rain tonight, but it's going to be sunny tomorrow.

W That sounds great! Can I go with you?

M Sure. But you should go to sleep early tonight. We will leave at 6 a.m. tomorrow.

W Okay. Thanks, Dad.

여 아빠, 뭐하세요?

남 짐을 싸고 있단다. 나는 내일 네 삼촌과 캠핑하러 갈 거야.

여 멋져요! 하지만 내일 날씨를 확인하셨어요? 하늘 좀 보세요. 비가 올 것 같아요!

남 벌써 일기 예보를 확인했단다. 오늘 밤에는 비가 오지만 내일은 맑을 거라고 했어.

여 잘됐네요! 저도 같이 가도 될까요?

남 물론이지. 하지만 오늘밤에 일찍 자야 해. 우리는 내일 아침 6시에 출발할 거야.

여 네. 감사합니다, 아빠.

[해설] 오늘 밤에는 비가 오지만 내일은 맑을 것이라고 했다.

[어휘] pack 짐을 싸다 go camping 캠핑하러 가다 check 확인하다 weather 날씨 forecast 예보, 예측 leave 출발하다

02 ⑤

(Cellphone rings.)

M Kate, where are you? Are you on your way home?

W I'm still at the office. I had a meeting, and it has just ended now.

M Then you will be late for Dad's birthday party.

W Yeah, I think so. Can you tell Dad that I'm on my way?

M Sure. I'll tell him.

W I think it will take about 40 minutes to get home. I'll hurry.

(휴대 전화가 울린다.)

남 Kate, 어디야? 집에 오고 있는 중이야?

여 아직 사무실이야. 회의가 있었는데 지금 막 끝났어.

남 그러면 아버지 생신 파티에 늦겠네.

여 응, 그럴 것 같아. 아버지께 내가 가는 중이라고 말씀드려 줄래?

남 그래. 말씀드릴게.

여 집에 도착하는 데 40분 정도 걸릴 것 같아. 서두를게.

[해설] 여자는 아버지의 생신 파티에 늦게 도착하게 되어 지금 가고 있다는 것을 아버지께 말씀드려 달라고 부탁했다.

[어휘] on one's way home 집에 오는 길에 office 사무실 meeting 회의 end 끝나다 hurry 서두르다

03 ④

W Excuse me. Can you help us?

M Sure. What can I do for you?

W We want to take the train to Busan. But I'm not sure we're on the right platform.

M Let me see your ticket. (Pause) Oh, you should go to platform 4.

W Platform 4? How can we get there quickly?

M It's easy. Just go up those stairs and turn left.

W Thank you so much.

여 실례합니다. 저희 좀 도와주시겠어요?

남 물론이죠. 무엇을 도와드릴까요?

여 부산행 기차를 타려고 하는데요. 그런데 우리가 맞는 플랫폼에 있는지 잘 모르겠어요.

남 표 좀 보여주세요. (잠시 후) 아, 4번 플랫폼으로 가셔야 합니다.

여 4번 플랫폼이요? 어떻게 그곳에 빨리 갈 수 있나요?

남 쉬워요. 저 계단으로 올라가셔서 왼쪽으로 가세요.

여 정말 감사합니다.

[해설] 부산행 기차를 타는 플랫폼이 어디인지 묻고 답하고 있으므로 대화가 이루어지는 장소는 기차역이다.

[어휘] platform 플랫폼, 승강장 quickly 빠르게 stairs 계단 turn left 왼쪽으로 돌다

04 ⑤

① M Watch out! There is wet paint.
  W Oh, thank you.
② M Can you help me carry these boxes?
  W Sure. Let's lift them together.
③ M What's wrong? You look sick.
  W I have a fever and runny nose.
④ M How can I help you?
  W Can I reserve a table for two for dinner tonight?
⑤ M What seems to be the problem?
  W I think Roger has a stomachache. It vomited three times yesterday.

① 남 조심하세요! 젖은 페인트가 있어요.
  여 아, 감사합니다.
② 남 이 상자들 나르는 것 좀 도와주시겠어요?
  여 네. 그것들을 함께 들어요.
③ 남 무슨 일이야? 너 아파 보여.

여 열이 나고 콧물이 흘러.
④ 남 무엇을 도와드릴까요?
　여 오늘밤 저녁 식사를 위해 두 명 자리를 예약할 수 있나요?
⑤ 남 무엇이 문제인 것 같나요?
　여 Roger가 배탈이 난 것 같아요. 어제 세 번 토했어요.

해설 동물 병원에서 강아지가 진료를 받는 상황이다.

어휘 watch out 조심하다　wet 젖은　fever 열　runny nose 콧물이 흐르는　reserve 예약하다　problem 문제　stomachache 복통　vomit 토하다

05 ④

W May I help you?
M Yes, please. Can I get a refund for this T-shirt?
W Let me see. <u>Do you have the receipt</u>?
M Sure. Here it is.
W I'm sorry, but you bought this T-shirt over a month ago. In that case, we can't <u>give you a refund</u>.
M Why not? I didn't wear it and <u>the price tag is still on it</u>.
W I'm so sorry. But you must bring the item back within 15 days to get a refund. It's <u>our store policy</u>, and we inform all of our customers about it.
M Oh, I must have forgotten it.

여 도와드릴까요?
남 네. 이 티셔츠를 환불받을 수 있을까요?
여 제가 한번 볼게요. 영수증 있으신가요?
남 물론이죠. 여기 있어요.
여 죄송하지만, 이 티셔츠를 사신 지 한 달이 넘었네요. 그런 경우에는 환불해 드릴 수 없습니다.
남 왜 안 되죠? 저는 이것을 입지 않았고 아직 가격표도 있어요.
여 정말 죄송합니다. 하지만 환불을 받으시려면 15일 이내에 물건을 가져오셔야 합니다. 그것이 저희 가게의 방침이고, 저희는 모든 고객님께 그것에 대해 알려 드립니다.
남 아, 제가 그것을 잊었나 보네요.

해설 환불을 받으려면 15일 이내에 물건을 가져와야 하는데 한 달이 넘어서 환불이 안 된다고 했다.

어휘 refund 환불　receipt 영수증　in that case 그런 경우에　price tag 가격표　item 물건　policy 방침, 정책　inform 알리다　customer 고객, 손님

06 ③

(Telephone rings.)
W For a Better World Volunteer Center. How may I help you?
M Hello. I'd like to <u>do volunteer work</u>.
W Great. Can you tell me your name and phone number?
M I'm Minho Park, and my phone number is 010-1234-5678.
W Thank you. What kind of volunteer work <u>are you interested in</u>?
M I'd like to <u>work with children</u>.

W Okay. Can you volunteer this Friday afternoon at Little Angel Orphanage?
M Yes. <u>That would be great</u>.

(전화벨이 울린다.)
여 Better World Volunteer Center입니다. 무엇을 도와드릴까요?
남 여보세요. 저는 자원봉사를 하고 싶습니다.
여 좋습니다. 이름과 전화번호를 말씀해 주시겠어요?
남 저는 박민호이고, 전화번호는 010-1234-5678입니다.
여 감사합니다. 어떤 종류의 자원봉사에 관심 있으신가요?
남 저는 아이들과 함께 하는 일을 하고 싶습니다.
여 알겠습니다. 이번 주 금요일 오후에 Little Angel Orphanage에서 자원봉사하실 수 있으세요?
남 네. 그거 좋겠네요.

해설 남자는 아이들과 함께 하는 자원봉사를 하고 싶다고 했다.

어휘 volunteer 자원봉사자; 자원봉사하다　be interested in ~에 관심이 있다　orphanage 고아원

07 ③

① W Is it okay if I <u>use your laptop</u>?
　M Okay. How long do you need it for?
② W Do you think I <u>should apologize first</u>?
　M Yes, I think you should.
③ W Can you do me a favor?
　M Sure, I really <u>needed your help</u>.
④ W Long time, no see. How have you been?
　M Good. How about you?
⑤ W <u>What time shall we meet</u>?
　M How about at 7 o'clock?

① 여 네 노트북 컴퓨터를 사용해도 되니?
　남 응. 얼마나 오래 필요하니?
② 여 넌 내가 먼저 사과해야 한다고 생각하니?
　남 응. 나는 그래야 한다고 생각해.
③ 여 나 좀 도와줄래?
　남 물론, 네 도움이 정말 필요했어.
④ 여 오랜만이야. 어떻게 지냈니?
　남 잘 지냈어. 너는?
⑤ 여 몇 시에 만날까?
　남 7시 어때?

해설 ③ 도와 달라는 말에 도움이 필요했다고 답하는 것은 어색하다.

어휘 laptop 노트북 컴퓨터　apologize 사과하다　first 먼저　Long time, no see. 오랜만이다.

08 ⑤

M I want to <u>attach a file to an email</u>, but I don't know how to do it. Can you help me?
W Sure. That's easy. Did you <u>log in to your account</u>?
M Yes. And I've finished the email.
W Just click the "attach files" button and then double-click on the file you <u>want to attach</u>.

M (Click sound) Oh, I did it!

W Yes. Then click the "send" button, and that's it.

M Thank you so much.

남 이메일에 파일을 첨부하고 싶은데 어떻게 하는 건지 모르겠어. 도와줄 수 있니?

여 물론이야. 그것은 쉬워. 네 계정에 로그인했니?

남 응. 그리고 이메일을 다 썼어.

여 '파일 첨부' 버튼을 클릭하고, 그러고 나서 네가 첨부하고 싶은 파일을 더블 클릭해.

남 (클릭 소리) 오, 했어!

여 좋아. 그러고 나서 '보내기' 버튼을 클릭해. 그러면 돼.

남 정말 고마워.

[해설] 남자는 이메일에 파일을 첨부하는 방법을 잘 모르겠다고 말하며 여자에게 도와 달라고 부탁했다.

[어휘] attach 첨부하다   log in 로그인하다   account 계정
finish 완성하다   button 버튼, 단추   send 보내다

09 ④

M Welcome to Good Health Fitness Center. Our center offers a variety of exercise programs. On the first floor, there is a weight room so you can strengthen your muscles with trainers. On the second floor, you can take yoga classes every hour. On the ground floor, you can enjoy our swimming pool. If you want to take swimming lessons, please talk to the manager. Thank you so much for choosing our center.

남 Good Health Fitness Center에 오신 것을 환영합니다. 저희 센터는 다양한 운동 프로그램을 제공합니다. 1층에서는, 체력 단련실이 있어서 트레이너와 함께 근육을 강화하실 수 있습니다. 2층에서는, 매시간 요가 수업을 받으실 수 있습니다. 지하에서는, 수영장을 즐기실 수 있습니다. 수영 수업을 받고 싶으시면, 매니저에게 이야기해 주세요. 저희 센터를 선택해 주셔서 정말 감사합니다.

[해설] 피트니스 센터에서 제공하는 다양한 운동 프로그램을 안내하는 방송이다.

[어휘] offer 제공하다   a variety of 다양한   weight room
체력 단련실   strengthen 강화하다   muscle 근육   trainer
트레이너, 훈련시키는 사람   ground floor 지하   choose
선택하다

10 ①

M I'd like to buy some flowers for my wife.

W What kind of flowers do you have in mind?

M I don't know. How much are the red roses?

W They are $2 each. How about the pink tulips? They go well with red roses.

M I like them. How much are they?

W They are $3 each, but if you buy five, you can get them for $12.

M Then I will take five red roses and five pink tulips.

Can you wrap them?

W Sure. Wait a minute.

남 아내를 위해 꽃을 좀 사고 싶어요.

여 어떤 종류의 꽃을 생각하고 계신가요?

남 잘 모르겠어요. 빨간색 장미는 얼마인가요?

여 한 송이에 2달러입니다. 분홍색 튤립은 어떠세요? 그것은 빨간색 장미와 잘 어울려요.

남 마음에 드네요. 그것은 얼마인가요?

여 한 송이에 3달러인데, 다섯 송이를 사시면 12달러에 사실 수 있습니다.

남 그러면 빨간색 장미 다섯 송이와 분홍색 튤립 다섯 송이를 주세요. 포장해 주실 수 있나요?

여 네. 잠시만 기다리세요.

[해설] 2달러짜리 장미 다섯 송이와, 다섯 송이에 12달러인 튤립 다섯 송이를 산다고 했으므로 남자가 지불할 금액은 22달러이다.

[어휘] have in mind ~을 염두에 두다(생각하다)   go well with
~와 잘 어울리다   wrap 포장하다

11 ⑤

(Telephone rings.)

M AP Service Center. How can I help you?

W Hello. I bought one of your company's printers, but I think something's wrong with it.

M Oh, what's the problem?

W I connected the printer to my computer, but nothing happened.

M Oh, I see. Did you install the printer driver program on your computer?

W No. How can I install the program?

M Open our company's website and download the program and install it.

W Oh, I see. I'll do that now.

(전화벨이 울린다.)

남 AP Service Center입니다. 무엇을 도와드릴까요?

여 안녕하세요. 저는 귀사에서 프린터를 샀는데, 무언가 잘못된 것 같아요.

남 아, 무슨 문제인가요?

여 프린터를 컴퓨터에 연결했는데, 아무 반응이 없었어요.

남 아, 알겠습니다. 컴퓨터에 프린터 드라이버 프로그램을 설치하셨나요?

여 아니요. 어떻게 프로그램을 설치할 수 있나요?

남 저희 회사의 홈페이지를 열고 프로그램을 다운로드하신 후 설치하세요.

여 오, 알겠습니다. 지금 할게요.

[해설] 남자가 프린터 드라이버 프로그램을 설치하라고 안내하자 여자는 지금 하겠다고 했다.

[어휘] company 회사   wrong 잘못된   connect 연결하다
happen 일어나다   install 설치하다   download 다운로드하다

12 ④

W Hello. This is Suzie. Do you remember that we

made plans to throw a surprise party for Irene this Saturday? But I heard that Irene won't be back in town until Sunday as she is spending three days with her family in Busan. So we've changed the plans and will throw the party on Monday at her house. Call me back when you get this message. Bye.

여 안녕, 나 Suzie야. 너 이번 주 토요일에 Irene을 위한 깜짝 파티를 열기로 계획한 것을 기억하고 있지? 하지만 나는 Irene이 부산에서 가족과 3일을 보내기 때문에 일요일까지 돌아오지 않을 거라고 들었어. 그래서 우리는 계획을 바꿔서 월요일에 그녀의 집에서 파티를 열기로 했어. 이 메시지 받으면 전화해 줘. 안녕.

해설 친구를 위한 깜짝파티를 토요일에서 월요일로 변경했다는 내용의 메시지이다.

어휘 make a plan 계획하다　throw a party 파티를 열다 spend (시간을) 보내다　change 바꾸다, 변경하다

13 ③

W What are you doing?
M I'm writing an essay for tomorrow's English writing class.
W Oh, what's it about?
M It's about my future job.
W I know you've always wanted to help others.
M Right. I want to help people in need and do volunteer work in foreign countries.
W Then are you going to be a volunteer?
M No, I'm planning to be a doctor and give medical help to people in need.

여 너 뭐 하고 있니?
남 내일 영어작문 수업을 위한 에세이를 쓰고 있어.
여 아, 무엇에 관한 건데?
남 나의 미래 직업에 관한 거야.
여 나는 네가 항상 다른 사람들을 돕고 싶어 했다는 걸 알아.
남 맞아. 나는 어려운 사람들을 도우면서 외국에서 자원봉사를 하고 싶어.
여 그러면 너는 자원봉사자가 될 거니?
남 아니, 나는 의사가 되어서 어려운 사람들에게 의학적인 도움을 줄 계획이야.

해설 남자는 의사가 되어 어려운 사람들을 돕고 외국에서 자원봉사를 하고 싶다고 했다.

어휘 essay (짧은 논문식) 과제물　in need 어려움에 처한, 궁핍한　volunteer 자원봉사자　foreign 외국의　medical 의학의

14 ⑤

M Let me introduce our latest model HC120 to you. The screen is a good size for watching movies. And the battery lasts longer than ever. When you make calls with this new model, it will sound as if the person is right next to you! It has an amazing camera, so you can take pictures you'll want to keep forever. You can get a 10% discount if you buy one this week.

남 저희 최신 모델인 HC120을 여러분께 소개합니다. 화면은 영화를 보기에 충분한 사이즈입니다. 그리고 배터리는 전보다 더 오래 갑니다. 당신은 이 새 모델로 통화할 때, 마치 그 사람이 당신 바로 옆에 있는 것처럼 들릴 것입니다! 그것은 놀라운 카메라를 가지고 있어서, 영원히 간직하고 싶은 사진들을 찍을 수 있습니다. 이번 주에 사시면 10퍼센트 할인을 받으실 수 있습니다.

해설 영화를 보거나 통화를 하고 사진을 찍을 수 있는 것은 스마트폰이다.

어휘 introduce 소개하다　latest 최신의　screen 화면 battery 배터리　last 지속하다　as if 마치 ~처럼　take a picture 사진을 찍다　forever 영원히　discount 할인

15 ②

W Hi, John. What are you doing?
M Hey, Jessy. I'm looking at the school website. Do you have any plans for this summer vacation?
W Actually, I want to learn Chinese this summer vacation.
M Oh, there is a Chinese class offered through the school vacation program! And there are several other classes.
W Oh, really? Which classes are you going to take?
M I will take the robot class.
W That sounds interesting! Do you think I can take both classes?
M Perhaps. Let's check the schedule.

여 안녕, John. 뭐 하고 있니?
남 안녕, Jessy. 난 학교 홈페이지를 보고 있어. 너 이번 여름 방학에 무슨 계획 있니?
여 사실, 나는 이번 여름 방학에 중국어를 배우고 싶어.
남 오, 학교 방학 프로그램에서 제공하는 중국어 수업이 있네! 그리고 몇 가지 다른 수업들도 있어.
여 아, 그래? 너는 어떤 수업을 들을 거니?
남 나는 로봇 수업을 들을 거야.
여 그거 재미있겠다! 내가 두 수업을 다 들을 수 있을 것 같니?
남 아마도. 시간표를 확인해 보자.

해설 남자는 방학 동안 로봇 수업을 들을 것이라고 했다.

어휘 plan 계획　vacation 방학　actually 사실은　offer 제공하다　several 몇 개의　both 둘 다　schedule 시간표, 스케줄

16 ④

W What were you doing?
M I was listening to Jenny's podcast. It's about new books.
W Sounds interesting. Do you usually listen to it?
M Yes. She uploads a new podcast every Monday.
W What do you like about the podcast?

M I can find out about new books. Also, I really <u>like</u> <u>the special segments</u>.

W The special segments? What are they about?

M A guest speaker reads a book, and <u>that person is usually a celebrity</u>!

W That's interesting! I'll have to download the podcasts.

여 너 뭐 하고 있었니?

남 나는 Jenny의 팟캐스트를 듣고 있었어. 이건 새로운 책에 관한 거야.

여 재미있겠다. 너는 그걸 자주 듣니?

남 응. 매주 월요일마다 새 팟캐스트를 업로드해 줘.

여 너는 그 팟캐스트의 어떤 점이 좋니?

남 새로 나온 책들에 대해 알 수 있어. 또한, 나는 특별 부분을 정말 좋아해.

여 특별 부분? 그건 뭐에 관한 거야?

남 게스트가 책을 읽어 주는데, 그 사람은 대개 유명인이야!

여 흥미로운걸! 나도 그 팟캐스트를 다운로드해야겠어.

[해설] 팟캐스트를 업로드하는 시각은 언급되지 않았다.

[어휘] podcast 팟캐스트(인터넷망을 통해 다양한 콘텐츠를 제공하는 서비스) upload 업로드하다 special 특별한 segment 부분 guest 게스트, 특별 출연자 celebrity 유명인사

17 ⑤

M Hi. <u>I'd like to check in</u>.

W Okay. Can you tell me your name, please?

M My name is Dan Brown.

W Thank you. You're <u>staying</u> <u>for</u> <u>two</u> <u>nights</u> in a deluxe room with a king bed.

M That's correct.

W Here is your key. <u>Do you have any questions</u>?

M Where can I have breakfast?

W <u>In the Garden Restaurant. It's next to the lobby.</u>

남 안녕하세요. 체크인하고 싶습니다.

여 네. 이름을 말씀해 주시겠어요?

남 제 이름은 Dan Brown입니다.

여 감사합니다. 손님은 킹 사이즈 침대가 있는 디럭스 룸에서 이틀 밤을 머무실 예정이시군요.

남 맞습니다.

여 여기 열쇠가 있습니다. 궁금한 점이 있으신가요?

남 아침 식사는 어디에서 할 수 있죠?

여 Garden Restaurant에서요. 그것은 로비 옆에 있습니다.

[해설] 남자가 아침 식사를 어디서 할 수 있는지 물었으므로 식당의 위치를 알려 주는 응답이 와야 한다.

① 손님의 방은 전망이 아주 좋습니다.

② 저희 호텔에 머물러 주셔서 감사합니다.

③ 손님은 아침 식사와 저녁 식사를 하실 수 있습니다.

④ 화장실은 복도 끝에 있습니다.

[어휘] check in 체크인하다 stay 머무르다 correct 옳은 question 질문 view 전망 restroom 화장실 hall 복도 lobby 로비

18 ①

M Mom, <u>I'm leaving for school</u> in a minute.

W This early? What about your breakfast? I'm making egg sandwiches.

M I have no time. I have to <u>discuss our science project</u> with my group members before class.

W They're almost ready. It wouldn't take long to have one.

M Yeah, but <u>I'm in a hurry</u>. A glass of milk will be enough.

W Then take the sandwiches to school.

M Okay. I can <u>share them with my friends</u>.

W Good idea. Just give me a minute to pack them.

M Okay. <u>I'll wait until you're done.</u>

남 엄마, 저 곧 학교에 가요.

여 이렇게 일찍? 아침은 어떻게 하고? 달걀 샌드위치를 만들고 있는데.

남 시간이 없어요. 수업 전에 조원들과 과학 프로젝트에 대해 토론해야 해요.

여 거의 다 준비됐어. 먹는 데 오래 안 걸릴 거야.

남 네, 하지만 서둘러야 해요. 우유 한 잔이면 충분해요.

여 그럼 학교에 샌드위치를 가져가렴.

남 알겠어요. 친구들과 나눠 먹을게요.

여 좋은 생각이야. 그것들을 싸 줄 테니 잠시만 기다려.

남 네. 끝내실 때까지 기다릴게요.

[해설] 여자가 샌드위치를 싸 주겠다고 했으므로 준비될 때까지 기다리겠다는 응답이 가장 적절하다.

② 네. 저는 햄샌드위치를 가장 좋아해요.

③ 물론이에요. 저는 10분 후에 그것들을 끝낼 수 있어요.

④ 아니에요. 저는 오늘 학교에 일찍 갈 필요가 없어요.

⑤ 죄송해요. 저는 아침에 우유 마시는 걸 좋아하지 않아요.

[어휘] leave for ~을 향해 떠나다 discuss 토론하다 class 수업 ready 준비된 in a hurry 서둘러, 급히 share 나누다, 공유하다 pack 싸다 wait 기다리다

19 ⑤

W Hi, David. What are you looking at?

M Oh, sorry. <u>I didn't notice you</u>. I'm looking at a brochure about Thailand.

W Are you planning to go on a vacation? I'm so jealous of you!

M I'm just thinking about taking a break for a while. I <u>feel so tired of working</u> these days.

W I think you need to be refreshed. <u>Lying on the beach</u> in the sunshine would be good for you.

M Do you know any good places to rest <u>without getting disturbed</u>?

W There are lots of quiet and beautiful beaches in Phuket.

여 안녕, David. 무엇을 보고 있니?

남 아, 미안. 네가 온 줄 몰랐어. 나는 태국에 관한 안내 책자를 보고 있어.

여 휴가 갈 계획이니? 네가 정말 부럽구나!

남 나는 잠시 휴식을 취할 생각이야. 나는 요즘 일하는 데 너무 피곤함을 느껴.

여 나는 네가 원기를 회복할 필요가 있다고 생각해. 햇볕을 받으며 해변에 누워 있는 게 너에게 좋을 거야.

남 방해 받지 않고 휴식을 취할 수 있는 좋은 장소를 아니?

여 푸껫에 조용하고 아름다운 해변들이 많이 있어.

해설 남자가 휴식을 취하기에 좋은 장소를 아는지 물었으므로 그와 관련된 정보를 주는 응답이 적절하다.
① 너는 그녀를 깨우면 안 돼.
② 나는 덥고 습한 날씨를 좋아하지 않아.
③ 넌 일하기 위해 노트북을 가져가야 해.
④ 하루 종일 일을 하는 것은 네 건강에 해로워.

어휘 notice 알아차리다 brochure (안내) 책자 jealous 질투하는 refresh 원기를 회복시키다, 생기를 되찾게 하다 rest 쉬다 disturb 방해하다 humid 습한 be bad for ~에 해롭다 beach 해변

20 ⑤

W Jessica is at the theater to watch a musical. When she gets inside the theater, most people are already in their seats. She goes to her seat, but finds that it's already taken by a man. She checks her seat number again and confirms that she is not wrong. The musical is about to start. In this situation, what would Jessica most likely say to the man?

Jessica Sorry, but I think you're sitting in my seat.

여 Jessica는 뮤지컬을 보러 극장에 왔다. 그녀가 극장 안에 들어갔을 때, 대부분의 사람들은 이미 착석해 있었다. 그녀는 자신의 자리로 갔지만, 이미 어떤 남자가 앉아 있는 것을 알게 된다. 그녀는 좌석 번호를 다시 확인하고 자신이 틀리지 않았음을 확인한다. 뮤지컬이 막 시작하려고 한다. 이 상황에서, Jessica는 그 남자에게 무엇이라고 말할 것 같은가?

Jessica 죄송하지만, 제 자리에 앉아 계신 것 같아요.

해설 뮤지컬이 막 시작하려고 하는데 자신의 자리에 다른 사람이 잘못 앉아 있는 상황이다.
① 우리가 전에 만난 적이 없나요?
② 당신도 뮤지컬을 좋아하세요?
③ 신분증 좀 볼 수 있을까요?
④ 실례합니다. 당신 옆에 앉아도 될까요?

어휘 theater 극장 inside ~ 안에 seat 좌석 confirm 확인하다, 확증하다 wrong 틀린 ID card(= identity card) 신분증

01 ③	02 ①	03 ④	04 ③	05 ④
06 ⑤	07 ③	08 ⑤	09 ②	10 ④
11 ③	12 ⑤	13 ①	14 ②	15 ⑤
16 ④	17 ④	18 ⑤	19 ③	20 ④

01 ③

W Jake, you need a new bag before the semester begins next month?

M Yes, I do. My bag is quite old.

W There are many kinds of bags here. How about a striped bag or a check bag?

M I don't want any pattern. And I want to buy one with a shoulder strap.

W Then how about that bag with pockets on the sides?

M Hmm... it looks good, but I don't like the round bag.

W Oh, I found one. Look at the sqaure bag with a pocket on the front.

M It's perfect. Let's get it.

여 Jake, 다음 달에 학기가 시작되기 전에 새 가방이 필요하니?

남 네, 맞아요. 제 가방은 너무 오래됐어요.

여 여기 많은 종류의 가방들이 있구나. 줄무늬 가방이나 체크무늬 가방은 어떠니?

남 전 무늬를 좋아하지 않아요. 그리고 전 어깨끈이 있는 가방을 사고 싶어요.

여 그럼 양 옆에 주머니가 있는 저 가방은 어떠니?

남 음… 좋아 보이지만, 저는 둥근 가방은 싫어요.

여 아, 찾았다. 앞에 주머니가 있는 사각형 모양 가방 좀 봐.

남 완벽해요. 그걸로 사요.

해설 남자는 무늬가 없고 어깨끈이 달려 있으며 앞에 주머니가 있는 사각형 모양의 가방을 구입하기로 했다.

어휘 semester 학기 striped 줄무늬의 check 체크무늬의 pattern 무늬 strap 끈 side 옆 square 사각형의 front 앞 perfect 완벽한

02 ①

(Telephone rings.)

M Hello, Janet. This is Brian.

W Oh, hi. What's up?

M Are you busy tomorrow afternoon? I really need your advice on something.

W Hmm... how about meeting around 4:00? I have a doctor's appointment at 2:00, so we can meet after that.

M I have a class at 4 o'clock. Are you busy at 5:30?

W I have a badminton lesson at 5. Then how about having lunch together?

M That sounds good. Then let's meet at Joe's Café at

noon.

W Great. See you tomorrow.

(전화벨이 울린다.)

남 여보세요, Janet. 나 Brian이야.

여 오, 안녕. 무슨 일이야?

남 내일 오후에 바쁘니? 무언가에 대해 네 조언이 정말 필요해.

여 음… 4시쯤에 만나는 게 어때? 2시에 병원 진료 예약이 있어서, 그 후에 만날 수 있어.

남 나는 4시에 수업이 있어. 5시 30분에는 바쁘니?

여 나는 5시에 배드민턴 수업이 있어. 그러면 같이 점심을 먹는 게 어때?

남 좋아. 그러면 Joe's Café에서 정오에 만나자.

여 좋아. 내일 보자.

해설 두 사람은 내일 정오에 Joe's Café에서 만나서 함께 점심을 먹기로 했다.

어휘 advice 조언, 충고 busy 바쁜 appointment 약속, 예약 together 함께

03 ④

① W Where can I find the dairy products?
　 M They're right over there, in section two.
② W What's the matter with your puppy?
　 M He hasn't eaten anything since yesterday.
③ W How often do you exercise here?
　 M I work out here three times a week.
④ W When are the books due?
　 M You should return these by next Thursday.
⑤ W Hi. Would you like to order?
　 M Yes, please. I'd like one cheeseburger and a coke.

① 여 유제품은 어디에 있나요?
　 남 바로 저기, 2번 구역에 있습니다.
② 여 강아지한테 무슨 문제가 있나요?
　 남 어제 이후로 아무것도 먹지 않고 있어요.
③ 여 여기서 얼마나 자주 운동하시나요?
　 남 일주일에 세 번 이곳에서 운동을 해요.
④ 여 그 책들을 언제 반납해야 하죠?
　 남 다음 주 목요일까지 반납하셔야 합니다.
⑤ 여 안녕하세요. 주문하시겠어요?
　 남 네. 치즈버거 한 개와 콜라 하나 주세요.

해설 도서관에 온 여자와 사서가 대화를 나누는 상황이므로 도서 반납 기일을 묻고 답하는 대화가 적절하다.

어휘 dairy product 유제품 right 바로 work out 운동하다 due 마감인 return 반납하다

04 ③

W Good morning, Happy Fitness Center. How can I help you?
M Hi. I'd like to join your fitness center. I heard your center has good facilities.
W You've visited the right place.

M How much is the membership fee?
W It's $30 a month. But if you get an annual membership, it's just $170.
M Wow! The annual fee is less than the fee for 6 months.
W Yes. And if you get an annual membership, it also includes a personal training session once a week.
M Sounds perfect. I will sign up for an annual membership.

여 안녕하세요, Happy Fitness Center입니다. 무엇을 도와드릴까요?
남 안녕하세요. 이 피트니스 센터에 가입하고 싶어요. 이 센터가 시설이 좋다고 들었습니다.
여 제대로 찾아오셨네요.
남 회비는 얼마인가요?
여 한 달에 30달러입니다. 그런데 연간 회원이 되시면 겨우 170달러입니다.
남 와! 연회비가 6개월 회비보다 싸네요.
여 네. 그리고 연간 회원이 되시면 일주일에 한 번 개인 훈련 수업이 포함됩니다.
남 완벽하네요. 연간 회원으로 등록할게요.

해설 남자는 연간 회원으로 등록하기로 했으므로 연회비인 170달러를 지불할 것이다.

어휘 facility 시설 membership 회원 fee 요금 annual 매년의, 연례의 include 포함하다 personal 개인의, 개인적인 session 수업 sign up for ~을 신청하다(가입하다)

05 ④

M Hi, Susan. Is this your dog?
W Yes, he's a dachshund, a German dog.
M Dachshunds are usually dark chocolate but your dog is a light cream color.
W That's why we call him Creamy.
M Oh, I see. Does he eat a lot?
W Yes, all the time. He eats almost 3 kilograms of dog food a week.
M Wow. How old is he?
W He is three years old. Do you want to pet him?
M Yes. He's so cute. I'd like to have a pet, too.

남 안녕, Susan. 네 개니?
여 응, 닥스훈트라고 독일 개야.
남 닥스훈트 종은 보통 진한 초콜릿색인데 너희 강아지는 밝은 크림색이구나.
여 그래서 우리가 그것을 Creamy라고 불러.
남 아, 그렇구나. 그것은 많이 먹니?
여 응, 항상. 일주일에 사료를 거의 3킬로그램 정도 먹어.
남 와. 그것은 몇 살이니?
여 세 살이야. 쓰다듬어 볼래?
남 그래. 너무 귀엽다. 나도 애완동물을 키우고 싶어.

해설 Creamy의 몸무게는 언급되지 않았다. 일주일에 먹는 사료의 양을 몸무게로 혼동하지 않도록 한다.

어휘 German 독일의 usually 보통, 대개 dark 진한, 어두운

light 밝은, 가벼운   all the time 항상   pet 쓰다듬다; 애완동물

06 ⑤

M What did you think of the movie?
W Well, I thought it was not bad, but I think I <u>expected too much</u>.
M What do you mean? I thought it <u>had a dramatic story</u> and great music.
W Well, the concert scene was kind of exciting. But there were some unrealistic scenes.
M Oh, I really <u>agree with you about that</u>.
W And some special effects in the movie were not very impressive.
M Yeah, I know what you mean.

남 그 영화에 대해 어떻게 생각했니?
여 글쎄, 나쁘지는 않았는데, 내가 너무 기대했었나 봐.
남 무슨 말이니? 난 스토리가 극적이고 음악이 아주 좋다고 생각했는데.
여 음, 콘서트 장면은 약간 신났어. 하지만 몇몇 비현실적인 장면들이 있었잖아.
남 아, 그건 네 말에 아주 동의해.
여 그리고 영화에 사용된 몇몇 특수 효과들이 별로 인상적이지 않았어.
남 그래, 무슨 뜻인지 알겠어.

해설 여자는 영화를 보기 전에 기대를 많이 했는데 비현실적인 장면들도 있었고 특수 효과가 좋지 않았다고 말했으므로 실망했음을 임을 알 수 있다.

어휘 expect 기대하다   dramatic 극적인   scene 장면   kind of 약간, 어느 정도   unrealistic 비현실적인   special effect 특수 효과   impressive 인상적인

07 ③

① **M** May I <u>have your passport</u> to check your visa?
　W Okay. Here you are.
② **M** Have you ever <u>tried any extreme sports</u>?
　W Yes. I went bungee jumping last summer.
③ **M** Are we allowed to take pictures in here?
　W Thank you so much for <u>taking my picture</u>.
④ **M** Where do you want to spend the coming vacation?
　W Well, I would like to go anywhere cooler than here.
⑤ **M** Do you mind if <u>I use your pen</u>?
　W No, not at all. Here you are.

① **남** 비자 확인을 위해 여권을 좀 볼 수 있을까요?
　여 네. 여기 있어요.
② **남** 익스트림 스포츠를 해 본 적이 있나요?
　여 네. 작년 여름에 번지 점프하러 갔었어요.
③ **남** 여기에서 사진을 찍어도 되나요?
　여 사진을 찍어 주셔서 정말 감사합니다.
④ **남** 다가오는 휴가를 어디에서 보내고 싶으세요?
　여 글쎄요, 여기보다 더 시원한 곳에 가고 싶어요.

⑤ **남** 당신 펜을 좀 사용해도 될까요?
　여 네, 물론이죠. 여기 있습니다.

해설 ③ 사진 촬영이 허용되는지 묻는 말에 사진을 찍어 줘서 고맙다고 답하는 것은 어색하다.

어휘 passport 여권   visa 비자   extreme sports 익스트림 스포츠(부상이나 위험을 무릅쓰고 다양한 묘기를 펼치는 스포츠)   go bungee jumping 번지 점프를 하러 가다   be allowed to ~하는 것이 허용되다   spend (시간을) 보내다   anywhere 어디든지

08 ⑤

W Mark, if you're not busy, can you help me?
M Why not? What do you <u>want me to do</u>?
W Do you remember that your grandma is coming to visit tomorrow?
M Sure. So do you want me to <u>clean the house</u>?
W No, I'll do that. I'm wondering what time the first train from Busan gets in tomorrow.
M Is she taking the first train? I'll <u>look up the arrival time</u> on the computer.
W Thanks. That's all I need you to do.

여 Mark, 바쁘지 않으면, 나 좀 도와줄래?
남 당연하죠. 제가 뭘 하면 되죠?
여 할머니께서 내일 오시는 거 기억하고 있지?
남 그럼요. 그래서 제가 집 청소를 하길 원하세요?
여 아니, 그건 내가 할게. 내일 부산발 첫 열차가 몇 시에 도착하는지 궁금하구나.
남 할머니께서 첫 열차를 타신대요? 제가 컴퓨터로 도착 시각을 찾아볼게요.
여 고맙구나. 그게 바로 네가 해 줄 일이란다.

해설 여자는 남자에게 내일 부산발 첫 열차의 도착 시각을 알아봐 달라고 부탁했다.

어휘 busy 바쁜   remember 기억하다   wonder 궁금하다   look up 찾아보다   arrival 도착

09 ②

M Last week, we surveyed <u>180 third-grade students</u> on the activities they enjoy doing in their spare time. Among the 180 students, <u>99 students responded</u> that they spend most of their spare time playing computer games. 45 students said they watch TV or go to the movies, and 23 students read books in their spare time. And <u>the least number of students</u> said they spend time outside exercising such as playing soccer or basketball.

남 지난주, 180명의 3학년 학생들을 대상으로 여가 시간에 즐기는 활동에 대해 설문 조사를 했습니다. 180명의 학생들 중, 99명의 학생들이 대부분의 여가 시간을 컴퓨터 게임을 하는 데 쓴다고 답했습니다. 45명의 학생들은 TV를 보거나 영화를 보러 간다고 말했고, 23명의 학생들은 그들의 여가 시간에 책을 읽는다고 말했습니다. 가장 적은 수의 학생들이 축구나 농구

같은 야외 운동을 하면서 시간을 보낸다고 말했습니다.

해설 학생들이 여가 시간에 즐겨 하는 활동에 대한 설문 조사 결과이다.

어휘 survey 설문 조사하다 activity 활동 spare time 여가시간 respond 응답하다 least 가장 적은 outside 밖에서 exercise 운동하다

10 ④

W Do you have any special plans this weekend?
M No. I might just stay at home and read some books.
W Hey, why don't we go swimming?
M Sorry, I can't. I skinned my left knee while playing badminton yesterday.
W Did you go to see a doctor?
M No, I just put some ointment on the area.
W Oh, I see. Then how about watching a musical?
M That's a good idea. Then I'll search for a good one online and book tickets.

여 이번 주말에 특별한 계획 있니?
남 아니. 아마도 그냥 집에 있으면서 책이나 읽겠지.
여 얘, 수영하러 가는 게 어때?
남 미안하지만, 안 돼. 난 어제 배드민턴을 치다가 왼쪽 무릎이 까졌어.
여 병원 다녀왔니?
남 아니, 그냥 상처 부분에 연고를 발랐어.
여 오, 그렇구나. 그럼 뮤지컬 볼래?
남 좋은 생각이야. 그럼 내가 온라인으로 좋은 것을 검색해서 표를 예매할게.

해설 남자는 어제 배드민턴을 치다가 무릎이 까졌다고 말했다.

어휘 special 특별한 skin 까지다 knee 무릎 ointment 연고 search for ~을 찾다, 검색하다 book 예약하다

11 ③

M Hi, Ms. Kim.
W Hi, John. What's up?
M Well, could you please do me a favor?
W Sure, what is it?
M I heard that it will rain this afternoon, but I forgot to bring my umbrella.
W Aha, so you want me to lend you one, right?
M Exactly. Can I borrow an umbrella later?
W No problem. Drop by my office again after school.
M Thank you so much.

남 안녕하세요, 김 선생님.
여 안녕, John. 무슨 일이니?
남 저, 부탁 하나 들어주시겠어요?
여 물론이지, 뭔데?
남 오늘 오후에 비가 온다고 들었는데, 우산을 가져오는 것을 잊었어요.
여 아하, 그래서 우산을 빌려달라는 거구나, 그렇지?
남 맞아요. 나중에 우산 하나를 빌릴 수 있을까요?

여 문제없어. 방과 후에 교무실에 다시 들르렴.
남 정말 감사합니다.

해설 여자가 남자에게 방과 후에 자신의 사무실에 다시 들르라고 했으므로 여자가 말한 사무실은 교무실을 뜻하며, 대화가 이루어지는 장소는 학교임을 알 수 있다.

어휘 do ~ a favor ~의 부탁을 들어주다 bring 가져오다 lend 빌려주다 exactly 정확히 borrow 빌리다 drop by 잠깐 들르다

12 ⑤

W Good afternoon, everyone. Let me tell you about our annual Fresh Farm Festival. It will take place in Seoul Square from 10 a.m. to 6 p.m. this Saturday. You can buy fresh fruit and vegetables from all over the country. You should bring your own shopping bags and cups. The admission will be $3, and children under 5 will be admitted free. Thank you.

여 안녕하세요, 여러분. 해마다 열리는 Fresh Farm Festival에 대해 말씀 드리겠습니다. 축제는 이번 주 토요일 오전 10시부터 오후 6시까지 서울 광장에서 개최됩니다. 여러분은 전국에서 온 신선한 과일과 채소를 구입하실 수 있습니다. 여러분은 자신의 장바구니와 컵을 가져오셔야 합니다. 입장료는 3달러이고, 5세 미만 어린이는 무료로 입장됩니다. 감사합니다.

해설 예매 방법은 언급되지 않았다.

어휘 annual 매년의, 연례의 take place 개최되다, 일어나다 admission 입장료 admit 입장을 허락하다 free 무료로

13 ①

M Why the long face, Judy?
W I'm disappointed with my grade in English. I got 75. How about you, John?
M I got 85. How about Korean? You're very good at it.
W I got 93. I honestly was expecting that I would get at least 95.
M Well, it's a high grade. What about your other grades? You always struggle with math and science.
W I have no problem with an 85 in math and science. I think they are both fair.
M Then did you get over 90 only in Korean?
W No. I got a 97 in history. I studied history really hard.

남 왜 시무룩하니, Judy?
여 내 영어 점수에 실망했어. 난 75점 받았어. 넌 어떠니, John?
남 난 85점 받았어. 국어는 어때? 넌 국어를 아주 잘하잖아.
여 93점이야. 난 솔직히 최소한 95점 받을 거라고 기대하고 있었어.
남 뭘. 높은 점수네. 다른 점수들은 어때? 넌 항상 수학과 과학을 힘들어하잖아.
여 수학과 과학은 85점으로 별 문제없어. 둘 다 적당하다고 생각해.
남 그럼 국어에서만 90점 넘은 거야?

여 아니. 역사에서 97점 받았어. 역사 공부 정말 열심히 했거든.

해설 여자는 국어 성적을 95점 이상 받을 것으로 예상했지만 실제 성적은 93점이라고 했다.

어휘 be disappointed with ~에 실망하다 be good at ~을 잘하다 expect 기대하다 grade 점수 at least 최소한, 적어도 struggle 힘겹게 하다, 고군분투하다

14 ②

M This is one of the most popular drinks in the world. Its color is very dark, and it tastes bitter and slightly sour. This can prevent you from getting a good sleep due to its caffeine content. But it can also help you feel less tired and increase your energy level. Roasting its beans is a very important process because that has a big influence on how it tastes.

남 이것은 세계에서 가장 인기 있는 음료 중 하나입니다. 이것의 색은 매우 진하고, 맛이 쓰며 약간 신맛도 납니다. 이것은 카페인 성분 때문에 당신이 숙면을 취하는 것을 방해할 수 있습니다. 하지만 이것은 당신이 피로를 덜 느끼게 해 주고 에너지 수준을 증가시켜 주는 데 도움이 될 수도 있습니다. 이것의 콩을 볶는 것은 이것이 어떤 맛이 나는지에 큰 영향을 주기 때문에 매우 중요한 과정입니다.

해설 진한 색, 쓴맛과 신맛, 카페인으로 인한 장단점, 콩을 볶는 과정의 내용으로 보아 커피에 관한 설명임을 알 수 있다.

어휘 popular 인기 있는 bitter 맛이 쓴 slightly 약간 sour 신, 시큼한 prevent A from ~ing A가 ~하는 것을 방해하다 due to ~ 때문에 caffeine 카페인 content 내용물, 함유량 increase 증가시키다 level 수준 roast 볶다, 굽다 process 과정 influence 영향

15 ⑤

M My wallet is gone. It's not inside my bag.
W You must have left it at home. Why don't you call your mom and check?
M I had it with me in the morning. I remember taking it out to buy a Sprite from the vending machine before I entered the classroom.
W Have you checked the places you went earlier?
M I have, but I couldn't find it. What should I do now?
W Why don't you check with lost and found?
M Okay. I hope somebody has picked it up and taken it there.

남 내 지갑이 사라졌어. 가방 안에 없어.
여 집에 두고 왔겠지. 어머니께 전화해서 확인해 보는 게 어떠니?
남 아침에는 가지고 있었어. 교실에 들어오기 전에 자동판매기에서 스프라이트를 사려고 지갑을 꺼냈던 기억이 나.
여 네가 전에 갔던 장소들을 확인해 봤어?
남 그랬는데, 못 찾았어. 이제 어떻게 해야 하지?
여 분실물 보관소를 확인해 보는 게 어때?
남 그래. 누군가가 주워서 그곳에 가져다 놓았으면 좋겠다.

해설 남자는 여자의 조언대로 분실물 보관소를 확인해 보겠다고 했다.

어휘 wallet 지갑 must have p.p. ~했음이 틀림없다 take out 꺼내다 vending machine 자동판매기 enter 들어가다 lost and found 분실물 보관소 pick up 줍다

16 ④

M Hi, Jessy. I want to apologize to you.
W Hey, Tim. I was surprised that you left in the middle of the performance, but I heard your mom had an accident! What happened?
M My mom fell down at the station and broke her leg.
W You must have been really upset yesterday. Is she okay?
M Yes, she's better. She was treated at a hospital yesterday, and she's resting at home now.
W What a relief! I hope your mom will get better soon.
M Thank you. Once again, I'm really sorry for leaving the theater without saying anything.

남 안녕, Jessy. 너에게 사과하고 싶어.
여 안녕, Tim. 나는 네가 공연 중간에 없어져서 놀랐는데, 너희 어머니께서 사고를 당하셨다고 들었어! 무슨 일이니?
남 어머니께서 역에서 넘어지셔서 다리가 부러지셨어.
여 어제 정말 속상했겠구나. 어머니는 괜찮으시니?
남 응, 더 좋아지셨어. 어제 병원에서 치료 받으시고 지금은 집에서 쉬고 계셔.
여 다행이다! 어머니께서 빨리 나으시면 좋겠다.
남 고마워. 다시 한 번, 아무 말 없이 극장을 떠나서 정말 미안해.

해설 남자는 어제 공연 중간에 말 없이 극장을 떠난 것에 대해 여자에게 사과하고 있다.

어휘 apologize 사과하다 surprised 놀란 performance 공연 have an accident 사고를 당하다 fall down 넘어지다 break 부러지다 treat 치료하다 rest 휴식을 취하다 relief 안심, 안도

17 ④

W Steve, can I ask you something?
M Yes. What is that?
W I think I told the students to study the wrong lesson for the vocabulary test.
M I wrote it down. Just a second. You said the test covers lesson 5.
W It's actually lesson 6. I made a mistake.
M Oh, no. Then we should tell the students right away.
W Can you help me post a notice on the board?
M I think sending text messages would be better.

여 Steve, 내가 뭐 좀 물어봐도 되겠니?
남 네. 무슨 일이신데요?
여 내가 학생들에게 잘못된 어휘 시험 범위를 공부하라고 알려 준 것 같아.
남 제가 적어 놨어요. 잠시만요. 시험이 5과까지라고 말씀하셨어요.

여 사실은 6과목야. 내가 실수했어.

남 아, 저런. 그럼 당장 학생들에게 알려 줘야 해요.

여 게시판에 공지 사항 올리는 것 좀 도와줄래?

남 문자 메시지를 보내는 게 더 좋을 것 같아요.

해설 여자가 남자에게 게시판에 공지 사항을 올리는 것을 도와 달라고 부탁했으므로 이에 응하거나 다른 방법을 제안하는 응답이 적절하다.

① 신경 쓰지 마세요. 그건 선생님 잘못이 아니에요.

② 시험을 연기해 주셔서 감사합니다.

③ 제가 시험공부를 더 열심히 했다면 좋았을 텐데요.

⑤ 죄송하지만, 모든 과목을 다 다룰 충분한 시간이 없어요.

어휘 vocabulary 어휘   write down 기록하다, 쓰다   cover 다루다, 포함시키다   make a mistake 실수하다   post 게시하다   notice 공지 사항   board 게시판   fault 잘못 postpone 연기하다   subject 과목

18 ⑤

M Tell me more about the girl you want to introduce me to.

W Okay. She's my best friend from elementary school.

M What does she like to do?

W She likes dancing. She was in the school dance club in middle school.

M I see. I hope she likes sports, too.

W Yeah. She enjoys watching sports. Her favorite sport is basketball.

M Cool. Then we can go to watch basketball games together.

W I think the two of you have much in common.

남 네가 나한테 소개해 주고 싶어 하는 여자 아이에 대해 좀 더 얘기해 줘.

여 알았어. 그녀는 초등학교 때부터 나의 가장 친한 친구야.

남 그녀는 뭐 하는 걸 좋아하니?

여 춤추는 걸 좋아해. 그녀는 중학교에서 학교 댄스 동아리에 있었어.

남 그렇구나. 그녀가 스포츠도 좋아하면 좋겠다.

여 응. 그녀는 스포츠 경기 보는 걸 좋아해. 그녀가 가장 좋아하는 스포츠는 농구야.

남 잘됐다. 그럼 함께 농구 경기를 보러 갈 수 있겠다.

여 내 생각에 너희 둘은 공통점이 많은 것 같아.

해설 남자는 자신이 소개 받을 여자 아이도 스포츠를 좋아한다는 것을 알고 기대감에 차 있으므로, 두 사람은 공통점이 많은 것 같다는 말이 이어지는 것이 자연스럽다.

① 난 그녀가 너랑 사귀지 않을까 봐 걱정돼.

② 스포츠를 직업으로 삼는 건 잊어버려.

③ 그녀는 네가 찾고 있는 여자 아이가 아니야.

④ 내가 Michael Jordan의 열렬한 팬이라고 말했잖아.

어휘 introduce 소개하다   elementary school 초등학교 favorite 매우 좋아하는   go with ~와 사귀다, 어울리다 profession 직업   fan 팬   have in common 공통으로 갖다

19 ③

W Jerry is angry with me. I don't know what I should do.

M Oh, did anything happen between you?

W Actually, I made a joke about his dark skin.

M That wasn't very thoughtful of you.

W But I did it just for fun.

M Hey, what's funny to some may not be funny to others.

W I thought it was okay because we are best friends.

M You can't be rude to your friends.

여 Jerry가 나한테 화가 났어. 어떻게 해야 할지 모르겠어.

남 오, 너희 둘 사이에 무슨 일이라도 있었니?

여 사실은 내가 그의 어두운 피부색을 놀렸어.

남 너 정말 사려 깊지 못했구나.

여 하지만 난 그냥 장난으로 했던 거야.

남 얘, 누군가에게 재미있는 일이 다른 사람들에게는 재미있지 않을 수도 있는 거야.

여 난 우리가 가장 친한 친구 사이라서 괜찮다고 생각했어.

남 친구들에게 무례해서는 안 돼.

해설 남자는 여자가 친구에게 한 농담이 부적절하다고 생각하므로, 괜찮을 줄 알았다는 여자의 말에 대해 충고를 하는 것이 자연스럽다.

① 우리는 다시 가장 친한 친구 사이가 될 수 있어!

② 너는 약속을 지켜야 해.

④ 천만에. 친구 좋다는 게 뭐니?

⑤ 사람을 외모로 판단하지 마라.

어휘 happen 일어나다, 발생하다   actually 사실   make a joke 농담을 하다   thoughtful 사려 깊은   keep one's promise 약속을 지키다   rude 무례한   What are friends for? 친구 좋다는 게 뭐야?   judge 판단하다   appearance 외모

20 ④

W Mark and David are close friends. Mark tells David that he doesn't understand science class very well, but he wants to understand it better. David knows that Mark likes reading. So David thinks that once Mark enjoys reading stories related to science, science itself will become more interesting. In this situation, what would David most likely say to Mark?

David Mark, why don't you read science fiction books?

여 Mark와 David는 친한 친구이다. Mark는 David에게 과학 수업을 잘 이해하지 못하지만, 자신이 과학을 더 잘 이해하고 싶다고 말한다. David는 Mark가 읽기를 좋아한다는 것을 안다. 그래서 David는 일단 Mark가 과학 관련 이야기를 즐겨 읽으면 과학 자체가 더 흥미로워질 것이라고 생각한다. 이 상황에서, David는 Mark에게 뭐라고 말할 것 같은가?

David Mark, 공상 과학 소설책을 읽어 보는 게 어때?

해설 David는 Mark가 책 읽기를 좋아해서 과학 관련 책을 읽으

면 과학에 흥미가 생길 것이라고 생각하고 있으므로 그와 관련된 조언을 하는 것이 적절하다.

① 내가 전공을 어떻게 바꾸지?
② 나는 네가 훌륭한 과학자가 될 거라고 믿어.
③ 네가 그것을 포기하는 게 좋을 것 같아.
⑤ 나는 네가 과학에 흥미가 있는 줄 몰랐어.

어휘 close 가까운, 친한   understand 이해하다   once 일단 ~하면   related to ~와 관련 있는   change 바꾸다   major 전공   science fiction 공상 과학 소설   give up 포기하다

Review Test

pp.150~151

Word Check

13회

01 회사	02 환불
03 나누다, 공유하다	04 자원봉사자; 자원봉사를 하다
05 알리다	06 예약하다
07 최신의	08 영원히
09 계단	10 전망
11 ~을 염두에 두다(생각하다)	12 강화하다
13 muscle	14 orphanage
15 customer	16 vomit
17 attach	18 policy
19 discuss	20 price tag
21 jealous	22 install
23 ground floor	24 medical

Expression Check

25 on, way home	26 tired of
27 go well with	28 in need
29 throw a, party	30 connected, to

Word Check

14회

01 야외의	02 신
03 직업	04 연기하다
05 비현실적인	06 인상적인
07 연고	08 판단하다
09 끈	10 특수 효과
11 앞	12 유제품
13 treat	14 passport
15 content	16 influence
17 rude	18 annual
19 board	20 provide
21 appearance	22 roast
23 drop by	24 facility

Expression Check

25 have, in common	26 fell down
27 disappointed with	28 Have you ever
29 prevent, from	30 take place

실전 모의고사 **15**회

pp.152~159

01 ③	02 ⑤	03 ①	04 ④	05 ⑤
06 ③	07 ②	08 ⑤	09 ④	10 ⑤
11 ③	12 ②	13 ②	14 ①	15 ②
16 ⑤	17 ④	18 ⑤	19 ②	20 ⑤

01 ③

M How can I help you?
W My computer is so slow these days, so I want to buy a new one.
M Do you want to buy a desktop computer?
W No, I want to try a laptop this time.
M That's right. These three laptops are the most popular ones.
W I want one that is light to carry around.
M Then how about this one? It weighs only 1 kilogram and it costs $900. It's our newest model.
W It looks great. I'll take it.

남 무엇을 도와드릴까요?
여 요즘 제 컴퓨터가 너무 느려서 새로운 것을 사고 싶어요.
남 데스크톱 컴퓨터를 사고 싶으신가요?
여 아니요. 이번에는 노트북 컴퓨터를 써 보고 싶어요.
남 좋습니다. 이 세 가지 노트북 컴퓨터가 가장 인기 있는 것들입니다.
여 저는 들고 다니기에 가벼운 것을 원해요.
남 그러시면 이것은 어떠세요? 이것은 1킬로그램밖에 안 나가고 가격은 900달러입니다. 최신 모델이에요.
여 좋아 보이네요. 그걸 살게요.

해설 여자는 1킬로그램이고 900달러인 노트북 컴퓨터를 사겠다고 했다.

어휘 these days 요즘   desktop computer 데스크톱 컴퓨터   laptop 노트북 컴퓨터   popular 인기 있는   carry around 들고 다니다, 휴대하다   weigh 무게가 ~이다

02 ⑤

W Look at the girl with the white helmet and blue jacket! She's really fast!
M Yeah, I think she's one of the best skaters here.
W I want to be fast like her. But I don't think I am improving.
M Come on, you only started skating three months ago.
W I know. But it's really difficult for me to keep practicing.
M Practice makes perfect. I'm sure you will improve quickly.
W Thanks.

여 저기 흰색 헬멧과 파란색 재킷을 입은 소녀 좀 봐. 그녀는 정말 빠르다!

남 맞아, 나는 그녀가 여기에서 가장 스케이트를 잘 타는 사람들 중 한 명이라고 생각해.

여 나는 그녀처럼 빨라지고 싶어. 하지만 난 나아지고 있는 것 같지 않아.

남 이런, 너는 겨우 석 달 전에 스케이트를 타기 시작했잖아.

여 알아. 하지만 계속 연습하는 건 나에게 정말 힘들어.

남 연습이 완벽을 만들잖아. 나는 네가 실력이 빠르게 향상될 거라고 확신해.

여 고마워.

해설 두 사람이 스케이트를 타는 소녀를 보면서 이야기하고 있으므로 대화가 이루어지는 장소는 스케이트장이다.

어휘 helmet 헬멧   improve 향상하다   skate 스케이트를 타다   practice 연습하다; 연습   perfect 완벽한

03 ①

M Hi. Are you free this Saturday?

W Well, I guess so. Why do you ask?

M I have tickets to see the Berlin Philharmonic Orchestra at the Art Center. Do you want to go?

W Definitely! What time is it?

M Let me see. It starts at 7:00 p.m. Let's meet thirty minutes earlier.

W Why don't we have dinner together before that?

M Good idea. Then how about 6:00 p.m.?

W Oh, I don't want to hurry to the concert. Let's meet two hours before the concert.

M Okay. See you then.

남 안녕. 이번 주 토요일에 시간되니?

여 글쎄, 그럴 것 같은데. 왜 물어보니?

남 나에게 Art Center에서 Berlin Philharmonic Orchestra를 관람할 수 있는 표가 있어. 너 가고 싶니?

여 물론이지! 몇 시니?

남 어디 보자. 오후 7시에 시작이야. 30분 더 일찍 만나자.

여 연주회 전에 같이 저녁 먹을래?

남 좋은 생각이야. 그러면 오후 6시 어때?

여 오, 난 공연에 급하게 가고 싶지 않아. 연주회 두 시간 전에 만나자.

남 좋아. 그때 보자.

해설 연주회는 오후 7시에 시작하는데 두 사람은 연주회 두 시간 전에 만나기로 했다.

어휘 guess 추측하다   definitely 분명히, 틀림없이

04 ④

W Hey, Jason. Long time, no see.

M Hi, Katie. It's good to see you again. How are you?

W I'm good. Where are you going?

M Actually, I'm going to a new restaurant to eat lunch.

W Oh, really? Are you meeting someone there?

M No, I'm alone. Do you want to have lunch with me?

W Why not? What kind of restaurant is it?

M It's a Vietnamese restaurant. I heard their rice noodles are delicious.

W I love Vietnamese food! Let's go!

여 Jason, 안녕. 오랜만이야.

남 안녕, Katie. 다시 만나서 반가워. 어떻게 지내니?

여 잘 지내. 너 어디에 가는 중이니?

남 사실, 나는 새로운 식당에 점심 먹으러 가고 있어.

여 오, 정말? 거기서 누구 만나니?

남 아니, 나 혼자야. 나랑 같이 점심 먹을래?

여 좋아. 그곳은 어떤 종류의 식당이니?

남 베트남 식당이야. 그곳의 쌀국수가 맛있다고 들었어.

여 난 베트남 음식을 아주 좋아해! 가자!

해설 오랜만에 만난 두 사람은 함께 베트남 식당에 가서 점심을 먹기로 했다.

어휘 actually 사실은   alone 혼자의   Vietnamese 베트남의   noodles 국수   delicious 맛있는

05 ⑤

M How can I help you?

W I want to get a refund on this sweater.

M I can help you with that. Can I ask you the reason why you want to return it?

W I ordered this online, but the color is different from what I saw on the screen.

M Oh, we're really sorry about the problem. Actually, this sweater comes in six different colors, so why don't you look at the other colors and consider an exchange first?

W Okay, I can do that.

M Good. This way, please.

남 무엇을 도와 드릴까요?

여 저는 이 스웨터를 환불받고 싶습니다.

남 제가 도와드리겠습니다. 환불받고 싶으신 이유를 여쭤봐도 될까요?

여 저는 이것을 온라인으로 주문했는데, 색이 제가 화면에서 본 것과 달라서요.

남 아, 그 문제에 대해 정말 죄송합니다. 사실, 이 스웨터는 여섯 가지 색으로 나오는데, 먼저 다른 색상을 보시고 교환을 고려해 보시는 게 어떨까요?

여 네, 그렇게 할게요.

남 좋습니다. 이쪽으로 오세요.

해설 여자는 온라인으로 구입한 스웨터의 색상이 화면에서 본 것과 달라서 환불받으려고 했다.

어휘 refund 환불   reason 이유   return 반환하다   online 온라인으로   screen 화면   consider 고려하다   exchange 교환; 교환하다

06 ③

① W Let me carry your luggage for you.
   M Thank you so much.

② W Do you think I should eat less to lose weight?
   M I think you should exercise more.

③ W What did you do during summer vacation?

M I'm planning to visit my grandmother.
④ **W** What time do you go to bed?
M Normally around 11 p.m.
⑤ **W** What would you like to do in the future?
M I want to become a photographer and take pictures of nature.

① 여 제가 짐을 들어드릴게요.
남 정말 감사합니다.
② 여 제가 살을 빼기 위해 덜 먹어야 할까요?
남 당신은 운동을 더 해야 한다고 생각합니다.
③ 여 너는 여름 방학 동안 무엇을 했니?
남 할머니를 찾아뵐 계획이야.
④ 여 너는 몇 시에 잠자리에 드니?
남 보통, 11시쯤에 자.
⑤ 여 너는 미래에 무엇을 하고 싶니?
남 사진작가가 되어 자연 사진을 찍고 싶어.

해설 ③ 여름 방학 동안 무엇을 했는지 묻는 말에 앞으로의 계획을 답하는 것은 어색하다.

어휘 luggage 짐 lose weight 체중을 줄이다 exercise 운동하다 normally 보통 in the future 미래에 photographer 사진작가 nature 자연

07 ②

① **W** Excuse me. Can you tell me where the subway station is?
M No problem. Go straight and turn left. It's on your right.
② **W** Are we there yet? I'm exhausted!
M We are almost there. You can do it!
③ **W** We're late. I think we should take a taxi.
M No, I don't think so. We should take the subway.
④ **W** The flowers are so beautiful. I want to take some home.
M You should not pick the flowers.
⑤ **W** Why don't you go hiking this afternoon?
M I'd love to, but I can't. I have to help my mom.

① 여 실례합니다. 지하철역이 어디인지 말씀해 주시겠어요?
남 물론이죠. 곧장 가시다가 왼쪽으로 도세요. 그것은 오른쪽에 있어요.
② 여 아직 도착 안했니? 나 너무 지쳤어!
남 거의 다 왔어. 너는 할 수 있어!
③ 여 우리 늦었어. 택시를 타야 할 것 같아.
남 아니야, 나는 그렇게 생각하지 않아. 우리는 지하철을 타야 해.
④ 여 꽃이 참 아름답다. 집에 좀 가져가고 싶어.
남 너는 꽃을 꺾으면 안 돼.
⑤ 여 오늘 오후에 하이킹하러 가는 게 어때?
남 그리고 싶지만, 안 돼. 난 엄마를 도와드려야 해.

해설 등산을 하다가 여자가 힘들어하자 남자가 거의 다 왔다고 여자를 격려하는 내용의 대화가 적절하다.

어휘 subway station 지하철역 go straight 직진하다 exhausted 지친 pick 꺾다 go hiking 하이킹하러 가다

08 ⑤

(Cellphone rings.)
W Hey, Jim. It's me.
M What's up, Kate? Did you arrive at the market?
W Yes, I did. But I think I left my shopping list on the table at home.
M Do you make a shopping list every time you go to the market?
W Yes. Can you look on the table and see if it's there?
M Sure. Let me see. *(Pause)* Oh, I found it. It says tomatoes, cheese, coffee beans, and dish soap.
W Can you take a picture of the list and send it to me?
M Sure. I will send it to you right away.

(휴대 전화가 울린다.)
여 여보세요, Jim. 저예요.
남 무슨 일이에요, Kate? 시장에 도착했어요?
여 네. 하지만 집 탁자 위에 쇼핑 목록을 두고 온 것 같아요.
남 당신은 시장에 갈 때마다 쇼핑 목록을 작성하나요?
여 네. 탁자를 한번 보고 거기에 목록이 있는지 봐 줄래요?
남 물론이죠. 어디 보자. (잠시 후) 아, 찾았어요. 토마토, 치즈, 커피 원두, 그리고 주방용 세제라고 적혀 있어요.
여 그 목록을 사진으로 찍어서 보내 줄래요?
남 네. 바로 보낼게요.

해설 여자는 남자에게 자신이 집에 두고 온 쇼핑 목록을 사진으로 찍어서 보내 달라고 부탁했다.

어휘 arrive 도착하다 leave 두고 오다[가다] make a shopping list 쇼핑 목록을 작성하다 every time ~할 때마다 dish soap 주방용 세제 take a picture 사진을 찍다

09 ④

M Welcome to our volunteer training program. This program lasts for three days, and each day you have to take five hours of classes. After you finish the program, you will get a certificate and can participate in any volunteer work organized by Good Will Foundation. If you have any questions, feel free to ask one of our staff members. Now, let me introduce our first lecturer.

남 저희 자원봉사자 교육 프로그램에 오신 것을 환영합니다. 이 프로그램은 3일간 지속되며, 매일 5시간 동안 수업을 들어야 합니다. 이 프로그램이 끝난 후에, 여러분은 수료증을 받게 될 것이고 Good Will Foundation이 주최하는 어떤 자원봉사 활동에도 참여할 수 있습니다. 질문이 있으면, 저희 직원 중 한 명에게 편하게 질문해 주세요. 자, 첫 번째 강사를 소개하겠습니다.

해설 재단에서 주최하는 자원봉사자 교육 프로그램에 관한 안내 방송이다.

어휘 volunteer 자원봉사자 last 지속하다 certificate 수료증 participate in ~에 참여하다 organize 조직하다, 편성하다 foundation 재단 feel free to 자유롭게 ~하다 staff 직원 lecturer 강사

10 ⑤

M Hey, Kate. What are you doing?
W I'm making the new poster for our club.
M Oh, can I see it?
W Sure. I put the photos of us working together on the poster.
M I like them. And I like the way you highlighted the name of our club.
W Thanks. Is there anything missing or anything that should be corrected?
M Let me see. (Pause) Oh, you should change the interview date to January 15.
W Okay. What about the contact number?
M That is correct. Nice work.

남 안녕, Kate. 뭐 하고 있니?
여 우리 동아리의 새로운 포스터를 만들고 있어.
남 오, 내가 봐도 될까?
여 물론이지. 난 우리가 함께 작업하는 사진들을 포스터에 넣었어.
남 마음에 들어. 그리고 난 우리 동아리의 이름을 강조한 방식이 좋아.
여 고마워. 놓치거나 고쳐야 할 부분이 있을까?
남 어디 보자. (잠시 후) 아, 면접 날짜를 1월 15일로 바꿔야 해.
여 알았어. 연락처는 어때?
남 그것은 정확해. 잘했어.

해설 남자는 동아리 포스터의 내용 중 면접 날짜를 바꿔야 한다고 했다.

어휘 photo 사진　highlight 강조하다　miss 놓치다
correct 고치다　change 바꾸다, 변경하다　interview 면접
contact number 연락처

11 ③

M What are you doing?
W I'm knitting a sweater. It's nearly finished.
M Oh, I can't imagine you knitting something. Is this your new hobby?
W No, you know I'm not really good at making things.
M Then what made you decide to knit a sweater?
W My brother broke up with his girlfriend recently. I want to give him a present to cheer him up.
M Wow, great. It's a kind of surprise present then.
W Can you try it on for me?
M No problem. Your brother and I have a similar build.

남 너 뭐 하고 있니?
여 스웨터 뜨고 있어. 거의 끝났어.
남 오, 난 네가 뭔가를 뜨개질한다는 걸 상상할 수가 없어. 이것이 네 새로운 취미니?
여 아니, 내가 뭘 만드는 데 소질이 없다는 건 너도 알잖아.
남 그런데 왜 스웨터를 뜨기로 결정했니?
여 오빠가 최근에 여자 친구와 헤어졌어. 오빠에게 힘내라고 선물을 주고 싶어서.
남 와, 대단하다. 그러면 일종의 깜짝 선물이구나.
여 날 위해 한번 입어 봐 줄래?
남 좋아. 네 오빠랑 내가 체격이 비슷하니까.

해설 여자는 오빠와 체격이 비슷한 남자에게 자신이 뜬 스웨터를 입어 봐 달라고 부탁했다.

어휘 knit 뜨다, 짜다　nearly 거의　imagine 상상하다
break up with ~와 헤어지다　recently 최근에　cheer up
힘내다　similar 비슷한　build 체격

12 ②

W Excuse me. I'm looking for the food court. Do you know where it is?
M Sure. It's near the bakery.
W Where is the bakery?
M Turn right at the first corner and go straight until you see the information desk.
W And then?
M Across from the information desk, you will see the bakery. The food court is right next to the bakery.
W Thank you so much.

여 실례합니다. 저는 푸드 코트를 찾고 있어요. 그것이 어디에 있는지 아세요?
남 물론이죠. 그것은 제과점 근처에 있어요.
여 제과점은 어디에 있나요?
남 첫 번째 모퉁이에서 오른쪽으로 돌아서 안내 데스크가 보일 때까지 직진하세요.
여 그런 다음에는요?
남 안내 데스크 건너편에 제과점이 보일 거예요. 푸드 코트는 제과점 바로 옆에 있어요.
여 정말 감사합니다.

해설 여자가 가려는 푸드 코트는 안내 데스크 맞은편에 있는 제과점(①) 바로 옆에 있다고 했다.

어휘 look for ~을 찾다　food court 푸드 코트, 식당가
corner 모퉁이　until ~할 때까지　across from ~ 건너편에
information desk 안내 데스크

13 ②

W How can I help you?
M I'd like to get these clothes dry-cleaned.
W Let me see. You have two shirts and a coat.
M Yes, right. How much is it?
W It's $3 for each shirt and $10 for the coat.
M I have a discount coupon. Can I use this?
W Sure, you can get $2 off with this coupon.
M Thanks.

여 무엇을 도와드릴까요?
남 이 옷들을 드라이클리닝 하고 싶어요.
여 어디 볼게요. 셔츠 두 장과 코트 한 벌이네요.
남 네, 맞아요. 얼마인가요?
여 셔츠는 한 장에 3달러이고 코트는 10달러입니다.
남 저는 할인 쿠폰이 있어요. 이것을 사용할 수 있을까요?
여 물론이죠, 이 쿠폰으로 2달러를 할인받으실 수 있습니다.
남 고맙습니다.

해설 셔츠 두 장의 세탁비(각 3달러)와 코트 한 벌의 세탁비(10달

러)를 합하면 총 16달러이다. 여기에 2달러 할인 쿠폰을 사용할 수 있으므로 14달러를 지불하면 된다.

[어휘] clothes 옷　dry-clean 드라이클리닝을 하다　discount 할인　coupon 쿠폰　off 할인되어

14 ①

W This sport is played by two teams. Each team has 9 players. The offensive team hits the ball with a bat and runs around the bases. On the other hand, the defensive team tries to prevent batters from running around the bases by catching the ball and throwing it to the bases. When a batter advances around four bases and reaches the last base, or home plate, the team scores.

여 이 스포츠는 두 팀에 의해 진행된다. 각 팀의 선수는 9명이다. 공격 팀은 방망이로 공을 쳐서 베이스를 돌며 뛴다. 반대로, 수비 팀은 타자가 베이스를 돌며 뛰지 못하도록 공을 잡아서 그것을 베이스로 던진다. 타자가 네 개의 베이스를 돌아서 전진하고 마지막 베이스인 본루에 도달하면 그 팀이 득점한다.

[해설] 한 팀에 9명의 선수들이 있고 타자가 방망이로 공을 쳐서 베이스로 뛰는 스포츠는 야구이다.

[어휘] offensive 공격하는　bat 방망이　on the other hand 반대로, 한편　defensive 수비의　prevent A from ~ing A가 ~하는 것을 막다　catch 잡다　throw 던지다　advance 전진하다　reach 닿다, 이르다　score 득점하다

15 ②

W Did you see the poll in the school newspaper?
M No, I didn't. What's it about?
W It's about the most popular Christmas presents.
M Oh, what was the most popular present?
W It was toys. Twelve students chose toys. What do you want to get as a Christmas gift?
M I want to get a bicycle.
W Four students chose bicycles, and eight students chose accessories.
M That's interesting.
W Five students chose smartphones, and the smallest number of students chose books.

여 너 학교 신문에서 여론 조사를 봤니?
남 아니. 무엇에 관한 건데?
여 가장 인기 있는 크리스마스 선물에 관한 거야.
남 아, 가장 인기 있는 선물은 뭐였니?
여 그것은 장난감이었어. 12명의 학생들이 장난감을 선택했어. 너는 크리스마스 선물로 무엇을 받고 싶니?
남 나는 자전거를 받고 싶어.
여 4명의 학생들이 자전거를 선택했고, 8명의 학생들이 액세서리를 선택했어.
남 흥미롭구나.
여 5명의 학생들이 스마트폰을 선택했고, 가장 적은 수의 학생들이 책을 선택했어.

[해설] 크리스마스 선물로 액세서리를 선택한 학생들은 8명이라고 했다.

[어휘] poll 여론 조사　newspaper 신문　popular 인기 있는 present 선물　choose 선택하다

16 ⑤

M Can you tell me what you saw that night?
W I was getting out of a taxi, and I saw someone leaving Mr. Bell's house through the window.
M Can you remember what he looked like?
W He was wearing a black baseball cap and blue jacket. He looked tall and skinny.
M Did you see anyone get hurt or anything on fire?
W No, I didn't see or hear anything else. The house was so quiet.
M I see. Thank you for your time.

남 그날 밤에 보신 것을 말씀해 주시겠습니까?
여 저는 택시에서 내리고 있었고, 누군가가 Bell 씨의 집의 창문을 통해서 나오는 것을 보았어요.
남 그가 어떻게 생겼는지 기억하시나요?
여 그는 검은색 야구모자를 쓰고 파란색 재킷을 입고 있었어요. 그는 키가 크고 비쩍 말라 보였어요.
남 누군가 다치거나 불이 난 것을 보셨나요?
여 아니요, 다른 어떤 것도 보거나 듣지 못했어요. 그 집은 정말 조용했어요.
남 알겠습니다. 시간 내 주셔서 감사합니다.

[해설] 여자가 목격한 것을 자세히 묻는 것으로 보아 남자는 경찰관임을 알 수 있다.

[어휘] remember 기억하다　look like ~처럼 보이다　skinny 비쩍 마른　get hurt 다치다

17 ④

M Good afternoon. Show me your driver's license, please.
W Did I do something wrong, officer?
M Yes, I'm afraid you violated a traffic rule. You're not supposed to turn right while the light is red.
W Oh, I didn't know that. I'm sorry. Here is my license.
M I will have to give you a ticket.
W How much is the fine?
M The fine for a traffic signal violation is $70.

남 안녕하세요. 운전면허증 좀 보여 주세요.
여 제가 잘못한 게 있나요, 경관님?
남 네, 유감이지만 교통 규칙을 위반하셨습니다. 빨간 불일 때는 우회전을 하시면 안 됩니다.
여 오, 그걸 몰랐어요. 죄송합니다. 여기 면허증이 있습니다.
남 제가 딱지를 드려야 겠네요.
여 벌금이 얼마인가요?
남 교통 신호 위반 벌금은 70달러입니다.

[해설] 벌금이 얼마인지 물었으므로 벌금의 액수에 대한 응답이 적절하다.

① 나는 경찰관이 되고 싶어.
② 나는 지난주에 할머니를 찾아뵈었어.
③ 여기에 차를 주차하시면 안 됩니다.
⑤ 그 도시를 방문할 때는 차를 빌려야 합니다.

18 ⑤

W I'm hungry. Let's eat something.
M Okay. What do you want to eat?
W I want to have a burger and fries.
M Again? You ate a cheeseburger yesterday! Eating fast food like hamburgers every day is not good for your health.
W But I love hamburgers! Why can't I have them every day?
M As teens, we need to have nutritious food to grow, but fast food is not nutritious!
W Okay, you win. Let's eat something else.

여 나 배고파. 뭐 좀 먹자.
남 그래. 너는 무엇을 먹고 싶니?
여 나는 햄버거와 감자튀김을 먹고 싶어.
남 또? 너 어제 치즈버거 먹었잖아! 햄버거 같은 패스트푸드를 매일 먹는 것은 건강에 좋지 않아.
여 하지만 난 햄버거가 정말 좋단 말이야! 왜 그것들을 매일 먹으면 안 되는데?
남 우리 같은 십 대들은 성장하기 위해 영양가 있는 음식을 먹어야 하는데, 패스트푸드는 영양가가 없어!
여 알았어, 네가 이겼어. 다른 것을 먹자.

해설 남자가 패스트푸드를 매일 먹는 것은 좋지 않다고 거듭하여 충고하고 있으므로, 알겠다고 답하며 다른 것을 먹자는 응답이 가장 적절하다.
① 너는 어디에 머물 예정이니?
② 제가 그것들을 살게요. 그것들은 얼마인가요?
③ 나는 피자를 먹을래. 너는?
④ 대신에 따뜻한 차 좀 드실래요?

19 ②

M What's the matter? You look upset!
W I'm so angry at my sister.
M Why?
W Yesterday, she wore my skirt without telling me and ended up leaving a stain on it.
M Oh, that's terrible.
W And today, she told me she lost my camera! I'm tired of her using my things without my permission!
M You should tell her how you feel.

남 무슨 일 있니? 화나 보여!
여 내 여동생 때문에 너무 화가 나.
남 왜?
여 어제, 그녀는 나에게 말도 하지 않고 내 치마를 입더니 결국 치마에 얼룩을 남겼어.
남 오, 정말 안됐다.
여 그리고 오늘 그녀는 나에게 내 카메라를 잃어버렸다고 말했어. 나는 그녀가 허락 없이 내 물건을 쓰는 것이 지긋지긋해.
남 너는 그녀에게 너의 감정을 말해야겠다.

해설 여자가 허락 없이 자신의 물건을 사용하는 여동생 때문에 화가 나 있으므로 그에 대한 조언의 말을 하는 것이 적절하다.
① 나는 네가 빨리 낫기를 바라.
③ 너는 그녀에게 사실을 말하지 않는 게 좋겠어.
④ 새로운 카메라를 사는 게 어때?
⑤ 나는 네가 그녀에게 사실을 말해야 한다고 생각해.

20 ⑤

M Steve and Kate had a great meal at a fancy restaurant. The food was very good, and they had a great time together. As the price of the meal was a little expensive, they agree to go Dutch. They are about to leave the restaurant, and they want to get their bill. What will Steve say to the waiter?
Steve Can you give us separate bills, please?

남 Steve와 Kate는 고급 식당에서 훌륭한 식사를 했다. 음식은 정말 만족스러웠고, 그들은 함께 즐거운 시간을 보냈다. 식사 비용이 약간 비쌌기 때문에, 그들은 비용을 각자 내는 것에 동의한다. 그들은 식당을 막 떠나려고 하고 있고, 그들의 계산서를 받고 싶어 한다. Steve는 웨이터에게 무엇이라고 말하겠는가?
Steve 계산서를 나눠서 주시겠어요?

해설 식사 비용을 각자 내기로 한 상황이므로 계산서를 분리해 달라고 말하는 것이 적절하다.
① 제 코트를 가져다주시겠어요?
② 음식을 가져갈 수 있도록 포장해 주시겠어요?
③ 식당의 위치가 어디인가요?
④ 음식이 매우 실망스러웠습니다.

01 ④	02 ⑤	03 ⑤	04 ①	05 ①
06 ⑤	07 ②	08 ④	09 ④	10 ④
11 ③	12 ②	13 ①	14 ②	15 ②
16 ③	17 ③	18 ⑤	19 ⑤	20 ⑤

01 ④

M I'm looking for a card for my younger brother.
W How about this one? This superhero character is <u>very popular with kids</u>.
M Well, he loves robots and cars, not superheroes.
W Sure. What about this one with three small cars?
M Oh, can I see that car-shaped one <u>instead</u>?
W Okay. You can get that card <u>with two different messages</u> in it. One is "Happy Birthday," and the other is "I Love You."
M I'll buy the one that says "Happy Birthday."

남 남동생에게 줄 카드를 찾고 있어요.
여 이건 어떠세요? 이 슈퍼히어로 캐릭터가 아이들에게 인기가 많아요.
남 음, 그 애는 슈퍼히어로가 아니라 로봇과 자동차를 좋아해요.
여 네. 작은 자동차 세 대가 있는 이 카드는 어떠세요?
남 아, 대신에 저 자동차 모양 카드를 볼 수 있을까요?
여 알겠어요. 그 카드에는 두 개의 다른 메시지가 있어요. 하나는 'Happy Birthday'이고, 다른 하나는 'I Love You'예요.
남 'Happy Birthday'라고 쓰인 카드를 살게요.

해설 남자는 'Happy Birthday'라는 메시지가 쓰인 자동차 모양의 카드를 사겠다고 했다.

어휘 character 캐릭터 popular 인기 있는 car-shaped 자동차 모양의 instead 대신에 message 메시지, 문구 the other (둘 또는 여럿 중) 나머지 하나

02 ⑤

M You were late for school again today. Did you oversleep?
W No, I got up early and <u>took the bus on time</u>, but there was heavy traffic.
M I used to have that problem, too. So I decided to just bike to school.
W <u>How long does it take</u> you to get here?
M Only fifteen minutes. Why don't you do <u>the same</u>?
W But I'm not sure if I can <u>ride my bike to school</u> by myself. Can I ride with you?
M No problem. Let's meet at 8:20 in front of the apartment bike rack tomorrow morning.

남 너 오늘 학교에 또 지각했지. 늦잠 잤니?
여 아니, 일찍 일어나서 제시간에 버스를 탔는데, 차가 많이 막혔어.

남 나도 그런 문제를 겪었었지. 그래서 나는 그냥 자전거를 타고 등교하기로 결정했어.
여 여기까지 얼마나 걸리는데?
남 15분밖에 안 걸려. 너도 그렇게 하는 게 어때?
여 하지만 난 내가 자전거로 혼자 등교할 수 있을지 모르겠어. 네가 나와 함께 타고 가 줄래?
남 문제없어. 내일 아침 아파트 자전거 보관대 앞에서 8시 20분에 만나자.

해설 여자는 남자에게 자신과 함께 자전거를 타고 등교할 것을 부탁했다.

어휘 oversleep 늦잠 자다 on time 제시간에 heavy traffic 극심한 교통량 used to ~하곤 했다 problem 문제 decide 결정하다 do the same 똑같이 하다 by oneself 혼자서 bike rack 자전거 보관대

03 ⑤

M I'd like to make a reservation.
W When would you like to make a reservation for?
M This Friday, at seven in the evening.
W That will be on October 30 at 7 p.m. <u>How many people are there</u> in your party?
M Six people. Four adults and two kids.
W All right. Are there any specific dishes you would like us to <u>prepare for you</u>?
M Well, we would like 4 servings of smoked duck for the adults and 2 servings of bacon fried rice for the kids.
W Sure. Could you <u>tell me your name</u> and contact number, please?
M My name is Tony Brown, and my number is 010-234-5678.

남 예약하고 싶은데요.
여 언제 예약해 드릴까요?
남 이번 주 금요일, 저녁 7시요.
여 10월 30일 오후 7시가 되겠군요. 일행이 몇 분이신가요?
남 여섯 명이요. 어른 네 명과 아이 두 명입니다.
여 알겠습니다. 특별히 저희가 준비해야 할 음식이 있나요?
남 음. 어른용 훈제 오리 4인분과 어린이용 베이컨 볶음밥 2인분요.
여 네. 이름과 연락처를 알려 주시겠어요?
남 제 이름은 Tony Brown이고, 전화번호는 010-234-5678입니다.

해설 남자가 주문한 음식은 훈제 오리 4인분과 베이컨 볶음밥 2인분이다.

어휘 make a reservation 예약하다 party 일행 adult 어른, 성인 specific 특정한 dish 요리 prepare 준비하다 serving (음식의) 1인분 smoked 훈제한 contact number 연락처 전화번호

04 ①

M Attention, students. This is an announcement from

the science department. Dr. Bruce Phillips' speech on endangered species was supposed to be at 5 p.m. today. But I'm sorry to announce that today's speech has been canceled due to his sudden illness. Instead, there will be a documentary movie titled *Saving Polar Bears*. Again, we're very sorry for this change in schedule.

남 학생 여러분, 주목해 주십시오. 과학부에서 알려 드립니다. 오늘 멸종 위기의 종에 관한 Bruce Phillips 박사님의 강의가 오후 5시에 예정되어 있었습니다. 하지만 박사님의 갑작스러운 병환 때문에 오늘 강의가 취소되었음을 알려 드리게 되어 죄송합니다. 그 대신, 〈Saving Polar Bears〉라는 제목의 다큐멘터리 영화가 있을 것입니다. 다시 한 번, 일정상 변경이 생기게 되어 매우 죄송합니다.

해설 강사의 갑작스러운 병환 때문에 예정된 강의가 취소되었음을 알리는 방송이다.

어휘 announcement 공지, 알림 department 부서 speech 강의 endangered 멸종 위기에 처한 species 종(種) announce 알리다 cancel 취소하다 due to ~ 때문에 sudden 갑작스러운 illness 병 instead 대신에 documentary 다큐멘터리 change 바꾸다, 변경하다 schedule 일정

05 ①

M Suji, your shoes look very nice.
W Do they? I bought this pair at Claire's Choice. They're having a big sale right now.
M Really? How much did you pay for them?
W The original price was $40, but all shoes are on sale at 50% off.
M Fifty percent? Then you got them for just $20, right?
W Actually, I got a bigger discount than that.
M Even more? How?
W Well, I used a five-dollar discount coupon I got from the flyer.

남 수지야, 네 신발 정말 멋지다.
여 그래? Claire's Choice에서 이것을 샀어. 지금 할인을 많이 하고 있거든.
남 정말? 얼마를 냈는데?
여 원래 가격은 40달러였는데, 모든 신발이 50퍼센트 할인 중이야.
남 50퍼센트? 그럼 20달러에 산 거네, 그렇지?
여 사실, 나는 그보다 할인을 더 많이 받았어.
남 거기서 더? 어떻게?
여 응, 전단지에 있던 5달러짜리 할인 쿠폰을 사용했거든.

해설 여자는 원래 40달러였던 신발을 50퍼센트 할인받았고, 여기에 5달러 할인 쿠폰을 사용했으므로 15달러를 지불했다.

어휘 original 원래의 price 가격 on sale 할인 중인(*cf.* for sale 판매 중인) actually 사실은 discount 할인 flyer 전단지

06 ⑤

W Do you have any baggage to check in?
M Just this one.
W Please place your bag on the scale.
M Okay. One bag is free, right?
W Yes. The free checked baggage allowance is one bag, but it must not exceed 20 kilograms in weight.
M I didn't know that regulation.
W Sorry, but the overweight charge for your bag is $50.

여 부치실 짐이 있으십니까?
남 이거 하나예요.
여 저울 위에 가방을 올려 주시기 바랍니다.
남 알겠습니다. 가방 하나는 무료인 거죠, 그렇죠?
여 네. 무료 수하물 허용은 가방 하나입니다만, 무게가 20킬로그램이 초과하면 안 됩니다.
남 그런 규정은 몰랐어요.
여 죄송합니다만, 고객님 가방에 대한 중량 초과 요금은 50달러입니다.

해설 비행기 탑승 전에 짐을 부치는 과정에서 나누는 대화이므로 두 사람의 관계는 항공사 직원과 승객이다.

어휘 baggage 짐, 수하물 check ~ in (비행기 등을 탈 때 짐을) 부치다 scale 저울 allowance 허용(량) exceed 초과하다 weight 무게 regulation 규정 overweight 중량 초과의 charge 요금

07 ②

① M Did you finish writing your report?
　W Yes, I finished it yesterday.
② M Why didn't you come to Chinese class?
　W Okay. Let's make it at five.
③ M Do you have any seat preference?
　W Please let me have a window seat.
④ M Did you buy a present for her?
　W Not yet. I'm just thinking about that.
⑤ M Can you tell me the way to the post office?
　W Go straight two blocks. It's on your left.

① 남 리포트 작성 끝마쳤니?
　여 네, 어제 끝냈어요.
② 남 중국어 수업에 왜 안 왔니?
　여 좋아. 5시에 만나자.
③ 남 선호하는 좌석이 있으신가요?
　여 창가쪽 좌석으로 주세요.
④ 남 그녀에게 줄 선물을 샀니?
　여 아직. 그것에 대해 생각 중이야.
⑤ 남 우체국에 가는 길을 알려 주시겠어요?
　여 두 블록 직진하세요. 그것은 왼쪽에 있어요.

해설 ② 수업에 오지 않은 이유를 물었는데 약속 시간을 정하는 말을 하는 것은 어색하다.

어휘 preference 선호 seat 좌석 present 선물 post office 우체국 straight 곧장, 똑바로

08 ④

(Cellphone rings.)

M Hello, Mom. It's me.

W Steve, what's up?

M I'm suffering from a terrible headache, so I have to leave school early.

W Oh, no! Your voice sounds bad. Did you get permission from your teacher?

M Yes. And the school nurse told me to see a doctor right away. So could you come to the school and take me to the doctor's?

W I really want to, but I have an important meeting. Instead, I'll call your dad and ask him if he can pick you up now.

M Okay. I'll be in the nurse's office.

(휴대 전화가 울린다.)

남 여보세요, 엄마. 저예요.

여 Steve, 무슨 일이니?

남 저 두통이 심해서 학교에서 조퇴해야겠어요.

여 오, 저런! 목소리가 안 좋구나. 선생님께 허락받았니?

남 네. 그리고 보건 선생님이 당장 병원에 가 보라고 말씀하셨어요. 그러니까 엄마가 학교에 오셔서 저 좀 병원에 데려가 주실래요?

여 정말 그러고 싶은데, 나는 중요한 회의가 있단다. 대신에, 내가 네 아빠한테 전화해서 지금 널 데리러 가실 수 있는지 여쭤볼게.

남 알겠어요. 전 보건실에 있을게요.

> **해설** 여자는 회의 때문에 남자(아들)를 데리러 갈 수 없어서 남자의 아빠, 즉 여자의 남편에게 전화해서 갈 수 있는지 물어보겠다고 했다.

> **어휘** suffer from ~로 고통받다 terrible 끔찍한 headache 두통 voice 목소리 permission 허락 school nurse 보건 선생님 pick up ~을 (차에) 태우러 가다 nurse's office 보건실

09 ④

M Hi, Jenny. My family moved to a new apartment.

W Oh, how's the new house?

M The place is not that large but the view is great. My house is on the 27th floor.

W Wow, you live in a high-rise apartment. How's your neighborhood?

M People are very kind. But one disadvantage is that it's far from school.

W How far?

M Well, it used to take about fifteen minutes to go to school, but now it takes double the time.

W Oh, you must be busy in the morning.

남 안녕, Jenny. 우리 가족이 새로운 아파트로 이사를 했어.

여 오, 새 집은 어때?

남 공간이 그렇게 넓지는 않지만 전망이 아주 좋아. 우리 집이 27층이거든.

여 와, 고층 아파트에 사는구나. 이웃은 어떠니?

남 사람들은 매우 친절해. 그런데 한 가지 단점은 학교에서 멀다는

거야.

여 얼마나 먼데?

남 음, 예전에는 학교에 가는 데 15분 정도 걸렸는데, 지금은 두 배가 걸려.

여 오, 너 아침에 바쁘겠구나.

> **해설** 관리비는 언급되지 않았다.

> **어휘** place 공간, 장소 high-rise 고층의 disadvantage 불리한 점, 약점 double 두 배

10 ④

W Hello. My name is Joan Brown. I'm going to teach English Literature to you this semester. We are going to meet every Thursday from 10 a.m. to 12 p.m. If you're late for the class, I will deduct a class participation point. You will have two reports to write: one is an individual report, and the other is a group assignment. Plus, you will take a final exam at the end of the semester. Are there any questions?

여 안녕하세요. 제 이름은 Joan Brown입니다. 저는 이번 학기에 여러분에게 영문학을 가르칠 것입니다. 우리는 매주 목요일 오전 10시부터 오후 12시까지 만날 것입니다. 만약 여러분이 수업에 늦는다면, 수업 참여 점수에서 감점을 할 것입니다. 여러분은 두 개의 리포트를 써야 하는데, 하나는 개인 과제이고 다른 하나는 조별 과제입니다. 게다가, 여러분은 학기말에 기말고사를 보게 될 것입니다. 질문 있나요?

> **해설** 조별 과제의 주제는 언급되지 않았다.

> **어휘** literature 문학 semester 학기 be late for ~에 늦다, 지각하다 deduct 공제하다, 감하다 participation 참가, 참여 individual 개인의 assignment 과제 plus 게다가 final exam 기말고사 at the end of ~의 말에

11 ③

M Is she your grandmother? Wow! She looks so young.

W Yes, many people say that. She really does not look her age.

M Do you know what her secret is? Does she eat only healthy food?

W I don't think so. She just exercises regularly.

M Oh, does she?

W Yeah, she goes to the gym at 6 a.m. every morning.

M Now I see. Regular exercise is her secret.

W Yeah, I think so.

남 저분이 너희 할머니시니? 우와! 정말 젊어 보이신다.

여 응, 많은 사람들이 그렇게 말해. 할머니는 정말 그 연세로 안 보이셔.

남 너희 할머니의 비결이 뭔지 아니? 할머니께서 건강식만 드시니?

여 그렇진 않으신 것 같아. 할머니는 규칙적으로 운동을 하실 뿐이야.

남 아, 그러시니?
여 응, 할머니는 매일 아침 6시에 체육관에 가셔.
남 이제 알겠다. 규칙적인 운동이 할머니의 비결이구나.
여 맞아, 그런 것 같아.

해설 여자의 할머니가 젊어 보이는 이유는 매일 규칙적으로 운동을 하시기 때문인 것 같다고 했다.

어휘 age 나이   secret 비밀, 비결   healthy 건강한, 건강에 좋은   regularly 규칙적으로   gym 체육관

12 ②

M Welcome to this season's first performance at Wilson Youth Theater. The play will last about three hours and we'll have a fifteen-minute break after one and a half hours. A snack shop is on the third floor, next to the elevator. We'd also like to remind you that both photography and recording are forbidden. Now, please turn off your cellphones. We shall begin shortly.

남 Wilson Youth Theater의 이번 시즌 첫 번째 공연에 오신 것을 환영합니다. 연극은 약 세 시간 동안 진행되며 1시간 30분 후에 15분간 휴식 시간을 갖겠습니다. 매점은 3층 엘리베이터 옆에 있습니다. 저희는 또한 여러분께 사진 촬영과 녹화가 모두 금지됨을 상기시켜 드립니다. 자, 이제 휴대 전화를 꺼 주세요. 곧 시작하겠습니다.

해설 휴식 시간은 15분이라고 했다.

어휘 performance 공연   last 지속되다   break 휴식   snack shop 매점   remind 상기시키다   photography 사진 촬영   record 녹화하다   forbid 금지하다   turn off ~을 끄다

13 ①

W Which movie do you want to see?
M What about Spider-Man?
W Sorry, I've already seen it with my brother. It's a really exciting movie.
M Then what about Free Solo?
W Don't you think it finishes too late? I have to be home by 9 o'clock.
M So the movie should finish before 8. Then there are only two movies left we can see.
W How about this one that got five stars from the critics?
M Okay. I don't think it'll disappoint us.

여 너는 어느 영화를 보고 싶니?
남 〈Spider-Man〉 어때?
여 미안하지만, 내 남동생이랑 이미 봤어. 정말 재밌는 영화야.
남 그럼 〈Free Solo〉는 어떠니?
여 너무 늦게 끝나는 것 같지 않니? 난 9시까지는 집에 가야 해.
남 그럼 영화가 8시 전에는 끝나야겠구나. 그러면 우리가 볼 수 있는 건 딱 두 편만 남았어.
여 비평가들로부터 별 다섯 개를 받은 이 영화 어때니?
남 좋아. 우리를 실망시키지 않을 것 같아.

해설 〈Spider-Man〉은 여자가 이미 봤고, 8시 전에 끝나는 두 편 중에서 별 다섯 개의 평점을 받은 영화는 〈The Grinch〉이다.

어휘 already 이미, 벌써   exciting 재미있는, 흥미진진한   critic 평론가, 비평가   disappoint 실망시키다

14 ②

W This is a department in a hospital, and it operates 24 hours a day. People who have severe injuries or sudden illnesses are taken there for urgent treatment. It is not necessary to make an appointment first. If you need to get there really fast, you can call 119 for an ambulance. We often call it ER, which is the short form for this.

여 이것은 병원에 있는 부서이고, 하루 24시간 운영한다. 심각한 부상이나 갑작스러운 질병이 생긴 사람들이 긴급한 치료를 받기 위해 그곳으로 후송된다. 먼저 예약을 할 필요 없다. 만약 당신이 아주 빨리 그곳에 도착해야 한다면, 당신은 구급차를 부르기 위해 119에 전화할 수 있다. 우리는 종종 그것을 ER이라고 부르는데, ER은 이것의 줄임말이다.

해설 병원에 있고 하루 24시간 운영되며 심각한 부상이나 갑작스러운 질병이 생긴 환자가 후송되는 곳은 응급실이다.

어휘 department 부서   operate 운영하다   severe 심각한   injury 부상   sudden 갑작스런   urgent 긴급한   treatment 치료   necessary 필수적인   appointment 약속, 예약   ambulance 구급차   ER(= emergency room) 응급실

15 ②

(Cellphone rings.)
M Hello, Sally. It's Eric.
W Hi, Eric! What's up?
M Are you still at the cafeteria?
W Yes, but I am just about to leave.
M Whew, that's good. Then could you check if my bag is still there?
W Your bag? What does it look like?
M It's a small blue bag with two short handles on the top.
W Let me check. (Pause) Oh, here it is! Your name is on it.
M Yes! Could you bring it back to the dorm? Call me when you get back, and I'll go and get it.

(휴대 전화가 울린다.)
남 안녕, Sally. 나 Eric이야.
여 안녕, Eric! 무슨 일이니?
남 너 아직 식당에 있니?
여 응, 하지만 지금 막 떠나려던 참이야.
남 휴, 다행이다. 그럼 내 가방이 아직 그곳에 있는지 확인해 줄래?
여 네 가방? 어떻게 생겼는데?
남 작은 파란색 가방인데 위에는 짧은 손잡이가 두 개 달려 있어.
여 한번 볼게. (잠시 후) 오, 여기 있어! 가방에 네 이름이 있어.
남 맞아! 기숙사에 돌아오는 길에 그것 좀 가져다줄래? 돌아오면 내게 전화해 줘, 그러면 내가 가지러 갈게.

해설 남자는 식당에 가방을 놓고 와서 여자에게 기숙사에 돌아오는 길에 자신의 가방을 가져다 달라고 부탁했다.

어휘 cafeteria 셀프 서비스식 식당, 구내식당   be about to 막 ~하려고 하다   look like ~처럼 보이다   handle 손잡이   dorm(= dormitory) 기숙사

16 ③

W Jason, it's already 11 o'clock. You should go to bed.

M I know, Mom. But I've not finished my report yet. I have to hand in this report tomorrow.

W Why don't you get up early tomorrow and finish it? You look so tired.

M Okay. I'm so tired. Can you wake me up an hour before I usually leave for school?

W Sure. You leave for school at 8, so I will wake you up at 7.

M Now that I think about it, that's too late. You'd better wake me up at 6.

W Okay, I will.

여 Jason, 벌써 11시야. 너는 자러 가야 해.

남 알아요, 엄마. 하지만 아직 리포트를 못 끝냈어요. 내일 이 리포트를 제출해야 해요.

여 내일 일찍 일어나서 끝내는 게 어떠니? 너 정말 피곤해 보여.

남 그럴게요. 저는 너무 피곤해요. 제가 보통 학교에 가기 한 시간 전에 깨워 주시겠어요?

여 물론이지. 너는 학교에 8시에 가니까, 7시에 깨워 줄게.

남 생각해 보니, 너무 늦은 것 같아요. 6시에 깨워 주시는 게 좋겠어요.

여 좋아, 그렇게 할게.

해설 남자는 내일 아침 학교에 가기 전에 리포트를 완성하기 위해 6시에 일어나려고 한다.

어휘 hand in 제출하다   wake up 깨우다   leave 출발하다, 떠나다   now that ~이므로

17 ③

W Hi, Brian! How's your leg?

M Hi, Jenny. It hurts a lot. But thanks for coming here.

W How can't I come when you're injured? When will you leave here?

M I'll be out of here tomorrow. I can use crutches to move around.

W That sounds good. Anyway, how did you break your leg?

M I broke it while playing soccer last Friday.

W You must have got tackled hard by an opponent.

M Yes, I was. But he apologized to me.

여 안녕, Brian! 다리는 좀 어떠니?

남 안녕, Jenny. 많이 아파. 그런데 와줘서 고마워.

여 네가 다쳤는데 어떻게 내가 안 올 수 있니? 이곳에서 언제 나가니?

남 내일 이곳에서 나갈 거야. 목발을 사용해서 돌아다닐 수 있어.

여 잘됐다. 그런데, 어쩌다가 다리가 부러졌니?

남 지난 금요일에 축구하다가 부러졌어.

여 상대편에게 태클을 심하게 당한 모양이구나.

남 응, 그랬어. 하지만 그가 내게 사과했어.

해설 여자는 축구를 하다가 다리가 부러진 남자를 보며 상대편이 남자를 태클한 것이 틀림없다고 확신했으므로, 이에 대한 사실 여부를 답하는 것이 가장 적절하다.
① 결국, 난 레드카드를 받았어.
② 넌 재미있는 경기를 보지 못했어.
④ 아니야. 이번엔 내 잘못이 아니라고 생각해.
⑤ 맞아. 난 한 주 더 병원에 있고 싶지 않아.

어휘 injure 다치게 하다   crutch 목발   must have p.p. ~했음이 틀림없다   tackle 태클하다   opponent 상대편   fault 잘못   apologize 사과하다

18 ⑤

W Hi, Seho. You missed an important exam last week. Why?

M My grandmother suddenly passed away last week. I was at her funeral.

W Oh, I'm really sorry to hear that.

M Thanks. I am worried about my father. He is having a hard time.

W Her sudden death must have shocked your father.

M It is hard for me to watch him feel sad and depressed.

W Cheer up. It will take some time for him to accept her death.

여 안녕, 세호야. 너 지난주에 중요한 시험을 놓쳤지. 왜 그랬니?

남 지난주에 할머니께서 갑자기 돌아가셨거든. 난 할머니 장례식에 갔었어.

여 아, 그 말을 들으니 정말 유감이다.

남 고마워. 난 아버지가 걱정돼. 아버지는 힘든 시간을 보내고 계셔.

여 할머니께서 갑자기 돌아가셔서 너희 아버지께서 충격을 받으셨나 봐.

남 아버지가 슬퍼하고 우울해하시는 걸 보는 게 힘들어.

여 힘내. 너희 아버지께서 할머니의 죽음을 받아들이시는 데 시간이 필요하실 거야.

해설 남자는 할머니께서 돌아가신 후 아버지께서 우울해하시는 모습을 보는 게 힘들다고 했으므로 남자를 위로하는 말을 하는 것이 가장 적절하다.
① 기운 내. 너는 빠르게 회복할 거야.
② 너는 너희 아버지께서 말씀하신 대로 하는 게 좋겠어.
③ 넌 할머니 장례식에 가야 할 것 같아.
④ 시험을 놓치다니 네가 어리석었어.

어휘 miss 놓치다   important 중요한   suddenly 갑자기   pass away 돌아가시다   funeral 장례식   be worried about ~에 대해 걱정하다   death 죽음   shock 충격을 주다   depressed 우울한   recover 회복하다   stupid 어리석은   accept 받아들이다

19 ⑤

W Why the long face, Mark?

M I failed the singing audition for the school band.

W That's too bad. The club is very popular.

M I really wanted to join it, so I practiced hard for a few days.

W I'm sorry to hear that. Well, how about trying out for the musical club?

M Is there a musical club in our school?

W Sure. I believe you're interested in acting as well as singing.

M I am! That's exactly the club I'm looking for.

여 왜 그렇게 우울해 보이니, Mark?

남 학교 밴드부의 노래 오디션에서 떨어졌어.

여 정말 안됐구나. 그 동아리 정말 인기 많더라.

남 난 정말 그 동아리에 들어가고 싶어서 며칠 동안 열심히 연습했어.

여 그 말을 들으니 유감이다. 그런데, 너 뮤지컬 동아리에 지원해 보는 건 어때?

남 우리 학교에 뮤지컬 동아리가 있어?

여 응. 너는 노래뿐만 아니라 연기에도 관심 있잖아.

남 맞아! 그게 바로 내가 찾고 있는 동아리야.

[해설] 여자는 밴드부 오디션에 떨어져 낙심한 남자에게 뮤지컬 동아리에 지원해 보라고 권유했으므로 이에 대한 긍정적인 응답이 가장 적절하다.

① 넌 내가 연습을 더 해야 한다고 생각하니?

② 나는 학교 밴드부의 보컬리스트였어.

③ 난 음악과 관련된 어떤 것에도 관심 없어.

④ 하지만 난 많은 사람들 앞에서 노래 못 불러.

[어휘] audition 오디션   popular 인기 있는   try out for ~에 지원하다   be interested in ~에 관심이 있다   *A* as well as *B* B뿐만 아니라 A도   practice 연습   be into ~에 관심이 많다, ~을 좋아하다   related to ~와 관련된

20 ⑤

M Minho is going to take a trip to Jeju-do with his family this Saturday. On Wednesday afternoon, Minho is having lunch with Sandra, a transfer student from India. Sandra asks him to show her around Seoul this Saturday. Minho would love to show her around, but he has to refuse because of his plan to take a trip to Jeju-do that day. In this situation, what would Minho most likely say to Sandra?

Minho Sandra, I'd love to, but I can't. We're taking a family trip that day.

남 민호는 이번 주 토요일에 가족과 함께 제주도로 여행을 갈 것이다. 수요일 오후에, 민호는 인도에서 전학 온 학생 Sandra와 점심을 먹고 있다. Sandra는 그에게 이번 토요일에 서울 구경을 시켜 줄 수 있는지 묻는다. 민호는 그녀에게 구경시켜 주고 싶지만, 그날 제주도 여행 계획 때문에 거절해야 한다. 이런 상황에서, 민호는 Sandra에게 뭐라고 말할 것 같은가?

민호 Sandra, 그러고 싶지만 할 수가 없어. 우리는 그날 가족 여행을 갈 예정이거든.

[해설] 미리 계획한 가족 여행 때문에 여자의 제안을 거절해야 하는 상황이므로 거절과 함께 그 이유를 설명하는 것이 적절하다.

① 토요일에는 수업이 없어.

② 난 제주도보다 서울이 더 좋아.

③ 왜 안 되겠니? 3시에 만나자.

④ 네가 가고 싶은 곳 어디든지 데려갈게.

[어휘] take a trip 여행하다   transfer student 전학생   refuse 거절하다   because of ~ 때문에

Review Test   pp.168~169

Word Check   15회

01 수비의
02 짐
03 수료증
04 지친
05 위치하고 있는
06 조직하다, 편성하다
07 전진하다
08 계산서
09 고급의, 일류의
10 ~에 동의하다
11 체중을 줄이다
12 좋아지다
13 truth
14 violate
15 nutritious
16 lecturer
17 separate
18 poll
19 permission
20 choose
21 highlight
22 traffic rule
23 skinny
24 go Dutch

Expression Check

25 on fire
26 about to
27 participate in
28 broke up with
29 ended up
30 every time

Word Check   16회

01 금지하다
02 상대편
03 특정한
04 운영하다
05 회복하다
06 평론가, 비평가
07 멸종 위기에 처한
08 중량 초과의
09 공제하다, 감하다
10 ~ 때문에
11 초과하다
12 ~하곤 했다
13 refuse
14 weight
15 treatment
16 urgent
17 depressed
18 disadvantage
19 department
20 regulation
21 literature
22 funeral
23 high-rise
24 transfer student

Expression Check

25 check in
26 hand in
27 passed away
28 as well as
29 at the end of
30 One, the other

01 ④	02 ⑤	03 ②	04 ⑤	05 ②
06 ④	07 ②	08 ②	09 ②	10 ③
11 ②	12 ①	13 ⑤	14 ⑤	15 ③
16 ④	17 ⑤	18 ①	19 ④	20 ①

01 ④

M Is that a class picture from your field trip? Who's your best friend?

W It's Elsie. Guess who she is.

M Umm... is she the tall girl standing next to your teacher?

W No, she isn't wearing a cap. She is wearing glasses.

M Then is she next to the boy wearing a baseball cap?

W No, she is near that boy. Elsie always enjoys listening to music.

M Oh, I found her. She must be the girl wearing big headphones.

W Yes, exactly. That's my best friend Elsie.

남 그것은 현장학습에서 찍은 학급 사진이니? 누가 너의 가장 친한 친구니?

여 Elsie예요. 누군지 맞춰 보세요.

남 음… 너희 선생님 옆에 서 있는 키 큰 여학생이니?

여 아니에요, 그녀는 모자를 쓰고 있지 않아요. 안경을 쓰고 있어요.

남 그렇다면 야구 모자를 쓴 남학생 옆에 있는 애니?

여 아니요, 그녀는 그 남학생 근처에 있어요. Elsie는 항상 음악을 즐겨 들어요.

남 아, 그녀를 찾았어. 큰 헤드폰을 끼고 있는 여학생이 틀림없어.

여 네, 정확해요. 그녀가 저의 가장 친한 친구 Elsie예요.

해설 안경을 쓰고 큰 헤드폰을 낀 여학생이 Elsie이다.

어휘 field trip 현장학습   guess 알아맞히다   next to ~ 옆에   glasses 안경   near ~ 근처에   exactly 정확하게

02 ⑤

M What do you want to do this coming Christmas?

W Well, why don't we just stay home?

M Really? You don't want to eat out?

W There were so many people everywhere last year. So let's just celebrate it at home.

M Okay, then I'm going to make you some delicious food.

W Thanks. Then I'll decorate the Christmas tree with lights and a big star on top.

M I'm sure the tree will look fantastic!

남 다가오는 이번 크리스마스에 무엇을 하고 싶어요?

여 음, 그냥 집에 있는 게 어때요?

남 정말로요? 외식하고 싶지 않나요?

여 작년에는 모든 곳에 사람들이 너무 많았어요. 그러니까 그냥 집에서 기념해요.

남 알았어요, 그러면 내가 맛있는 음식을 만들어 줄게요.

여 고마워요. 그럼 나는 조명과 큰 별을 맨 위에 올려서 크리스마스트리를 장식할게요.

남 틀림없이 트리가 환상적일 거예요!

해설 남자는 요리를 하기로 했고 여자는 크리스마스트리를 장식하기로 했다.

어휘 eat out 외식하다   everywhere 모든 곳에   celebrate 기념하다, 축하하다   decorate 장식하다   light 전등, 조명   fantastic 환상적인

03 ②

① W May I pet the puppy?

　 M Sure. She won't bite you.

② W Can I bring my dog with me in here?

　 M No. For the safety of your pet, no animals are allowed.

③ W Did you take the dog out for a walk today?

　 M Not yet. I usually walk the dog in the evening.

④ W I wonder what your dog looks like.

　 M It has black hair and short legs.

⑤ W What kind of pet would you like to have?

　 M A dog. Dogs are my favorite pets.

① 여 강아지를 쓰다듬어도 될까요?

　 남 물론이죠. 물지 않을 거예요.

② 여 여기에 개를 데리고 가도 되나요?

　 남 아니요. 애완동물의 안전을 위해서, 동물은 허용되지 않습니다.

③ 여 오늘 개를 데리고 나가서 산책했니?

　 남 아직. 나는 보통 저녁에 개를 산책시켜.

④ 여 나는 네 개가 어떻게 생겼는지 궁금해.

　 남 검은색 털과 짧은 다리를 갖고 있어.

⑤ 여 어떤 종류의 애완동물을 갖고 싶으세요?

　 남 개요. 개가 제가 가장 좋아하는 애완동물이에요.

해설 여자가 개를 데리고 들어갈 수 있는지 묻자 남자가 애완동물은 출입할 수 없다고 답하는 상황이다.

어휘 pet 쓰다듬다; 애완동물   bite 물다   safety 안전   allow 허락하다   wonder 궁금하다

04 ⑤

W Did you finish your report on the Space Race?

M No, I'm reading a book on the development of space rockets for the report.

W It sounds interesting. I'd like to read it.

M Okay. I'll lend it to you after I'm finished.

W Thanks. When is the report deadline?

M I have to hand in the report by Wednesday.

W Then can you bring it to the writing club meeting on Saturday?

M No problem.

여 너 Space Race에 관한 보고서 마쳤니?

남 아니, 보고서 쓰려고 우주 로켓의 발전에 관한 책을 읽고 있어.

여 재미있겠다. 나도 그것을 읽고 싶어.

남 좋아. 내가 다 읽은 후에 너에게 빌려줄게.

여 고마워. 보고서 마감이 언제니?

남 수요일까지 보고서를 제출해야 해.

여 그럼 토요일 작문 동아리 모임에 그 책을 가져올래?

남 문제없어.

해설 여자가 토요일 동아리 모임에 책을 가져다 달라고 하자 남자는 그러겠다고 했다.

어휘 Space Race 우주 경쟁(미국과 구소련이 우주에서의 업적을 놓고 벌인 경쟁)   development 발전   lend 빌려주다   deadline 기한, 마감 일자   hand in 제출하다   writing 작문

05 ②

(Telephone rings.)

M Hello. This is Chicken Heaven. Is this Ms. Park?

W Yes. Is there a problem?

M Yes. We're not <u>sure of the</u> <u>exact</u> <u>address</u> to deliver the chicken to. Your school isn't on the map.

W Oh, our school <u>has a</u> <u>new name</u>. We used to be Seowon Middle School.

M All right. We'll be there in a few minutes.

W Oh, <u>could you bring</u> a 1.5-liter bottle of coke, too?

M No problem. We'll add that to your order of two fried chickens.

(전화벨이 울린다.)

남 여보세요. Chicken Heaven입니다. 박 선생님이신가요?

여 네. 문제가 있나요?

남 네. 치킨을 배달할 정확한 주소를 알 수가 없어서요. 손님 학교가 지도에 없어요.

여 아, 저희 학교 이름이 바뀌었어요. 예전에는 서원중학교였어요.

남 알겠습니다. 곧 가겠습니다.

여 저, 1.5리터 콜라 한 병도 가져다주실 수 있나요?

남 네. 주문하신 프라이드치킨 두 마리와 함께 보내드리겠습니다.

해설 남자는 치킨을 배달할 주소가 지도에 나와 있지 않아서 여자의 주소를 확인하기 위해 전화했다.

어휘 exact 정확한   address 주소   deliver 배달하다   map 지도   used to (예전에는) ~이었다   bottle 병   add 추가하다, 더하다

06 ④

W Hi. I'm here for an appointment at 3 o'clock.

M Let me see. Oh, Ms. Jessica Anderson. Please <u>take a seat here</u>.

W Thank you. I'd like my hair dyed light brown.

M Okay, and I think a wavy perm might <u>look good on you</u>.

W No, I don't like perms. How long do you think it will take to dye my hair?

M Probably two hours. Do you want to grab anything <u>before we get started</u>?

W Yes. I think I'll <u>grab</u> a <u>glass of water</u> and some magazines.

여 안녕하세요. 저는 3시 예약으로 여기에 왔는데요.

남 어디 봅시다. 아, Jessica Anderson님이시군요. 여기 앉으세요.

여 감사합니다. 저는 머리를 밝은 갈색으로 염색하고 싶어요.

남 네, 그리고 손님에게 웨이브 파마가 잘 어울리실 것 같아요.

여 아니에요. 전 파마를 안 좋아해요. 염색하는 데 얼마나 걸릴 것 같으세요?

남 아마도 두 시간쯤이요. 시작하기 전에 뭐 좀 챙겨드릴까요?

여 네. 물 한 잔과 잡지 좀 챙겨놔야겠어요.

해설 머리를 염색하러 온 손님과 미용사가 나누는 대화이므로 대화가 이루어지는 장소는 미용실이다.

어휘 appointment 약속, 예약   take a seat 자리에 앉다   dye 염색하다   wavy 웨이브가 있는   perm 파마; 파마하다   look good on ~에게 잘 어울리다   grab 손에 넣다(이용하다, 먹다)   magazine 잡지

07 ②

① M Can I talk to Mr. Brown, please?

   W I'm sorry, but he's <u>on the other line</u> now.

② M Did you watch *Christmas in Paris* last night?

   W I wanted to, but I couldn't. It was the best movie ever.

③ M I was late for school this morning.

   W Really? <u>You should have left</u> home earlier.

④ M Do you mind if I close the window?

   W Not at all. <u>I feel a little chilly</u>, too.

⑤ M Can you help me do my math homework today?

   W I'm afraid I can't. <u>I already have plans</u>.

① 남 Brown 씨와 통화할 수 있을까요?

   여 죄송하지만, 지금 통화 중이십니다.

② 남 어젯밤에 〈Christmas in Paris〉 봤니?

   여 보고 싶었지만 못 봤어. 이제껏 중 최고의 영화였어.

③ 남 오늘 아침에 학교에 지각했어요.

   여 정말? 넌 좀 더 일찍 집을 나섰어야 했어.

④ 남 창문을 닫아도 될까요?

   여 그럼요. 저도 약간 춥네요.

⑤ 남 오늘 내 수학 숙제하는 것 좀 도와줄래?

   여 안 될 것 같아. 난 이미 계획이 있거든.

해설 ② 영화를 봤는지 묻는 말에 못 봤다고 대답한 후 그것이 역대 최고의 영화였다고 이어서 말하는 것은 어색하다.

어휘 be on the other line 통화 중이다   should have p.p. ~했어야 했다   a little 약간   chilly 쌀쌀한   plan 계획

08 ②

M Where are you going, Jenny?

W I'm <u>going to the grocery</u> store.

M Are you going to the store on Main Street?

W Yes. Mom will be late today, so <u>I'm thinking about cooking curry</u> for dinner.

M Good. Could you get some digestive medicine for me?

W Oh, Dad, do you still <u>have a stomachache</u>? Shouldn't you see a doctor?

M No, <u>it's nothing serious</u>.

W All right. I'll get it for you.

남 Jenny, 어디 가려고 하니?

여 식료품점에 가려고요.

남 Main Street에 있는 그 가게에 갈 거니?

여 네. 오늘 엄마가 늦으신대요. 그래서 제가 저녁 식사로 카레를 만들어 볼 생각이에요.

남 좋아. 소화제를 좀 사다 줄 수 있겠니?

여 어머, 아빠, 아직도 배가 아프세요? 병원에 가 보셔야 하지 않을까요?

남 아니야, 심각한 건 아니야.

여 알겠어요. 제가 사 올게요.

<u>해설</u> 남자는 식료품점에 가는 여자에게 소화제를 사다 달라고 부탁했다.

<u>어휘</u> grocery store 식료품점 digestive medicine 소화제 stomachache 복통 see a doctor 진료를 받다 serious 심각한

09 ②

W I got a part-time job for this winter vacation.

M <u>Good for you</u>! What kind of work will you do?

W I'm going to work in my uncle's bakery.

M So are you going to work <u>all day long</u>?

W No. I'll work just four hours a day. From eight to noon.

M You'll have to get up early in the morning.

W I don't think so. The bakery is only five minutes on foot <u>from my apartment</u>.

여 나 이번 겨울방학에 할 시간제 일자리를 구했어.

남 잘됐구나! 어떤 종류의 일을 하는 거니?

여 나의 삼촌 제과점에서 일할 거야.

남 그러면 하루 종일 일하는 거니?

여 아니. 하루에 4시간만 일할 거야. 8시부터 정오까지.

남 아침에 일찍 일어나야겠구나.

여 그러지 않아도 돼. 그 제과점이 우리 아파트에서 걸어서 5분밖에 안 걸려.

<u>해설</u> 급여는 언급되지 않았다.

<u>어휘</u> part-time 시간제의 all day long 하루 종일 on foot 걸어서

10 ③

M I need to return these two books.

W Oh, it appears these books are <u>four days late</u>.

M I forgot they were overdue. Sorry.

W You know you <u>must pay a late fee</u>, right? The late fee is 25 cents a day.

M So I have to pay 25 cents for each day for each book? That's a lot.

W And what happened to this one?

M I <u>dropped it by mistake</u>, and the cover tore off.

W Hmm... you have to pay $2 <u>for the damage</u>.

남 이 책 두 권을 반납하려고 합니다.

여 오, 이 책들은 4일 연체된 것 같은데요.

남 기한이 지났다는 것을 잊었어요. 죄송합니다.

여 연체료를 지불해야 한다는 건 아시죠, 그렇죠? 연체료는 하루에 25센트입니다.

남 하루에 한 권당 25센트를 지불해야 한다고요? 많네요.

여 그리고, 이 책은 어떻게 된 거죠?

남 제가 실수로 떨어뜨렸는데, 표지가 찢어졌어요.

여 음… 손상에 대한 비용 2달러를 지불하셔야겠네요.

<u>해설</u> 책 한 권당 하루 연체료가 25센트인데 두 권을 4일간 연체했으므로 연체료는 총 2달러이다. 여기에 책이 훼손된 것에 대한 배상으로 2달러를 내야 하므로, 남자가 지불할 금액은 4달러이다.

<u>어휘</u> return 반납하다 appear ~인 것 같다 overdue 기한이 지난 pay 지불하다 late fee 연체료 drop 떨어뜨리다 by mistake 실수로 tear off 찢어내다 damage 손상

11 ②

W Today, I'll tell you about <u>the famous writer</u> Hans Christian Andersen. He was born on April 2, 1805, in Odense, Denmark. <u>His father was a shoemaker</u> and his mother a washerwoman. Although Andersen wrote novels, poems, plays, and travelogues, he is best remembered for his fairy tales. Some of <u>his most famous fairy tales</u> include *The Little Mermaid*, *The Nightingale*, and *The Ugly Duckling*.

여 오늘은 유명한 작가인 한스 크리스티안 안데르센에 대해 말씀드리겠습니다. 그는 1805년 4월 2일에 덴마크의 오덴세에서 태어났습니다. 그의 아버지는 구두 수선공이었고 어머니는 세탁업자였습니다. 안데르센은 소설, 시, 희곡, 그리고 여행기를 썼지만, 동화로 가장 잘 기억되고 있습니다. 그의 가장 유명한 동화에는 〈인어공주〉, 〈나이팅게일〉, 〈미운오리새끼〉가 포함됩니다.

<u>해설</u> 안데르센의 형제자매는 언급되지 않았다.

<u>어휘</u> famous 유명한 writer 작가 be born 태어나다 novel 소설 poem 시 play 희곡 travelogue 여행기 fairy tale 동화 include 포함하다 mermaid 인어 duckling 새끼 오리

12 ①

W <u>It feels like</u> the air is different in Jeju-do.

M I agree. Mom, what are we going to do tomorrow morning?

W The weather forecast says we will have a strong wind tomorrow morning, so <u>we'd better stay inside</u>.

M Ah, it's too bad I can't go sea fishing.

W Come on. Let's <u>find some fun indoor activities</u> in

the guidebook. How about the aquarium?

M Um... I think it's too far from the hotel. Why don't we go shopping nearby the hotel instead?

W Good idea. Let's go out for dinner now.

M Okay. I'd like to have some seafood dishes.

여 제주도는 공기가 다른 것 같구나.

남 맞아요. 엄마, 우리 내일 아침에 뭐 할까요?

여 일기 예보에서 내일 아침에 강풍이 불 거라고 하니까, 실내에 있는 게 좋겠어.

남 아, 바다낚시 하러 못 가서 너무 아쉬워요.

여 얘야. 안내 책자에서 재미있는 실내 활동을 좀 찾아보자. 수족관은 어떠니?

남 음… 그건 호텔에서 너무 먼 것 같아요. 대신에 호텔 근처에서 쇼핑하러 가는 게 어때요?

여 좋은 생각이구나. 이제 저녁 먹으러 나가자.

남 좋아요. 전 해산물 요리를 먹고 싶어요.

해설 두 사람은 내일 아침에 강풍이 분다는 일기 예보 때문에 호텔 근처에서 쇼핑하기로 했다.

어휘 air 공기   weather forecast 일기 예보   strong wind 강풍   had better ~하는 것이 좋겠다   inside 실내에서   activity 활동   guidebook 안내 책자   aquarium 수족관   far from ~에서 먼   nearby 근처의   instead 대신에   seafood 해산물   dish 요리

13 ⑤

M Central Park Zoo has a special program designed to connect you to nature. Please join us for our one-day zoo camp experience. During this one-day camp, you'll explore the Tropic Zone and learn about animals living in the tropics. Campers will also enjoy a jungle safari. It's filled with hands-on investigations and up-close animal encounters. The camp requires pre-registration. Don't miss this chance. Thank you.

남 Central Park Zoo에는 여러분을 자연과 연결시켜 드리기 위해 고안된 특별 프로그램이 있습니다. 저희 동물원 일일 체험 캠프에 참여하세요. 일일 캠프 동안에, 여러분은 열대 지역을 탐험하고 열대 지방에서 사는 동물들에 대해 배우게 될 것입니다. 캠프 참여자들은 밀림 사파리 여행도 즐기게 될 텐데요. 직접 해 보는 조사와 근거리에서의 동물들과의 만남을 만끽하게 됩니다. 캠프는 사전 등록이 필수입니다. 이번 기회를 놓치지 마세요. 감사합니다.

해설 동물원에서 제공하는 일일 캠프 프로그램을 소개하는 안내 방송이다.

어휘 designed 계획된, 고안된   connect 연결하다   nature 자연   explore 탐험하다   tropic zone 열대 지역   be filled with ~로 가득 차 있다   hands-on 직접 해 보는   investigation 조사, 연구   up-close 근거리의   encounter 만남, 조우   require 필요하다, 요구하다   pre-registration 사전 등록   chance 기회

14 ⑤

W These people work on a beach or at a swimming pool. They supervise the safety of swimmers, surfers, and people participating in other water sports. They are excellent swimmers, and they are trained in a variety of life-saving skills including first aid. They always wear a whistle around their necks and have important rescue or communication equipment close at hand.

여 이 사람들은 해변이나 수영장에서 일합니다. 그들은 수영하는 사람들, 파도타기 하는 사람들, 그리고 다른 수상 스포츠에 참여하는 사람들의 안전을 관리합니다. 그들은 수영을 아주 잘하며, 응급 처치를 포함한 다양한 인명 구조 기술 훈련을 받습니다. 그들은 항상 목에 호루라기를 걸고 있고 중요한 구조 장비나 통신 장비를 가까이에 두고 있습니다.

해설 해변이나 수영장에서 사람들의 안전을 관리하며 다양한 인명 구조 기술 훈련을 받은 사람은 인명 구조 요원이다.

어휘 supervise 관리하다, 감독하다   safety 안전   participate in ~에 참여하다   a variety of 여러 가지의   life-saving 인명 구조의   skill 기술   including ~을 포함한   first aid 응급 처치   whistle 호루라기   rescue 구조   equipment 장비   close at hand 쉽게 손닿는 곳에

15 ③

M Look at this notice. The community center provides free exercise classes for residents.

W Oh, there are many good classes. Dad, I'd really like to take a yoga class.

M But I think the class is too late. You should come back home earlier for dinner.

W Oh, that's too bad.

M How about aerobics? The classes are from 5:00 to 6:00 in the afternoon.

W Dad, I usually come home at 5:30. And every Monday I don't have time to exercise.

M Then you have only one option left. Would you like to take it?

W Sure. I have to do something to get in shape.

남 이 안내문 좀 보렴. 지역 문화 센터에서 주민들을 위한 무료 운동 수업을 제공하는구나.

여 어머, 좋은 수업이 많네요. 아빠, 전 요가 수업을 정말 받고 싶어요.

남 하지만 수업이 너무 늦은 것 같구나. 너는 저녁 시간 전에는 집에 돌아와야 해.

여 아, 너무 아쉽네요.

남 에어로빅은 어떠니? 수업이 오후 5시부터 6시까지 있구나.

여 아빠, 저는 보통 5시 30분에 집에 오잖아요. 그리고 매주 월요일에는 운동할 시간이 없다고요.

남 그럼 한 가지 선택만 남았구나. 그걸 듣겠니?

여 네. 몸매를 유지하기 위해서 뭔가를 해야 해요.

해설 여자는 너무 늦게 끝나는 요가를 제외하고, 5시 30분 이후에 시작하며 월요일을 제외한 수업을 신청하기로 했다.

16 ④

(Cellphone rings.)

M Hello? Shelly, are you there already?

W Yeah, I'm in front of the theater. Where are you?

M Sorry. I'm on my way. I missed the train, and I had to wait for twenty minutes to get the next one.

W Oh, my. The movie starts at 6:00 and it's already 5:40.

M I'm really sorry. I think it will take half an hour for me to get there.

W Then I'll change the tickets to a later movie.

M Sounds perfect. A movie starting after 6:20 should be okay.

W All right. See you soon.

(휴대 전화가 울린다.)

남 여보세요? Shelly, 너 벌써 도착했니?

여 응. 극장 앞이야. 넌 어디야?

남 미안해. 난 가는 중이야. 기차를 놓쳐서, 다음 기차를 타느라 20분을 기다려야 했어.

여 오, 저런. 영화가 6시에 시작인데 벌써 5시 40분이야.

남 정말 미안해. 내가 그곳에 도착하려면 30분 정도 걸릴 것 같아.

여 그러면 내가 더 늦은 영화로 표를 바꿀게.

남 아주 좋은 생각이야. 6시 20분 이후에 시작하는 영화면 괜찮을 것 같아.

여 알았어. 곧 보자.

해설 현재 시각은 5시 40분인데 남자는 30분 후에 도착한다고 했으므로 남자가 도착할 시각은 6시 10분이다.

어휘 be on one's way 가는 중이다   miss 놓치다   half an hour 30분   change 바꾸다   perfect 완벽한

17 ⑤

W Mike, didn't you hear me?

M Oh, Mom. I'm sorry. I couldn't hear you.

W What were you doing? I called you several times.

M I was studying while listening to music on my earphones.

W I told you before that it's not helpful for you to study while listening to music.

M Yes, I know. But some good music makes me feel good when I study.

W Music can help you relax, but it makes it more difficult to focus.

여 Mike, 내 말 못 들었니?

남 오, 엄마. 죄송해요. 못 들었어요.

여 뭐 하고 있었니? 너를 여러 번 불렀는데.

남 이어폰으로 음악을 들으면서 공부하고 있었어요.

여 음악을 들으면서 공부하는 건 도움이 되지 않는다고 전에 말했잖니.

남 네, 알아요. 하지만 공부할 때 좋은 음악을 들으면 기분이 좋아지는걸요.

여 음악이 네가 긴장을 푸는 데 도움을 줄 수 있지만, 그것은 집중하기 더 어렵게 만든단다.

해설 남자는 여자의 충고와는 달리 공부할 때 좋은 음악을 들으면 기분이 좋아진다고 대꾸했으므로 이에 대한 충고의 말이 이어지는 것이 자연스럽다.

① 우리는 음악 취향이 다르구나.

② 너는 네 선생님의 말씀을 들어야 해.

③ 저 이어폰 좀 가져다줄래?

④ 공부할 때 빠른 음악을 들어 보렴.

어휘 several times 여러 번   helpful 도움이 되는   relax 긴장을 풀다   focus 집중하다   taste 취향

18 ①

W Jack, did you buy a textbook?

M A textbook? What do you mean?

W We need to buy a new science textbook for Thursday's class.

M Oh, I totally forgot about it.

W Then let's go to the bookstore together.

M Well, why don't we just order the books online? They are delivered very quickly these days.

W Really? How long does it take?

M It only takes one business day.

여 Jack, 교재 구입했니?

남 교재? 무슨 말이야?

여 우리는 목요일 수업을 위해 새 과학 교재를 사야 하잖아.

남 오, 그것에 대해 완전히 잊어버렸어.

여 그러면 같이 서점에 가자.

남 음, 그냥 온라인으로 책을 주문하는 게 어때? 요즘에는 아주 빨리 배송돼.

여 그래? 얼마나 걸리는데?

남 영업일로 하루밖에 안 걸려.

해설 여자가 책이 배송되는 데 얼마나 걸리는지 물었으므로 소요 시간을 말하는 응답이 와야 한다.

② 온라인으로 사면 훨씬 더 저렴해.

③ 서둘러! 시간이 충분하지 않아.

④ 온라인으로 이용 가능한 책들이 많아.

⑤ 너는 아침에 서점을 가는 게 좋겠어.

어휘 textbook 교과서, 교재   totally 완전히   online 온라인으로   deliver 배달하다   these days 요즘   business day 영업일, 평일   available 이용할 수 있는   had better ~하는 것이 좋겠다

19 ④

M What are you thinking about?

W Yena's birthday is coming up soon. But I have no idea what to buy for her.

M Me neither! We need to think about what she might

구성하다   translate *A* into *B* A를 B로 번역하다   in charge of ~을 담당해서, ~을 맡아서   role 역할   improve 향상시키다   take part in ~에 참여하다   meaningful 의미 있는

like.

W You're right. What are her interests?

M If I remember right, she likes music, swimming, and reading.

W Maybe we could get her some concert tickets.

M Good idea. Who would know her favorite groups?

W I think her roommate might know about that.

남 무슨 생각 하고 있니?

여 예나의 생일이 곧 다가오고 있어. 그런데 그녀에게 뭘 사 줘야 할지 모르겠어.

남 나도 그래. 우린 그녀가 뭘 좋아할지 생각해야 해.

여 맞아. 그녀의 관심사가 뭐지?

남 내 기억이 맞다면, 그녀는 음악, 수영, 그리고 독서를 좋아해.

여 우리가 그녀에게 콘서트 표를 사 줄 수 있겠다.

남 좋은 생각이야. 그녀가 가장 좋아하는 그룹을 누가 알고 있을까?

여 그녀의 룸메이트가 그것에 대해 알 것 같아.

[해설] 예나가 좋아하는 그룹을 누가 알고 있을지 물었으므로 그와 관련된 응답이 와야 한다.

① 나는 왜 그녀가 그들을 좋아하는지 모르겠어.

② 미안해. 너에게 말해 줄 수 없어. 그건 비밀이야.

③ 넌 네 생일에 무엇을 원하니?

⑤ 나는 그녀가 콘서트에 가고 싶은지 궁금해.

[어휘] Me neither. (부정문에 대해) 나도 그래.   interest 관심사   secret 비밀   roommate 룸메이트   wonder 궁금하다

20 ①

M Jisu is interested in volunteer work. Recently, she decided to form a school volunteer club. The volunteer work in the club is to translate some Korean storybooks into English for African children. But she learns that every club needs a teacher to be in charge of it. So Jisu wants to ask her English teacher Mr. Philip to take that role. In this situation, what would Jisu most likely say to Mr. Philip?

Jisu Mr. Philip, would you lead our volunteer club?

남 지수는 자원봉사 활동에 관심이 있다. 최근에, 그녀는 학교 자원봉사 동아리를 만들기로 결심했다. 그 동아리의 자원봉사 활동은 아프리카 어린이들을 위해 한국의 동화책을 영어로 번역하는 일이다. 하지만 그녀는 모든 동아리에는 그것을 담당할 교사가 필요하다는 것을 알게 된다. 그래서 지수는 그녀의 영어 선생님이신 Philip 선생님께 그 일을 맡아 줄 것을 부탁하고 싶어 한다. 이런 상황에서, 지수는 Philip 선생님께 뭐라고 말하겠는가?

지수 Philip 선생님, 저희 자원봉사 동아리를 이끌어 주시겠어요?

[해설] Philip 선생님께 자신이 만들려고 하는 자원봉사 동아리의 담당 교사가 되어 달라고 부탁하려는 상황이다.

② 왜 자원봉사를 하시는지 말씀해 주시겠어요?

③ 제 영어 실력을 향상시키는 방법을 알려 주세요.

④ 이 책을 영어로 번역해 주시겠어요?

⑤ 좀 더 의미 있는 일에 참여하시는 게 어떠세요?

[어휘] volunteer 자원봉사; 자원봉사를 하다   form 만들다.

01 ②	**02** ③	**03** ②	**04** ④	**05** ③
06 ⑤	**07** ③	**08** ⑤	**09** ①	**10** ③
11 ②	**12** ⑤	**13** ④	**14** ④	**15** ③
16 ①	**17** ④	**18** ④	**19** ⑤	**20** ④

01 ②

① W What's the matter? You look upset.
　M I can't find my book. I think I left it on the bus.
② W Can you show me these sandals in a size 8?
　M Sorry. They were sold out.
③ W Excuse me, but where can I find the diapers?
　M They're in aisle 7.
④ W Are you going to drink your coffee here or take it out?
　M I'll take it out.
⑤ W I will have the seafood spaghetti.
　M Okay, do you want anything to drink?

① 여 무슨 일이니? 너 화나 보여.
　남 내 책을 찾을 수가 없어. 버스에 두고 내린 것 같아.
② 여 이 샌들을 8 사이즈로 보여주시겠어요?
　남 죄송합니다. 품절입니다.
③ 여 실례지만, 기저귀를 어디에서 찾을 수 있나요?
　남 기저귀는 7번 통로에 있습니다.
④ 여 커피를 여기서 마실 건가요, 가져가실 건가요?
　남 가져갈게요.
⑤ 여 저는 해산물 스파게티를 먹을게요.
　남 네, 마실 것을 원하세요?

해설 신발 가게에서 손님이 점원에게 자신이 원하는 사이즈의 신발을 요청하는 상황이다.

어휘 find 찾다　leave ~을 두고 오다　sold out 다 팔린, 매진된　diaper 기저귀　aisle 통로

02 ③

W May I help you?
M Yes, please. I'm looking for the latest edition of Charles Brown's novel, *A New Life*.
W Okay, let me check. (*Pause*) It's in section E, next to the foreign language section. Do you want me to get it for you?
M Oh, thank you so much.
W Here is your book.
M Can I use this coupon?
W Sure, you can get a 10% discount with this coupon.

여 도와드릴까요?
남 네. 저는 Charles Brown의 소설 〈A New Life〉의 최신판을 찾고 있습니다.
여 네, 찾아볼게요. (*잠시 후*) 그것은 E 구역, 외국어 부문 옆에 있

어요. 제가 가져다 드릴까요?
남 아, 정말 감사합니다.
여 여기 책이 있습니다.
남 제가 이 쿠폰을 쓸 수 있나요?
여 물론이죠, 이 쿠폰으로 10퍼센트 할인받으실 수 있습니다.

해설 할인 쿠폰을 사용하여 소설책을 구입하고 있으므로 대화가 이루어지는 장소는 서점이다.

어휘 latest 최신의　edition 판, 호　section 부문, 구역 foreign language 외국어　discount 할인

03 ②

(*Cellphone rings.*)
W Hi, Patrick. This is Lisa.
M Oh, hi, Lisa.
W I heard you're in the hospital. What happened?
M I fell down the stairs and broke my leg last week. But I'm doing better now.
W Well, Jerry and I are thinking of visiting you this afternoon. Would you like your favorite snack?
M No, thanks. But can you bring me some books to read? I'm so bored in here.
W No problem. We'll bring you some fiction books and magazines.

(*휴대 전화가 울린다.*)
여 안녕, Patrick. 나 Lisa야.
남 아, 안녕, Lisa.
여 네가 병원에 있다고 들었어. 무슨 일이니?
남 나는 지난주에 계단에서 넘어져서 다리가 부러졌어. 하지만 이제 나아지고 있어.
여 음, Jerry와 내가 오늘 오후에 너한테 가려고 해. 네가 좋아하는 간식 좀 가져다줄까?
남 아니, 괜찮아. 그런데 읽을 책 좀 몇 권 가져다줄래? 이곳이 너무 지루하네.
여 물론이지. 소설책과 잡지 몇 권 가져다줄게.

해설 남자는 병문안을 오려는 여자에게 간식 대신 읽을 책을 가져다 달라고 부탁했다.

어휘 fall down 넘어지다　stairs 계단　break 부러뜨리다 snack 간식　bored 지루한　fiction 소설　magazine 잡지

04 ④

W Welcome to Magic Shoes. It has been 5 years since we opened our store, and we want to show our gratitude to all of our customers. We are having a BUY ONE PAIR, GET ONE FREE sale from today until next Tuesday. In addition to this sale, you can use your store points or any coupons you have to save even more money. Thank you again for shopping here.

여 Magic Shoes에 오신 것을 환영합니다. 저희가 가게를 개점한 지 5년이 되어서 모든 고객님들께 감사의 뜻을 보이고 싶습니다. 오늘부터 다음 주 화요일까지 한 켤레를 사시면 한 켤레

를 무료로 받으실 수 있는 할인 행사를 실시합니다. 이 할인 행사 이외에도, 여러분이 훨씬 더 많은 돈을 절약하실 수 있도록 여러분의 가게 적립금이나 가지고 계신 어떤 쿠폰도 사용하실 수 있습니다. 저희 가게를 이용해 주셔서 다시 한번 감사드립니다.

해설 개점 5주년 기념 할인 행사에 관한 안내 방송이다.

어휘 gratitude 감사   customer 고객, 손님   free 무료로   sale (할인) 판매   in addition to ~ 이외에, ~에 더하여

05 ③

W There are a lot of movies playing. What do you want to see?
M How about *Flying Man*? It's an action movie.
W Good. How much is a ticket?
M It's $8 a ticket for the 2D movie, and $15 for the 4D movie.
W Let's see it in 4D! It'll be more exciting!
M Okay. Do you want to have popcorn?
W Let's buy one bucket and share it.
M Okay. It's $6 for a bucket, so here's $3. While you're buying the popcorn, I will buy the tickets.
W Okay, I'll give you the money for my ticket.

여 상영 중인 영화가 많네. 넌 무엇을 보고 싶니?
남 〈Flying Man〉은 어때? 액션 영화야.
여 좋아. 표는 얼마야?
남 2D 영화는 8달러이고, 4D 영화는 15달러야.
여 4D 영화를 보자! 더 재미있을 거야!
남 그래. 팝콘 먹을까?
여 한 통 사서 나눠 먹자.
남 좋아. 한 통에 6달러니까, 여기 3달러 줄게. 네가 팝콘을 사고 있는 동안, 내가 표를 살게.
여 좋아, 내 표 값을 줄게.

해설 4D 영화표 한 장은 15달러이고, 한 통에 6달러인 팝콘은 남자와 3달러씩 나눠 내기로 했으므로 여자가 사용한 금액은 총 18달러이다.

어휘 play 상영되다, 공연되다   action movie 액션 영화   bucket 양동이, 들통   share 나누다

06 ⑤

① W Did you see the soccer match last night?
　 M Yes, I'm really upset. The team I like lost again.
② W I would like to open a new account.
　 M Okay, can you fill out this form?
③ W You're from Busan, right?
　 M Yes, I have lived there for 18 years.
④ W Are there any seats left?
　 M Yes, two seats in the front row are available now.
⑤ W Do you have a charger?
　 M I'm afraid not. I don't have time.

① 여 어젯밤에 축구 경기를 봤니?
　 남 응, 정말 속상해. 내가 좋아하는 팀이 또 졌어.

② 여 저는 새로 계좌를 만들고 싶어요.
　 남 네, 이 양식을 작성해 주시겠어요?
③ 여 당신은 부산 출신이시죠, 그렇죠?
　 남 네, 저는 그곳에서 18년 동안 살았어요.
④ 여 남은 자리가 있나요?
　 남 네, 앞쪽의 두 자리가 지금 이용 가능합니다.
⑤ 여 충전기 있으신가요?
　 남 안될 것 같아요. 저는 시간이 없습니다.

해설 ⑤ 충전기가 있는지를 묻는 말에 시간이 없다고 답하는 것은 어색하다.

어휘 match 경기   account 계좌   fill out 작성하다, 기입하다   form 양식, 서식   row 줄, 열   available 이용할 수 있는   charger 충전기

07 ③

M I would like to book a flight to Tokyo on Friday, August 13.
W We only have a six-thirty flight on Friday morning.
M Oh, really? That's too early. How about on Thursday, August 12?
W We only have a 2 o'clock flight on Thursday afternoon.
M That's better. I'll take it.
W Which class would you like?
M Economy class, please. And can I get a window seat?
W Sure.

남 8월 13일 금요일에 도쿄행 항공편을 예약하고 싶어요.
여 금요일 아침에는 6시 30분 항공편만 있습니다.
남 오, 정말요? 너무 이르네요. 8월 12일 목요일은 어떤가요?
여 목요일 오후에는 2시 항공편만 있습니다.
남 그게 더 낫네요. 그걸로 할게요.
여 어느 좌석으로 드릴까요?
남 일반석으로 주세요. 그리고 창가석에 앉을 수 있을까요?
여 물론이죠.

해설 남자는 8월 12일 목요일 오후 2시에 출발하는 항공편을 예약했다.

어휘 book 예약하다   flight 항공편   economy class 일반석 (항공 좌석 등급 중 기본석)   window seat 창가석   gate 게이트(탑승구)   departure 출발

08 ⑤

W Dad, I've got some good news.
M Tell me. What is it?
W Do you remember the musical that I auditioned for last month?
M Yeah. Unfortunately, you failed the audition.
W Right. But I got a phone call from the director and he suggested another role for me.
M Congratulations! Is there anything I can help you with?
W Actually, there is. It would be really great if you

could record me practicing.

M　No problem.

여　아빠, 좋은 소식이 있어요.
남　말해 보렴. 그게 뭐니?
여　제가 지난달에 오디션 본 뮤지컬 기억하세요?
남　그래. 유감스럽게도, 넌 그 오디션에 떨어졌잖아.
여　맞아요. 그런데 감독님한테 전화를 받았는데 저에게 다른 역할을 제안하셨어요.
남　축하한다! 내가 도울 수 있는 일이 있니?
여　사실, 있어요. 제가 연습하는 것 좀 녹화해 주시면 정말 고맙겠어요.
남　문제없단다.

해설　여자는 남자에게 자신의 뮤지컬 연습 장면을 녹화해 달라고 부탁했다.

어휘　audition 오디션을 보다; 오디션　unfortunately 유감스럽게도　fail (시험 등에) 떨어지다　director 감독　suggest 제안하다　role 역할　record 녹화하다　practice 연습하다

09 ①

(Telephone rings.)

W　Jamie's Flower Shop. May I help you?
M　Hi. I bought a dozen tulips this morning at your store. Do you remember me?
W　Sure. Is there any problem?
M　No. But I think I accidently dropped one of my credit cards at your store.
W　Oh, really? Where do you think you dropped it?
M　Can you look around the front door near the stack of flowerpots? It's blue with my name, Jonathan White on it.
W　Yes, I found it.
M　Thank you so much. I'll come by this evening to get it.

(전화벨이 울린다.)

여　Jamie's Flower Shop입니다. 도와드릴까요?
남　안녕하세요. 저는 오늘 아침에 당신의 가게에서 튤립 열두 송이를 샀습니다. 저를 기억하시나요?
여　물론이죠. 무슨 문제가 있으신가요?
남　아니요. 그런데 제가 실수로 당신의 가게에 제 신용 카드 한 장을 떨어뜨린 것 같아요.
여　오, 정말요? 어디에 떨어뜨리신 것 같나요?
남　화분 더미 근처 정문 주변을 둘러봐 주시겠어요? 제 이름 Jonathan White가 쓰여 있는 파란색 카드입니다.
여　네, 그것을 찾았어요.
남　정말 고맙습니다. 그것을 가지러 오늘 저녁에 들를게요.

해설　남자는 아침에 꽃을 사면서 꽃집에 자신의 신용 카드를 떨어뜨렸는지 확인하기 위해 전화했다.

어휘　dozen 열두 개의　problem 문제　accidently 실수로, 잘못하여　drop 떨어뜨리다　stack 더미　flowerpot 화분　come by 잠깐 들르다

10 ③

W　Sam, how was your pasta?
M　Great. All the food was really good. How about your dish, Mom?
W　I'm really satisfied, and I think the service is great, too.
M　That's true. I like the quiet atmosphere and the simple interior.
W　Yeah, the white walls and ceilings look neat.
M　I'd like to come back again soon. It's extremely close to our house.
W　Yeah, it's just a five-minute walk from the house.

여　Sam, 파스타 어땠니?
남　좋았어요. 모든 음식이 정말 좋았어요. 엄마 음식은 어떠셨어요?
여　정말 만족스럽고 서비스도 훌륭한 것 같구나.
남　맞아요. 전 조용한 분위기와 단순한 인테리어가 마음에 들어요.
여　그래, 흰 벽과 천장이 깔끔해 보이네.
남　조만간 다시 오고 싶어요. 우리 집과 아주 가깝잖아요.
여　그래, 집에서 걸어서 겨우 5분 거리지.

해설　음식의 가격은 언급되지 않았다.

어휘　satisfied 만족하는　atmosphere 분위기　simple 단순한　interior 인테리어, 실내 장식　wall 벽　ceiling 천장　neat 깔끔한　extremely 매우, 극도로

11 ②

W　Hi, Brian. You look great!
M　Thanks. How was your vacation? You went to Europe, right?
W　Yeah, it was good. But I didn't have the best vacation there.
M　Why not? Didn't you like the cities in Europe?
W　I liked them. I enjoyed the gorgeous churches and interesting markets. And the people were kind there.
M　Then what was the problem?
W　I had food poisoning and had to go to the emergency room because of that.
M　Oh, I'm sorry to hear that.

여　안녕, Brian. 너 아주 좋아 보여!
남　고마워. 휴가는 어땠니? 너는 유럽에 갔었잖아, 그렇지?
여　응, 좋았어. 하지만 그곳에서 최고의 휴가를 보내진 못했어.
남　왜? 유럽의 도시들이 좋지 않았니?
여　좋았어. 나는 멋진 교회들과 재미있는 시장들을 즐겼어. 그리고 그곳의 사람들은 친절했어.
남　그러면 문제가 뭐였니?
여　난 식중독에 걸려서 응급실에 가야 했어.
남　오, 그 말을 들으니 안됐구나.

해설　여자는 유럽 여행 중 식중독에 걸려서 최고의 휴가를 보내지 못했다고 했다.

어휘　vacation 휴가, 방학　gorgeous 멋진　food poisoning 식중독　emergency room 응급실　because of ~ 때문에

12 ⑤

M It feels like the yellow dust season is getting longer and more severe.
W I agree. We hardly have any days with clear skies.
M I have a sore throat and itchy eyes all the time.
W That's too bad. Do you wear a mask when you go out?
M Yes. I try to wear one when I go out.
W And you should not exercise outside when the air quality is bad.
M I know, but I really enjoy playing soccer with my friends in my free time.
W But it's really bad for your health.

남 황사 기간이 더 길어지고 더 심해지는 것 같아.
여 맞아. 맑은 하늘이 있는 날이 거의 없어.
남 나는 항상 목이 아프고 눈이 간지러워.
여 그것 참 안됐다. 너 외출할 때 마스크를 쓰니?
남 응. 나는 외출할 때 마스크를 쓰려고 노력해.
여 그리고 너는 공기 질이 안 좋을 때는 밖에서 운동을 하면 안 돼.
남 알아, 그런데 나는 여가 시간에 친구들과 축구하는 것을 정말 좋아해.
여 하지만 그것은 네 건강에 정말 안 좋아.

해설 여자는 남자에게 공기 질이 안 좋을 때 밖에서 운동을 하면 안 된다고 충고했다.

어휘 yellow dust 황사 severe 심한 clear 맑은, 깨끗한 hardly 거의 ~ 않다(없다) sore 아픈, 쓰린 throat 목, 목구멍 itchy 간지러운 all the time 항상 go out 외출하다 outside 실외에서 free time 여가 시간

13 ④

W Look! There's something on the street.
M It's a wallet. Somebody must have lost it.
W We should take this to the police station.
M Do you know where the police station is?
W Yes, there is one next to Seoul Station.
M Then let's pick up Grandma first at the station, and then take the wallet to the police station.
W That's a good idea. Grandma must be waiting for us.
M We should hurry. Let's go.

여 저기 봐! 길에 뭔가가 있어.
남 지갑이야. 누군가가 그것을 잃어버린 게 틀림없어.
여 우리는 이것을 경찰서에 가져다줘야 해.
남 너는 경찰서가 어디에 있는지 아니?
여 응, 서울역 옆에 하나 있어.
남 그러면 먼저 역에서 할머니를 모시고 오고, 그러고 나서 경찰서에 지갑을 가져가자.
여 좋은 생각이야. 할머니께서 우리를 기다리고 계실 거야.
남 서둘러야 해. 가자.

해설 두 사람은 먼저 역에서 할머니를 모시고 온 후에 길에서 주운 지갑을 경찰서에 가져다주기로 했다.

어휘 wallet 지갑 must have p.p. ~했음에 틀림없다 police station 경찰서 pick up ~을 (차에) 태우러 가다 hurry 서두르다

14 ④

W There are so many marks on your calendar!
M Yes, right. There are a lot of family events in May.
W I know it's Children's Day on May 5. What's the occasion a week after that?
M That's my mother's birthday.
W I see. You've also got the date circled two days after that.
M That's my wedding anniversary!
W You do have lots of things to celebrate in May!
M Yeah, it's a really busy month for me.

여 달력에 정말 많은 표시가 있구나!
남 응, 맞아. 5월에는 가족 행사가 많이 있어.
여 5월 5일이 어린이날인 것은 알아. 그날 일주일 후는 무슨 날이니?
남 그날은 우리 어머니의 생신이야.
여 그렇구나. 그날의 이틀 뒤에도 동그라미가 있네.
남 그날은 나의 결혼기념일이야!
여 너는 5월에 기념해야 할 일이 많이 있구나!
남 맞아, 나에게 정말 바쁜 달이야.

해설 5월 5일의 일주일 후(5월 12일)는 어머니 생신이고, 어머니 생신의 이틀 뒤(5월 14일)는 남자의 결혼기념일이라고 했다.

어휘 calendar 달력 event 행사 occasion 때, 행사 wedding anniversary 결혼기념일 celebrate 축하하다, 기념하다

15 ③

(Cellphone rings.)
M Hi, Jennifer. What's up?
W I just called to invite you to a party. It's our church's Christmas party.
M That sounds great. When is it?
W It's this Friday. The main event starts at 5:00. Can you come?
M Sure, I'd love to. All our classes are finished at 4:30. Let's meet 20 minutes after the last class.
W Then let's make it ten to five in front of the church.
M Okay. See you then.

(휴대 전화가 울린다.)
남 안녕, Jennifer. 무슨 일이야?
여 너를 파티에 초대하려고 전화했어. 우리 교회에서 하는 크리스마스 파티야.
남 좋지. 언젠데?
여 이번 주 금요일이야. 주요 행사는 5시에 시작해. 올 수 있니?
남 물론, 가고 싶어. 우리 수업은 4시 30분에 모두 끝나. 마지막 수업 끝나고 20분 후에 만나자.
여 그러면 교회 앞에서 5시 10분 전에 만나자.
남 좋아. 그때 보자.

해설 남자가 4시 30분에 수업이 모두 끝난다고 말하며 마지막 수업 20분 후에 만나자고 했고, 여자가 동의하며 5시 10분 전에 만나자고 했다.

어휘 invite 초대하다   church 교회   main event 주요 행사   last 마지막의   finish 끝나다   make it 약속을 정하다, 만나다   in front of ~ 앞에

16 ①

W Hello, Mr. Smith. Can I ask you something?
M Sure, Jane. What is it?
W I'm thinking about running for student president, but I don't know what I should do.
M Oh, that's great! Why do you want to be student president?
W I want to help the students who are in trouble.
M Well, think about how you can really listen to them, and make a specific plan to help them.
W I got it. That could be my campaign speech.
M That's right. But first of all, you must submit a letter of self-introduction.
W Oh, then I'll have to write that first. Thank you so much.

여 안녕하세요, Smith 선생님. 뭐 좀 여쭤봐도 될까요?
남 물론이지, Jane. 그게 뭐니?
여 저는 학생회장에 출마하는 것에 대해 생각 중인데요, 무엇을 해야 할지 모르겠어요.
남 오, 훌륭하구나! 넌 왜 학생회장이 되고 싶니?
여 저는 어려움에 처한 학생들을 돕고 싶어요.
남 음, 네가 그들의 말을 잘 들을 수 있는 방법을 생각해 보고, 그들을 도울 수 있는 구체적인 계획을 세워 보렴.
여 알겠습니다. 그것이 저의 선거 연설이 될 수 있겠네요.
남 맞아. 하지만 가장 먼저, 너는 자기소개서를 제출해야 한단다.
여 아, 그러면 그것 먼저 써야겠네요. 정말 감사합니다.

해설 남자가 학생회장에 출마하기 위해서는 가장 먼저 자기소개서를 제출해야 한다고 하자 여자는 그것을 먼저 써야겠다고 했다.

어휘 run for ~에 출마하다   student president 학생회장   be in trouble 어려움에 처하다   specific 구체적인   campaign speech 선거 연설   first of all 우선, 가장 먼저   submit 제출하다   self-introduction 자기소개

17 ④

M Are you watching the drama, *Summer Story*?
W Yes, the story is really interesting, isn't it?
M I agree with you. I've heard that the drama is based on a real story.
W Really? That's why the drama is so realistic. I can't wait to see the next episode.
M You're really into that drama.
W You're right. What do you think about the actors and actresses?
M All of the characters are great. I like them all.

남 너 〈Summer Story〉라는 드라마 보니?

여 응, 이야기가 정말 재미있어, 그렇지 않니?
남 네 말에 동의해. 나는 그 드라마가 실제 이야기를 바탕으로 한다고 들었어.
여 정말? 그래서 그 드라마가 그렇게 현실적이구나. 나는 다음 회를 빨리 보고 싶어.
남 너 정말 그 드라마에 빠져 있구나.
여 맞아. 너는 그 배우들에 대해 어떻게 생각하니?
남 모든 등장인물들이 훌륭해. 나는 그들 모두가 좋아.

해설 드라마에 출연하는 배우들에 대해 어떻게 생각하는지 물었으므로 그들에 대한 의견을 말하는 응답이 와야 한다.
① 나는 어젯밤에 영화를 보러 갔어.
② 나는 전에 그들을 식당에서 만났어.
③ 나는 그 드라마를 여러 번 봤어.
⑤ 나는 그 주인공처럼 전 세계를 여행할 수 있으면 좋겠어.

어휘 agree with ~에 동의하다   be based on ~을 기반으로 하다   realistic 현실적인   episode 1회 방송분   be into ~에 관심이 많다, ~을 좋아하다   character 등장인물   main character 주인공

18 ④

W Welcome to Safari World. Can I help you?
M Yes, please. I'd like to buy tickets. Two adults and two children.
W How old are your children?
M One is 7 years old, and the other is 5 years old.
W It's $10 for an adult and $5 for children under 12.
M And how much is the tour bus?
W It's $4 for each person.
M Can I get a discount for the children?
W I'm afraid not. It's the same for children.

여 Safari World에 오신 것을 환영합니다. 도와드릴까요?
남 네. 입장권을 사고 싶어요. 성인 두 명과 어린이 두 명입니다.
여 아이들은 몇 살인가요?
남 한 명은 일곱 살, 다른 한 명은 다섯 살입니다.
여 성인은 10달러이고, 12세 미만의 어린이는 5달러입니다.
남 그리고 투어 버스는 얼마인가요?
여 1인당 4달러입니다.
남 어린이 할인을 받을 수 있나요?
여 죄송하지만 안 됩니다. 어린이도 똑같습니다.

해설 어린이 할인을 받을 수 있는지 물었으므로 어린이 할인 여부에 대한 응답이 와야 한다.
① 그 다리는 공사 중입니다.
② 버스 정류장에 어떻게 가나요?
③ 그들이 걷기에는 먼 거리입니다.
⑤ 버스에 남은 자리가 있나요?

어휘 adult 성인, 어른   tour 여행, 관광   discount 할인   bridge 다리   under construction 공사 중인   distance 거리   available 이용할 수 있는

19 ⑤

M John's Pizza Delivery. How may I help you?

W Hi. I want a large pepperoni pizza and a meatball spaghetti.

M Okay. Do you want extra toppings?

W Yes, I want extra cheese and olives.

M I got it. Anything to drink?

W A bottle of coke, please. How long will it take?

M It will take about half an hour.

남 John's Pizza Delivery입니다. 무엇을 도와드릴까요?

여 안녕하세요. 페퍼로니 피자 큰 사이즈와 미트볼 스파게티 주세요.

남 네. 추가 토핑을 원하시나요?

여 네, 저는 추가 치즈와 올리브를 원합니다.

남 알겠습니다. 마실 것은요?

여 콜라 한 병 주세요. 얼마나 걸릴까요?

남 약 30분 걸릴 겁니다.

해설 피자를 주문하면서 시간이 얼마나 걸리는지 물었으므로 소요 시간을 말하는 응답이 와야 한다.

① 전부 50달러입니다.
② 저는 치즈피자를 더 좋아합니다.
③ 네, 저는 피자를 가져갈 거예요.
④ 오늘 추가 토핑은 무료입니다.

어휘 delivery 배달   extra 추가의   topping 토핑, 고명   total 총, 합계   half an hour 30분

20 ④

M Cindy and Sam are sitting in the theater to watch a musical. As the musical starts, all the lights turn off and the curtains open. In the middle of the show, Cindy notices that Sam keeps taking out his cellphone to send text messages. Cindy knows that they're not allowed to use cellphones during the performance. She thinks that she should tell him to stop using his cellphone. In this situation, what would Cindy most likely say to him?

Cindy Sam, we're not supposed to use cellphones during the show.

남 Cindy와 Sam은 뮤지컬을 보기 위해 극장에 앉아 있다. 뮤지컬이 시작되자, 모든 불이 꺼지고 커튼이 열린다. 공연 도중에, Cindy는 Sam이 문자 메시지를 보내기 위해 휴대 전화를 계속 꺼내는 것을 알아차린다. Cindy는 공연 도중에 휴대 전화를 사용할 수 없다는 것을 알고 있다. 그녀는 그에게 휴대 전화 사용을 그만하라고 말해야 한다고 생각한다. 이 상황에서, Cindy는 그에게 무엇이라고 말할 것 같은가?

Cindy Sam, 우리는 공연 도중에 휴대 전화를 사용해서는 안 돼.

해설 Sam에게 뮤지컬 공연 도중에는 휴대 전화를 사용하면 안 된다고 말해 주려는 상황이다.

① 너는 언제 휴대 전화를 샀니?
② 내가 사진을 찍어줄까?
③ 이것은 지금껏 내가 본 것 중 가장 훌륭한 공연이야.
⑤ 내가 네 전화를 사용해서 문자 메시지를 보내도 되니?

어휘 light 전등, 조명   turn off 꺼지다   in the middle of ~의 도중에   notice 알아차리다   take out 꺼내다   text

message 문자 메세지   be allowed to ~하는 것이 허용되다   during ~ 동안에   performance 공연   be supposed to ~하기로 되어 있다

Review Test pp.186~187

Word Check   **17회**

01 탐험하다	02 번역하다
03 관리하다, 감독하다	04 환상적인
05 기한이 지난	06 손상
07 만남, 조우	08 조사, 연구
09 소화제	10 열대 지역
11 쉽게 손닿는 곳에	12 ~에 참여하다
13 rescue	14 nature
15 fairy tale	16 decorate
17 dye	18 meaningful
19 deadline	20 require
21 resident	22 late fee
23 taste	24 role

Expression Check

25 by mistake	26 should have left
27 in shape	28 was born
29 a variety of	30 in charge of

Word Check   **18회**

01 거리	02 현실적인
03 분위기	04 ~에 열광하다
05 멋진	06 간지러운
07 줄, 열	08 감사
09 식중독	10 때, 행사
11 아픈, 쓰린	12 어려움에 처하다
13 aisle	14 accidently
15 interior	16 main character
17 dozen	18 performance
19 self-introduction	20 invite
21 window seat	22 emergency room
23 pick up	24 under construction

Expression Check

25 come by	26 fill out
27 ten, five	28 is based on
29 running for	30 In addition to

01 ⑤	02 ③	03 ⑤	04 ③	05 ④
06 ④	07 ⑤	08 ①	09 ③	10 ②
11 ⑤	12 ⑤	13 ②	14 ③	15 ⑤
16 ①	17 ③	18 ⑤	19 ②	20 ③

01 ⑤

M Sally, I need your help with the cover design of the school magazine.
W Why don't you put our school logo in the middle of the page?
M But I'm afraid it might look too simple.
W Then you can put students' photo in the middle.
M That sounds like a great idea.
W Then you'd better move the school logo to the top right-hand corner.
M You're right. Where should I put the title?
W I think under the photo would be better.
M I agree. Thank you for your help.

남 Sally, 교내 잡지 표지 디자인에 네 도움이 필요해.
여 페이지 중앙에 우리 학교 로고를 넣는 게 어때?
남 그런데 너무 단순해 보일까 봐 걱정돼.
여 그러면 가운데에 학생들의 사진을 넣으면 되잖아.
남 그거 좋은 생각인 것 같아.
여 그럼 학교 로고를 오른쪽 위 모퉁이로 옮기는 게 좋겠다.
남 맞아. 제목은 어디에 놓아야 할까?
여 사진 아래가 더 좋을 것 같아.
남 나도 그렇게 생각해. 도와줘서 고마워.

해설 페이지 중앙에 학생들 사진을 넣고, 오른쪽 위에는 학교 로고를, 사진 아래에는 제목을 배치했다.

어휘 design 디자인, 모양 magazine 잡지 logo 로고 in the middle of ~의 중앙에 simple 단순한 move 옮기다 top 맨 위 right-hand 오른쪽의 corner 모퉁이 title 제목

02 ③

W Hi, Daniel. Are you going to be busy later today?
M I don't have any plans for later today. Why do you ask?
W I need your help. Do you know about our club's photo exhibition?
M Yes. Do you need help in arranging a display?
W Actually, Jina is already going to help with that. What I need help with is the music.
M Music? Oh, I've got a big collection to choose from. You can borrow whatever you need.
W I have a bigger favor than that. Can you be in charge of the music during the exhibition?
M Sure. I just need to return these books to the library then I'll come right back.
W Thank you so much.

여 안녕, Daniel. 오늘 이따가 바쁘니?
남 오늘 이따가는 계획이 없어. 왜 물어보니?
여 네 도움이 필요해서. 우리 동아리 사진 전시회에 대해 알고 있지?
남 응. 전시물 정돈하는 데 도움이 필요하니?
여 사실은, 지나가 이미 그 일을 도와주기로 했어. 도움이 필요한 건 음악이야.
남 음악? 오, 나는 고를 만한 곡을 많이 가지고 있어. 네가 필요한 건 무엇이든 빌려줄게.
여 그보다 더 큰 부탁이 있어. 전시회가 열리는 동안 음악을 담당해 줄 수 있을까?
남 물론이지. 나는 지금 이 책들을 도서관에 반납해야 하니까 그러고 나서 바로 돌아올게.
여 정말 고마워.

해설 여자는 남자에게 전시회가 열리는 동안 음악을 담당해 줄 것을 부탁했다.

어휘 exhibition 전시회 arrange 배열하다, 정돈하다 display 전시물 collection 모음, 소장품 choose 선택하다 borrow 빌리다 favor 부탁 during ~ 동안에 be in charge of ~을 담당하다 return 반납하다

03 ⑤

① W How much is this swimming cap?
　M It's for rent, not for sale. It's $3 for the day.
② W What's your secret to keeping in shape?
　M I swim every day so that I can stay healthy.
③ W What if I fall into the deep water?
　M Don't worry. A lifeguard will rescue you.
④ W The life vest will let you float.
　M Oh, no. It doesn't really help me.
⑤ W Sorry. You can't go in the pool unless you are wearing a cap.
　M Oh, I didn't know that.

① 여 이 수영모자 얼마죠?
　남 그건 판매용이 아니라 대여용입니다. 하루에 3달러예요.
② 여 당신의 건강 유지의 비결은 뭔가요?
　남 전 건강을 유지하기 위해 매일 수영을 해요.
③ 여 제가 만약 깊은 물에 빠지면 어떻게 하죠?
　남 걱정하지 마세요. 안전 요원이 당신을 구해 줄 거예요.
④ 여 구명조끼를 입으시면 물에 떠요.
　남 오, 저런. 그건 정말로 저에게 도움이 안돼요.
⑤ 여 죄송합니다. 모자를 쓰지 않으면 수영장에 들어가실 수 없어요.
　남 오, 몰랐어요.

해설 수영장에서 여자 안전 요원이 모자를 착용하지 않은 남자에게 모자를 써야 한다고 말하는 상황이다.

어휘 rent 대여 sale 판매 secret 비밀, 비결 keep in shape 몸매를(건강을) 유지하다 What if ~하면 어쩌지? lifeguard 안전 요원, 인명 구조 요원 rescue 구조하다 life vest 구명조끼 float 뜨다 unless 만약 ~하지 않으면

04 ③

(Telephone rings.)

W Shogun Restaurant. May I help you?

M Hi. I'd like to make a reservation for this Saturday evening.

W I'm sorry, sir, but all the tables are already booked on Saturday evening.

M Oh, really? What about on Sunday?

W On Sunday, we have a few tables available at 6 p.m. and at 8 p.m.

M Then I'll book a table at 6 p.m.

W Okay. How many people is the reservation for?

M There will be four of us.

W All right. May I have your name, please?

M My name is Jason Foster.

(전화벨이 울린다.)

여 Shogun Restaurant입니다. 도와드릴까요?

남 안녕하세요. 이번 주 토요일 저녁에 예약을 하고 싶습니다.

여 죄송하지만, 손님, 토요일 저녁에는 모든 테이블이 이미 예약되었습니다.

남 아, 정말요? 일요일은 어떤가요?

여 일요일에는 저녁 6시와 8시에 몇몇 테이블이 있습니다.

남 그러면 6시 테이블을 예약할게요.

여 알겠습니다. 몇 명 예약해 드릴까요?

남 4명입니다.

여 네. 이름을 알려 주시겠어요?

남 제 이름은 Jason Foster입니다.

> **해설** 토요일 저녁은 이미 예약이 다 되어 있어서 남자는 일요일 저녁 6시로 예약했다.

> **어휘** make a reservation 예약하다   book 예약하다
> available 이용할 수 있는

05 ④

W John, what are you looking at?

M Hi, Amy. I'm looking at a poster for the World Food Festival.

W The World Food Festival? Is there really food from around the world?

M Yes, visitors can taste over a hundred different kinds of food from all around the world.

W Wow, that sounds very interesting! When is it?

M It's May 28 at the World Culture Center.

W Are you going there?

M Of course. Since we are students, we can get a 40% discount.

W That's cool. I'd like to go with you.

여 John, 무엇을 보고 있니?

남 안녕, Amy. 난 World Food Festival을 위한 포스터를 보고 있어.

여 World Food Festival? 정말 전 세계 음식이 있는 거니?

남 응. 방문객들은 세계 각지의 100여 가지 다양한 종류의 음식을 맛볼 수 있어.

여 와, 정말 흥미롭다! 그게 언제니?

남 5월 28일 World Culture Center에서 있어.

여 너 거기에 갈 거니?

남 당연하지. 우리는 학생이니까, 40퍼센트 할인을 받을 수 있어.

여 그거 좋다. 너와 함께 가고 싶어.

> **해설** 축제의 주최 기관은 언급되지 않았다.

> **어휘** visitor 방문객   taste 맛보다   all around the world 전 세계의   culture 문화   get a discount 할인을 받다

06 ④

W Sejin, I need your help.

M What is it?

W My friend Julia is coming to Korea next week. Can you give me some ideas where I can take her?

M Is there anything about Korea that she is particularly interested in?

W She did say that she likes Korean royal palaces.

M Why don't you take her to Changdeokgung? It's one of the most famous palaces in Korea.

W Sounds good. Umm, are there any Korean restaurants near the palace that serve *bulgogi*?

M Yeah, there's one right behind the palace.

W Wow. Please let me know the location of the restaurant.

M Okay. I'll share the location in a text message.

여 세진아, 네 도움이 필요해.

남 뭔데?

여 내 친구 Julia가 다음 주에 한국에 올 예정이야. 내가 그녀를 어디에 데려가면 좋을지 아이디어 좀 줄래?

남 그녀가 한국에 대해 특별히 관심 있는 게 있니?

여 그녀는 한국의 왕궁을 좋아한다고 말했어.

남 그녀를 창덕궁에 데려가는 게 어때? 그곳은 한국에서 가장 인기 있는 궁전들 중 하나잖아.

여 좋은 것 같아. 음, 그 궁 근처에 불고기 파는 한국 식당이 있니?

남 응, 궁 바로 뒤에 하나 있어.

여 와. 그 식당 위치 좀 알려 줘.

남 알았어. 내가 문자 메시지로 위치를 공유할게.

> **해설** 남자가 창덕궁 뒤에 있는 한국 식당을 소개하자 여자는 식당의 위치를 알려 달라고 부탁했다.

> **어휘** particularly 특별히   be interested in ~에 관심이 있다
> royal 왕의   palace 궁전   famous 유명한   behind ~ 뒤에
> share 공유하다   location 위치   text message 문자 메시지

07 ⑤

① **M** Do you know how long it takes to get there?
　W Well, it depends on how you go there.

② **M** Why don't we go shopping this Saturday?
　W Sorry. I have a previous engagement.

③ **M** Do you have any special plans for this coming holiday?
　W Yeah, I'm planning to go camping with friends.

④ **M** When did you come back from your trip to Europe?

W Last Friday. I'm sorry. I should have let you know I was back.

⑤ M The printer is broken again. How will I print the report?

W I don't think it matters what kind of paper you print the report on.

① 남 거기까지 가는 데 얼마나 걸리는지 아세요?
여 글쎄요, 어떻게 가는지에 따라 다르죠.

② 남 이번 주 토요일에 쇼핑하러 갈래?
여 미안해. 난 선약이 있어.

③ 남 다가오는 휴일에 어떤 특별한 계획이라도 있니?
여 응, 난 친구들과 캠핑하러 갈 계획이야.

④ 남 유럽 여행에서 언제 돌아왔니?
여 지난 금요일에. 미안해. 내가 돌아왔다고 알려 줬어야 했는데.

⑤ 남 프린터가 또 고장이네. 보고서 출력을 어떻게 하지?
여 내 생각엔 어떤 종류의 종이에 보고서를 출력하는지는 중요하지 않아.

해설 ⑤ 보고서 출력을 어떻게 해야 하는지 묻는 말에 어떤 종이에 출력하는지는 중요하지 않다고 답하는 것은 어색하다.

어휘 depend on ~에 달려 있다 previous 앞의, 사전의 engagement 약속 should have p.p. ~했어야 했다 broken 고장 난, 부서진

08 ①

W What is special about April 22? It is Earth Day. Our Earth is suffering from pollution, but many people don't care enough about the environment. Here are several things we can do to save the Earth. First, we can ride a bike or walk to school instead of taking a car. We can also stop using paper cups and use something reusable instead. When we go shopping, we can take a reusable shopping bag. Finally, by using less water, we can reduce wastewater.

여 4월 22일은 왜 특별할까요? 지구의 날입니다. 우리 지구는 오염으로 고통받고 있지만, 많은 사람들이 환경에 대해 충분히 신경 쓰지 않습니다. 여기에 우리가 지구를 구하기 위해 할 수 있는 몇 가지 일들이 있습니다. 우선, 우리는 학교에 차를 타고 가는 대신에 자전거를 타고 가거나 걸어갈 수 있습니다. 우리는 또한 종이컵을 사용하지 않고 대신에 재사용할 수 있는 것을 사용할 수 있습니다. 쇼핑하러 갈 때는, 재사용할 수 있는 장바구니를 가지고 갈 수 있습니다. 마지막으로, 물을 더 적게 사용함으로써, 버려지는 물을 줄일 수 있습니다.

해설 나무 심기는 언급되지 않았다.

어휘 special 특별한 suffer from ~로 고통받다 pollution 오염 care 신경 쓰다 enough 충분히 environment 환경 several 몇 가지의 instead of ~ 대신에 reusable 재사용할 수 있는 reduce 줄이다 wastewater 폐수

09 ③

M Good afternoon, everyone. This is an announcement about our school sports day. This year's sports day

was going to be held this Friday, but there is a change in the schedule. Because of concern about the amount of fine dust for this entire week, we have decided to reschedule the event for your health. We are expecting the air quality to get better next week, so we will inform you of the rescheduled date as soon as possible. Please be prepared for your regular classes this Friday. Thank you.

남 여러분, 안녕하십니까. 우리 학교 체육 대회에 대해 알려 드립니다. 올해 체육 대회는 이번 주 금요일에 열릴 예정이었지만, 일정상 변동이 있습니다. 이번 주 내내 미세 먼지의 양에 대한 염려 때문에, 여러분들의 건강을 위해 행사 일정을 변경하기로 결정했습니다. 다음 주에는 공기 질이 더 좋아질 것으로 예상되므로 가능한 한 빨리 변경된 날짜를 알려 드리겠습니다. 이번 주 금요일에는 정규 수업을 준비해 주십시오. 감사합니다.

해설 미세 먼지로 인해 체육 대회가 연기되었음을 알리는 안내 방송이다.

어휘 announcement 공지, 알림 change 변경 concern 염려 fine dust 미세 먼지 entire 전체의 reschedule 일정을 변경하다 health 건강 expect 예상하다 inform 알리다 prepare 준비하다 regular class 정규 수업

10 ②

W Good afternoon. May I help you?

M I bought these pants here last week. I'd like to exchange them for a bigger pair.

W Sorry, but I can't seem to find a bigger size in the same style.

M Then can I get a refund?

W Sure. You can get a full refund of $27.

M Hmm... do you have another style of pants in a size 28?

W Sure. How about this pair? I think they will look good on you.

M They are the right size. I'll take them.

W They are $29 and the pants you are returning are $27. You just need to pay the difference.

여 안녕하세요. 도와드릴까요?
남 지난주에 여기에서 이 바지를 샀는데요. 더 큰 바지로 교환하고 싶어요.
여 죄송하지만, 같은 스타일로는 더 큰 사이즈가 없는 것 같아요.
남 그러면 환불 받을 수 있나요?
여 그럼요. 27달러 전액 환불받으실 수 있어요.
남 음… 28 사이즈로 다른 스타일의 바지가 있나요?
여 네. 이 바지는 어떠세요? 손님께 잘 어울리실 것 같아요.
남 맞는 사이즈네요. 이걸로 할게요.
여 그건 29달러이고 손님이 다시 가져오신 바지는 27달러입니다. 차액만 지불해 주시면 됩니다.

해설 남자가 교환하려고 가져온 바지는 27달러였고 새로 구입할 바지는 29달러이므로 차액인 2달러를 지불해야 한다.

어휘 exchange A for B A를 B로 교환하다 refund 환불 look good on ~와 잘 어울리다 return 반납하다

difference 차이

11 ⑤

W James, you look so down. What's wrong?
M Well, my mom won't allow me to join the music band.
W Really? That's too bad.
M Yeah. You know how much I want to join it.
W Of course. Why won't she let you?
M She keeps saying that I won't be able to play in the band and study at the same time.
W Then why don't you make a study plan and show it to her? That would help change her mind.
M That's a good idea! I'll make one right away.

여 James, 기분이 정말 안 좋아 보이네. 무슨 일이니?
남 음, 우리 엄마가 내가 음악 밴드에 가입하는 걸 허락하지 않으셔.
여 정말? 정말 안됐다.
남 응. 내가 얼마나 가입하고 싶어 하는지 너도 알잖아.
여 물론이지. 너희 엄마는 왜 허락을 안 하시니?
남 엄마는 내가 밴드 활동과 공부를 동시에 못 할 거라고 계속 말씀하셔.
여 그러면 공부 계획서를 작성해서 너희 엄마께 보여드리는 게 어때? 엄마 마음을 바꾸는 데 도움이 될 거야.
남 그거 좋은 생각이다! 당장 작성해야겠어.

[해설] 남자는 공부 계획서를 작성해서 엄마를 설득해 보라는 여자의 제안을 따르기로 했다.

[어휘] down 우울한 allow A to B A가 B하는 것을 허락하다 keep ~ing 계속 ~하다 at the same time 동시에 change one's mind ~의 마음을 바꾸다 right away 지금 바로, 당장

12 ⑤

W Excuse me. Can I get a map for this area?
M Sure. Which language would like to have?
W Korean, please.
M Here you are. Do you need anything else?
W Can you recommend some places to visit around here?
M Sure. You should definitely visit the Modern Art Museum. Let me show you on the map. It's right here next to this church.
W Great! That looks easy to get to.
M If you need further information for this area, just call this center.
W Thank you so much.

여 실례합니다. 이 구역 지도를 구할 수 있을까요?
남 그럼요. 어느 언어로 드릴까요?
여 한국어로 주세요.
남 여기 있습니다. 다른 필요하신 것이 있으세요?
여 이 근처에 방문할 만한 곳 좀 추천해 주시겠어요?
남 네. Modern Art Museum에 꼭 가 보세요. 지도에서 보여드릴게요. 이 교회 옆 바로 여기에 있습니다.
여 좋아요! 가기 쉬워 보이네요.

남 이 구역에 대한 더 많은 정보가 필요하시면 이 센터로 전화 주세요.
여 정말 감사합니다.

[해설] 다양한 언어의 지도를 구할 수 있고, 지역에 대한 정보를 물어볼 수 있는 곳은 관광 안내소이다.

[어휘] map 지도 language 언어 recommend 추천하다 definitely 반드시, 꼭 modern 현대의 further 더 많은 information 정보

13 ②

M Jimin, have you decided on a Chinese course for this summer?
W No, not yet. Let's take one together. Which one do you think we should take?
M Well, we have two options: a 5-week course or a 10-week course.
W I prefer the shorter one. I don't want to spend my whole vacation studying.
M Okay. But then let's take the course that is 3 hours a day. One hour seems too short.
W I agree. It's an intermediate level, like last winter's course, right?
M Yes. And the class will be delivered by a Korean instructor.
W Good. Do you know when registration starts?
M From next Monday.

남 지민아, 이번 여름 중국어 수업 결정했니?
여 아니, 아직 안 했어. 같이 듣자. 우리가 어떤 수업을 들어야 한다고 생각해?
남 음, 우리에게는 두 가지 선택 사항이 있어. 즉, 5주 수업과 10주 수업 중에서 선택할 수 있어.
여 나는 짧은 게 더 좋아. 방학을 통째로 공부하는 데 쓰고 싶지는 않아.
남 그래. 하지만 하루에 3시간짜리 수업을 듣자. 1시간은 너무 짧아 보여.
여 동의해. 레벨은 지난 겨울 수업처럼 중급이지, 그렇지?
남 응. 그리고 수업은 한국인 강사가 할 거야.
여 좋아. 등록은 언제 시작하는지 아니?
남 다음 주 월요일부터야.

[해설] 두 사람은 5주 과정, 하루 세 시간, 중급 난이도, 한국인 강사에 해당하는 수업을 듣기로 했다.

[어휘] decide 결정하다 option 선택 prefer 선호하다 whole 전체의 intermediate 중급의 deliver (강연을) 하다 instructor 강사 registration 등록

14 ③

M This is something you carry in your hand or in your bag. You need this on rainy or snowy days because it keeps your hair and clothes from getting wet. You probably carry this on a cloudy day as well just in case it rains. But even on a very bright day, you can also use this to protect your skin from the sun.

You shouldn't open this indoors. In Western culture, there is a superstition that says opening this indoors <u>will bring bad luck</u>.

남 이것은 당신이 손에 들거나 가방 속에 가지고 다니는 것입니다. 당신은 이것을 비나 눈이 오는 날에 필요로 하는데 왜냐하면 그것이 당신의 머리와 옷이 젖는 것을 막아 주기 때문입니다. 당신은 아마 흐린 날에도 비가 올 경우를 대비해서 이것을 가지고 다닐지도 모릅니다. 하지만 아주 화창한 날에도, 당신은 태양으로부터 피부를 보호하기 위해 이것을 사용할 수도 있습니다. 실내에서는 이것을 펼쳐서는 안 됩니다. 서구 문화에서는, 이것을 실내에서 펴는 것이 불운을 가져다준다는 미신이 있습니다.

해설 비나 눈이 오는 날에 머리와 옷이 젖지 않도록 해 주고, 태양으로부터 피부를 보호하기 위한 목적으로도 사용할 수 있는 것은 우산이다.

어휘 keep A from ~ing A가 ~하는 것을 막다　get wet 젖다　probably 아마도　as well 또한　just in case 만약을 위해서, 혹시나 해서　bright 화창한, 밝은　protect 보호하다　skin 피부　indoors 실내에서　culture 문화　superstition 미신

15 ⑤

W Hey, Mike. Do you have a minute?
M Of course. What's up, Soyoung?
W One of my friends is writing a book about Korea. She's looking for some foreigners <u>who can share their experiences</u> in Korea.
M Really? That's interesting.
W I think <u>you're the best person</u> for it. Can you tell her about your experiences?
M Well, I don't know <u>if I can be that helpful</u>.
W Oh, you don't have to worry about anything. All you need to do is just to tell her about your everyday life in Korea.
M Okay, <u>if you say so</u>.
W Thank you. I'll give her your phone number.

여 Mike, 안녕. 잠깐 시간 좀 있니?
남 물론이지. 무슨 일이니, 소영아?
여 내 친구들 중 한 명이 한국에 관해 책을 쓰고 있어. 그녀는 한국에서의 자신의 경험을 공유할 수 있는 외국인들을 찾고 있어.
남 정말? 재미있겠다.
여 나는 네가 거기에 가장 적합한 사람인 것 같아. 네 경험을 그녀에게 말해 줄 수 있니?
남 음, 내가 그렇게 도움이 될지는 모르겠어.
여 아, 넌 아무것도 걱정하지 않아도 돼. 네가 할 일은 한국에서의 네 일상생활에 대해 내 친구에게 말해 주기만 하면 돼.
남 알겠어, 네가 그렇게 말한다면야.
여 고마워. 그녀에게 네 전화번호를 줄게.

해설 여자는 인터뷰할 외국인을 찾고 있는 자신의 친구에게 남자의 전화번호를 주겠다고 했다.

어휘 foreigner 외국인　share 공유하다　experience 경험　helpful 유용한, 도움이 되는　worry about ~에 대해 걱정하다

16 ①

(Telephone rings.)

M Good morning. I'd like to book a flight to Chicago.
W <u>What date and what time</u>, please?
M I would like to travel on May 15 in the morning.
W Yes, sir. I'll check the flight schedule for you. <u>Will you hold</u>, please?
M Sure.
W <u>There is a direct flight</u> leaving Incheon at 10:40 a.m.
M What time does it arrive in Chicago?
W It arrives at 8:30 a.m. <u>local time</u>.
M That sounds good. What time should I <u>arrive at the airport</u>?
W You have to be at the terminal by 7:00 a.m. at the latest.

(전화벨이 울린다.)

남 안녕하세요. 시카고행 항공편을 예약하고 싶은데요.
여 날짜와 시간은요?
남 5월 15일 아침에 가려고 해요.
여 알겠습니다. 손님. 비행 일정을 확인해 보겠습니다. 잠시만 기다려 주시겠어요?
남 네.
여 오전 10시 40분에 인천에서 출발하는 직항 항공편이 있습니다.
남 시카고에 몇 시에 도착하나요?
여 현지 시각으로 오전 8시 30분에 도착합니다.
남 그거 좋네요. 제가 공항에 몇 시에 도착해야 하죠?
여 늦어도 터미널에 아침 7시까지는 도착하셔야 합니다.

해설 여자는 남자에게 오전 7시까지는 공항 터미널에 도착해야 한다고 했다.

어휘 book 예약하다　flight 항공편　hold (전화를 끊지 않고) 기다리다　direct 직항의　local time 현지 시각　airport 공항　at the latest 늦어도

17 ③

W Excuse me. Do you need any help? You look like you're lost.
M Yes. <u>I've been looking around here</u> for half an hour, but I still can't find the museum.
W Really? What museum do you want to go to?
M The History Museum. It says it's on Redwood Street <u>on the map</u>.
W Oh, that one is the Modern Art Museum. The History Museum is on Oak Street.
M Then do you know <u>how I can get there</u>?
W Go straight up Pine Street for two blocks and then <u>turn left at the corner</u>.
M Okay. Is it on my left or right?
W It will be on your left. You can't miss it.

여 실례합니다. 도움이 필요하신가요? 길을 잃으신 것 같아요.
남 네. 이 주변을 30분 동안 찾아보고 있는데, 아직도 박물관을 못 찾겠어요.
여 그래요? 어떤 박물관에 가시려고 하는데요?

남 History Museum이요. 지도에는 Redwood Street에 있다고 되어 있어요.

여 오, 그건 Modern Art Museum이에요. History Museum은 Oak Street에 있어요.

남 그러면 그곳에 가는 길을 아시나요?

여 Pine Street 쪽으로 두 블록 직진하신 다음 모퉁이에서 왼쪽으로 도세요.

남 알겠습니다. 그것은 제 왼쪽에 있나요, 오른쪽에 있나요?

여 <u>왼쪽에 있을 거예요. 찾기 쉬워요.</u>

해설 박물관이 왼쪽에 있는지 오른쪽에 있는지 물었으므로 어느 쪽에 있는지를 알려 주는 응답이 와야 한다.

① 당신의 방문 목적을 말씀해 주세요.

② 저는 전에 박물관에 가방을 두고 왔어요.

④ 당신은 다른 종류의 지도를 가져왔어야 했어요.

⑤ Modern Art Museum을 방문하시면 정말 재미있을 거예요.

어휘 be lost 길을 잃다   look around 찾아다니다   half an hour 30분   map 지도   turn left 왼쪽으로 돌다   purpose 목적   visit 방문   miss 놓치다   different 다른

18 ⑤

M Jina, how was your exam today?

W It was <u>harder than I expected</u>.

M Do you think you will <u>get a good grade</u>?

W Dad, I think I tried hard. But the result will not be good.

M Oh, that's too bad. But <u>the process is more important</u> than the result.

W But <u>I've lost all my desire</u> to study because I really tried hard this time.

M Come on. Hang in there. You just need to <u>keep a positive attitude</u>.

W Can I do well?

M Sure. Try to think <u>"I can and will do better than this."</u>

남 지나야, 오늘 시험이 어땠니?

여 예상했던 것보다 더 어려웠어요.

남 좋은 성적을 받을 것 같니?

여 아빠, 전 열심히 노력했다고 생각해요. 하지만 결과는 좋지 않을 거예요.

남 오, 정말 안됐구나. 하지만 결과보다 과정이 더 중요한 거란다.

여 하지만 이번에 정말 열심히 노력했기 때문에 공부할 모든 의욕을 상실했어요.

남 진정해. 힘을 내렴. 넌 긍정적인 태도를 가져야 해.

여 제가 잘할 수 있을까요?

남 물론이지. "나는 이번보다 더 잘할 수 있고 잘할 거야."라고 생각해 봐.

해설 여자는 노력했지만 결과가 나쁠 것이라는 생각에 낙담하고 있으므로 남자는 격려의 말을 하는 것이 적절하다.

① 선생님께 도움을 청해 봐.

② 그건 네 잘못이 아니라는 걸 확실히 해 두거라.

③ 그래. 너는 작년보다 더 좋은 결과를 기대할 수 있어.

④ 당연하지. 네가 어떤 결정을 내리든지, 난 항상 네 편이야.

어휘 expect 기대하다, 예상하다   grade 성적   result 결과   process 과정   desire 의욕, 욕구   positive 긍정적인   attitude 태도   fault 잘못   decide 결정하다

19 ②

W Excuse me. Could you help me?

M Sure, what can I do for you?

W I have just <u>missed my train</u> back to London Station. I don't know what to do.

M I'm sorry to hear that. Could you <u>show me your train ticket</u>?

W Here you are.

M The next train to London Station will arrive in 30 minutes and you can <u>take that one</u>.

W That's great. Do I need to <u>pay any extra</u>?

M No. You are allowed to <u>switch your reservation</u> to any later train leaving within 2 hours.

W <u>That's a relief. Thank you so much.</u>

여 실례합니다. 저 좀 도와주시겠어요?

남 네, 무엇을 도와드릴까요?

여 런던역으로 돌아가는 기차를 막 놓쳤어요. 어떻게 해야 할지 모르겠어요.

남 안됐군요. 기차표 좀 보여 주시겠습니까?

여 여기 있습니다.

남 런던역으로 가는 다음 기차는 30분 후에 도착할 예정인데 그걸 타시면 됩니다.

여 잘 됐네요. 추가 요금을 내야 하나요?

남 아니요. 두 시간 이내에 떠나는 후발 기차 중 어느 것으로든 예약 변경이 가능합니다.

여 다행이네요. 정말 감사합니다.

해설 여자는 기차를 놓쳐서 당황했지만 추가 요금 없이 두 시간 이내의 다른 기차편으로 예약을 변경할 수 있다는 말을 들었으므로, 안도의 말과 함께 감사의 인사를 하는 것이 적절하다.

① 굉장해요! 잠깐 쉽시다.

③ 예상했던 것보다 더 비싸네요.

④ 온라인으로 표를 예매하시는 게 더 낫습니다.

⑤ 서두르세요! 시간이 충분하지 않아요.

어휘 miss 놓치다   pay 지불하다   extra 추가되는 것   be allowed to ~하는 것이 허용되다   switch 변경하다, 바꾸다   take a break 휴식을 취하다   relief 안도, 안심

20 ③

W Suji is <u>shopping for a new dress</u> at a department store. She finally finds a cute pink dress she likes. She likes its style because it is not too long and not too short. She can also save money <u>since it's on sale</u>. But when she tries it on in the fitting room, she finds that the dress is <u>a little small</u>. She wants to try on another size, but <u>she can't find one</u>. In this situation, what would Suji say to the salesperson?

Suji <u>Excuse me. Do you have this dress in a bigger size?</u>

여 수지는 백화점에서 새 원피스를 사기 위해 쇼핑하고 있다. 마침내 그녀는 자신이 좋아하는 귀여운 분홍색 원피스를 발견한다. 그녀는 그것이 너무 길지도 짧지도 않아서 그 스타일을 마음에 들어 한다. 할인 판매 중이어서 돈을 절약할 수 있다. 하지만 탈의실에서 옷을 입어 봤을 때, 원피스가 약간 작다는 것을 알았다. 그녀는 다른 사이즈를 입어 보고 싶지만 찾을 수가 없다. 이러한 상황에서, 수지는 판매 직원에게 무엇이라고 말할 것인가?

수지 실례합니다. 이 원피스로 더 큰 사이즈 있나요?

[해설] 입어 본 원피스가 약간 작아서 더 큰 사이즈가 있는지 물어보려는 상황이다.

① 탈의실이 어디에 있나요?
② 이 원피스 할인받을 수 있나요?
④ 이 원피스 다른 색도 있나요?
⑤ 이 원피스와 잘 어울리는 신발을 추천해 주시겠어요?

[어휘] department store 백화점 save 절약하다 on sale 할인 중인 fitting room 탈의실 a little 약간 salesperson 판매 직원 discount 할인 recommend 추천하다

01 ④	02 ⑤	03 ②	04 ⑤	05 ②
06 ④	07 ①	08 ④	09 ③	10 ①
11 ②	12 ③	13 ②	14 ⑤	15 ③
16 ②	17 ④	18 ④	19 ④	20 ②

01 ④

M Mom, have you seen my science report? I can't find it in my room.
W Well, have you checked on the tea table? I think I saw a piece of paper on it.
M Really? No, this paper is just a computer company's advertisement. Would you check the kitchen, Mom?
W I cleaned the kitchen this morning, and it wasn't there.
M I checked on the couch and piano. But I still can't find it.
W Why don't you check under the couch? Maybe you dropped it after you read it.
M Okay. Let me see. You're right. I found it.
W That's good. Please be more careful where you put your things the next time.

남 엄마, 제 과학 보고서 보셨어요? 제 방에서 찾을 수가 없어요.
여 글쎄, 티 테이블 확인해 봤니? 내가 그 위에서 종이 한 장을 본 것 같은데.
남 정말요? 아니에요, 이 종이는 그냥 컴퓨터 회사 광고예요. 엄마, 부엌 좀 확인해 주실래요?
여 오늘 아침에 부엌 청소를 했는데, 부엌에는 없었어.
남 소파와 피아노 위에도 확인해 봤어요. 그런데 여전히 못 찾겠어요.
여 소파 밑을 확인해 보는 게 어떠니? 네가 보고서를 읽은 후에 떨어뜨렸을지도 모르잖아.
남 알겠어요. 어디 보자. 엄마 말씀이 맞았어요. 찾았어요.
여 잘됐다. 다음에는 네 물건을 어디에 둘지 더 신경 쓰렴.

[해설] 남자는 여자의 제안대로 소파 밑에서 과학 보고서를 찾았다.

[어휘] a piece of ~ 한 장 company 회사 advertisement 광고 couch 소파 drop 떨어뜨리다 careful 조심하는

02 ⑤

W Mike, shouldn't you be leaving for your lunch date with Lisa?
M I still have time, Mom.
W Where are you going for lunch?
M We're meeting at Thai Table. It's just a ten-minute walk.
W Thai Table is a chain restaurant. Are you meeting at the one in our neighborhood?
M What? Is there another Thai Table?

W Yeah, I heard there's a new Thai Table next to the theater downtown.

M Oh my! We are going to a movie after lunch. She might think that we are meeting at the restaurant nearby the theater.

W I'm afraid so. I think you'd better check with her.

M You're right. I'll give her a call now.

여 Mike, 너 Lisa와 점심 약속을 위해 출발해야 하지 않니?

남 아직 시간 있어요, 엄마.

여 점심 먹으러 어디로 가니?

남 Thai Table에서 만날 거예요. 걸어서 겨우 10분 거리예요.

여 Thai Table은 체인 식당이잖아. 우리 동네에 있는 식당에서 만날 거니?

남 뭐라고요? Thai Table이 또 있어요?

여 그래, 시내 극장 옆에 새로운 Thai Table이 생겼다고 들었단다.

남 맙소사! 우리는 점심 먹고 영화를 볼 거예요. 그녀가 극장 가까이에 있는 식당에서 만날 거라고 생각할지도 모르겠어요.

여 그럴지도 모르겠네. 그녀에게 확인하는 게 좋겠구나.

남 맞아요. 그녀에게 지금 전화해야겠어요.

해설 남자는 Lisa와 만나기로 한 식당의 정확한 위치를 확인하기 위해 그녀에게 전화하겠다고 했다.

어휘 neighborhood 동네, 이웃   downtown 시내에
nearby 근처의   check 확인하다   give a call 전화하다

03 ②

① **W** The light bulb in my room just burned out.

  M I'll check if we have an extra light bulb in the closet.

② **W** Hold the chair tightly while I change this bulb.

  M Don't worry. I'm holding it firmly.

③ **W** Would you put away those dangerous items?

  M Sure. Just sit down and relax while I put them away.

④ **W** I like the atmosphere of this restaurant.

  M Yes. The classical music and the colorful lighting are good.

⑤ **W** Did you see the lightning last night?

  M Yes, I was scared to death.

① 여 내 방 전구가 방금 나갔어.
  남 벽장에 여분의 전구가 있는지 확인해 볼게요.

② 여 내가 전구를 교체하는 동안 의자를 꽉 잡고 있어.
  남 걱정 마세요. 단단히 잡고 있으니까요.

③ 여 저 위험한 물건들 좀 치워 줄래?
  남 물론이죠. 그것들을 치우는 동안 앉아서 좀 쉬세요.

④ 여 이 식당 분위기 마음에 들어.
  남 맞아요. 클래식 음악과 화려한 조명이 좋아요.

⑤ 여 어젯밤에 번개 봤니?
  남 네, 무서워 죽는 줄 알았어요.

해설 여자가 의자 위에 올라가 전구를 교체하고 있고 남자가 의자를 붙잡고 있는 상황이다.

어휘 (light) bulb 전구   burn out (전구가) 나가다, 꺼지다

extra 여분의   closet 벽장   hold 붙잡다   firmly 단단히
put away 치우다   dangerous 위험한   atmosphere 분위기
lightning 번개   scared 무서운   to death 극도로

04 ⑤

(*Telephone rings.*)

M Hello. Daehan Library.

W Hi. I want to know if a book is available.

M Okay, which book?

W Kevin Lee's new book.

M You mean *The Red Cup's Secret* that was published last week?

W Yes, I've been looking forward to reading it.

M Well, I'm sorry, but it has already been checked out.

W That's too bad. Then can I put a hold on it?

M Sure. I'll contact you when the book is returned. May I have your name and number?

W It's Julie Jang. My number is 010-123-4567.

(전화벨이 울린다.)

남 안녕하세요. Daehan Library입니다.

여 안녕하세요. 책을 빌릴 수 있는지 알고 싶어요.

남 네. 어느 책이요?

여 Kevin Lee의 신간이요.

남 지난주에 출간된 〈The Red Cup's Secret〉 말씀하시는 건가요?

여 네, 저는 그 책을 읽는 것을 기대해 왔거든요.

남 음, 죄송하지만, 그 책은 이미 대출되었습니다.

여 아쉽네요. 그러면 제가 그것을 예약할 수 있나요?

남 물론이죠. 책이 반납되면 연락 드릴게요. 이름과 전화번호가 어떻게 되시나요?

여 Julie Jang입니다. 제 번호는 010-123-4567입니다.

해설 여자는 Kevin Lee의 신간을 대출할 수 있는지 물어보기 위해 전화했다.

어휘 available 이용할 수 있는   publish 출판하다   check out 대출하다   put a hold on (도서관 책을) 예약하다
contact 연락하다   return 반납하다

05 ②

W The Moai Statues are located in Easter Island. There are more than 900 statues throughout the island. They are human figures carved from rocks and almost all of them have overly large heads. The ratio between the head and the trunk is three-to-five. The average height of the moai statues is about four meters. They are one of the most mysterious statues in the world. It is unknown by whom or when they were created. In 1995, UNESCO named Easter Island a World Heritage Site.

여 모아이 상은 이스터 섬에 위치해 있다. 섬 전체에 900여 개의 조각상들이 있다. 그것들은 돌을 깎아 만들어진 인간의 형상이고 대부분은 머리가 매우 크다. 머리와 몸통의 비율은 3대 5이

다. 모아이 상의 평균 높이는 약 4미터이다. 그것들은 세상에서 가장 신비한 조각상들 중 하나이다. 그것들이 누구에 의해서 또는 언제 만들어졌는지 알려지지 않았다. 1995년에 유네스코는 이스터 섬을 세계 문화유산으로 지정했다.

해설 모아이 상을 제작한 이유는 언급되지 않았다.

어휘 statue 조각상 be located in ~에 위치하다 island 섬 throughout ~ 전체에 걸쳐서 figure 형상 carve 깎아서 만들다, 조각하다 overly 몹시, 지나치게 ratio 비율 trunk 몸통 average 평균(의) height 높이 mysterious 신비한 create 창조하다, 만들다 name 명명하다, 지정하다

06 ④

M Welcome back, viewers! The first item that I'm going to show you is this fashionable bag. It comes in blue and red. It's waterproof so you don't have to worry about your bag in the rain. It also has two inner pockets that make it easy for you to carry many small things. It usually sells for $50, but just for today we're offering it for only $30. You'll get an extra discount if you download our app on your smartphone and order it there. Don't miss this great opportunity!

남 시청자 여러분, 환영합니다! 여러분께 보여드릴 첫 번째 상품은 멋진 가방입니다. 파란색과 빨간색이 있습니다. 방수가 되어서 비가 와도 가방 걱정을 하실 필요가 없습니다. 안쪽에 주머니가 두 개 있어서 작은 물건들을 많이 갖고 다니시기 편합니다. 보통 50달러에 판매하는데, 오늘만 단지 30달러에 제공합니다. 스마트폰에 앱을 다운로드해서 주문하시면 추가 할인을 받으실 수 있습니다. 이렇게 좋은 기회를 놓치지 마세요!

해설 평소에는 50달러인데 오늘만 30달러에 판매한다고 했다.

어휘 fashionable 멋진 waterproof 방수의 don't have to ~할 필요 없다 offer 제공하다 discount 할인 app 앱 opportunity 기회

07 ①

① M Excuse me. Could you help me find a book?
  W Me, too. I have already read the book.
② M Could you tell me how I can get to J Art Center?
  W It is near here. You can walk there.
③ M How about having some tea before you leave?
  W Absolutely. I'd love a cup.
④ M Which color do you prefer, white or black?
  W I prefer white to black.
⑤ M Did you find it hard to accept your illness?
  W No, it wasn't too difficult to accept.

① 남 실례합니다. 책 찾는 것 좀 도와주시겠어요?
  여 저도요. 저는 그 책을 이미 읽었어요.
② 남 J Art Center에 가는 방법 좀 알려 주시겠어요?
  여 이 근처에 있습니다. 걸어가실 수 있어요.
③ 남 떠나기 전에 차 좀 드시겠어요?
  여 물론이죠. 한 잔 마시고 싶어요.

④ 남 흰색과 검은색 중에서 어느 색이 더 좋으세요?
  여 검은색보다는 흰색이 더 좋아요.
⑤ 남 당신의 병을 받아들이기 힘들었죠?
  여 아니에요, 받아들이는 것이 그렇게 힘들지 않았어요.

해설 ① 책 찾는 것을 도와 달라는 말에 그 책을 이미 읽었다는 응답은 어색하다.

어휘 already 이미, 벌써 absolutely 전적으로, 틀림없이 prefer ~을 더 좋아하다 hard 어려운, 힘든 accept 받아들이다 illness 병, 질병

08 ④

W James, you seem to be happy today. What's up?
M Molly finally agreed to go on a date with me.
W Good for you. What are your plans for the date?
M I'm not sure yet, but I'm thinking of taking her to a flower exhibition and then dinner.
W Sounds good. What restaurant do you have in mind?
M That's the problem. I can't decide where to eat.
W Have you ever been to Orga Garden next to the police station downtown? I'm sure Molly would love it.
M Oh, then please let me know the phone number.
W Sure. You'd better call and make a reservation.

여 James, 너 오늘 기분이 좋아 보인다. 무슨 일이니?
남 Molly가 마침내 나와 데이트하는 데 동의했어.
여 잘됐네. 네 데이트 계획은 무엇이니?
남 아직 확실하지 않지만, 꽃 박람회에 간 후에 저녁 식사를 할 생각이야.
여 좋은 생각이야. 어느 식당을 생각하고 있니?
남 그게 문제야. 어디서 식사를 할지 못 정하겠어.
여 시내 경찰서 옆에 있는 Orga Garden에 가 봤니? 틀림없이 Molly가 그곳을 좋아할 거야.
남 오, 그럼 전화번호 좀 알려 줘.
여 그래. 전화해서 예약하는 게 좋을 거야.

해설 남자는 여자 친구와 함께 저녁 식사를 할 식당의 전화번호를 알려 달라고 부탁했다.

어휘 agree to ~에 동의하다 go on a date with ~와 데이트하다 exhibition 박람회 have in mind 염두에 두다 〔생각하다〕 decide 결정하다 downtown 시내에 make a reservation 예약하다

09 ③

M Good morning. Can you recommend a good vacation package?
W Certainly. When would you like to leave?
M At the beginning of the lunar New Year's holiday.
W Well, you'd better book soon. Air tickets and hotel rooms at that time are almost fully booked.
M Really? Are there any package tours left to a warm place?
W Yes, look at this brochure. How about this one? It's

a five-day package tour to Thailand.
M Oh, it looks good. I'd like to book it.
W Good. Then I need your passport number for the reservation.
M Okay. Here you are.

남 안녕하세요. 괜찮은 휴가 패키지여행을 추천해 주시겠어요?
여 물론이죠. 언제 출발하기를 원하세요?
남 구정 연휴 초예요.
여 그럼 빨리 예약하시는 게 좋습니다. 그때는 비행기 표와 호텔이 거의 다 예약되었어요.
남 정말요? 따뜻한 곳으로 가는 패키지여행이 있나요?
여 네, 이 안내 책자를 보세요. 이 상품은 어떠세요? 5일간 태국 패키지여행입니다.
남 아, 좋네요. 그걸 예약하고 싶어요.
여 좋습니다. 그럼 예약을 위해 고객님의 여권 번호가 필요합니다.
남 네. 여기 있어요.

해설 안내 책자를 보면서 패키지여행 상품을 고르고 예약할 수 있는 곳은 여행사이다.

어휘 recommend 추천하다 the lunar New Year 구정 fully 완전히 package tour 패키지여행 brochure (안내·광고용) 책자 passport 여권 reservation 예약

10 ①

(Telephone rings.)
W Hello.
M Hello. I'm calling about the ad for a library assistant. Is the job still available?
W Yes. Are you a student?
M Yes, I am. I'm looking for a part-time job during the winter vacation.
W Okay. Do you know the working conditions?
M As far as I know, the working hours are from one to five, and it's $10 per hour.
W Right. You're supposed to work five days a week, but if you want, you can work on Saturdays, too.
M Sorry. I don't want to work on weekends.
W Okay. I don't think it's a problem. You'll hear from us pretty soon.

(전화벨이 울린다.)
여 여보세요.
남 여보세요. 도서관 보조 구인 광고를 보고 전화 드립니다. 아직 자리 있나요?
여 네. 학생이신가요?
남 네, 맞습니다. 저는 겨울 방학 동안에 할 시간제 일자리를 찾고 있는 중이에요.
여 좋아요. 근무 조건은 알고 있나요?
남 근무 시간은 1시부터 5시까지이고, 시간당 10달러라고 알고 있어요.
여 맞습니다. 일주일에 5일 근무하시면 되는데요, 원하시면 토요일에도 근무하실 수 있어요.
남 죄송합니다. 주말에는 일하고 싶지 않아요.
여 알겠습니다. 문제될 건 없어요. 곧 저희에게서 연락을 받으실 거예요.

해설 시급은 10달러이고 하루 4시간씩 주 5일 근무이므로 주급으로 200달러를 받을 것이다.

어휘 ad(= advertisement) 광고 assistant 조수, 보조 available 이용할 수 있는 condition 조건 as far as ~하는 한 be supposed to ~하기로 되어 있다 problem 문제

11 ②

W Take a look at this. There are some interesting sports classes at Central Sports Center.
M I have taken a few classes there, and they were all good. I especially liked the tennis and swimming classes.
W Did you? I'm interested in playing ball sports.
M Then why don't you take a tennis class?
W I will. Which instructor would you recommend, Jonathan or Natalia?
M Natalia. She's excellent.
W Okay. I'll take her class. But why is the Friday class shorter than the others?
M The Friday one doesn't have a group practice session. There's only a lesson.
W I see. I'll choose the longer one. I want to practice with my partners, too.

여 이것 좀 봐. Central Sports Center에 재미있는 스포츠 수업들이 있어.
남 나 거기에서 몇 가지 수업을 들었는데, 전부 괜찮았어. 나는 특히 테니스와 수영 수업이 좋았어.
여 그랬니? 나는 구기 종목에 관심이 있는데.
남 그러면 테니스 수업을 듣는 게 어때?
여 그래야겠어. 너는 Jonathan과 Natalia 중 어느 강사를 추천하니?
남 Natalia. 그녀는 최고야.
여 알겠어. 그녀의 수업을 들어야겠어. 그런데 왜 금요일 수업이 다른 것들보다 더 짧니?
남 금요일 수업은 단체 연습 시간이 없거든. 레슨만 있어.
여 그렇구나. 나는 더 긴 것을 선택해야겠어. 파트너랑 연습도 하고 싶거든.

해설 여자는 Natalia가 가르치는 테니스 수업 중 시간이 긴 수업을 선택했다.

어휘 especially 특히 be interested in ~에 관심이 있다 instructor 강사 recommend 추천하다 excellent 훌륭한 practice 연습(하다) session 시간, 시기 choose 선택하다

12 ③

W Jason, you've been to ST Ski Resort before, right?
M Yes, several times. It usually takes only an hour from Seoul.
W Do you know how many slopes there are?
M Over 20. If you are a beginner, the green slopes are the best choice.
W Thanks. Are there any ski lessons for beginners?
M Sure, the ski school provides various lessons for

beginners. When are you thinking of going?

W I'm going with some friends this weekend. It will be really crowded, right?

M I don't think so. The resort only admits 7,000 skiers every day.

W Wow, I didn't know there was a limit on the number of visitors. Thank you so much.

여 Jason, 너 전에 ST Ski Resort에 가 봤지, 그렇지?

남 응, 여러 번. 서울에서 보통 한 시간밖에 안 걸려.

여 슬로프가 몇 개나 되는지 아니?

남 20개가 넘어. 네가 초급자라면, 그린 슬로프가 가장 잘 맞아.

여 고마워. 초급자들을 위한 스키 강습도 있니?

남 물론이야, 그 스키 학교는 초급자를 위한 다양한 수업들을 제공해. 너는 언제 갈 생각이니?

여 이번 주말에 친구들과 갈 거야. 엄청 붐비겠지, 그렇지?

남 그렇게 생각하지 않아. 그 리조트는 매일 7천 명의 이용객만 허용하거든.

여 우와, 방문객 수에 제한이 있는 건 몰랐어. 정말 고마워.

해설 대기 시간은 언급되지 않았다.

어휘 resort 리조트 slope (스키장의) 슬로프 beginner 초급자 choice 선택 provide 제공하다 crowded 붐비는 admit 허용하다 limit 제한

13 ②

W You remember this Saturday is Mom's birthday, right?

M Sure. Have you decided the place for dinner?

W Yeah. I called Shelly's Restaurant and made a reservation for a big family room.

M Good. Our grandparents are coming that day, too. Did you order a birthday cake?

W Yes. I ordered a cake and a flower basket. You know she loves flowers.

M Great. Is there anything else that we have to do?

W We should wrap her present and buy a birthday card.

M I'm not good at wrapping things. I'll buy a beautiful card.

W Okay. I'll take care of the wrapping.

여 너 이번 주 토요일이 엄마 생신인 거 기억하지, 그렇지?

남 물론이지. 저녁 식사할 장소는 결정했어?

여 응. Shelly's Restaurant에 전화해서 큰 패밀리 룸을 예약했어.

남 잘했어. 그날 할아버지 할머니도 오시잖아. 생일 케이크는 주문했니?

여 응. 케이크와 꽃바구니를 주문했어. 알다시피 엄마가 꽃을 좋아하시잖아.

남 정말 잘했네. 우리가 해야 할 다른 일이 있을까?

여 엄마 선물을 포장해야 하고 생일 카드를 사야 해.

남 난 물건 포장하는 걸 잘 못해. 내가 예쁜 카드를 살게.

여 좋아. 내가 포장을 할게.

해설 남자는 생일 카드를 사기로 했고 여자는 선물을 포장하기로 했다.

어휘 decide 결정하다 make a reservation 예약하다 wrap 포장하다 present 선물 be good at ~을 잘하다 take care of (일·책임 등을) 맡다

14 ⑤

W This is a reference book. This has a lot of information about many subjects. The information is usually arranged in alphabetical order and sometimes classified by topics. This has such reliable information that you can find this book in libraries, schools and other educational institutions. This is not limited to simple definitions of a word or topic. This provides wide knowledge on subjects. This also often includes many maps and illustrations.

여 이것은 참고 서적입니다. 이것은 다양한 주제에 관한 많은 정보를 담고 있습니다. 그 정보는 보통 알파벳순으로 정리되어 있고 때로는 주제별로 분류되기도 합니다. 이것은 매우 믿을 수 있는 정보를 담고 있어서 도서관, 학교, 그리고 다른 교육 기관에서 찾아볼 수 있습니다. 이것은 한 단어나 주제의 단순한 정의에 국한되지 않습니다. 이것은 주제에 관해 광범위한 지식을 제공합니다. 이것은 또한 종종 많은 지도와 삽화를 포함합니다.

해설 어떤 주제에 대해 광범위하고 믿을만한 정보가 담긴 책으로, 알파벳순이나 주제별로 정보가 분류되어 있는 것은 백과사전이다.

어휘 reference 참고, 참조 information 정보 subject 주제 arrange 배열하다 order 순서 classify 분류하다 reliable 믿을 만한 institution 기관 limit 제한하다 definition 정의 provide 제공하다 knowledge 지식 include 포함하다 map 지도 illustration 삽화

15 ③

M What do you feel like having for dinner?

W I don't know. I want to try something new.

M Okay. Let's look for some recipes on the Internet.

W Good idea. Let's see what we can find.

M Oh, how about this chicken curry? We both like chicken and curry.

W That looks delicious and it doesn't look too hard to make.

M Yeah. Do we have all the ingredients?

W We're out of potatoes. Can you wash all the vegetables? I'll go get some potatoes.

남 저녁으로 뭐 먹고 싶어요?

여 모르겠어요. 뭔가 새로운 걸 먹고 싶어요.

남 좋아요. 인터넷으로 조리법을 찾아봅시다.

여 좋은 생각이에요. 어떤 게 있는지 찾아봐요.

남 오, 이 닭고기 카레 어때요? 우리 둘 다 닭고기와 카레를 좋아하잖아요.

여 맛있어 보이고 만들기도 어려워 보이지 않네요.

남 네. 재료는 모두 있나요?

여 감자가 떨어졌어요. 채소 좀 씻어 줄래요? 내가 가서 감자를 사 올게요.

16 ②

W What are you doing on the computer?
M I'm looking for running shoes on the Internet. But I don't think I can get them before my trip.
W When do you leave?
M Next Friday, July 10.
W Today is already July 5. Why don't you go to Mary's Shoes on Main Street?
M I think that store is too expensive.
W I heard that Mary's Shoes is having a sale until tomorrow.
M Then we'd better go right now.
W But the store closes at 7 p.m. and it's already 8. Let's go tomorrow.
M Okay. I have no choice.

여 컴퓨터로 뭐 하고 있니?
남 인터넷으로 운동화를 찾고 있어요. 그런데 여행 전에는 받지 못할 것 같아요.
여 언제 출발하지?
남 다음 주 금요일, 7월 10일이에요.
여 오늘이 벌써 7월 5일이네. Main Street에 있는 Mary's Shoes에 가 보는 게 어떠니?
남 그 가게는 너무 비싼 것 같아요.
여 Mary's Shoes가 내일까지 할인 판매한다고 들었단다.
남 그러면 지금 당장 가는 게 좋겠어요.
여 그런데 그 가게는 7시에 문을 닫는데 벌써 8시야. 내일 가자.
남 알았어요. 어쩔 수 없네요.

17 ④

M Hi, Ella. What's up?
W Well, I've just had a regular checkup.
M Oh, how was it? Is everything okay?
W Not so good. The doctor said I have high blood pressure, and it can cause other diseases.
M Oh, no. What should you do to prevent those diseases?
W The doctor advised me to lose some weight.
M Then you need to exercise regularly.
W Yeah, but I've been swimming every morning for several years now.
M Then what about eating healthier foods?

남 안녕, Ella. 어떻게 지내니?
여 음, 난 방금 정기 건강 검진을 받았어.

남 오, 어땠니? 모든 게 괜찮니?
여 별로 좋지 않아. 의사 선생님이 내가 고혈압이 있는데, 그것이 다른 병을 일으킬 수 있다고 말씀하셨어.
남 오, 저런. 너는 그런 질병들을 예방하기 위해 뭘 해야 하니?
여 의사 선생님은 내게 살을 좀 빼라고 충고하셨어.
남 그럼 너는 규칙적으로 운동해야겠구나.
여 그래, 하지만 나는 지금 몇 년째 매일 아침 수영을 하고 있어.
남 그러면 좀 더 건강에 좋은 음식을 먹는 게 어때?

18 ④

W Have you read Janet Jones' new book?
M Is she the author of *Magic Castle*?
W Yes. Her new book *Silent Village*, was released recently. I've already read it.
M What's the story about?
W It's about an orphaned boy who has to understand a secret message to save his village.
M Sounds interesting. What do you think of it?
W It's just fascinating. He travels all over the world and fights against every evil.
M It must be thrilling. I think I should read it myself.
W You should. I think this book is her best work ever.

여 Janet Jones의 신간 읽어 봤니?
남 〈Magic Castle〉의 저자 말하는 거니?
여 응. 그녀의 신간 〈Silent Village〉가 최근에 발간됐어. 난 벌써 그것을 읽었어.
남 무엇에 관한 이야기니?
여 마을을 구하기 위해 비밀 메시지를 알아야 하는 고아 소년에 관한 이야기야.
남 재미있겠다. 넌 그것에 대해 어떻게 생각해?
여 대단히 재미있어. 그 소년이 전 세계를 여행하면서 모든 악과 맞서 싸워.
남 아주 재미있겠는데. 나도 그 책을 읽어 봐야겠어.
여 꼭 읽어 봐. 이 책은 그녀의 작품 중 역대 최고인 것 같아.

19 ④

M Kate, are you tired?
W No, Mr. Benson. Why do you think so?
M You cannot concentrate on the lesson, and you are dozing off during the class.
W Oh, I'm sorry. I'm not getting much sleep these days.
M What time do you usually go to bed?
W I usually go to bed before midnight, but I stayed awake until 3 o'clock last night.
M Are you worried about something?
W No. I was just surfing the Internet on my smartphone and didn't realize what time it was.
M Try not to use your phone in bed at night.

남 Kate, 피곤하니?
여 아니에요, Benson 선생님. 왜 그렇게 생각하세요?
남 너는 수업에 집중하지 못하고 수업 중에 졸더구나.
여 아, 죄송해요. 저는 요즘 잠을 충분히 못 자고 있어요.
남 보통 몇 시에 잠자리에 드니?
여 대개 자정 전에 잠자리에 드는데, 어젯밤에는 3시까지 깨어 있었어요.
남 걱정거리가 있니?
여 아니요. 단지 스마트폰으로 인터넷 검색을 하다가 몇 시인지 깨닫지 못했어요.
남 밤에 잠자리에서 스마트폰을 사용하지 않도록 하렴.

해설 여자가 밤늦게까지 스마트폰을 사용하다가 잠이 부족하여 수업 시간에 조는 상황이므로 잠자리에서 스마트폰 사용을 자제하라는 조언이 적절하다.
① 한숨 자고 나면 괜찮아질 거야.
② 운동을 하는 것이 낮잠을 자는 것보다 더 나아.
③ 너는 밤늦게까지 공부해야 해.
⑤ 수업 중에 휴대 전화 사용은 금지란다.

어휘 concentrate on ~에 집중하다   doze off 졸다   midnight 자정, 밤 12시   awake 깨어 있는   realize 깨닫다   take a nap 낮잠을 자다   stay up late at night 밤늦게까지 깨어 있다

20 ②

M Jennifer is a student from England studying in Korea. Today, her Korean friend, Jiyoon, takes her to a Korean restaurant for lunch. The restaurant specializes in *cheonggukjang*, and Jennifer hasn't tried it before. Jiyoon explains that it is made from soybean and healthy food. Jennifer thinks it smells bad at first. But after having some, Jennifer is surprised to find it's delicious. Jiyoon asks Jennifer how it tastes. In this situation, what would Jennifer most likely say to Jiyoon?

Jennifer Jiyoon, it's much better than I expected.

남 Jennifer는 한국에서 공부하는 영국 출신 학생이다. 오늘, 그녀의 한국인 친구 지윤이가 점심 식사를 하러 그녀를 한국 식당에 데려간다. 그 식당은 청국장을 전문으로 하는데, Jennifer는 전에 그것을 먹어 본 적이 없다. 지윤이는 그것이 콩으로 만든 것이며 건강에 좋은 음식이라고 설명한다. Jennifer는 처음에 안 좋은 냄새가 난다고 생각한다. 하지만 조금 먹어 본 후, Jennifer는 그것이 맛있다는 것을 알고 놀란다. 지윤이는 Jennifer에게 맛이 어떤지 묻는다. 이 상황에서, Jennifer는 지윤이에게 뭐라고 말할 것 같은가?

Jennifer 지윤아, 내가 예상했던 것보다 훨씬 더 맛있어.

해설 처음에는 좋지 않은 냄새가 났지만 조금 먹어 본 후 맛있어서 놀랐다고 했으므로, 맛이 어떤지 묻는 말에 대해 긍정적인 응답이 와야 한다.
① 이 음식은 내 입맛엔 안 맞아.
③ 다음엔 내가 점심 살게.
④ 난 이 음식을 항상 먹어 보고 싶었어.
⑤ 어디로 갈지 선호하는 곳은 없어.

어휘 specialize 전문으로 하다   explain 설명하다   soybean 콩   healthy 건강에 좋은   smell 냄새가 나다   at first 처음에   suit (음식, 기호 등에) 맞다   taste 맛이 ~하다; 맛   expect 예상하다   preference 선호

Word Check

19회

01 줄이다	02 염려
03 선택	04 앞의, 사전의
05 일정을 변경하다	06 오른쪽의
07 위치	08 뜨다
09 탈의실	10 ~와 잘 어울리다
11 또한	12 휴식을 취하다
13 attitude	14 intermediate
15 modern	16 positive
17 purpose	18 arrange
19 save	20 superstition
21 reusable	22 fine dust
23 local time	24 at the same time

Expression Check

25 What if	26 suffering from
27 keeps, from	28 at the latest
29 instead of	30 one of, palaces

Word Check

20회

01 악	02 기관
03 고아가 된	04 무서운
05 광고	06 분류하다
07 발표하다, 공개하다	08 믿을 만한
09 정의	10 (전구가) 나가다, 꺼지다
11 극도로	12 저자
13 specialize	14 carve
15 island	16 name
17 statue	18 crowded
19 ratio	20 subject
21 disease(illness)	22 doze off
23 take a nap	24 reference

Expression Check

25 out of	26 feel like
27 have in mind	28 go on a date
29 concentrate on	30 As far as

LISTENING CLEAR
중학영어듣기 모의고사 20회

3

영역	브랜드	초1~2	초3~4	초5~6	중1	중2	중3	고1	고2	고3
독해	[중등] 기본서 READING CLEAR				READING CLEAR 1	READING CLEAR 2	READING CLEAR 3			
	[고등] 기본서 Supreme 구문독해 / 유형독해							Supreme 구문독해	Supreme 유형독해	
	[중·고등] 문장독해 공식으로 통하는 문장독해 기본 완성							공통문 기본	공통문 완성	
듣기	[중등] 듣기모의고사 LISTENING CLEAR 중학영어 듣기모의고사				LISTENING CLEAR 1	LISTENING CLEAR 2	LISTENING CLEAR 3			
	[고등] 듣기모의고사 Supreme 수능 영어 듣기 모의고사 기본 실전							Supreme	Supreme	
기출	[중등] 기출예상문제집 특급기출 (중간, 기말) 윤정미, 이병민				특급기출	특급기출				
어휘	[초·중·고등] 영단어, 영숙어 뜯어먹는 시리즈	뜯어먹는 필수 영단어 1	뜯어먹는 필수 영단어 2		뜯어먹는 1200	뜯어먹는 1800	뜯어먹는 중학 1000	뜯어먹는 1800	뜯어먹는 1800	뜯어먹는 1200
	[중·고등] 영단어 보카클리어				보카클리어	보카클리어	보카클리어	보카클리어 고교필수편	보카클리어 수능편	

영어 실력과 내신 점수를 함께 높이는
중학 영어 클리어 시리즈

문법 영문법 클리어 | LEVEL 1~3

최신
개정판

문법 개념과 내신을 한 번에 끝내다!

- 중등에서 꼭 필요한 핵심 문법만 담아 시각적으로 정리
- 시험에 꼭 나오는 출제 포인트부터 서술형 문제까지 내신 완벽 대비

쓰기 문법+쓰기 클리어 | LEVEL 1~3

영작과 서술형을 한 번에 끝내다!

- 기초 형태 학습부터 문장 영작까지 단계별로 영작 집중 훈련
- 최신 서술형 유형과 오류 클리닉으로 서술형 실전 준비 완료

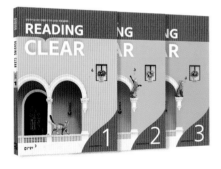

독해 READING CLEAR | LEVEL 1~3

문장 해석과 지문 이해를 한 번에 끝내다!

- 핵심 구문 32개로 어려운 문법 구문의 정확한 해석 훈련
- Reading Map으로 글의 핵심 및 구조 파악 훈련

듣기 LISTENING CLEAR | LEVEL 1~3

듣기 기본기와 듣기 평가를 한 번에 끝내다!

- 최신 중학 영어듣기능력평가 완벽 반영
- 1.0배속/1.2배속/받아쓰기용 음원 별도 제공으로 학습 편의성 강화